Advanced Information and Knowledge Processing

Series Editors
Professor Lakhmi Jain
Lakhmi.jain@unisa.edu.au
Professor Xindong Wu
xwu@cems.uvm.edu

T0140588

For other titles published in this series, go to
http://www.springer.com/4738

Richard Chbeir · Youakim Badr · Ajith Abraham
Aboul-Ella Hassanien
Editors

Emergent Web Intelligence: Advanced Information Retrieval

 Springer

Editors
Dr. Richard Chbeir
Université de Bourgogne
LE2I-UMR CNRS 5158
Fac. de Sciences Mirande
21078 Dijon Cedex
France
richard.chbeir@u-bourgogne.fr

Dr. Ajith Abraham
Norwegian University of Science
    & Technology
Center for Quantifiable Quality
    of Service in Communication Systems
O.S. Bragstads plass 2E
7491 Trondheim
Norway
ajith.abraham@ieee.org

Dr. Youakim Badr
INSA de Lyon
Université de Lyon
Département Informatique
7 avenue Jean Capelle
69621 Villeurbanne CX
France
youakim.badr@insa-lyon.fr

Dr. Aboul-Ella Hassanien
Kuwait University
College of Business & Administration
Dept. Quantitative Methods
    & Information Systems
PO Box 5486
13055 Safat
Kuwait
abo@cba.edu.kw

AI&KP ISSN: 1610-3947
ISBN: 978-1-4471-2549-5   ISBN: 978-1-84996-074-8 (eBook)
DOI: 10.1007/978-1-84996-074-8
Springer London Dordrecht Heidelberg New York

British Library Cataloguing in Publication Data
A catalogue record for this book is available from the British Library

Cover design: KuenkelLopka GmbH

Printed on acid-free paper

Springer is part of Springer Science+Business Media (www.springer.com)

Editorial Preface

Richard Chbeir, Youakim Badr, Ajith Abraham, and Aboul-Ella Hassanien

Abstract As the Web continues to grow and evolve, more and more data are becoming available. Particularly, multimedia and XML-based data are produced regularly and in increasing way in our daily digital activities, and their retrieval and access must be explored and studied in this emergent web-based era. This book provides reviews of the cutting-edge technologies and insights of various topics related to XML-based and multimedia information access and retrieval under the umbrella of Web Intelligence and reporting how organizations can gain competitive advantages by applying new different emergent techniques in the real-world scenarios. The primary target audience for the book includes researchers, scholars, postgraduate students and developers who are interested in advanced information retrieval on the web research and related issues.

1 Introduction

Since the last two decades, Internet has changed our daily life by redefining the meanings and processes of business, commerce, marketing, finance, publishing,

R. Chbeir
Université de Bourgogne, LE2I-UMR CNRS 5158, Fac. de Sciences Mirande, 21078 Dijon Cedex, France
e-mail: richard.chbeir@u-bourgogne.fr

Y. Badr
INSA de Lyon, Université de Lyon, Département Informatique, 7 avenue Jean Capelle, 69621 Villeurbanne CX, France
e-mail: youakim.badr@insa-lyon.fr

A. Abraham
Norwegian University of Science & Technology, Center for Quantifiable Quality of Service in Communication Systems, O.S. Bragstads plass 2E, 7491 Trondheim, Norway
e-mail: ajith.abraham@ieee.org

A.-E. Hassanien
Kuwait University, College of Business & Administration, Dept. Quantitative Methods & Information Systems, PO Box 5486, 13055 Safat, Kuwait
e-mail: abo@cba.edu.kw

education, research, etc. and by revolutionizing the way we produce, store, process, retrieve and use information. This has participated to the emergence of the Web Intelligence.

Web Intelligence (WI) explores the impact of Artificial Intelligence (AI) and advanced information technologies representing the next generation of Web-based systems, services, and environments, and designing hybrid web systems that serve wired and wireless users more efficiently.

In addition, multimedia and XML data have become increasingly available on the web (considered as the largest multimedia database to date). Its applications include video-on-demand systems, video conferencing, social tagging, medical imaging, on-line encyclopedia, cartography, etc. Since the value of this complex content depends on how easy it is to search and manage, the need to efficiently index, store, and particularly retrieve these data is becoming very high. Although Web-based information retrieval systems and search engines are regularly being deployed and used, they are currently inappropriate to handle the retrieval of complex data. The need for new more relevant and intelligent techniques and approaches for developing and benefiting from collective Web Intelligence is obvious more than ever to help users fetch data and avoid irrelevant web search results (pages, links, etc.), fraud e-business and email transactions, non-personalized Web information, even wrong web decisions, etc. It goes without saying that the novel intelligent Web theory needs to exploit advanced information technology and AI to explore the next generation of web-empowered systems, services, and environments, and to design and provide hybrid web systems that serve wired and wireless users more efficiently. This book assesses the current status and technologies describing major challenges and proper solutions for effective Advanced Information Retrieval under the umbrella of Web Intelligence along the Web evolution trajectory. The included chapters cover different facets of the Advanced Information Retrieval ranging from the access control and security to information retrieval and adaptation of complex information that are a step forward towards a full-fledged intelligent web age.

Why This Book Is Interesting?

In order to meet the industrial and technological demand at present, universities across the world are striving to develop curriculum in this area. Almost every computer science and engineering department is now introducing Web Intelligence and XML-based and multimedia information retrieval into their curriculum. Moreover, many research-oriented departments are conducting research in this area to attract funding. As a result, the interest in the field of Advanced Information Retrieval under the umbrella of Web Intelligence is growing. The number of journals in this area has increased and the number of related conferences organized in the last 10 years is overwhelming. There are very few books on Web Intelligence retrieval and unfortunately do not cover features of XML-based and multimedia information retrieval as a new paradigm. Thus, there is a need for such a book to meet this increasing demand in the academia and research organizations and to introduce and explore the related techniques and methodologies to scholars, postgraduates, developers and researchers and help them grasp the basic and advanced concepts. This book is written at a comprehensible level for students who have some basic knowledge in web-based retrieval. Due to the emphasis on case-studies, systems and applications, the book should be appropriate for computer engineering students as well as computer and information science ones. The book should also serve already-practicing engineers and scientists who intend to study the emerging areas of advanced Web intelligence retrieval.

2 Book Organization

The book is organized in self-contained chapters to provide greatest reading flexibility. It is organized into three main categories as follows.

The first six chapters are related to *Web and Multimedia Information Querying*.

The first chapter is entitled "Contextual and Conceptual Information Retrieval and Navigation on the Web." Its goal is to propose a methodology and tools to enhance information retrieval and navigation on the Web through contextual and conceptual help. This methodology provides users with an extended navigation space by adding a conceptual and a semantic layer above Web data. The conceptual layer is made of Galois lattices which cluster Web pages into concepts according to their common features (in particular their textual content). These lattices represent the Global Conceptual Context of Web pages. An additional navigation layer is provided by ontologies which are connected to the conceptual level through specific concepts of the lattices. Users may navigate transparently within each of these three layers and go from one to another very easily. However, the navigation within Galois lattices may be difficult as the number of concepts grows very fast with the number of Web pages. The second contribution of this chapter consists in providing tools to help users navigate within a complex conceptual lattice. A new similarity measure is proposed to find the most relevant concept to start a navigation or to choose the most relevant concept to visit from a given navigation point. This similarity measure is based on Jiang and Conraths measure used for ontology matching, extended to reflect conceptual information. This chapter illustrates these methodology and tools for Web information retrieval and navigation through example experimentations and presents future research directions-visualization in particular.

Entitled "Automatic Invocation Linking for Collaborative Web-Based Corpora", the second chapter attempts to provide a solution to help a user understand a particular concept in collaborative online encyclopedias and knowledge bases (e.g., Wikipedia, PlanetMath, etc.) becoming increasingly popular because of their open access, comprehensive and interlinked content, rapid and continual updates, and community interactivity. To do that, it is essential to link the content so a user can learn about related and underlying concepts. After presenting the problems and challenges of (automatic) invocation linking for collaborative web corpus and reviewing the state of the art for invocation linking in current online systems, the NNexus approach is provided which is an abstraction and generalization of the automatic linking component used by PlanetMath.org. The chapter emphasizes both research problems and practical design issues through discussion of real world scenarios.

The third chapter addresses the problem of querying Web Services.[1] It is entitled "WS-Query A Framework to Efficiently Query Semantic Web Service" where a query framework is proposed to efficiently query semantic Web services using Quality of Web Service (QoWS). QoWS consists of a set of criteria that characterize the behavior of Web services in delivering their functionalities. Service querying is enabled by a novel service query model where declarative service queries are resolved by multi-level Web service invocations. Quality of Web Service is used as a key parameter to select the best services. To adjust the different QoWS parameters, dynamic rating and multimode matching are adopted. The dynamic rating provides a quantitative assessment of the Web services in achieving the promised QoWS throughout their interactions with the query infrastructure while the multimode matching expands the solution space by enabling similar/partial answers and allows assigning a degree of precision for each matching mode.

The fourth chapter focuses on querying the Resource Description Framework (RDF).[2] It provides an "RDF-GL: A SPARQL[3]-Based Graphical Query Language for RDF". The proposed query language is based on SPARQL, and allows the graphical design of SPARQL Select queries, that are then translated into pure SPARQL. RDF-GL is unique as it represents the only graphical query language for RDF that is based on the state-of-the-art query language for RDF: SPARQL. Additionally, SPARQLinG, an application that enables the design of graphical RDF-GL queries, is also presented.

The fifth chapter is entitled "Semantics-Based Intelligent Indexing and Retrieval of Digital Images – A Case Study". It assesses on the recent proliferation of digital media leading to a huge interest in classifying and indexing media objects for generic search and usage. It is true that the colossal growth in digital image repositories makes them difficult to navigate using free-text search mechanisms, which often return inaccurate matches as they typically rely on statistical analysis of query keyword recurrence in the image annotation or surrounding text. In this chapter, a semantically enabled image annotation and retrieval engine is presented. It has been designed to satisfy the requirements of the commercial image collections market in terms of both accuracy and efficiency of the retrieval process. The proposed search engine relies on methodically structured ontologies[4] for image annotation, thus allowing for more intelligent reasoning about the image content and subsequently obtaining a more accurate set of results and a richer set of alternatives matchmaking the original query. Also, explicit and implicit semantic-based query expansion is studied here.

---

[1] A Web service is a software system designed to support interoperable machine-to-machine interaction over a network. It has an interface described in a machine-processable format (specifically WSDL). Other systems interact with the Web service in a manner prescribed by its description using SOAP messages, typically conveyed using HTTP with an XML serialization in conjunction with other Web-related standards.

[2] Developed under the auspices of the World Wide Web Consortium (W3C), RDF is a general framework for how to describe any Internet resource such as a Web site and its content. An RDF description, often referred to as metadata or "data about data", uses an XML-based syntax and can include the authors of the resource, date of creation or updating, the organization of the pages on a site (the sitemap), information that describes content in terms of audience or content rating, key words for search engine data collection, subject categories, and so forth. It is a triple consisting of a subject, a predicate, and an object. It is represented as a directed node-arc-node link. A set of such triples is called an RDF graph.

[3] SPARQL is an RDF query language. It was standardized by the RDF Data Access Working Group (DAWG) of the W3C, and is considered as a key semantic web technology. SPARQL allows for a query to consist of triple patterns, conjunctions, disjunctions, and optional patterns.

[4] An ontology defines the vocabulary with which queries and assertions are written. It can be a guarantee of consistency, but not completeness, with respect to queries and assertions. It is often equated with taxonomic hierarchies of classes.

The sixth chapter is dedicated to "Harvesting Intelligence in Multimedia Social Tagging Systems". As more people adopt tagging practices, social tagging systems (Flickr, YouTube, Del.icio.us, etc.) tend to form rich knowledge repositories that enable the extraction of patterns rejecting the way content semantics is perceived by the web users. This is of particular importance, especially in the case of multimedia content, since the availability of such content in the web is very high and its efficient retrieval using textual annotations or content-based automatically extracted metadata still remains a challenge. It is argued that complementing multimedia analysis techniques with knowledge drawn from web social annotations may facilitate multimedia content management. This chapter focuses on analyzing tagging patterns and combining them with content feature extraction methods, generating, thus, intelligence from multimedia social tagging systems. Emphasis is placed on using all available tracks of knowledge, that is tag co-occurrence together with semantic relations among tags and low-level features of the content. Towards this direction, a survey on the theoretical background and the adopted practices for analysis of multimedia social content are presented. A case study from Flickr illustrates the efficiency of the proposed approach.

The following six chapters focus on *User-Profile[5] Modeling and User Interactions in Information Retrieval Systems*.

An interesting technique for "User Profiles Modeling in Information Retrieval Systems" is explored in the seventh chapter. With the explosion of Internet technologies and data, the requirements imposed on information retrieval systems are increasing steadily in rapid manner. Of course, the vast number of documents in today's large databases and especially on the Web which causes notable problems when searching for concrete information making sometimes difficult to find satisfactory information that accurately matches user information needs even if it is present in the database. One of the key elements when searching the web is proper formulation of user queries. Search effectiveness can be seen as the accuracy of matching user information needs against the retrieved information. Personalized search applications can notably contribute to the improvement of web search effectiveness. It has been shown, that genetic programming can evolve search queries towards users interests captured by the means of relevance. In this chapter, the proposed user modelling technique is based on relevance estimation. The experimental results in web search framework with evolutionary query optimization is also detailed.

Another interesting study is provided in the eighth chapter entitled "Human–Web Interactions" addressing the human behavior on the web. In is worthy to mention that early conceptions of human web behavior essentially assumed a random nature of human actions. However, the recent findings revealed that human behavior in electronic environments exhibits bursts of activity followed by longer inactivity periods. This is being attributed to the conceptual prioritization of cognitive processes. In this chapter, web interactions are divided into segments of tasks having varying complexities and represented through a novel model that accurately captures them. The segmentation of human web interactions enables to observe and elucidate several pertinent behavioral aspects. One can observe how users form elemental and complex browsing patterns, how their behavior habituates, and how they utilize the web navigation space.

In Web Recommender Agents with Inductive Learning Capabilities, the issue of generating user-oriented Web recommendations is explored. It is true that early recommendations techniques have been based mainly on content-based and collaborative-filtering algorithms, that exploit a prefixed users profile to compare the interests of a user with the content of a

---

[5] A user profile (or simply profile when used in-context) is a collection of personal data, preferences and characteristics associated to a specific user. It refers therefore to the explicit digital representation of a person's identity.

Web site and with the profiles of other users. However, some recent proposals introduced the possibility to automatically construct the users profile by software agents able to monitor "over the shoulders" the users behaviour. This way, the profile can contain some useful information about not only the users interest but also the users behaviour. In this chapter, a new type of agent, called CILWEB, is provided with an inductive learning capability and an additional implication-based recommendation algorithm. The introduction of the implication-based recommendations gives to CILWEB agent the capability of better performing with respect to the traditional recommendation systems, as it is shown by some experimental results.

The chapter, "Capturing the Semantics of User interaction: A Review and Case Study", addresses the problematic gap between what computers can describe and what humans are capable of perceiving. This gap is most evident in the indexing of multimedia data such as images, video and sound where the low-level features are too semantically deficient to be of use from a typical users' perspective. On the other hand, users possess the ability to quickly examine and summarize these documents, even subconsciously. Examples include specifying relevance between a query and results, rating preferences in film databases, purchasing items from online retailers, and even browsing web sites. Data from these interactions, captured and stored in log files, can be interpreted to have semantic meaning, which proves indispensable when used in a collaborative setting where users share similar preferences or goals. In this chapter, several techniques for efficiently exploiting user interaction in its many forms for the generation and augmentation of semantic data in large databases are explored. A case study is presented which applies a popular technique, Latent Semantic Analysis, to improve retrieval on an image database.

The 11th chapter in this book is "Analysis of Usage Patterns in Large Multimedia Web Sites". As mentioned previously, user behavior in a website is a critical indicator of the web site's usability and success. Therefore, an understanding of usage patterns is essential to website design optimization. In this context, large multimedia websites pose a significant challenge for comprehension of the complex and diverse user behaviors they sustain. This is due to the complexity of analyzing and understanding user-data interactions in media-rich contexts. In this chapter, a novel multi-perspective approach for usability analysis of large media rich websites is presented. It consists of combining multimedia web content analysis with elements of web-log analysis and visualization/visual mining of web usage metadata. Multimedia content analysis allows direct estimation of the information-cues presented to a user by the web content. Analysis of web logs and usage-metadata, such as location, type, and frequency of interactions provides a complimentary perspective on the site's usage. The entire set of information is leveraged through powerful visualization and interactive querying techniques to provide analysis of usage patterns, measure of design quality, as well as the ability to rapidly identify problems in the web-site design. Experiments on media rich sites including the SkyServer – a large multimedia web-based astronomy information repository, demonstrate the efficacy and promise of the proposed approach.

"An Adaptation Framework for Web Multimedia" is provided in the 12th chapter. Here, a multimedia document is considered as composed of several media-objects that are presented to user/application with respect to certain spatio-temporal relationships defined over them (called also multimedia presentation). In Web environments, those media objects could be located onto different servers and hence pose the problem of delivering multimedia documents with respect to those constrains. In many situations, it is not always possible to support the presentation spatio-temporal constraints. This is due to noisy problems such as low bandwidth, or user preferences/prole as the lack of audio devise. One interesting alternative consists in adapting the presentation by substituting media elements by others media that are semantically equivalent. This adaptation is not obvious and could lead, if it is not carried out carefully, to a misunderstood presentation. This chapter deals with the problem of finding adequate multimedia presentation that fulfils spatio-temporal constraints.

More precisely, it first provides a spatio-temporal algebra for the composition of multimedia presentations before presenting a semantic adaptation strategy by means of substitution of media elements that preserves presentation semantics.

The last six chapters focus on *Advanced Information Security and Access Control Models.*

The 13th chapter is related to authentication protocols and is entitled "A Multifactor Secure Authentication System for Wireless Payment". Since organizations are deploying wireless based online payment applications to expand their business globally, the growing need of regulatory requirements for the protection of confidential data, and especially in internet based financial areas is increasing. Existing internet based authentication systems often use either the Web or the Mobile channel individually to confirm the claimed identity of the remote user. The vulnerability is that access is based on only single factor authentication which is not secure to protect user data. This chapter proposes a new protocol based on multifactor authentication system that is both secure and highly usable. It uses a novel approach based on Transaction Identification Code and SMS to enforce another security level with the traditional Login/password system. The system provides a highly secure environment that is simple to use and deploy with in a limited resources that does not require any change in infrastructure or underline protocol of wireless network. This Protocol for Wireless Payment is extended as a two way authentications system to satisfy the emerging market need of mutual authentication and also supports secure B2B communication which increases faith of the user and business organizations on wireless financial transaction using mobile devices.

Similarly, in "A Lightweight Authentication Protocol for Web Applications in Mobile Environments" chapter, another authentication approach is proposed for mobile environments. Here, the context is a bit different and is related to saving power and requiring reduced computation resources without loss of security due to the emergence of ubiquitous (mobile) Web applications, where the user works on wireless devices possibly with limited computation capacities and poor energy autonomy. Here, a new authentication scheme is explored requiring neither cryptographic algorithms nor one-way hash functions, as all the methods existing in the literature do, but resisting to all the major known attacks, thus improving the state of the art on the authentication schemes.

The 15th chapter "Developing Access Control Model of Web OLAP[6] over Trusted and Collaborative Data Warehouses",[7] proposes the design and development of Role-Based Access Control (RBAC) model for the Single Sign-On (SSO) Web-OLAP query spanning over multiple data warehouses (DWs). The model is based on Public Key Infrastructure (PKI) Authentication and Privilege Management Infrastructure (PMI); it presents a binding model of RBAC authorization based on dimension privilege specified in attribute certificate and user identification. Particularly, the way of attribute mapping between DW user authentication and privilege of dimensional access is illustrated. Here, a multi-agent system is applied to automate flexible and effective management of user authentication, role delegation as well as system accountability. The chapter culminates in the prototype system A-Cold (Access Control of web-OLAP over multiple DWs) that incorporates the OLAP features and authentication and authorization enforcement in the multi-user and multi-data warehouse environment.

In the 16th chapter entitled "Security in Distributed Collaborative Environments: Limitations and Solutions", the issue of establishing secure collaboration between heterogeneous

---

[6] OnLine analytical processing.

[7] Data warehouse is a repository of an organization's electronically stored data. Data warehouses are designed to facilitate reporting and analysis.

environment is explored where nomadic users with ubiquitous access to digital information and surrounding resources. The problem here is that the constraints of mobility and heterogeneity arise a number of crucial issues related to security, especially authentication access control and privacy. In this chapter, the trust paradigm is deeply explored, especially the transitive capability to enable a trust peer to peer collaboration and so that each organization sets its own security policy to recognize (authenticate) users of a trusted community and to provide them a local access (access control). The trust transitivity between peers will allow users to gain a broad, large and controlled access inside the pervasive environment. In addition, the problem of user's privacy is studied. In fact, in pervasive and ubiquitous environments, nomadic users gather and exchange certificates or credentials allowing them to have rights to access, by transitivity, unknown and trusted environments. These signed documents embeds increasing number of attributes that require to be filtered out according to such contextual situation. A new morph signature is proposed enabling each certificate owner to preserve his/her privacy by disclosing or blinding some sensitive attributes according to a particular situation.

In the 17th chapter, entitled "A Low-Cost and Secure Solution for E-Commerce", a new architecture for remote banking and e-commerce applications is provided. The proposed solution is designed to be low cost and provides some good guarantees of security for a client and his bank issuer. Indeed, the main problem for an issuer is to identify and authenticate one client (a cardholder) using his personal computer through the web when this client wants to access to remote banking services or when he wants to pay on a e-commerce site equipped with 3D-secure payment solution. The proposed solution described in this chapter is MasterCard Chip Authentication Program compliant and was experimented in the project called SOPAS. The main contribution of this system consists in the use of a smartcard with a Inter Integrated Circuit (I2C)[8] bus that pilots a terminal only equipped with a screen and a keyboard. During the use of services, the user types his PIN code on the keyboard and all the security part of the transaction is performed by the chip of the smartcard. None information of security stays on the personal computer and a dynamic token created by the card is sent to the bank and verified by the front end.

The last chapter in the book is entitled "Hyperchaotic Encryption for Secure E-Mail Communication". In this chapter, secure computer communication based on synchronized hyperchaotic maps is presented. In particular, a model-matching approach from nonlinear control theory is adopted to synchronize the outputs of two coupled hyperchaotic Rössler maps. An application to secure e-mail communication for confidential information is given. By using a hyperchaotic encryption scheme, the output synchronization of hyperchaotic Rössler maps looks indeed suitable for encryption, transmission, and decryption of information.

3 Acknowledgment

We hope this book motivates lot of people to take the next steps beyond building models to implementing, evaluating, comparing, and extend proposed approaches and applications. Many people helped us that this book becomes a reality. We

---

[8] It a simple bi-directional 2-wire bus for efficient inter-IC control. It is used for performing communication functions between intelligent control devices (e.g., microcontrollers), general-purpose circuits (e.g., LCD drivers, remote I/O ports, memories) and application-oriented circuits (e.g., digital tuning and signal processing circuits for radio and video systems).

would first like to gratefully acknowledge and sincerely thank all the reviewers for their timely and insightful valuable comments and criticism of the manuscripts that greatly improved the quality of the final chapter versions. Of course, thanks are also due to the authors, who provided excellent chapters and timely revisions. Finally, we are grateful to the editors of the Advanced Information and Knowledge Processing (AI and KP) series of Springer Verlag for their trust in us, their efforts, patience, and editorial work during the production of this book.

4 About the Editors

Richard Chbeir received his Ph.D. in Computer Science from the INSA DE LYON-FRANCE in 2001. He is member of IEEE and ACM since 1999. He is currently an Associate Professor in the Computer Science Department of the Bourgogne University, Dijon, France. His research interests are in the areas of distributed multimedia database management, XML similarity and rewriting, spatio-temporal applications, indexing methods, and multimedia access control models. Dr. Chbeir has published (more than 40 peer-reviewed publications) in international journals and books (IEEE Transactions on SMC, Information Systems, Journal on Data Semantics, Journal of Systems Architecture, etc.), conferences (ER, WISE, SOFSEM, EDBT, ACM SAC, Visual, IEEE CIT, FLAIRS, PDCS, etc.), and has served on the program committees of several international conferences (SOFSEM, AINA, IEEE SITIS, ACM SAC, IEEE ISSPIT, EuroPar, SBBD, etc.). He has been organizing many international conferences and workshops (ACM SAC, ICDIM, CSTST, SITIS, etc.). He is currently the Vice-Chair of the ACM SIGAPP and the Chair of its French Chapter.

Youakim Badr received his Ph.D. in Information Systems from the French National Institute for Applied Sciences in Lyon (INSA of Lyon). In 2004, he joined the faculty of the INSA of Lyon as Assistant Professor of Computer Science. Dr. Badr has worked extensively in the field of coupling XML documents and Object-Relational Databases. Through his research he has acquired skills in fields such as Interoperability, Modeling, System Architectures and Networking, and their application to various domains such as Business Processes, Supply Chains, Productions Systems and Virtual Enterprises. His current academic research interests include systems in both the service sector and ICT. In particular, he studies the ecosystem of services and the multidisciplinary modeling approach to design services through the integration of ICT, strategy and processes. He leads the Service-Oriented Enterprise research team which combines industrial and computer engineering approaches. Dr. Badr is vigorously involved in a series of international conferences. He served as General Co-Chair of ICDIM'07, CSTST'08, Programme Chair of INCOS'09, Track chair of IEEE DEST10, AINA10, ICETET'09, ICITST08 and International Program Member of IAS'08, SITIS'07, JFO'07, WCNC'07 and ECWS'06. He is a professional member of ACM, IEEE Services Computing Community, MILRLabs/

France coordinator, IEEE-SMC Technical Committee on Soft Computing, Digital Ecosystems Community, a member of OW2 and the Service Sciences working group of the Networked European Software and Services Initiative (NESSI).

Ajith Abraham received his Ph.D. degree in computer science from Monash University, Melbourne, Australia. His research and development experience includes over 18 years in the Industry and Academia. He works in a multidisciplinary environment involving machine intelligence, network security, sensor networks, e-commerce, Web intelligence, Web services, computational grids, data mining, and applications to various real-world problems. He has given more than 30 plenary lectures and conference tutorials in these areas. He authored or coauthored more than 500 publications. He works with the Norwegian University of Science and Technology, Norway and also coordinate the activities of the Machine Intelligence Research Labs (MIR Labs), which has representation in 47 countries. He is the Co-Chair of the IEEE Systems Man and Cybernetics Society Technical Committee on Soft Computing. He is the founder of several conference series, which are now sponsored by IEEE and also serves the editorial board of over 30 international Journals.

Aboul Ella Hassanien received his B.Sc. with honours in 1986 and M.Sc. degree in 1993, both from Ain Shams University, Faculty of Science, Ain Sham University, Egypt. On September 1998, he received his doctoral degree from the Department of Computer Science, Graduate School of Science and Engineering, Tokyo Institute of Technology, Japan. He is currently a Professor at Cairo University, Faculty of Computer and Information. He has authored/coauthored over 120 research publications in peer-reviewed reputed journals and conference proceedings. He serves on the editorial board and reviewer of number of journals and on the program committee of several international conferences and he has editing/written more than 18 books. He has received the excellence younger researcher award from Kuwait University. He has also guest edited several special issues on various topics. His research interests include, rough set theory, wavelet theory, medical image analysis, multimedia data mining, and cyber security.

5 List of Reviewers

Ahmed El Oualkadi (Universit Catholique de Louvain, Belgium)
Akira Asano (Hiroshima University, Japan)
Alfredo Cuzzocrea (University of Calabria, Italy)
Andries Engelbrecht (University of Pretoria, South Africa)
Bernard Grabot (LGP-ENIT, France)
Carlos Alberto Reyes-Garcia (IInstituto Nacional de Astrofisica Optica Y Electronica-INAOE, Mexico)
Chi Shen (University of Kentucky, USA)
Chrisa Tsinaraki (Technical University of Crete, Greece)
Christine Verdier (University of Grenoble, France)

Contents

Chapter 1
Contextual and Conceptual Information Retrieval and Navigation on the Web

Bénédicte Le Grand, Marie-Aude Aufaure, and Michel Soto

Abstract The goal of this chapter is to propose a methodology and tools to enhance information retrieval and navigation on the Web through contextual and conceptual help. This methodology provides users with an extended navigation space by adding a conceptual and a semantic layer above Web data. The conceptual layer is made of Galois lattices which cluster Web pages into concepts according to their common features (in particular their textual content). These lattices represent the *Global Conceptual Context* of Web pages. An additional navigation layer is provided by ontologies which are connected to the conceptual level through specific concepts of the lattices. Users may navigate transparently within each of these three layers and go from one to another very easily.

However, the navigation within Galois lattices may be difficult as the number of concepts grows very fast with the number of Web pages. The second contribution of this chapter consists in providing tools to help users navigate within a complex conceptual lattice. A new similarity measure is proposed to find the most relevant concept to start a navigation or to choose the most relevant concept to visit from a given navigation point. This similarity measure is based on Jiang and Conrath's measure used for ontology matching, extended to reflect conceptual information. This chapter illustrates these methodology and tools for Web information retrieval and navigation through example experimentations and presents future research directions-visualization in particular.

B. Le Grand (✉)
LIP 6 Laboratory – Université Pierre et Marie Curie – 104, rue du Président Kennedy – 75016 Paris, France
e-mail: Benedicte.Le-Grand@lip6.fr

M.-A. Aufaure
Ecole Centrale Paris, MAS Laboratory, SAP Business Objects Chair on Business Intelligence, Grande Voie des Vignes 92295 Chatenay-Malabry, France
e-mail: Marie-Aude.Aufaure@ecp.fr

M. Soto
Université René Descartes (Paris 5) – 45, rue des Saints Pères – 75006 Paris, France
e-mail: Michel.Soto@lip6.fr

R. Chbeir et al., *Emergent Web Intelligence: Advanced Information Retrieval*, Advanced Information and Knowledge Processing, DOI 10.1007/978-1-84996-074-8_1,
© Springer-Verlag London Limited 2010

1

1.1 Introduction: Goals and Challenges

This chapter presents a contextual and conceptual methodology to enhance information retrieval and navigation on the Web. The complexity of these tasks is due to many factors, among which the volume of data as well as its lack of structure and semantics. This chapter therefore proposes to use conceptual analysis in conjunction with semantics in order to provide contextual answers to users' queries and to help their information retrieval and their navigation on the Web. Galois lattices and ontologies are good candidates to address the structure and the semantic issues respectively. Both the textual content of data and additional information provided by ontologies are taken into account in this approach. Moreover, a new similarity measure is defined in order to help selecting relevant concepts for navigation and information retrieval.

The proposed architecture [19] provides users with an extended navigation environment consisting of raw resources (i.e. Web pages), and two additional layers: the conceptual and the semantic layers, as shown on Fig. 1.1.

The lower layer is made of Web pages (or images, specific sections of Web pages, etc.).

The intermediate layer is the conceptual layer, made of Galois lattices built from these pages. Galois lattices contain concepts which cluster Web pages according to their common features. This layer is directly connected to the original data and provides them with a structure they do not necessarily have as Web pages.

Finally, on top of this architecture, the semantic layer contains general or domain-specific ontologies whose ontological concepts are related to concepts of Galois lattices through a semantic coordination as described in Section 1.2.3.3.

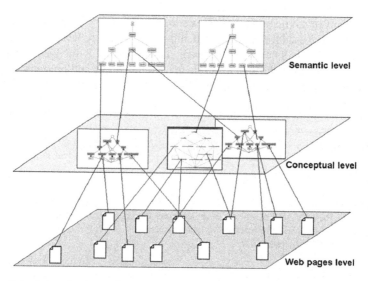

Fig. 1.1 Extended navigation environment

With this approach, users may navigate at a more abstract level than original Web pages, by easily traveling within the conceptual or semantic levels – and go from one to another transparently. Two types of information retrieval may be distinguished depending on whether the research goal is precisely formulated or not (both cases are addressed in this chapter, see Section 1.4.4). The information provided by Galois lattices and ontologies is complementary to intrinsic information about Web pages. Moreover, ontologies are a potential bridge between non overlapping Galois lattices.

This chapter is organized as follows. Section 1.2 formalizes the joint use of Galois lattice and ontologies as *conceptual contexts*. A new methodology to enhance information retrieval and navigation on the Web based on these conceptual contexts is proposed in Section 1.3. In order to further help navigation within the conceptual layer, a similarity measure among concepts of the lattice is defined in Section 1.4. Finally, this chapter concludes with perspectives towards lattices' *visual footprints*.

1.2 Conceptual Contexts and Relationship with Ontologies

This section briefly introduces Galois lattices, before defining *global* and *instantaneous conceptual contexts*, based on Formal Concept Analysis (FCA) and Galois lattices in particular.

1.2.1 Introduction to Formal Concept Analysis and Galois Lattices

FCA is a mathematical approach to data analysis which provides information with structure. FCA may be used for conceptual clustering as shown in [9] and [33].

The notion of Galois lattice to describe a relationship between two sets is the basis of a set of conceptual classification methods. This notion was introduced by [2] and [1]. Galois lattices group objects into classes that materialize concepts of the domain under study. Individual objects are discriminated according to the properties they have in common. This algorithm is very powerful as it performs a semantic classification. The algorithm we implemented is based on [13].

First, Galois lattices basic concepts are introduced. Consider two finite sets D (a set of objects) and M (the set of these objects' properties also called attributes), and a binary relation $R \subseteq D \times M$ between these two sets. Let o be an object of D and p a property of M. We have $o R p$ if the object o has the property p. According to Wille's terminology [34]:

$$Fc = (D, M, R) \tag{1.1}$$

is a formal context which corresponds to a unique Galois lattice, representing natural groupings of G and M elements.

Let P(D) be a powerset of D and P(M) a powerset of M. Each element of the lattice is a couple, also called concept, noted (O, A). A concept is composed of two sets $O \in P(D)$ and $A \in P(M)$ which satisfy the two following properties (1.2):

$$A = f(O) \, where \, f(O) = \{a \in M \,|\, \forall o \in O, oRa\}$$
$$O = f'(A) \, where \, f'(A) = \{o \in D \,|\, \forall a \in A, oRa\} \qquad (1.2)$$

O is the *extent* of the concept and A is its *intent*.

A partial order on concepts is defined as follows (1.3):

$$Let \, C1 = (O_1, A_1) \, and \, C2 = (O_2, A_2),$$
$$C1 < C2 \Leftrightarrow A1 \subseteq A_2 \Leftrightarrow O_2 \subseteq O1 \qquad (1.3)$$

In the context of the Web, *objects* may be pages or images and *properties* the most frequent terms contained in these pages or annotations related to these images. The corresponding Galois lattice therefore consists of concepts comprising sets of Web pages and images (objects) described by the common terms they contain or their common metadata (common properties). The term *concept* has been formally defined previously in this section but it can be intuitively understood as an abstraction built on multiple objects sharing common properties.

1.2.2 Related Work on FCA and Ontologies

The previous section introduced Galois lattices which play an important role in the proposed methodology for information retrieval and navigation on the Web as described later in this chapter. Ontologies are the other essential actors as they constitute the semantic layer in this conceptual and contextual architecture.

In computer science, the word *ontology*, borrowed from philosophy, represents a set of precisely defined terms (vocabulary) about a specific domain, accepted by this domain's community, as well as the properties of these terms and the relationships among them. Ontologies may also comprise reasoning capabilities for inference purposes. An ontology thus enables people to agree upon the meaning of terms used in a precise domain, knowing that several terms may represent the same concept (synonyms) and several concepts may be described by the same term (ambiguity). Ontologies are at the heart of information retrieval from nomadic objects, from the Internet and from heterogeneous data sources; languages have been developed such as OWL in the Semantic Web initiative [25].

With regard to the state of the art, many research works apply concept lattices to information retrieval [26] and to association rules extraction [15]. Formal concepts can be seen as relevant documents for a given query.

The introduction of a domain ontology, combined with concept lattices to enhance information retrieval is more recent. The authors of [22, 23] propose an approach based on Formal Concept Analysis to classify and search relevant data sources for a given query; this work is applied to bioinformatics data. A concept lattice is built according to the metadata associated to data sources. Then, a concept built from a given query is classified in this concept lattice. In this approach, query refinement is performed using domain ontology.

The refinement process of OntoRefiner, dedicated to Semantic Web Portals [29], is based on the use of a domain ontology to build a Galois Lattice for the query refinement process. The domain ontology avoids building the whole lattice.

The CREDO system [8] allows the user to query Web documents and to see the results in a browsable concept lattice. This system is useful to quickly retrieve items with the intended meaning, and to highlight the documents' content.

Finally, in [11], the authors investigate methods for automatically relaxing over-constrained queries based on domain knowledge and user preferences. Their framework combines query refinement and relaxation in order to provide a personalized access to heterogeneous RDF data.

Most approaches presented above address precise queries. On the contrary, the method proposed here is also adapted to imprecise and user-centered queries. Moreover, it is not only dedicated to information retrieval or navigation: it can also be used to populate ontologies, compare documents through their lattices or provide a personalized navigation among heterogeneous documents. It is also an interesting means to connect several non-overlapping Galois lattices, using the semantic layer as a bridge.

1.2.3 Definition of Conceptual Context

This section first introduces the general term of *context*. The notions of *global* and *instantaneous conceptual contexts* are then defined, which rely on Galois lattices and ontologies.

1.2.3.1 Notion of Context

Context is an abstract notion and cannot be precisely defined as it only makes sense when it is linked to a particular situation. Human beings implicitly associate a context to a set of actions, an attitude, etc. In situations of everyday life, context surrounds and gives meaning to something else. Some definitions of context have emerged in cognitive psychology, philosophy and areas of computer science like natural language processing.

The concept of formal context was introduced by McCarthy [20, 21]. According to [12], "a context is a theory of the world which encodes an individual's subjective perspective about it". This theory is partial, incomplete, and approximate as the world is never described in full detail. Context is a key issue for many research communities like artificial intelligence, mobile computing or problem solving

[7, 32]. In artificial intelligence, means to interact between contexts are defined by rules allowing navigation from one context to another [14]. Contexts can be represented by various formalisms such as conceptual graphs, topic maps, description logics with OWL extensions, etc.

As for the Semantic Web, context is often used either as a filter for disambiguation in information retrieval [11], to define contextual Web services [24] or as a means to integrate or merge different ontologies [6, 10].

In the following, the *conceptual context* is defined, with a distinction between the *global* and the *instantaneous* conceptual contexts. The global context (Gc) is intended to describe the data individually as well as the relationships between data. Whereas the global context focuses on the conceptual level, the instantaneous context (Ic) is directly related to user's queries and navigation and involves both the conceptual and the semantic layers.

1.2.3.2 Global Conceptual Context

In order to comply with the role described above, the global conceptual context (Gc) of a selection of heterogeneous data sources is defined as the Galois Lattice constructed from them.

Let W, a set of heterogeneous data sources with $W \neq \emptyset$ and K an arbitrary function applied to W for the extraction of W's properties.

From (1.1), the global contextual context of W is defined as:

$$Gc = (K(W), K(W)', R) \qquad (1.4)$$

where $D = K(W)$ and $M = K(W)'$ and $K(W) \subseteq W$.

Thus $K(W)$ is the set of data sources from which K has extracted properties.

For example, the properties extracted by K on textual documents are the most frequent and significant nouns. In this example, $K(W)$ is the set of documents and $K(W)$' is the set of the most frequent and significant nouns found in these documents.

Properties:

- Uniqueness

A global conceptual context is unique since:

$$Gci = Gcj \Leftrightarrow (Ki = Kj \text{ and } Wi = Wj) \qquad (1.5)$$

Thus, changing K and/or W leads to a different global conceptual context.

- Overlapping

$$Overlap\,(Gci, Gcj) \Rightarrow Wi \cap Wj \neq \emptyset \qquad (1.6)$$

Overlapping reflects the semantic proximity between several global conceptual concepts. Two lattices, Gc_i and Gc_j, overlap, if there are objects which belong both to some concepts of Gc_i, and some concepts of Gc_j. Thus, existing overlapping allows context switching for a better fit with the instantaneous user's needs.

1.2.3.3   Instantaneous Conceptual Context

As explained above in Section 1.2.1, Galois lattices are built in order to represent the content of heterogeneous data sources and provide them with a structure. These lattices may be linked to ontologies thanks to a semantic coordination performed by matching Galois concepts with the semantic concepts from the ontology(ies) according to the common terms contained in their intents.

The semantic layer provides alternative ways of traveling from one global conceptual context to another, with the instantaneous context (Ic). It also makes it possible to reach isolated global contexts.

The *instantaneous conceptual context* represents the current position of a user in the navigation process, within the semantic or the conceptual levels. The user's initial instantaneous context corresponds to the result of a *query*. The definition of a *query* is quite large and represents a user's information need in general: it may be a *mapping query* or a *navigating query*. Users formulate their queries with mapping queries in order to get a starting point of navigation. They might then refine or generalize the result of a mapping query using a navigating query.

Let CGc the set of all the formal concepts of a global conceptual context Gc and Q a non finite set of user's queries on CGc.

Let M an arbitrary function, for the mapping of a user's query to a concept of Gc:

$$M : Q \rightarrow C_{Gc}$$
$$M(q) = c \tag{1.7}$$

Whatever the query language is, the M function processes the query and returns a concept of Gc answering this query. Mapping queries are typically formulated with keywords. In this case, the M function computes the intent's best match with these keywords.

Let N an arbitrary function, for the navigation from one concept of Gc to another:

$$N : C_{Gc} \rightarrow C_{Gc}$$
$$N(c) = c' \tag{1.8}$$

with $c \neq c'$.

The concept c' is either more general or more specific than the concept c if users respectively generalize or refine the result of their last query. Navigating in a Galois lattice is critical, thus the fundamental purpose of N is to help users navigate from a concept to another. For example, c' might be the semantically nearest concept from c, as proposed in Section 1.4.

From this starting point, the user may navigate within the global context: her instantaneous context changes every time she travels to another concept through the generalization or specialization links of the global context; the instantaneous context may thus be seen as a vehicle which enables the user to go from one global context to another.

An instantaneous conceptual context (Ic) is defined by:

$$Ic_i = (q_i, c_i) \tag{1.9}$$

with $q_i \in Q$ and $c_i \in C_{Gc}$ and where c_i is the answer to q_i.
Properties:

- Because of the explorative and iterative features of the information retrieval process, the main property of this instantaneous conceptual context is that it evolves every time the user modifies, refines or generalizes his/her query.
- The variation of the instantaneous conceptual context is bounded by the global conceptual context. A semantic layer is therefore needed to enable users to travel from a conceptual context to another.

1.3 Methodology for a Conceptual and Contextual Information Retrieval and Navigation on the Web

This methodology illustrated on Fig. 1.2 is divided into two steps:

- Offline pre-treatment of heterogeneous data sources (Galois lattices and semantic coordination with ontologies).
- Online contextual processing of users' information needs and provision of navigation help (similarity measure).

The pre-treatment phase consists in computing a conceptual lattice from Web pages in order to build the global conceptual context. Each concept of the lattice corresponds to a cluster of Web pages with common properties. This methodology is presented here for the Web but it can be applied to any type of data sources such as databases, email, personal documents and images, etc.

Whereas the processing of data sources is achieved offline, information retrieval is performed in real-time: users formulate queries with terms from the ontology. This cluster of terms is compared to the concepts' labels and the best-matching concepts are returned. A similarity measure may also be used in order to get more relevant answers as explained in Section 1.4. Users may then navigate within the enhanced navigation environment illustrated on Fig. 1.1.

This method has several advantages:

- Ontologies enable enhanced query formulation and help return more relevant results.
- The added semantics may be adapted to the target user(s).
- Results are provided according to available data. In particular, query refinements depend on underlying data.

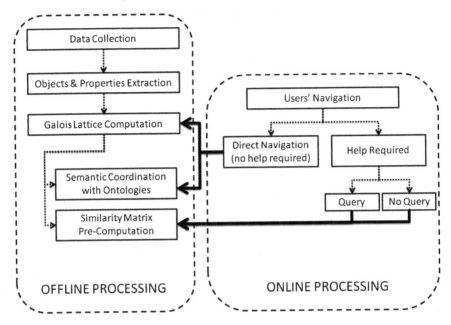

Fig. 1.2 Methodology

1.3.1   Step 1: Offline Pre-treatment

This first step consists in:

- Selecting a set of heterogeneous data sources.
- Parsing data sources: generation of input for the Galois lattice (generation of objects and properties, if possible normalized terms from a thesaurus or an ontology).
- Building the Galois lattice (i.e. the global conceptual context).
- Performing the semantic coordination between Galois lattices' concepts and ontological concepts. The normalized label of a concept consists in the normalized labels of all its extent's objects.

1.3.2   Step 2: Online Contextual Processing of Users' Queries

Once the global conceptual context is built, the initial instantaneous conceptual context is computed online for each user's query.

If the information need is precisely formulated with keywords (through a mapping query) the answer is the concept in the lattice whose properties contained in the intent best match the query's keywords. If no concept provides a perfect match, the more relevant concepts are proposed to the user through a refinement

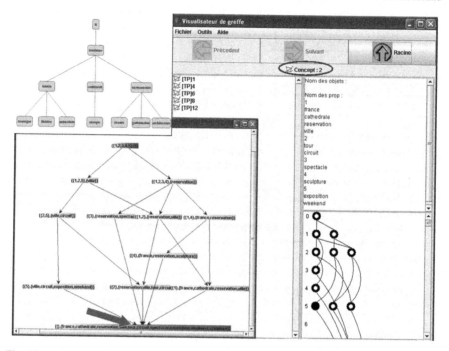

Fig. 1.3 Example of navigation environment

or a generalization of the query, according to available data. The answer to a user's query gives the initial position of the instantaneous context. Then, the user is free to navigate either within other nodes of the lattice – and thus go to more specific or more general concepts – or within the ontology(ies) as explained in Section 1.1. Figure 1.3 shows an example of navigation environment which combines the conceptual (bottom left corner of the figure) and the semantic (upper left corner of the figure) levels.

If the user's information need is not precisely defined, the system should propose a relevant starting point for the navigation. This is precisely one of the goals of the similarity measure proposed in the following section.

1.4 Enhancing Navigation in the Lattice – Similarity Measure

This section presents the requirements for a similarity measure between concepts of a Galois lattice as well as a state of the art of existing similarity measures for ontology matching. The similarity measure proposed in this chapter is an extension of one of those allowing the exploitation of both semantic and topological information provided by the ontology and the lattice respectively. Finally the use of this metric to enhance navigation within a Galois lattice is explained.

1.4.1   Requirements

The three-tier architecture presented earlier (see Fig. 1.1) provides a relevant and contextualized answer to users' information needs. They may navigate transparently through these levels and may go easily from one to another. Galois lattices are very interesting in this context as explained in Section 1.2.3.3. Nevertheless, finding the initial navigation point (i.e. the initial instantaneous conceptual context in the lattice) or navigating within a Galois lattice may be difficult. Indeed, the number of concepts increases with the number of objects and properties, which makes them very complex and difficult to interpret beyond a certain size. In order to cope with this complexity, some help is necessary to guide users in their choice for the navigation starting point and for the next visited concept, in terms of relevance to their current position. One possible approach consists in reducing the size of the lattice [16, 31]. However, the semantically "closest" concept from a given navigation point may not be one of the parent or children nodes. In order to provide this help, a similarity measure between the concepts of the lattice is necessary and an adequate similarity measure is therefore needed.

1.4.2   State of the Art on Semantic Similarity Measures

This section briefly presents a selection of similarity measures used for ontology matching. In particular, approaches based on *distances* and on *Informational Content* are introduced.

In the ontology domain, semantic similarity measures may rely on distances using hierarchical links of the ontology. Two widely used similarity measures [27, 35] are presented here. Their computation is based on the minimum number of edges which separate a concept from another.

Rada [27] specifies a distance between two concepts c_1 and c_2 by counting the minimum number of arcs from c_1 to c_2. The similarity is measured as follows:

$$Sim_{Rada}(c_1, c_2) = 1/1 + dist(c_1, c_2) \qquad (1.10)$$

where $dist(c_1, c_2) = minPath(c_1, c_2)$.

In the same direction, Wu and Palmer [35] define the similarity as a function of the distance of these concepts (and of their smallest generalizing concept) to the root:

$$Sim_{W \& P}(c_1, c_2) = 2^* depth(sgc(c_1, c_2))/depth(c_1) + depth(c_2) \qquad (1.11)$$

where $depth(c)$ is the number of edges separating $sgc(c_1, c_2)$, the smallest concept generalizing c_1 and c_2, from the root and $depth(c_i)$ the number of edges separating c_i from the root using a path containing $sgc(c_1, c_2)$.

These measures are easy to implement and give an idea on the semantic relationship between concepts. However, they do not take into account the content of the concept itself and this might minimize concepts' contributions in terms of information.

Another direction to define a similarity measure is therefore to consider the *Informational Content (IC)* and jointly use the ontology and the corpus. The informational content expresses the relevance of the concept in the corpus by taking into account its generality or specificity. Thus, the frequency is obtained by the frequency of the concept occurrence and the subsumed concepts. Two widely used measures in this category are presented here.

Resnik [28] defines the semantic similarity between two concepts by the shared informational content, which is obtained by the informational content of the most specific concept subsuming the two concepts in the ontology (the smallest generalizing concept). It is defined as follows:

$$Sim_{Resnik}(c_1, c_2) = IC(sgc\ (c_1, c_2)) \qquad (1.12)$$

where $IC(c) = -log(P(c))$, $P(c)$ the probability of finding a concept based on frequency calculations among all concepts and $sgc(c_1, c_2)$ the smallest generalizing concept of c_1 and c_2.

The measure of Jiang and Conrath [17] considers the information content of the two concepts and the information content of their most specific common subsumer:

$$Sim_{J\ \&\ C}(c_1, c_2) = 1/dist(c_1, c_2) \qquad (1.13)$$

where $dist(c_1, c_2) = IC(c_1) + IC(c_2) - (2.IC(sgc(c_1, c_2)))$.

In recent studies, other similarity measures have been derived from these measures. Among them, Zargayouna and Salotti's measure [36] extends Wu and Palmer's by adding a specificity component and Blanchard et al.'s [3] take into account the taxonomy and the notion of *quantity of information*.

1.4.3 Conceptual Similarity Measure

The similarity measure proposed in this chapter aims at evaluating the similarity between concepts from a Galois lattice built for Web pages clustering purposes. This measure is an extension of Jiang and Conrath's measure used for ontological concepts, adapted to get a better insight of the Galois lattice.

The objective of this similarity measure is both to enhance navigation in the lattice and to reduce the number of visited concepts; it also helps users choose their starting navigation point in the lattice. In particular, the information brought by the intent of a concept is quantified. The evaluation of the context shared by two concepts is based on the frequency of their common elements.

The conceptual similarity proposed in this chapter between two concepts of a lattice depends on their content (based on *Average Information* defined below), their topological neighborhood and their depth in the Galois lattice. This similarity measure is adapted to Galois lattices' concepts only – and not to ontological concepts. The reason for this focus on conceptual concepts is that they are directly associated to actual Web pages, which is not necessarily the case of ontological concepts. The initial navigation point is therefore selected among the concepts of the Galois lattice (rather than concepts from the ontologies) in order to be related to actual data.

The similarity measure proposed in this chapter takes into account concepts' content as it relies on the notion of *Average Information* (*AI*). The Average Information is based on the *Informational Content* (*IC*) defined in Section 1.4.2 and evaluates the weight of terms within pages of a Web site.

As explained in Section 1.2.1, each concept in Galois lattice consists of a couple (extent, intent). The Average Information of each concept is based on the frequency of the intent's terms. Let a concept c with an extent E and an intent I. The Average Information of c is defined as the IC of c's intent (I):

$$AI(c) = IC(I) = -log(P(I)) \qquad (1.14)$$

where $P(I)$ is the probability to find the intent's terms (i.e. frequent terms) simultaneously in the Web pages corpus.

This similarity measure also takes into account the position of the concepts within the lattice (i.e. a topological information) with the $depth(c_i)$ parameter i.e. the number of edges from c_i to the most specific concept of the lattice. The integration of this depth parameter exploits the generalization/specialization property of a Galois lattice: the lower a concept is in the lattice the more specialized it is. The Galois lattice structure is also taken into account through the use of the average information of the nearest common ancestor of the two involved concepts.

Let c_1 and c_2 two concepts of the Galois lattice. The similarity measure between c_1 and c_2 is defined as (16):

$$Sim(c_1, c_2) = \frac{1}{AI(c_1). depth(c_1) + AI(c_2). depth(c_2) - 2AI(sgc(c_1, c_2. depth(sgc(c_1, c_2)))} \qquad (1.15)$$

where $sgc(c_1, c_2)$ is the smallest generalizing concept of the two concepts c_1 and c_2 i.e. the nearest common ancestor of c_1 and c_2.

1.4.4 Navigation Help

The similarity measure presented in this chapter facilitates users' navigation within a Galois lattice. Two phases may be distinguished: navigation initialization and navigation itself.

1.4.4.1   Navigation Initialization

This phase calculates the most significant concept (noted SC for *Starting Concept*), to be used as an entry point in the Galois lattice. This concept has an extent (E_{SC}), and an intent (I_{SC}). Users may perform either an exploration without a specific query or an accurate information research. In the following these two situations are described.

Without a User's Query

This is the main added value of the proposed similarity measure: from a given Galois lattice, it defines an *analytical conceptual footprint* of the lattice by finding the most significant concept of the lattice.

   This analytical conceptual footprint, corresponding to SC, is defined as the concept which is, in average, the nearest concept from all other concepts of the lattice (i.e. the most similar). This Starting Concept is therefore the most "central" concept, which makes it a relevant starting point for navigating in the lattice.

   Thus if the user does not formulate any query and only wants to explore a set of Web pages, SC is the concept having the highest total average similarity with the all the objects of the lattice:

$$SC = c_i \ such \ as \ Sim_i^{ta} = Max \ (Sim_j^{ta}) \ for \ j = 1 \ to \ G, \qquad (1.16)$$

with $Sim_i^{ta} = Average(Sim(c_i, c_k))$ for $k = 1$ to G and $k \neq i$.

With a User's Request

In this case, the user has formulated a query with R terms from the ontology $((p_1, p_2, \ldots, p_R)$, as explained in Section 1.3). The set of keywords chosen by the user constitutes the intent of the *Target Concept* noted TC. In the lattice, the starting concept SC, selected to start the navigation, is the concept whose intent contains the maximum number of elements in common with TC's intent. This intent is made of all the terms of the user's query and noted $I_{TC} = \{p_1, p_2, \ldots, p_R\}$.

   If several concepts in the lattice have the same number of researched properties, SC is chosen among these candidate concepts according to the importance of these properties for the user (in this case, the user needs to rank these properties e.g. by assigning weights to them).

1.4.4.2   Navigation

During the navigation in the lattice, users may follow the generalization and specialization links of the lattice from their current navigation point (noted CC: *Current Concept*). However, users might need a hint when leaving CC to explore other concepts. The objective is thus to indicate the semantically nearest concept from CC.

Indeed, the most similar concept from *CC* seems to be the most relevant next step for the navigation (and it might be neither a parent nor a child node from *CC*). Similarity between each couple of concepts of the lattice can be pre-calculated. It is then possible to indicate to the user the value of the similarity of *CC* with all the other concepts of the lattice, in descending order for example. During navigation, uniqueness of the proposed concept is not necessary like in the initialization phase. Thus, several concepts may be proposed to the user provided ergonomic constraints are satisfied.

1.4.5 Experimentation

In this section, the two-steps methodology presented above is illustrated with a corpus of Web pages related to tourism.

Step 1: Offline Pre-treatment

- The selected data sources are a corpus of Web pages related to tourism.
- The *K* function (defined in Section 1.2.3.2) extracts to the most frequent terms which appear in Web pages of the corpus. A thesaurus dedicated to tourism (the World-Tourism Organization thesaurus) was used to perform the most frequent terms' extraction. The result of *K* applied to the corpus is a set of pages and, for each page, a set of most frequent terms found in the page. In the Galois terminology each Web page is an *object* and each term of the page is a *property* of this object. The extracted objects and properties are gathered in a database used for the construction of a Galois lattice. An incremental algorithm based on [13] was implemented to build a lattice where each concept is described by its extent (a set of Web pages) and its intent (common terms among the extent's Web pages). The Hasse diagram of the resulting lattice is illustrated on Fig. 1.4.

Step 2: Online Contextual Processing of Users' Queries Let a user query formulated with the following keywords: *holiday*, *trip* and *renting*. The intent of the

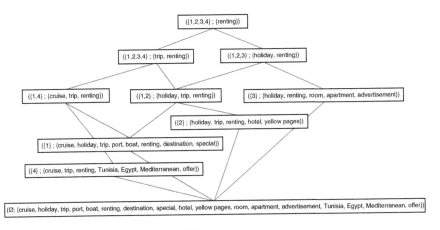

Fig. 1.4 Galois lattice built from tourism Web pages

target concept is thus $I_{TC} = \{holiday, trip, renting\}$. In this case, one of the lattice's concepts matches exactly: $(\{1, 2\}; \{holiday, trip, renting\})$, which will thus become the navigation starting point.

If the user wants to navigate from this concept, she can choose a link of the lattice to go to a more specific or a more general concept. In this example, she can choose between two parent concepts:

- $(\{1, 2, 4\}, \{trip, renting\})$,
- $(\{1, 2, 3\}, \{holiday, renting\})$

and between two children concepts:

- $(\{2\}, \{holiday, trip, renting, Hotel, yellow pages\})$,
- $(\{1\}, \{cruise, holiday, trip, harbor, boat, renting, destination, promotion\})$.

Several questions arise: how choose between several parent concepts without having to select some properties? How choose between several children without having to select some pages? Moreover, could the most relevant concept to carry on the navigation be neither a child nor a parent of the current node, i.e. a concept which is not linked to the current concept by a link of the lattice? (e.g. a sibling such as the concept $(\{1, 4\}, \{cruise, trip, renting\})$)?

In order to answer these questions, the value of the similarity measure between the current concept and all other concepts of the lattice is computed in order to help the user make a choice to carry on her navigation. All these values are presented in a decreasing order as shown on the bottom right corner of Fig. 1.5. In this case, the

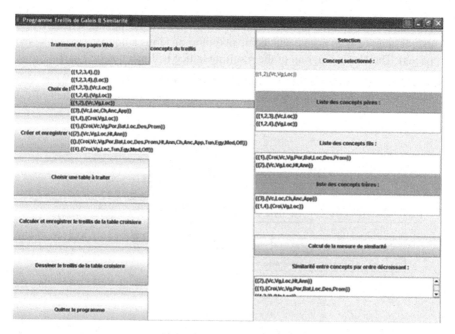

Fig. 1.5 Computation of the similarity measure from the current concept

most similar concept from the current concept is *({2), {holiday, trip, renting, hotel, yellow pages})*.

All similar values between each concepts pair can be pre-computed in order to optimize the response time.

1.5 Perspectives: Towards Galois Lattices' Visual Footprints

A challenging perspective related to this work consists in finding an intuitive representation of a lattice, i.e. a kind of *visual footprint* allowing users to interpret it at a glance. Among the state of the art, some works generate a map resulting from a query and may represent several hundreds or thousands of documents [5, 30].

The methodology used in this chapter to generate 2D spatial visualizations of Galois lattices is the same as in [4], based on the pixelization paradigm [18]. This approach consists in representing data as coloured pixels placed in the 2D space along to a Peano-Hilbert curve. This method was not applied to data itself but to its conceptual context (the Galois lattice). The dimensions of a concept are all properties of its intent. A Principal Component Analysis (PCA) is performed to reduce this number to three dimensions, as a colour has three components Red, Green and Blue. The values of the obtained (X, Y, Z) triples are usually low. In order to get more satisfying values, the inverse Ohta's transform was used which approximates the three components of PCA for a natural colour image as in [4]. This inverse transform is applied to each concept and the values are normalized to be well distributed between 0 and 255. This algorithm also transforms decimal values into entire as RGB components are entire numbers. Finally, concepts are ordered according to their RGB vector in order to cluster concepts with similar colours on a straight line (i.e. a 1D space). Each pixel is placed in the 2D space along a Peano-Hilbert curve. This curve places the points of a straight line on a plane by minimizing the Euclidian distance of points which are close on the straight line. Figure 1.6 shows an example of Galois lattice's pixelized visualization.

From a first visual analysis of this pixelization, some clusters of pixels may be identified. Each cluster reflects a cluster of concepts of the lattice. The Euclidian and colorimetric proximity of pixels symbolizes the semantic proximity of the corresponding concepts in the lattice. These clusters show how the lattice's concepts get organized, which would be impossible from a Hasse diagram, considering the size of the lattice. This cartography thus allows to consider one or several exploration strategies for the lattice and consequently for the data from which it was computed.

Fig. 1.6 Example of Galois lattice's pixelized visualization

1.6 Conclusion

Knowledge extraction can be performed with numerical or conceptual clustering. Dealing with heterogeneous data, numerical techniques are difficult to use due to an initial data recoding and to the choice of a proximity measure. Conceptual clustering computes groups of objects according to their common properties and offers an interesting representation structure. In order to deal with real heterogeneous data, a semantic level must be added to a conceptual level.

This chapter showed how the use of conceptual lattices in conjunction with semantics could provide interesting results in the context of navigation and context-aware information retrieval. One interest is to perform a more relevant and refined information retrieval, closer to users' expectations.

The methodology presented in this chapter is divided into two steps; the first one consists in an offline pre-treatment of heterogeneous data sources where a conceptual lattice is built. Each concept corresponds to a cluster of data sources having common properties. Then, a matching is performed between the data sources' relevant terms and an ontology, in order to label each concept in a normalized way and achieve a semantic coordination between the Galois lattices and ontologies. The second step is an online contextual processing of users' information need. If the query is formulated with keywords, the request's terms are compared with the concepts' labels. Users can then navigate within the lattice through the generalization/specialization links; they may also navigate within the semantic structure – thesaurus or ontology – if they need domain knowledge.

A new similarity measure between the concepts of a lattice was also proposed to help users during their navigation by indicating a starting point in the concept lattice and/or the closest concept – and thus the most relevant – from their current navigation point. This similarity measure takes into account semantic relations between the concept and the lattice structure (content and position in the lattice, as well as the smallest generalizing concept). It orders neighbor concepts of a given concept according to their relevance as next visited concepts. Experimentation results on Web pages in the tourism domain have been described.

This methodology can also be used for other purposes, e.g. to populate ontologies. It may also be applied to compare data sources through their respective lattices. The query's terms correspond to an entry point in one or more lattices. Then, the user may navigate from one lattice to others to refine his/her query. Another possible application is to help web site designers, as the lattice reflects the Web site's content: this method makes it easy to compare the resulting Web site/lattice with the original goals of the Web site designer. In the future this work will be extended to the spatial visualization of documents associated to the concept lattice. New visualization paradigms may indeed enhance the interpretation of Galois lattices.

One general perspective for the future is to conduct larger-scale evaluations of this methodology and evaluate more precisely to what extent these new navigation environment and similarity measure help users during the navigation and information retrieval process. In particular, the recall and precision of visited Web pages with regard to users' search objectives will be studied.

Another challenging perspective of this work is to apply it to other contexts than the Web. Its use for the analysis of online social networks such as *Facebook* or *Myspace* is currently being experimented. Such tools could further enhance the potential of these networks by helping users find matching profiles and content, as well as providing advances search and personalization features.

References

1. Barbut, M., Monjardet, B., Ordre et classification, Algebre et combinatoire, Tome 2, Hachette, 1970
2. Birkhoff, G., Lattice Theory, First Edition, Amer. Math. Soc. Pub. 25, Providence, RI, 1940
3. Blanchard, E., Harzallah, M., Kuntz, P. and Briand, H. Une nouvelle mesure sémantique pour le calcul de la similarité entre deux concepts d'une même ontologie. Revue nationale des nouvelles technologies de l'information, 2006
4. Blanchard, F., Herbin, M., Rousseaux, F. Compendium de données multidimensionnelles par une image couleur. Atelier "Visualisation des connaissances" des journées Extraction et Gestion des Connaissances EGC 2005, Paris, 19–21 janvier 2005
5. Börner, K., Chen C., Boyak K. W. Visualizing Knowledge Domains. Annual review of information science and technology, vol. 37, pp. 179–255, 2003
6. Bouquet P., Giunchiglia F., Van Harmelen F., Serafini L., Stuckenschmidt H.: Contextualizing Ontologies. Journal of Web Semantics, 1(4):1–19, 2004
7. Brézillon, P., Context in Artificial Intelligence: I. A survey of the literature. Computer and Artificial Intelligence. 18(18): 321–340. 1999
8. Carpineto, C., Romano, G., Exploiting the Potential of Concept Lattices for Information Retrieval with CREDO. Journal of Universal Computer Science, vol. 10, no. 8, pp. 985–1013, 2004
9. Carpineto, C., Romano, G., Galois: An order-theoretic approach to conceptual clustering, Proc. of the 10th Conference on Machine Learning, Amherst, MA, Kaufmann, pp. 33–40, 1993

10. Doan, A., Madhavan, J., Domingos, P., Learning to Map between Ontologies on the Semantic Web. In the 11th International World Wide Web Conference (WWW'2002), May 7–11, Hawaii, 2002

11. Dolog, P., Stuckenschmidt, H., Wache, H., Robust Query Processing for Personalized Information Access on the Semantic Web. FQAS 2006: 343–355

12. Giunchiglia F., Contextual reasoning. Epistemologia, special issue on I Linguaggi e le Macchine, XVI:345–364, 1993

13. Godin, R, Chau, T.-T., Incremental concept formation algorithms based on Galois Lattices, Computational intelligence, 11, n° 2, pp. 246–267, 1998

14. Guha, R., McCarthy, J., Varieties of contexts. 4th International and Interdisciplinary Conference, CONTEXT 2003. Lecture Notes in Computer Science, vol. 2680, pp. 164–177, 2003

15. Guigues, J.L. and Duquenne V., Familles minimales d'implications informatives résultant d'un tableau de données binaires, Math. Sci. Hum. N° 95, Pp. 5–18, 1986

16. Jay, N., Kohler, F. and Napoli, A.: Analysis of Social Communities with Iceberg and Stability-Based Concept Lattices. ICFCA 2008: 258–272

17. Jiang, J. and Conrath, D. Semantic similarity based on corpus statistics and lexical taxonomy. In. Proceedings on International Conference on Research in Computational Linguistics, Taiwan, 1997

18. Keim, D. A., Schneidewing, J., Sips, M. Scalable pixel based visual data exploration. Pixelization Paradigm, First Visual Information Expert Workshop, Springer, vol. 4370, pp. 12–24, 2007

19. Le Grand, B., Aufaure, M.-A., Soto, M. Semantic and Conceptual Context-Aware Information Retrieval, the IEEE/ACM International Conference on Signal-Image Technology & Internet-Based Systems (SITIS'2006), pp. 322–332, Hammamet, Tunisie, 2006

20. McCarthy, J., The advice taker. In M. Minsky, editor, Semantic Information Processing. MIT Press, Cambridge, MA, 1968

21. McCarthy J., Generality in Artificial Intelligence. Communications of ACM, 30(12):1030–1035, 1987

22. Messai, N., Devignes, M-D., Napoli, A. and Smaïl-Tabbone, M., Querying a Bioinformatic Data Sources Registry with Concept Lattices. 13th International Conference on Conceptual Structures - ICCS 2005. (Kassel, Germany). Springer, 2005. Lecture Notes in Computer Science. vol. 3596. pp. 323–336

23. Messai N., Devignes M-D., Napoli A., and Smaïl-Tabbone M. "BR-Explorer: An FCA-based Algorithm for Information Retrieval". 4th International Conference on Concept Lattices and their Applications, CLA 2006, Hammamet, Tunisia, 2006

24. Mrissa, M., Ghedira, C., Benslimane, D., Maamar, Z., A Context Model for Semantic Mediation in Web Services Composition. 25th International Conference on Conceptual Modeling (ER2006) November 6–9 2006, Tucson, Arizona, USA. 2006

25. OWL Web Ontology Language, W3C Recommendation 10 February 2004

26. Priss, U., "Lattice-based Information Retrieval." Knowledge Organization, Vol. 27, 3, 2000, p. 132–142

27. Rada, R., Mili, H., Bicknel, E., Blettner, M. Development and application of a metric on semantic nets. IEEE Transaction on Systems, Man, and Cybernetics, 19(1):17–30, 1989

28. Resnik, P. Using information content to evaluate semantic similarity in a taxonomy. In Proceedings of the 14th International Joint Conference on Artificial Intelligence, Montreal, 1995

29. Safar, B., Kefi, H., Reynaud, C., OntoRefiner, a user query refinement interface usable for Semantic Web Portals, Application of Semantic Web Technologies to Web Communities (ECAI'2004) August 23rd, Spain, 16th European Conference on Artificial Intelligence, August 22–27, 2004, Valencia (Spain), p65–p79

30. Skupin, A. S., Fabrikant, I. Spatialization methods: a cartographic research agenda for non-geographic information visualization. Cartography and Geographic Information Sciences, vol. 30 (2), pp. 95–115, 2003

31. Snášel, V., Horák, Z., Abraham, A., Understanding Social Networks Using Formal Concept Analysis, wi-iat, pp.390–393, 2008 IEEE/WIC/ACM International Conference on Web Intelligence and Intelligent Agent Technology, 2008

32. Theodorakis M. & Spyratos N. Context in artificial intelligence and information modelling. Proceedings of the second Hellenic Conference on Artificial Intelligence (SETN'02), Thessalonique, 2002

33. Wille, R., Line diagrams of hierarchical concept systems, Int. Classif. 11, pp. 77–86, 1984

34. Wille, R., Concept lattices and conceptual knowledge systems, Computers & Mathematics Applications, 23, n° 6–9, pp. 493–515, 1992

35. Wu, Z. and Palmer, M. Verb Semantics and Lexical Selection, Proceedings of the 32nd Annual Meetings of the Associations for Computational Linguistics, pp. 133–138, 1994

36. Zargayouna, H. and Salotti, S. Mesure de similarité sémantique pour l'indexation de documents semi-structurés dans 12ème Atelier de Raisonnement à Partir de Cas, 2004

Chapter 2
Automatic Invocation Linking for Collaborative Web-Based Corpora

James Gardner, Aaron Krowne, and Li Xiong

Abstract Collaborative online encyclopedias or knowledge bases such as Wikipedia and PlanetMath are becoming increasingly popular because of their open access, comprehensive and interlinked content, rapid and continual updates, and community interactivity. To understand a particular concept in these knowledge bases, a reader needs to learn about related and underlying concepts. In this chapter, we introduce the problem of invocation linking for collaborative encyclopedia or knowledge bases, review the state of the art for invocation linking including the popular linking system of Wikipedia, discuss the problems and challenges of automatic linking, and present the NNexus approach, an abstraction and generalization of the automatic linking system used by PlanetMath.org. The chapter emphasizes both research problems and practical design issues through discussion of real world scenarios and hence is suitable for both researchers in web intelligence and practitioners looking to adopt the techniques. Below is a brief outline of the chapter.

Problem and Motivation. We first introduce the problem of invocation linking for online collaborative encyclopedia or knowledge bases. An online encyclopedia consists of multiple entries. An *invocation link* is a hyperlink from a term or phrase in an entry representing a concept to another entry that defines the concept. It allows a reader easily "jump" to requisite concepts in order to fully understand the current one. We refer to the term or phrase being linked from as *link source* and the entry being linked to as *link target*. The problem of *invocation linking* is how to add these invocation links in an online encyclopedia in order to build a semantic concept network.

State of the Arts. We review the state of arts for the invocation linking in current online encyclopedia and knowledge bases. The existing approaches can be mainly

J. Gardner (✉) and L. Xiong
Department of Mathematics and Computer Science, Emory University, 400 Dowman Dr. Atlanta, GA 30322
e-mail: jgardn3@emory.edu; lxiong@mathcs.emory.edu

A. Krowne
PlanetMath.org, 4336 Birchlake Ct. Alexandria, VA 23309
e-mail: akrowne@gmail.com

R. Chbeir et al., *Emergent Web Intelligence: Advanced Information Retrieval*, Advanced Information and Knowledge Processing, DOI 10.1007/978-1-84996-074-8_2,

classified into: 1) *manual linking* where both the link source and link target are explicitly defined by the user (such as blog software), 2) *semi-automatic linking* where the link source are explicitly marked by the user but the link target is determined automatically (such as Wikipedia), and 3) *automatic linking* where both the link source and link target are determined automatically. We discuss the representative systems for each approach and illustrate their advantages and disadvantages. We will also review potential technologies such as web search and recommender systems and discuss their applicability for invocation linking.

Automatic Invocation Linking. We advocate in this chapter the automatic linking approach as we believe that the manual and semi-automatic approaches are an unnecessary burden on contributors, and in addition, require continuous re-inspection of the entire corpus by writers or other maintainers for a growing and dynamic corpus. We discuss the challenges and design goals for developing such an automatic linking system including linking quality, efficiency and scalability, and generalization to multiple corpus.

NNexus Approach. In particular, we present the NNexus system, an automatic linking system that we have developed as an abstraction and generalization of the linking component of PlanetMath (planetmath.org), PlanetPhysics(planet-physics.org), and other sites. We discuss a number of key features and design ideas of NNexus in addressing the challenges for invocation linking. NNexus provides an effective linking scheme utilizing metadata to automatically identify link sources and link targets. It achieves good linking quality with a classification-based link steering approach and an interactive entry filtering component. It achieves good efficiency and scalability by its efficient data structures as well as a mechanism for efficiently updating the links between entries that are related to newly defined or modified concepts in the corpus. Finally, its implementation utilizes OWL and has a simple interface, which allows for an almost unlimited number of online corpora to interconnect for automatic linking.

Conclusions and Open Issues. We close the chapter by discussing a set of interesting issues and open problems for invocation linking.

2.1 Introduction

Collaborative online encyclopedias or knowledge bases such as Wikipedia[1] and PlanetMath[2] are becoming increasingly popular because of their open access, comprehensive and interlinked content, rapid and continual updates, and community interactivity.

To understand a particular concept in these knowledge bases, a reader needs to learn about related and underlying concepts. Thus, a knowledge based should

---

[1] http://www.wikipedia.org

[2] http://www.planetmath.org

contain the appropriate links for all of the concepts to the appropriate definitions or articles. These links should allow browsing to all the concepts that are evident to the reader's intuition.

The popularity of these encyclopedic knowledge bases has also brought about a situation where the availability of high-quality, canonical definitions and declarations of educationally useful concepts have outpaced their usage (or *invocation*) in other educational information resources on the web. Instead, the user must execute a new search (either online or offline) to look up an unknown term when it is encountered, if it is not linked to a definition. For example, blogs, research repositories, and digital libraries quite often do not link to definitions of the concepts contained in their texts and metadata, even when such definitions are available. This is generally not done because of the lack of appropriate software infrastructure and the extra work creating manual links entails. When such linking is actually done, it tends to be incomplete and is quite laborious.

2.1.1   Problem Definition

In this chapter, we study the problem of invocation linking to build a semantic network for collaborative online encyclopedia. We first define a number of terminologies and define our problem to facilitate our discussion.

A *collaborative online encyclopedia* is a kind of knowledge base containing "encyclopedic" (standardized) knowledge contributed by a large number of participants (typically but not necessarily in a volunteer capacity). Any article submitted by a user in such a collaborative corpus is an *entry* or an *object*. We say *invocation* referring to a specific kind of semantic link: that of *concept invocation*. Any statement in a language is composed of concepts represented by tuples of words. Such a statement invokes these concepts, as evidenced by the inclusion of word tuples that correspond to common labels for the concepts. We call these tuples of words *concept labels*. A *invocation link* is a hyperlink from these tuples of words in an entry that represent a concept to an entry that defines the concept. We refer to the tuples of words being linked from as *link source* and the entry being linked to as *link target*. The problem of *invocation linking* is how to add these invocation links in an collaborative online encyclopedia.

The table in Fig. 2.1 shows a list of entries (objects) in an example online encyclopedia[3] corpus with their object ID and metadata including what concepts each entry defines and the Mathematical Subject Classification (MSC) for each entry. It also shows an example entry[4] with links to concepts that are defined in the same corpus. The terms underlined indicate terms that need to be linked based on the meta-data in the table. For example, *planar graph* in the example entry needs to

---

[3] http://planetmath.org

[4] Extracted from http://planetmath.org/encyclopedia/PlaneGraph.html

ObjectId	Concepts defined	MSC
1	Triangle, right triangle, ...	51-00
2	Planar, planar graph, ...	05C10
3	Connected, ...	05C40
4	Geometry, Euclidean geometry, ...	01A16
5	Graph, graph theory, edge, ...	05C99
6	Graph, function graph	03E20

A *planar graph* is a *graph* which can be drawn on a plane (a flat 2-d surface) or on a sphere, with no *edges* crossing. When drawn on a sphere, the *edges* divide its area in a number of regions called faces (or "countries", in the context of map *coloring*). Even if . . .

Fig. 2.1 Example document corpora with meta-data and example entry

be linked to object (entry) 2 that defines the concept *planar graph*. We will use this example to explain the concepts discussed in this chapter.

While it is possible to extend the problem definition and the techniques we will discuss for other types of linking such as links to articles with a similar or different point of view, it is our focus in this chapter to study *concept* or *definitional* linking.

2.1.2 Chapter Overview

In this chapter, we study the problem of invocation linking for collaborative encyclopedia or knowledge bases, review the state of the art for invocation linking, discuss the problems and challenges of automatic linking, and present the NNexus approach, an abstraction and generalization of the automatic linking system used by PlanetMath.org. The chapter emphasizes both research problems and practical design issues through discussion of real world scenarios and hence is suitable for both researchers in web intelligence and practitioners looking to adopt the techniques. Below is a brief outline of the chapter.

Section 2.2 reviews the state of arts for the invocation linking in current online encyclopedia and knowledge bases. We discuss the representative systems and illustrate their advantages and disadvantages and motivate the automatic linking approach. We will also review potential technologies such as web search, recommender systems and machine learning and discuss their applicability for invocation linking. In Section 2.3, we discuss a set of general challenges and design goals for an automatic linking system to achieve including linking quality, efficiency and scalability, and generalization to multiple corpus. In Section 2.4, the main part of the chapter, we present the NNexus system, an automatic linking system that we have developed as an abstraction and generalization of the linking component of PlanetMath (planetmath.org), PlanetPhysics(planetphysics.org), and other sites [4]. We discuss a number of key features and design ideas of NNexus in addressing the challenges for invocation linking. Finally, we close the chapter in Section 2.6 by discussing a set of interesting issues and open problems for invocation linking.

2.2   State of the Art

We briefly survey the existing and potential solutions for invocation linking and motivate the automatic linking approach. We also review a number of technologies that are related or applicable to the invocation linking problem.

2.2.1   Invocation Linking

The existing and potential approaches for invocation linking can be mainly classified into the following three categories, namely, *manual linking, semi-automatic linking*, and *automatic linking*.

2.2.1.1   Manual Linking

Manual linking refers to the linking technique where both the link source and link target are explicitly defined, e.g., anchor tags in html documents. Most web pages use the manual approach. Blog software (such as Wordpress) generally requires writers create links manually.

2.2.1.2   Semi-automatic Linking

Semi-automatic linking refers to the technique where the terms at the source are explicitly marked for linking, but the link target is determined by the collaborative online encyclopedia system. Many current online encyclopedias (including Wikipedia) use the semi-automatic approach.

Wikipedia (which is powered by the Mediawiki software) uses a semi-automatic approach. That is, the links are manually delimited by authors when the author invokes a concept that they believe should be defined in the collection, but the system disambiguates between the possible destinations for the link. If an entry for a concept is present only by an alternate name, the link might fail to be connected. Links to non-existent entries are rendered specially as "broken" links, and the Mediawiki system makes it easy to start a new entry for that term. However, this is inherently somewhat distracting to those uninterested in creating a new entry. Mediawiki and other systems that take a similar approach also fail to provide systemic treatment of homonymy. The Wikipedia convention is to manually create "disambiguation nodes," which contain links to all homonymous concepts with a particular label. Such nodes add an extra step to navigation, require ongoing maintenance, and can contain an extremely random and distractive jumble of topics.

2.2.1.3 Automatic Linking

Automatic invocation linking refers to the technique where the terms at the source and link target are both automatically determined by the system. This is the approach that we advocate in order to build the semantic network with minimal manual effort [4, 9].

Our primary viewpoint is that the manual and semi-automatic approaches are an unnecessary burden on contributors, since the knowledge management environment (or Wiki) should contain the data for which concepts are present and how they should be cited. By contrast, authors will usually not be aware of all concepts which are already present within the system – especially for large or distributed corpora.

In addition, a more challenging problem with the manual and semi-automatic linking strategy is that a growing, dynamic corpus will generally necessitate links from existing entries to new entries as the collection becomes larger. To attend to this reality would require continuous re-inspection of the entire corpus by writers or other maintainers, which is an $\mathcal{O}(n^2)$-scale problem (where the corpus contains n entries). To keep an evolving corpus correctly and completely linked, it would be necessary for maintainers to search it upon each update (or at least periodically) to determine if the links in the constituent articles should be updated. When generalizing to inter-linkage across separate corpora, the task would potentially be even more laborious, as authors would have to search across multiple web sites to determine what new terms are available for linking into their entries.

The optimal end product of an automatic invocation linking system should be a fully connected network of articles that will enable readers to navigate and learn from the corpus almost as naturally as if was interlinked by painstaking manual effort. Without understanding the invoked concepts in a statement, the reader cannot attain a complete understanding of the statement, and by extension the entry it appears in. This is why node interlinkage is so important in hypertexts being used as knowledge bases, and why an automated system is of such utility. There are two feasible approaches to automatic linking including rule-based systems and machine learning-based systems. The main focus of this chapter is on rule-based systems but the next section includes a brief introduction to the latest machine learning-based approaches.

2.2.2 Related Technologies

There are a number of technologies that are related or applicable to the *automatic invocation linking* problem. We briefly review them below and discuss their implications and relations to our problem.

2.2.2.1   Semantic Knowledge Bases

There are several efforts [10, 13, 14] towards using a wiki for collaboratively editing semantic knowledge bases where users can specify semantic information including links in addition to standard wiki text. Most of them focus on improving usability and integrating machine readable data and human-readable editable text. PowerMagpie [5] is a tool that was developed that extends browsing by automatically selecting a wide range of online ontologies for a term in a web page that allows users to browse through the ontology and through the entities of the ontology. The system will automatically determine the correct ontology for a term and allow the user to browse that ontology using a browser plugin.

Among the semantic information, links are arguably the most basic and also most relevant markup within a wiki and are interpreted as semantic relations between two concepts described within articles. Völkel et al. [10] provide an extension to be integrated in Wikipedia, that allows users to specify typed links in addition to regular links between articles and typed data inside the articles.

2.2.2.2   Information Retrieval and Web Search

In our automatic linking problem, both the link target and the link source need to be identified and linked automatically. One part of this problem for identifying the best linking target for a concept label bears similarity to the web search problem in finding the most relevant documents based on a keyword. For the most part the work in information retrieval [3] has not been explored in the collaborative semantic linking context [8]. Typical information retrieval issues such as plurality, homonyms, and polysemy are all relevant for the linking process. Some of the information retrieval and web search techniques also provide potential solutions for the linking problem. In particular, the term-frequency and inverse document-frequency (TFIDF) based document ranking may be applied to rank relevant linking targets given a concept label. However, the entries that define a particular concept may not contain the actual concept label (terms) and thus the TFIDF-based approach alone may not yield a good linking quality.

2.2.2.3   Recommender Systems

Another related technology is recommender systems [1] that aim to predict ratings of a particular item for a particular user using a set of similar users based on a user-item rating matrix. At an initial glance, we can model our problem as an entry–entry link matrix where each cell represent a link or non-link from a certain entry to another entry and use entry similarities to help determine the best entry to link to for a term that belongs to a certain entry. While this approach is more appropriate for relevance linking and may help to narrow down the potential link targets, it alone is not sufficient for the invocation or concept linking problem. Nevertheless, it remains an interesting research question to adapt the collaborative filtering technologies to enhance the linking precision by incorporating entry similarities and user feedback into the linking process.

2.2.2.4 Machine Learning

The popularity of Wikipedia has recently produced an interest in the machine learning community for the problem of automatic linking. Wikipedia is a very large data source with hyperlinks manually created by the authors of the wiki. The links in Wikipedia are highly accurate [15]. We can use the existing manually linked pages as a training set for machine learning based automatic linking. The most successful machine learning based technique for automatically linking Wikipedia is described in [11]. We briefly summarize their work. Two different classifiers can be trained for disambiguation and link detection. In the disambiguation phase they use the commonness of each candidate sense and the relatedness to the surrounding context. The commonness of a sense is the probability it is used as a the link destination in Wikipedia. The relatedness or semantic similarity of two pages is based on comparing their incoming and outgoing links. In the detection phase the link detector is trained based on the link probability, the disambiguation confidence, the depth of the article in the Wikipedia classification tree, and the location and spread of the topics mentioned in the page. After using both of the classifiers links can be added to the appropriate location in an entry.

2.3 Challenges and Design Goals

In this section, we discuss the computing challenges and identify a set of design goals for building an automatic invocation linking system.

2.3.1 Linking Quality

The main analytic challenges lie in how to determine which terms or phrases to link and which entries to link to. Typical information retrieval and natural language processing issues such as plurality, homonyms, and polysemy are all relevant for the linking process and bear on the quality of linking. In light of all these challenges, the linking process is necessarily imperfect and so *linking errors* may be present. We characterize many such forms of errors as follows.

- *Mislinking* refers to the error that a term or phrase is linked to an incorrect link target, e.g., an incorrect homonym from a group of homonyms. For example, in our sample entry shown in Fig. 2.1, if "graph" is linked to object 6 instead of 5, then we have a mislink.

- *Overlinking* refers to the error that a term or phrase is linked when there should be no link at all. Note that overlinking also contributes to mislinking because the term is mislinked. For example, if the term "even" is used as a common term (not in a mathematics sense) but was linked to an entry that defines "even number", we have an overlink.
- *Underlinking* refers to the error that a term or phrase is not linked when there should be a link because it invokes a concept that is defined in the corpus. For example, consider our sample entry shown in Fig. 2.1 again, if "planar graph" is not linked, then we have a underlink.

An important goal of designing the automatic linking system is to reduce the above errors and improve the *link precision* (perfect link precision means every link is linked to the correct link target) while maintaining high *link recall* (perfect link recall means a link is created for every concept label that should be linked given the present state of the corpus).

2.3.2 Efficiency and Scalability

Another important design goal of an automatic linking system is its efficiency so the links can be created near-real time during rendering of the entries and its scalability so it can handle the large size of an online encyclopedia corpora. In addition, most collaborative corpora change frequently, an automatic invocation linking system needs to efficiently update the links between entries that are related to newly defined or modified concepts in the corpus. A continually changing corpus must be dealt in such a way that the analysis and processing of automatic links is tractable and scalable.

2.3.3 Generalization to Multiple Corpora

It is also necessary and important that an automatic linking system is easy to use for the adoption by a large user base and easy to setup for the widespread adoption for linking various materials across multiple sites.

To help users learn more quickly it is now generally accepted that knowledge bases should leverage each others' content (or metadata) to increase the scope of the available learning materials. This is the reason for the development of Semantic Web standards such as the Web Ontology Language (OWL). An important design goal of an automatic linking system should be to leverage these standards so that the system would not only enable intra-linking collaborative encyclopedias, such as PlanetMath.org, but also allow for linking educational materials such as lecture notes, blogs, abstracts in research and educational digital libraries. Such usage aids researchers and students in the better understanding of abstracts and full texts, and also helps them find related articles quickly.

2.4 NNexus Approach

We designed and developed NNexus (Noosphere Networked Entry eXtension and Unification System) [4], a system used to automate the process of automatically linking encyclopedia entries (or other definitional knowledge bases) into a semantic network of concepts using metadata of the entries. NNexus is an abstraction and generalization of the automatic linking component of the Noosphere system [9], which is the platform of PlanetMath (planetmath.org), PlanetPhysics (planetphysics.org), and other Noosphere sites. To the best of our knowledge, it is the first automatic linking system that links articles and concepts using the metadata of entries, to make linking almost a "non-issue" for writers, and completely transparent to readers.

NNexus has a number of key features addressing the challenges we outlined above. First, it provides an effective indexing and linking scheme that utilizes metadata to automatically identify link sources and link targets. It achieves perfect link recall without *underlinking* error. It uses a classification-based link steering approach to address the mislinking problem and enhance the link precision. It also provides an interactive entry filtering component to address overlinking problem and further enhance the link precision for a minority of "tough cases." Second, NNexus achieves good efficiency and scalability by its efficient data structures and algorithm design. It has mechanisms for efficiently updating the links between entries that are related to newly defined or modified concepts in the corpus. Lastly, NNexus utilizes OWL and has a simple interface, which allows for an almost unlimited number of online corpora to interconnect for automatic linking.

In this section, we first give an overview of the model and functionalities behind NNexus, then present its key components and techniques.

2.4.1 Overview

Users of NNexus apply the following basic functionality to their corpus: when an entry is rendered either at display time or during offline batch processing, the text is scanned for words or concept labels (*link source*) and they are ultimately turned into hyperlinks to the corresponding entries (*link target*) in the output rendering.

There are two basic steps in performing the invocation linking. The engine breaks the text of an entry into a single words/tokens array to iterate through. The tokens and token tuples (phrases) that invoke concepts defined in other entries are then used for *link target identification* to determine the entries to link to.

Figure 2.2 illustrates the conceptual flow of the automatic linking process. In order to determine which entry to link to for a concept label, NNexus indexes the entries by building a *concept map* that maps all of the concept labels in the corpus to the entries which define these concepts. The tokens and token tuples (phrases) that are identified as link sources are searched to retrieve the candidate links using the concept map (see Section 2.4.2). After the candidate links are determined they are

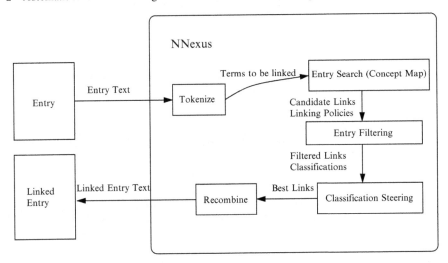

Fig. 2.2 Linking Diagram: When an entry is linked through NNexus the candidate links are found in the concept map. These candidates are then compared against the linking policies and sent through the classification module. The top candidate links are then recombined into the original text and returned to the user

filtered based on linking policies (see Section 2.4.4). The candidates are then compared by "classification proximity" and the object with the closest classification is then selected as the link target (see Section 2.4.3). The "winning" candidate for each position are then substituted into the original text and the linked document is then returned.

In addition, when new concepts are added to the collection (or the set of concept labels otherwise changes), entries containing potential invocation of these concept labels can be *invalidated*. This allows entries to be re-scanned for links, either at invalidation time or before the next time they are displayed. NNexus uses a special structure called the *invalidation index* to facilitate this (see Section 2.4.5).

This automatic system almost completely frees content authors from having to "think about links." It addresses the problems of both outgoing and incoming links, with respect to a new entry or new concepts. However, it is not completely infallible, and in an epistemological sense, there is only so much that a system can infer without having a human-level understanding of the content. Because of this, the user can ultimately override the automatic linking, create their own manual links, or specify link policies for steering the automatic linker (see Section 2.4.4). While complemented and enhanced by the interactive learning components, NNexus is a completely automatic system and we show in next section that NNexus performs well even without any human efforts.

2.4.2 Entry Search

In order to determine which entry to link to for a concept label, NNexus indexes the entries by building a *concept map* that maps all of the concept labels in the corpus to the entries which define these concepts. Below we present the details of how to build the concept map and how it is used for entry search.

When adding a new object (entry) to NNexus, a list of terms the object defines, synonyms, and a title are provided (the concept labels) by the author as metadata. The concept labels are kept in a chained-hash index structure, called the *concept map*. This structure contains as keys the words that occur as the first word of some concept label. Following these words (retrieving the value for the key) leads to a list of full concept labels starting with that particular word. To facilitate efficient scanning of entry text to find concept labels, the map is structured as a chained hash, keyed by the first word of each phrase placed in it. This structure is shown graphically in Fig. 2.3.

NNexus also performs *morphological transformations* on concept labels when building concept map in order to handle morphological invariances and ensure they can be linked to in most typical usages. The first, and most important transformation, has the effect of invariance of pluralization. The second invariance is due to possessiveness. Another morphological invariance concerns international characters. When a token is checked into the index, NNexus will ensure that the token is singular and non-possessive, with a canonicalized encoding.

We now discuss how the concept map is used for entry search. When searching for candidate links for a given entry, the entry is represented as an array of word tokens (concept labels). The tokenized text of the entry is iterated over and searched in the concept map. If a word matches the first word of an indexed concept label in the concept map, the following words in the text are checked to see if they match the longest concept label starting with that word. If this fails, the next longest concept

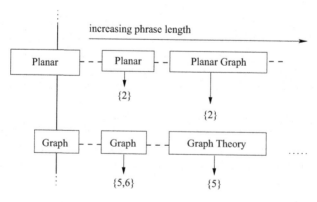

Fig. 2.3 *Concept map:* a fast-access (chained-hash-based) structure filled with all the concept labels for all included corpora, used for determining available linking targets as the text is being scanned. This figure contains a subset that would be generated based on our example corpus

label is checked, and so on. NNexus always performs *longest phrase match*. For example, if an author mentions the phrase "orthogonal function" in their entry and links against a collection defining all of "orthogonal," "function," and "orthogonal function," then NNexus links to the latter. This is based on a nearly universally consistent assumption of natural language, which is that longer phrases semantically subsume their shorter atoms.

When a matching concept label is found, it is included in the *match array*. In our example "graph", "plane", and "connected components" are all defined in the corpus. All possible link targets of the terms or phrases are added to the match array. The match array is then iterated over and the possible link targets are then disambiguated to determine the best link target for each term or phrase. Classification based link steering is the main technique used in disambiguation and is discussed in the next section.

2.4.3 Classification Steering

As we discussed in Section 2.3, one of the main challenges of building an automatic linking system is to cope with possible mislinking errors. Online encyclopedias are typically organized into a classification hierarchy, and this ontological knowledge can be utilized to increase the precision of automatic linking by helping identifying the best link targets that are closely related to the link source in the ontological hierarchy. Below we present our classification steering approach that is designed to reduce mislinking errors and to enhance link precision.

2.4.3.1 Classification Hierarchy

Each object in the NNexus corpus may contain one or more classifications. The classification table maps entries (by object ID) to lists of classifications which have been assigned to them by users. The classification hierarchy is represented as a tree. A subtree of the Mathematical Subject Classification (MSC) hierarchy is shown as an example in Fig. 2.4. Each class is represented as a node in the tree. Edges represent parent/child relationships between the classes. In order to select the most relevant link target for a link source, NNexus compares the classes of the candidate link targets to the classes of the link source and selects the closest object with the shortest *distance* in the classification tree. Algorithm 2.1 presents a sketch of the classification steering algorithm.

2.4.3.2 Distance Computation

The key to the algorithm is how to compute the distance between two classes (nodes) in the classification tree. Note that when there are multiple classes associated with

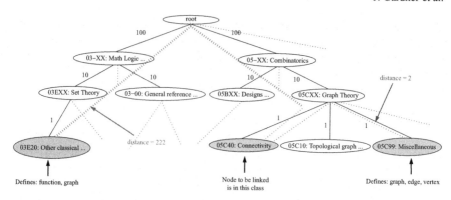

Fig. 2.4 Example Classification Tree: This is the MSC subject classification represented as a weighted graph. The shaded nodes indicates the classification of the source node (where "graph" is to be linked") and the classifications of the two target nodes. The weights are assigned with base 10

Algorithm 2.1 Algorithm of classification steering: it returns the target objects that are closest in classification to the link source in the NNexus classification graph

1: *sourceclasses* ← list of classes of source object
2: *targetobjects* ← list of candidate target objects
3: **for all** *object$_i$* ∈ *targetobjects* **do**
4:    *targetclasses$_i$* ← list of classes of *object$_i$*
5:    *distance$_i$* ← minimum distance between all *sourceclasses* and *targetclasses$_i$* pairs
6: **end for**
7: **return** {*object$_i$*|*distance$_i$* = min$_i$ *distance$_i$*}

---

the link source or link target, the minimum distance of all possible pairs of classes are used. We adopt two approaches, namely *non-weighted approach* and *weighted approach*, for computing the distance between two classes and discuss each them below.

In the *non-weighted approach*, the distance between two classes are simply the length of the shortest path between two classes. Intuitively, a node further away is less related to a given node in the tree. NNexus uses Johnson's All Pairs Shortest Path algorithm to compute the distances between all classes at startup.

In the *weighted approach*, each edge is assigned a weight. This is motivated by the observation that classes at the same level and in the same subtree should be considered closer than classes at a higher level in the same subtree and classes deeper in a subtree are more closely related than classes higher in the same subtree. For example, in Fig. 2.4, 05C10 (Connectivity) and 05C40 (Topological graph ...) are more closely related than the node 05CXX (Graph theory) and 05BXX (Designs ...). Based on this observation, we assign a weight to each edge that is inversely proportional to their depth in the tree. We define a weight of an edge in the graph as

$$w(e) = b^{height-i-1}$$

where b is the chosen base weight (default is 10), *height* is the height of the tree (or in general the distance of the longest path from the designated root node), and i is the distance of the edge from the root. The distance is computed as the weighted shortest path between two nodes. Please note that when the base weight is 1, it becomes the non-weighted approach.

Figure 2.4 also illustrates a scenario of the classification steering algorithm and the distance computation using our example in Fig. 2.1. The MSC classification of our source entry 05C40. The term to be linked, "graph", has two possible link targets: objects 5 with classification 05C99 and object 6 with classification 03E20. We examine the weighted distance (with weight base 10) between the source class and the two target classes to determine which is a better link target. As the weighted distance from 05C99 to 05C40 is shorter in the weighted classification graph than 03E20, "graph" is linked to object 5.

It is worth mentioning that this methodology presents problems when attempting to link across multiple sites (or *across domains*), as different knowledge bases may not use the same classification hierarchy. To address the general problem of inter-linking multiple corpora it is necessary to consider mapping (or otherwise combining) multiple, differing classification ontologies. We are currently investigating the techniques discussed in [2, 12] and implementing this type of functionality in our system.[5]

2.4.4   Entry Filtering

NNexus achieves perfect link recall without underlinking errors as every linkable terms will be linked in an entry. However, it is possible to have overlinking errors when a term that should not be linked (at all) is linked to an entry in the corpus (recall Section 2.3). For example, many articles will contain the word "even." In many cases this is not used in mathematical context and should be forbidden from linking to the entry defining "even number."

In order to combat this overlinking problem and those rare cases where the classification of target articles does not completely disambiguate the link targets, NNexus includes an interactive learning component, entry filtering by linking policies, that is designed to complement and further enhance the link precision by allowing users to specify linking policies. *Linking policies* are a set of directives controlling linking based on the subject classification system within the encyclopedia. The linking policy of an article describes, in terms of subject classes, where links may be made or prohibited. Thus, the entry for "even number" would forbid all articles from linking to the concept "even" unless they were in the number theory category. The author need only supply a linking policy for those terms that the article defines that are used commonly in language and are not meant in a mathematical sense.

---

[5] For more information on ontology mapping, we recommend the survey in [6].

For each object there is stored text chunk representing the user-supplied linking policy. The linking policy table is keyed by object ID. The linking policies can be specified by the author but administrators also have the ability to modify the linking policies.

We note that the linking policy component requires minimal work from the users and we will show in the experiment section later that by adding linking policies for a very small number (percentage) of entries, the precision for the overall corpus is enhanced significantly.

We are also exploring automatic keyword extraction techniques in order to extract those terms that should be or should not be linked in an automatic way. In addition, we also have a few efforts in progress exploring various ranking techniques by integrating multiple factors such as domain class, priority, pedagogical level, and reputation of the entries to handle the over-linking problem in a more automatic way.

2.4.5 Invalidation

Since NNexus operates on a dynamic and growing corpus we need to know when articles need to be re-linked. As an optimization technique to further enhance the efficiency and performance of the system, NNexus also includes an invalidation component. When a new object is added, NNexus utilizes an *invalidation index* to determine which articles may possibly link to the new object and need to be "invalidated" (marked for re-processing before being displayed again). The invalidation index stores term and phrase *content* information for all entries in the corpus. It is an adaptive index in that longer phrases are only stored if they appear frequently in the collection. There is no limit to how long a stored phrase can be; however, very long phrases are extremely unlikely to appear.

The invalidation index is a variation on a standard text document inverted index structure and works in the usual way for lookups. However, instead of just being keyed on single-word terms, it is keyed on phrases (which are usually but not always single-word). For each term or phrase in the index, there is a list of objects which contain that term or phrase. These lists are called *postings lists*. Since the falloff in occurrence count by phrase length in a typical collection follows a Zipf distribution, the invalidation index tends to be around twice the size of a simple word-based inverted index.

The invalidation index has a special property that for every phrase indexed, all shorter prefixes of that phrase are also indexed for every occurrence of the longer phrase. This allows us to guarantee that occurrences of the shorter phrases or single terms will be noticed if we do a lookup using these shorter tuples as keys.

The invalidation index exists for a single purpose: so that when concept labels are added to the collection (or when they change), we can determine a minimal superset of entries effected by the change – that is, they likely link to the newly added concept. The invalidation index allows us to do this in a way that never misses an entry that should be re-examined, but does not catch too many irrelevant entries (false positives).

2.5   Case Studies

We have implemented NNexus as a general, open source tool and deployed NNexus in a variety of settings including the online encyclopedia web site PlanetMath.org. In this section, we briefly introduce some implementation features and the interface of NNexus, present some statistics of its deployment in the PlanetMath corpus, and discuss a few other scenarios illustrating the deployability and effectiveness of NNexus. Figure 2.5 shows a sample architecture linking to multiple corpora.

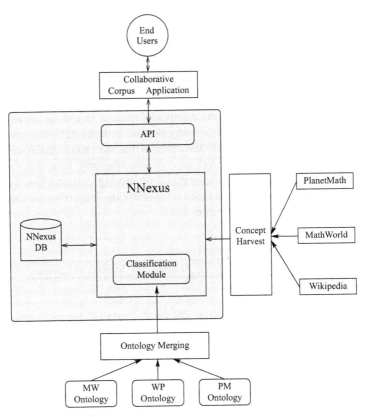

Fig. 2.5 NNexus System Architecture (in an example deployment): The shaded region denotes NNexus proper. The classification module provides classification-invariant link steering between multiple ontologies

2.5.1 PlanetMath

The core methods of NNexus have proven their large-scale applicability in the PlanetMath[6] site, a collaborative and dynamic mathematics encyclopedia in existence on the web for about 7 years now. As of this writing PlanetMath had more than 7,145 entries defining more than 12,171 concepts. We present a set of statistics of the linking system for the PlanteMath Corpus in terms of linking quality, efficiency and scalability.

2.5.1.1 Linking Quality

In order to evaluate the linking quality and the effect of the different system components of NNexus, we performed a study on the live PlanetMath collection examining the linking precision with basic lexical matching (without classification steering and linking policies) vs. lexical matching with classification steering (without linking policies) vs. lexical matching with classification steering and linking policies. The experiment was performed over the entire PlanetMath corpus but the statistics were estimated from a sample of 50 random entries in the corpus.

Table 2.1 presents the link precision for the three cases respectively. Link *precision* is defined as the number of *correct* links (those to the appropriate destination) divided by the number of created links. Note that NNexus system was designed for near-perfect link *recall* defined as the number of created (retrieved) links divided by the number of concepts invoked the entry that are actually defined in the corpus and thus we do not report link recall. We observe that the classification steering as well as linking policies improve the link precision significantly. Note that these policies were supplied by real-world users with no prompting, and no effort was made to tackle the remaining problematic cases of overlinking. Nevertheless, the linking policies drove precision up to more than 92%.[7]

Table 2.1 Linking quality for PlanetMath

Statistic	Basic	Steering	Steering and policies
Number of links	761	761	701
Good links	630	672	646
Mislinks	131	89	55
Overlinks	69	69	36
% mislink	17.2	11.7	7.8
% overlink	9.1	9.1	5.1
Precision	82.8	88.3	92.2

---

[6] Visit PlanetMath on the web at http://www.planetmath.org

[7] Likely this number could exceed 95% with a little bit of targeted effort, and given that these policies have been available on PlanetMath for less than 2 years, the numbers will likely continue to improve on their own.

We believe these results provide compelling support for our hypothesis that NNexus with classification-based link steering achieves good linking quality. Further, overlinking, which represents at least two-thirds of the precision shortfall in our collection, can be largely eliminated by adding linking policies to a small subset of it. The results also indicate that by adding the linking polices the mislinking percentage was reduced. Thus a small subset of homonyms in the corpus contribute not only to overlinking by also to much of the mislinking.

2.5.1.2 Scalability and Efficiency

To study the scalability and efficiency of our approach, we ran experiments on a modest Mac machine running OS X with a 1.83 GHz Intel Core Duo and 512MB DDR2 SDRAM. We selected random subsets of size 200–7,132 from the Planet-Math corpus and kept track of the number of seconds to link every object in the subset corpora.

Table 2.2 and Fig. 2.6 show the performance results for different corpus sizes. We can see that the time per link quickly falls off and then hovers around a constant value as the collection grows. This indicates that NNexus is not only efficient but also scalable to very large corpus sizes. All overhead quickly amortizes and diminishes relative to productive linking work done by the system, meaning that NNexus automatic linking is a legitimate feature to build into expanding collections and growing ensembles of interlinked collections on the web.

2.5.1.3 Comparison to Wikipedia

A survey in [15] shows that about 97–99% of Wikipedia links are accurate. However, this study is not directly comparable to our survey for a number of reasons. First, because it relies on the convention of "disambiguation nodes" (which NNexus allows one to avoid) and second, it doesn't take into account link recall (underlinking). In other words, links in Wikipedia tend to be accurate, but some of

Table 2.2 Linking scalability for PlanetMath

Corpus size	Number of links	Total time (s)	Time/link
200	640	126	0.197
500	2,067	290	0.140
1,000	5,837	617	0.106
2,000	17,757	1,218	0.069
3,000	35,682	1,972	0.055
4,000	52,030	2,881	0.055
5,000	79,139	3,737	0.047
6,000	101,787	4,487	0.044
7,132	127,430	5,599	0.044

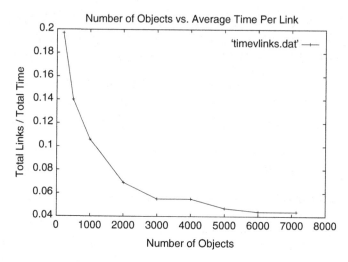

Fig. 2.6 Scalability study: time-per-link for progressively larger corpora, showing clearly that the automatic linking process is sub-linear in time complexity

this "accuracy" is due to the presence of disambiguation nodes, and some is likely due to the fact that many links simply aren't being made.

Most significantly, from a usability and productivity standpoint, no formal comparison of the *effort* required for link maintenance in the manual/semi-automatic vs. automatic paradigms has been made. However, anecdotal evidence suggests our approach to linking is less work for authors and more appreciated by them; and with classification and linking steering, precision approaches that achieved on Wikipedia with manual effort and disambiguation nodes. It is interesting to note that artificial hubs are created in the Wikipedia network because of disambiguation pages. This may have impact on some algorithms that use the link structure of a semantic network such as HITS [7]. Disambiguation pages paradoxically add ambiguity to the data because the link structure is modified and it encourages authors not to find the correct target for a link.

2.5.2 Lecture Notes

In addition to enabling intra-linking in an single encyclopedic knowledge base such as PlanetMath, NNexus also provides a generalized automatic linking solution to a variety of potential applications. One such application is the linking of lecture notes to math encyclopedia sites (including PlanethMath and MathWorld, but potentially extending to others, such as Wikipedia, the Digital Library of Mathematical Functions [DLMF], and more). Figure 2.7 demonstrates this sort of use, showing screenshots of automatically linked notes from a probabilities course taught by

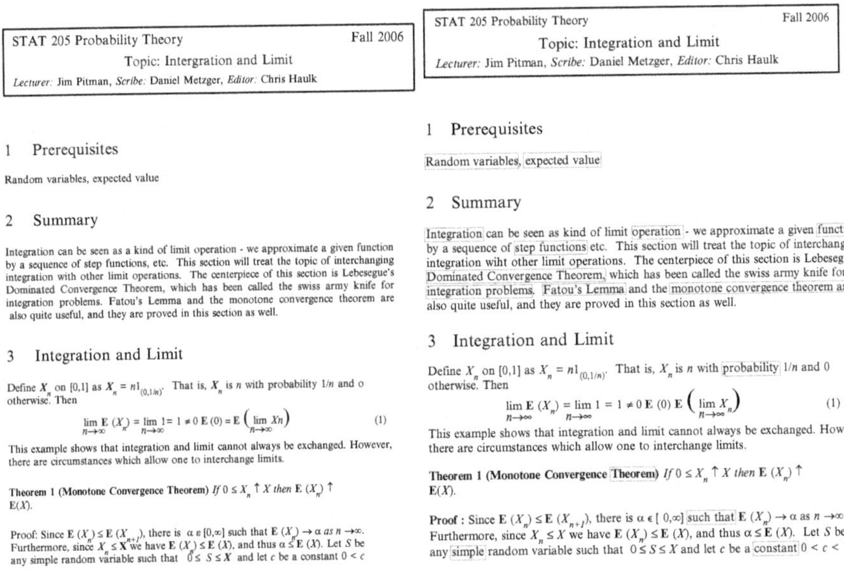

STAT 205 Probability Theory   Fall 2006
          Topic: Intergration and Limit
Lecturer: Jim Pitman, *Scribe:* Daniel Metzger, *Editor:* Chris Haulk

1   Prerequisites

Random variables, expected value

2   Summary

Integration can be seen as a kind of limit operation - we approximate a given function by a sequence of step functions, etc. This section will treat the topic of interchanging integration with other limit operations. The centerpiece of this section is Lebesegue's Dominated Convergence Theorem, which has been called the swiss army knife for integration problems. Fatou's Lemma and the monotone convergence theorem are also quite useful, and they are proved in this section as well.

3   Integration and Limit

Define X_n on [0,1] as $X_n = n1_{(0,1/n)}$. That is, X_n is n with probability $1/n$ and 0 otherwise. Then

$$\lim_{n\to\infty} E(X_n) = \lim_{n\to\infty} 1 = 1 \neq 0 = E(0) = E\left(\lim_{n\to\infty} Xn\right) \tag{1}$$

This example shows that integration and limit cannot always be exchanged. However, there are circumstances which allow one to interchange limits.

Theorem 1 (Monotone Convergence Theorem) *If* $0 \le X_n \uparrow X$ *then* $E(X_n) \uparrow$ $E(X)$.

Proof: Since $E(X_n) \le E(X_{n+1})$, there is $\alpha \in [0,\infty]$ such that $E(X_n) \to \alpha$ as $n \to \infty$. Furthermore, since $X_n \le X$ we have $E(X_n) \le E(X)$, and thus $\alpha \le E(X)$. Let S be any simple random variable such that $0 \le S \le X$ and let c be a constant $0 < c$

STAT 205 Probability Theory   Fall 2006
          Topic: Integration and Limit
Lecturer: Jim Pitman, *Scribe:* Daniel Metzger, *Editor:* Chris Haulk

1   Prerequisites

Random variables, expected value

2   Summary

Integration can be seen as kind of limit operation - we approximate a given function by a sequence of step functions etc. This section will treat the topic of interchanging integration wiht other limit operations. The centerpiece of this section is Lebesegue's Dominated Convergence Theorem, which has been called the swiss army knife for integration problems. Fatou's Lemma and the monotone convergence theorem are also quite useful, and they are proved in this section as well.

3   Integration and Limit

Define X_n on [0,1] as $X_n = n1_{(0,1/n)}$. That is, X_n is n with probability $1/n$ and 0 otherwise. Then

$$\lim_{n\to\infty} E(X_n) = \lim_{n\to\infty} 1 = 1 \neq 0 = E(0) = E\left(\lim_{n\to\infty} X_n\right) \tag{1}$$

This example shows that integration and limit cannot always be exchanged. However, there are circumstances which allow one to interchange limits.

Theorem 1 (Monotone Convergence Theorem) *If* $0 \le X_n \uparrow X$ *then* $E(X_n) \uparrow$ $E(X)$.

Proof : Since $E(X_n) \le E(X_{n+1})$, there is $\alpha \in [0,\infty]$ such that $E(X_n) \to \alpha$ as $n \to \infty$. Furthermore, since $X_n \le X$ we have $E(X_n) \le E(X)$, and thus $\alpha \le E(X)$. Let S be any simple random variable such that $0 \le S \le X$ and let c be a constant $0 < c < 1$.

Fig. 2.7 Screenshot of original (*left*) and automatically linked (*right*) lecture notes using NNexus. The links in this example are to definitions on both MathWorld and PlanetMath, depending on which site had each particular definition available, and in the case both did, a collection priority configuration option determined the outcome. Concepts were "imported" from MathWorld using that site's OAI repository

Professor Jim Pitman at UC Berkeley – before and after automatic linking with NNexus (the links in this example are to both PlanetMath and MathWorld).

Due to the ease-of-use and success of linking lecture notes we are confident that we can extend NNexus to other applications with diminishing additional effort. Another interesting application is the linking of abstracts in research and educational digital libraries. This would enable learners (students or researchers) to quickly find related articles and also would help the user better understand the underlying concepts in the abstracts.

It would also be useful to apply automatic linking to educational blogs, which are of increasing prevalence and impact on the web, and are being embraced by large-scale efforts such as the NSDL.[8]

The modular design of NNexus allows developers to use NNexus as a web plugin for on-demand text linking and for various document authoring applications. NNexus could be deployed as a web service to allow third parties to link arbitrary documents to particular corpora.

---

[8] For their "Expert Voices" service. See http://www.nsdl.org/

2.6 Conclusion and Open Issues

We have introduced the problem of automatic invocation linking for collaborative web-based corpora and outlined the design goals that any automatic linking system should strive to achieve. We presented NNexus, an automatic linking system that we have developed as a potential solution and presented a few case studies demonstrating the effectiveness and efficiency of the NNexus approach. NNexus is now available for general use as open source software[9] and we look forward to working with others to improve it and apply it more widely to enhance the semantic quality of the web in general.

There are a number of open research directions remaining with the automatic linking problem. First, in order to achieve perfect link recall yet avoiding overlinking problem, automatic keyword extraction technique is a promising direction to investigate to better extract concept labels to be linked. Second, in order to further enhance link precision, it is a fruitful research direction to combine content based information retrieval techniques and collaborative filtering techniques [1] with the metadata based approach in NNexus to enhance the ranking of potential link targets and address issues of "competing" entries and different needs and preferences of authors. This especially becomes an issue when one goes beyond a single collaborative corpus, as would typically be the case in linking to them by third parties. Finally, it remains a major research and development item to generalize any linking system for inter-linking of multiple corpus across domains with expansion of ontology mapping capabilities.

Acknowledgements This work has been partially supported by the Google Summer of Code Program. We would also like to thank the editors of the special issue and the anonymous reviewers for their valuable comments that improved this paper.

References

1. G. Adomavicius and A. Tuzhilin. Toward the next generation of recommender systems: a survey of the state-of-the-art and possible extensions. *IEEE Transactions on Knowledge and Data Engineering*, 17(6), 2005.
2. Zharko Aleksovski and Michel Klein. Ontology mapping using background knowledge. In *K-CAP '05: Proceedings of the 3rd international conference on Knowledge capture*, 2005.
3. Ricardo A. Baeza-Yates and Berthier A. Ribeiro-Neto. *Modern Information Retrieval*. ACM Press / Addison-Wesley, 1999.
4. J. Gardner, A. Krowne, and L. Xiong. NNexus: An Automatic Linker for Collaborative Web-Based Corpora In *IEEE Transactions on Knowledge and Data Engineering*, 21(6), 2009.
5. L. Gridinoc, M. Sabou, M. dAquin, M. Dzbor, and E. Motta Semantic Browsing with Power-Magpie In *ESWC '2008: 5th European Semantic Web Conference*, pages 802–806, 2008.

---

[9] http://aux.planetmath.org/nnexus/

6. Yannis Kalfoglou and Marco Schorlemmer. Ontology mapping: The state of the art. In Y. Kalfoglou, M. Schorlemmer, A. Sheth, S. Staab, and M. Uschold, editors, *Semantic Interoperability and Integration*, number 04391 in Dagstuhl Seminar Proceedings. Internationales Begegnungs- und Forschungszentrum fuer Informatik (IBFI), Schloss Dagstuhl, Germany, 2005.

7. Kleinberg, Jon *Authoritative sources in a hyperlinked environment* In *Journal of the ACM 46* (5):604632. 1999.

8. J. Kolbitsch and H. Maurer. Community building around encyclopeadic knowledge. *Journal of Computing and Information Technology*, 14, 2006.

9. Aaron Krowne. An architecture for collaborative math and science digital libraries. Master's thesis, Virginia Polytechnic Institure and State University, Blacksburg, VA, 2003.

10. Max Völkel, Markus Krötzsch, Denny Vrandecic, Heiko Haller, and Rudi Studer. Semantic wikipedia. In *WWW '06: Proceedings of the 15th international conference on World Wide Web*, pages 585–594, New York, NY, USA, 2006. ACM Press.

11. D. Milne and I. Witten. Learning to Link with Wikipedia. In *CIKM '2008: 17th Conference on Information and Knowledge Management*, 2008.

12. Natalya Fridman Noy and Mark A. Musen. PROMPT: Algorithm and Tool for Automated Ontology Merging and Alignment. In *Proceedings of the Seventeenth National Conference on Artificial Intelligence and Twelfth Conference on Innovative Applications of Artificial Intelligence*, 2000.

13. S. E. Roberto Tazzoli and Paolo Castagna. Towards a semantic wiki web. In *In Demo Session at ISWC2004*, 2004.

14. Adam Souzis. Building a semantic wiki. *IEEE Intelligent Systems*, 20(5):87–91, 2005.

15. G. Weaver, B. Strickland, and G. Crane. Quantifying the accuracy of relational statements in wikipedia: a methodology. In *JCDL '06: Proceedings of the 6th ACM/IEEE-CS joint conference on Digital libraries*, 2006.

Chapter 3
WS-Query – A Framework to Efficiently Query Semantic Web Service

Mourad Ouzzani, Athman Bouguettaya, and Ahmed Elmagarmid

Abstract We propose a query framework, called *WS-Query*, to efficiently query semantic Web services using *Quality of Web Service* (QoWS). Service querying is enabled by a novel service query model where declarative service queries are resolved by multi-level Web service invocations. Quality of Web Service is used as a key parameter to select the best services. QoWS consists of a set of criteria that characterize the behavior of Web services in delivering their functionalities. We adjust the different *QoWS* parameters through dynamic rating and multimode matching. The dynamic rating provides a quantitative assessment of the Web services in achieving the promised *QoWS* throughout their interactions with the query infrastructure. The proposed multimode matching expands the solution space by enabling similar/partial answers and allows assigning a degree of precision for each matching mode.

3.1 Introduction

Service computing and semantic Web services have undeniably taken ground in many industries and academia as the technology of choice for building complex applications over the Web. Many organizations are now using semantic Web services to interact with each others and give access to their business to internal users and external customers. Even the scientific community has embarked in similar endeavors

M. Ouzzani (✉)
Cyber Center, Purdue University, West Lafayette, IN
e-mail: mourad@cs.purdue.edu

A. Bouguettaya
CSIRO, Canberra, ACT 2601, Australia
e-mail: athman.bouguettaya@csiro.au

A. Elmagarmid
Department of Computer Science and Cyber Center, Purdue University, West Lafayette, IN
e-mail: ake@cs.purdue.edu

R. Chbeir et al., *Emergent Web Intelligence: Advanced Information Retrieval*, Advanced
Information and Knowledge Processing, DOI 10.1007/978-1-84996-074-8_3,

where analysis tools and access to databases are offered through web services. Semantic Web services offer an ideal framework to leverage the huge investments in application development over the Web. They provide a standard framework for interoperating independently developed Web applications. Simply defined, a Web service is a set of related functionalities that can be programmatically accessed through the Web. As the *Service Web* starts to take shape, we anticipate that the business model will include a whole community of Web service *providers* that will compete to provide similar and different services. Therefore, the expected querying paradigm shift will be from a *data-centric querying* to a *service-centric querying* where *first-class* objects are Web services.

Fully delivering on the potential of Web services will require a foundation to provide a sound design for efficiently publishing, discovering, composing, monitoring, and optimizing access to Web services. The proposed Web service foundation will enable the ubiquitous deployment of *Web Service Management Systems* (WSMSs) [33]. Web services would be treated as *first-class* objects, i.e., they would be the focus of manipulation and reasoning tasks. This paper focuses on the *service query optimization* aspect of WSMSs. Because we are witnessing a growing pace in Web service deployments (e.g., IBM, Google, BEA, and Microsoft), it will soon be common for Web service providers to offer the same or similar user-requested functionality (*aka* service). Thus, there is an urgent need to provide a uniform *foundational framework* for defining the *criteria* used in service query optimization along with the development of a *selection process* for obtaining the *"best"* Web services that fulfill the requested functionality (service). In this framework, it is assumed that service requesters can either be human users or other Web services. Users would typically be represented by a Web service proxy. In this paper, we present a comprehensive query infrastructure, called *WS-Query*, that relies on a user-oriented set of criteria to determine the *Quality of Web Service (QoWS)* of the requested service. Central to this approach is the use of a three-level service query refinement approach that implements a novel user-centric optimization process.

Querying *simple* Web services typically consists of invoking one or more operations using messages. Querying multiple Web services that would form a *composite Web service*, like a travel package, requires finding all relevant Web services and their corresponding operations, and combining these operations under several constraints including feasibility, e.g., do we have all inputs to invoke a given operation, and efficiency, is it the best choice with respect to a given objective function. *WS-Query* offers a novel multi-level service query model to address such needs. In such a framework, users formulate their requests for services through *declarative service queries*. These queries are resolved by *orchestrating* the invocation of several Web service operations. Without loss of generality, we assume that each Web service is represented by one single operation. In our framework, users typically formulate declarative queries against *abstract relations*. Abstract relations are a means to represent *meta-service* information. Query processing and optimization is a three-phase process that corresponds to three levels, namely, *query level*, *mediator level*, and *concrete level*, to obtain an efficient *service execution plan*. In the first level, i.e., *query level*, the use of *abstract relations* allows for easy query formulation.

The second level, i.e., *mediator level*, consists of mapping the message invocations from the abstract relations to generic operations' invocations of a particular domain application. In the third level, i.e., *concrete level*, a mapping is performed from generic operations to *concrete operations* implemented in actual Web services. The proposed three-level query infrastructure allows different degrees of matching, thus enabling a broader range of choices and more flexibility in resolving a given service query. The matching process involves the use of *ontologies* to express the semantics of both requests and Web service offerings.

The *optimization model* of *WS-Query* is based on the use of *Quality of Web Service (QoWS)* which captures users' requirements (i.e., expectations) for acceptable performance. In contrast, traditional database query optimization techniques are usually system-oriented. In our proposed query infrastructure, *QoWS* is key in distinguishing between competing Web services [31, 34]. QoWS includes different quality parameters that characterize the behavior of a Web service in delivering its functionalities. Examples of such parameters include *availability*, *latency*, and *fees*. Since several fluctuations may occur during a Web service lifetime leading to situations where the promised *QoWS* may not be fulfilled, we propose to *monitor QoWS* when Web service operations are invoked. This monitoring measures the fluctuations of *QoWS* parameters to be able to accurately assess the Web service's behavior.

The work described here builds upon the preliminary work presented in [20] and extends it in several major ways. Our contributions in this article are: First, we propose a three-level service query model where users formulate declarative queries against abstract relations (i.e., abstract services). These queries are then transformed into invocations of different Web service operations. As part of this model, a flexible matching scheme is used to allow partial answers. Second, a comprehensive characterization of non-functional properties of Web services is proposed. The result is a model where *QoWS* parameters are classified based on the Web service behavior they characterize. In this paper, we assume that the values of these parameters are available from either the service providers (as part of the Web service descriptions in the service registry) or from other third parties. We do not delve into how these *QoWS* parameters are actually computed. Third, we propose to monitor Web service invocations to measure *QoWS* parameters' fluctuations and rate the Web services accordingly. These ratings will be used in the optimization process. Fourth, we propose different optimization algorithms to efficiently query Web services based on the use of *QoWS*. The two basic premises for our query infrastructure are that (i) multiple Web services compete to offer similar functionalities, and that (ii) service providers may be engaged in business partnerships. Finally, we provide an implementation of the proposed infrastructure in the context of a real-life digital government application. We conducted an extensive experimental study of the different proposed algorithms. While our scenario examples focus on the social services for senior citizens application which lends itself to the type of on-demand, customized, and outsourced services considered in this work, the proposed query infrastructure is generic enough to be applicable to a wide range of other domains such as e-commerce (B2B, B2C, etc.), grid services, bioinformatics, etc.

3.1.1 Motivating Scenario

To illustrate the need for a comprehensive query infrastructure over Web services, we consider the case of social benefits for senior citizens. The scenario illustrates how getting those benefits for senior citizens is difficult and highlights the many challenges facing social workers throughout this process. The goal of *WS-Query* is to overcome such difficulties and help achieve the maximum efficiency and the best services for senior citizens.

Let us assume that Maria, an indigent senior citizen, would like to receive social benefits. She would have to visit a local social service agency for an interview (Fig. 3.1). There, Peter, a social worker, finds out that Maria is potentially qualified for several benefits, most of which are sub-contracted from outside organizations. As several potential providers may be candidate, Peter needs to contact them to check if they meet the agency requirements (e.g., budget) and are actually able to serve Maria's needs. This may not be an easy task for the social worker.

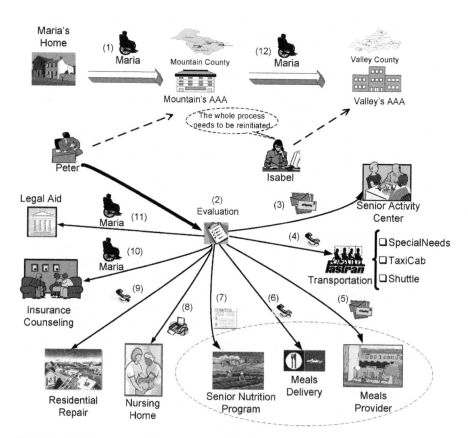

Fig. 3.1 A typical scenario for senior citizens services

For example, the *transportation* service may be provided by different transportation companies: County Shuttle – a county service that provides free rides for senior citizens but has limited coverage, Vans Shuttle – a private shuttle company that charges a monthly fee, TaxiCab – offers flat fee for any use of a taxi cab, SpecialNeeds – a specialized transportation company for the handicapped. Although all these providers offer transportation services, the conditions (e.g., price, quality) under which these services are offered may differ. For instance, the Vans Shuttle company may be the least expensive but may not provide the same level of service for handicapped persons as SpecialNeeds. Furthermore, caring for the nutritional needs of Maria may require three types of services *Meals Provider*, *Meals Delivery*, and *Senior Nutrition Program*. In this case, individual providers should be selected in a way that optimizes their combination. For instance, the choice of Meals@Home as a *meals provider* may reduce costs if combined with MealsOnTime as the *meals delivery* since these two providers are in business partnership.

In summary, for any particular service that Maria is qualified for, several potential providers may exist. Although they may offer similar services, the conditions (e.g., price, quality) under which those services are offered may differ. Manually looking for the appropriate providers is an error-prone process that may lead to sub-optimal outcomes for both the agency and the senior citizens. In addition, as Maria's situation changes, it might be necessary to modify existing services and add new ones. Furthermore, as provider quality changes over time and new providers are available or become unavailable, the agency may need to change Maria's providers for better efficiency.

The remainder of this paper is organized as follows. In Section 3.2, we present a novel query model for Web services where the *Web service space* is abstracted into three levels, namely *query*, *mediator*, and *concrete*. In Section 3.3, we describe WS-Query's optimization strategy for Web services. We mainly focus on the non functional properties (*QoWS*) to select and combine Web services. We propose a monitoring technique to assess the behavior of Web services. We then present several algorithms for optimizing queries based on *QoWS*. In Section 3.4, we present the implementation of our approach in an e-government application. We also describe experiments conducted using the proposed optimization algorithms. In Section 3.5, we overview the related work. We provide the concluding remarks in Section 3.6.

3.2 Service Query Model

Given a query, its resolution involves the invocation of various Web service operations and the combination of their results. The proposed service query model enables users to express their requests through simple declarative queries.

3.2.1 Three-Level Service Model

To facilitate the manipulation of Web services as first-class objects, we propose a three-level service model where queries only specify the requested information and functionalities without referring to specific Web services or the way to combine them. More precisely, we define at the top level, *relations* to allow for easy query formulation. At the second level, we define *generic operations* which are usually specific to a given application domain. The third level represents *concrete operations* from actual Web services. The three-level model acts as a layered schema for the service space. Although our Web service model is inspired from database concepts, we note some major differences. In databases, the requested data is well-known, static, and owned and managed by a central authority. In the query infrastructure, relevant Web services need first to be located for each query. These a priori unknown Web services are independent entities that compete against each other to solve a query. In addition, the same query may be answered by different Web services if executed twice due to the dynamic nature of the Web service space. The three-level service model is defined in more details as follows:

- *Query Level* Defines a set of *relations* that allow the formulation and submission of declarative queries over Web services. Different sets of relations may be defined over the generic operations using different *mapping rules*. Examples of relations include *transportation_options*, and *food_provider_menu*.
- *Mediator Level* Defines *generic operations* typically offered in a particular application domain. Theses generic operations determine, along with the relations, the kind of queries that are supported by the query infrastructure. Examples of generic operations include *Transportation*, *LegalAid*, and *MealsProvider*.
- *Concrete Level* Represents actual Web services and their concrete operations offered on the Web. These are the potential candidates to answer queries. Web services are a priori unknown; they need to be discovered and their operations need to be *matched* with generic operations.

A typical scenario for building the three-level query model would be of a "designer" willing to provide query capabilities over Web services in a target application domain, e.g., social services. The designer starts by defining a set of generic operations that represent basic operations usually offered by Web services in this application using some domain expertise. These generic operations are not related to any existing Web services. This is crucial since Web services are continuously evolving and the system is always looking for the best deals for users' queries. Next, the designer defines a set of relations tailored for a particular user group that is interested in some specific part of the service space (by adding conditions, composing generic operations, etc.) For example, citizens will not have access to the same set of generic operations as social workers. Finally, a user-friendly interface is provided to allow users pose queries using those relations.

In Fig. 3.2, we illustrate the three level scheme for the senior citizens scenario. For example, a social worker could get services for providing meals in a given

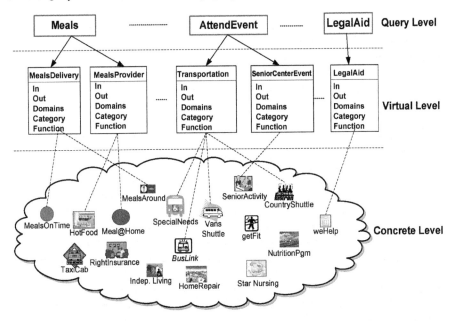

Fig. 3.2   The three-level query model for the senior citizens scenario

area and fulfilling some conditions (price, quantity, etc.) by simply formulating a query that uses the relation Meals. This relation is then mapped to its corresponding generic operations *DeliverMeal* and *PrepareMeal*. Each of these generic operations could then be matched to various operations from the concrete level. For example, *DeliverMeal* could be matched to operations from two potential Web services *MealsOnTime* and *FoodAround*.

3.2.2   Mapping Relations to Generic Operations

Different views can be obtained over the service space by defining different relations at the query level and varying the way they relate to generic operations. A given relation is obtained by "invoking" one or several generic operations. Output parameters of the concrete operations that will be matched to those generic operations will feed the tuples of that relation. We represent relations at the query level as a sort of "conjunctive queries" over generic operations. Conjunctive queries or select-project-join queries are simply a conjunction of atoms, where each atom is built out of relation symbols and existentially quantified variables. Let $\mathcal{R}$ be the set of relations defined at the query level and $\mathcal{G}$ the set of generic operations, which are defined in more details in the next subsection, the mapping between relations and generic operations is defined as follows:

Definition 3.1. For any relation $R_i \in \mathcal{R}$,

$$(R_i(x_1, x_2, \ldots, x_n)) : - \bigwedge_j Gop_j(y_{j_1}, \ldots, y_{j_m}), \bigwedge_k C_k)$$

where x_i are the parameters of R_i, $Gop_j \in \mathcal{G}$, and y_j are input/output parameters of the corresponding operation. C_k's represent conditions on parameters appearing in Gop_j. Their form is: $C_k = x_k \; op \; c$, where x_k is an input/output parameter from any Gop_j, c a constant, and $op \in \{=, \neq, <, >, \geq, \leq, \in\}$.   □

The :- is the transcription of an implication arrow. It means that to obtain R_i, we need to invoke the different operations Gop_j. The $\bigwedge$ refers to a conjunction. Multiple occurrences of a parameter express equality. This definition does not mandate any order on the concrete operation invocations. The order is obtained during the processing and optimization phase of complete queries. This enables more flexibility in deciding which Web services to use to solve a query. Furthermore, this definition captures the process of going from a static entity, the relations, to a dynamic entity, the generic operations, in order to populate the former with the results of the invocation of the latter.

Here is an example of a mapping rule:

> *Meals(Zipcode, MealType, MealPrice, DeliveryPrice)* :-
> *DeliverMeals(Area, DeliveryPrice),*
> *PrepareMeals(ProviderZip, MealType, MealPrice),*
> *Zipcode* $\in$ *Area, ProviderZip* $\in$ *Area*

The relation *Meals* is defined through two generic operations: *DeliverMeals* returns a meals delivery service in a certain area and *PrepareMeals* returns a meal provider. *Area* is a set of zip codes where the delivery service operates. In addition, the mapping rule states conditions to make sure that the meal delivery service's area includes both the meal provider and the zip code specified in the relation.

3.2.3 Generic Operations Representation

For any generic operation in a query, we need to locate relevant concrete operations from an a priori unknown service space. These are *matching operations* that provide the "same" functionality as the generic operation. The description of generic operations should contain enough information to decide if a match is possible. It should be also flexible enough to allow a wide range of concrete operation selections. Thus, a semantic description is required in addition to syntactic attributes.

In general, it is not possible to assume that "all" existing Web services would agree on a common ontology. However, queries usually target specific applications domains or communities of Web services which would agree on some common ontology. In this case, the target ontology will be known a priori and selecting Web services from those communities would be possible. On the contrary, if a query targets multiple ontologies, semantics reconciliation, ontology mapping and alignment techniques [9] should be used to enable matching. Using such techniques will not have a major impact on our query infrastructure; if a common ontology exists direct matching occurs, otherwise a "semantics reconciliation" module will be transparently added without modifying the rest of the infrastructure. Discussions of reconciliation techniques and the corresponding module are outside the scope of this paper. In WS-Query, we use the ontology-based description of Web services proposed in [16] to describe concrete and generic operations. This ontology-based description has been specified using DAML+OIL [12]. While the semantic description of Web services is still work in progress, there are two emerging specifications that are of interest: (1) OWL-S [14] (previously DAML-S), built on top of OWL, provides a set of markup language constructs to describe Web services. (2) The Web service modeling ontology (WSMO) [11] focuses on describing various aspects related to Semantic Web Services. However, we choose to use our in-house semantic description for the sake of simplicity and since there is no accepted standard.

We assume that each operation, either generic or concrete, is semantically described through its *Purpose* and *Category*. *Purpose* contains two attributes: *functionality* and *synonyms*. The functionality represents the business functionality provided by the operation. Examples of functionalities include *eligibility screening* and *listing*. The synonyms attribute contains a set of alternative functionality names for the operation. For example, *eligibility screening* is synonym of *eligibility check*. *Category* contains also two attributes: *domain* and *synonyms*. The domain gives the area of interest of the operation. Examples of domains include *food*, *legal*, and *counseling*. Synonyms attributes are similar to those defined for purpose. Web services and their concrete operations are usually described using WSDL which does not provide support for semantic description. We assume that the different semantic attributes are either added to the WSDL description or advertised in the service registry with the Web service using, for example, UDDI tModels.

Operations may have parameters that play either the role of input or output. There may be situations where in Web service operations offering similar functionalities, the same parameter is used as input in some concrete operations and output in others. For example, two transportation services may specify a parameter related to pricing type (per use, per ride, monthly, etc.) as an input in one case and output in another. Thus, we propose to define parameters that can be either input or output (*InOut*). The actual nature, i.e., input or output, of these parameters is determined at processing time, when actual Web services are located and their concrete operations are matched against generic operations. We should note that Web services do not include, in their basic definition, this concept of *InOut*. However, we introduced this concept at the abstract level only when we define generic operations. This will allow us to match a given generic operation to a larger set of concrete operations.

Definition 3.2. A generic operation is formally represented by a tuple $Gop = (In, Out, InOut, Category, Purpose)$ where In is the set of input parameters, Out the set of output parameters, $InOut$ the set of parameters that may be either input or output, $Category$ describes the domain of interest, and $Purpose$ describes the business functionality. □

The following is an example of a generic operation:

TransportationOptions = (*In, Out, InOut, Category, Purpose*)

where   *In* = {DepartureZip,   ArrivalZip},   *Out* = {Rules,   PricingType,   Price}
InOut = {PricingType},   *Category* = (Travel,   {Transportation,   Voyage}),   and
Purpose = (Listing, {Fare, Time Table}).

3.2.4   Web Service Query Specification

Usually, users pose their queries through some user-friendly graphical interface.
However, queries are manipulated internally as conjunctive queries over relations
from the query level.

Definition 3.3. Q is a conjunctive (select-project-join) query over $\mathcal{R}$:

$$Q(X) : - \bigwedge_i R_i(X_i), \bigwedge_k C_k$$

where R_i are relations from the query level. X and X_i are tuples of parameters such
that $\forall x \in X, \exists x \in X_i$. C_k's represent conditions on parameters appearing in the
query. Their form is: $C_k = x \; op \; c$, where x is a parameter appearing in any X_i, c a
constant, and $op \in \{=, \neq, <, >, \geq, \leq, \in\}$.   □

To illustrate the use of our service model, we present a sample query from the
senior citizens scenario. Here are the generic operations used in this example:

- Transportation(In(DepartureZip, ArrivalZip), Out(Rules, PricingType, Price)) –
Returns transportation services provided between two zip codes.
- ArtGallery(In(Zipcode), Out(OperationHours)) – Information on an art gallery
in a zip code.

For example, Maria is looking for the best Web services for transportation and
art gallery. She may submit either two different queries for each service or one
single query for both. In the latter case, she may take advantage of some potential
discounts that may be offered by an art gallery in partnership with a transportation
service. Without loss of generality, we assume that the query is expressed directly
over generic operations.

Query(Rules, PricingType, Price, Zipcode, OperationHours) :-
        Transportation(DepartureZip, ArrivalZip, Rules,
                        PricingType, Price),
        ArtGallery(Zipcode, OperationHours),
        Price < 30, *DepartureZip* = 22044, *ArrivalZip* = 22311,
        Zipcode = 22311

3.2.5 Multimode Matching for Generic Operations

Different providers compete by offering "similar" functionalities while differing on the required input, returned output, etc. Thus, it would not be always possible to find an exact match for a given request. In addition, users may be inclined to accept similar or close answers. Hence, instead of looking only for concrete operations that match exactly the generic operations appearing in a query, a more flexible matching scheme would allow having generic and concrete operations' attributes not necessarily identical. The idea is to vary the way that the different attributes (e.g., input, category) from generic and concrete operations are compared to each other. This results in different levels of "*precision*" for the matching process. While the matching scheme described below overlaps with some existing techniques like those in [7, 15, 24, 26, 29], our focus in this paper is mostly on defining different levels of matching precision and being able to quantify their influence on optimization. In fact, we could replace the proposed scheme by another as long as we can define levels of matching precision and assign a matching degree to each level.

We define a function *similar* to check whether two parameters of two operations are the same. $similar(x, y)$ is *True* if x and y correspond exactly to the same concept with respect to the common ontology defined in the application domain, i.e., same meaning and same data type. For example, the attribute "cost" and "price" represent the same concept; both correspond to the sale price of an item in US\$ before tax. It is also possible to relax the condition on data types provided that there is a mechanism to relates different data types. Other option for defining similarity are possible but are outside the scope of this paper. For any generic operation op_g, we assume that $InOut(op_g)$ has been divided into two sets $InOut_i(op_g)$ and $InOut_o(op_g)$ that correspond to parameters from $InOut$ that have been matched to input parameters and output parameters from the concrete operation op_c respectively. We can now present two potential comparisons between the input and output parameters of a generic operation op_g and a concrete operation op_c that we are using when defining the matching levels.

(a) **Equality** $In(op_c) = In(op_g) \cup InOut_i(op_g)$ ($Out(op_c) = Out(op_g) \cup InOut_o(op_g)$ is defined similarly) if

- (i) $In(op_c)$ and $In(op_g) \cup InOut_i(op_g)$ have the same number of parameters and
- (ii) $\forall x \in In(op_c)$ (resp. $In(op_g) \cup InOut_i(op_g)$), $\exists y \in In(op_g) \cup InOut_i(op_g)$ (resp. $In(op_c)$) such that $similar(x, y)$ is *True*.

(b) **Subsumption** $In(op_c) \subset In(op_g) \cup InOut_i(op_g)$ ($Out(op_c) \subset Out(op_c) \cup InOut_o(op_g)$ is defined similarly) if

- (i) The number of parameters in $In(op_c)$ is smaller than in $In(op_g) \cup InOut_i(op_g)$ and
- (ii) $\forall x \in In(op_c)$, $\exists y \in In(op_g) \cup InOut_i(op_g)$ such that $similar(x, y)$ is *True*.

Let op_g and op_c be two generic and concrete operations respectively. We define four matching levels obtained by varying the way the different attributes are compared. Other classifications of the matching levels are possible by introducing other variations in comparing the different attributes. We assume that $Category(op_c) = (Domain_c, Cat\_Synonyms_c)$, $Category(op_g) = (Domain_g, Cat\_Synonyms_g)$, $Purpose(op_c) = (Functionality_c, Pur\_Synonyms_c)$, and $Purpose(op_g) = (Functionality_g, Pur\_Synonyms_g)$.

1. *Exact Match* The concrete operation op_c matches the generic operation op_g with respect to all attributes. op_c *matches exactly* op_g if they have the same *Category* and *Purpose*, and the conditions of the *equality* case are fulfilled.

2. *Overlapping Match* Corresponds to the case of a concrete operation offering *close* functionalities to that of the generic operation. op_c and op_g *overlap* if the conditions of the *equality* case are fulfilled and their *Category* and *Purpose* overlap:

$$(\{Domain_c\} \cup Cat\_Synonyms_c) \cap (\{Domain_g\} \cup Cat\_Synonyms_g) \neq \emptyset$$
and
$$(\{Functionality_c\} \cup Pur\_Synonyms_c) \cap (\{Functionality_g\} \cup Pur\_Synonyms_g) \neq \emptyset.$$

3. *Partial Match* Corresponds to the case where the input and output parameters are not identical. Two operations op_g and op_c *match partially* if they have the same *Category* and *Purpose*, and the conditions of the *subsumption* case as presented above are fulfilled. Examples of such subsumption include a concrete operation that does not return all the output parameters expected by the generic operation (this may be an acceptable answer for some users) or a concrete operation that uses only a subset of the input provided by the generic operation. A simple example for the second case is of two operations busFare1(<Other Inputs>, Age, Cost) and busFare2(<Other Inputs>, Cost). Both operations return bus fares except that the second operation does not take into account the age information which can is used by the second operation to get a lower Cost.

4. *Partial and Overlap Match* This level is a combination of the *overlap* and *partial* matches. Two operations op_g and op_c match partially and by overlap if the conditions of the *subsumption* case as presented above are fulfilled and their *Category* and *Purpose* attributes overlap as defined in the *overlap* case.

A query may lead to several candidate service execution plans and each plan may have operations matched using one of the above modes. Since these different matching modes do not offer the same matching precision, it is important to be able to distinguish between them in selecting the best service execution plan. For this purpose, we assign a *matching degree* to each level and use the matching degree of each operation in computing the objective function of the overall service execution plan. This is done in a way that a matching level with a high value for the matching degree will give a better value for the objective function and thus the corresponding service execution plan will be most likely selected as the optimal plan. Hence, we define four matching degrees for the above levels; the default values are 1, 9/10, 8/10, and 7/10 respectively. It is important to notice that our goal is to distinguish between the different matching modes and use this information in the objective function of the optimizer. Using other matching degrees will either decrease or increase the contribution of the *QoWS* of the corresponding operation to the overall objective function. Thus, the default values can be changed depending on the intended weight to be given for each matching mode.

We define the following simple guidelines for the matching degrees:

1. Matching_degree(Exact) = 1.
2. Matching_degree(Exact) > matching_degree(Overlapping) > matching_degree (Partial) > matching_degree(Partial & Overlap).
3. If a given mode is not desirable then the matching degree of that mode will be set to zero (0) or to a very low value making it less likely to be selected by the optimizer, while keeping rule 2 satisfied.

3.3 Quality of Web Service-Aware Optimization

A query may be potentially solved by several service execution plans using different Web services. Thus, it is necessary to set appropriate criteria to select the "best" service execution plan amongst all possible ones. Recent literature [8, 23, 31] shows that *QoS* (or *QoWS*) of individual Web services is crucial for their competitiveness. The concept of *QoWS* captures more accurately users and applications' requirements for efficiency and hence for query optimization on the Web. The challenge is to define appropriate metrics to characterize *QoWS* and devise techniques to optimize service-based queries. In our approach, *QoWS* consists of a number of parameters (non-functional properties) that characterize the Web service performance in delivering its functionalities.

We define *QoWS* parameters for individual Web services and for service execution plans composed of several Web services. Since *QoWS* parameters may be subject to various fluctuations during a Web service's life time, we propose a monitoring scheme that assesses *QoWS* advertised by service providers based on their actual behavior. We then present several optimization algorithms based on the proposed *QoWS* model that take into account the presence of different constraints.

3.3.1 Quality of Web Service Model

The concept of QoS has been mostly used in networking and multimedia applications. In [30], quality of service is defined as the "collective effect of service performance, which determines the satisfaction of a user of a service. It is characterized by the combined aspects of performance factors applicable to all services." To a certain extent, this definition holds also in the context of WS-Query. However, in the case of Web services, we need to go beyond classical system-centric quality metrics. Different aspects that influence the user experience with the Web service should be taken into account. We base our model on some of the criteria that have been proposed for Web services as in [34]. While more criteria can be added, we focus on those that are more likely to influence the selection of a given Web service. In this section, we present the different *QoWS* parameters that we are using in our framework and categorize them based on the behavioral aspects they characterize.

Each Web service would advertise its *QoWS* parameters in a service registry, for example UDDI. Some of the *QoWS* parameters may be obtained from third parties, e.g., rating systems like *epinions.com* could be used for the *reputation* parameter. Our focus in this paper is not on how these parameters are computed but on defining and categorizing these parameters and more importantly using them for optimizing Web service queries. We are assume that we are dealing with fixed values parameters that do not depend on the parameters of the specific Web service operation being invoked.

Definition 3.4. The *QoWS* of a Web service is represented by a vector of *QoWS* parameters. Each *QoWS* parameter is defined by a pair: QoWSp = (Name, Value). Name is the name of the *QoWS* parameter. Value may represent a probability, a scalar, or an enumeration. □

We assume that the meaning of *QoWS* parameters is common to all Web services. Our goal is to focus on defining those parameters and use them for optimization. As a result, the query infrastructure does not have to deal with issues of interpreting and/or mapping the meaning of *QoWS* parameters as specified by every single Web service. Furthermore, a given *QoWS* criterion could be generic enough to be used across domains or application specific. For example, response time or latency are inherent to any operation invocation. However, a transportation service, as those used in the senior citizens scenario, could be characterized with its *on time rate*. This is clearly not applicable to all Web service. In our work, we focus on generic parameters. However, our *QoWS* model should be easily extensible to include other application specific parameters without changing the underlying optimization model. We consider two main categories of generic *QoWS*: *computational behavior* and *business behavior*.

Computational QoWS Computational *QoWS* characterizes the invocation of Web service operations as perceived by a service consumer. It is further organized into three sub-categories:

- *Execution* Includes performance parameters while interacting with the Web service. We consider the following parameters:

  - *Latency* It represents the average time for an operation to return results after its invocation.
  - *Availability* It represents the probability that a service is available. In general, availability refers to the probability that the system is operating at any given moment and is available to perform its functions on behalf of its users [27].
  - *Accessibility* It represents the degree that a Web service is capable of serving a request. It may be measured by the ratio between the number of requests

being sent to the Web service and the number of requests that are effectively served. There could be situations when a Web service is available but not accessible.

- *Security*   Relates to the ability of the Web service in providing appropriate security mechanisms. The following (binary-valued) parameters are considered:

  - *Encryption*   Whether the Web service supports encryption of received and sent messages.
  - *Authentication*   Whether the Web service provides mechanisms to identify the invoking party (i.e., service consumer) to allow operation invocation.
  - *Access Control*   Whether the Web service supports access control by restricting operation invocation and access to information to authorized parties.

- *Privacy*   Relates to the ability of the Web service of preserving the privacy of the information it obtains from invokers. This includes the following (binary-valued) parameters:

  - *Privacy Policy*   Specifies whether the Web service has a privacy policy.
  - *Information Sharing*   Specifies whether the Web services shares collected information with third parties without explicit permission.

Business QoWS   Business *QoWS* includes the following parameters:

- *Usage Fee*   It represents units of money that a service consumer needs to pay to use the Web service, i.e., invoke operations.
- *Reputation*   Measures the reputation of the Web service based on user feedbacks. Users are prompted to rate Web services on a [1, 10] scale after the end of a query session. The reputation corresponds to the average of collected ratings.

QoWS parameters are also characterized as being either *negative* or *positive*. In negative parameters, the higher the value, the worse the quality. They include latency and usage fees. In positive parameters, the lower the value, the worse the quality. They include availability, accessibility, reliability, authentication, encryption, access control, privacy policy, information sharing, information disclosure, and reputation.

3.3.2   Rating QoWS Claims Through Monitoring

Depending of the resources allocated at the service provider side, server load, and other parameters, *QoWS* may fluctuate over time. The values that Web services advertise may necessarily reflect the actual *QoWS* they are delivering when they are invoked. Thus, it is important to assess the claims in terms of the *QoWS* that these Web services are promising to their clients. Our goal is to be able to *rate* Web services in terms of their *QoWS* parameters and use this rating in the optimization process.

Accurately assessing the behavior of Web services in terms of their *QoWS* depends on the nature of the *QoWS* to monitor and how easy is it to obtain information to asses this $QoWS$ parameter. For the $QoWS$ parameters in the execution category and the usage fee $QoWS$ parameter, WS-Query can simply measure the actual values of the $QoWS$ being delivered by collecting various information during the invocation of a Web service operation. For the security and privacy categories, we need to learn if there was any security breach or privacy violation. This may not be feasible by simply monitoring the invocations of Web service operations. Two approaches can be used in this case: (1) cooperative monitoring where cooperating peers share information about Web services to form a "common opinion" on how a specific Web service is behaving with respect to a given $QoWS$ and (2) community-based monitoring where Web services report the occurrence of security breaches or privacy violations.

In the latter case, we need to find out if there were any security or privacy breaches

3.3.2.1 Monitoring Execution and Business QoWS

We assume that all interactions with Web services occur through WS-Query. Hence, it is possible to collect different kinds of information about these interactions and use them in rating Web services. To avoid a high overhead on the system, monitoring or the process of collecting information is conducted periodically. In the following, we give more details on the information that WS-Query collects for each the execution and business $QoWS$ parameters. We will then explain how the collected information is used to rate Web services.

Execution Parameters The collected information relates to the behavior of the actual invocations of Web service operations.

- *Latency* Actual latency values are collected during operation invocations and their average is computed over a given time period θ_{lat}.
- *Availability* The number of successful and failed connection attempts to Web services are accumulated. A connection is successful if the Web service accepted the invocation but did not necessarily fulfill it successfully. Their ratio is computed for a given time period θ_{av} and collected values are discarded.
- *Accessibility* The number of successful and failed operation invocations are recorded. Their ratio is computed for a given time period θ_{acc} and the collected values are discarded.

Business Parameters

- *Usage Fee* The usage fee does not generally change from the published value and the actual value at invocation time. However, there may be cases where the Web service asks for a different usage fee (e.g., hidden costs) at execution time from the one that has been published in the service registry. In this case, we compute the difference between these two values.
- *Reputation* This parameter is obtained by WS-Query from a third party and is not subject to monitoring. This can be used as a summary rating for the other $QoWS$ parameters as an alternate to monitoring.

The value of the different time periods $\theta_{<p_i>}$ and the frequency of information collections depend mainly on the monitored $QoWS$ and the application domain. For example, the value of θ_{fee} should be long enough to allow the detection of changes in the usage fee parameter. In addition, if the load on the query infrastructure is very high, short time periods and low collection frequency may be sufficient.

3.3.2.2 Monitoring Security and Privacy QoWS

For the security category, we need to know if a certain security parameter has been breached. In the cooperative monitoring approach, cooperating peers would share with each other whatever they have been able to learn about security violations and use this shared knowledge to rate the security of the Web service. If this is not feasible, then community-based monitoring should be used. Web services will need to report the occurrence of security breaches. This reporting can be possible as part of obligations of the Web services in being part in the community of services that QS-Query uses to answer queries.

For the privacy category, we need to check if the Web service is keeping its promises in terms of the stated privacy and information sharing policies. Finding out about such privacy violations can be either achieved by having Web services voluntarily report such events (community-based monitoring) or through cooperating monitoring along the lines of the approach that we described in [22]. In a nutshell, collaborating peers would share specific data they have been able to access from the Web service and contrast this data with each other based on the privacy and disclosure policies advertised by the Web service. This may reveal whether the Web service is adhering to its privacy policies.

3.3.2.3 Rating Computation

To rate Web services, we need to compute for each $QoWS$ parameter, a $QoWS$ distance ($QoWSdist_{parameter}$) that quantifies the Web service behavior in delivering the promised $QoWS$ ($pQoWS_{parameter}$). The $QoWS$ distance depends on the meaning of the parameter, whether the parameter is negative or positive, the advertised or promised value, and the information being collected through monitoring. The value of this distance is used to either increase or decrease the rating assigned to each $QoWS$. The following formulas give the $QoWSdist$ for the execution and usage fee parameters:

$$QoWSdist_{lat} = pQoWS_{lat} - \mu_{lat}$$
$$QoWSdist_{av} = \rho_{av} - pQoWS_{av}$$
$$QoWSdist_{acc} = \rho_{acc} - pQoWS_{acc}$$
$$QoWSdist_{fee} = pQoWS_{fee} - dQoWS_{fee} \quad (dQoWS_{fee} \text{ is what is}$$
$$\text{effectively requested})$$

Without loss of generality, we assume that ratings take values in the interval [0, 1]. For the sake of homogenization and fairness, parameters not subject to monitoring are assigned a fixed rating which is the highest value. Web services receive initially the highest ratings. As the query infrastructure evolves and a new *QoWSdist* value is available, the corresponding rating is re-evaluated. Thus, whenever the *QoWSdist* goes beyond a certain threshold, τ_{QoWS}, the rating is either increased or decreased. This reflects how good or bad the Web service is behaving. For each *QoWS* parameter, we define a constant $\delta_{parameter}$ by which the rating is increased or decreased. Note that any increase or decrease of a rating is bound by the maximum and minimum values 1 and 0 respectively. The following formula illustrate how rating is computed for latency, the other distances are computed similarly:

$$ rat_{lat} = \begin{cases} max(rat_{lat} + \delta_{lat}, 1) & \text{if } QoWSdist_{lat} > \tau_{lat} > 0 \\ min(0, rat_{lat} - \delta_{lat}) & \text{if } QoWSdist_{lat} < -\tau_{lat} \end{cases} $$

Ratings will be used to weigh the *QoWS* in determining an optimal service execution plan. Our rating scheme evolves in a way that privileges Web services that respect their promises in terms of *QoWS*. However, its dynamic nature gives a chance to Web services with low ratings to catch up. These Web services may improve their ratings by either changing their promised *QoWS*, putting more efforts to achieve them, or both.

3.3.2.4 Fine Tuning Monitoring

The proposed monitoring and the ratings it produces depend on several parameters including collected information, collection policy, number of values collected, collection frequency, and threshold values for distance checks. These parameters determine the level of aggressiveness and degree of tolerance of monitoring and rating. Using a too aggressive approach (e.g., allowing very small thresholds) may deliver more precise ratings. However, this may put a heavy burden on the query infrastructure. A less aggressive approach will put less burden on the query infrastructure but may deliver poor quality ratings. We could still follow such approach with some *QoWS* parameters. For example, we may be tolerant in terms of availability but more reluctant to tolerate degradation of latency. A fair approach is to have a configurable monitoring where the different parameters are adjusted depending on users' requirements in terms of rating precision.

3.3.3 Service Execution Plan

Queries are subject to several transformations as explained before until a service execution plan that contains concrete operations is obtained along with the order in which they need to be invoked. Operation invocations may occur either in sequence or in parallel depending on potential constraints that may exist between the different operations. For example, for the query presented in Section 3.2.4, we can invoke both concrete operations corresponding to `Transportation` and `ArtGallery` concurrently to get the query Q executed. We represent a service execution plan by a directed graph. This allows a simple expression of sequence and concurrency of operation invocations. While this representation allows us to focus on optimization, the actual execution requires the detailed description of the service execution plan using service composition language like *BPEL4WS* [4] including the list of concrete operations, mappings between messages and parameters, and the flow of control and data between the different concrete operations.

Definition 3.5. A service execution plan *SEP* is represented by a directed graph $G = (V, E)$ called *execution graph*. $V = (op_s, op_t, OP)$ where OP is the set of operations being invoked by the service execution plan. op_s and op_t are two special nodes that do not correspond to any actual operation. They represent the starting and termination of *SEP*. E is a set of edges that represent the control flow of *SEP*. An edge will be drawn from a node op_i to a node op_j, if op_j has to be executed after op_i. Operations with no connecting paths can be executed concurrently. □

3.3.3.1 Operation Dependencies

To invoke an operation, it is necessary to have all its input parameters bound, i.e., assigned a value. For example, in the senior citizens scenario, a query may contain an operation, e.g., `checkEligibility`, that first checks if Maria is eligible for benefits, e.g., receiving food stamps, before being able to invoke the operation, e.g., `getFoodStamps`, related to that benefit. `checkEligibility` will be invoked first and produce an output parameter that will be used by `getFoodStamps` to proceed. We capture this requirement by defining, for any operation, a *dependency* set containing all operations which output parameters are used as input parameters by that operation. For example, if we define three operations in a given service execution plan as $op_1(x^i, y^i, z^o)$, $op_2(x^i, z^i, t^o)$, and $op_3(z^i, t^i, v^o)$ then *dependency*$(op_2) \supseteq \{op_1\}$ and *dependency*$(op_3) \supseteq \{op_1, op_2\}$. The notation x^i means that x is an input parameter (denoted with a superscript i) and z^o means that z is an output parameter (denoted with a superscript o). Bound parameters provided by the query are available to all operations. Operations that draw all their required input from bound parameters specified in the query can be the first to be invoked in the service execution plan.

Definition 3.6. For any operation *op* in a service execution plan, we define its *dependency set* as: *dependency*$(op) = \{op_i \mid op_i$ is an operation in the service execution plan and $\exists x \in Out(op_i), x \in In(op)\}$. □

We also define a *dependency graph*, DG_Q for any query Q. This is a directed graph that is initially built based on binding requirements of generic operations.

As the query is processed, this graph is updated to reflect dependencies amongst concrete operations. With this graph we can easily know which operations are missing any input parameter.

Definition 3.7. For any query Q, we define a dependency graph DG_Q, $DG_Q = (op_Q, op_\emptyset, V, E)$. op_Q represents a node acting as an operation whose output parameters are all bindings provided initially by the query. $op_\emptyset$ represents a node acting as an operation that does not provide any output parameter. Vertices in V are the different operations in the query Q including op_Q and $op_\emptyset$. Edges in E represent dependency relationships between operations. An edge is drawn from op_i to op_j if $op_i \in dependency(op_i)$. An edge is drawn from $op_\emptyset$ to op_i if op_i requires an input parameter that is not provided by any other node in the graph.   □

Dependency graphs allow to check if a query is answerable or not based on binding requirements. Thus, if a query is found to be non answerable, we could instruct the service locator to match the corresponding generic operation (with an edge to $op_\emptyset$) to a concrete operation that does not require the missing input parameters. This may not lead to an exact answer for the query. However, such partial answers may be acceptable for the user.

3.3.3.2 Discount Relationships

In an era of high competition and shared interests, it is often the case that service providers engage in partnerships that are a crucial parameter when determining the composition of Web services. These partnerships are usually translated through some privileges to customers who use both partners in achieving some needs. In the case of WS-Query, this means that a user will get a "better" *QoWS* if a query is resolved by using two specific Web services. For example, in the scenario presented in the introduction, caring for the nutritional needs of Maria required three types of services *meals provider*, *meals delivery*, and *senior nutrition program*. For instance, the choice of Meal@Home as a *meals provider* may reduce costs if combined with MealsOnTime as the *meals delivery* provider. These two providers are in business partnership to provide discounts for their common customers. This concept is captured by the following definition.

Definition 3.8. If a Web service ws_1 has a *discount relationship* with a Web service ws_2, then there exists a *QoWS* parameter P_i of ws_1 for which the system will use a better value (discounted value) when both ws_1 and ws_2 are involved in resolving a query; the default value of P_i, *defaultP_i*, is replaced by (discount(ws_1, ws_2) * defaultP_i) where discount(ws_1, ws_2) gives the amount of the discount.   □

Discount relationships are defined and their values decided by service providers who engage in some business partnerships. This information is advertised in the service registry. A given service provider may engage in more than one *discount relationship*. In this case, the best discounted value for its *QoWS* parameter is used if more than one partner is involved in resolving a given query. Without loss of generality, we assume that the *discount relationship* is non-symmetric.

3.3.3.3 Feasibility of a Service Execution Plan

In addition to finding the best service execution plan, the optimizer has to ensure that the execution plan is effectively executable or *feasible*. This is captured in the following definition.

Definition 3.9. A service execution plan is *feasible* if (i) for any operation op_i in *SEP*, all required input bindings for op_i can be provided as output by the operations op_j's which nodes in the direct graph representing *SEP* are ancestors to op_i, i.e., $\forall op_j$, there is a path from op_j to op_i, and (ii) if a Web service has been selected using a discounted *QoWS*, its partners in the discount relationship are in *SEP*. □

3.3.3.4 QoWS for Service Execution Plans

A given Web service ws_i is characterized by a vector of *QoWS* parameters,

$$QoWS(ws_i) = (lat(ws_i), av(ws_i), acc(ws_i), enc(ws_i), aut(ws_i), act(ws_i),$$
$$pp(ws_i), is(ws_i), id(ws_i), fee(ws_i), rep(ws_i)).$$

where *lat* (latency) and *fee* (usage fee) take scalar values ($\Re^+$), *av* (availability) and *acc* (accessibility) represent a probability (a real value between 0 and 1), *enc* (encryption), *aut* (authentication), *act* (access control), *pp* (privacy policy), *is* (information sharing), and *id* (information disclosure) are Boolean values (0 or 1). Finally, *rep* (reputation) ranges over the interval [0,10].

For each *QoWS* parameter, we define the following aggregation functions to compute *QoWS* of service execution plans (assumed to have *N* operations). We assume that Web services are independent with respect to their *QoWS*. This would allow to easily aggregate parameters representing a probability.

- *Latency* We need to determine the longest path, in terms of latency, in the execution graph between the starting and ending nodes. The latency of the service execution plan corresponds to the sum of latencies of Web services being executed in sequence along this path.
- *Availability* The service execution plan depends on the availability of all Web services it accesses. Thus, its availability corresponds to the probability that all Web services are available. As we assume that Web services are independent in terms of *QoWS* it is equal to $\prod_{i=1}^{N} av(ws_i)$.
- *Accessibility* Accessibility is computed similarly to availability. It corresponds to the probability that all Web services are accessible: $\prod_{i=1}^{N} acc(ws_i)$.
- *Encryption* This *QoWS* takes a Boolean value (0 or 1) for individual Web services. We could either assume that the service execution plan has a 0 value for encryption if at least one of the Web service has a 0 value, or we consider the ratio of encrypted Web services. Both options may be desirable. Thus, we leave it up to the user to select the appropriate option.
- *Authentication, Access Control, Privacy Policy, Information Sharing, and Information Disclosure* These parameters are treated similarly to encryption.

- *Usage Fee* Accessing all Web services appearing in the service execution plan requires paying access fees for all of them. This parameter corresponds to the sum of all usage fees of all invoked Web services: $\sum_{i=1}^{N} fee(ws_i)$.
- *Reputation* The reputation of a service execution plan depends on the reputation of all its Web services. It corresponds to the average of the reputation of all invoked Web services: $\frac{1}{N} \sum_{i=1}^{N} rep(ws_i)$.

3.3.4 Cost Model

Selecting an optimal service execution plan is at the core of WS-Query. This challenging task is exacerbated by the large number of competing Web services to select from. Different service execution plans using different Web services could be used to solve the same query. However, they may differ according to the *QoWS* they deliver. These differences can be several orders of magnitude large. Thus, it is necessary to devise appropriate techniques to select the "best" execution plan. This requires first defining a cost model to compare service execution plans solving the same query. We then need to build search strategies based on this cost model.

We propose a cost model based on the concept of *QoWS* as introduced earlier. The overall idea is to define what constitutes an "optimal" service execution plan based on *QoWS*. A service execution plan is built by first mapping relations to generic operations, then locating actual Web services with concrete operations that can be matched to those generic operations, and finally combining the different operation invocations in a way to answer the query. The first step is straightforward and does not involve any optimization decision. However, the two last steps are key in producing an optimal plan. Furthermore, users may have preferences on how their queries are answered. They may specify as part of a query which *QoWS* parameters are important to them and how important they are. This is achieved by assigning *weights* (ranging from 0 to 1) to each *QoWS* parameter. WS-Query uses default values for these weights if users do not specify them.

One approach to rank service execution plans is to aggregate all its *QoWS* parameters in one single formula. An interesting method is the *Simple Additive Weighting* [32] widely used in decision making. Its ranking results are usually very close to results of more sophisticated methods [19]. This method comprises three basic steps: (i) scale the different parameters (*QoWS*) to make them comparable, (ii) apply user-supplied weights to each parameter, and (iii) sum up the weighted and scaled *QoWS* parameters. Service execution plans are then ranked based on the scores they obtain in the last step.

Generic operations are matched to concrete ones using one of the different matching modes that we have defined in Section 3.2.5. As each mode delivers a different matching "precision", we assigned a *matching degree* to each level to quantify this precision. These matching degrees will be used to adjust the values of the different *QoWS*. Similarly, ratings obtained through monitoring will be also included in the cost model as they enable adjusting advertised *QoWS* according to the actual behavior of Web services.

More precisely, for negative $QoWS$, the value used in computing the aggregated $QoWS(SEP)$ is replaced by $QoWS(ws_j)/(matching\_degree(ws_j) * rating(ws_j))$ for all Web services ws_j used in SEP. For positive $QoWS$, the value used in computing the aggregated $QoWS(SEP)$ is replaced by $QoWS(ws_j) * matching\_degree(ws_j) * rating(ws_j)$ for all Web services ws_j used in SEP. The corresponding values are either lowered or increased to reflect the effect of the matching level and the ratings.

Based on the previous discussion, we can now specify the targeted optimization problem. Given a query Q expressed using relations from the query level, find concrete operations from the concrete level that form a feasible service execution plan SEP that maximizes the objective function F:

$$F(SEP) = \left(\sum_{i \in neg} W_i \frac{Q_i^{max} - Q_i}{Q_i^{max} - Q_i^{min}} + \sum_{i \in pos} W_i \frac{Q_i - Q_i^{min}}{Q_i^{max} - Q_i^{min}} \right)$$

Where neg and pos are the set of negative and positive $QoWS$ respectively. W_i is the weight assigned by users to each parameter. Q_i is the value of the ith $QoWS$ of the service execution plan obtained through the corresponding aggregation functions adjusted to the rating and matching degree obtained by individual Web services. Q_i^{max} is the maximum value for the $Q i^{th}$ $QoWS$ parameter for all potential service execution plans and Q_i^{min} is the minimum value. These two values can be computed by considering matching concrete operations with the highest and lowest values for the ith $QoWS$ adjusted to ratings and matching degrees. We do not have to generate all potential execution plans.

3.3.5 Optimization Strategies

The optimization strategy has three main tasks: (1) Selecting for each generic operation a concrete operation amongst all potential ones obtained from the service registry using the different matching modes. The resulting service execution plan should maximize the objective function. (2) Ensuring that whenever a given Web service is selected using a discounted $QoWS$ then a concrete operation from its partner Web service should be present in the plan. (3) Ordering the concrete operations in such a way that the obtained plan is feasible. This optimization problem is similar to a resource allocation problem that is NP-hard [13] and a such cannot be solved in a polynomial time. Indeed, in a exhaustive strategy, we need to generate all possible service execution plans and select the best one. This strategy does not miss the optimal plan but it is achieved at a prohibitive cost. If we assume that the query is translated to N generic operations and that each generic operation could be matched to as many as M concrete operations. The total number of potential service execution plans is in this case M^N. This is clearly not an option if we consider the ever expanding service space where a single functionality could be offered by a large number of Web services. On the other side if we use a local selection strategy, the best concrete operation is selected for each generic operation in the query. Such strategy may lead to sub-optimal or non feasible solutions if some constraints need to be enforced. This is especially true for the case of *discount relationships* where we need to check that two concrete operations involved in a discount relationship are used in the selected service execution plan.

Our objective now is to select an optimal or a near optimal solution in a realistic time scale. This means a time much less than that needed to examine all solutions. In the following, we present heuristics-based algorithms that take into account constraints on binding requirements and discount relationships. These algorithms have been designed in a way to balance between finding the optimal plan and processing a query in an acceptable time. The main issue when optimizing queries in the presence of discount relationships is to make sure that both partners are present in the plan. The optimizer will be faced with several global constraints, called the *presence test*, to be checked against the service execution plan. In the following sections, we present three different algorithms: two based on the use of heuristics and the third on the simulated annealing optimization method [1].

For each of these algorithms, we assume the availability of a function *lookupBest-Operation* that returns the best matching concrete operation given a generic operation. This function has several options: use the discount relationships and in this case return the set of corresponding partners (the variable *partner* below), ignore discount relationships, and ignore multimode matching and returns the best exact match. The *lookupBestOperation(genericOp, concrOp, DiscRel, partner, exactMatchOnly)* function returns a concrete operation (*concOP*) with the highest value for the objective function we have defined applied to individual operation. It starts by looking for relevant Web services through a UDDI service registry using the Category and Function attributes of the generic operation. We use these semantic attributes to build a keyword query directed to UDDI. For each returned Web service, its description is searched for operations that match the virtual operation using the different levels previously defined or just the exact match if the corresponding parameter, *exactMatchOnly*, is set *True*. The function then selects the operation with the highest value for the objective function taking into account discount relationships if required (*DiscRel* set to *True*).

3.3.5.1 Local Bi-Selection Algorithm

The *Local Bi-Selection* algorithm is based on a simple heuristic. It starts with a local selection and then replaces the operations that do not satisfy the presence test for discount relationships.

Local Bi-Selection Algorithm
Input: Conjunctive query (X) : $-\, R_1(X_1), R_2(X_2), ..., R_n(X_n), C_1, C_2, ..., C_m$
Output: A dependency graph representing a feasible service execution plan.
   • **Initialization**
1:    $V = \emptyset$ /* Set of generic operations */
2:    $DRCop = \emptyset$ /* Set of concrete operations selected based on discounted
                   $QoWS$ that do not have their partners in the plan */
3:    *missingPartners* $= \emptyset$ /* Set of missing partners */

```
4:      For each R_i in Q
5:          V = V ∪ {Gop | Gop is obtained from the mapping rule of R_i}
6:      EndFor
7:      DG = buildDG(V) /* Build the dependency graph */
```
  ● **Local Selection**
```
8:      For each Gop ∈ V
                /* Lookup best concrete operation Cop taking into account*/
                /* discount relationships */
9:          lookupBestOperation(Gop, Cop, True, partner, False)
10:         If Cop = Null Then
11:             return(∅) /* The query is not answerable*/
12:         EndIf
13:         If Cop ∈ missingPartners Then
14:             missingPartners = missingPartners − Cop
                /* Remove corresponding partners from DRCop */
15:             DRCop = DRCop − {op | op is partner of Cop}
16:         EndIf
17:         DG = DG + Cop /* Update DG by replacing Gop with Cop */
18:         If partner ≠ ∅ and partner ∉ DG  Then
19:             DRCop = DRCop + Cop
20:             missingPartners = missingPartners + partner
21:         EndIf
22:     EndFor
```
  ● **Second Local Selection**
```
23:     For Cop ∈ DRCop /* Remove a Cop if partner not present */
24:         Gop = matchOf(Cop) /* Get generic operation corresponding to Cop */
                /* Lookup the best Cop without considering discount relationships */
25:         lookupBestOperation(Gop, Cop', False, partner, False)
26:         If Cop' ∈ missingPartners Then
27:             missingPartners = missingPartners − Cop'
28:             remove corresponding partner(s) from DRCop
29:         EndIf
                /* Update DG by removing Cop and replacing it by Cop' */
30:         DG = DG − Cop + Cop'
31:     EndFor
```
  ● **End**
```
32:         return(DG)
```

The *Local Bi-Selection Algorithm* has three phases. The first phase $(1-7)$ consists of initializing the variables needed by the algorithm, unfolding queries into generic operations, and building the dependency graph based on generic operation dependencies. In the second phase $(8-22)$, a local selection takes place taking into account discount relationships between Web services using the *lookupBestOperation* function. Each generic operation is replaced by the best concrete operation using the objective function F (applied to individual operations). Since the returned concrete operation may require the presence of a partner, we test if that partner is present. We test also whether the located concrete operation is a partner of concrete operations $(13-16)$ that have been already included in the service execution plan. In the third phase $(23-31)$, any concrete operation missing its partners will be replaced by a concrete operation that does not require one. This operation is the next best match selected without taking into account discount relationships. Finally (23), the dependency graph which represents the service execution plan is returned.

3.3.5.2   Iterative Algorithm

We present now the *Iterative Algorithm* that, in contrast to the *Bi-Selection Algorithm*, does not stop looking for the a feasible service execution plan. Instead, it keeps trying to find a feasible plan taking into account discount relationships. More specifically, the algorithm iterates over an initial service execution plan by replacing one concrete operation until finding a feasible plan that satisfies the presence test or reaching a threshold. We propose two different replacement policies for selecting the concrete operation to be replaced. To address the issue of binding requirements, we build the dependency graph based on generic operations thus ensuring that the inclusion of a concrete operation will still give us a feasible plan. The lookup will only fetch those concrete operations that satisfy input requirements as specified by the dependency graph.

Iterative Algorithm
Input: Conjunctive query (X) $: - R_1(X_1), R_2(X_2), ..., R_n(X_n), C_1, C_2, ..., C_m$
Output: A dependency graph representing a feasible service execution plan.
   • **Initialization**
1:     $V = \emptyset$ /* Set of generic operations */
2:     $C = \emptyset$ /* Set of matching concrete operations */
3:     $DRCop = \emptyset$ /* Set of concrete operations selected based on discounted */
                      $QoWS$ that do not have their partners in the plan */
4:     $missingPartners = \emptyset$ /* Set of missing partners */
5:     For each R_i in Q
6:         $V = V \cup \{Gop \mid Gop$ is obtained from the mapping rule of $R_i\}$
7:     EndFor
8:     $DG = $ buildDG(V) /* Build the dependency graph */
   • **Local Selection**
9:     For each $Gop \in V$
                 /* Lookup the best concrete operation
                 taking into account discount relationships */
10:    lookupBestOperation$(Gop, Cop, True, partner, False)$
11:    If $Cop = $ Null Then
12:        return$(\emptyset)$ /* The query is not answerable */
13:    EndIf
14:    If $Cop \in missingPartners$ Then
15:        $missingPartners = missingPartners - Cop$
                 /* Remove corresponding partners from $DRCop$*/
16:        $DRCop = DRCop - \{op \mid op$ is partner of $Cop\}$
17:    EndIf
18:    $DG = DG + Cop$ /* Update DG by replacing Gop with Cop */
19:    If $partner \neq \emptyset$ and $partner \notin DG$ Then
20:        $DRCop = DRCop + Cop$
21:        $missingPartners = missingPartners + partner$
22:    EndIf
23:   EndFor
   • **Iterative Selection (first version)**
    /* Iterate until finding a feasible solution or reaching a threshold */
    /* Set the threshold such that the total computation time is acceptable */
24:    /* Sort $DRCop$ to facilitate subsequent selection of concrete operations */
24:    While $missingPartners \neq \emptyset$ and $threshold \neq 0$
        /* Remove the concrete operation that may have the least effect */

```
         /* on the QoWS of the service execution plan */
25:      Cop = getWorst(DRCop)
         /* Get the generic operation corresponding to that concrete operation */
26:      Gop = getMatch(Cop)
         /* Get the next best concrete operation */
27:      lookupNextBestDR(Gop, Cop', partner)
28:      If Cop' = Null Then /* No more concrete operation to match */
29:          return(∅) /* Give up, the query may not be answerable */
30:      EndIf
31:      If Cop ∈ missingPartners Then
32:          missingPartners = missingPartners − Cop
33:          remove corresponding partner(s) fromDRCop
34:      EndIf
         /* Update DG by removing Cop and replacing it by Cop' */
35:      DG = DG − Cop + Cop'
36:      If partner ≠ ∅ and partner ∉ DG Then
37:          DRCop = DRCop + Cop /* Respect the sort while updating DRCop
38:          missingPartners = missingPartners + partner
39:      EndIf
40:      threshold = threshold - 1
41:  EndFor
  • End /* Return execution graph if any */
43:  If missingPartners = ∅ Then
44:      return((DG))
45:  Else
         /* Either the query is unanswerable or the threshold has been reached */
46:      return(∅)
47:  EndIf
```

After the usual initialization phase (1–8), the *Iterative Algorithm* proceeds with a local selection of the service execution plan (9–23). If the plan is not feasible with respect to discount relationships (i.e., some partners are missing), then the algorithm goes through an iterative process based on a simple heuristic (24–41): The heuristic consists in selecting the concrete operation that has a missing partner that may have the least effect on the *QoWS* of the service execution plan by invoking the function *getWorst* (25). This operation corresponds to the operation that has the worst *QoWS* when compared to other concrete operations with missing partners (*DRCop*). The algorithm then replaces it by its next best match. This process is repeated until a feasible plan is found or a threshold is reached. The threshold could be set in such a way that the total computation time is still acceptable. For efficiency reasons, we assume that both functions *lookupBestOperation* and *lookupNextBestDR* share common information to avoid extra computation. This would allow the *lookupBestDR* to find the next best operation based on the work done by *lookupBestOperation*.

Below is another option for the iteration phase of the previous algorithm. Instead of replacing only one concrete operation from *DRCop*, all concrete operations in that set are replaced.

   • **Iterative Selection (second version)**
```
         /* Iterate until finding a feasible solution or reaching a threshold
            based on a different replacement policy */
24:  While missingPartners ≠ ∅ and threshold ≠ 0
```

```
25:       For all Cop ∈ DRCop
          /* Get the corresponding generic operation */
26:          Gop = getMatch(Cop)
          /* Get the next best concrete operations */
27:          lookupNextBestDR(Gop, Cop', partner)
          /* Update DG by removing Cop and replacing it by Cop' */
28:          DG = DG − Cop + Cop'
29:          If Cop' ∈ missingPartners Then
30:             missingPartners = missingPartners − Cop'
31:             remove corresponding partner(s) from DRCop
32:          EndIf
33:          If partner(Cop') ≠ ∅ and partner ∉ C Then
34:             DRCop = DRCop + Cop
35:             missingPartners = missingPartners + partner(Cop')
36:          EndIf
37:       EndFor
38:   EndWhile
```

3.3.5.3 Simulated Annealing Based Algorithm

We present now a simulated annealing based algorithm to optimize queries over Web services. The simulated annealing method draws a correspondence between complex optimization problems and statistical mechanics [1]. Given an initial solution, a controlled perturbation is introduced to reach a global optimum while avoiding to be trapped in a local one. This perturbation is reduced as the optimality of the solution improves. In our case, the initial solution is obtained through local selection without considering discount relationships and making sure that binding requirements are satisfied. The current solution (starting from the initial one) is perturbed by changing concrete operation(s) for one or several generic operations. The new service execution plan is tested for feasibility in terms of binding requirements and discount relationships. Only feasible plans are considered. The objective function is computed for the new plan and compared to the current one. The current execution plan is replaced by the new one if it leads to a better solution otherwise the replacement takes place with a probability $\exp^{(F(SEP_1)-F(SEP_2))/T}$ as defined in the original simulated annealing algorithm.

Simulated Annealing Algorithm
Input: Conjunctive query $(X) : − R_1(X_1), R_2(X_2), ..., R_n(X_n), C_1, C_2, ..., C_m$
Output: A dependency graph representing a feasible service execution plan.
  • **Initialization**
```
1:    V = ∅ /* Set of generic operations */
2:    For each R_i in Q
3:        V = V ∪ {Gop | Gop is obtained from the mapping rule of R_i}
4:    EndFor
5:    DG = buildDG(V)
```
  • **Local Selection**
```
6:    For each Gop ∈ V
          /* Lookup the best concrete operation without taking into account
          discount relationships and requiring exact match */
7:        lookupBestOperation(Gop, Cop, False, partner, True)
```

```
8:          DG_0 = DG_0 + Cop
9:       EndFor
```
   • **Annealing Iterations**
```
10:      T = T_0
11:      While (T > T_f)
12:          For max_iteration
13:              DG_1 = Perturb(DG_0)
14:              If (F(DG_1) > F(DG_0)) or exp^{(F(DG_1)-F(DG_0))/T} > random(0,1)
14:              Then
15:                  DG_0 = DG_1
16:              EndIf
17:          EndFor
18:          T = T * α
19:      EndWhile
```
   • **End**
```
20:          return(DG_0)
```

The *Simulated Annealing Algorithm* has three main phases. After the initialization phase (1–5), an initial feasible solution (6–9) is built using local selection and ignoring discount relationships. In the third phase, the algorithm continuously iterates (10–19) by perturbing the initial solution until reaching the final temperature T_f. The algorithm is guaranteed to stop since the current temperature T is decreased by a cooling rate $\alpha < 1$. There are several parameters that need to be determined for the algorithm. These include the *initial temperature* T_0, the *final temperature* T_f, the number of iterations *max_iteration*, the *cooling rate alpha*, and the perturbation function. For the perturbation of the current solution, we need to identify the most appropriate way to modify the solution while making sure that it is still feasible (discount relationships and binding requirements). The feasibility check may require looking at more than one potential service execution plan. For the kind of perturbation to be applied, we need to characterize the neighborhood structure for a given execution plan. This can be done, for example, by selecting a random number of generic operations for which we seek another matching concrete operation. We have two options to decide which concrete operation to take: (i) randomly pick up a concrete operation from all potential matches for a given Gop, or (ii) get the next best Cop.

3.4 Implementation

In this section, we present the implementation of WS-Query and experiments on the different optimization algorithms. The implementation is conducted in the context of an e-government prototype that provides access to e-government databases and services [17].

3.4.1   A Middleware for Querying E-Government Services

WS-Query is part of the WebDG project, an e-government platform transparently querying data and applications alike. The system is implemented across a network of *Solaris* workstations. Citizens and case officers access the system via a *Graphical User Interface* (GUI) implemented using HTML/Servlet (Fig. 3.3). We currently included seven (7) applications implemented in Java (JDK 1.3). These applications are wrapped by WSDL descriptions. WSDL service descriptions are published into UDDI registry. We adopt *Systinet's WASP UDDI Standard 3.1* as our UDDI toolkit. *Cloudscape* (4.0) database is used as a UDDI registry. The system uses the *service management client* provided within *Apache SOAP* (2.2) to deploy e-government services. *Apache SOAP* provides not only server-side infrastructure for deploying and managing services, but also client-side API for invoking those services. Each service has a *deployment descriptor*. The descriptor includes the unique identifier of the Java class to be invoked, session scope of the class, and operations in the class available for the clients. Each service is deployed using its descriptor and the URL of the *Apache SOAP servlet rpcrouter* as input arguments.

The *Service Query Engine* is responsible for the correct and optimal execution of Web service queries through the interaction of several modules: The *Service Locator* discovers WSDL descriptions by accessing the UDDI registry. It implements *UDDI Inquiry Client* using WASP UDDI API. The *Operation Matchmaker* interacts with the *Service Locator* to retrieve the services' descriptions and determine the concrete operations to use in the service execution plan. WSDL descriptions (along with semantic attributes as defined earlier) are parsed and concrete operations are matched to generic operations using one of the matching modes. The *Monitoring Agent* is

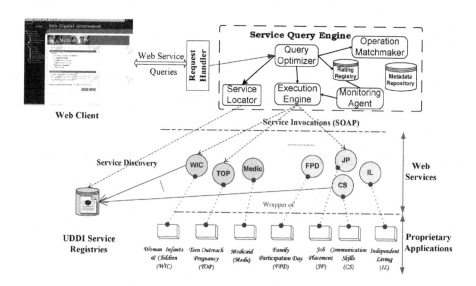

Fig. 3.3   WS-query architecture

responsible for monitoring Web service invocations. It maintains a local repository for ratings and other information to compute those ratings. An entry is added to this repository the first time a given Web service is being used by WS-Query. The *Query Optimizer*'s task is to determine the best service execution plan for a given query. It uses one of the algorithms that we presented earlier and interacts with all other modules. After the optimizer generates an efficient service execution plan, the plan is handed over to the *Execution Engine*. The execution engine enacts the service execution plan by actually invoking Web services using SOAP. We use *SOAP Binding Stubs* which are implemented using Apache SOAP API for this purpose. Finally, the Metadata Repository stores different metadata information required by other modules including the definition of relations and generic operations and their mappings.

3.4.2 Complete Example Unfolding

We present now a complete example showing how a query is processed until obtaining an optimal service execution plan. We assume that the following generic operations have been defined:

- *DetermineMealType* = (*In, Out, InOut, Category, Purpose*) where *In* = {Age, Sex, SpecialDietType, Allergies}, *Out* = {MealType}, *InOut* = {}, *Category* = (Nutrition, {Diet}), and *Purpose* = (Counseling, {Advising}).
- *PrepareMeals* = (*In, Out, InOut, Category, Purpose*) where *In* = {ProviderZip}, *Out* = {MealPrice}, *InOut* = {MealType}, *Category* = (Meal Preparation, {Restaurant, Meal Provider, Catering}), and *Purpose* = (Pricing, {Cost, Fees, Quote}).
- *DeliverMeals* = (*In, Out, InOut, Category, Purpose*) where *In* = {Area}, *Out* = {DeliveryPrice}, *InOut* = {}, *Category* = (Meal Delivery, {Delivery, Transporting, Carryover}), and *Purpose* = (Pricing, {Cost, Fees, Quote}).

Based on the above generic operations, we define the following relations with their corresponding mappings:

> *Meals(*Zipcode, MealType, MealPrice, DeliveryPrice*) :-*
> *DeliverMeals(Area, DeliveryPrice),*
> *PrepareMeals(ProviderZip, MealType, MealPrice),*
> *Zipcode* ∈ *Area, ProviderZip* ∈ *Area*

> *MealType(*Age, Sex, SpecialDietType, Allergies, MealType*) :-*
> *DetermineMealType(Age, Sex, SpecialDietType,*
> *Allergies, MealType)*

Let now assume that the following query has been submitted to WS-Query:

> *Query(Zipcode, MealType, MealPrice, DeliveryPrice) :-*
> *MealType(Age, Sex, SpecialDietType, Allergies, MealType),*

$Meals(ZipCode, MealType, MealPrice, DeliveryPrice)$,
$Age = 68, Sex =$ "M", $SpecialDietType =$ "$LowSodium$",
Allergies = "None", $MealPrice + DeliveryPrice < 15$,
$Zipcode = 22043$

The first step would be to unfold the query in terms of generic operations:

$Query_2 (Zipcode, MealType, MealPrice, DeliveryPrice)$:-
$DetermineMealType(Age, Sex, SpecialDietType,$
$Allergies, MealType)$,
$PrepareMeals(ProviderZip, MealType, MealPrice)$,
$DeliverMeals(Area, DeliveryPrice)$,
$Age = 68, Sex =$ "M", $SpecialDietType =$ "$LowSodium$",
$Allergies =$ "$None$", $MealPrice + DeliveryPrice < 15$,
$Zipcode \in Area, ProviderZip \in Area, Zipcode = 22043$

In the second step, for each generic operation appearing in the query, WS-Query needs to find all matching concrete operations. This would require first to query the UDDI service registry which would return all potential matches. We use the different semantic attributes of the generic operation to build a keyword query directed to UDDI. These potential matches are then filtered using our multimode matching. Each Web service is assigned to one of the different matching modes. It is obvious that more semantic-aware techniques are needed to search for services in a UDDI registry. The keyword search we are using may return too many irrelevant results and may also miss some relevant ones. Looking at such techniques is outside the scope of our work.

Note that there is a dependency between *DetermineMealType* and *PrepareMeals* through the parameter *MealType* that needs to be taken into account. Assume now that the following concrete operations match, based on one of the four modes, their generic operation counterparts as listed below (for the sake of space, we omit their attributes.)

- *DetermineMealType* can be matched to `EatHealthy` or `NutriExpert`.
- *PrepareMeals* can be matched to `Meals@Home`, `HealthyChoice`, or `DeliForLess`.
- *DeliverMeals* can be matched to `MealsOnTime`, `FastMeals`, or `MealsAround`, or `WeDeliver`.

By using one of the optimization algorithms that we proposed, specific concrete operations are selected and combined in a way to get the optimal plan. In addition to the dependency condition mentioned above, if the candidate Web services are in business partnerships through discount relationships, these need also to be taken into account by the optimization algorithm.

3.4.3 Experiments

For the purpose of the experiments, we assess our approach using a large number of synthetically generated Web services. The major objective is to measure the cost of the different algorithms and the quality of the service execution plans they generate. We focus on computing the time it takes each algorithm to reach a decision. The quality of their results is simply the objective function, F, as defined previously. The different algorithms are run under different scenarios and their results are compared. Given a generic operation, we assume that it is already matched (using different matching levels) to a given set of concrete operations. We focus then on generating $QoWS$ values for these concrete operations (or their Web services). The general form of the experiments is:

- Queries are varied by the number of generic operations or query size.
- For each query, we consider different situations by varying the number of potential concrete operations per generic operations.
- Randomly generate values of $QoWS$ parameters for the different concrete operations.
- Randomly generate discount relationships including the number of concrete operations involved in partnerships, $QoWS$ subject to discount, and the values of the discounts.
- Process the query using the different algorithms.
- Collect the values of the objective function obtained by the service execution plan and the time it takes for the algorithm reach a decision.

We used the following settings. The number of generic operations per query is varied from 2 to 30. The number of matching concrete operations per generic operation takes three distinct values 5, 10, and 15. $QoWS$ are generated in their respective domains (scalar, [0, 1], or {0, 1}). The number of concrete operations involved in discount relationships is varied between 0 and 1/3 of the available concrete operations. We assume that one third of the service space is involved in partnerships. We assume that a Web service is involved in at most one discount relationship. Each algorithm is run on the same generated sample data. For each run, we collect the values of the objective function and the processing time. Table 3.1 gives the values of the different parameters used to generate the sample service space based on our three-level service model.

Figures 3.4 and 3.5 show the time it takes for the *iterative-selection* and *simulated annealing* respectively, to reach a decision on the optimal solution. The results consistently show that the processing time increases with the average number of concrete operations per generic operations and the size of the query. Indeed, even if the different algorithms do not do an exhaustive search, they still have to explore a large space of possible solutions. In particular, for an average number of 15 concrete operation per generic operations, the processing time increases considerably, 50% more than for an average number of 10 concrete operation per generic operations.

In Fig. 3.6, we compare the processing time for the two algorithms: *iterative* (first version) and *simulated annealing*. The different algorithms are run under different

Table 3.1 Experimental parameters

Parameter	Value	Notes
maxNbrGops	100	Maximum number of generic operations
maxNbrCops	3,500	Maximum number of concrete operations
maxNbrDiscountOperations	500	Maximum number of operations in a discount relationship
maxNbrInputAttributes	10	Maximum number of input parameters per operation
maxNbrOutputAttributes	10	Maximum number of output parameters per operation
maxNbrCategoryAttributes	10	Maximum number of Category attributes operation
maxNbrPurposeAttributes	10	Maximum number of Purpose attributes per operation
iterativeAlgorithmThreshold	10	Threshold for the iterative algorithm
poolInputOutputAttributes	12	Number of potential values for input/output parameters
poolCategoryAttributes	12	Number of potential values for the Category attribute
poolPurposeAttributes	12	Number of potential values for the Purpose attribute
nbrQoWS	5	Number of QoWS parameters
nbrNegativeQoWS	2	Number of negative QoWS parameters
nbrPositiveQoWS	3	Number of positive QoWS parameters

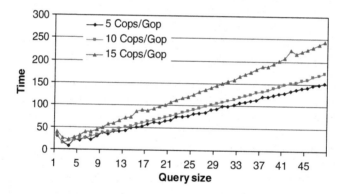

Fig. 3.4 Simulated annealing algorithm

average numbers of concrete operations per generic operations, namely 5, 10, and 15, and the size of the query (number of generic operations) is varied. The results that we show are obtained by consolidating results for the three cases. The *simulated annealing* spends a much greater time to find a solution. It is almost double the time spent by the *iterative* algorithm. This is predictable as the annealing algorithm has to go through a much larger number of iterations to reach an equilibrium state or optimal solution.

In Fig. 3.7, we compare the value of the aggregated cost (objective function) of the two algorithms: *iterative* (first version) and *simulated annealing*. The results that we show are obtained by consolidating results for the three cases (5, 10, and 15

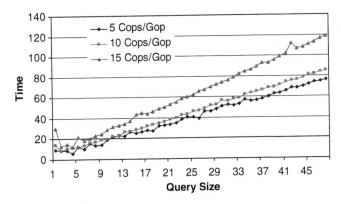

Fig. 3.5   Iterative algorithm (Form 1)

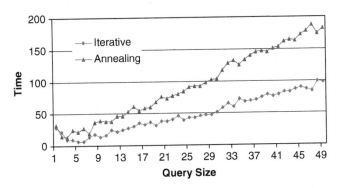

Fig. 3.6   Processing time comparison

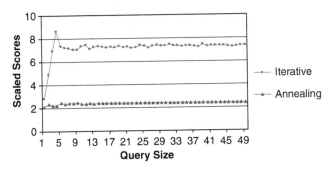

Fig. 3.7   Aggregated costs comparison

concrete operations per generic operation). The *simulated annealing* algorithm achieves poor results compared to the *iterative* algorithm. This may be due to the choice of the perturbation procedure that is causing the current solution to diverge from the optimal solution or be trapped in some local optimum. Based on these results, part of our future work would be twofold on one side we need to study different perturbation procedures and on another side we need to look at different optimization approaches like genetic algorithms.

3.5 Related Work

In this section, we review a number of research efforts that have some overlap with our service query infrastructure research. These efforts can be classified into five categories: Web service composition and optimization, integrating Web services and XML querying, Web service request language, Web service matching, and Web service search engine.

In [34], a technique based on linear programming to optimize service composition is proposed. This work is part of the Self-Serv prototype for service composition [5]. The optimization is based on several *QoWS* criteria (e.g., duration, price, reliability). Composite services are represented as a state-chart where a task could be matched to several Web services belonging to the same community. A community is a collection of Web services offering the same functionality but eventually differing in terms of *QoWS*. The optimization problem of finding the best Web services to execute a composite service is expressed in the form of a linear programming problem. This work differs with our approach in that it does not provide an end-to-end query infrastructure for querying Web services. The constraints being considered are only those introduced by the computation of the *QoWS* of the composite service plan. This work does not take into account global constraints imposed by the application like the existence of partnerships between Web services. The optimization does not consider discount relationships on *QoWS* that may increase the overall quality of the composite service. The work in [28] describes a composition and optimization of bioinformatics Web services. They use the concept of tuple filtering to reduce the load on Web service providers. There is no attempt to provide a more generic optimization solution. It uses the traditional system performance criteria for plan selection and no QoWS is used. The WSMS project at Stanford [25] also focuses on Web service optimization. In [6], a more general method of optimization that was introduced in [25] is introduced. However, the proposed optimization process is purely performance based focusing on the data aspects using traditional database techniques to generate execution plans. No user-centric Quality of Web service is assumed.

Active XML (AXML) [2] enables querying XML documents based on Web services. AXML documents are defined as XML documents with portions corresponding to operation invocations. These invocations could be defined explicitly or declaratively as XQuery queries over AXML documents. AXML focuses on different issues related to the evaluation of Web service invocations within an AXML document [18]. These include activation time determination, invocation's arguments discovery, output validity over time, etc. Different techniques drawn from databases and XML research are proposed to address these issues. A major difference with our work is that we view Web services as first class objects while Active XML uses Web services as a mean to "update" XML documents. The object of querying in AXML is the XML documents themselves. Additionally, AXML does not support QoWS or any type of optimization in selecting Web services.

In [3], a Web service request language (XSRL) based on XML and AI planning techniques is proposed. The authors proposed also a framework to handle and execute XSRL requests. The aim is to provide planning actions under uncertainty on the basis of refinement and revision as new service-related information is acquired (via interaction with the user or UDDI) and as the execution context change. The focus is on defining a language specification for requests for Web services. This includes specifying the core entities of the request and user's scheduling preferences and dependencies among requested Web services. XSRL requests are translated to generic plans based on AI planning techniques. The plan executor produces instantiated plans by interacting with UDDI, users, and Web services. This work has some overlapping with WS-Query, especially the planning part. However, it is not clear, from the available literature, how the global planning is conducted. There is no details on how a generic plan is obtained. Furthermore *QoWS* and efficiency issues are not addressed.

Matching algorithms for Web services have been the target of several research efforts [7, 15, 26, 29]. In [26], the authors propose a matching engine that contains five filters that incrementally refine the matching of two specifications. These specifications are expressed in an agent description language called LARKS. Li and Horrocks [15] proposes a matchmaking prototype based on DAML-S that uses ontology and a Description Logic reasoner. The authors present different levels of matching including exact, plugin, subsume, intersection, and disjoint. Matching in [29] is based on matching RDF graphs describing the two entities to be matched. The authors of [7] proposes an extensive matching scheme where a service object (representing the Web service) and a service template (representing the intent of the designer) are compared at syntactic, operational, and semantic levels. Different similarity functions are defined for each level. The semantic integration function is defined for the same ontology or distinct ontologies. As we mentioned earlier, our matching scheme has some overlaps with these efforts, however our work focuses mostly on how different modes of matching influence optimization. We could also use one of the existing matching schemes as long as we can assign degrees (of precision) to different matching levels or modes.

Woogle [10] is a search engine for Web services. The goal is to support keyword and similarity search in Web services like finding similar Web service operations and operations that can eventually compose with some given operation. Similarity is defined on input and output parameters. Woogle adopts machine learning mechanisms to determine the similarity between the desirable operations and targeted operations. An important component of this work is to analyze collections of Web services and clustering their parameter names into semantically meaningful concepts. Thus, the focus of this work is on finding the right criteria for clustering Web services and producing high precision and recall on similarity search. Woogle does not support high level query capabilities and corresponding

QoWS-aware optimization as in our query infrastructure. However, Woogle may be leveraged by our infrastructure to find concrete operations and matching them to generic ones.

Database integration has been the subject of a sustained research effort [21]. Query optimization in this context is still a major challenge. A fundamental difference between database query optimization and our approach lies in the manipulated objects. The first class objects in our approach are *services* while *data* is the first class object in databases. In our approach, optimization focuses on *QoWS* parameters related to the behavior of the Web services while in most existing techniques, optimization concerns only the response time of the query execution plan. Efficiently ordering Web service operations in the service execution plan has some similarities with the classical problem of processing queries over sources with limited capabilities. However, there are several differences with the classical problem found in databases. First, concrete operations need to be discovered and matched against generic operations. Second, for any generic operation, there may be several choices of concrete operations which complicates more query processing and optimization. Finally, our matching strategy allows certain types of matching that may change the binding requirements from those of the corresponding generic operations.

3.6 Conclusions

This paper addressed key issues to enable efficient access to Web services. We presented WS-Query, a comprehensive query infrastructure for the emerging concept of Web services. Treating Web services as first class objects is a major milestone towards materializing the *Service Web*. We proposed a novel service query model where declarative queries are resolved through a novel three-level service model that provides an easy way for developers to represent the service space and for users to formulate and submit queries. We proposed an optimization strategy based on aggregating quality of Web service (*QoWS*) of different Web services. *QoWS* is adjusted through a dynamic rating scheme and multimode matching. Web service ratings provide an assessment of their behavior. The multimode matching allows a larger solution space by enabling similar and partial answers.

There are many possible extensions to this work. One direction is to investigate other optimization strategies like genetic algorithms or using techniques from linear programming. Another direction is replace the monitoring portion for *QoWS*, which may not be always practical, by a reputation-based mechanism that collect trust scores from the different participants and aggregates this for each specific *QoWS* parameter. Finally, the service querying we introduced could be extended to other service models like Web API and REST-based services.

References

1. E. Aarts and J. Korst. *Simulated Annealing and Boltzman Machines: : A Stochastic Approach to Combinatorial Optimization and Neural Computing.* John Wiley and Sons, New York, USA, January 1989.
2. S. Abiteboul, O. Benjelloun, and T. Milo. Web Services and Data Integration. In *International Conference on Web Information Systems Engineering*, pages 3–6, Singapore, December 2002.
3. M. Aiello, M. P. Papazoglou, M. Carman J. Yang, M. Pistore, L. Serafini, and P. Traverso. A Request Language for Web-Services Based on Planning and Constraint Satisfaction. In *Proceedings of the 3rd International Workshop on Technologies for E-Services*, pages 76–85, Hong Kong, China, August 2002.
4. BEA, IBM, and Microsoft. *Business Process Execution Language for Web Services (BPEL4WS).* http://xml.coverpages.org/bpel4ws.html, 2003.
5. B. Benatallah, Q. Z. Sheng, A. H. H. Ngu, and M. Dumas. Declarative Composition and Peer-to-Peer Provisioning of Dynamic Web Services. In *Proceedings of the 18th International Conference on Data Engineering*, pages 297–308, San Jose, California, USA, February 2002.
6. J. Burge, K. Munagala, and U. Srivastava. Ordering Pipelined Query Operators with Precedence Constraints. Technical report, Stanford University, October 2005. http://infolab.stanford.edu/~usriv/papers/precconst.pdf.
7. J. Cardoso and A. Sheth. Semantic E-Workflow Composition. *Journal of Intelligent Information Systems*, 21(3):191–225, 2003.
8. M. Conti, M. Kumar, S. K. Das, and B. A. Shirazi. Quality of Service Issues in Internet Web Services. *IEEE Transactions on Computers*, 51(6):593–594, June 2002.
9. A. Doan. *Learning to Map between Structured Representations of Data.* PhD thesis, University of Washngton, Seattle, 2002.
10. X. Dong, A. Halevy, J. Madhavan, E. Nemes, and Jun Zhang. Similarity Search for Web Services. In *Proceedings of the 30th International Conference on Very Large Data Bases*, Toronto, Canada, August-Septmeber 2004.
11. The WSMO Workign Group. *Web Service Modeling Ontology.* http://www.wsmo.org.
12. I. Horrocks. DAML+OIL: a Description Logic for the Semantic Web. *IEEE Data Engineering Bulletin*, 25(1):4–9, March 2002.
13. T. Ibaraki and N. Katoh. *Resource allocation problems: algorithmic approaches.* MIT Press, Cambridge, MA, USA, 1988.
14. The DARPA Agent Markup Language. *OWL-S.* http://www.daml.org/services/owl-s.
15. Lei Li and Ian Horrocks. A Software Framework for Matchmaking based on Semantic Web Technology. In *Proceedings of the Twelfth International World Wide Web Conference, WWW2003, Budapest, Hungary*, pages 331–339, May 2003.
16. B. Medjahed, A. Bouguettaya, and A. Elmagarmid. Composing Web Services on the Semantic Web. *The VLDB Journal*, 12(4):333–351, November 2003.
17. B. Medjahed, M. Ouzzani, and A. Bouguettaya. Using Web Services in E-Government Applications. In *Proceedings of the 2002 National Sciences Foundation Conference on Digital Government Research*, pages 371–376, Los Angeles, California, USA, May 2002.
18. T. Milo, S. Abiteboul, B. Amann, O. Benjelloun, and F. Dang Ngoc. Exchanging Intensional XML Data. In *Proceedings of the ACM SIGMOD International Conference on Management of Data*, pages 289–300, San Diego, California, USA, June 2003.
19. F. Naumann. Data Fusion and Data Quality. In *Proceedings of the New Techniques and Technologies for Statistics Seminar*, pages 147–154, Sorrento, Italy, May 1998.
20. M. Ouzzani and A. Bouguettaya. Efficient Access to Web Services. *IEEE Internet Computing*, 8(2), March/April 2004.
21. M. Ouzzani and A. Bouguettaya. Query Processing and Optimization on the Web. *Distributed and Parallel Databases, an International Journal*, 15(3):187–218, May 2004.
22. A. Rezgui, A. Bouguettaya, and Z. Malik. A Reputation-based Approach to Preserving Privacy in Web Services. In *Proceedings of the 4th International Workshop on Technologies for E-Services*, pages 91–103, Berlin, Germany, September 2003.

23. A. Ruiz, R. Corchuelo and. Duran, and M. Toro. Automated Support for Quality Requirements in Web-Based Systems. In *Proceedings of the 8th IEEE Workshop on Future Trends of Distributed Computing Systems*, pages 48–55, Bologna, Italy, October-November 2001.

24. N. Srinivasan, M. Paolucci, and Katia Sycara. *An Efficient Algorithm for OWL-S Based Semantic Search in UDDI* . Lecture Notes in Computer Science, Springer, 2005.

25. U. Srivastava, J. Widom, K. Munagala, and R. Motwani. Query Optimization over Web Services. In *Proceedings of the 32nd International Conference on Very Large Data Bases*, Seoul, Korea, September 2006.

26. K. Sycara, M. Klusch, S. Widoff, and J. Lu. Dynamic Service Matchmaking Among Agents in Open Information Environments. *SIGMOD Record*, 28(1):47–53, 1999.

27. A. S. Tannenbaum and M. van Steen. *Distributed Systems: Principles and Paradigms*. Prentice Hall, New Jersey, USA, 2002.

28. S. Thakkar, J.L. Ambite, and C.A. Knoblock. Composition, optimizing, and executing plans for bioinformatics Web services. *The VLDB Journal*, 15(3), 2005.

29. D. Trastour, C. Bartolini, and J. Gonzalez-Castillo. A Semantic Web Approach to Service Description for Matchmaking of Services. In *Proceedings of SWWS'01, The first Semantic Web Working Symposium, Stanford University, California, USA*, pages 447–461, July 30-August 1 2001.

30. International Telecommunication Union. *ITU-T Recommendation E.800: Terms and Definitions Related to Quality of Service and Network Performance Including Dependability, ITU-T*, 1994.

31. S. Vinoski. Service Discovery 101. *IEEE Internet Computing*, 7(1):69–71, January/February 2003.

32. K. Yoon and C. Hwang. *Multiple Attribute Decision Making: An Introduction*. Thousand Oaks: Sage, Thousand Oaks, California, USA, January 1995.

33. Q. Yu, X. Liu, A. Bouguettaya, and B. Medjahed. Deploying and Managing Web Services: Issues, Solutions, and Directions. *VLDB Journal*, 2006.

34. L. Zeng, B. Benatallah, A.H.H. Ngu, M. Dumas, J. Kalagnanam, and H. Chang. QoS-Aware Middleware for Web Services Composition. *IEEE Transactions on Software Engineering*, 30(5):311–327, May 2004.

Chapter 4
RDF-GL: A SPARQL-Based Graphical Query Language for RDF

Frederik Hogenboom, Viorel Milea, Flavius Frasincar, and Uzay Kaymak

Abstract This chapter presents RDF-GL, a graphical query language (GQL) for RDF. The GQL is based on the textual query language SPARQL and mainly focuses on SPARQL SELECT queries. The advantage of a GQL over textual query languages is that complexity is hidden through the use of graphical symbols. RDF-GL is supported by a Java-based editor, SPARQLinG, which is presented as well. The editor does not only allow for RDF-GL query creation, but also converts RDF-GL queries to SPARQL queries and is able to subsequently execute these. Experiments show that using the GQL in combination with the editor makes RDF querying more accessible for end users.

4.1 Introduction

In an era of ever-increasing information needs, the ability to query large databases quickly and efficiently has come to play a major part. For a large share, this growing need is addressed by tools and languages aimed at performing complex queries on distributed data. However, the intuitiveness of designing such complex queries has only been addressed to a limited extent, making such tools available solely for technical users.

The realm of such tools, aimed at the intuitiveness of query design, though rather limited, presents some interesting applications. Examples of interfaces aimed at the non-technical user include EROS [19] and SPARQLViz [4]. Additionally, several graphical query languages (GQL) enable users to create queries only by arranging and connecting symbols on a virtual canvas. Therefore, complete knowledge of a normal query language is not necessary, as GQL's are mainly focused on intuitiveness of use.

F. Hogenboom (✉), V. Milea, F. Frasincar, and U. Kaymak
Econometric Institute, Erasmus University Rotterdam, P.O. Box 1738, 3000 DR, Rotterdam, The Netherlands
e-mail: fhogenboom@ese.eur.nl; milea@ese.eur.nl; frasincar@ese.eur.nl; kaymak@ese.eur.nl

R. Chbeir et al., *Emergent Web Intelligence: Advanced Information Retrieval*, Advanced Information and Knowledge Processing, DOI 10.1007/978-1-84996-074-8_4,
© Springer-Verlag London Limited 2010

Next to intuitive queries, the representation of knowledge is gaining importance, especially in the context of Web-based applications. New standards are being developed for this purpose under a common denominator – the Semantic Web [3]. One of the state-of-the-art languages put forward by this initiative is the Resource Description Framework (RDF) [5]. The language enables representations centered around the meaning of data, rather than the presentation hereof, and allows the inference of implicit knowledge from explicitly modeled data. The state-of-the-art query language for RDF is SPARQL [14].

Graphical query languages have already been developed for different types of relational representations, but no SPARQL-based GQL is available yet for querying RDF models. Our main focus is to propose one such GQL for RDF, based on SPARQL. For this purpose we introduce RDF-GL, our graphical query language for RDF. Additionally, we present SPARQLinG, an application aimed at the design of graphical RDF-GL queries.

After discussing approaches related to our current goal in Section 4.2, we move on to presenting our main contribution, the SPARQL-based graphical query language for RDF, RDF-GL, in Section 4.3. The application developed for designing RDF-GL queries, SPARQLinG, is presented in Section 4.4. We conclude in Section 4.5.

4.2 Related Work

This section is aimed at providing an overview of current research efforts related to graphical query languages. Although none of the presented approaches is built around RDF and SPARQL simultaneously, we deem some of the ideas presented relevant for the current goals, as outlined in the following sections. A summarizing overview of the main features of the presented graphical query languages is provided in Table 4.1. The four attributes considered in this overview consist of whether the considered approach (i) is a true graphical query language, (ii) shows a graphical user interface, (iii) the query language on which the tool is based, and (iv) the data language for which it is intended.

Table 4.1 GQL features summary

	GQL	GUI	Query language	Data language
DERI	Yes	No	–	RDF
XML-GL	Yes	No	–	XML
GLOO	Yes	No	nRQL	OWL ontologies
EROS	No	Yes	RQL	RDFS
SPARQLViz	No	Yes	SPARQL	RDFS
GRQL	No	Yes	RQL	RDFS
SEWASIE	Yes[a]	Yes	–	Unknown

[a] Queries cannot be drawn by hand, but are generated through a visual interface to the ontology.

Fig. 4.1 RDF GQL graphical
query example [11]

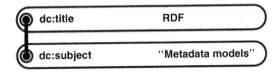

Fig. 4.2 The example query
in N3 query syntax

```
<> q1:select {
     ?subject1 ?p ?o .
}; q1:where {
     ?subject1 dc:title ?keyword .
     ?keyword yars:keyword ''RDF'' .
     ?subject1 dc:subject ''Metadata models'' .
     ?subject1 ?p ?o .
} .
```

An approach aimed at the graphical representation of RDF queries, developed by the Digital Enterprise Research Institute (DERI) at the National University of Ireland, is presented in [11]. The DERI graphical query language for RDF is built around facets – filter conditions over RDF graphs. The developed graphical language addresses however only a limited set of RDF queries.

Figure 4.1 presents a simple query, consisting of two facets, as enabled by the RDF graphical query language introduced in [11]. The purpose of this query consists of retrieving resources that have the keyword "RDF" in their title and address the subject of "metadata models". It should further be noted that the output of DERI RDF GQL queries consists of regular RDF triples, which may serve as input to other queries, thus providing closure for the proposed graphical query language.

Although the language presented in [11] does not provide semantics for the introduced graphical constructs, the graphical queries may always be translated to N3 [2] query syntax. For the example query depicted in Fig. 4.1, the translation is shown in Fig. 4.2.

XML-GL [8] is a graphical language for querying XML documents. The Graphical Data Model (GDM) introduced by the language addresses objects, properties, and relationships, represented as rectangles, circles, and arcs, respectively. Based hereon, XML-GL queries are then defined as consisting of four parts: (i) the extract part, (ii) the match part, (iii) the clip part, (iv) the construct part. Upon identifying the scope of the query in the *extract* part, the *optional* match part aims at representing additional logical conditions that should be imposed on the result set. The *clip* part specifies the focus of the query (relating to entities) in a similar way the *select* clause is used in SQL queries. Finally, the optional *construct* part of an XML-GL query specifies the new elements to be included in the result document and their relationships to the extracted elements [8].

Figure 4.3 depicts a graphical representation of an XML-GL query. The aim of this query is to select all (CD) items for which the product of the price and the quantity is less than 50. As can be observed from this figure, arithmetical operators may also be employed in the language, for the construction of complex queries such as the one presented here.

Fig. 4.3 XML-GLgraphical
query example [8]

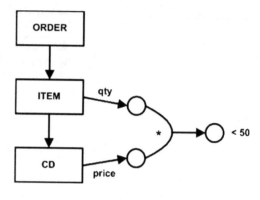

Fig. 4.4 GLOO example
query [9]

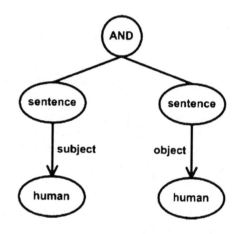

Despite fulfilling most of the requirements defined in [8], the language still lacks a precise definition of the semantics for the graphical symbols. Relevant to the current context, XML-GL is designed for XML, rather for more expressive knowledge representation languages such as RDF or OWL.

A graphical query language for OWL-DL ontologies (GLOO) is presented in [9]. The main focus of GLOO consists of translating visual, diagrammatic queries to DL-based query languages. The proposed version maps the graphical queries to the new Racer Query Language (nRQL) [10], but without matching the full expressive power of the latter language.

GLOO allows for construction of queries based on classes, individuals, and roles. Additionally, a number of operators may be employed: negation (true classical negation), complement (negation as failure), disjunction and conjunction. An example GLOO query is depicted in Fig. 4.4. The aim of this query is in selecting those sentences which have a human as subject and object (both conditions must be simultaneously satisfied), where *sentence* is a variable.

The authors argue for the formality of the proposed language, employing as main argument the connectivity syntax on which GLOO is based, and that is defined based on a formal grammar [9]. Additionally, the way in which elements of a query are placed into space has no influence on the semantics of that query.

The EROS tool [19], is aimed at simplifying queries on RDFS models. The main focus of the tool is to combine the advantages of a tree-based approach and a graph-based approach for visualizing RDFS, as both approaches present advantages and shortcomings. A tree view has the downside of being somewhat limited, due to the fact that multiple inheritance is not visible, while a graph view is limited because of its hierarchical structure that is hard to discover. On the positive side, a tree view provides increased clarity when visualizing the relevant entities. However, one can express more complex structures with graphs than is possible by using trees. The combination of the two approaches has resulted in an interface with two hierarchy trees: one domain tree and one range tree. Properties are depicted as arrows from left to right between tree nodes. The property-centric view of EROS is in line with the RDF philosophy.

Despite the fact that EROS is developed for visualizing ontologies, it also offers a built-in query generator [19]. This generator is based on RQL [13] – a query language for RDF descriptions. RQL uses SELECT, FROM and WHERE clauses. The EROS user is able to generate queries by selecting nodes in the graph and assigning properties to them using normal buttons, listboxes, etc. in the interface. The user can specify which variables should be visible in the results.

Summarizing, EROS does not implement a graphical query language, but visualizes ontologies and enables the user to query RDFS models using a normal graphical interface. Vdovjak et al. claim that an effective visual representation of ontologies is vital for users, since querying models without a clear view of the ontology is cumbersome [19]. EROS provides an interface in which the user is able to view the ontology both from the viewpoint of classes and that of properties.

SPARQLViz [4] is a query editor centered around graphical query composition and natural language processing in an RDF visualization interface. This tool is an extension for IsaViz, a visual interaction tool for RDF. SPARQLViz implements graphical query composition by using a graphical user interface for generating SPARQL queries. The user has to click through different menus to compose a query, as presented in screenshots in [4]. The tool demonstrates that it is possible to cover a great part of the SPARQL syntax with a simple user interface. However, no graphical query language is implemented, which makes the understanding of the relationships between different query parts difficult.

In [1], GRQL is introduced. GRQL is an intuitive interface which is able to construct RQL queries (like EROS) by using inputs from the user via a graphical interface (for screenshots, see [1]). GRQL is a graphical query generator in a way that it uses a graphical user interface. GRQL does not implement a graphical query language and thus does not support drawing queries. With GRQL, the user is able to browse through an RDFS model and to generate a lot of different queries graphically. GRQL's tree-based interface offers many functionalities. It is able to handle a lot of different actions, varying from browsing RDFS models towards all directions and the possibility to translate a sequence of browsing actions into an RQL query.

The SEWASIE project (which stands for SEmantic Webs and AgentS in Integrated Economies) [6] shows us it is possible to create a tool with which a user can generate a query using an integrated ontology. The tool's main purpose is to offer functionality to generate conjunctive queries ready to be executed by some evaluation engine associated to the information system. With the SEWASIE tool, a user is able to compose a query using drop-down menus and input fields (shown in screenshots in [6]). The composed query can be viewed in a natural language-like form and in a graphical form. The authors, however, remain unclear on how query execution works with the application, and only demonstrate the capabilities of the query editor.

One of the main conclusion supported by the approaches presented in this section is that, currently, no graphical query language based on SPARQL exists for RDF. In the following section we introduce one such language in the form of RDF-GL, aimed at querying RDF ontologies through a translation of graphical queries to the state-of-the-art RDF query language – SPARQL.

4.3 RDF-GL

In this section we introduce RDF-GL, the first SPARQL-based graphical language for RDF. The main constructs of the language are presented in Section 4.3.1, whereas Section 4.3.2 elaborates on the subset of SPARQL which is covered by RDF-GL. Sections 4.3.3 and 4.3.4 present how SPARQL queries are mapped to RDF-GL, and how the latter can be converted into SPARQL queries, respectively.

4.3.1 Language Constructs

The constructs of RDF-GL, which shall be denoted as *elements*, can be divided into three main groups: boxes, circles and arrows. All elements can be found in the example query presented in Figs. 4.5 and 4.6. The elements of RDF-GL queries are assigned meaning based on their shape and color. In what follows, we provide an informal overview hereof.

Boxes can have an orange, pink or green color, each color representing different SPARQL query elements. An orange box, which is called a result box or simply *BR*, contains information about the execution of the query, e.g., the type of query and the way result variables are ordered. A pink box (referred to as an subject/object box or as *BSO*) represents a subject or an object of a triple in a SPARQL query, whereas a green box, the filtered subject/object box (*BFSO*), is used to depict filtered subjects or objects.

```
PREFIX j.1: <http://www.daml.org/2003/09/factbook/factbook-ont#>
SELECT DISTINCT ?name ?oil
WHERE
{
    ?country j.1:localShortCountryName ?name .
    ?country j.1:grossDomesticProductPerCapita ?gdp .
    {
        FILTER (?gdp < 1500) .
    }
    UNION
    {
        FILTER (?gdp > 2500) .
    }
    OPTIONAL
    {
        ?country j.1:oilProvedReserves ?oil .
    }
}
ORDER BY ASC(?gdp)
```

Fig. 4.5 Example SPARQL query

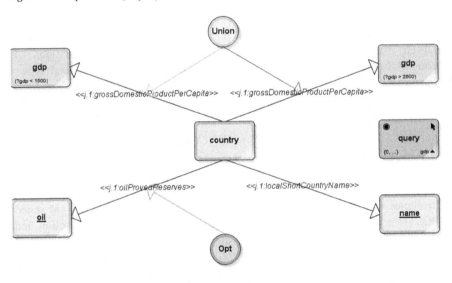

Fig. 4.6 Example RDF-GL query

We do have two types of circles. Blue circles, called union circles (*CU*), are used in an RDF-GL query to define or-relationships, similar to SPARQL UNION blocks. Purple circles – to which we refer to as optional circles (*CO*) – are used for RDF-GL's equivalents of SPARQL OPTIONAL blocks, in order to identify statements which are optional.

RDF-GL uses four colors for arrows. Black arrows, labeled with a property, depict a SPARQL triple predicate and are referred to as property arrows (*AP*), since they can be interpreted as a property relationship between two elements (a subject and an object), whereas grey arrows (also known as optional arrows, or *AO*) are used to indicate optional statements. Yellow and red arrows point to relationships belonging to a SPARQL UNION block, where yellow arrows point to the first part of the block and the red arrows to the second part. Two types of UNION arrows are used, because it is implied by SPARQL, as SPARQL makes a distinction between the two block parts to be joined. Yellow and red arrows are also called union arrows (*AU1* and *AU2*).

The use of the different elements of an RDF-GL query can best be illustrated by means of an example. Let us assume we want to search the CIA World Factbook [7] for countries that have a gross domestic product per capita of less than $1,500 or greater than $2,500. We want to know the name of every country matching this criterion. Furthermore we want to know the oil supply of every resulting country, if any data about oil supply is stored in the database for these countries. The SPARQL query used for retrieving this data is presented in Fig. 4.5, whereas the RDF-GL graphical representation of this query is presented in Fig. 4.6. Note that from now on, we will refer to the ontology as *j.1* in our RDF-GL graphs to maintain readability. This prefix is declared in the SPARQL query and does not need to be declared explicitly in RDF-GL. In our RDF-GL, the prefix is thus considered given, as well as the prefixes RDF, RDFS, and XSD.

We next move on to a more formal presentation of the different elements of RDF-GL queries. In general, we denote an RDF-GL query by Q. Equations 4.1 through 4.4 give an overview of all possible elements of Q, and their different types:

$$Q = \{BOX, CRC, ARR\}, \tag{4.1}$$
$$BOX = \{BR, BSO, BFSO\}, \tag{4.2}$$
$$CRC = \{CU, CO\}, \tag{4.3}$$
$$ARR = \{AP, AO, AU1, AU2\}. \tag{4.4}$$

The different types of boxes (*BR*, *BSO*, and *BFSO*) are grouped in the *BOX* set. The circles joined in set *CRC* are referred to as *CU* and *CO*, which are – as stated earlier – the blue and purple circle, respectively. Finally, the black, grey, yellow and red arrows (*AP*, *AO*, *AU1*, and *AU2*, respectively) are stored in set *ARR*.

Tables 4.2 and 4.3 give an overview of the constructs of RDF-GL introduced in this section. For each construct we give its shape name, acronym, and color, as well as a short description.

Table 4.2 Constructs of RDF-GL: shapes, properties and names

Subset	Name	Acronym	Color
Box (*BOX*)	Result box	*BR*	Orange
	Subject/object box	*BSO*	Pink
	Filtered subject/object box	*BFSO*	Green
Circle (*CRC*)	Union circle	*CU*	Blue
	Optional circle	*CO*	Purple
Arrow (*ARR*)	Property arrow	*AP*	Black
	Optional arrow	*AO*	Grey
	Union arrow 1	*AU1*	Yellow
	Union arrow 2	*AU2*	Red

Table 4.3 Constructs of RDF-GL: descriptions

Element	Description
BR	Contains information about query execution
BSO	Subject or object in a SPARQL triple
BFSO	Filtered subject or object in a SPARQL triple
CU	SPARQL UNION block
CO	SPARQL OPTIONAL block
AP	Predicate in a SPARQL triple
AO	Points to an optional element
AU1	Points to an alternative element (part 1)
AU2	Points to an alternative element (part 2)

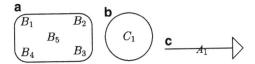

Fig. 4.7 Basic shapes of RDF-GL. (**a**) Box, (**b**) Circle, (**c**) Arrow

In what follows, we focus on giving a more precise description for each type of element of an RDF-GL query, given in Fig. 4.7. We start with describing drawing rules for boxes and continue by elaborating on circles. Finally, arrows are discussed.

4.3.1.1   Boxes

In general, box shapes have five positions where properties can be defined. There is one position in each corner, and one position in the center of the figure. Figure 4.7a shows a basic box shape. The positions are indicated with B_1 to B_5. The different types of boxes in our graphical query language not only differ in color, but also in the positions they use and how they use them. We continue with describing each type of box separately.

The *BR* box contains information about the execution of the query. In an RDF-GL query, exactly one *BR* box should be present. Also, its properties are bound to rules and restrictions. The box can be neither a child of another element in the query (i.e., being on the receiving end of a property relationship) nor parent of another element in the query (i.e., having a property relationship). Additionally, some graphic rules apply.

First of all, the *BR* box should be orange. Furthermore, a query name should be depicted, which is the centered text on position B_5 in the example. Subsequently, the corners of the box may each contain information.

The upper-left corner (B_1) states whether the query should return only distinct values or not. The upper-right corner (B_2) contains information about the SPARQL query type, which can be only SELECT for the moment, and the lower-right corner (B_3) is reserved for ordering the results. The names of the variables by which the

Table 4.4 Overview of symbols used in a *BR* box in RDF-GL

Corner	Symbol	Explanation
Upper-left	◯	Display all results
	◉	Display only distinct results
Upper-right	➤	SELECT query
Lower-right	▲	Ascending ordering
	▼	Descending ordering
Lower-left	{ , }	Range of results

query results should be ordered (zero or more) are displayed in this corner, where each name is followed by a symbol indicating an ascending or descending ordering. The lower-left corner (B_4) contains information about the result range, displayed as *{from, to}*. For example, if the range is set to *{5, 8}*, results 5, 6, 7 and 8 will be displayed as results. It should be noted that ending the range with "..." indicates infinity (for result set length). Table 4.4 shows all *BR* symbols with their descriptions.

The other boxes do not use all positions. The *BSO* box is a pink rectangle, which represents a subject or object in a SPARQL triple. In RDF-GL, the subject and object types are limited to a (new) variable, a blank node, an ontology object, or data type. A variable is displayed as bold text on position B_5 (representing the variable name), with or without underline. By underlining the variable name, one can express the variable will be visible in the query results. In case the box lacks a name, it represents a blank SPARQL node. Finally, one can denote an object or data type as a *BSO* box by placing its type on position B_5, for example ≪*type*≫. A *BSO* box can be a child of another *BSO* or *BFSO* box and can also be parent of another *BSO* or *BFSO* box.

The same rules apply to the *BFSO* box, which represents a filtered subject or object, except for the color, which is green instead of pink. Also, *BFSO* boxes cannot have empty names (i.e., cannot represent a blank SPARQL node) and their types are restricted to (new) variables. The content of the applied filter is displayed on position B_4, which is the lower-left corner of the rectangle shaped construct.

4.3.1.2 Circles

Circles only have one position which can be given a property. This position, C_1 (shown in Fig. 4.7b), should always be used and is located in the shape's center.

A *CU* circle is used for representation of a SPARQL UNION block, which models alternatives. In the center of this blue circle, "Union" is depicted. Restrictions of the *CU* are that it can only be a child and/or parent of both elements from the *CRC* set. Also, a *CU* can be parent of an *AP* arrow. Finally, *AU1* and *AU2* are associated with this circle. Note that conjunctions are implicit in SPARQL and thus are not included in RDF-GL as a *CU*-like symbol.

The purple colored *CO* circles, which are all labeled with "Opt", represent a SPARQL OPTIONAL block. These circles can be a child and/or a parent of another circle in *CRC*. Also, *CO* circles can be parent of an *AP* arrow. Grey arrows, *AO*, are used in combination with the *CO* circle. Note that RDF-GL elements which are connected by arrows have parent–child relationships. Children are on the receiving end of an arrow, while parents are on the other side of an arrow. Using circles, one can create nested OPTIONAL and UNION blocks, simply by pointing an *AO, AU1*, or *AU2* arrow from one circle to another circle. If an arrow points from a circle to an arrow, it represents a SPARQL triple inside an OPTIONAL or UNION block.

4.3.1.3   Arrows

Figure 4.7c shows the basic shape of an arrow. Each arrow is constructed with a transparent, closed head. As is the case with circles, arrows have only one property position in their center: A_1.

Four types of arrows can be distinguished, which are included in the *ARR* set. The black arrow, *AP*, should be read as a property relationship between two elements, for example: a resulting country has a gross domestic product per capita of less than \$2,500. The arrow represents a SPARQL triple predicate. Property types can be object or data types from ontologies, variables previously defined in the query and new variables. The property type is specified as a label located in the center of the arrow (position A_1). An *AP* arrow can be drawn from and to *BSO* and *BFSO* boxes.

An *AO* arrow indicates a SPARQL OPTIONAL relationship between two elements. Just like the *AP* arrow, the *AO* arrow should be read as a property relationship between two elements, but an *AO* arrow can only be drawn between a *CO* circle and the two types of circles or between a *CO* circle and an *AP* arrow.

As mentioned earlier, *AU1* and *AU2* arrows can be used in combination with the *CU* circles. With *AU1* arrows, one is able to define which relationships belong to the first part of the SPARQL UNION block and with *AU2* arrows one can define which belongs to the second part of the SPARQL UNION block. These two arrows can only be drawn from a *CU* circle to both circle types or from a *CU* circle to a black arrow.

An important point relates to the fact that arrows cannot be drawn from and to every element in a query. Also, it is not possible for an element to have children of every type. Tables 4.5 and 4.6 summarize the ways in which various RDF-GL elements may be connected.

Table 4.5 shows the allowed directions for every arrow type (displayed as columns) with respect to every element type (displayed as rows). Allowed directions are: from an element (from), to an element (to), and none (–).

As we can see, no arrows can be drawn from or to *BR* boxes. In RDF-GL, one is allowed to draw *AP* arrows from and to *BSO* and *BFSO* boxes. Furthermore, *AO* arrows cannot be drawn from or to other *AO, AU1*, or *AU2* arrows, as well as from

Table 4.5 Overview allowed arrow directions RDF-GL

Element	Arrow			
	AP	AO	AU1	AU2
BR	–	–	–	–
BSO	From/to	–	–	–
BFSO	From/to	–	–	–
CU	–	To	From/to	From/to
CO	–	From/to	To	To
AP	–	To	To	To
AO	–	–	–	–
AU1	–	–	–	–
AU2	–	–	–	–

Table 4.6 Overview allowed parent–child relationships RDF-GL

Child	Parent								
	BR	BSO	BFSO	CU	CO	AP	AO	AU1	AU2
BR	–	–	–	–	–	–	–	–	–
BSO	–	+	+	–	–	–	–	–	–
BFSO	–	+	+	–	–	–	–	–	–
CU	–	–	–	+	+	–	–	–	–
CO	–	–	–	+	+	–	–	–	–
AP	–	–	–	+	+	–	–	–	–
AO	–	–	–	–	–	–	–	–	–
AU1	–	–	–	–	–	–	–	–	–
AU2	–	–	–	–	–	–	–	–	–

or to other boxes. However, these arrows can be drawn to both types of circles and AP arrows, and can also be drawn from CO circles. The AU1 and AU2 arrows have equal restrictions to those of the AO arrows. However, the shapes differ in that AO arrows may only be drawn from CO circles, whereas AU1 and AU2 arrows may only be drawn from CU circles.

Since arrows indicate parent–child relationships, we can deduce Table 4.6 from Table 4.5. Table 4.6 shows every possible parent–child relationship. Possible parents are all types of boxes and circles, which are displayed in the columns of the table. Possible children are all elements of an RDF-GL query, which are displayed in the rows of the table. In Table 4.6 we summarize the valid parent–child relationships, where (+) denotes a valid relationship and (−) an invalid (not allowed) one.

As can be observed from this table, the orange box cannot be parent of any element in an RDF-GL query. The BSO and BFSO boxes can only be parent of other BSO and BFSO boxes. Furthermore, both types of circles can be parent of AP arrows and both types of circles. Finally, AO, AU1 and AU2 arrows cannot have any parents and none of the arrows can have children.

4.3.2 The SPARQL Subset of RDF-GL

In what follows, we define the subset of SPARQL which can be covered using the elements of the RDF-GL query language by means of Extended BackusNaur Form (EBNF) [15] rules, which are similar to the ones defined for SPARQL in [14]. Most of the rules in [14] can be maintained. However, since RDF-GL only covers a subset of SPARQL, we need to alter some of the grammar rules in order to define the covered SPARQL subset adequately.

First of all, SPARQL queries can be either ASK, CONSTRUCT, DESCRIBE, or SELECT queries. Usually, a query can be defined as a prologue, followed by a query type. This prologue contains BASE and PREFIX statements. In RDF-GL, currently only SELECT queries are covered, and thus we can define our first rule, which differs from SPARQL in that the prologue and all query types but the SELECT query are removed.

Query : := SelectQuery

Normally, in SPARQL, a SELECT query consists of the string "SELECT", optionally followed by the string "DISTINCT" or "REDUCED", followed by one or more variables which have to be selected to be returned in the result set, zero or more data set clauses containing FROM and NAMED elements, a WHERE clause, and solution modifiers. The subset of SPARQL which covers RDF-GL does not include all the elements of a regular SPARQL SELECT query [14]. The string "REDUCED" is not supported, as well as the data set clause (FROM and NAMED). Therefore, our second rule also differs from the rule presented in the SPARQL grammar.

```
SelectQuery : : = 'SELECT' 'DISTINCT'? ( Var+ | '*' ) WhereClauseSolutionModifier
```

SPARQL implements two types of variables, which have a name preceded by either a "?" or a "$" (type 1 and 2, respectively). RDF-GL can currently only represent the former type, and thus we define another rule which differs from the one presented in the SPARQL grammar.

Var ::= VAR1

Continuing defining the grammar rules of the SPARQL subset, we can state that the WHERE clause is not fully supported by RDF-GL. Normally, this clause would contain triples, FILTER elements, and graph patterns which are not triples, i.e., OPTIONAL, UNION, and GRAPH elements. RDF-GL's SPARQL subset does not contain GRAPH elements, but the triples and FILTER elements as defined in the clause are fully included. Therefore, we can add three rules to our rule set. The first two rules are exactly the same as in the grammar of SPARQL, but the last rule is redefined so that it cannot contain GRAPH elements. The rules are the following.

```
WhereClause            : : =   'WHERE'? Group Graph Pattern
GroupGraphPattern      : : =   '{' Triples Block? ((Graph Pattern Not Triples|
                               Filter )' . ' ? Triples Block? )*'}'
GraphPatternNotTriples : : =   Optional Graph Pattern | Group Or Union Graph Pattern
```

[1]	Query	::=	SelectQuery
[2]	SelectQuery	::=	'SELECT' 'DISTINCT'? (Var+ | '*') WhereClause SolutionModifier
[3]	WhereClause	::=	'WHERE'? GroupGraphPattern
[4]	SolutionModifier	::=	OrderClause? LimitOffsetClauses?
[5]	LimitOffsetClauses	::=	(LimitClause OffsetClause? | OffsetClause LimitClause?)
[6]	OrderClause	::=	'ORDER' 'BY' OrderCondition+
[7]	OrderCondition	::=	(('ASC' | 'DESC') BracketedExpression) (Constraint | Var)
[8]	LimitClause	::=	'LIMIT' INTEGER
[9]	OffsetClause	::=	'OFFSET' INTEGER
[10]	GroupGraphPattern	::=	'{' TriplesBlock? ((GraphPatternNotTriples | Filter) '.'? TriplesBlock?)* '}'
[11]	TriplesBlock	::=	TriplesSameSubject ('.' TriplesBlock?)?
[12]	GraphPatternNotTriples	::=	OptionalGraphPattern	GroupOrUnionGraphPattern
[13]	OptionalGraphPattern	::=	'OPTIONAL' GroupGraphPattern
[14]	GroupOrUnionGraphPattern	::=	GroupGraphPattern ('UNION' GroupGraphPattern)*
[15]	Filter	::=	'FILTER' Constraint
[16]	Constraint	::=	BracketedExpression	BuiltInCall	FunctionCall
[17]	FunctionCall	::=	IRIref ArgList
[18]	ArgList	::=	(NIL	'(' Expression (',' Expression)* ')')
[19]	TriplesSameSubject	::=	VarOrTerm PropertyListNotEmpty	TriplesNode PropertyList
[20]	PropertyListNotEmpty	::=	Verb ObjectList (';' (Verb ObjectList)?)
[21]	PropertyList	::=	PropertyListNotEmpty?
[22]	ObjectList	::=	Object (',' Object)*
[23]	Object	::=	GraphNode
[24]	Verb	::=	VarOrIRIref	'a'
[25]	TriplesNode	::=	Collection	BlankNodePropertyList
[26]	BlankNodePropertyList	::=	'[' PropertyListNotEmpty ']'
[27]	Collection	::=	'(' GraphNode+ ')'
[28]	GraphNode	::=	VarOrTerm	TriplesNode
[29]	VarOrTerm	::=	Var	GraphTerm
[30]	VarOrIRIref	::=	Var	IRIref
[31]	Var	::=	VAR1
[32]	GraphTerm	::=	IRIref	RDFLiteral	NumericLiteral	BooleanLiteral	BlankNode	NIL

Fig. 4.8 Rules in RDF-GL's subset of SPARQL (non-terminals)

Furthermore, the solution modifiers of the SELECT query (i.e., ORDER BY, LIMIT, and OFFSET) belong to the subset of SPARQL that can be represented by elements of RDF-GL.

When all non-terminal rules are refined using the rules of the SPARQL grammar, which of course all apply to some extent to our subset, the obtained rule set is as given in Fig. 4.8. Figure 4.9 shows all terminals.

4.3.3 Mapping SPARQL to RDF-GL

This section explains how the most common features of a SPARQL SELECT query look like in RDF-GL, or in other words, how SPARQL is mapped to RDF-GL. We try to create a mapping using the main rules of Fig. 4.8, as discussed in Section 4.3.2.

```
[33] Expression                ::= ConditionalOrExpression
[34] ConditionalOrExpression   ::= ConditionalAndExpression ( '||'
                                   ConditionalAndExpression )*
[35] ConditionalAndExpression  ::= ValueLogical ( '&&' ValueLogical )*
[36] ValueLogical              ::= RelationalExpression
[37] RelationalExpression      ::= NumericExpression ( '=' NumericExpression | '!='
                                   NumericExpression | '<' NumericExpression | '>'
                                   NumericExpression | '<=' NumericExpression | '>='
                                   NumericExpression )?
[38] NumericExpression         ::= AdditiveExpression
[39] AdditiveExpression        ::= MultiplicativeExpression ( '+'
                                   MultiplicativeExpression | '-'
                                   MultiplicativeExpression |
                                   NumericLiteralPositive |
                                   NumericLiteralNegative )*
[40] MultiplicativeExpression  ::= UnaryExpression ( '*' UnaryExpression | '/'
                                   UnaryExpression )*
[41] UnaryExpression           ::= '!' PrimaryExpression | '+' PrimaryExpression |
                                   '-' PrimaryExpression | PrimaryExpression
[42] PrimaryExpression         ::= BrackettedExpression | BuiltInCall |
                                   IRIrefOrFunction | RDFLiteral | NumericLiteral |
                                   BooleanLiteral | Var
[43] BrackettedExpression      ::= '(' Expression ')'
[44] BuiltInCall               ::= 'STR' '(' Expression ')' |
                                   'LANG' '(' Expression ')' |
                                   'LANGMATCHES' '(' Expression ',' Expression ')' |
                                   'DATATYPE' '(' Expression ')' |
                                   'BOUND' '(' Var ')' |
                                   'sameTerm' '(' Expression ',' Expression ')' |
                                   'isIRI' '(' Expression ')' |
                                   'isURI' '(' Expression ')' |
                                   'isBLANK' '(' Expression ')' |
                                   'isLITERAL' '(' Expression ')' |
                                   RegexExpression
[45] RegexExpression           ::= 'REGEX' '(' Expression ',' Expression ( ','
                                   Expression )? ')'
[46] IRIrefOrFunction          ::= IRIref ArgList?
[47] RDFLiteral                ::= String ( LANGTAG | ( '^^' IRIref ) )?
[48] NumericLiteral            ::= NumericLiteralUnsigned | NumericLiteralPositive |
                                   NumericLiteralNegative
[49] NumericLiteralUnsigned    ::= INTEGER | DECIMAL | DOUBLE
[50] NumericLiteralPositive    ::= INTEGER_POSITIVE | DECIMAL_POSITIVE |
                                   DOUBLE_POSITIVE
[51] NumericLiteralNegative    ::= INTEGER_NEGATIVE | DECIMAL_NEGATIVE |
                                   DOUBLE_NEGATIVE
[52] BooleanLiteral            ::= 'true' | 'false'
[53] String                    ::= STRING_LITERAL1 | STRING_LITERAL2 |
                                   STRING_LITERAL_LONG1 | STRING_LITERAL_LONG2
[54] IRIref                    ::= IRI_REF | PrefixedName
[55] PrefixedName              ::= PNAME_LN | PNAME_NS
[56] BlankNode                 ::= BLANK_NODE_LABEL | ANON
```

Fig. 4.8 (continued)

4.3.3.1   Query Type and Sequence Modifiers

As stated in Section 4.3.2, RDF-GL uses a subset of SPARQL, which results in
the fact that only SELECT queries can be performed to a certain extent. The main
elements of this query which are implemented in the RDF-GL language, are sequence modifiers, variables to include in the result set, and a WHERE clause (Rules
1 and 2). These sequence modifiers, i.e., DISTINCT, LIMIT, OFFSET, and ORDER

[57]	IRI_REF	::=	'<' ([^<>"{}|^`\]-[#x00-#x20])* '>'
[58]	PNAME_NS	::=	PN_PREFIX? ':'
[59]	PNAME_LN	::=	PNAME_NS PN_LOCAL
[60]	BLANK_NODE_LABEL	::=	'_:' PN_LOCAL
[61]	VAR1	::=	'?' VARNAME
[62]	LANGTAG	::=	'@' [a-zA-Z]+ ('-' [a-zA-Z0-9]+)*
[63]	INTEGER	::=	[0-9]+
[64]	DECIMAL	::=	[0-9]+ '.' [0-9]*	'.' [0-9]+
[65]	DOUBLE	::=	[0-9]+ '.' [0-9]* EXPONENT	'.' ([0-9])+ EXPONENT	([0-9])+ EXPONENT
[66]	INTEGER_POSITIVE	::=	'+' INTEGER
[67]	DECIMAL_POSITIVE	::=	'+' DECIMAL
[68]	DOUBLE_POSITIVE	::=	'+' DOUBLE
[69]	INTEGER_NEGATIVE	::=	'-' INTEGER
[70]	DECIMAL_NEGATIVE	::=	'-' DECIMAL
[71]	DOUBLE_NEGATIVE	::=	'-' DOUBLE
[72]	EXPONENT	::=	[eE] [+-]? [0-9]+
[73]	STRING_LITERAL1	::=	"'" (([^#x27#x5C#xA#xD])	ECHAR)* "'"
[74]	STRING_LITERAL2	::=	'"' (([^#x22#x5C#xA#xD])	ECHAR)* '"'
[75]	STRING_LITERAL_LONG1	::=	"'''" (("'" | "''")? ([^'\] | ECHAR))* "'''"
[76]	STRING_LITERAL_LONG2	::=	'"""' (('"' | '""')? ([^"\] | ECHAR))* '"""'
[77]	ECHAR	::=	'\' [tbnrf\"']
[78]	NIL	::=	'(' WS* ')'
[79]	WS	::=	#x20	#x9	#xD	#xA
[80]	ANON	::=	'[' WS* ']'
[81]	PN_CHARS_BASE	::=	[A-Z]	[a-z]	[#x00C0-#x00D6]	[#x00D8-#x00F6]	[#x00F8-#x02FF]	[#x0370-#x037D]	[#x037F-#x1FFF]	[#x200C-#x200D]	[#x2070-#x218F]	[#x2C00-#x2FEF]	[#x3001-#xD7FF]	[#xF900-#xFDCF]	[#xFDF0-#xFFFD]	[#x10000-#xEFFFF]
[82]	PN_CHARS_U	::=	PN_CHARS_BASE	'_'
[83]	VARNAME	::=	(PN_CHARS_U | [0-9]) (PN_CHARS_U | [0-9] | #x00B7 | [#x0300-#x036F] | [#x203F-#x2040])*
[84]	PN_CHARS	::=	PN_CHARS_U	'-'	[0-9]	#x00B7	[#x0300-#x036F]	[#x203F-#x2040]
[85]	PN_PREFIX	::=	PN_CHARS_BASE ((PN_CHARS | '.')* PN_CHARS)?
[86]	PN_LOCAL	::=	(PN_CHARS_U | [0-9]) ((PN_CHARS | '.')* PN_CHARS)?

Fig. 4.9 Rules in RDF-GL's subset of SPARQL (terminals)

BY (Rules 4, 5, 6, 8, 9), all can be defined using a *BR* box and the symbols from Table 4.4. Furthermore, the variables that have to be selected are denoted as pink or green (filtered) boxes with an underlined, centered label.

Figure 4.10 shows the translation from a SPARQL SELECT query that uses all sequence modifiers to an RDF-GL query. The displayed query asks for all distinct elevations of countries in the CIA World Factbook. Results 5, 6, 7 and 8 are returned in a descending order. The SPARQL triple (*?country j.1:elevation ?elevation* .) is drawn using two *BSO* boxes, both representing variables. Solely information on elevation will be returned in the result set, which is denoted by the underlining of the variable name in the RDF-GL query. In the *BR* box, all corners have been used to display the sequence modifiers.

```
PREFIX j.1: <http://www.daml.org/2003/09/factbook/factbook-ont#>
SELECT DISTINCT ?elevation
WHERE
{
     ?country j.1:elevation ?elevation .
}
ORDER BY DESC(?elevation) OFFSET 5 LIMIT 4
```

(a) SPARQL

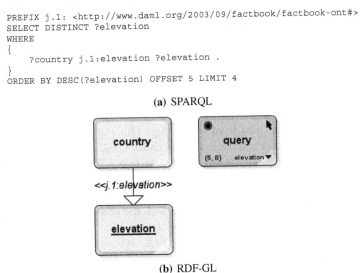

(b) RDF-GL

Fig. 4.10 Mapping query type and sequence modifiers

```
FILTER (?gdp > 1250) .
```

(a) SPARQL

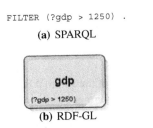

(b) RDF-GL

Fig. 4.11 Mapping filters

4.3.3.2 Filtered Variables

One element that is included in the WHERE clause (Rules 3 and 10) of a SPARQL query in general, as well as in our implemented subset of SPARQL, is the FILTER element (Rule 15). RDF-GL has full functionality with respect to filtering, as the SPARQL filter condition is embedded in the graphical representation.

In RDF-GL, filtering variables used in a query can be done by denoting the filtered variable as a *BFSO* box with a variable name and filter. This box is equal to a FILTER statement in a query written in SPARQL syntax. Figure 4.11 shows how a filter is applied to a variable called *gdp* in SPARQL and how the same filter can be applied to a variable in a RDF-GL query. In RDF-GL, the filter is displayed in the lower-left corner of the box representing the variable and the box has been colored green.

4.3.3.3 Triples

Another important element in the WHERE clause is the triple. Each query contains one or more triples. According to Rule 11 and 19 and their refinements, a triple typically consists of a variable or term, followed by a property and another variable or reference to an IRI from an ontology. A term can either be a reference to an IRI from an ontology, some literals (data types), or a blank node. A property is defined as a variable, IRI, or data type from an ontology (Rule 20 and some of the rules after it). The three elements of a triple are also called subject, predicate and object.

With RDF-GL, these elements are denoted as two *BSO* or *BFSO* boxes (representing the subject and object) and an *AP* arrow between them (representing the predicate). The arrow points from the box representing the triple's subject to the box representing the triple's object and is labeled with the predicate name. Both boxes and arrows are able to represent all required elements.

Figure 4.12 shows a single triple in SPARQL syntax and the same triple in RDF-GL. This triple asks for the classes of which the class *EthnicGroup* is a subclass and stores them in a variable called *class*. Two *BSO* boxes and one arrow have been used to construct this triple in RDF-GL. The upper box represents the subject, and the lower box represents the object, which in this case is a variable. The arrow depicts the triple's predicate.

4.3.3.4 Alternatives

A third part of the WHERE clause of the full SPARQL set is not entirely covered by RDF-GL: the graph patterns which are not triples (Rule 12 shows what is covered). One of those patterns is called the UNION graph pattern (Rule 14), which is nothing more than an element which groups 2 query blocks (containing for example triples) and takes the union of both groups. This way one is able to represent alternatives.

```
j.1:EthnicGroup rdfs:subClassOf ?class .
```

(a) SPARQL

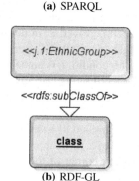

(b) RDF-GL

Fig. 4.12 Mapping triples

Fig. 4.13 Mapping
alternative triples

```
?country j.1:highwaysTotal ?hw .
{
    FILTER (?hw < 20000) .
}
UNION
{
    FILTER (?hw > 150000) .
}
```

(a) SPARQL

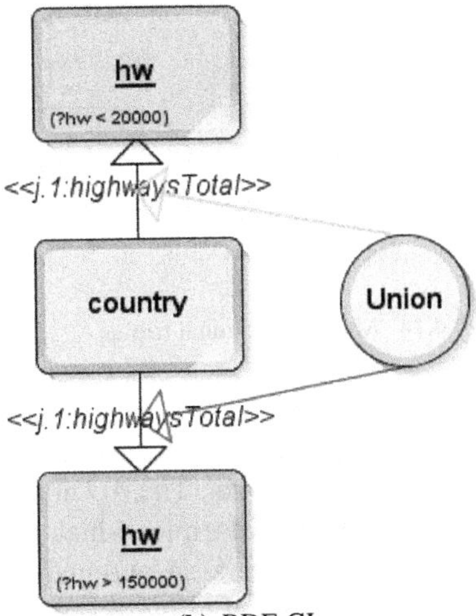

(b) RDF-GL

In RDF-GL, a *CU* circle and *AU1* and *AU2* arrows are used to point to elements (triples and other graph patterns) which represent a union part. The user decides which triples belong to which part of the union, and draws the arrows accordingly. Whichever elements belong to the first group (at least 1) will be pointed at with a yellow arrow (*AU1*), and the other elements (also at least 1) will be pointed at with a red arrow (*AU2*). These arrows point from a *CU* circle to *AP* arrows (predicates of triples), other *CU* circles, or *CO* circles. In case circles are being pointed at, it can lead to nested alternatives or options, which will be discussed shortly.

Figure 4.13 shows an alternative in SPARQL and how the same alternative is represented in RDF-GL. The UNION depicted in Fig. 4.13 joins a variable which is filtered in two different ways. The countries which have a total highway kilometers of less than 20,000 km as well as the countries which have a total highway kilometers of more than 150,000 have to be selected.

4.3.3.5 Options

The rules we have defined for our SPARQL subset indicate that not only the UNION element is included in RDF-GL, but also the OPTIONAL element. In SPARQL, one is able to provide additional triples by using the OPTIONAL block (Rule 13).

```
OPTIONAL
{
        ?country j.1:heliports ?heli .
}
```

(a) SPARQL

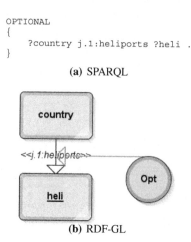

(b) RDF-GL

Fig. 4.14 Mapping optional triples

In RDF-GL, a *CO* circle and *AO* arrows are used to point to triples which have to be marked as optional. The *AO* arrows point from *CO* circles to *AP* arrows (representing predicates of triples which have to be added to the set of additional triples).

Figure 4.14 shows an optional triple in SPARQL and how the same triple is marked as additional in our developed GQL. The triple depicted in Fig. 4.14 asks for the number of helicopter ports in a resulting country and stores it in a variable called *heli*.

4.3.3.6 Nested Options and Alternatives

In SPARQL, it is possible to create nested options and alternatives. By looking at the defined grammar rules carefully, it becomes clear that UNION and OPTIONAL blocks not only include triples, but also other graph patterns which are not triples. Recalling our implementation of those graph patterns, we see that these patterns are in fact UNION and OPTIONAL blocks and thus it is possible to nest several options and alternatives in one query. This is also possible in RDF-GL. One can denote nested options and/or alternatives in RDF-GL by letting one or more *AO*, *AU1*, or *AU2* arrows point to circle(s). These arrows are not only allowed to point to *AP* arrows, but also to both types of circles.

Figure 4.15 combines the queries from Figs. 4.13 and 4.14 by nesting the option from Fig. 4.13 in the second union part of the query from Fig. 4.14. The order in which the union parts are specified is not relevant. Arrows pointing from the *CU* circle to the *AP* arrows indicate the triples to which these arrows belong should be regarded as alternatives. The circle to which an *AU2* arrow is pointing should also be added to the same alternative. The *AO* arrow pointing to an *AP* arrow indicates that the triple to which this arrow belongs should be optional.

```
?country j.1:highwaysTotal ?hw .
{
    FILTER (?hw < 20000) .
}
UNION
{
    FILTER (?hw > 150000) .
    OPTIONAL
    {
        ?country j.1:heliports ?heli .
    }
}
```

(a) SPARQL

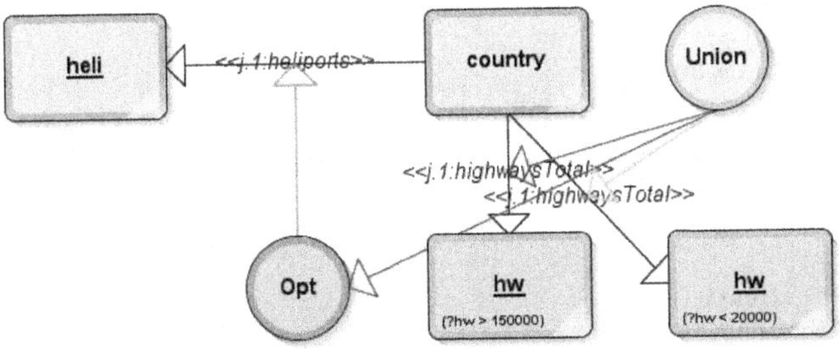

(b) RDF-GL

Fig. 4.15 Mapping nested triples

4.3.4 Converting RDF-GL to SPARQL

RDF-GL queries can be converted to SPARQL queries, using the algorithms presented in Figs. 4.16 and 4.17. These algorithms generate SPARQL queries based on drawing order. The SPARQL query is generated in a fixed order. First the default prefixes for RDF, RDFS, and XSD are generated, as well as for the ontology currently used (1). Subsequently, the query type is determined (2), after which the complete WHERE clause is generated (3). Finally, the ORDER BY (7) and the LIMIT and OFFSET (8) statements are determined. These main steps are directly related to some of the basic rules we defined in Section 4.3.2 (Rules 1 and 2, as well as 3 and 7).

Generating the prefixes and fetching the query type (with or without DISTINCT parameter and variables to select) is quite straightforward. Generating the complete WHERE clause, however, involves more complex actions. First, all *ARR* elements are read and converted to triples (4). We have seen in Rules 10, 11, and 19, that many types of triple configurations exist. If these triples do not belong to a UNION or OPTIONAL block, they are added to the SPARQL query (5). Subsequently, all *CU* circles and *CO* circles with their children (triples or other circles) are added to the query (6), using the recursive algorithm shown in Fig. 4.17. The generation of the ORDER BY, LIMIT and OFFSET is trivial and is solely based on the Rules 6–9.

Data: all elements from drawing
Result: RDF-GL converted to SPARQL
query = "";
query += prefixes;   (1)
query += BR.type;   (2)
if BR.type = SELECT **then**
  if BR.distinct = *true* **then**
    | query += DISTINCT;
  foreach arrow *in* ARR *and* box *in* BOX **do**
    if show = *true and* type = *variable and is not in* SELECT **then**
    | query += name;

  end
query += WHERE;   (3)
foreach arrow *in* ARR **do**
  triple = "";   (4)
  //Subject
  foreach box *in* BOX **do**
    if box.id = arrow.fromId **then**
      triple += box.name, blank or box.objectType;
      if filter *present and* box.type = *variable* **then**
      | store filter;

  end
  //Predicate
  triple += arrow.name or arrow.objectType;
  //Object
  foreach box *in* BOX **do**
    if box.id = arrow.toId **then**
      triple += box.name, blank or box.objectType;
      if filter *present and* box.type = *variable* **then**
      | store filter;

  end
  store triple with filter in triples;
end
foreach triple *in* triples **do**
  search for references in AU1, AU2, and AO;   (5)
  if *no references found* **then**
    query += triple;
    if triple *has* filter **then**
    | query += filter;

end
foreach circle *in* CU *and* CO **do**
  search for parentless circle;   (6)
  if *found* **then**
  | query += getChildren(id);

end
query += BR.orderBy;   (7)
convert BR.range to limit and offset;   (8)
query += limit;
query += offset;
return query;

Fig. 4.16 Generating a SPARQL query (generateQuery)

Result: triples and children's triples
Input: id of circle
query = "";
store all circle children which are triples in triples;
forall triple *in* triples **do**
| query += triple;
end
store all circle children which are other circles in CRC;
forall circle *in* CRC **do**
| query += getChildren(circle.id);
end
return query;

Fig. 4.17 Generating a SPARQL query (getChildren)

4.4 SPARQLinG

This section introduces our RDF-GL editor: SPARQLinG. We elaborate on the technical details of this editor and provide an overview of the application's functionality. Finally, we present experimental results on the SPARQLinG tool.

4.4.1 Design

The SPARQLinG RDF-GL editor is a Java-based editor, which is able to read an RDF file (which contains both schema and instance data) and interpret the ontologies used, and offers users with little knowledge of SPARQL and some knowledge on the domain of the RDF file tools to draw RDF-GL queries in an intuitive way. Furthermore, RDF-GL queries can be converted into SPARQL queries and can be executed.

Although quite a few Java libraries for drawing graphs are around, such as JGraph [17], Piccolo [12], and Prefuse [18], none of these are suitable for SPARQLinG, since real-time drawing mostly is not supported and it is difficult to store non-standard information in the graph elements of the libraries. Also, these libraries cause a lot of overhead. Therefore, both the functionality of the graphical user interface and the graphics are created without using any existing libraries. Reading and interpreting RDF files however, is done using the Jena [16] library. The latter library is also used for executing SPARQL queries.

At an abstract level, we distinguish between three main components of SPARQLinG: (i) Ontology Management, (ii) Query Drawing, and (iii) Query Execution. In what follows, we describe the main functionality hereof and discuss the interactions between components, which is also illustrated in Fig. 4.18.

An RDF file which has to be queried is fed into the *Ontology Management* component. The RDF Schema ontology used in the RDF file is extracted, so that it can be used in the *Query Drawing* component. Also, the RDF instances which populate the RDF Schema ontology are extracted. Both RDF instances and RDF Schema are used in the *Query Execution* component.

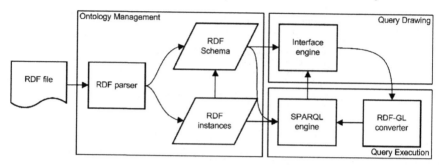

Fig. 4.18 Design of SPARQLinG

After loading an RDF file, the *Query Drawing* component offers the user tools to draw RDF-GL queries and handles all interface tasks. RDF-GL elements can be drawn using all elements stored in the ontology. The RDF-GL query is fed into the third module, the *Query Execution* module.

The *Query Execution* module handles two tasks. The first task is converting an RDF-GL query into a SPARQL query, which is done using the algorithms elaborated on in Section 4.3.4. The second task is executing this SPARQL query, using the ontology and RDF instances read from the input file. The query results are returned to the *Query Drawing* component.

4.4.2 Using SPARQLinG

The SPARQLinG RDF-GL editor is a tool like many other drawing applications. The user interface contains floating windows, which can be moved and toggled on and off. These windows contain drawing tools, settings, and query results. Furthermore, hot-keys are implemented for several actions, such as opening and saving files and executing queries. Figure 4.19 shows the user interface of SPARQLinG.

The background of the SPARQLinG tool is a large canvas, which can contain a grid – if desired – making it easier to draw and align RDF-GL elements. Elements can be drawn by selecting the appropriate drawing tool and by clicking and dragging on the canvas. SPARQLinG implements a sketch mode, so that users can see a sketch-like representation of an element while holding the mouse, before actually drawing the element (when the mouse is released). Figure 4.20 shows how a box is drawn in SPARQLinG.

Other features related to drawing RDF-GL queries are moving, resizing, and deleting elements. Whereas boxes can be drawn anywhere on the canvas and their dimensions can be manipulated, arrows can only be drawn from one (valid) element to another – forcing the user to actually touch both elements while drawing the arrow – and their dimensions cannot be changed, since the tool automatically optimizes the location of arrows between two elements. All properties of boxes and arrows can

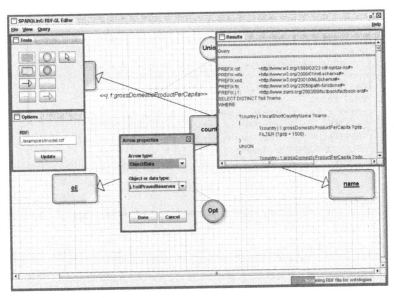

Fig. 4.19   User interface of SPARQLinG

Fig. 4.20   Drawing a box

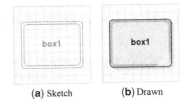

(a) Sketch   (b) Drawn

be edited intuitively by means of a property window, which appears when the user clicks on an element.

SPARQLinG's features with respect to file input and output are rather basic. Entire RDF-GL drawings can be saved and loaded using dialogs, just like regular graphical applications support saving and loading. Also, drag and drop is supported for loading RDF-GL files. Furthermore, the user can specify the RDF file which is to be queried. After the user specifies the RDF file, the tool automatically parses the file, so that the ontology can be used for drawing RDF-GL queries and queries can be executed immediately. For RDF-GL queries to be executed, the tool is also able to convert RDF-GL to SPARQL. Query results are displayed in a result window, along with the RDF-GL query represented in SPARQL, as shown in Fig. 4.21.

Despite the fact that prefixes currently are not fully supported in RDF-GL, SPAR-QLinG automatically assigns a prefix to the ontology used and to default RDF, RDFS, and XSD elements, to make it easier for users to browse through the available IRIs and to ensure readability of the diagrams. In case full paths (IRIs) are used, labels would get hard to read. Future versions of RDF-GL are likely to support prefixes and thus this functionality eventually will become obsolete.

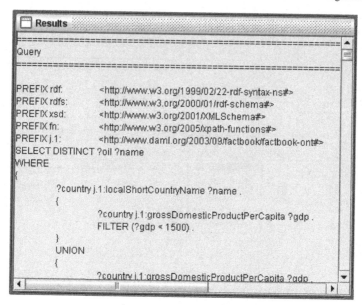

Fig. 4.21 Results of an executed RDF-GL query

4.4.3 Experiments with RDF-GL and SPARQLinG

A usability experiment held under a small group of students with fair knowledge on SPARQL querying shows that the combination of RDF-GL and an RDF-GL editor such as SPARQLinG enables one to create and execute complex queries in a convenient and intuitive way. The participants are chosen randomly from a group of students who are indicative of a cross-section of potential end users.

The participants are given a complex query related to the CIA World Factbook ontology (as described earlier), which they need to translate into a SPARQL query and an RDF-GL query. Performance is measured with how much time each user needs to complete each of the two queries. Also, accuracy is measured by means of the number of mistakes each member of the test group makes.

The students need to query the CIA World Factbook for countries which have an import or export to neighbors worth more than \$10,000,000,000 a year. The query needs to return the names of both countries and their neighboring trading partners, as well as the percentages of imports and exports and optionally, the inflation rate of the neighboring partners. Only the first 20 results are desired and should be ordered by country name (ascending). In SPARQL, a query which returns the requested results is given in Fig. 4.22, whereas its RDF-GL query equivalent is presented in Fig. 4.23.

Results show that about 60% of the students state that creating a complex query using RDF-GL takes (slightly) less time than manually inserting a SPARQL query (for SPARQL experts). Converting the (natural language) search assignment to a valid query takes about as much time with both query languages, but actually

```
PREFIX j.1: <http://www.daml.org/2003/09/factbook/factbook-ont#>
SELECT DISTINCT ?nameC ?nameN ?percentExp ?percentImp ?inflation
WHERE
{
    ?country j.1:conventionalShortCountryName ?nameC .
    ?country j.1:border ?border .
    ?border j.1:country ?neighbor .
    ?neighbor j.1:conventionalShortCountryName ?nameN .
    ?country j.1:exportPartner ?partnerExp .
    ?partnerExp j.1:percent ?percentExp .
    ?partnerExp j.1:country ?neighbor .
    ?country j.1:importPartner ?partnerImp .
    ?partnerImp j.1:percent ?percentImp .
    ?partnerImp j.1:country ?neighbor .
    {
        ?country j.1:imports ?imports .
        FILTER (?imports > 10000000000) .
    }
    UNION
    {
        ?country j.1:exports ?exports .
        FILTER (?exports > 10000000000) .
    }
    OPTIONAL
    {
        ?neighbor j.1:inflationRate ?inflation .
    }
}
ORDER BY ASC(?nameC) LIMIT 20
```

Fig. 4.22 Complex SPARQL query

drawing this query in RDF-GL sometimes is more time consuming than manually inserting a SPARQL query. The SPARQLinG or RDF-GL user especially benefits from the expressive power of RDF-GL when reusing variables, changing or adding relations between variables, and changing query characteristics (e.g., query type, variables to select). The more complex a query is, the more a user can benefit from RDF-GL over SPARQL.

Although manually inserting a SPARQL query might be faster than drawing an RDF-GL query in some cases, about 80% of the participants indicate that querying becomes easier to do with RDF-GL, because a clear overview of the complex construction of the query can easily be maintained, since an RDF-GL query usually gives more insight in relations between variables and the entire construction of the query. Problems with respect to easily understanding the expected results of a query and the way a query is constructed will arise when complex queries in SPARQL syntax become larger, whereas RDF-GL's symbols support the understanding and the construction of the query visually, which is more natural for the average end user.

The same 80% of participants that state that querying becomes easier to do using RDF-GL, indicate that the SPARQLinG editor simplifies query creation, because it only allows syntactical correct drawing actions, so that (drawing) errors related to RDF-GL elements occur less. Furthermore, the SPARQLinG editor's functionality of offering all available IRIs from the ontology which is being used, is deemed valuable, as well as the ease with which one can edit the properties of the RDF-GL elements.

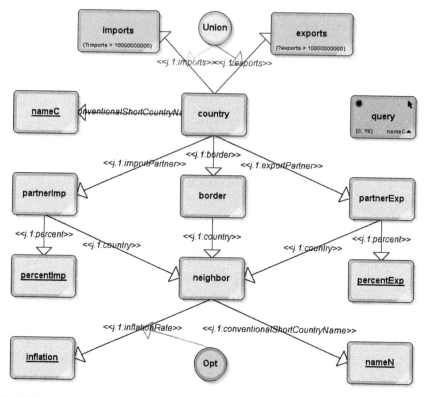

Fig. 4.23 Complex RDF-GL query

All participants agree on the fact that SPARQLinG is able to convert the RDF-GL query to a SPARQL query within acceptable time (less than one second). It should be noted that, while converting RDF-GL to SPARQL and querying the RDF file is done very fast, emptying large result buffers could take up quite some time. Furthermore, the students state that the interface of the tool runs smoothly and works intuitively enough to let a user with fair knowledge of SPARQL be able to draw his or her first RDF-GL query in only a few minutes.

4.5 Conclusions and Further Research

The main aim of RDF-GL is to cover as much of SPARQL expressivity as possible while maintaining simplicity and intuitiveness. For best results, a graphical query language such as RDF-GL should be combined with a tool, such as SPARQLinG. This way, complexity of a textual query language (i.e., SPARQL) is hidden by using symbols, text and menus. Not every aspect of a textual query language can be covered by symbols of a graphical query language, and thus some text elements have to be added to the GQL. Drawing (recognizable) query elements is difficult and this is where the user interface comes to play a major part. A user interface should offer the user convenient menus and windows to edit properties of symbols in a query. The combination of RDF-GL and SPARQLinG, makes one able to create and execute complex queries in a convenient and intuitive way.

RDF-GL is the first graphical query language based on SPARQL, designed for RDF. The focus of the language is on SPARQL SELECT queries. Although RDF-GL can handle almost every SELECT query, it currently offers no support for FROM, FROM NAMED and GRAPH elements. However, the design of RDF-GL allows for extensions, and this should form the main focus of future research.

For the design of graphical RDF-GL queries, we have introduced the SPARQLinG application, a Java-based framework that comprises all the required components for the design as well as the generation of queries on any RDF data sources. Currently, the editor lacks a converter from SPARQL queries to RDF-GL queries, which is to be investigated in further research. Naturally, any syntactic/semantic extension of RDF-GL should be mirrored in the application, and this constitutes an inevitable attention point of future development.

References

1. Nikos Athanasis, Vassilis Christophides, and Dimitris Kotzinos. Generating On the Fly Queries for the Semantic Web: The ICS-FORTH Graphical RQL Interface (GRQL). In *International Semantic Web Conference (ISWC 2004)*, pages 486–501. Springer, 2004.
2. Tim Berners-Lee. Notation 3 (N3) A readable RDF syntax, 1998.
3. Tim Berners-Lee, James Hendler, and Ora Lassila. The Semantic Web. *Scientific American*, 284(5):28–37, 2001.
4. Jethro Borsje and Hanno Embregts. Graphical Query Composition and Natural Language Processing in an RDF Visualization Interface. Bachelor Thesis, Erasmus University Rotterdam, 2006. http://www.jborsje.nl/publications/bachelor-thesis.pdf.
5. Dan Brickley and R.V. Guha. RDF Vocabulary Description Language 1.0: RDF Schema - W3C Recommendation 10 February 2004, 2004.
6. Tiziana Catarci, Paolo Dongilli, Tania Di Mascio, Enrico Franconi, Giuseppe Santucci, and Sergio Tessaris. An Ontology Based Visual Tool for Query Formulation Support. In *Sixteenth European Conference on Artifical Intelligence (ECAI 2004)*, volume 110 of *Frontiers in Artificial Intelligence and Applications*, pages 308–312, Amsterdam, The Netherlands, 2004. IOS Press.
7. Central Intelligence Agency. The CIA World Factbook, 2008. See https://www.cia.gov/library/publications/the-world-factbook/index.html, last visited Oct. 2008.
8. Stefano Ceri, Sara Comai, Ernesto Damiani, Piero Fraternali, Stefano Paraboschi, and Letizia Tanca. XML-GL: A Graphical Language for Querying and Reshaping XML Documents. *Computer Networks*, 31(11–16):1171–1187, 1999.
9. Amineh Fadhil and Volker Haarslev. GLOO: A Graphical Query Language for OWL Ontologies. In *OWL: Experience and Directions (OWLED 2006)*. CEUR-WS, 2006.
10. Volker Haarslev, Ralf Möller, and Michael Wessel. Querying the Semantic Web with Racer + nRQL. In *Third International Workshop on Applications of Description Logics (ADI 2004)*. CEUR-WS, 2004.

11. Andreas Harth, Sebastian Ryszard Kruk, and Stefan Decker. Graphical Representation of RDF Queries. In *Fifteenth International Conference on World Wide Web (WWW 2006)*, pages 859–860, New York, NY, USA, 2006. ACM Press.
12. Human-Computer Interaction Lab, University of Maryland. Piccolo, 2007. See http://www.cs. umd.edu/hcil/jazz/index.shtml, last visited Oct. 2008.
13. Gregory Karvounarakis, Sofia Alexaki, Vassilis Christophides, Dimitris Plexousakis, Forth Vassilika Vouton, and Michel Scholl. RQL: A Declarative Query Language for RDF. In *Eleventh International World Wide Web Conference (WWW 2002)*, pages 592–603, New York, NY, USA, 2002. ACM Press.
14. Eric Prud'hommeaux and Andy Seaborne. SPARQL Query Language for RDF - W3C Recommendation 15 January 2008, 2008.
15. Roger S. Scowen. Extended BNF – A generic base standard. ISO 14977.
16. SourceForge. Jena, 2008. See http://jena.sourceforge.net/, last visited Oct. 2008.
17. SourceForge. JGraph, 2008. See http://www.jgraph.com/, last visited Oct. 2008.
18. SourceForge. Prefuse, 2008. See http://prefuse.org/, last visited Oct. 2008.
19. Richard Vdovjak, Peter Barna, and Geert-Jan Houben. EROS: Explorer for RDFS-Based Ontologies. In *Eigth International Conference on Intelligent User Interfaces (IUI 2003)*, pages 330–330, New York, NY, USA, 2003. ACM Press.

Chapter 5
Semantics-Based Intelligent Indexing and Retrieval of Digital Images – A Case Study

Taha Osman, Dhavalkumar Thakker, and Gerald Schaefer

Abstract The proliferation of digital media has led to a huge interest in classifying and indexing media objects for generic search and usage. In particular, we are witnessing colossal growth in digital image repositories that are difficult to navigate using free-text search mechanisms, which often return inaccurate matches as they typically rely on statistical analysis of query keyword recurrence in the image annotation or surrounding text. In this chapter we present a semantically enabled image annotation and retrieval engine that is designed to satisfy the requirements of commercial image collections market in terms of both accuracy and efficiency of the retrieval process. Our search engine relies on methodically structured ontologies for image annotation, thus allowing for more intelligent reasoning about the image content and subsequently obtaining a more accurate set of results and a richer set of alternatives matchmaking the original query. We also show how our well-analysed and designed domain ontology contributes to the implicit expansion of user queries as well as presenting our initial thoughts on exploiting lexical databases for explicit semantic-based query expansion.

5.1 Introduction

Affordable access to digital technology and advances in Internet communications have contributed to an unprecedented growth of digital media repositories (audio, images, and video). Retrieving relevant media from these ever-increasing collections

T. Osman (✉)
School of Computing and Informatics, Nottingham Trent University, Nottingham NG11 8NS, UK
e-mail: taha.osman@ntu.ac.uk

D. Thakker
PA Photos, Nottingham, UK
e-mail: dhavalkumar.thakker@ntu.ac.uk

G. Schaefer
Department of Computer Science, Loughborough University, Loughborough LE11 3TU, UK
e-mail: gerald.schaefer@ieee.org

R. Chbeir et al., *Emergent Web Intelligence: Advanced Information Retrieval*, Advanced
Information and Knowledge Processing, DOI 10.1007/978-1-84996-074-8_5,
© Springer-Verlag London Limited 2010

is an impossible task for the user without the aid of appropriate search tools. Whether considering public media repositories such as Google^{TM} images and YouTube^{TM} [23] or commercial photo-libraries such as PA Photos^{TM} [15], some kind of search engine is required to matchmake the user query and the available media. In this chapter we focus on images/photos as media.

Most public image retrieval engines rely on analysing the text accompanying the image to matchmake it with a user query. Various optimisations were developed including the use of weighting systems where for instance higher regard can be given to the proximity of the keyword to the image location, or advanced text analysis techniques that use term weighting methods which rely on the proximity between the anchor to an image and each word in an HTML file [7]. Similar relevance-analysis and query expansion techniques [10] are used in annotation-enriched image collections, where usually a labour-intensive annotation process is utilised to describe the images with or without the aid of some domain-specific schema [8].

Despite optimisation efforts, these search techniques remain hampered by the fact that they rely on free-text search which, while cost-effective to perform, can return irrelevant results as they primarily rely on the recurrence of exact words in the image caption or the text surrounding the image in an HTML page. The inaccuracy of the results increases with the complexity of the query. For instance, while performing this research we used the Yahoo^{TM}search engine to look for images of the football (soccer) player Zico. The search engine returned some good pictures of the player, mixed with photos of cute dogs as apparently Zico is also a popular name for pet dogs. However, when we added the action of "scoring a goal" to the search text, this seems to completely confuse the search engine and only one picture of Zico was returned, in which he is standing still.

Any significant contribution to improve the accuracy of matchmaking results can be achieved only if the search engine can "comprehend" the meaning of the data that describe the stored images, for example that scoring is an act associated with sport activities performed by humans. Semantic annotation techniques have gained wide popularity in associating plain data with "structured" concepts that software programs can reason about [21]. In this chapter we present a comprehensive semantics-based solution to image annotation and retrieval while further deploying query expansion techniques for improving the recall rate. We claim that shrewd analysis of the application domain characteristics, coupled with a subsequently well-designed ontology can significantly contribute to the user query expansion process via direct term replacement or by modifying the domain taxonomy we build for the query. We also present our initial research into using lexical databases to analyse free-entry queries in our effort to make them compatible with the requirements of our semantic search engine.

The remainder of the chapter is organised as follows. We begins with an overview of semantic web technologies in Section 5.2. Section 5.3 reviews the case study that was the motivation for our work. Sections 5.4–5.7 then detail the implementation roadmap of our semantic-based retrieval system, i.e., ontology engineering, annotation, retrieval, and query expansion. Conclusions are presented in Section 5.8.

5.2 Semantic Web

5.2.1 Ontologies

The fundamental premise of the semantic web is to extend the web's current human-oriented interface to a format that is comprehensible to software programmes. This requires a standardised and rich knowledge representation scheme or ontology. One of the most comprehensive definitions of ontologies is that expressed in [8]: Ontology is a shared conceptualisation of a domain and typically consists of a comprehensive set of concept classes, relationships between them, and instance information showing how the classes are populated in the application domain. This comprehensive representation of knowledge from a particular domain allows reasoning software to make sense of domain-related entities (images, documents, services, etc.) and aid in the process of their retrieval and use.

5.2.2 Caption-Based Semantic Annotation

Applied to image retrieval, the semantic annotation of images allows retrieval engines to make more intelligent decisions about the relevance of the image to a particular user query, especially for complex queries. For instance, to retrieve images of the football star David Beckham expressing anger, it is natural to type the keywords "David Beckham angry" into the Google™ Image Search engine. However, at the time of the experiment, the search engine returned 14 images of David Beckham and he looks upset in only two of them. The other retrieved images were completely irrelevant with one of them displaying an angry moose!

The use of semantic technologies can significantly improve the computer's understanding of the image objects and their interactions by providing a machine-understandable conceptualisation of the various domains that the image represents. This conceptualisation integrates concepts and inter-entity relations from different domains, such as Sport, People and Emotions relation to the query above [1], thus allowing the search engine to infer that David Beckham is a person and thus likely to express emotions, and that he is also an English footballer playing for LA Galaxy.

5.2.3 Content-Based Semantic Annotation

The success of caption-based semantic image retrieval largely depends on the quality of the semantic caption (annotation) itself. However, the caption is not always available largely because annotation is a labour intensive process. In such situations, image recognition techniques are applied, which is better known as content-based retrieval. However, the best content-based techniques deliver only partial success as image recognition is an extremely complex problem [11], especially in the absence of accompanying text that can aid inferring in the relationship between the recognised objects in the image. Moreover, from a query composition point of view, it is much easier to use a textual interface rather than a visual interface (e.g., by providing a sample image or a sketch) [13].

5.3 Case Study

PA Photos is a Nottingham-based company which is part of the Press Association Photo Group Company [15]. As well as owning a huge image database in excess of 4 million annotated images which date back to the early 1900s, the company processes a large amount of images each day from varying events ranging from sport to politics and entertainment. The company also receives annotated images from a number of partners that rely on a different photo indexing schema. Importantly, initial investigation has proven that the accuracy of the results sets that match the user queries do not measure up to the rich repository of photos in the company's database.

The goal of the case study is twofold. Initially, we intend to investigate the use of semantic technology to build a classification and indexing system that unifies the annotation infrastructure for all the sources of incoming stream of photos. Subsequently, we conduct a feasibility study aiming to improve the end-user experience of their images search engine. At the moment, PA Photos's search engine relies on free-text search to return a set of images matching the user requests. Therefore, the returned results can go off-tangent if the search keywords do not exactly recur in the photo annotations. A significant improvement can result from semantically enabling the photo search engine. Semantic-based image search will ultimately enable the search engine software to understand the "concept" or "meaning" of the user request and hence return more accurate results (images) and a richer set of alternatives.

It is important here to comment about the dynamics of the retrieval process for this case study as it represents an important and wide-spread application domain where there is a commercial opportunity for exploiting semantic technologies:

1. The images in the repository have not been extracted from the web. Consequently, the extensive research into using the surrounding text and information in HTML documents for improving the quality of the annotation such as in [13,21] is irrelevant.
2. A significant sector of the market relies on fast relay of images to customers. Consequently, this confines advanced but time-consuming image analysis techniques [11] to off-line aid with the annotation of caption-poor images.
3. The usually colossal amount of legacy images annotated to particular (non-semantic) schema necessitates the integration of these heterogeneous schemas into any new, semantically enabled and more comprehensive ontologies.

5.4 Ontology Development

5.4.1 Domain Analysis

Our domain analysis started from an advanced point as we had access to the photo agency's current classification system. Hence, we adopted a top-down approach to ontology construction that starts by integrating the existing classification with published evidence of more inclusive public taxonomies [12]. At the upper level, two ontological trees were identified. The first captures knowledge about the event (objects and their relationships) in the image, while the second is a simple upper class that characterises the image attributes (frame, size, creation date, etc.), which is extensible in view of future utilisation of content-based recognition techniques.

Building knowledge-management systems using ontologies and reasoning engines is a more cumbersome task than the traditional database-based approach. Hence, it is wise to be prudent with the scale of semantic-based projects until feasibility of the semantic approach is ascertained, particularly in commercial contexts, where emphasis is on deliverables rather than the methodology. At the initial stages of the research, we made the following decisions to:

1. Limit the domain of investigation to sport-related images.
2. Address the sports participants' "actions" and "emotions" in our ontology to demonstrate the advantage of using semantics in expressing relationships between objects in the image.
3. Defer research into content-based methods, which mainly targets aid in annotating legacy images, until the feasibility of caption-based semantic retrieval proves successful.

A bottom-up approach was used to populate the lower tiers of the ontology class structure by examining the free-text and non-semantic captions accompanying a sample set of sport images. Domain terms were acquired from approximately 65,000 image captions. The terms were purged of redundancies and verified against publicly available related taxonomies such as the media classification taxonomy detailed in [12]. An added benefit of this approach is that it allows existing annotations to be seamlessly parsed and integrated into the semantic annotation.

Wherever advantageous, we integrated external ontologies (e.g., [18, 19]) into our knowledge representation. For instance, the property *hasNationality* is an object property referring to the publicly available ontology in [18] where useful information about the specific country can be found. However, bearing in mind the responsiveness requirements of on-line retrieval applications, we applied caching methods to localise the access in order to reduce its time overhead. Figure 5.1 represents a subset of our ontology.

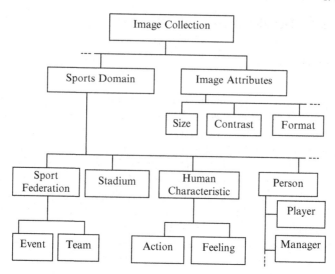

Fig. 5.1 Subset of the derived ontology tree

5.4.2 Datatype vs. Object Properties

All semantic models use two types of properties to build relationships between individuals (classes), datatype properties, and object properties. When assigning properties to a class, all its sub-classes inherit their parent's class properties. Deciding on the appropriate type of property to use is not a trivial task. Whereas object properties link individuals of different classes together, datatype properties can only point to immediate values (e.g., text strings), which are meaningless to a reasoning software except for performing a string-based search. For example, allocating datatype properties to the person *class* in order to give each new instance a last name is a correct use of datatype properties because they cannot be reused by another individual. On the other hand, object properties are required to assign someone a nationality since a country is an autonomous object that can have properties such as currency, capital city, language, etc. Hence, a country needs to be an instance that can be reused from an already existing ontology [18].

5.4.3 Consistency Check

Unlike database structures, ontologies represent knowledge not data, hence any structural problems will have detrimental effect on their corresponding reasoning agents especially as ontologies are open and distributed by nature, which might cause wide-spread propagation of any inconsistencies [16]. For instance, in traditional structuring of methodologies, usually the *part-of* relationship is adopted to ex-

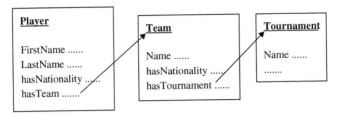

Fig. 5.2 Traditional *part-of* relationship

Fig. 5.3 Reorganisation of the player classification

press relationships between interdependent concepts. So, for players that are *part-of* a team performing in a particular event, the approach in Fig. 5.2 is commonly taken.

However logical this approach might appear at first sight, further analysis reveals inconsistency problems. When a player plays for two different teams at the same time (e.g., his club and his national team) or changes clubs every year, it is almost impossible to determine which team the player plays for. Hence, the order of definition (relationship direction) should always be the reversal sequence of the part-of relationship as redesigned in Fig. 5.3.

5.4.4 Coverage

Although consistent, the structural solution in Fig. 5.3 is incomplete as a player's membership is temporal. The same problem occurs with tournaments as from one year to another teams taking part in a tournament change. This problem can be solved by adding a start and end date for the tournament as in Fig. 5.4, rather than by engineering more complex object property solutions. Hence, as far as the semantic reasoner is concerned, the "FIFA World Cup 2002" is a different instance from "FIFA World Cup 2006". The same reasoning can be applied to the class team, as players can change team every season. These considerations, although basic for human reasoning, need to be explicitly defined in the ontology.

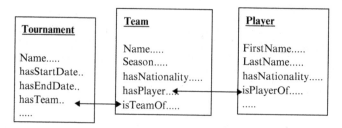

Fig. 5.4 Resolving coverage problems in the ontology

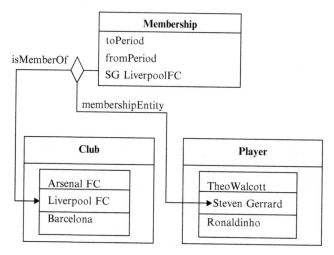

Fig. 5.5 Membership class in final ontology

5.4.5 Normalisation

The objective of normalisation is to reduce redundancy. In ontology design, re-dundancy is often caused by temporal characteristic that can generate redundant information and negatively affect the performance of the reasoning process.

Direct adoption of the ontology description in Fig. 5.4 will result in creating new teams each season, which is rather inefficient as the team should be a non-temporal class regardless of the varying player's membership or tournament participation every season. Hence, Arsenal or Glasgow Rangers Football clubs need to remain abstract entities. Our approach is to introduce an intermediary temporal *member-ship* concept that serves as an indispensable link between teams and players, as well as between teams and tournaments as illustrated in Fig. 5.5.

The temporal instances from the *Membership* class link instances from two perpetual classes as follows:

- *memberEntity* links to a person (Player, Manager, Supporter, Photographer, etc.).
- *isMemberOf* refers to the organisation (Club, Press Association, Company, etc.).
- *fromPeriod* and *toPeriod* depict membership temporal properties.

5.5 Image Annotation

The Protégé® Ontology Editor was utilised to construct the sport domain ontology. Protégé uses frame-based knowledge representation [14] and adopts the Web Ontology language (OWL) as ontology language. OWL [4] has become the de-facto standard for expressing ontologies. OWL adds extensive vocabulary to describe properties and classes and express relations between them (such as disjointness), cardinality (for example, "exactly one"), equality, richer typing of properties, and characteristics of properties (such as symmetry). The Jena Java API [2] was used to build the annotation portal to the constructed ontology.

The central component of the annotation are the images stored (as OWL descriptions) in the image library as illustrated in Fig. 5.6. Each image comprises an object, whose main features are stored within an independent object library. Similarly, object characteristics, event location, etc. are distinct from the image library. This highly modular annotation model facilitates the reuse of semantic information and reduces redundancy.

Taking into account the dynamic motion nature of the sport domain, we conclude that a variation of the sentence structure suggested in [9] is best suited to design our annotation template. We opted for an *"Actor – Action/Emotion – Object"* structure that will allow the natural annotation of motion or emotion-type relationships without the need to involve NLP techniques [3]. For example, *"Beckham – Smiles – null"*, or *"Gerrard – Tackles – Henry"*. An added benefit of this structure is that it simplifies the task of the reasoner in matching actor and action annotations with entities that have similar characteristics.

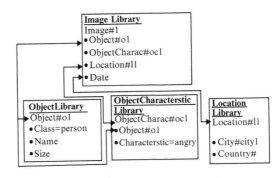

Fig. 5.6 Architecture of the annotation

5.6   Image Retrieval

The developed image retrieval user interface is illustrated in Fig. 5.7. The search
query can include sentence-based relational terms (Actor – Action/Emotion – Object) and/or key domain terms (such as tournament or team). In case multiple terms
were selected for the query, the user needs to specify which term represents the
main search criterion. For example, in Fig. 5.7 the relational term (Gerrard – Tackle
– Rooney) is the primary search term and team Liverpool the secondary search term.
The preference setting is used to improve the ranking of retrieved images. By default all secondary search terms have the same priority, unless additional weighing
is applied. Weighting is defined by users and stored persistently in their profiles.

Figure 5.8 gives a high level view of the annotation and retrieval mechanism.
The semantic description generator allows the annotator to transparently annotate
new images, and also transforms the user query into OWL format. The semantic
reasoning engine applies our matchmaking algorithm in two phases: the first phase
retrieves images with annotations matching all concepts in the query, while in the
second phase further matchmaking is performed to improve the ranking of the retrieved images in response to user preferences.

Our reasoning engine uses a variation of the nearest neighbour matchmaking
algorithm [17] to serve both the semantic retrieval and the ranking phases. Our algorithm continues traversing back to the upper class of the ontology and matching
instances until there are no super classes in the class hierarchy, i.e., the leaf node for

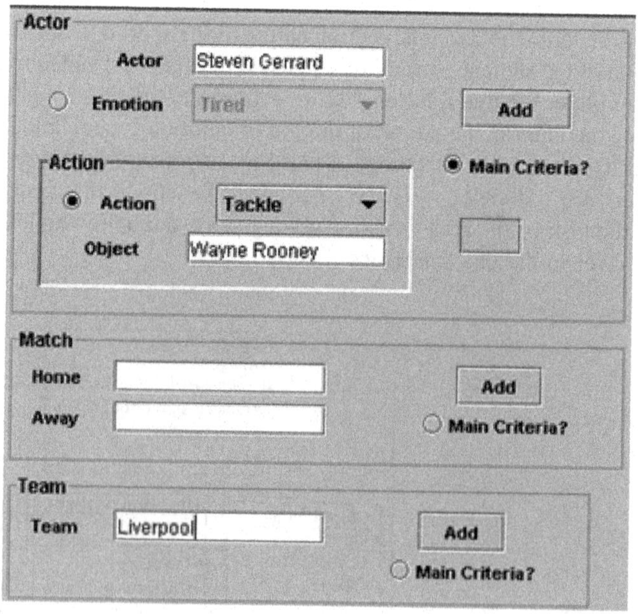

Fig. 5.7 Snapshop of the retrieval interface

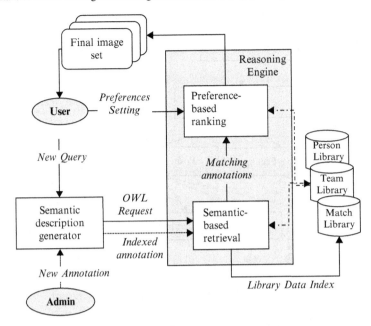

Fig. 5.8 Schematic diagram of the semantic web image retrieval software

the tree is reached, giving a degree of match equal to 0. The degree of match DoM is calculated according to

$$DoM = \sum_{i=1}^{N} W_i \frac{MN_i}{GN_i} \quad \forall W_i \in [0; 1] \tag{5.1}$$

where MN is the total number of matching nodes in the selected traversal path, and GN is the total number of nodes in the selected traversal path for a particular search criterion i such as "Wayne Rooney", or "Zidane receives red card". Each criterion is scaled with the importance factor W according to the user preferences that are attached to the user profile.

The example in Fig. 5.9 illustrates the operation of the algorithm for a single criterion only, where the query is: Object – hasCharacteristic-happy, and image1 and image2 are annotated with Object – hasCharacteristic-happy and Object – hasCharacteristic-smile respectively. The DoM for image1 is 1 as all the nodes match as we traverse the ontology tree from the root (characteristic) to the leaf (happy) nodes, i.e., $5/5 = 1$. However, for image2 instances match to the level of Positive Feeling-Mild class, resulting in matching 4 nodes out of five from the root node, hence the $DoM = 4/5 = 0.8$.

Although not demonstrated in the example of Fig. 5.9, the importance factor W can be used to scale the criticality of the emotion concept against other similarity factors such as the player's name or team.

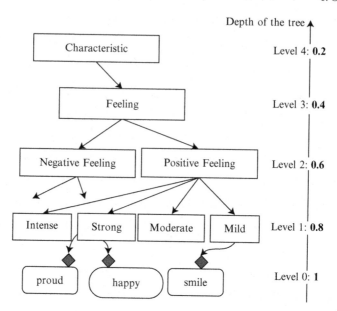

Fig. 5.9 Traversing the ontology tree

5.7 Query Expansion

Recently, query expansion (QE) techniques have gained a lot of attention in attempting to improve the recall of document and media queries. Query expansion is traditionally considered as a process of supplementing a query with additional terms as the assumption is that the initial query as provided by the user may be an inadequate representation of the user's information needs [6].

QE methods fit naturally into our image retrieval technology as we rely on computing the aggregate degree of match for the semantic relations describing a particular image to determine its match to the original query. Hence, we can easily determine the quality of the returned results in terms of accuracy and volume and decide whether to apply QE techniques to replace or improve the query concepts to improve the quality of recall. This is particularly feasible for semantic-based knowledge bases as they provide language expressiveness for specifying the similarity of the concepts (implicit and explicit) at different granularity.

Query expansion techniques can be broadly classified into two categories. The first category uses statistical and probabilistic methods to extract frequently occurring terms from successfully recalled documents and image annotations [22]. These terms are then used to expand the keyword set of similar future queries. The main shortcoming of statistics-based QE techniques is that they are only as good as the statistics they rely on and have similar disadvantages as free-text based search engines in that they lack structure and are difficult to generalise or to reuse for other domains. The second category utilises lexical databases to expand user queries [20]. A lexical database similar to WordNet [5] is employed, in which language nouns, verbs, adjectives and adverbs are organised into synonym sets that can potentially replace or expand the original query concepts. However, when independently deployed, lexical databases lack the semantic conceptualisation necessary to interrelate concepts in complex queries and render them comprehensible to search engines.

Our semantic relations-based QE technique expands the query with related concepts rather than simple terms. In the following we discuss the design of both the implicit and explicit elements of our QE algorithm.

5.7.1 Implicit Query Expansion

Taking into account the domain knowledge hardwired into the ontologies, our implicit query expansion mechanism can be considered as a by-product of a well-researched and designed domain ontology. The "Actor – Action/Emotion – Object" semantic format allows to naturally employ the ontology in order to find related terms via simple equivalence relations as that of equating the action of smiling to the emotion of happiness. Taking into account the limited vocabulary of the sport domain, and in consultation with the domain experts, we decided against the automatic expansion of directly related terms from a lexical public database such as WordNet. Our initial experiments have shown that while that expansion improved image recall, the accuracy of returned results suffered significantly, particularly for complex queries where partial replacement of terms might invalidate the semantics of the query.

Using our ontology structure we are also able to expand queries implicitly by analysing more complex relations as in inferring that Liverpool is a possible replacement for Chelsea as both are teams playing football in the Premier League in England. Moreover, we are able to scale the relatedness of each term in the query tree according to the importance weighting set by the user/domain manager as explained earlier. The explicit query expansion algorithm is implemented in three consecutive steps.

Step 1 If a query has concept C^p as the primary search concept and C^s as the secondary search concept provided by the searcher then we define query expansion on C^p as follows. For each concept C_i^p, assuming $C_i^{p'}$ is the alternative concept, δ_i is the distance between C_i^p and $C_i^{p'}$ and Ψ_i is the expected distance between these two implying them related, the expansion function is:

$$\sum_{i=1}^{N} \left(C_i^p \xrightarrow{\delta_i, \Psi_i} C_i^{p'} \right), \, \delta_i \geq \Psi_i \qquad (5.2)$$

which implies that concepts $C_i^{p'}$ are related to C^p if they are at an acceptable distance from C^p.

5.7.1.1   Relatedness Between Concepts

A major concern in QE techniques is the formalisation of relatedness between two concepts in order to select an optimal set of alternatives. For the benefit of the discussion, let's first revisit the following components of semantic web formalism and their representation in the OWL ontology language:

- Taxonomy relationships (TR): Taxonomy is the concepts classification system facilitated by Semantic Web. Class and Individual are the two main elements of this structure where a class is simply a name and collection of properties that describe a set of individuals. Examples of relationships between concepts at the taxonomy level are *class, subclass, superclass, equivalent class, individual, sameAs, oneOf, disjointWith, differentFrom, AllDifferent*.
- Rule based relationships (RR): Semantic Web Rule Language (SWRL) defines rule based semantics using subset of OWL with the sublanguages of Rule Markup Language. SWRL extends OWL with horn-like First Order Logic rules to extend the language expressivity of OWL.

We use this relationship formalism to identify explicit and implicit relatedness of concepts. To evaluate implicit relationships we use *subsumption* and *classification* to perform semantic tree traversal and compare the concepts with respect to the semantic network tree as detailed in our image retrieval algorithm earlier. Contrarily, explicit relationship between two concepts always has a DoM of 0 or 1 as they explicitly equate or distinct two individuals. For example the *owl:sameAs* equates two individuals to unify two distinct ontology elements, while *owl:differentFrom* has the exact opposite effect where it makes individuals mutually distinct.

If the taxonomy and rule-based implicit and explicit relationship results in n equivalent concepts represented by $\{C_1, C_2, C_3, ..., C_n\}$ or $C_i^{p'}$, then in order to calculate DoM for these likely replacement concepts we employ another semantic web relationship formalism, which we will refer to as property-based relationship:

- Property Relationships (PR): Properties can be used to state relationships between individuals or from individuals to data values. These relationships are achieved through the data or object type properties (e.g., *hasTeam, hasTournament, isMemberOf*).

Step 2   Assuming query preference concept C^p has properties R_i which has value instances I_i^R and the annotation matching the alternative concept $C^{p'}$ has properties R'^i and the value instances $I_i^{R'}$, then we can compare I_i^R and $I_i^{R'}$ semantically using Equation 5.2.

5.7.1.2   Example

In the following we illustrate how our QE algorithm works by discussing the following case: if a user is searching for images with *England Team* possibly in the *2006*

Table 5.1 Preference concept for England Team (C^p)

C^p has properties R_i	I_i^R (properties value)
hasNationality	Country (England)
hasSport	Sport (Football)
isWinnerOf	Tournament(Fifawc66)
hasNationalTeamTournament	FifaWC66, WC70, etc.

Table 5.2 Comparing relationship

	Query	Team Brazil		Team Chelsea	
hasNationality	England	Brazil	0	England	1
hasSport	Football	Football	1	Football	1
isWinnerOf	FifaWC 06	FifaWC 70	0.5	Prem. 06	0
hasNationalTeamTournament	Fifawc 66, 70, ...	Fifawc 66, 70, ...	1	Prem. 93, 94, ...	0
DoM		Brazil	2.5	Chelsea	2

Table 5.3 Analysing secondary terms in query

	Query	Image 1		Image 2	
hasTournament	FifaWC 06	FifaWC 06	1	Prem. 07	0
DoM		Brazil	2.5	Chelsea	2

FIFA World Cup Tournament, the system treats *England Team* as the user's primary search criterion and *2006 FIFA World Cup Tournament* as secondary search criterion in the query.

Without expanding the query, the retrieval algorithm returns zero results if there are no images annotated with Team England (Table 5.1). In our sports domain ontology implicit subsumption relationship is applied to find relevant primary concepts. For instance, to find alternative terms for *Team England*, the reasoner first retrieves siblings of the *National Team* such as *Team Brazil*, *Team Spain*, and then less adjacent siblings of the *Team* instances such as *Team Chelsea* and *Team Barcelona*.

We compare the relationship as defined in Step 2 as illustrated in Table 5.2.

Step 3 If the ranked images in Step 2 are $\{X_1, X_2, X_3, \ldots\}$, C^s is the secondary search term in the query provided by the searcher, these ranked images have C^s present in their annotation C_X^s then repeat Step 2 where $C^p = C^s$ and $C^{p'} = C_X^s$.

In our image database this results in images retrieved for the first stage associated with the relevant concepts and they are (see Table 5.3): Image 1 (Image with Team Brazil in 2006 FIFA world cup), Image 2 (Chelsea-Premiership 2007).

5.7.2 Explicit Query Expansion

Explicit query expansion involves direct replacement of terms in the user query with terms that were identified as identical by the knowledge domain administrator or the end user. These replacement terms are not part of the ontology infrastructure, but are kept in a separate synonym dictionary that contains one-to-many (USE_FOR) relations between the ontology term and the possible synonyms. For instance, the domain administrator might use the ontology term "Manchester United" to replace the popular term "Man UTD". Similarly, users are allowed to cache (USE_FOR) terms on the client-side for exclusive expansion of their queries. The domain administrator has access to the most popular cached nicknames/synonyms and can choose to enter them into the main synonym dictionary.

We considered adding synonyms to the ontology using OWL's *owl:sameAs* property, but decided against it, primarily because of the performance penalties in processing RDF data as opposed to simple text strings. Our initial experiments have shown that the search time increases by a factor of 2.5 if the synonyms are deployed in the ontology. We also think that from a pure semantic engineering point of view, nicknames such as "Man UTD" should not exist as an RDF individual.

5.8 Conclusions

In this chapter, we have presented a comprehensive solution for image retrieval applications that takes full advantage of advances in semantic web technologies to coherently implement the annotation, retrieval and query expansion components of an integrative framework. We claim that our solution is particularly attractive for commercial image providers where emphasis is on the efficiency of the retrieval process as much as on improving the accuracy and volume of returned results. For instance, we shied from employing expensive content-based recognition techniques at the retrieval stage and deployed public ontology caching to reduce the reasoning overhead, while designing an efficient query expansion algorithm to improve the quality of the image recall.

The first stage of the development was producing ontologies that conceptualise the objects and their relations in the selected domain. We methodically verified the consistency of our ontology, optimised its coverage, and performed normalisation methods to eliminate concept redundancies. Our annotation approach was based on a variation of the "sentence" structure to obtain the semantic-relational capacity for conceptualising the dynamic motion nature of the targeted sport domain. This careful analysis of the domain features allowed us to hardwire application domain knowledge into the ontology and hence implicitly perform query expansion either by simple replacement of equivalent terms or by traversing the ontology tree to modify more complex queries.

The retrieval algorithm is based on a variation of the nearest-neighbour search technique for traversing the ontology tree and can accommodate complex, relationship-driven user queries. The algorithm also provides for user-defined weightings to improve the ranking of the returned images and was extended to embrace query expansion technology in a bid to improve the quality of the recall.

Our efforts in implicit query expansion were greatly aided by our well-structured domain ontology that can be seamlessly deployed to find related terms via simple equivalence relations without compromising the semantics of the overall query.

References

1. T. Berners-Lee and M. Fischetti. *Weaving the Web: the original design of the World Wide Web by its inventor.* Harper Collins, 2000.
2. J. J. Carroll, I. Dickinson, C. Dollin, D. Reynolds, A. Seaborne, and K. Wilkinson. Jena: implementing the semantic web recommendations. In *13th Int. World Wide Web Conference*, pages 74–83, 2004.
3. H. Chen. Machine learning for information retrieval: Neural networks, symbolic learning and genetic algorithms. *Journal of the American Society for Information Science and Technology*, 46(3):194–216, 1995.
4. W3C Corporation. OWL web ontology language overview, 2004. http://www.w3.org/TR/owl-features.
5. C. Fellbaum. *WordNet: An Electronic Lexical Database and Some of its Applications.* MIT Press, 1998.
6. G. Fu, C.B. Jones, and A.I. Abdelmoty. Ontology-based spatial query expansion in information retrieval. In *Int. Conference on Ontologies, Databases and Applications of Semantics*, 2005.
7. A. Fujii and T. Ishikawa. Toward the automatic compilation of multimedia encyclopedias: Associating images with term descriptions on the web. In *2005 IEEE/WIC/ACM International Joint Conference on Web Intelligence*, pages 536–542, 2005.
8. J.S. Hare, P.H. Lewis, P.G.B. Enser, and C.J. Sandom. Mind the gap: another look at the problem of the semantic gap in image retrieval. In *Multimedia Content Analysis, Management, and Retrieval*, volume 6073 of *Proceedings of SPIE*, 2006.
9. L. Hollink, G. Schreiber, J. Wielemaker, and B. Wielinga. Semantic annotation of image collections. In *Workshop on Knowledge Markup and Semantic Annotation*, 2003.
10. J. Jeon, V. Lavrenko, and R. Manmatha. Automatic image annotation and retrieval using cross-media relevance models. In *26th Annual Int. ACM SIGIR Conference on Research and Development in Information Retrieval*, pages 119–126, 2003.
11. T. Lam and R. Singh. Semantically relevant image retrieval by combining image and linguistic analysis. In *Int. Symposium on Visual Computing*, pages 1686–1695, 2006.
12. A. Maedche, B. Motik, and L. Stojanovic. Managing multiple and distributed ontologies on the semantic web. *The VLDB Journal*, 12(4):286–302, 2003.
13. E. W. Maina, M. Ohta, K. Katayama, and H. Ishikawa. Semantic image retrieval based on ontology and relevance model: A preliminary study. *Journal of Digital Information Management*, 3(4):227–230, 2005.
14. N. F. Noy, M. Crubézy, R. W. Fergerson, H. Knublauch, S. W. Tu, J. Vendetti, and M. A. Musen. Protégé-2000: An open-source ontology-development and knowledge-acquisition environment. In *AMIA Annual Symposium*, page 953, 2003.
15. PA Photos. http://www.paphotos.com/.
16. A. Rector. Modularisation of domain ontologies implemented in description logics and related formalisms including OWL. In *2nd Int. Conference on Knowledge Capture*, pages 121–128, 2003.
17. T. Osman, D. Thakker, and D. Al-Dabass. Semantic-driven matchmaking of web services using case-based reasoning. In *IEEE Int. Conference on Web Services*, pages 29–36, 2006.
18. Advanced Knowledge Technologies. Portal ontology. http://www.aktors.org/ontology/portal#.
19. Advanced Knowledge Technologies. Support ontology. http://www.aktors.org/ontology/support#.

20. E. Voorhees. Query expansion using lexical-semantic relations. In *17th Annual Int. ACM SIGIR Conference on Research and Development in Information Retrieval*, pages 61–69, 1994.
21. H. Wang, S. Liu, and L.-T. Chia. Does ontology help in image retrieval?: a comparison between keyword, text ontology and multi-modality ontology approaches. In *14th Annual ACM Int. Conference on Multimedia*, pages 109–112, 2006.
22. J. Xu and W. Croft. Query expansion using local and global document analysis. In *19th Annual Int. ACM SIGIR Conference on Research and Development in Information Retrieval*, pages 4–11, 1996.
23. K-P. Yee, K. Swearingen, K. Li, and M. Hearst. Faceted metadata for image search and browsing. In *SIGCHI Conference on Human factors in Computing Systems*, pages 401–408, 2003.

Chapter 6
Harvesting Intelligence in Multimedia Social Tagging Systems

Eirini Giannakidou, Foteini Kaklidou, Elisavet Chatzilari,
Ioannis Kompatsiaris, and Athena Vakali

Abstract As more people adopt tagging practices, social tagging systems tend to form rich knowledge repositories that enable the extraction of patterns reflecting the way content semantics is perceived by the web users. This is of particular importance, especially in the case of multimedia content, since the availability of such content in the web is very high and its efficient retrieval using textual annotations or content-based automatically extracted metadata still remains a challenge. It is argued that complementing multimedia analysis techniques with knowledge drawn from web social annotations may facilitate multimedia content management. This chapter focuses on analyzing tagging patterns and combining them with content feature extraction methods, generating, thus, intelligence from multimedia social tagging systems. Emphasis is placed on using all available "tracks" of knowledge, that is *tag co-occurrence* together with *semantic relations* among tags and *low-level features* of the content. Towards this direction, a survey on the theoretical background and the adopted practices for analysis of multimedia social content are presented. A case study from Flickr illustrates the efficiency of the proposed approach.

6.1 Introduction

Participating users in the web act as co-developers and their actions and interactions with one another have produced a valuable, quite difficult to handle, though, information repository, enhanced with social characteristics, derived from the communication and the collaboration among them. This social dimension was emphasized

E. Giannakidou (✉) and A. Vakali
Informatics Department, Aristotle University of Thessaloniki, Thessaloniki 540.06, Greece
e-mail: eirgiann@csd.auth.gr; avakali@csd.auth.gr

E. Giannakidou, F. Kaklidou, E. Chatzilari, and I. Kompatsiaris
Informatics & Telematics Institute, CERTH, Thermi, Thessaloniki 57001, Greece
e-mail: igiannak@iti.gr; fkaklid@iti.gr; ehatzi@iti.gr; ikom@iti.gr

R. Chbeir et al., *Emergent Web Intelligence: Advanced Information Retrieval*, Advanced
Information and Knowledge Processing, DOI 10.1007/978-1-84996-074-8_6,
© Springer-Verlag London Limited 2010

in the next generation of web, namely Web 2.0 or Social Web technologies and applications [1], resulting in a remarkable bursting of web usage and content availability, and addressing, at the same time, the need for efficient techniques' deployment for exploiting this collective knowledge.

Central to this new web is the concept of tagging (i.e., users attaching keywords to describe digital data sources). The process of having end-users adding their own metadata to internet resources, namely *social* or *collaborative tagging*, introduces a new way of digital data sources' organization and retrieval in the web that constitutes the core process in a number of web 2.0 applications that have received tremendous attention lately, such as Flickr,[1] Del.icio.us,[2] YouTube,[3] Technorati[4] and so on. The remarkable with tagging activity is that although completely subjective and without relying on a controlled vocabulary, it has dynamics similar to those of a *complex system* [2, 3], i.e., knowledge is built incrementally in an evolutionary and decentralized manner, yielding stable and knowledge-rich patterns, namely Emergent Semantics [4]. Thus, unlike earlier static knowledge representation structures, social tagging systems are dynamic and have a noteworthy ability in capturing the community' s point of view of the specific data sources and the general trends, at a given time. Additionally, they capture social relations between the community members. Therefore, they constitute promising data structures for knowledge mining.

In this chapter, we study social tagging systems that host multimedia data sources. We argue that the metadata given by users in social tagging systems (i.e., tags) form a valuable knowledge source which has a social dimension and is extremely dynamic, since users add content and tags all the time. Towards this direction, we focus on analyzing tagging patterns and combining them with content feature extraction methods, in order to get useful knowledge about the content, that will facilitate its retrieval. This knowledge can be regarded as a first basic step towards intelligence generation from multimedia social tagging systems. The problem to be analyzed in this chapter is how to exploit this source and overcome, at the same time, the intrinsic limitations these systems have and are summarized in (i) *tag redundancies and ambiguities*, raised by the complete lack of structure and hierarchical relations, and (ii) *metadata questionable validity*, as users are prone to make mistakes.

Our methods are based on developing solutions for linking descriptive semantics, yielded by tag processing, with the low-level features of the media assets. In order to derive such semantics from tags and get information interpretable by the end user, a clustering procedure takes place. Clustering is often employed in the bibliography of social tagging systems as a way of grouping together tags related to a certain topic. Here, we put emphasis on using all available "tracks" of knowledge,

---

namely *social knowledge* (i.e., knowledge that can be derived from tagging systems, e.g., tag co-occurrence), *semantic knowledge* (i.e., knowledge about the meaning of the concepts, e.g., hierarchical relations among them), and *content-based knowledge* (i.e., the low-level features of the multimedia data). Our goal is to yield useful knowledge from the multitude of user annotations, which, especially in the case of multimedia data, can be used to semantically enrich the specified content and facilitate the retrieval task, promoting, thus, its exploitation. A case study on 10,000 and 3,000 resources from Flickr is used to demonstrate that the exploitation of users' annotations produces semantic metadata and provides added-value to the available multimedia content.

The structure of this chapter is as follows. Section 6.2 gives a short overview to the multimedia content annotation approaches and introduces multimedia social tagging systems, emphasizing on the reasons of their popularity. An extended state-of-the-art follows, in Section 6.3, including (i) approaches that analyze and/or cluster social tagging systems, (ii) content-based multimedia techniques, and (iii) cases in which the two methods are combined. In Section 6.4 our approach, which joins tagging and content-based knowledge, is presented. Next, experimental results and use cases of the proposed approach are quoted in Sections 6.5 and 6.6, respectively. Finally, Section 6.7 concludes the chapter.

6.2 Multimedia Content Annotation

Multimedia is, increasingly, gaining popularity in the web with several technologies supporting the use of images, animation, video and audio to supplement the traditional medium of text. The basic reason behind the vast quantity of multimedia web data was the rapid technological growth, together with some quality traits that the combined use of multiple modalities gives to the content, such as natural design, interactivity and pleasure to work with. In order for that enhanced-valued content to be easily found and accessible, special design/management discipline is required. Unconstrained use of multimedia results in a chaotic web environment that confuses users and makes it hard for them to locate the information they are interested in.

There is a growing number of research methods for analyzing, understanding and delivering multimedia content which are based on content-based features extracted from the multimedia data. These methods rely on extracting low-level features of the digital objects either for retrieval by visual similarity or for associating them with high-level concepts. While automatic extraction of low-level features and mapping to high-level concepts is possible in many applications, their major drawback, lies in the distance between the high-level concepts that describe the multimedia content and the extracted low-level features, a problem that is known as the *semantic gap* [5]. Semantic gap is a serious concern in these methods, as it makes retrieval by semantic relevance a very difficult task. Therefore challenging methods for efficient mapping to a large number of high-level concepts are needed.

Another approach to multimedia content handling is based on utilizing additional knowledge about the content, given in the form of *metadata*. Metadata is defined in [6] as *"structured information that describes, explains, locates, or otherwise helps in retrieving, using or managing a resource"*. Thus, retrieval of multimedia content may be based on its metadata, exclusively, or on complementing existing content-based approaches with accompanying content metadata. However adding metadata to content still remains an expensive and difficult to maintain and evolve process, as it requires a group of experts spending human-hours in manually annotating the content. Moreover, the defined metadata reflect the experts' point of view of the particular content, which is not always identical with the users' perception of it. With the enormous growth of multimedia content and the rapid changes in the web environment, a more dynamic approach is needed that ensures that the metadata provided encompass the user community's awareness and understanding of the available content. We argue that such metadata can be drawn from multimedia social tagging systems, which are web-based applications that allow users upload/share/browse multimedia content and annotate it by completely freely chosen metadata. A more detailed description of multimedia social tagging systems follows.

6.2.1　Multimedia Social Data Sources

Given the warm embrace of tagging activity by web users,currently a variety of social tagging systems prevail in the web map. These systems are web-based applications in which users add textual descriptions (i.e., tags) to digital content (i.e., resources), enriching it, thus, with ready-to-use metadata and making its retrieval more efficient. Users may participate as atoms or, more commonly, as members of communities. The resources of these systems are specified/uploaded by users and may be available to the entire web community, along with their metadata. There is no restriction on the selection of tags; any user may choose any term that is meaningful to him/her and thinks as appropriate for the resource description. This rough description illustrates the three-partite structure of social tagging systems, which is depicted in Fig. 6.1.

Adding keywords (i.e., tags) to data sources is not something new. Librarians and indexers have been using keywords to facilitate the retrieval of their resources, a long time ago. Ever since many professionals have adopted the tagging technique in an effort to organize and enhance searching in their data [7]. The feature that is new in social tagging systems and promoted their endorsement by the majority of web community is that tagging is now performed by everyone, not only by a small group of experts, and that the tags are being made public and shared to anyone. This high participatory nature urged users in adapting them as a form of information organization and exchange of content and experience with other users.

Here, we focus on these systems that facilitate the storage and sharing of multimedia content. Currently, millions of users participate in multimedia social tagging

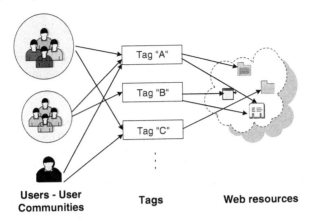

Fig. 6.1 A web-based social tagging system

systems, uploading content, adding tags or just browsing for tracking interesting content. The increased popularity of such sites can be traced by a rapidly increasing number of multimedia resources posted. Indicatively, we quote that YouTube reported in July 2006 100 million video viewings and 65,000 video uploads per day and Flickr is valued to have an upload rate of approximately 3,000 images per minute, which yields 1.6 billion images per year. This realization is largely attributed to the widespread adoption of high quality but relatively low-cost digital media technology, which resulted in an enormous growth of readily available multimedia content.

Social tagging systems have played a crucial role in the improvement of handling and utilization of multimedia resources. In fact, this was a key factor for their wide spread and adoption by the web community, since the retrieval of such resources has long been extremely difficult, without proper metadata. As mentioned earlier, employing experts to perform annotations is an expensive and practically immutable procedure. On the same time, despite the recent progress in content-based automatic extraction of semantic metadata from multimedia, such techniques are far from being perfect and generic applicable [8].

This can be overcome by exploiting the annotations (tags) given in a multimedia social tagging system and hence receiving readily and without cost user generated metadata that best fits the community point of view of the specific resources. In this way, handling of multimedia data becomes a tag-oriented procedure and the extraction of their context (i.e., semantics) for their analysis turns into the problem of extracting the semantics and analyzing of their corresponding tags. In many cases the concepts involved in the tags are ambiguous and there is subjectivity introduced by the users. Consequently the use of information extracted from visual features of the data can improve the accuracy of the method. Complementing the knowledge from tags with knowledge extracted from the content of the images is shown that can result in collecting valuable metadata that enhance the multimedia content exploitation.

6.3 State of the Art

Currently, there is a growing number of research efforts that have focused on exploiting knowledge stored and often "hidden" in social tagging systems. However, in most of them, the resource management is a transparent process, which does not rely on the varying nature of digital resources (i.e., text or multimedia). Each resource is associated only with user-generated metadata (produced through the tagging activity), regardless of the specific nature of it. These involve: (i) context information, such as the user who uploaded the specified resource, the users who annotated it, the time when each of the above tasks occurred, etc., and (ii) the group of tags assigned to it. In some approaches, though, analysis techniques for intrinsic feature extraction are employed, in order to achieve a better insight to the annotated content. Here, as outlined in the Introduction, we present an approach of web knowledge emergence, in which all tracks of knowledge (i.e., social, semantic and content-based) regarding the social content are taken into account. We give emphasis on multimedia content and especially on the knowledge that can be derived through low-level content-based multimedia analysis.

Towards that direction, the rest of this section is organized as follows. At first, a description of approaches that implement knowledge retrieval in social tagging systems, without employing content information is given. Then, a state-of-the-art on multimedia content-based related literature follows. The section ends with a presentation of approaches relevant to our technique in utilizing both tagging and content-based information for better retrieval.

6.3.1 Knowledge Retrieval in Social Tagging Systems

The dynamics of social tagging systems have turned a big part of scientific community into analyzing them and examining the emergent knowledge that derives from them. More specifically, in [2, 3] the authors demonstrate that the structure and dynamics of social tagging systems are similar to those of a *complex system*, i.e., knowledge is built incrementally in an evolutionary and decentralized manner, yielding stable and knowledge-rich patterns, namely Emergent Semantics [4]. Likewise in [9] the authors show that the tag proportions each resource receives crystallizes after about 100 annotations, attributing this behavior to users common background and their tendency for imitation of other users' tagging habits. They reach to this conclusion after examining and analyzing the tagging behavior in del.icio.us and identifying tagging patterns and kind of tags people tend to use.

Clustering is often introduced in the bibliography of social tagging systems as a way of overcoming the intrinsic limitations these systems have and, at the same time, generating knowledge from the mass activity. The authors in [10–12] rely solely on tagging information and tag co-occurrence to derive semantically-related groups of tags and resources, out of social tagging systems. Each group of tags involves a certain topic and encompasses the users' understanding and vocabulary describing this topic. Flickr photo-sharing system implements tag clusters, based on tag co-occurrence, as well, and handles quite well the tag ambiguity issue, managing to separate different senses of ambiguous tags in different cluster. For instance the ambiguous tag *"jaguar"* yields three clusters. The first cluster contains images and tags that describe the animal, the second one involves car-related material, while the last one includes tags and photos related to music. However, the described methodologies involve only tag statistical analysis and they lack of any semantic information that could guide the clustering process. Thus, they quite often yield clusters of co-occurring tags, which cannot be mapped to an actual topic and cannot be interpreted by a user. Additionally, they do not always tackle quite well the tag synonymy issue, since synonymous tags are commonly given by different users and they seldom co-occur.

To address the problem of lack of relations and semantics in the tag space, many researchers claim that the application of mature semantic web technologies (e.g., ontology usage, reasoning) on social data could add great value to the latter, as it may render a kind of structure to them. More specifically, in [13], the author proposes the building of an ontology that formalizes the activity of tagging, so to as enable the exchange, comparison and reasoning over the tag data acquired from varied tagging applications. Likewise, in [14, 15] the authors present their own OWL ontologies that aim at achieving a common formal conceptualization for the representation of tagging. Moreover, a step towards semantics' inclusion in a tagging system is the use of Simple Knowledge Organization System (SKOS) vocabulary [16], which allows to declare relationships between the terms used by users (e.g., broader term, narrower term, etc.). Despite the fact that interoperability between tagging systems is a subject of research, these approaches have not found widespread application and, so far, there is no common agreement on a formal representation of tagging activity between social tagging systems.

Another trend for social data exploitation is the exploration of the tag space and the detection of emergent relations in social data that can be exploited for ontology building and/or evolution. It is expected that merging the Semantic Web with natural language and concepts used by ordinary people is a right step in the direction of making Semantic Web dynamic and bridging the gap between knowledge applications and common users. Towards that direction Schmitz, in [17], analyzes a model that employs natural language processing techniques to induce an ontology from Flickr tags. In [18], Mika proposes a model to extend the traditional bipartite model of ontologies with the social context in which each concept or instance is produced. He extracts community-based ontologies or evolves defined ones, based on emergent semantics from the underlying social tagging activities and claims that when social actions of a community are taken into consideration, the extracted ontology has greater potential to closely match the conceptualization of the corresponding community. Another approach of eliminating the lack of semantics in tagging systems can be found in [19], where the authors employ association rule mining, in order to analyze and structure the tag space. Likewise, they use the mining results for ontology learning. In [20], the authors try to tackle the shortcomings of a tagging system and extract semantics by clustering of tag data based on co-occurrence and mapping of tags to ontology concepts with the use of semantic web engines. In the same way in [21], the authors use statistical analysis of co-occurrence of objects (in unsupervised learning, i.e., clustering) to infer a global semantic model. This semantic model can help in tag disambiguation and attempts to tackle the synonymy problem by grouping synonymous tags together. Finally, in [22] Zhou et al. present a clustering method for exploring hierarchical relations in social data.

The aforementioned overview of existing approaches indicates that clustering is, quite often, employed as a technique to overcome the limitations and improve the retrieval efficiency of social tagging systems.

6.3.2 Content-Based Multimedia Retrieval

Multimedia information has replaced in recent years the traditional forms of storing knowledge, as printed text or still graphics. A wide variety of content forms is used nowadays: text, audio, still images, animation, video, interactivity. Consequently methods for multimedia retrieval and mining are necessary for the effective use of multimedia information. Content-based multimedia analysis is necessary, because even though text in many cases is present, it is ambiguous. In addition, there is subjectivity introduced by the human annotator. While both visual, audio and other content-related features can be used in content-based methods to improve retrieval accuracy, in this work we focus on the use of visual information. Lew et al have made an excellent work in gathering all research trends in their survey paper [23] where they also pinpoint what is to be expected from new research efforts in the field.

New features and similarity measures are proposed and used in order to efficiently describe multimedia information and consequently help to fulfill the goals of multimedia information retrieval. MPEG-7 is an ISO/IEC standard developed by MPEG (Moving Picture Experts Group) that standardizes object-based audiovisual description tools, including the metadata elements and their structure and relationships that create descriptions enabling effective and efficient access to multimedia content. MPEG-7 allows fast and efficient content searching, filtering and identification, and addresses a large range of applications [24].

Lew [25] and Gevers [26] propose new color features that are applied in fields such as lighting invariance, intuitiveness and perceptual uniformity. Research on texture understanding has been done by Ojala et al. in [27] that outline the effectiveness of using simple texture histograms. Additionally a new texture feature based on the Radon transform orientation is introduced in [28]. Novel approaches on learning shape have been proposed in [29–31]. In [32] Vretos et al. propose several classes to extend the MPEG-7 standard and describe the digital video content in a more homogeneous and anthropocentric way.

In content-based multimedia retrieval, similarity measures have an equally important role as the visual features. In [33] Sebe et al. provide a method for selecting the appropriate metric given a training dataset and propose the Cauchy metric as an alternative to the commonly used distance measures. Jacobs et al. [34] evaluate the performance of nonmetric distances in classification. New methods of measuring image similarity based on graph matching and time and pictorial content are suggested in [35] and [36] respectively.

Lindeberg [37] presents a scale selection methodology, using the Laplacian-of-Gaussian function. The computation of the size of image structures can be done from the scales at which normalized differential geometric descriptors assume maxima over scales. Scale-invariant feature transform (SIFT) [38] is an algorithm in computer vision to detect and describe local features in images. This algorithm in the first step constructs a scale space pyramid using difference-of-Gaussian filters. The Laplacian-of-Gaussian can be approximated using the difference-of-Gaussian. From the local 3D maxima, a robust descriptor is built for matching purposes. The localization of the features that are detected using difference-of-Gaussian and Laplacian-of-Gaussian may not be very accurate. This disadvantage is due to the fact that they respond to high gradients and consequently the repeatability is not the best possible.

In the field of evaluation, TRECVID [39] has been the most complete evaluation initiative during the last decade and has benchmarked detection of a variety of semantic and low-level video features. Additionally, in recent years, there has been an extended utilization of explicit knowledge with formal semantics which within the SW initiative translates to the use of ontologies [40–42].

6.3.3 Integrating Social with Content-Based Knowledge

Recently, there has been an increasing interest by the research community towards approaches that utilize both tagging information and content-based features.

In [43], the authors claim that the intrinsic shortcomings of collaborative tagging are tackled by employing content-based image retrieval technique. Such techniques facilitate image database browsing and retrieval by exploiting both the two aforementioned technologies in a supplementary way. Indeed, it is shown that the visual features can support the suggestion of new tags and contribute to the emergence of interesting (semantic) relationships between data sources. Through the use of a navigation map, these emergent relationships between users, tags and data may be explored. The visual features employed for the content-based image retrieval are *Color* and *Texture*. For the extraction of texture features they use *Oriented Gaussian Derivatives*[44].

Our original approach for coupling tagging information with content-based features was introduced in [45]. A number of varied clustering techniques were employed and applied to a dataset from Flickr. The clustering was tag-oriented and occurred in two steps. In the first step the resources were assigned to clusters, depending on the similarity of their accompanying tags. The similarity between tags yields based on their co-occurrence in tagging activities of users and their semantic vicinity. For every cluster an emergent topic was extracted based on the most frequent tags used to describe the resources assigned to this cluster. In the second step, visual features were employed, in an effort to increase the purity of already created clusters. For instance, if an image assigned to the cluster "sea" was found quite dissimilar to the rest images, it was removed from the specified cluster as an outlier. The second step of the process could be regarded as a "*misleading tags tracking phase*". The evaluation showed that the resulted clusters were very good, each one containing images and tags about the topic it has been extracted from the specified cluster. This approach was extended and presented in the next section of the chapter. Another work that combines user data with feature-based approaches, in order to rank the results of a video retrieval system is presented in [46]. The authors use this knowledge, along with a multimedia ontology to build a learning personalized environment.

A number of works have addressed the problem of identifying photos from social tagging systems that depict a certain object, location or event [47–49]. In [47] they analyze location and time information from geotagged photos from Flickr, in order to track tags that have place semantics (i.e., they refer to an object in a restricted location) or event semantics (i.e., they are met in specified time periods). Then, they employ tag-based clustering on these specific tags, followed by visual clustering, in order to capture distinct viewpoints of the object of interest. The same authors in [50] combine tags with content analysis techniques, in order to get groups of music events photos. Likewise, in [48, 49] the authors use various modalities of photos (i.e., visual, textual, spatial, temporal proximity), in order to get photo collections in an unsupervised fashion. Apart from the obvious retrieval application, the outcome of these methods can be used for training of multimedia algorithms and for tag recommendations. Another approach towards this direction, that deploys the visual annotations, also known as "notes" in Flickr is described in [51], where it is shown that the retrieval of content in a social tagging system improves significantly by combining tags and visual analysis techniques.

The problem of tag recommendation has been studied in [52], where the authors suggest an approach for recommending tags by analyzing existent tags, visual context and user context in a multimedia social tagging system. Tag recommendation techniques were, also, proposed in [53], where the authors suggest four methods for ranking candidate tags and in addition, they present the semantics of tags in flickr.

Other efforts to design tools that employ simple image analysis algorithms and apply them on Flickr images have appeared in [54, 55], yet they are not intended for semantic similarity extraction or integrated navigation in the social tagging system.

6.4   Content and Tag-Based Clustering Approach

In this section we present a two-step method for clustering on multimedia social sources. As highlighted in Section 6.3.1, clustering is often introduced in the bibliography of social tagging systems as an approach to overcome their intrinsic limitations and derive knowledge regarding their content or their users. The main approach is: divide the resources into semantically related clusters (i.e., meaningful groups of resources) and exploit the shared understanding about tags and resources fostered in each cluster. The division is performed according to some *metric of similarity* and each extracted cluster would ideally correspond to a specific topic. The expected benefit of the whole process is that the collective activity of tagging will isolate erroneous tags and illustrate the dominant tags in each cluster, expressing, thus, the community's point of view around the corresponding topic.

In order for the clustering to be effective and yield pure clusters, an appropriate metric of similarity between the resources needs to be employed. In an effort to capture knowledge in all its forms, a *two-step process* is adopted. In the *first step* the textual knowledge about the resources is considered. This involves capturing social and semantic similarity of the resources' accompanying tags. The intuition here is that if the similarity among the tags of two resources is high, then the resources are possible related to one another. In the *second step* of the process, content-based methods are employed, so as to get additional insight into the multimedia content. While both visual, audio and other content-related features can be used in content-based methods to improve retrieval accuracy, in this work we focus on the use of visual information.

Based on these, the rest of this section is organized as follows. At first, a problem formulation is quoted, to emphasize the required concept definitions and the mathematical notations used throughout the rest of the chapter. Then, an analytical description of each step of the process follows.

6.4.1 Problem Formulation

We define a Social Tagging System as the finite sets U, R, T, A which describe the set of users, resources, tags and user annotations (i.e., tag assignments), respectively. Table 6.1 summarizes the basic symbols' notation used in this paper.

Table 6.1 Main symbols' notation

Symbol	Definition
m, n, l	Number of users, resources, tags (respectively)
d, p	Number of attributes and user annotations (respectively)
K	Number of clusters
U	Users' set $\{u_1, \ldots, u_m\}$
R	Resources' set $\{r_1, \ldots, r_n\}$
U	Tags' set $\{t_1, \ldots, t_l\}$
A	User annotations' set $\{a_1, \ldots, a_p\}$
AS	Attributes' set $\{at_1, \ldots, at_d\}$
MA	Manual annotations' set $\{ma_{r_1}, \ldots, ma_{r_n}\}$

We consider that the context of each resource is captured by the manifold annotations it has received. Hence, we characterize and define resources by their corresponding tags, as follows:

Definition 6.1 (RESOURCE'S REPRESENTATION). Each resource $r_j \in R$, where $j = 1, \ldots, n$, is represented by aggregating the tags assigned to it by all users. Thus:

$$r_j = (h_1 \times tag_{j1}, h_2 \times tag_{j2}, \ldots, h_z \times tag_{jz}) \qquad (6.1)$$

where z is the number of tags assigned to r_j by all users and the coefficients $h_i, i = 1, \ldots, z$ denote the number of times the tag_{ji} has been used in r_j's annotation.

Our purpose is to create groups of related resources by taking into consideration textual annotations and content-based information and, thus, we need to provide solution to the following JOINT SOCIAL, SEMANTIC & CONTENT-BASED DATA CLUSTERING problem.

Problem 6.1 (JOINT SOCIAL, SEMANTIC & CONTENT-BASED DATA CLUSTERING). Given a set R of n resources, an integer k and a *Similarity* function, find a set C of k subsets of resources, $C = \{C_1, \ldots, C_k\}$, such that $\sum_{x=1}^{k} \sum_{r_i, r_j \in C_x} Similarity(r_i, r_j), i, j = 1, \ldots, n$ and $i \neq j$, is maximized.

The *Similarity* function must be defined in a way to sufficiently capture the association between two resources by jointly considering the social and semantic aspects of their accompanying tags, together with the low-level visual features of the involved resources. These two types of data have very different characteristics: while textual data (i.e., tags) is typically sparse and high-dimensional, visual data is usually dense and low-dimensional. Due to this heterogenous representation of the two modalities involved in the feature space, a *two-step* process is followed, in each step of which, each modality is treated separately.

Out of each final extracted cluster a *tag cluster* and a *cluster topic* are extracted, as follows.

Definition 6.2 (TAG CLUSTER). Given a resource cluster C, we call Tag Cluster, TC, the set with the user-assigned tags that describe the resources in C.

Definition 6.3 (CLUSTER TOPIC). Given a resource cluster C, we define its cluster topic as the tags that belong to its corresponding Tag Cluster, having frequency above a user-defined threshold τ.

The two steps of the proposed framework are shown in Fig. 6.2.

6.4.2 Tag-Based Resources Clustering

This section describes the first step of the proposed method, which aims at a tag-guided resources' clustering. As already discussed in Section 6.4.1, in our approach,

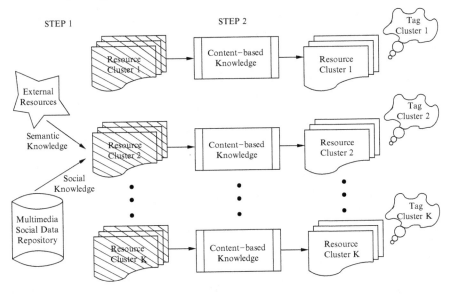

Fig. 6.2 Two-step content and tag-based clustering approach

each resource is expressed via the tags assigned to it (see Eq. 6.1). In practice, the number of tags used to represent all the resources in a social tagging system may grow in large scale and thus we need to employ a selection process of the most distinguishing tags which will form the resources' attribute set AS. In our approach we use the d most frequent tags to form the AS set which will guide our clustering process.

Definition 6.4 (THE ATTRIBUTE SET). Given the $T = \{t_1, \ldots, t_l\}$ set of tags, we define the attribute set $AS = \{at_1, \ldots, at_d\}$: $AS \subseteq T$ and AS contains the d most frequent tags $t_x \in T$.

Each attribute $at_y \in AS$ is related with a different degree to the various r_i, $1 \leq i \leq n$, resources, while two different resources may be indirectly related, if they present strong relation with the same set of attributes. To represent the relation of each resource to each attribute, we define a function, namely *Similarity Factor* sf_{ij} between a resource r_i and an attribute $attr_j$ that is evaluated by encompassing both social and semantic similarity between the resource's tags and the tag that corresponds to the specified attribute. We describe in the sequel how this similarity yields.

As introduced in Section 6.3.1, current approaches which employ clustering in social tagging systems, rely solely on tag co-occurrence to estimate tag closeness, and hence, resource closeness. We refer to such similarity between two tags as *social similarity*, *SoS*, and we define it as follows:

$$SoS(t_x, t_y) = \frac{\sum_{i=1}^{n} r_i : (u_w, r_i, t_x) \in A \text{ and } (u_z, r_i, t_y) \in A}{\max\left(\sum_{i=1}^{n} r_i : (u_w, r_i, t_x) \in A, \sum_{i=1}^{n} r_i : (u_z, r_i, t_y) \in A\right)} \quad (6.2)$$

where $u_w, u_j \in U, r_i \in R$.

However, considering the semantic aspect of tags, as well, is expected to be beneficial for the clustering process in a social tagging system, since it can contribute to eliminating the tag synonymy issue and avoiding separation of semantically related tags into different clusters. For the estimation of the *Semantic Similarity* between two tags, we need to use external resources (i.e., web ontologies, thesauri, etc.), available in the web. A mapping technique is applied to act as a bridge between a free-text tag and a structured concept of the used resource. There are a number of available measures that attempt to evaluate the semantic distance between ontology concepts and a thorough presentation of the most popular ones is given in [56]. In our work we adopted the Wu and Palmer measure, described in [57], due to its straightforward application to our data. According to this measure, the semantic distance between two concepts is proportional to the path distance between them. For example, let t_x and t_y be two tags for which we want to find the semantic similarity and $\overrightarrow{t_x}$, $\overrightarrow{t_y}$ be their corresponding mapping concepts via an ontology. Then, their *Semantic Similarity SeS* is calculated as:

$$SeS(t_x, t_y) = \frac{2 \times depth(LCS)}{\left[depth(\overrightarrow{t_x}) + depth(\overrightarrow{t_y}) \right]} \tag{6.3}$$

where $depth(\overrightarrow{t_x})$ is the maximum path length from the root to $\overrightarrow{t_x}$ and *LCS* is the least common subsumer of $\overrightarrow{t_x}$ and $\overrightarrow{t_y}$.

The total similarity between two tags will be estimated by considering both their social and semantic similarity, which are normalized in the interval [0..1] (Eqs. 6.2 and 6.3). In order to examine the impact that each kind of information has on the clustering process, we combine them in the form of a weighted sum. Specifically, a factor w is employed to define the effect each track has on the estimation of their joint similarity. Thus, we define the *Similarity Score SS* between two tags t_x and t_y in terms of both their social (Eq. 6.2) and semantic (Eq. 6.3) similarity as:

$$SS(t_x, t_y) = w * SoS(t_x, t_y) + (1 - w) * SeS(t_x, t_y) \tag{6.4}$$

where $w \in [0, 1]$ is a normalization parameter which adjusts the magnitude of the semantic similarity against the social one upon the final outcome. More specifically, at the one end when $w = 1$ we consider solely the *Social Similarity SoS*, while at the other end, when $w = 0$, only the *Semantic Similarity SeS* is considered. For any other value of w both similarities contribute to the *Similarity Score SS* of two tags.

Having specified the similarity metric between tags, we can proceed to the estimation of *similarity factors*, $sf_{i\,j}$, discussed in the beginning of the section.

Definition 6.5 (SIMILARITY FACTOR). Given a resource r_i, in which the users have assigned $|r_i|$ tags, and an attribute $attr_j$, we define as Similarity Factor, sf_{ij}, between the specified resource and the specified attribute, the maximum Similarity Score, SS between every tag assigned to resource r_i and the attribute $attr_j$. Thus:

$$sf(r_i, attr_j) = max_{x=1\ldots|r_i|}\{SS(t_x, at_j)\} \tag{6.5}$$

where $r_i \in R, t_x \in r_i, at_j \in AS$.

In the above definition, we assume that all the tags assigned to each resource are relevant to the content. Alternatively, taking the average *Similarity Score* could be more robust against tag-spamming, but it would be biased against resources which receive tags of different kinds (i.e., regarding a "sea" attribute, a resource with a tag "sea" would get higher score than another resource with tags "sea", "beach", "anna", "2007", although both of them involve sea). In the second step of the process (where content analysis is employed and described in the sequel), we take control of the tag-spamming issue and track the noisy tags that surpassed the first step, cleaning, thus, the clusters from resources with erroneous annotations.

The values of *similarity factors* between each of the N resources and d attributes are then used to form the $n \times d$ so-called Similarity Matrix, as follows:

$$SimMatrix(i, j) = sf(r_i, at_j) \qquad (6.6)$$

where $i = 1, \ldots, n$ and $j = 1, \ldots, d$.

The above resources *similarity matrix* is the input to the clustering procedure, out of which k resources clusters shall arise. As described above, the *similarity function* that is used to estimate the relation between two resources (in this phase) is based on both social and semantic aspects of their involving tags.

6.4.3   Cluster Refinement with MPEG-7 Visual Features

This section describes the second step of the proposed approach, which involves clustering of the resources, based on their visual features. Content-based approaches are often employed in the multimedia content retrieval, as can be seen in the bibliography presented in Section 6.3.2. Here, we exploit multimedia analysis as a means that gives additional insight into the content (apart from the present textual annotations) and is expected to minimize the intrinsic limitations of social tagging systems and potentially improve the retrieval accuracy.

In order to estimate the visual similarity, appropriate similarity metrics between numerical automatically extracted low-level features are used. Such features can be extracted from multimedia sources, using the MPEG-7 standard [58]. The MPEG-7 standard constitutes the greatest effort towards a common framework to multimedia description. It aims to provide a rich set of standardized tools for the description of multimedia content and additionally support some degree of interpretation of the information's meaning enabling thus smooth sharing and communication of multimedia metadata across applications and their efficient management, e.g., in terms of search and retrieval. MPEG-7 is implemented in the form of XML Schemas.

The MPEG-7 Standard consists of five main parts: the *Description Definition Language* that defines the syntax of the MPEG-7 Description Tools and new Description Schemes, the *Visual* and *Audio* parts that include the description tools for visual and audio content respectively, the *Multimedia Description Schemes* that

Table 6.2 MPEG-7 descriptors of visual features

Color	Texture	Shape	Motion
Color quantization	Texture browsing	Region shape	Motion activity
Dominant color	Edge histogram	Contour shape	GoF/GoP
Scalable color	Homogeneous texture		
Color layout			
Color structure			

comprise the set of Description Tools dealing with generic features and multimedia descriptions and the MPEG-7 Systems, the tools needed to prepare MPEG-7 descriptions for efficient transport and storage and the terminal architecture.

The MPEG-7 Visual Description Tools, that are included in the standard and are related to our approach, consist of basic structures and descriptors that cover the following basic visual features: color, texture, shape, motion, localization, and face recognition. In Table 6.2 there are the visual features and their corresponding MPEG-7 visual descriptors.

Color and texture descriptors are among the most expressive visual features. This is the reason why they are widely used and they were chosen in our own case in order to extract visual information from the images. In particular we used three Color Descriptors of MPEG-7: Scalable Color, Color Structure, Color Layout and two Texture Descriptors of MPEG-7: Homogeneous Texture and Edge Histogram [59]. An extended description of the five MPEG-7 descriptors that we used can be found in the Appendix 6.8.

MPEG-7 defines appropriate descriptors together with their extraction techniques and similarity matching distances. More specifically, the MPEG-7 eXperimentation Model, XM provides a reference implementation which can be used in our approach [60].

Therefore the second step of our approach is based on identifying low-level visual features of the multimedia resources, which are extracted from images and form an image feature vector. The image feature vector proposed in this work involves the descriptors of the MPEG-7 standard, mentioned above chosen due to their effectiveness in similarity retrieval. Their extraction is performed according to the guidelines provided by the MPEG-7 XM and then, an image feature vector is produced, for every resource, by encompassing the extracted MPEG-7 descriptors in a single vector. Thus, the *Content Similarity* between two resources is the similarity of their corresponding image feature vectors.The distance functions used to calculate the *content similarity* are according to the guidelines of MPEG-7 and they are provided by the MPEG-7 XM. Based on *content similarity*, an outlier analysis is performed in every cluster, aiming at removing the most distant objects (which surpassed Step 1, mostly due to noisy tags). By this way, we will show that we result in more homogeneous clusters.

6.5 Experimental Results

In this section, experimental results of the application of the proposed approach to a corpus of multimedia resources obtained from a social tagging system are presented.

To carry out the experimentation phase and the evaluation of the proposed clustering approach, two different datasets from Flickr were crawled using the wget[5] utility and Flickr API facilities. The first one consists of 3,000 images depicting cityscape, seaside, mountain, roadside, landscape, sport-side and locations (about 500 images from each domain). The second dataset comprises 10,000 images related to concepts: jaguar, turkey, apple, bush, sea, city, vegetation, roadside, rock, tennis. The particular selection was based on the fact that the above concepts are very commonly used by Flickr users and embed ambiguity that restricts their efficient retrieval. As a source of semantic information for tag concepts, we employ the lexicon WordNet [61], which stores English words organized in hierarchies, depending on their cognitive meaning.

Both image datasets were manually annotated in order to get the ground truth for the evaluation procedure. Even though manual annotation of 13,000 images is a big task both time consuming and tedious, it enables the testing of our method, using quantitative measures (like precision, recall and f-measure), rather than relying solely on qualitative observation of the data or on (often misleading) user tags. In addition, the gathered dataset together with the manual annotations is a valuable source for the training of multimedia analysis algorithms. Next, we describe the metrics that we used to evaluate our proposed approach.

6.5.1 Evaluation Metrics

To evaluate the quality of the extracted clusters of resources, for each technique described in the chapter, each image resource was manually annotated with respect to a predefined vocabulary V related to the visual and thematic content of the images. Thus, the *Manual Annotations Set* was created, which contains the manual annotations, each resource has received, i.e.:

$$MA = \{\cup ma_{r_x}\}, \forall r_x \in R \qquad (6.7)$$

Then, we use precision Pr and recall R as follows. Let, C_j be an extracted cluster and CT_j be the dominant tags assigned to resources of the specified cluster, above a user-defined threshold τ (see Definition 6.6.3 – CLUSTER TOPIC). We call *Relevant*

---

[5] wget: http://www.gnu.org/software/wget

Resources RR of the cluster C_j the set of resources in the corpus that at least one of the manual annotations they have received matches a tag in CT_j, i.e.:

$$RR(C_j) = \{\cup r_x\}, \forall r_x \in R : ma_{r_x} \cap CT_j \neq \emptyset \tag{6.8}$$

where $ma_{r_x} \in MA$.

It should be noted that in case we perform visual clustering in a tag-based cluster (this happens during the second step of our proposed method), the *RR* are computed on the resources in the tag-based cluster, and not in the entire dataset. Thus, if C_j is a tag-based cluster and VC_i is a visual cluster extracted from C_j, then the *RR* of the VC_i are the set of resources in the C_j that at least one of the manual annotations they have received matches a tag in the cluster topic of VC_i, i.e.:

$$RR(VC_i) = \{\cup r_x\}, \forall r_x \in C_j : ma_{r_x} \cap CT_i \neq \emptyset \tag{6.9}$$

where $ma_{r_x} \in MA$.

We define *precision* as the fraction of resources that belong to C_j and are also relevant resources:

$$Pr\left(C_j\right) = \frac{|C_j \cap RR(C_j)|}{|C_j|} \tag{6.10}$$

We define *recall* as the fraction of relevant resources which belong to C_j:

$$R\left(C_j\right) = \frac{|RR(C_j) \cap C_j|}{|RR(C_j)|} \tag{6.11}$$

The ideas of *precision* and *recall* are combined in *F-Measure* which is a broadly accepted and reliable index used in various clustering evaluation approaches [62]. Given the precision and recall definitions described in this section, the value of F-measure for a cluster C_j is defined as:

$$F\left(C_j\right) = \frac{2 * Pr\left(C_j\right) * R\left(C_j\right)}{Pr\left(C_j\right) + R\left(C_j\right)} \tag{6.12}$$

The values of F-measure fluctuate in the interval $[0..1]$ with higher values indicating a better clustering.

The user-defined threshold τ sets the frequency limit a tag should reach, in order to be member of the *Cluster Topic* of the specified cluster. It takes values in $[0..1]$, where $\tau = 1$ denotes that a tag should have been assigned in every resource in the cluster, so as to be part of the *Cluster Topic*, while $\tau = 0$ denotes that all the tags assigned to cluster resources are also members of the *Cluster Topic*. After testing varying values for τ, we concluded that the best value for the specified dataset was 0.6 (i.e., the *Cluster Topic* of every extracted cluster comprises tags that have been assigned to at least 60% resources of the specified cluster, as shown in Fig. 6.3).

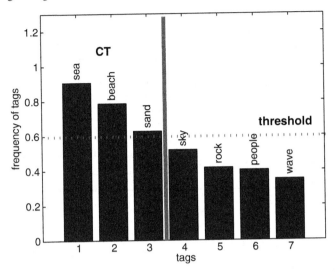

Fig. 6.3 Selection of τ value

6.5.2 Clustering Evaluation

To ensure the stability and robustness of clustering results, a variety of clustering algorithms were tested. Specifically, we used a partitional algorithm (K-means), a hierarchical (agglomerative) and a conceptual clustering process (Cobweb) [63]. In the second step of the process we conducted experiments using content-based information of the images. For all the images in both datasets (13,000 images) the low-level visual features were extracted. In order to remove the irrelevant images from each cluster we conducted experiments using different number and types of visual features. In particular, we evaluated the performance of each one of the 5 MPEG-7 Visual Descriptors mentioned in Section 6.4.3 separately and the performance of every possible combination of groups of 2, 3, 4 and 5 Descriptors.

In Tables 6.3 and 6.4 the precision (Pr) and recall (R) of the clustering algorithms, as defined in the previous Section 6.5.1, are quoted for different values of number of clusters that were extracted from the first dataset (3,000 images), respectively. In each table, the measure is calculated at each step of the procedure separately. It can be seen that K-means and Hierarchical had both satisfying performance, while Cobweb was worse. Furthermore, the outcome shows clearly that content-related knowledge (employed in step 2) improves the quality of the extracted clusters, without deteriorating the recall of the system (average of 15% improvement).

Likewise, in Tables 6.5 and 6.6, the precision and recall of each clustering algorithm on the second dataset (10,000) are shown.

As it can be seen for K = 20 the best clustering yields, for this specific dataset. For all algorithms the precision was satisfying, meaning that the extracted clusters were of good quality. It is amazing that the precision of the clusters on 10,000 im-

Table 6.3 Precision in each step for varying algorithms and varying number of clusters (K) (1st dataset 3,000 resources)

Algorithms	K = 14		K = 17		K = 20	
K-means	0.657	0.77	0.75	0.813	0.687	0.806
Hierarchical	0.679	0.842	0.744	0.85	0.675	0.752
Cobweb	0.552	0.723	0.65	0.708	0.589	0.673
	Step 1	*Step 2*	*Step 1*	*Step 2*	*Step 1*	*Step 2*

Table 6.4 Recall in each step for varying algorithms and varying number of clusters (K) (1st dataset 3,000 resources)

Algorithms	K = 14		K = 17		K = 20	
K-means	0.6	0.57	0.781	0.75	0.634	0.6
Hierarchical	0.71	0.69	0.566	0.566	0.694	0.6
Cobweb	0.749	0.539	0.805	0.78	0.78	0.732
	Step 1	*Step 2*	*Step 1*	*Step 2*	*Step 1*	*Step 2*

Table 6.5 Precision in each step for varying clustering algorithm and varying number of clusters (K) (second dataset 10,000 resources)

Algorithms	K = 10		K = 20		K = 30	
K-means	0.57	0.604	0.644	0.738	0.655	0.685
Hierarchical	0.801	0.497	0.542	0.78	0.693	0.764
Cobweb	0.71	0.712	0.7	0.7	0.696	0.7
	Step 1	*Step 2*	*Step 1*	*Step 2*	*Step 1*	*Step 2*

Table 6.6 Recall in each step for varying clustering algorithm and varying number of clusters (K) (second dataset 10,000 resources)

Algorithms	K = 10		K = 20		K = 30	
K-means	0.4	0.489	0.456	0.531	0.245	0.307
Hierarchical	0.2	0.223	0.121	0.354	0.025	0.482
Cobweb	0.04	0.299	0.388	0.359	0.383	0.41
	Step 1	*Step 2*	*Step 1*	*Step 2*	*Step 1*	*Step 2*

ages is on the same levels with the precision of the clustering on the smaller dataset. This holds for all the three clustering algorithms we tested and proves the scalability of our approach in extracting clean clusters. The low values of the recall are attributed to the big size of the dataset and they show that the proposed approach did not manage to capture all the relevant resources together. Finally, and in this dataset, in most cases there was an improvement from combining tag analysis with visual knowledge from the content.

It should be noted that all algorithms were applied for a certain number of times on our data (in order to avoid random assignments of data) and here we report the average performance.

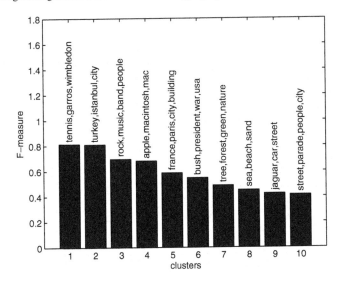

Fig. 6.4 Clusters' F-measure – 10,000 dataset, 10 clusters

6.5.3   Emergent Tag Clusters and Cluster Topics

Generally, most of the clusters the system generated were homogeneous and meaningful. The corresponding tag clusters were also very representative and highly informative. Indicatively F-Measure metric is presented for ten extracted clusters of the dataset of 10,000 images, along with the dominant tags for each cluster (i.e., its cluster topic) in Fig. 6.4. The values of F-measure fluctuate in the interval [0..1] with higher values indicating a better clustering.

6.5.4   Influence of w in the Extracted Clusters

In Section 6.4.2, the similarity between two tags was defined as a weighted sum of their social and semantic similarity (Eq. 6.4). The parameter w takes values in [0, 1] and is used to adjust the impact each kind of similarity measure (i.e., social or semantic) has on the overall outcome. More specifically, when w is close to 1, the social similarity is favored, while when w approximates 0, the semantic similarity is mostly considered in the total tag similarity calculation.

Here, we will examine how the values w takes, affects the quality of the extracted clusters. We will experiment with the following three indicative cases:

- $w = 0.2$: The similarity between two tags is mostly based on their co-occurrence.
- $w = 0.5$: Both co-occurrence and semantic affinity between two tags are counted equally in the estimation of their similarity.
- $w = 0.8$: The similarity between two tags is mostly based on their semantic affinity.

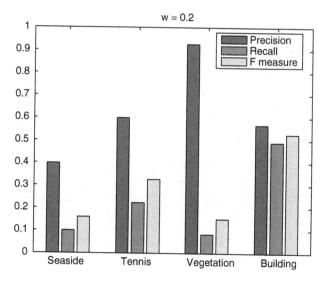

Fig. 6.5 F-measure of four clusters, taken from hierarchical algorithm with $w = 0.2$

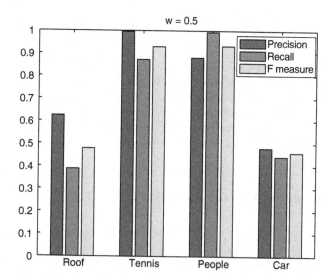

Fig. 6.6 F-measure of four clusters, taken from hierarchical algorithm with $w = 0.5$

The F-measure of four indicative clusters for each value of w is shown in Figs. 6.5, 6.6, and 6.7, respectively. The specified clusters were obtained with the hierarchical algorithm. It should be noted that these clusters are tag-based clusters (obtained during the first step of our proposed approach), since the value w affects the way we calculate tag affinity. The effect on the second step is indirect: that is, the better clusters yield during the first step, the higher the improvement in the overall procedure.

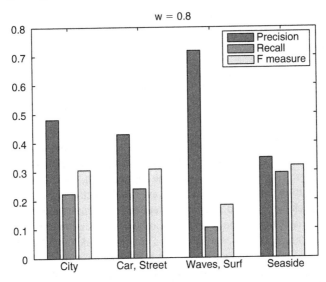

Fig. 6.7 F-measure of four clusters, taken from hierarchical algorithm with $w = 0.8$

As can be seen in all figures, the value of w affects the results. More specifically, we observe that, in most cases, for $w = 0.5$ both precision and recall have their highest values, meaning that the incorporation of both kinds of knowledge (social and semantic) is more advantageous towards relying solely on one of them.

In case of $w = 0.2$, where more weight is given to the *Social Similarity*, we can derive that the objects assigned by the algorithm in the same cluster have tags that co-occur in the users' annotations. For example the tags *forest, nature, green, tree* belong to the same cluster, because these tags are often used together for describing images related to sceneries of nature. The same holds for the cluster where *street, building, church, architecture* are assigned, since they constitute tags that occur frequently in the description of images referring to city places. In general, tag co-occurrence has proven to be more advantageous in the case of ambiguous tags (homonyms), since it is the context of such a tag (i.e., its co-occurring tags) that will help to disambiguate its meaning. However, lacking semantic information, the algorithm splits meaningful clusters into subclusters. This explains the low recall in the *sea* and *vegetation* clusters, in Fig. 6.5.

For $w = 0.8$ (Fig. 6.7), where the *Semantic Similarity* is favored, the algorithm assigns all semantically close tags in one cluster i.e., *sea, seaside, beach, sand* (*beach* and *sand* are grouped together). Despite the fact that all aforementioned tags are closely akin, in the previous described cases, they are split into different clusters, due to the fact that the users have not used all of them together in their annotations. However this method fails in disambiguating correctly tags like *rock* and *rocks*, to the same cluster even though in most cases they are not used in the same sense and they do not describe the same set of images. This results in clustering images having the tag *rock* but involving music themes together with images depicting stones. Thus, we can conclude that while this approach yields semantically meaningful clusters around a specific topic and it tackles well in case of synonyms (or tags with alike meaning), it fails to handle the tag ambiguity issue.

6.6   Use Cases – Scenarios

In this section we will show some indicative use cases and scenarios of our proposed approach. First of all, the proposed method tackles quite well the shortcomings of a social tagging system, described in the Introduction, resulting, thus, in better retrieval of multimedia content. Furthermore, the extracted clusters together with the cluster topics can be used as training sets for multimedia analysis learning algorithms [64]. Apart from the multimedia related application, our method has an ability in subdomain identification within a domain, which can be utilized in semantics extraction out of the raw tag data. Another potential use case of our method would be its integration by a recommender system, in order to support users of tagging systems by suggesting tags that have been already assigned to related content. In the following, some scenarios are demonstrated that justify our arguments. Due to space restriction only some snapshots are shown indicatively.

Tag Ambiguity   The clustering algorithms handled well the specified issue and distinguished different senses of the same tag, by dividing the corresponding resources into different clusters, by adjusting accordingly the value of w, as explained in the previous section (see Fig. 6.8).

Tag Questionable Reliability   It is expected that misleading tags in some annotations are practically overwhelmed by the massive activity of a large number of users. Nevertheless, in cases where a misleading tag may lead to the retrieval of irrelevant content, then the content similarity factor, employed in step 2 of the process, enhances the possibility that irrelevant content will be tracked and removed from a cluster, if the referred object has a visual appearance very different from the rest ones (e.g., Fig. 6.9). The cluster shown is a snapshot of the outcome of step 1 and the resource surrounded by a red box is removed during the step 2 of the process. The removed photo has been assigned with the tag "sea" which was a misleading tag and it was tracked.

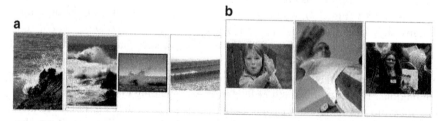

Fig. 6.8   Different clusters for the ambiguous tag: wave (**a**) members of cluster with CT = wave, sea, water (**b**) members of cluster with CT = wave, signal, hand, person (the photos are downloaded from Flickr photo sharing system)

CT
sea, beach, sand,
shore, ocean, rocks,
seashore, island

Fig. 6.9 Snapshot of a sea cluster with its emergent CT – Identification of a misleading tag in the sea cluster and rejection of the resource (surrounded by a *dotted box*) (the photos are downloaded from Flickr photo sharing system)

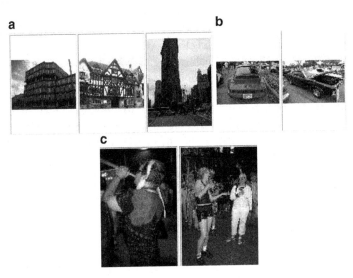

Fig. 6.10 Members of different clusters of roadside images (**a**) members of a cluster with CT = building, roof, street, (**b**) members of a cluster with CT = car, race, Porsche, street, (**c**) members of a cluster with CT = caribbean, carnival, festival, people, street (the photos are downloaded from Flickr photo sharing system)

Tag Redundancy and Lack of Hierarchical Relations   Since semantic similarity of tags is employed, tag redundancy is no more needed. The system inherits the structure of the external resource used (i.e., the structure of concepts of WordNet).

Identification of Subdomains (Semantics Extraction)   The proposed approach accomplishes to find meaningful sub-clusters, inside a generic cluster. For instance, the initial group of Roadside images is split by the process into three more specific clusters, depicted in Fig. 6.10, with (a) CT = building, roof, street, (b) CT = car, race, Porsche, street (c) CT = Caribbean, carnival, festival, people, street.

Tag Recommendation   The emergent cluster topic of each cluster can be suggested as candidate tags for the objects assigned inside the cluster. Furthermore, ranking mechanisms for candidate tags can be developed, based on the visual similarity of the content.

6.7 Conclusions

This paper introduces a joint approach for social data grouping that aims to enhance the multimedia social content exploitation. The proposed method considers the semantic in addition to the social aspect of resources accompanying tags in a balanced way, as well as the content-based information. It yields clusters consisting of both resources and user annotation tags. The proposed approach has been evaluated under two real datasets and the results proved its efficiency in extracting relevant tags and resources, illustrating the dominant tags in each cluster and expressing users' point of view around the corresponding topic. Moreover, the consideration of the visual aspect of the social resources enables the satisfying handling of common social tagging limitations, such as the tag ambiguity issue. The proposed approach has a number of potential applications. Apart from the obvious retrieval applications, the tag clusters produced can be used for semantics extraction and knowledge mining, in general and more specifically in automated multimedia content analysis, being used for example as training sets for specific concepts represented by tags. Future work includes the incorporation of visual features in the clustering procedure, based on using a common input vector resulting from all the available information per resource. In order to achieve this, appropriate normalization techniques need to be employed. In addition, the calculation of the similarities were relatively time consuming, so we plan to study ways to decrease the time spent and experiment with different metrics.

6.8 Appendix

6.8.1 Color Descriptors

6.8.1.1 Scalable Color

The Scalable Color Descriptor (SCD) is defined in the HSV color space (see HSV Color Space description below). It uses an encoding method, based on Haar transform on the color HSV histogram. The HSV space is uniformly quantized into histogram bins. The number of the bins can vary. The number of the bins depends on the required compactness – a low number of bins give a fast descriptor suitable for indexing and quick queries.

After the histogram values are extracted, there is a normalization and a nonlinear quantization into a four-bin integer representation. The Haar transform is applied to the four-bit integer values across the histogram bins. The output is the high and low-pass coefficients from the transform. In Fig. 6.11 it is described the process of SCD extraction process.

Fig. 6.11 Diagram of SCD generation

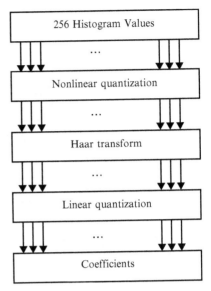

Haar transformation creates a scalable description, which is useful for image-to-image matching and retrieval based on color feature. In addition, SCD can be further used for group of frames or groups of pictures in video data.

6.8.1.2   Color Structure

The Color Structure Descriptor (CSD) represents the local color structure in an image. This descriptor enables it to distinguish both in which proportion each color exists and how uniformly color is distributed in the image. The CSD is a histogram and is computed by the use of an 8×8 structuring element, which visits all location in the image as shown in Fig. 6.12. In particular, CSD counts how many times a particular color is contained in all the pixels in the 8×8 window, as this window scans the image. Suppose $C_0, C_1, C_2, \ldots, C_{M-1}$ denote the M quantized colors. The value of each bin of the histogram represents the number of the structuring elements in the image that contain one or more pixels with the corresponding color Cm. In this way, unlike the color histogram, the CSD can help us to distinguish two pictures with the same amounts of color but with different color distribution. The CSD uses the HMMD color space, which is quantized non-uniformly into 32, 64, 128 or 256 bins. In our case the number of bins is 32. An 8-bit code represents each bin amplitude value.

As it is mentioned above, the size of the structuring element is 8×8. Their number is always 64, consequently the distance between the structuring points increases

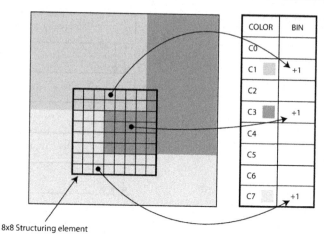

Fig. 6.12 CSD structuring element [65]

with the image size, as shown on Fig. 6.3. The spatial extent of the structuring element is computed by the following rule:

$$p = \max\{0, round(0.5 \log WH - 8)\} \tag{6.13}$$

$$K = 2^p, E = 8K \tag{6.14}$$

where

W, H image width and height;
$E \times E$ spatial extent of the structuring elements;
K sub-sampling factor.

For images smaller than 320×240 pixels, an 8×8 structure element with no subsampling is used, and for image size 640×480 (p = 1, K = 2, and E = 16) structuring element is 16×16 and subsampling is 2×2. The structuring element of size 8×8 is applied to a subsampled image.

6.8.1.3 Color Layout

The Color Layout Descriptor represents the spatial distribution of color of images in a very compact form. Its computation is based on the generation of an 8×8 thumbnail of the image. This 8×8 image is a result of DCT of the initial image and quantization. In particular the CLD extraction process consists of two parts. Firstly the input image is divided into 64 blocks (8×8). For each block of the grid, its average color is used as the representative color of the block. The average color is expressed in the YCbCr color space. An 8×8 DCT is performed in order to transform the derived average colors into a series of coefficients. After the transformation, the coefficients are zigzag scanned and few low-frequency coefficients are selected and quantized.

For matching two CLDs, $\{DY, DCr, DCb\}$ and $\{DY', DCr', DCb'\}$, the following distance measure is used:

$$D = \sqrt{\sum_i w_{yi}\left(DY_i - DY'_i\right)^2} + \sqrt{\sum_i w_{bi}\left(DCb_i - DCb'_i\right)^2}$$

$$+ \sqrt{\sum_i w_{ri}\left(DCr_i - DCr'_i\right)^2} \tag{6.15}$$

This descriptor provides an image-to-image or sketch-to-image search, which is high speed, accurate and requires minimum storage and transmission cost.

6.8.2 Texture Descriptors

6.8.2.1 Homogeneous Texture

The Homogeneous Texture Descriptor provides an accurate quantitative description of texture. The extraction method of the HTD is as follows: the frequency domain is partitioned into 30 channels as it is shown in Fig. 6.13. The partitioning of the frequency space is uniform in the angular direction (step size of 30°), but in the angular direction there is an unequal octave division. The individual feature channels are modeled by 2D-Gabor functions. The energy and the energy deviation of each channel is computed. Finally, mean and standard deviation of frequency coefficients are computed, resulting in a feature vector of 62 values as it is shown in Eq. 6.16. The HTD can be used for accurate search and retrieval.

$$TD = [f_{DC}, f_{SD}, e_1, e_2, \ldots, e_{30}, d_1, d_2, \ldots, d_{30}] \tag{6.16}$$

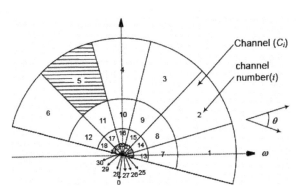

Fig. 6.13 Channels used in computing the HTD [66]

6.8.2.2 Edge Histogram

The Edge Histogram Descriptor represents the spatial distribution of five types of edges. In particular, the computation of the descriptor consists of four steps:

1. The image is divided in 4 × 4 sub-images.
2. Each of the sub-images that occur is divided in square blocks.
3. Each block is described by one edge type. There are four directional edges (horizontal, vertical, diagonal 45°, diagonal 135°) and one non-directional.
4. The edge histogram is extracted.

EHD represents local edge distribution in the image. However, the local histogram bins can be used in order to generate global and semi-local edge histograms, which increase the matching performance.

Acknowledgements The work presented in this paper was partially supported by the European Commission under contracts FP7-215453 WeKnowIt and FP6-26978 X-media.

References

1. O'Reilly T. (2005) What is Web 2.0, In http://www.oreillynet.com/pub/a/oreilly/tim/news/2005/09/30/what-is-web-20.html
2. Cattuto C, Loreto V, Petronero L. (2007) Semiotic dynamics and collaborative tagging. In Procceedings of the National Academy of Sciences, 104:14611464
3. Halpin H, Shepard H. (1990) Evolving ontologies from folksonomies: Tagging as a complex system. In Complex Systems Summer School Project, http://www.ibiblio.org/hhalpin/homepage/notes/taggingcss.html.
4. Steels L. (2006) Semiotic dynamics for embodied agents. IEEE Intelligent Systems, 21:3238
5. Smeulders A W M, Worring M, Santini S, Gupta A, Jain R. (2000) Content-Based Image Retrieval at the End of the Early Years, In IEEE Trans. Pattern Anal. Mach. Intell., vol. 22, number 12, pp. 1349–1380
6. National Information Standards Organization, (2004) Understanding Metadata. NISO Press, pp. 1-20
7. Wilensky R. (2000) Digital Library Resources as a Basis for Collaborative Work. Journal of The American Society for Information Science and Technology, 51(3):228245
8. Hobson P, Kompatsiaris Y. (2006) Advances in semantic multimedia analysis for personalised content access. Special Session on Advances in Semantic Multimedia Analysis for Personalised Content Access, IEEE International Symposium on Circuits and Systems
9. Golder S, Huberman A. (2006) The Structure of Collaborative Tagging Systems. Journal of Information Science
10. Begelman G, Keller Ph, Smadja F. (2006) Automated Tag Clustering: Improving search and exploration in the tag space. In Procceedings of Collaborative Web Tagging Workshop at the 15th WWW Conference, Edinburgh, Scotland
11. Grahl M, Hotho A, Stumme G. (2007) Conceptual Clustering of Social Bookmarking Sites. 7th International Conference on Knowledge Management, 356–364, KnowCenter,Graz, Austria.
12. Jaschke R, Hotho A, Schmitz Ch, Ganter B, Stumme G. (2006). TRIAS - An Algorithm for Mining Iceberg Tri-Lattices. In Proceedings of the 6th IEEE International Conference on Data Mining, 907–911
13. Gruber T. (2005) Folksonomy of Ontology: A Mash-up of Apples and Oranges. First On-Line conference on Metadata and Semantics Research MTSR

14. Knerr T. (2006) Tagging Ontology- Towards a Common Ontology for Folksonomies. Available at: http://code.google.com/p/tagont/
15. Newman R. (2005) Tag ontology design. Available at: http://www.holygoat.co.uk/projects/tags/
16. Brickley D, Miles A, (2005) SKOS Core Vocabulary Specification,W3CWorking Draft2. Available at: http://www.w3.org/TR/2005/WD-swbp-skos-core-spec-20051102
17. Schmitz P. (2006) Inducing Ontology from Flickr Tags. In Proceedings of the Collaborative Web Tagging Workshop at the 15th WWW Conference, Edinburgh, Scotland
18. Mika P. (2005) Ontologies are Us: A Unified Model of Social Networks and Semantics. In Proceedings of the 4th International Semantic Web Conference
19. Schmitz C, Hotho A, Jaschke R, Stumme G. (2006) Mining Association Rules in Folksonomies. In Proceedings of the (IFCS 2006), pages 261–270, Ljubljana
20. Specia L, Motta E. (2007) Integrating Folksonomies with the Semantic Web. In Proceedings of the 4th European Semantic Web Conference
21. Wu X, Zhang L, Yu Y. (2006) Exploring Social Annotations for the Semantic Web. In Proceedings of the 15th WWW Conference (WWW 2006), Edinnburgh, Scotland
22. Zhou M, Bao S, Wu X, Yu Y. (2007) An Unsupervised Model for Exploring Hierarchical Semantics from Social Annotations. In Proceedings of the 6th International Semantic Web Conference
23. Michael S. Lew and Nicu Sebe and Chabane Djeraba Lifl and Ramesh Jain (2006) Content-based Multimedia Information Retrieval: State of the Art and Challenges, ACM Transactions on Multimedia Computing, Communications, and Applications, 2(1): 1–19
24. Pereira F. and Koenen R. (2001) MPEG-7: A standard for multimedia content description, Int. J. Image Graph, 1, 3, 527546
25. Lew M.S. (2001) Principles of Visual Information Retrieval, Springer, London, UK
26. Gevers T. (2001) Color-based retrieval. In Principles of Visual Information Retrieval, M. S. Lew, Ed. Springer-Verlag, London, UK, 1149
27. Ojala T., Pietikainen M. and Hardwood D. (1996) Comparative study of texture measures with classification based on feature distributionsm, Patt. Recogn. 29, 1, 5159
28. Jafari-Khouzani K. and Soltanian-Zadeh H. (2005) Radon transform orientation estimation for rotation invariant texture analysis, IEEE Trans. Patt. Analy. Machine Intell. 27, 6, 10041008
29. Bartolini I., Ciaccia P. and Patella M. (2005) WARP: Accurate retrieval of shapes using phase of fourier descriptors and time warping distance, IEEE Trans. Patt. Analy. Machine Intellig. 27, 1, 142147
30. Srivastava A., Joshi S.H., Mio W. and Liu X. (2005) Statistical shape analysis: Clustering, learning, and testing, IEEE Trans. Patt. Analy. Mach. Intell. 27, 4, 590602
31. Sebastian T.B., Klein P.N. and Kimia B.B. (2004) Recognition of shapes by editing their shock graphs, IEEE Trans. Patt. Analy. Machine Intell. 26, 5, 550571
32. Vretos N., Solachidis V. and Pitas I. (2005) An MPEG-7 Based Description Scheme for Video Analysis Using Anthropocentric Video Content Descriptors, LECTURE NOTES IN COMPUTER SCIENCE, 3746, 725, Springer
33. Sebe N., Lew M.S. and Huijsmans D.P. (2000) Toward improved ranking metrics, IEEE Trans. Patt. Analy. Mach. Intell. 22, 10, 11321143
34. Jacobs D.W., Weinshall D. and Gdalyahu Y. (2000) Classification with nonmetric distances: Image hetrieval and class representation, IEEE Trans. Patt. Analy. Machine Intell. 22, 6, 583600
35. Beretti S., Del Bimbo A. and Vicario E. (2001) Efficient matching and indexing of graph models in content-based retrieval, IEEE Trans. Patt. Analy. Machine Intellig. 23, 10, 10891105
36. Cooper M., Foote J., Girgensohn A. and Wilcox L. (2005) Temporal event clustering for digital photo collections, ACMTrans. Multimedia Comput. Comm. Applica. 1, 3, 269288
37. Lindeberg T. (1998) Feature detection with automatic scale selection, Int. J. Comput. Vision, 30, 2, 79116
38. Lowe D. (2004) Distinctive image features from scale-invariant keypoints, Int. J. Comput. Vision 60, 2, 91110

39. Smeaton A. F., Over P. and Kraaij W. (2006) "Evaluation campaigns and TRECVid", In Proceedings of the 8th ACM International Workshop on Multimedia Information Retrieval (Santa Barbara, California, USA, October 26 - 27, 2006), MIR '06, ACM Press, New York, NY, 321–330

40. Maillot N., Thonnat M. and Boucher A. (2004) Towards ontology-based cognitive vision, Mach. Vis. Appl., 16, 1, 33–40

41. Hunter J., Drennan J. and Little S. (2004) Realizing the Hydrogen Economy through Semantic Web Technologies, IEEE Intelligent Systems, 19, 1, Jan.-Feb., 40–47

42. Dasiopoulou S., Heinecke J., Saathoff C. and Strintzis M.G. (2007) Multimedia Reasoning with Natural Language Support, 1st IEEE International Conference on Semantic Computing (ICSC), Irvine, CA, USA

43. Aurnhammer M, Hanappe P, Steels L. (2006) Augmenting navigation for collaborative tagging with emergent semantics. In Proceedings of the 5th International Semantic Web Conference

44. Alvarado P, Doerfler P, Wickel J. (2001) Axon2 a visual object recognition system for non-rigid objects. In Proceedings of the International Conference on Signal Processing, Pattern Recognition and Applications (SPPRA)

45. Giannakidou E, Kompatsiaris I, Vakali A. (2008) SEMSOC: Semantics Mining on Multimedia Social Data Sources. In Proceedings of the 2nd IEEE International Conference on Semantic Computing, Santa Clara, CA, USA

46. Ghosh H, . Poornachander P, Mallik A, Chaudhury S. (2007) Learning ontology for personalized video retrieval. In International Multimedia Conference, Workshop on multimedia information retrieval on The many faces of multimedia semantics, Augsburg, Bavaria, Germany

47. Kennedy L, Naaman M, Ahern S, Nair R, Rattenbury T. (2007) How flickr helps us make sense of the world: context and content in community-contributed media collections. In In Proceedings of the 15th international Conference on Multimedia, Augsburg, Germany

48. Quack T, Leibe B, Van Gool L. (2008) World-scale mining of objects and events from community photo collections. In Proceedings of the 2008 international Conference on Content-Based Image and Video Retrieval, Niagara Falls, Canada

49. Crandall D, Backstrom L, Huttenlocher D, Kleinberg J. (2009) Mapping the World's Photos. In Proceedings of the World Wide Web Conference, Madrid, Spain

50. Kennedy L, Naaman M. (2009) Less Talk, More Rock: Automated Organization of Community-Contributed Collections of Concert Videos. In Proceedings of the World Wide Web Conference, Madrid, Spain

51. Olivares X, Ciaramita M, van Zwol R. (2008) Boosting image retrieval through aggregating search results based on visual annotations. In Proceeding of the 16th ACM international conference on Multimedia, Vancouver, British Columbia, Canada

52. Lindstaedt S, Pammer V, Morzinger R, Kern R, Mulllner H, Wagner C. (2008) Recommending tags for pictures based on text, visual content and user context. In Proceedings of the Third International Conference on Internet and Web Applications and Services, Athens, Greece

53. Sigurbjornsson B, van Zwol R. (2008) Flickr tag recommendation based on collective knowledge. In Proceeding of the 17th international conference on World Wide Web, Beijing, China

54. Bumgardner J. (2006) Experimental colr pickr. Available at: http://www.krazydad.com/colrpickr/

55. Langreiter C. (2006) Retrievr. Available at: http://labs.systemone.at/retrie-vr/

56. Maguitman A, Lord P.W, Menczer F, Roinestad H, Vespignani A. (2005) Algorithmic Detection of Semantic Similarity. In Procceding of the 14th international conference on World Wide Web , (WWW'05), pages 107–116

57. Wu Z, Palmer M. (1994) Verm semantics and lexical selection. In Proceedings of the 32nd annual meeting of the association for computational linguistics, pages = 133–138. New Mexiko, USA.

58. Martnez J.M, "Overview of the MPEG-7 Standard (v4.0)", ISO/MPEG N3752

59. B. S. Manjunath, Philippe Salembier, Thomas Sikora (2002) Introduction to MPEG-7: Multimedia Content Description Interface, John Wiley & Sons, Inc. New York

60. MPEG-7 Visual Experimentation Model (XM), Version 10.0, ISO/IEC/JTC1/SC29/WG11, Doc. N4062, Mar., 2001.

61. Fellbaum C. (1990) WordNet, an electronic lexical database. The MIT Press
62. Larsen B. and Aone C. (1999) Fast and effective: Text mining using linear-time document clustering, Proc. of 5th ACM SIGKDD Int. Conf. on Knowledge Discovery and Data Mining, (KDD99), pages 1622, August
63. Xu R. (2005) Survey of Clustering Algorithms. In IEEE Transactions on Neural Networks, Vol. 16, No. 3, May
64. Chatzilari E, Nikolopoulos S, Giannakidou E, Vakali A, Kompatsiaris I. (2009) Leveraging Social Media For Training Object Detectors. In Proceedings of the 16th International Conference on Digital Signal Processing, Special Session on Social Media, Santorini, Greece
65. Buturovic Adis (2005) MPEG 7 Color Structure Descriptor for visual information retrieval project VizIR1. Institute for Software Technology and Interactive Systems, Technical University Vienna
66. B. S. Manjunath, Jens-Rainer Ohm, Vinod V. Vasudevan, and Akio Yamada (2001) Color and Texture Descriptors, IEEE Trans. On Circuits and Systemsfor Video Technology, vol. 11, No. 6

Chapter 7
User Profiles Modeling in Information Retrieval Systems

Václav Snášel, Ajith Abraham, Suhail Owais, Jan Platoš, and Pavel Krömer

Abstract The requirements imposed on information retrieval systems are increasing steadily. The vast number of documents in today's large databases and especially on the World Wide Web causes problems when searching for concrete information. It is difficult to find satisfactory information that accurately matches user information needs even if it is present in the database. One of the key elements when searching the web is proper formulation of user queries. Search effectiveness can be seen as the accuracy of matching user information needs against the retrieved information. As step towards better search systems represents personalized search based on user profiles. Personalized search applications can notably contribute to the improvement of web search effectiveness. This chapter presents design and experiments with an information retrieval system utilizing user profiles, fuzzy information retrieval and genetic algorithms for improvement of web search.

7.1 Introduction

Information retrieval activity is a derivation of real-world human communication. An information or knowledge, stored in a data repository by one person, is desired to be retrieved by another. Data repositories, emphasizing the Internet as the ultimate

V. Snášel (✉), J. Platoš, and P. Krömer
Department of Computer Science, Faculty of Electrical Engineering and Computer Science, VŠB, Technical University of Ostrava, 17. listopadu 15, 708 33 Ostrava, Poruba, Czech Republic
e-mail: vaclav.snasel@vsb.cz; jan.platos@vsb.cz; pavel.kromer.fei@vsb.cz

A. Abraham
Center of Excellence for Quantifiable Quality of Service, Norwegian University of Science and Technology, O.S. Bragstads plass 2E, 7491 Trondheim, Norway
e-mail: ajith.abraham@ieee.org

S. Owais
Department of Computer Science, Faculty of Information Technology, Applied Science University, Amman, 11931 Jordan
e-mail: dr_suhail@asu.edu.jo

R. Chbeir et al., *Emergent Web Intelligence: Advanced Information Retrieval*, Advanced Information and Knowledge Processing, DOI 10.1007/978-1-84996-074-8_7,
© Springer-Verlag London Limited 2010

one, are used for persisting information in both, time and space. Data available on the Internet might be accessed by users distant in time and space. Unfortunately, the omnipresence of data is not equal to instant availability of information. In general, data can be seen as a state of information used for storage purposes, encapsulating the information content itself. A speech is not information, it contains information. An article is not information, it contains information. An electronic document can be seen similarly. To exploit stored data, it is desired to access the contained information in an efficient way. Such *information retrieval* activity is not an easy task and its complexity depends specially on the dimension of searched data basis. Moreover, when we are trying to automate information search process, the requirement to understand is becomes crucial. To retrieve the information in document, its content should be understood. To present required information to inquirer, the requests must be understood and correctly interpreted. Advanced techniques of information retrieval are under investigation to provide both – better content representation and better query apprehension.

There is fuzziness in human mind. It involves the means of communication. Estimations and intuition are present. Vagueness, imprecision and mistakes occur. These facts influence both – information content of documents and search request formulations. Contrariwise, any automated search tool has rather crisp and rough picture (i.e., model) of the information content of data, providing satisfactory search service for data collections up to certain size. Inevitably, the enormous growth of data repositories and especially of the Internet brings up more and more problems when performing information retrieval tasks. The amount of regular users of search services is growing as well. One approach to improve information retrieval in such conditions is approximating reality better than before. To improve the efficiency of information retrieval, soft computing techniques with special emphasis on fuzzy technology are being intensively investigated. When modeling information and requests containing vagueness or imprecision, fuzzy set theory providing formal background to deal with imprecision, vagueness, uncertainty and similar concepts might be used, introducing significant improvements to the search results.

The requirements imposed on search applications are increasing steadily. The amount of available data is growing and user demands as well. The search application should provide the users with accurate, sensible responses to their requests. Unified consensual approach to search requirements of all inquirers becomes with growing amount of data and documents on the WWW inefficient to satisfy needs of large number of individuals desiring to retrieve particular information from Internet. Personalized approach to the needs of each user is general trend in state-of-the-art web applications including search engines. Personalization, based on stored knowledge of users general needs, area(s) of interest, usual behavior, long and short term context and search practices can be evaluated when improving web search applications, no matter if they are standalone search engines or more advanced meta-search systems lying on the top of individual search applications.

User profiles, personalization of web search tasks and soft information retrieval are current challenges. Information retrieval optimization based on knowledge of previous user search activities and fuzzy softening of both, search criteria and information models, aims at enriching document sets retrieved in response to user requests and helping user when she or he has no clear picture of searched information. In this paper we describe implicit user modeling algorithm based on click-through data analysis and introduce genetic and fuzzy oriented approach to query optimization with the goal to determine useful search queries describing documents relevant to users area of interest as deducted from previous searches as a tool helping user to fetch the most relevant information in his or her current context.

The rest of this chapter is organized as follows: In Section 7.2, some background on information retrieval and fundamentals of information retrieval systems is provided. Fuzzy logic is briefly technology and its application in the area of information retrieval is introduced. Section 7.3 summarizes the usage of Evolutionary Computation, Genetic Algorithms, Genetic Programming and its application to information retrieval tasks. In Section 7.4, we present our contribution extending the usage of genetic algorithms for search optimization in both, crisp and fuzzy information retrieval systems. Experiment results are presented in Section 7.5 and finally some conclusions are also provided.

7.2   Information Retrieval

The area of *Information Retrieval* (IR) is a branch of Computer Science dealing with storage, maintenance and information search within large amounts of data. The data could be all – textual, visual, audio or multimedia documents [7]. The rest of this chapter is devoted to information retrieval dealing with extensive collections of unstructured textual documents.

An *Information Retrieval System* (IRS) is a software tool for data representation, storage and information search. The amount of documents contained in data collections managed by IRS is usually very large and the task of easy, efficient and accurate information search is specially highlighted. General architecture of an information retrieval system is shown in Fig. 7.1 [7].

Documentary collection is for the search purposes analyzed and transformed into suitable internal representation in a process called indexing. The real world information need of an IRS user must be for the use with particular IRS expressed by the means of query language understandable to that system. A search query is then evaluated against the internal document representation and the system decides whether and how much are particular documents relevant to the query. The way of document indexing, structure of internal document representation, query language and document-query matching mechanism depends on certain IRS model which is a theoretical background below particular information retrieval system [7]. For regular users provides an IRS two main functions: data storage and information retrieval in order to satisfy users' information need.

An *information need* is a state in which ones own knowledge is insufficient for satisfying her or his demands. If an IRS is to be used for information search, the demanded information need must be expressed in query language of the particular IRS

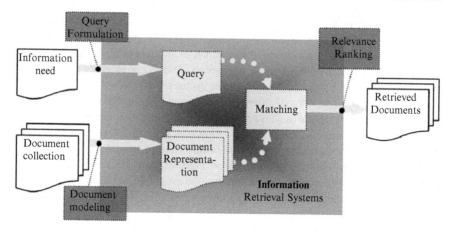

Fig. 7.1 An information retrieval system

Fig. 7.2 Documents
in collection classified
in response to a query

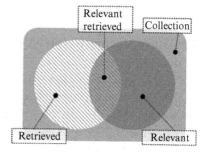

in a process called querying. The search system attempts to find in managed documentary collection entries relevant to the query. Ordered set of *retrieved* documents is then offered to the user. Retrieved documents are such subset of documentary collection that is considered by the information retrieval application to be *relevant* to the user query. Retrieved documents are presented in certain ordering as a source of information to satisfy information need stated in the query. The document ordering is based on particular ranking strategy which is realized by certain ranking function.

The typical allocation of documents within the collection in response to a query is illustrated in Fig. 7.2. We can see that not all relevant documents are usually retrieved and moreover, some non-relevant documents could be included in the set of retrieved documents. We may also legitimately consider different documents to be relevant to the query in a certain degree. One of the main goals in the research of IR systems is to improve the accuracy of retrieved document set. It means to maximize the subset of retrieved relevant documents and minimize the subset of retrieved non-relevant documents.

Documents classified against to a query as relevant and non-relevant, though the entire concept of relevance is a subject of discussion with no universal convergence yet. Objective relevance is an algorithmic measure of the degree of similarity between the query representation and the document representation. It is also referred to as a topicality measure, referring to the degree to which the topic of the retrieved information matches the topic of the request [12]. Subjective relevance is user-centric and deals with fitness for use of the retrieved information [29]. Subjective relevance involves intellectual interpretation by human assessors or users [5] and should be seen as a cognitive, dynamic process involving interaction between the information user and the information source. A general high-level relevance criterion is whether or not (and alternatively how much) the particular document contributes to the saturation of user's information need expressed by a query presented to the system at the beginning of search session. Different inquirers might be satisfied with different response to the same question. Among the most important factors having impact on the user request is long and short term context of the particular inquirer. When evaluating a search expression, the knowledge of user's area of interest, abilities, language capabilities, current needs, etc., can be important contribution to the search efficiency improvement. These are among the most fundamental reasons for personalized search research, user modeling and user profiling.

7.2.1   Information Retrieval Models

An *IR model* is a formal background defining internal document representation, query language and document-query matching mechanism. Consequently, the model determines document indexing procedure, result ordering and other aspects of particular information retrieval system. In the following, we will present two influential IR models – Boolean IR model and vector space IR model [7, 16].

7.2.1.1   Boolean IR Model

Boolean IR model belongs to the oldest but till nowadays widely used information retrieval models [2, 7]. It is based on set theory, Boolean logic and exact document-query match principle. The name Boolean comes from the fact that the query language uses as search expressions Boolean logic formulas composed of search terms and standard Boolean operators AND, OR and NOT [2]. The documents are represented as sets of indexed terms. The document indexing procedure distinguishes only whether a term is contained in the document or not and assigns to the term indexing weight 1 if the term is existed in the document or 0 if not. The inner representation of a documentary collection is a binary matrix composed of document representing vectors with term weights as coordinates. Therefore every column represents weight of certain term in all documents in the whole collection. Formally, an index of documentary collection containing n terms and m documents in Boolean IR model is described as shown in Eqs. 7.1 and 7.2, where d_i represents i^{th} document, t_{ij} the weight of jth term in i^{th} document and D denotes the index matrix.

$$d_i = (t_{i1}, t_{i2}, \ldots, t_{in}), \quad \forall t_{ij} \in \{0, 1\} \tag{7.1}$$

$$D = \begin{pmatrix} t_{11} & t_{12} & \cdots & t_{1n} \\ t_{21} & t_{22} & \cdots & t_{2n} \\ \vdots & \vdots & & \vdots \\ t_{m1} & t_{m2} & \cdots & t_{mn} \end{pmatrix} \tag{7.2}$$

The document-query matching procedure is based on the exact match principle. Only documents utterly satisfying all conditions stated by particular search query are considered to be relevant and thus retrieved in response to the query. When a document fully conforms to the search request, the query is against it evaluated, according to the Boolean algebra rules, as true. In the contrary case, when the document is in conflict with at least one of the clauses in the search request, the query is evaluated as false. In that way, the set of all documents in the collection is divided into two disjunctive subsets – retrieved and non-retrieved documents. There is no consideration of different degrees of document-query relevancy. All retrieved documents are supposed to be equally (fully) relevant to the query and all non-relevant documents are expected to be equally non-relevant. The ordering, in which are the results presented to the user, does not depend on the relevancy but on other factors such as date of last modification, document length, number of citations and so on [2, 7, 11]. There are numerous variations of basic Boolean IR model. Frequent modification relies on addition of advanced query operators – XOR implementing the logical exclusive OR operation, operator OF simplifying the notion of search formulas or, among others, operator NEAR expressing the requirement to retrieve documents having several terms near each other [11].

Apparently, the greatest advantage of Boolean IR model lies in exuberance and flexibility of its query language, allowing expressing very sophisticated and complex search requirements. On the other hand, to formulate such powerful search queries appropriately, the user should have at least minimal knowledge of Boolean algebra. Remarkable disadvantage of Boolean IR model is the crisp differentiation of documentary collection in response to query and therefore impossibility to use some relevance ranking technique to present retrieved documents sorted in relevance order. Because of this, a too restrictive query could cause denial of useful documents and contrariwise a too general query might retrieve additional non-relevant documents [15]. The Boolean IR model provides the basis for extended Boolean IR model introducing the principles of fuzzy set techniques and fuzzy logic to the area of information retrieval.

7.2.1.2 Vector Space Model

Vector space model (VSM) is based on interpretation of both, documents and queries, as points in a multidimensional document space [7, 11]. The dimension of the document space is given by the number of indexed terms in the documentary collection. Every term in every document assigned a weight representing the coordinate in multidimensional space. The weight is based on the importance of corresponding term in the document and in the scope of whole collection respectively. Greater weight means greater importance of particular term [2, 7, 16]. Formal description of VSM is almost identical to the description of Boolean model as provided in Eqs. 7.1 and 7.2. The domain of t_{ij} in VSM is the set of real numbers R. Query q is formalized as a vector of searched terms as shown in Eq. 7.3.

$$q = (t_{q1}, t_{q2}, \ldots, t_{qn}), \quad \forall t_{qj} \in R \qquad (7.3)$$

In Boolean IR, indexing procedure was due to the simplicity of internal document representation trivial task. In VSM, the matrix representing documentary collection composed of real values – the weights of terms in documents. The weight assessment can be done manually (this is too expensive and inefficient) or automatically [11]. Several automatic indexing approaches were proposed. They assign real weights to the terms in documents. The weighting algorithms are usually based on statistical distribution of the terms in particular document with respect to their distribution among all documents in the collection. Among the most popular and widely deployed indexing techniques takes significant place Gerard Salton's $TFIDF_t$ introduced in [26]. Consider normalised term frequency of term t in document d shown in Eq. 7.4 as the ratio of frequency of each term in the document to the maximum term frequency in that document. Therefore, the greatest frequency of particular term in the document, the greatest normalized frequency of such term in the document.

$$f_{dt} = \frac{freq(t, d)}{\max(freq(t_i, d))} \qquad (7.4)$$

Normalized inverse document frequency, defined as shown in Eq. 7.5, reflects the distribution of given term among all documents in the collection where, N is the number of all documents in the collection, N_t is number of documents containing at least one occurrence of the term t and g is some normalizing function. The rarer is the term in the scope of whole collection, the greater is its inverse document frequency. Finally, the weight of term t in document d according to $TFIDF_t$ is defined in Eq. 7.6.

$$IDF_t = g \left(\log \frac{N}{N_t} \right) \qquad (7.5)$$

$$F(d, t) = f_{dt} \cdot IDF_t \qquad (7.6)$$

Summarizing previous definitions, high weight will be assessed to the terms frequent in given document and rare in the scope of whole collection. It is obvious that such terms are good significant marks distinguishing current document from other documents. More indexing functions for VSM can be found, i.e., in [11]. Also queries have in VSM the form of documents (term vectors) and a term weighting function should be deployed. Query term weighting function example is shown in Eq. 7.7.

$$F(q,t) = \left(\frac{1}{2} + \frac{f_{qt}}{2}\right) \tag{7.7}$$

The document-query matching procedure in VSM based on best match principle. Both, document and query are interpreted as points in multidimensional space and we can evaluate similarity between them. Several formulas expressing numerically the similarity between points in the document space have been introduced [11]. Among the most popular are scalar product as shown in Eq. 7.8, and cosine measure as shown in Eq. 7.9 that can be interpreted as an angle between the query vector and document vector in m-dimensional document space.

$$Sim(q, d_i) = \sum_{j=1}^{m} t_{qj} \cdot t_{ij} \tag{7.8}$$

$$Sim(q, d_i) = \frac{\sum_{j=1}^{m} t_{qj} \cdot t_{ij}}{\sqrt{\sum_{j=1}^{m} t_{qj}^2 \cdot \sum_{j=1}^{m} t_{ij}^2}} \tag{7.9}$$

The similarity measure does not directly predicate document's relevance to the query. It is supposed that among documents similar to the query should be many relevant documents whereas among dissimilar documents is only few relevant ones [11]. Querying is in VSM based on the best match principle. All documents are during the query evaluation process sorted according their distance to the query and presented to the user. Omitting the vague relationship between point distance and document relevance, we can consider this ordering as relevance ranking.

VSM is more recent and advanced than Boolean IR model. Its great advantage lies in relevance based ordering of retrieved documents allowing easy deployment of advanced IR techniques such as document clustering, relevance feedback, query reformulation and topic evolution among others. Disadvantages are vague relationship between relevance and similarity and unclear query term explication. From the interpretation of query as a searched document prescription originates another significant disadvantage of VSM – the query language allows specifying only what should be searched and there are no natural means how to point out what should not be contained in retrieved documents.

7.2.2 IR Effectiveness Evaluation

When evaluating an information retrieval system, we are interested in the speed of search processing, user comfort, the possibilities of querying, result presentation and especially in the ability of *retrieving relevant documents*. As it was already noted, the concept of relevance is vague and uncertain. Though, it is useful to measure

IR effectiveness by the means of query-document relevance. Precision P and recall R are among the most used IR effectiveness measures as shown in Eq. 7.10. In the precision and recall definition, REL stands for the set of all relevant documents and RET for the set of all retrieved documents. Precision can be then understood as the probability of retrieved document to be relevant and recall as the probability of retrieving relevant document. For easier effectiveness evaluation were developed measures combining precision and recall into one scalar value. Among most popular of these measures are effectiveness E and F-score F [19] as shown in Eq. 7.11.

$$P = \frac{|REL \cap RET|}{|RET|} \quad R = \frac{|REL \cap RET|}{|REL|} \tag{7.10}$$

$$E = 1 - \frac{2}{\frac{1}{P} + \frac{1}{R}} \quad F = 1 - E = \frac{2PR}{P + R} \tag{7.11}$$

7.2.3   User Profiles in IR Systems

In previous section was shown that the concept of document-query relevance is highly subjective matter. Information need of particular user can be satisfied better if there are some knowledge about user specific needs, abilities, long and short term context. That is the field of personalized IR systems exploiting user profiles. A user profile (or user model) is a stored knowledge about particular user. Simple profile consists usually of keywords describing user's area of long time interest. Extended profile is replenished with information about the user such as name, location, mother tongue and so on. Advanced user profiles contain rather than set of keywords a list of queries characterizing user's behavior and habits [24].

User profile can be exploited to make the search task more personalized. Information retrieval system equipped with user profiles could utilize user-specific information from the profile for retrieving documents satisfying stated query with special respect to individual user, her or his preferences, needs, abilities, history, knowledge and context. User profile information might be evaluated when improving search process. Keywords from the profile can be used for query extension, query reformulation and for other techniques such as for improving search results. Such IR improvement techniques aim at retrieving information that satisfy users needs rather than information that was explicitly ask by potentially imprecise query [11]. User profile can be also exploited for document re-ranking according to individual preferences [24]. Advanced user profiles can instead of a set of keywords contain whole search expressions allocating areas of users long term interests and needs. Those queries are called persistent queries [9].

Explicit profiles, created by users or system administrators, are imprecise, not flexible enough and they do not reflect dynamic changes of user preferences. Instead, various techniques for automated creation and maintenance of user profiles are being investigated [6]. Automatically created and updated user profiles are referred as implicit user profiles. From the perspective of user profiling, IR systems can be divided into two categories: personalized IR systems providing personalized search services and consensual search system not aware of individual users [10].

7.2.3.1 Click-Through Data

Among the most promising methods, personalization techniques based on click-through data analysis attract attention [13, 30]. Click-through data recorded during web search activities might be seen as triplet (q, R, C) consisting of query q, ordered set of retrieved documents R and set of clicks C denoting documents user picked from the set of retrieved documents R, introducing individual search preferences [13].

The appeal of click-through data analysis for user profiling is based on several facts. It is omnipresent during web browsing click-through data is present in the web browsing activities always. The clicks are needed by the very essential structure of html documents and the WWW.

Click-through data is implicit user clicks are almost necessary to browse the web. Click-through data gathering must not be seen as an additional disturbing or obstructing activity. The clicks (or alternative link-following actions) are necessary to work with web. Additionally, click-through data has relevance feedback potential. The users click on links that he or she feels as relevant to his or her needs. Mostly, these links relevant by belief are really relevant to previous request although the essential information contained in click-through data is still under investigation.

Click-through is up-to-date and with appropriate analysis, the data gathered for sufficient time period could provide information on both, users long time interests and needs and immediate contemporary context. Finally, click-through data stored in query logs which can be used for many methods of information retrieval improvement, including offline techniques. Summarizing, most users click on rather relevant results and we should benefit from a large quantity of query logs. Experiments show that about 82% of the queries are in fact related to the topics of the clicked Web pages [31].

On the other hand, there are known issues with click-through data [13, 30]: it is usually noisy and rather incomplete piece of evidence about users relevance assessments. It is sparse since user clicks can cover only very small portion of WWW document space.

Click-through data collecting can be done on the top of current search systems and services. There could be a server based solution, observing user click behaviour from some central point like web application used as proxy for access to search services or client based solution tracking user clicks from, i.e., web browser. The web application is limited by its scope and as soon as the user leaves the application, the clicks are almost unrecordable. The client application is limited by the abilities of user workstations; the accommodation of such application must not be disturbing, i.e., it must not consume too much processor time, memory or disc space.

7.2.3.2 Document Relevance Estimation Based on Click-Through Data

Document relevance estimation model based on click-through data consists of recorded clicks committed by particular user. Each click c is captured a triplet (u, d, t), where $u \in U$ is particular user from the set of all users $U, d \in D$ is the clicked document and t is timestamp, describing moment in which the click was committed. $D = \{(u, n, s)\}$ is set of all documents known to the application. Consider $c_t : D \times U \to R^n$ as a set of timestamps describing clicks issued by particular user on certain document. For each document and user, the relevance $r : D \times U \to R$ is estimated by Eq. 7.12.

$$r(u, d) = \sum_{t \in c_t(u,d)} (f(t)) \qquad (7.12)$$

In the above, the function f enumerates the contribution of click issued at time t to relevance estimate of the document and t denotes age of the click. The contribution function used in this paper is reversed asymmetric sigmoid as defined in Eq. 7.13.

$$f(t) = 1 - \frac{1}{\left(1 + e^{\frac{t + c \cdot ln(2^{\frac{1}{g}} - 1) - b}{c}}\right)^g} \qquad (7.13)$$

Asymmetric reverse sigmoid as defined in Eq. 7.13 is highly customizable function. The parameter b denotes centre of the transition, c and g are used for enumeration of transition width w as specified in Eq. 7.14.

$$w = \left| c \cdot ln \left(4^{\frac{1}{g}} - 1\right) - c \cdot ln \left(4^{\frac{1}{g}} 3^{\frac{-1}{g}} - 1\right) \right| \qquad (7.14)$$

Figure 7.3 illustrates the reverse asymmetric sigmoid with $b = 5$, $c = -2$ and $g = 10$. The x axis unit is day and the transition width is 3.256. The scale of x axis in presented work is subject of further customization and it is variable parameter for different deployment cases of presented method.

Additionally, user model contains recorded recent user queries to be exploited later during query optimization process as an initial population for optimizing genetic algorithm.

7.3 Evolutionary Computation

Evolutionary algorithms (EAs) belongs to a family of iterative stochastic search and optimization methods based on mimicking successful optimization strategies observed in nature [3, 8, 14, 20]. The essence of EAs lies in the emulation of Darwinian evolution utilizing the concepts of Mendelian inheritance for the use in computer

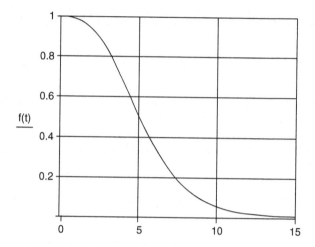

Fig. 7.3 Click contribution according to its age using reverse asymmetric sigmoid

science and applications [3]. Together with fuzzy sets, neural networks and fractals, evolutionary algorithms are among the fundamental members of the class of soft computing methods.

EAs operate with population (also known as pool) of artificial individuals (referred often as items or chromosomes) encoding possible problem solutions. Encoded individuals are evaluated using objective function which assigns a fitness value to each individual. Fitness value represents the quality (ranking) of each individual as solution of given problem. Competing individuals search the problem domain towards optimal solution [14]. In the following sections will be introduced general principles common for all methods belonging to the class of evolutionary algorithms.

7.3.1 Evolutionary Search Process

For the purpose of EAs, a proper encoding representing solutions of given problem as encoded chromosomes suitable for evolutionary search process, is necessary. Finding proper encoding is non-trivial problem dependent task affecting the performance and results of evolutionary search while solving given problem. The solutions might be encoded into binary strings, real vectors or more complex, often tree-like, hierarchical structures, depending on the needs of particular application.

The iterative phase of evolutionary search process starts with an initial population of individuals that can be generated randomly or seeded with potentially good solutions. Artificial evolution consists of iterative application of genetic operators, introducing to the algorithm evolutionary principles such as inheritance, survival of the fittest and random perturbations. Current population of problem solutions is modified with the aim to form new and hopefully better population to be used in next generation. Iterative evolution of problem solutions ends after satisfying specified termination criteria and especially the criterion of finding optimal solution. After terminating the search process, evolution winner is decoded and presented as the most optimal solution found.

7.3.2 Genetic Operators

Genetic operators and termination criteria are the most influential parameters of every evolutionary algorithm. All bellow presented operators have several implementations performing differently in various application areas. Selection operator is used for selecting chromosomes from population. Through this operator, selection pressure is applied on the population of solutions with the aim to pick more promising solutions to form following generation. Selected chromosomes are usually called parents. Crossover operator modifies the selected chromosomes from one population to the next by exchanging one or more of their subparts. Crossover is used for emulating sexual reproduction of diploid organisms with the aim to inherit and increase the good properties of parents for offspring chromosomes. Mutation operator introduces random perturbation in chromosome structure; it is used for changing chromosomes randomly and introducing new genetic material into the population.

Besides genetic operators, termination criteria are important factor affecting the search process. Widely used termination criteria are, i.e.:

- Reaching optimal solution (which is often hard, if not impossible, to recognize)
- Processing certain number of generations
- Processing certain number of generations without improvement in population

EAs are successful general adaptable concept with good results in many areas. The class of evolutionary techniques consists of more particular algorithms having numerous variants, forged and tuned for specific problem domains. The family of evolutionary algorithms consists of genetic algorithms, genetic programming, evolutionary strategies and evolutionary programming.

7.3.3 Genetic Algorithms

Genetic Algorithms (GA) introduced by John Holland and extended by David Goldberg are wide applied and highly successful EA variant. Basic workflow of original (standard) generational GA (GGA) is (see also Fig. 7.4):

```
1. Define objective function
2. Encode initial population of possible solutions as
   fixed length binary strings and evaluate
   chromosomes in initial population using objective
   function
```

Fig. 7.4 Iterative phase
of genetic algorithm

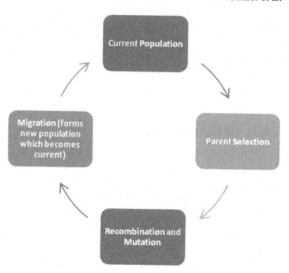

3. Create new population (evolutionary search for
   better solutions)
   a. Select suitable chromosomes for reproduction
      (parents)
   b. Apply crossover operator on parents with
      respect to crossover probability to produce
      new chromosomes (known as offspring)
   c. Apply mutation operator on offspring
      chromosomes with respect to mutation
      probability. Add newly constituted chromosomes
      to new population
   d. Until the size of new population is smaller
      than size of current population go back to (a).
   e. Replace current population by new population
4. Evaluate current population using objective
   function
5. Check termination criteria; if not satisfied go
   back to (3).

Many variants of standard generational GA have been proposed. The differences
are mostly in particular selection, crossover, mutation and replacement strategy [14].
Different high-level approach is represented by steady-state Genetic Algorithms
(SSGA). In GGA, in one iteration is replaced whole population [8] or fundamental part of population [28] while SSGA replace only few individuals at time and
never whole population. This method is more accurate model of what happens in the
nature and allows exploiting promising individuals as soon as they are created. However, no evidence that SSGA are fundamentally better than GGA was found [28].

7.3.4   Genetic Programming

Genetic Programming by John Koza is referred as special case [28] or an extension [18] to GA. Encoded individuals (chromosomes) have hierarchical structure, unlimited size and they are often modeled as tree structures. So can be modeled mathematical formulas, logical expressions or even whole computer programs (i.e., Lisp programs). Genetic programming is a native tool for modeling and artificial evolution of search queries.

7.4   Evolutionary Techniques and Fuzzy Logic Principles in IRS

Fuzzy theory, as a framework describing formally the concepts of vagueness, imprecision, uncertainty and inconsistency provide interesting extensions to the area of information retrieval. Imprecision and vagueness are present in natural language and take part in real-world human communication. User friendly and flexible advanced IRS should be able to offer user interface for non experienced users allowing natural deployment of these concepts in user-system interaction for more effective information retrieval.

IR models exploiting fuzzy techniques can overcome some of the limitations pointed out in first part of this chapter [15]. They support different grades of document-query relevance, cut inaccuracies and oversimplifications happening during document indexing and introduce the concepts of vagueness and imprecision in query language.

7.4.1   Genetic Algorithms in Information Retrieval

Multiple works have been recently published in the area of IR and search query optimization as this topic becomes increasingly challenging. The use of various evolutionary algorithms was proposed at multiple stages of the information retrieval process. Fan et al. [9] introduced genetic ranking function discovery framework. Nyongesa and Maleki-dizaji [21] used evolutionary interactive evolutionary learning for user modeling.

Yeh et al. [32] described in 2007 a genetic programming for IR ranking function discovery and introduced a set of numerical experiments demonstrating the contribution of proposed method to IR efficiency. Yeh et al. innovatively combined different types of evidences including classical IR content features, structure features, and query independent features to the ranking function.

Several contributions towards evolutionary optimization of search queries were introduced. Kraft et al. [15] used genetic programming to optimize Boolean search queries over a documentary database with an emphasis on the comparison of several

IR effectiveness measures as objective functions. Cordón et al. [6] introduced MOGA-P, an algorithm to deal with search query optimization as a multi-objective optimization problem and compared their approach with several other methods including Kraft's. Yoshioka and Haraguchi [33] introduced query reformulation interface to transform Boolean search queries into more efficient search expressions.

In one of the recent contributions to evolutionary query optimization, A. Aly [1] introduced a genetic algorithm for vector query reformulation based on vector space model of an IR system. The method is based on evolutionary learning of significant terms from search results to modify user queries. Snášel, Nyongesa et al. [27] used similar approach to learn user profiles in IRS based on click-through data and search engine expertness profiling.

This work aims to evaluate evolutionary learning of Boolean search queries in both, traditional crisp Information Retrieval frameworks and advanced fuzzy Information Retrieval systems.

7.4.2 Fuzzy Principles in Information Retrieval

Fuzzy concepts affect most phases of IR process. They are deployed during document indexing, query formulation and search request evaluation. Information retrieval is seen as fuzzy multi-criteria decision making in the presence of vagueness. In general, document is interpreted as a fuzzy set of document descriptors and queries as a composite of soft search constraints to be applied on documents. Document-query evaluation process is based on fuzzy ranking of the documents in documentary collection according to the level of their conformity to the soft search criteria specified via user queries. The document-query matching has to deal with the uncertainty arising from the nature of fuzzy decision making and from the fact that user information needs can be recognized, interpreted and understood only partially. Moreover, the document content is described only in a rough, imperfect way [4].

In the fuzzy enabled IR frameworks, soft search criteria could be specified using linguistic variables. User search queries can contain elements declaring level of partial importance of the search statement elements. Linguistic variables such as "probably" or "it is possible that", can be used to declare the partial preference about the truth of the stated information. The interpretation of linguistic variables is then among the key phases of query evaluation process. Term relevance is considered as a gradual (vague) concept. The decision process performed by the query evaluation mechanism computes the degree of satisfaction of the query by the representation of each document. This degree, called Retrieval Status Value (RSV), is considered as an estimate of the relevance of the document with respect to the query. $RSV = 1$ corresponds to maximum relevance and $RSV = 0$ denotes no relevance. The values within the range $(0, 1)$ correspond to particular level of document relevance between the two extremes 0 and 1 [4].

Possibility theory together with the concept of linguistic variable defined within fuzzy set theory provides a unifying formal framework to formalize the processing of imperfect information [4]. Inaccurate information is inevitably present in information retrieval systems and textual databases applications. The automatically created document representation based on a selection of index terms is invariably incomplete and far worse than document representations created manually by human experts who utilize their subjective theme knowledge when performing the indexing task. Automated text indexing deals with imprecision since the terms are not all fully significant to characterise the document content and their statistical distribution does not reflect their relevance to the information included in the document necessarily. Their significance depends also on the context in which they appear and on the unique personality of the inquirer. During query formulation, users might have only a vague idea of the information they are looking for therefore face difficulties when formulating their information needs by the means of query language of particular IR system. A flexible IRS should be designed to provide detailed and rich representation of documents, sensibly interpret and evaluate soft queries and hence offer efficient information retrieval service in the conditions of vagueness and imprecision [4].

In the next section, Extended Boolean IR model as the representative of fuzzy IR models will be discussed in details. Some other recent fuzzy IR models will be briefly presented.

7.4.3 Extended Boolean IR Model

Fuzzy generalizations of the Boolean model have been defined to extend existing Boolean IRSs without the need to redesign them. Classic Boolean model of IR represents documents as sets of indexed terms. Therefore we can for every term say whether it belongs to the set representing the document (then a weight 1 is assigned to the term for the particular document representation) or not (a weight 0 is assigned). The term weight is either 0 or 1 and multiple occurrences of the term in the document do not affect its internal representation.

Extended Boolean model of IR is based on fuzzy set theory and fuzzy logic. Documents are interpreted as fuzzy sets of indexed terms, assigning to every term contained in the document particular weight from the range of [0, 1] expressing the degree of significance of the term for document representation. Hence documents are modeled more accurately than in classic Boolean IR model. Formal collection description in extended Boolean IR model is shown in Eqs. 7.15 and 7.16.

$$d_i = (t_{i1}, t_{i2}, \ldots, t_{in}), \quad \forall t_{ij} \in \{0, 1\} \tag{7.15}$$

$$D = \begin{pmatrix} t_{11} & t_{12} & \cdots & t_{1n} \\ t_{21} & t_{22} & \cdots & t_{2n} \\ \vdots & \vdots & & \vdots \\ t_{m1} & t_{m2} & \cdots & t_{mn} \end{pmatrix} \tag{7.16}$$

Next new feature of extended Boolean IR model is fuzzy extension of query language aiming at providing apparatus to express more flexible and accurate search requests. Two techniques are being used for query enhancement query term weighting using numeric weights or linguistic variables and Boolean conjunction parameterization for expressing relationships among the extremes of AND, OR, NOT, etc. [15]. Choosing appropriate indexing procedure is essential for exploitation of extended Boolean IR model benefits. Internal documentary collection model should be as accurate as possible snapshot of the collection of textual documents in natural language and at the same time a basis for efficient and practical search. Fuzzy indexing function is defined as shown in Eq. 7.17, where D stands for the set of all documents and T for set of all indexed terms.

$$F : D \times T \to [0, 1] \tag{7.17}$$

Kraft in [15] used Salton's $TFIDF_t$ indexing formula introduced for VSM as textual document indexing mechanism in extended Boolean IR model. Query language is in extended Boolean model of IR upgraded by the possibility of weighting query terms in order to express different importance of those in search request and by weighting (parameterizing) aggregation operators to soften or blur their impact on query evaluation [7, 16]. Consider Q to be the set of user queries over a collection then the weight of term t in query q is denoted as $a(q, t)$ satisfying $a : Q \times T \to [0, 1]$. To evaluate atomic query of one term, stating therefore only one search criterion, will be used function $g : [0, 1] \times [0, 1] \to [0, 1]$. The value of $q(F(q, t), a)$ is called retrieval status value (RSV). For RSV enumeration is crucial the interpretation of query term weight a. The most used interpretations are to see query term weight as importance weight, threshold or ideal document description [7, 16]. The theorems for RSV evaluation in the case of importance weight interpretation and threshold interpretation are shown in Eqs. 7.18 and 7.19 respectively [7, 16], where $P(a)$ and $Q(a)$ are coefficients used for tuning the threshold curve. An example of $P(a)$ and $Q(a)$ could be as follows: $P(a) = \frac{1+a}{2}$ and $Q(a) = \frac{1+a^2}{4}$. The RSV formula in Eq. 7.19 is illustrated in Fig. 7.5a. Adopting the threshold interpretation, an atomic query containing term t of the weight a is a request to retrieve documents having $F(d, t)$ equal or greater to a. For documents satisfying this condition will be rated with high RSV and contrariwise documents having $F(d, t)$ smaller than a will be rated with small RSV.

$$RSV = \begin{cases} \min(a, F(d, t)) & \text{if t is operand of OR} \\ \max(1 - a, F(d, t)) & \text{if t is operand of AND} \end{cases} \tag{7.18}$$

$$RSV = \begin{cases} P(a) \frac{F(d,t)}{a} & \text{pro } F(d, t) < a \\ P(a) + Q(a) \frac{F(d,t)-a}{1-a} & \text{pro } F(d, t) \geq a \end{cases} \tag{7.19}$$

Query term weight a can be understood as ideal document term weight prescription. In that case, RSV will be evaluated according to Eq. 7.20, enumerating the distance between $F(d, t)$ and a in a symmetric manner as shown in Fig. 7.5b. This

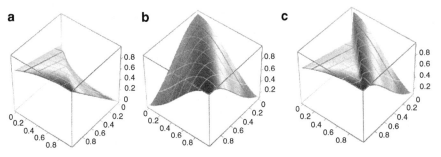

Fig. 7.5 Graphic representation of the three RSV functions. (**a**) PR-landscape for Eq. 7.19 (**b**) PR-landscape for Eq. 7.20 (**c**) PR-landscape for Eq. 7.21

means that a document with lower term weight will be rated with the same RSV as document with higher term weight, considering the same differences. Asymmetric version of Eq. 7.20 is shown in Eq. 7.21 and illustrated in Fig. 7.5c.

$$RSV = e^{K \cdot (F(d,t)-a)^2} \tag{7.20}$$

$$RSV = \begin{cases} e^{K \cdot (F(d,t)-a)^2} & \text{pro } F(d,t) < a \\ P(a) + Q(a)\frac{F(d,t)-a}{1-a} & \text{pro } F(d,t) \ge a \end{cases} \tag{7.21}$$

Single weighted term is basic element of fuzzified Boolean query. Aggregation operators concatenating query elements into more flexible and powerful search expressions might be weighted as well. The operator weight interpretation is another key part of fuzzy Boolean query evaluation. In general, various T-norm and T-conorm pairs might be used for fuzzy generalization of AND and OR operators while evaluating NOT as fuzzy complement. Operator weights are in these cases handled in the same manner as query term weight achieving higher flexibility and expressiveness of search expressions. Nevertheless, such approach does not reduce the complexity of Boolean logic needed to use the queries efficiently [16]. Alternatively, new definitions of aggregation operators for fuzzy queries have been introduced. Vague relationship among selection criteria is expressed using linguistic quantifiers such as all, most of, at least n, introducing blurred behaviour between AND and OR and allowing easier query formulation [7, 16].

7.4.4   Fuzzy IR Effectiveness Evaluation

When evaluating effectiveness of an IR system, precision and recall are among the most popular performance measures serving as a basis for numerous derived indicators such as effectiveness E or F-score F. For the enumeration of precision and recall in the framework of fuzzy IR systems cannot be used crisp precision and recall as specified in Eq. 7.10. New definitions were proposed on the basis of Zadehs cardinality (see Eq. 7.22; the function $\mu_A(x)$ assigns to every item x its fuzzy weight in fuzzy set A) as shown in Eqs. 7.23 and 7.24 [17].

$$card(A) = \|A\| = \sum_{x \in A} \mu_A(x) \tag{7.22}$$

$$\rho(X|Y) = \begin{cases} \frac{\|X \cap Y\|}{\|Y\|} & \|Y\| \neq 0 \\ 1 & \|Y\| = 0 \end{cases} \tag{7.23}$$

$$P = \rho(REL|RET) \text{ and } R = \rho(RET|REL) \tag{7.24}$$

7.5 Experimental Evaluation

This section describes computational experiments performed in order to validate presented search improvement and user modeling techniques. First, the experiments on Genetic Programming for query optimization will be presented Second, an online experiment comparing the efficiency of web search with and without query optimization and user profiling will be introduced.

7.5.1 Offline Query Optimization Experiments

A series of computer experiments was conducted in order to evaluate proposed GP enabled IR framework in both, crisp Boolean IR model and fuzzified Extended Boolean IR model [22, 23, 25, 27]. Experiments were executed using data taken from the LISA[1] collection. The collection was indexed for both Boolean IR and Extended Boolean IR systems, using Salton's indexing function based on normalized term frequency and normalized inverse document frequency in the latter case. Indexed collection contained 5999 documents and 18442 unique indexed terms.

Genetic Programming was used to evolve Boolean search queries. Boolean expressions were parsed and encoded into tree like chromosomes (see Fig. 7.6). Genetic operators were applied on nodes of the tree chromosomes. Several parameters were fixed for all experiments:

- Mutation probability $= 0.2$
- Crossover probability $= 0.8$
- Maximum number of generations $= 1000$
- Population of 70 individuals (queries)

We have used two scenarios for initial population. In the first case, all queries in initial population were generated randomly. In the second scenario, three better

---

[1] Available at: http://www.dcs.gla.ac.uk/idom/ir_resources/test_collections/

Fig. 7.6 Search query
(w₃ and w₄) xor ((w₅ and w₆)
or not w₈) encoded for GP

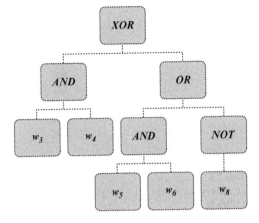

Table 7.1 Summary for experiments results

IR model	User query	Initial population enhancement
BIRM	(("EXTREMELY" AND "POOR") OR "FUNDS")	"FUNDS" OR "BIBLIOGRAPHIC" "EXTREMELY" AND "INNOVATORS" NOT ("POOR" XOR "FUNDS")
EBIRM	(("EXTREMELY":0.94 AND "POOR":0.50) OR:0.50 "FUNDS":0.90)	"FUNDS":0.9 OR "BIBLIOGRAPHIC":0.8 "EXTREMELY":0.3 AND "INNOVATORS" NOT ("POOR" XOR:0.03 "FUNDS":0.5)

ranked queries, created by the experiment administrators, were added to the initial population. Two selection strategies were investigated: elitary selection choosing parents among the best ranked individuals and probabilistic selection implementing the roulette wheel selection algorithm. Two mutation strategies were under investigation. Single point mutation performs random perturbation of one gene (i.e., one node) of the query chromosome and each point mutation attempts to apply mutation operator on every gene in the chromosome. Mutation is implemented as replacement of the node by an equivalent. This means that OR might be replaced by XOR and AND. NOT operator might be inserted or removed.

A user query was used to mark documents in the collection with some relevance degree. The user query (or its equivalent) represents in laboratory conditions desired output of the optimization algorithm. The experiments were conducted in crisp and fuzzy laboratory Information Retrieval framework. The crisp IR framework was marked as Boolean Information Retrieval Model (BIRM) and the fuzzy IR framework was denoted as Extended Boolean Information Retrieval Model (EBIRM). Due to the stochastic character of GP process, all experiments were executed several times and mean experimental results evaluated.

Table 7.1 lists the user query and better ranked queries injected into initial population in some experiments.

Tables 7.2 and 7.3 summarize the experimental results obtained for different scenarios. Experiments are labeled with the following flags: single point mutation **I**,

Table 7.2 Summary of experimental results in BIRM

Scenario	Precision	Recall	F-score
REI	0.04699	0.089552	0.0486915
REC	0.040411	0.11194	0.0621065
RPI	0.064519	0.074627	0.069205
RPC	0.053471	0.119403	0.0689775
SEI	1	0.985075	0.992481
SEC	1	0.985075	0.992481
SPI	1	0.985075	0.992481
SPC	1	0.985075	0.992481

Table 7.3 Summary of experimental results in EBIRM

Scenario	Precision	Recall	F-score
REI	0.078706	0.027165	0.04039
REC	0.078706	0.027165	0.04039
RPI	0.0765365	0.0760845	0.0754315
RPC	0.163975	0.0389625	0.060813
SEI	0.9933375	0.9045225	0.9454495
SEC	0.993873	0.968469	0.9810005
SPI	0.9138465	0.9696315	0.940731
SPC	0.9965815	0.968436	0.9823045

each point mutation **C**, elitism **E**, probabilistic selection **P**, seeded queries **S** and random initial population **R**. The results were taken as an average for fitness values for precision, recall and F-score.

From the experiments with Boolean queries we conclude the following results: Genetic Programming succeeded in optimization of Boolean and extended Boolean search queries. Crucial for the optimization process was the quality of initial population. For successful optimization, initial population must contain at least some quality queries pointing to documents related to user needs. This fact was especially significant when optimizing extended queries with weighted terms and operators. Weight assessment rapidly increases search domain of the problem.

F-score fitness was preferred as a measure combining precision and recall into one value by the means of information retrieval and therefore simplifying query optimization from multi-objective to a single-objective task. Figures 7.7–7.12 illustrate the improvements of F-score, *Precision* and *Recall* of the optimized queries in different experimental cases. Figures 7.13 and 7.14 respectively show the significant differences of optimization results when using random initial population and seeded initial population.

7.5.2 Online Experiments

To evaluate proposed user modeling method and search optimization technique, a set of experiments comparing search experience in different cases with and

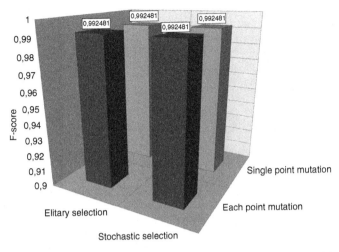

Fig. 7.7 The comparison of achieved F-score for different algorithm setups in BIRM with seeded initial population

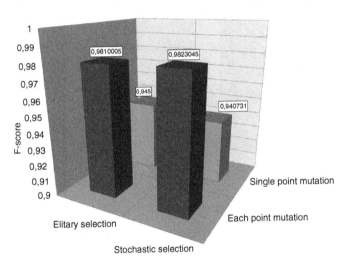

Fig. 7.8 The comparison of achieved F-score for different algorithm setups in EBIRM with seeded initial population

without query optimization support was designed and performed. Number of emitted queries, average click rate and length of mouse trajectory created before retrieving satisfactory information were traced as an objective measure of the efficiency of search task.

Intentionally, user queries were during experiments constructed from simple to more complex. In order to create initial user profile for optimized search, the participants performed common search activities focused on evolutionary algorithms

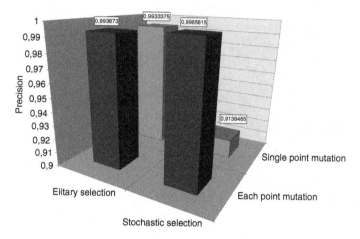

Fig. 7.9 The comparison of achieved precision for different algorithm setups in EBIRM with seeded initial population

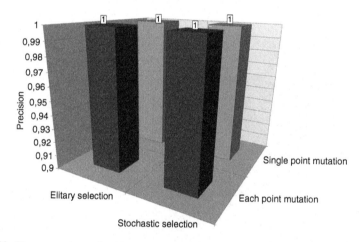

Fig. 7.10 The comparison of achieved precision for different algorithm setups in BIRM with seeded initial population

and optimization techniques. The resulting profile snapshot contained 1,044 terms in 120 documents and 25 queries such as:

- "genetic" AND "algorithm"
- "genetic" AND "operator"
- "dynamic" AND "optimization"
- "dynamic" AND "optimization" AND "task" AND NOT "dbm"

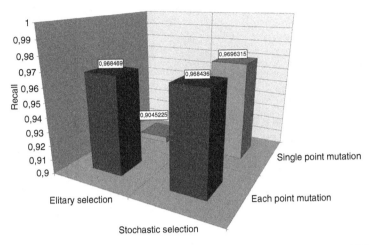

Fig. 7.11 The comparison of achieved recall for different algorithm setups in EBIRM with seeded initial population

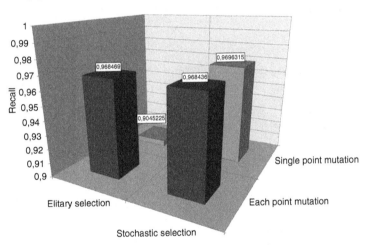

Fig. 7.12 The comparison of achieved recall for different algorithm setups in BIRM with seeded initial population

7.5.2.1 Online Experiments and Discussion

In the first experiment summarized in Table 7.4, the desired information should describe known evolutionary techniques for dynamic optimization problems which was searched during profiling phase. The submitted user query was

- "genetic" AND "algorithm"

In the first online experiment, the optimization process managed to modify query towards previously observed area of interest and the same document was retrieved

V. Snášel et al.

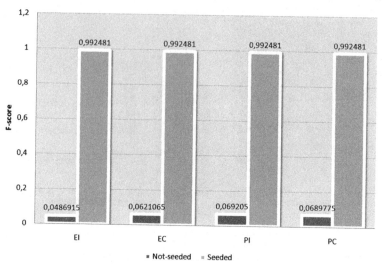

Fig. 7.13 The comparison of achieved F-score for used algorithm setups with seeded (S) and random (R) initial population in BIRM

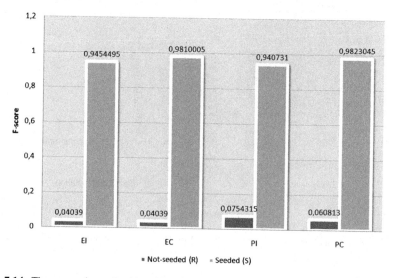

Fig. 7.14 The comparison of achieved F-score for used algorithm setups with seeded (S) and random (R) initial population in EBIRM

Table 7.4 Summary of first online experiment

Criterion	Search type	
	Non-optimized	Optimized
No. of queries	4	1
No. of clicks	55	7
Mouse trajectory [m]	12	1,8

Table 7.5 Summary
of second online experiment

Criterion	Search type	
	Non-optimized	Optimized
No. of queries	5	2
No. of clicks	22	14
Mouse trajectory [m]	4,6	2,20

Table 7.6 Summary of third
online experiment

Criterion	Search type	
	Non-optimized	Optimized
No. of queries	4	4
No. of clicks	92	104
Mouse trajectory [m]	14,44	17,21

in just one step. This was an expected result since the user profile was created when searching for exactly this information. Optimized search discovered the same document as un-optimized.

Second online experiment, as shown in Table 7.5, features search for new information from the same area, adaptive optimization via genetic programming. The submitted user queries were

- "adaptive" AND "optimization"
- "adaptive" AND "optimization" AND "genetic"

When searching information from an area covered by the user model, the optimization process helps to retrieve satisfactory information in fewer steps than non-optimized search. Different search types retrieved different documents but both documents were by the inquirer accepted as satisfactory.

The third online experiment covers situation when the searched information belongs to different area than the one captured by the user profile. The searched information is weather forecast for Ostrava, Czech Republic with aim to daylight period. The submitted queries were:

- "weather" AND "daylight"
- "weather" AND "daylight" AND "Ostrava"
- "weather" AND "daylight" AND "Ostrava" AND "year"
- "daylight" AND "Ostrava"

In the third online experiment, there was no improvement observed. The same number of queries was issued and the number of clicks and mouse trajectory were slightly higher for optimized search. This means, that when the search aims out of the known web region, the optimization process brings no benefits.

The performed experiments suggest that the method is able to improve (speed up) search in the areas covered by the user profile (Tables 7.4 and 7.5). It is not able to improve search process when aiming to totally new area of interest, however in real-life deployment; the application would be able to learn from every submitted query while in presented set of experiments the profile was constant (Table 7.6).

7.6 Conclusion

The area of information retrieval faces today enormous challenges. The information society in the age of Internet excels in producing huge amounts of data and it is often complicated to retrieve information retrieved in such data sources. Decades ago, sophisticated techniques and algorithms forming information retrieval systems were designed to handle document collections available at that time. Information retrieval systems have gone over an intensive evolution to satisfy increasing needs of growing data bases. In their mature form, they are still present in the heart of Internet search engines, one of the key communication hubs of our society.

Internet search allows exploitation of large amount of knowledge available in the ubiquitous multitude of data. Information search is one of the most important e-activities. The IR systems, despite their advanced features, need revision and improvement in order to achieve better performance and provide inquirer with more satisfactory answers. Aiming to achieve better performance, more flexible models and techniques are requested. Fuzzy set framework has been proved as suitable formalism for modeling and handling vagueness and imprecision, the hot topics of information retrieval. Numerous researches considering various applications of fuzzy set technology have been initiated and conducted, some recent summarized in this chapter. The deployment of fuzzy techniques in all phases of IR has brought improvement of IR results and therefore increases user satisfaction. Lotfi Zadeh once called fuzzy technology computing with words. Information retrieval performs real world computation with words for decades. The symbiosis of these two progressive areas promises exciting results for the coming years.

Evolutionary techniques are an excellent tool to extract non-explicit information from data. Their unique ability to estimate, evolve and improve can be used to model Internet search user. Implicit data, such as the click-stream, produced during the web browsing activities could be exploited to keep track of the preferences of every single user. Such model is accurate, flexible, and can be well exploited for query optimization. Simultaneous deployment of fuzzy set techniques for better document modeling and genetic algorithms for query optimization brings a significant contribution to the ultimate goal of web search: bringing knowledge to man.

References

1. Abdelmgeid A. Aly. Applying genetic algorithm in query improvement problem. *Int. Journal on Information Technologies and Knowledge*, 1(12):pp. 309–316, 2007.
2. Nicholas J. Belkin and W. Bruce Croft. Information filtering and information retrieval: two sides of the same coin? *Communications of the ACM*, 35(12):pp. 29–38, December 1992.
3. Ulrich Bodenhofer. *Genetic Algorithms: Theory and Applications*. Lecture notes, Fuzzy Logic Laboratorium Linz-Hagenberg, Winter 2003/2004.
4. Gloria Bordogna and Gabriella Pasi. Modeling vagueness in information retrieval. pages 207–241, 2001.
5. Pia Borlund and Peter Ingwersen. Measures of relative relevance and ranked half-life: performance indicators for interactive IR. In *SIGIR'98*, pages 324–331, Melbourne, Australia, August 1998.

6. Oscar Cordón, Félix de Moya, and Carmen Zarco. Fuzzy logic and multiobjective evolutionary algorithms as soft computing tools for persistent query learning in text retrieval environments. In *IEEE International Conference on Fuzzy Systems 2004*, pages 571–576, Budapest, Hungary, 2004.

7. Fabio Crestani and Gabriella Pasi. Soft information retrieval: Applications of fuzzy set theory and neural networks. In N. Kasabov and R. Kozma, editors, *Neuro-Fuzzy Techniques for Intelligent Information Systems*, pages 287–315. Springer Verlag, Heidelberg, DE, 1999.

8. Mehrdad Dianati, Insop Song, and Mark Treiber. An introduction to genetic algorithms and evolution strategies. Technical report, University of Waterloo, Ontario, N2L 3G1, Canada, July 2002.

9. Weiguo Fan, Michael D. Gordon, and Praveen Pathak. A generic ranking function discovery framework by genetic programming for information retrieval. *Inf. Process. Manage*, 40(4):pp. 587–602, 2004.

10. Weiguo Fan, Michael D. Gordon, Praveen Pathak, Wensi Xi, and Edward A. Fox. Ranking function optimization for effective web search by genetic programming: An empirical study. In *HICSS*, 2004.

11. E. Greengrass. *Information retrieval: A survey*. DOD Technical Report TR-R52-008-001, 2001.

12. Stephen P. Harter. Psychological relevance and information science. *JASIS*, 43(9):602–615, 1992.

13. Thorsten Joachims. Optimizing search engines using clickthrough data. In *Proceedings of the ACM Conference on Knowledge Discovery and Data Mining (KDD)*. ACM, 2002.

14. Gareth Jones. Genetic and evolutionary algorithms. In Paul von Rague, editor, *Encyclopedia of Computational Chemistry*. John Wiley and Sons, 1998.

15. D. H. Kraft, F. E. Petry, B. P. Buckles, and T. Sadasivan. Genetic Algorithms for Query Optimization in Information Retrieval: Relevance Feedback. In E. Sanchez, T. Shibata, and L.A. Zadeh, editors, *Genetic Algorithms and Fuzzy Logic Systems*, Singapore, 1997. World Scientific.

16. Donald H. Kraft, Gloria Bordogna, and Gabriella Pasi. Fuzzy set techniques in information retrieval. In J. C. Bezdek, D. Didier, and H. Prade, editors, *Fuzzy Sets in Approximate Reasoning and Information Systems*, volume 3 of *The Handbook of Fuzzy Sets Series*, pages 469–500, MA, 1999. Kluwer Academic Publishers.

17. Henrik L. Larsen. Retrieval evaluation. In *Modern Information Retrieval course*. Aalborg University Esbjerg, 2004.

18. Gondy Leroy, Ann M. Lally, and Hsinchun Chen. The use of dynamic contexts to improve casual internet searching. *ACM Transactions on Information Systems*, 21(3):pp. 229–253, 2003.

19. Robert M. Losee. When information retrieval measures agree about the relative quality of document rankings. *Journal of the American Society of Information Science*, 51(9):pp. 834–840, 2000.

20. Melanie Mitchell. *An Introduction to Genetic Algorithms*. MIT Press, Cambridge, MA, 1996.

21. H. O. Nyongesa and S. Maleki-Dizaji. User modeling using evolutionary interactive reinforcement learning. *Inf. Retr.*, 9(3):343–355, 2006.

22. Suhail Owais, Pavel Kromer, Vaclav Snasel, Dusan Husek, and Roman Neruda. Implementing GP on optimizing both boolean and extended boolean queries in IR and fuzzy IR systems with respect to the users profiles. In Gary G. Yen, Lipo Wang, Piero Bonissone, and Simon M. Lucas, editors, *Proceedings of the 2006 IEEE Congress on Evolutionary Computation*, pages 5648–5654, Vancouver, BC, Canada, 6–21 July 2006. IEEE Computer Society.

23. Suhail S. J. Owais, Pavel Krömer, and Václav Snášel. Evolutionary Learning of Boolean Queries by Genetic Programming. In Johann Eder, Hele-Mai Haav, Ahto Kalja, and Jaan Penjam, editors, *ADBIS Research Communications*, volume 152 of *CEUR Workshop Proceedings*, pages 54–65. CEUR-WS.org, 2005.

24. Suhail S. J. Owais, Pavel Krömer, and Václav Snášel. Query Optimization by Genetic Algorithms. In Karel Richta, Václav Snášel, and Jaroslav Pokorný, editors, *DATESO*, volume 129 of *CEUR Workshop Proceedings*, pages 125–137. CEUR-WS.org, 2005.

25. Suhail S. J. Owais, Pavel Krömer, and Václav Snášel. Implementing gp on optimizing boolean and extended boolean queries in irs with respect to users profiles. In H. M. A. Fahmy, A. M. Salem, M. W. El-Kharashi, and A. M. B. El-Din, editors, *Proceedings of the 2006 International Conference on Computer Engineering & Systems (ICCES06)*, pages 412–417, Cairo, Egypt, November 2006. IEEE Computer Society. ISBN: 1-4244-0272-7.

26. Gerard Salton and Chris Buckley. Term-weighting approaches in automatic text retrieval. *Information Processing and Management*, 24(5):pp. 513–523, 1988.

27. Václav Snášel, Pavel Krömer, Suhail S. J. Owais, Henry O. Nyongesa, and S. Maleki-Dizaji. Evolving web search expressions. In *Third International Conference on Natural Computation (ICNC'07)*, volume 4, pages 532 – 538, Haikou, Hainan, China, August 2007. IEEE Computer Society Press. ISBN: 0-7695-2875-9, IEEE CS Order Number: P2875, Library of Congress: 2007926988.

28. H. A. R. Townsend. *Genetic Algorithms - A Tutorial*, 2003.

29. P. Vakkari and N Hakala. Changes in relevance criteria and problem stages in task performance. *Journal of Documentation*, 5(56):540562, 2000.

30. Gui-Rong Xue, Hua-Jun Zeng, Zheng Chen, Yong Yu, Wei-Ying Ma, WenSi Xi, and WeiGuo Fan. Optimizing web search using web click-through data. In *CIKM '04: Proceedings of the thirteenth ACM international conference on Information and knowledge management*, pages 118–126, New York, NY, USA, 2004. ACM Press.

31. R. R. Yager. On ordered weighted averaging aggregation operators in multicriteria decision-making. In D. Dubois, H. Prade, and R. R. Yager, editors, *Readings in Fuzzy Sets for Intelligent Systems*, pages 80–87. Kaufmann, San Mateo, CA, 1993.

32. Jen-Yuan Yeh, Jung-Yi Lin, Hao-Ren Ke, and Wei-Pang Yang. Learning to rank for information retrieval using genetic programming. In *SIGIR*, 2007.

33. Masaharu Yoshioka and Makoto Haraguchi. An Appropriate Boolean Query Reformulation Interface for Information Retrieval Based on Adaptive Generalization. In *WIRI*, pages 145–150, 2005.

Chapter 8
Human–Web Interactions

Peter Géczy, Noriaki Izumi, Shotaro Akaho, and Kôiti Hasida

Abstract Investigation of human behavior in electronic environments is rapidly gaining eminent position in web research. The driving forces of this endeavor originate from both commercial and scientific spheres. The commercial sector is eagerly exploring the human web behavior characteristics for amplifying and expanding the revenue generating possibilities. Novel trends in web development, as well as internet business models, unavoidably incorporate the elements of human–web interactions. The scientific inquiry into human web behavior is fundamentally oriented toward exploring, analyzing, understanding, modeling, and applying the findings.

Early conceptions of human web behavior essentially assumed a random nature of human actions. The recent findings, however, revealed that human behavior in electronic environments exhibits bursts of activity followed by longer inactivity periods. This is being attributed to the conceptual prioritization of cognitive processes. We tend to divide our web interactions into segments of tasks having varying complexities. The presented perspective on the human–web interactions reflects this fundamental nature of our web behavior. The segmentation of human web interactions enables us to observe and elucidate several pertinent behavioral aspects. We can observe how users form elemental and complex browsing patterns, how their behavior habituates, and how they utilize the web navigation space. Human web navigation displays significant long tail characteristics in all analyzed topological aspects. A novel model that accurately captures it has been presented. Results of human–web interaction research have been applied to advanced systems improving our experience in web environments.

Future web will be increasingly user-conscious and user-centered. The human–web interaction research will play a primary role in this endeavor. Engineering challenges for the future web will lead to numerous scientific and commercial opportunities. Communities of academics and practitioners will greatly benefit from the human web behavior findings. Reaching the future potentials and ambitious goals, however, will demand broader interdisciplinary orientation and collaboration.

P. Géczy (✉), N. Izumi, S. Akaho, and K. Hasida
National Institute of Advanced Industrial Science and Technology (AIST),
2-3-26 Aomi Koto-ku, Tokyo 135-0064, Japan

R. Chbeir et al., *Emergent Web Intelligence: Advanced Information Retrieval*, Advanced
Information and Knowledge Processing, DOI 10.1007/978-1-84996-074-8_8,
© Springer-Verlag London Limited 2010

8.1 Introduction

World wide web has evolved during the past few decades into a global medium. The early web was predominantly static [1]. Information was presented via hypertext documents that were formatted using a set of predefined elements. Users were mainly passive receivers of displayed information.

More recently, web has become significantly more interactive. Dynamically generated documents, animations, vector graphics, rich internet applications, and other technologies have become common in web design. The new interactive technologies enrich user experiences and enable two-way interaction: human↔web.

The relative novelty of the web as a major world wide interaction medium presents numerous research opportunities and challenges. It also highlights an enormous commercial potential. Emergent web research and intelligence substantially benefits from observation, analysis, and deeper understanding of human web behavior. The evolution of the world wide web itself will inevitably adopt the findings from human–web interaction research.

Study of human–web interactions has been attracting significant attention from both academic and corporate spheres [2, 3]. The academics and researchers attempt to capture the underlying behavioral aspects, whereas the corporate sector aims at utilizing the findings in revenue generating opportunities of web-based e-commerce [4–7].

How can we, humans, interact with the web environment? Our interactions are largely determined by the modalities encompassed by the most commonly used input/output devices: display, keyboard, and mouse (with exception of some mobile devices that have touch-based interfaces instead of mouse-like ones). Novel devices may expand the interaction modes and enrich our interactive experiences in future digital environments.

What is the interaction-enabling mechanism of the web? The high-level perspective of the underlying mechanism is relatively straightforward. Encoded web document is rendered by a browser and shown on a display. The document may contain elements ranging from text to multimedia. The elements may permit one-way or two-way interactions. Within the document are embedded links to other documents and resources. Users can access these resources by preforming simple actions.

The prevailing human web behavior appears to be relatively simple. A user visits a web page containing information and links to other resources. After browsing throughout the information displayed on the page, a user decides on a follow-up resource – usually indicated by a hyperlink. Clicking on the hyperlink, the following resource is displayed. It may again contain hyperlinks to other resources. In this manner, the noticeable interaction pattern emerges: document display → click → document display → click → document display, and so on. It is often called a *click stream* (see Fig. 8.1). The seemingly simple click stream contains rich information about users' browsing patterns and habits. Its analysis provides vital knowledge for building advanced applications enhancing our web experience.

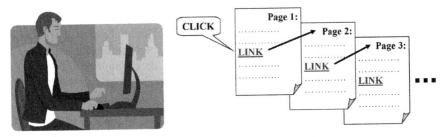

Fig. 8.1 Common users access the web environment via computers and/or mobile devices. The major interaction pattern reflects progression from the display of one page to the next. The transitions between pages are often initiated by actions – such as clicks – on the emphasized links

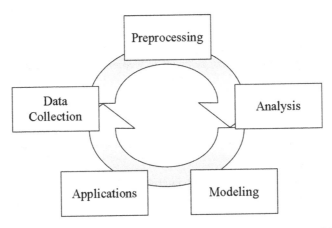

Fig. 8.2   Illustration of a single loop in progressive spiral of research on human–web interactions

8.1.1   *Elucidation of Human–Web Interactions*

Research on human–web interactions spans across several domains: data collection, preprocessing, analysis, modeling, and application of findings. These domains form a loop in a progressive research spiral – illustrated in Fig. 8.2.

Data Collection Acquiring reliable data on human–web interactions is the first step. The data acquisition methods may range from behavioral observations to automated non-invasive techniques. Each method has its advantages and disadvantages. Different data collection methods are suitable for different elucidation purposes. General trend in human web behavior research gravitates toward the automated non-invasive methods. The interaction data is collected automatically, in the background, without disturbing or restricting users. These methods often allow on-the-fly data processing.

Preprocessing Acquired data on human–web interactions is often contaminated. It contains elements or artifacts unsuitable for analytic purposes. Preprocessing of the acquired data is often required prior to the analysis. Preprocessing removes undesirable data components and/or artifacts that would affect the analysis. It also reduces the data volume. This is particularly beneficial in online data processing. Automated data collection techniques often generate substantial data volumes. Reducing the data volume helps to maintain efficiency in the subsequent processing stages.

Analysis Preprocessed and cleaned human–web interaction data is used for analysis. At the beginning of the analysis, the click stream sequences of user web navigation are reconstructed. The sequences are often long and contain interactions detected during the extensive time periods. For analytic purposes, it is desirable to observe shorter temporal segments of interactions. The long click streams are divided into smaller parts according to user activity and inactivity. The smaller activity segments, and their interrelations, are variously analyzed for individual users and/or groups.

Modeling Analytically observed features of human–web interactions are vital for creating viable models of human behavior in web environments. The models may encompass various aspects of human navigation and browsing characteristics. The modeling of human–web interactions generally targets verification of underlying behavioral aspects, or validation of concepts and algorithms for applications. Complexity and accuracy of models depend on the objectives. Deeper behavioral features require more complex models, whereas practical applicability demands computational efficiency.

Applications Findings in human–web interaction research are extensively utilized in numerous application domains; for instance: recommender systems, collaborative filtering engines, and personalization systems. Knowledge of users' browsing and behavioral characteristics helps to personalize the browsing experiences. Recommender systems provide suggestions to web users on various items of potential interest (ranging from search results to commercial goods). Collaborative filtering engines leverage similarities between 'like-minded/behaved' users.

In the following sections we look closer on these essential areas of human–web interaction research and provide a concise overview of our recent achievements. Data Collection and Preprocessing sections do not require formalisms. The formal approach is adopted from the Analysis section and utilized in the remaining sections.

8.2 Data Collection

Human–web interaction data can be collected by various methods. Generally, we can distinguish two classes of approaches: invasive and non-invasive. The former approaches introduce an invasive factor when acquiring the data. The latter approaches are transparent to users.

Methods in invasive data acquisition category utilize for example eye tracking devices [8, 9], or surveys and protocols [10, 11]. The eye tracking devices are capable of monitoring the user eye movement during the browsing experiences.

By superimposing the recorded eye movement data on the image displayed on the screen one can obtain a reasonable account of what a user has been looking at on a web page. Eye tracking approaches are useful when evaluating visual impression of elements displayed on the page. However, they are usually confined to controlled laboratory environments.

Surveys and protocol based studies collect data by administering surveys, questionnaires, interviews, and evaluation protocols to users. They can be administered prior to the browsing experiences, during the browsing, and/or after the browsing tasks. Administration can be done by humans or automated agents – adaptively modifying tests for self-administration by users [12]. Combinations of human observer, third-party ratings, and software agents have also been explored [13]. These behavioral approaches can acquire valuable data about the browsing experience that is otherwise unobtainable. Unfortunately, they are time and resource consuming.

The invasive techniques, although valuable, have either one or more of the following limiting issues: they can be perceived as disruptive (e.g., during browsing), they are difficult to perform on a large scale, and do not provide data for online processing. The interactive web applications, utilizing human behavioral data, require that data collection techniques be transparent to users during browsing, largely scalable, and provide data immediately for further processing. These properties are more practically important, event though the collected data might not be as feature rich and detailed.

The automated non-invasive data acquisition methods can be classified, depending on where the data is actually collected, as: client-side or server-side. The former collects data directly from user's computer via which he/she accesses the web. The latter collects data at the server serving the web documents.

Client-side data collection requires a code executable on user's computer. This is usually a script embedded in a web document the user accesses. When a user requests a web document from the server, the server sends to user both a web document and a script. The web document is rendered by a browser and the script is executed locally on the client. The script collects desired data and sends it to the specified data collection server that may store it in a database. The mechanism is illustrated in Fig. 8.3 (down).

Client-side data acquisition has both advantages and disadvantages. The major advantages include more accurate data collection, and less data loss. The main disadvantage is the requirement of enabled scripting. If the scripts are disabled (either globally or just for the specific site serving the script; or data collection server is otherwise blocked by the client) the mechanism simply does not work. [Note there may be other methods such as programs running directly on the client, or modules loaded in a browser that perform similar tasks.]

Server-side data collection functions as follows. Whenever client requests any document or resource from the web server, the transaction record is stored into files generated directly by the server. These files are called web log files, or simply web logs. The web server can store various kinds of log files – depending on the setup (e.g., access logs, error logs, script logs, rewrite logs, etc.). Intuitive illustration of this mechanism is presented in Fig. 8.3 (up).

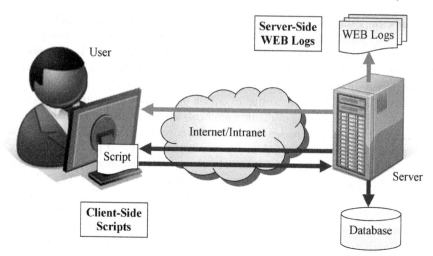

Fig. 8.3 Illustration of server-side and client-side data collection techniques. *Server-side:* whenever a user requests a document from the server, the server records the request in a web log file. *Client-side:* document requested by a user contains a script executed on user's computer that collects data and sends it to a database server. The database server can be different from the web server

Server-side data acquisition is more robust in a sense that it does not impose any additional requirements on the users' end. It works independently of the setup on the client side. Any requests arriving to the server are directly recorded by the server itself. The disadvantage of the server-side data acquisition approach is a partial data loss primarily due to caching and proxing.

Proxy server acts as an intermediary between a client and a web server. It collects the requests from multiple clients and forwards them to the servers. Hence the web server records the requests arriving from the proxy server rather than from the individual clients. Cache is a storage of duplicate data. It is usually implemented on both: a browser and a proxy server. It stores documents or resources already fetched by the server, or the ones likely to be requested – so-called pre-fetching. When a client requests a document that is already cached, it is served directly from the cache and not by the web server. This way, the server does not receive the request for the document and thus dose not generate the record in a log file.

8.3   Case Study: Data and Intranet Portal

This study uses server-side web log data. Server web logs contain records in a specified format. Format of log records is configurable. Administrator of a web server can choose which information should be recorded, in which order, and which log files should be generated. Following is an example of an access log recorded by Apache web server in combined log format.

```
127.0.0.1 - Peter [8/May/2008:20:55:36 +0700]
"GET /picture.gif HTTP/1.0" 200 1234
"http://www.example.com/start.html"
"Mozilla/5.0 (Linux; en-US) Firefox/2.0.0.14"
```

The log record contains several fields providing useful information about the request to the web server. Below is a concise description of individual fields:

127.0.0.1
IP address of the client from which the request originated.

-
Remote logname: not available – indicated by the 'hyphen'.

Peter
Identification of user requesting the document.

[8/May/2008:20:55:36 +0700]
Date and time stamp (with time zone at the end).

GET /picture.gif HTTP/1.0
Request line. It indicates that the request method used by the client was *GET*, the requested resource was */picture.gif*, and the used protocol was *HTTP/1.0*.

200
The status code sent by the server to the client (200 indicates a successful response).

1234
The size of the object returned to the client.

http://www.example.com/start.html
Referrer: the resource that the client reports having been referred from.

Mozilla/5.0 (Linux; en-US) Firefox/2.0.0.14
Client's browser identification (together with operating system and language).

Our web log data contained records accumulated during a 1 year period. The log records were in the combined format descried earlier. The records, however, did not include remote logname, user identification, and referrer information. The data was voluminous and spread across several thousand files. Each file held records of specific web server during 24 h period. A concise description of data is presented in Table 8.1.

The data was collected at the intranet portal of The National Institute of Advanced Industrial Science and Technology. The organizational portal has

Table 8.1 Information about web log data and intranet portal

Data volume	∼60 GB
Average daily volume	∼54 MB
Number of web servers	6
Number of log files	6,814
Average file size	∼9 MB
User population	∼10,000
Collection period	1 year

approximately ten thousand users. The majority of users are skilled knowledge workers. The users range from administrative and technical staff, to researchers and managers.

The intranet web portal has a load balancing architecture comprising of six servers providing extensive range of web services and documents vital to the organization. Intranet services supported managerial, administrative, and accounting processes (e.g., attendance verification, resource localization and utilization, search, etc.). The portal incorporates numerous databases (e.g., research achievements) and provides a bridge for research cooperation with industry and other institutes. It also hosts bulletin boards and other local networking platforms.

The institution has a number of branches at various locations throughout the country, thus certain services are decentralized. The size of visible web space was over 1 GB. Invisible web space was considerably larger, but difficult to estimate due to the distributed architecture and constantly changing back-end data.

Daily traffic was substantial and so was the data volume. It is important to note that the data was incomplete. Although some days were completely represented, every month there were missing logs from specific servers. Server side logs also suffered data loss due to caching and proxing. However, the missing data was estimated to be marginal in comparison to the overall volume.

8.4 Preprocessing

The initial preprocessing step was data fusion. Recall that the organizational intranet portal was served by six load balanced servers. Thus the clients' requests were distributed among the six servers depending on availability (and other conditions). Each web server generated its own records of served requests. The web logs from individual servers contained only a part of the overall traffic. Reconstruction of the complete image of portal traffic required proper fusion of log records from log files of individual web servers. The web log data was appropriately fused with respect to the temporal information and clients' IP addresses.

The portal traffic was both human and machine generated. The web servers do not distinguish between human and machine requests. They record every arrived and served request. The web log data was largely contaminated by records originating from automatic monitoring agents. Automatic monitors, verifying the responsiveness of the servers (and other aspects of the intranet portal), generated large number of log records that had to be filtered.

Additional cleaning of web log data was also performed. The data contained invalid requests to intranet resources (using various protocols and ports). These records were eliminated. There were also log records related to web graphics (in all major formats), cascading style sheets used for document formatting, and embedded client-side scripts uploaded to users' machines. These were removed as well.

All the other log records were preserved. The records encompassed wide ranging activity of human users in the web based intranet portal environment. Among them

Table 8.2 Essential data
statistics after preprocessing

Log records	315,005,952
Clean log records	126,483,295
Unique IP addresses	22,077
Unique URLs	3,015,848
Scripts	2,855,549
HTML documents	35,532
PDF documents	33,305
DOC documents	4,385
Others	87,077

were, for instance, accessed static pages as well as dynamically generated ones, used services, and retrieved syndicated resources. The interactions also included download of documents in various formats (e.g., PDF, DOC, XLS, PPT, etc.). The overall recorded scope of human–web interaction was relatively rich.

The cleaned server-side web log records were parsed for individual information fields and their derivatives. The extracted information included client IP address, complete URL, base URL, parameters passed via URL, date-time stamp, source identification, and several basic statistics. The obtained information was suitably structured and logged into a database. The database consisted of several tables appropriately linked. Database tables were further indexed and optimized for speedy data retrieval. Basic information summary of web log data after preprocessing is presented in Table 8.2.

Approximately 40.15% of the original log records remained after the preprocessing and cleaning (see Table 8.2). Significant portion of raw web log data (almost 60%) was not relevant to human–web interactions. Major access to intranet resources was via scripts (94.68%). Only relatively minor portions of accessible resources were static HTML documents (1.18%), PDF documents (1.1%), DOC documents (0.15%), and others (2.89%), such as downloadable software, updates, spreadsheets, syndicated resources, etc. Observed IP address space (22077 unique IPs) consisted of both statically and dynamically assigned IP addresses. Smaller portion of IP addresses were static, and relatively uniquely associable with users. Extensive use of dynamic addressing (DHCP) contributed to the larger portion of the IP address space. The detected number of the unique IP addresses proportionally corresponded to the number of users.

8.5   Analysis

Exploration of human interactions in web environments requires establishment of an analytic framework. The framework should effectively capture spatio-temporal dimensions of human–web interactions. It should have a broad analytic reach and a suitable depth. It must be extensible, and should deliver an actionable knowledge for wider spectrum of researchers and practitioners.

We start with a formalization of an analytic framework for exploration and modeling of human web behavior. The framework utilizes finer temporal segmentation of navigational sequences. It permits identification of the essential navigation points and behavioral abstractions. Furthermore, it enables observation elemental and complex browsing pattern formation. A detailed exploratory analysis of knowledge worker browsing behavior is presented. It highlights crucial behavioral features of users and usability aspects of the studied large organizational web portal.

The analytic framework is further expanded in the application section. The application domain necessitates closer observations of multitudes of short-range and long-range navigational pathways. Higher order browsing abstractions and identified navigation points are suitably utilized for the expansion. The extended construct is employed for derivation of an efficient and scalable algorithm that assists users during their navigation in web environments.

8.5.1 Analytic Framework Formulation

Recent elucidation of temporal dynamics of human behavior in electronic environments revealed various significant attributes [14]. The individual human actions appear to be strongly inhomogeneous. The temporal dynamics of human interactions in web environments exhibit periods of activity followed by longer periods of inactivity [15]. Individuals execute certain tasks rapidly, whereas other tasks are completed after a substantial delay. The timing of the task execution is being considered to be perceptually prioritized [16].

Implying from the observed human temporal dynamics in web environments, it is appropriate to partition the human web interactions according to the detected delays. This leads to the segmentation of human browsing behavior into the finer elements: sessions and subsequences [17]. Click stream sequences of page transitions are divided into sessions, and sessions are further divided into subsequences (Fig. 8.4). The division is done with respect to the user activity and inactivity. Consider the conventional time-stamp click stream sequence of the following form: $\{(p_i, t_i)\}_i$, where p_i denotes the visited page URL_i at the time t_i. For the purpose of analysis this sequence is converted into the form: $\{(p_i, d_i)\}_i$ where d_i denotes a delay between the consecutive views $p_i \rightarrow p_{i+1}$. User browsing activity $\{(p_i, d_i)\}_i$ is divided into subelements according to the periods of inactivity d_i satisfying certain criteria.

Definition 8.1 (Session and Subsequence).
Let $\{(p_i, d_i)\}_i$ be a sequence of pages p_i associated with delays d_i between consecutive transitions $p_i \rightarrow p_{i+1}$.
Browsing session is a sequence $B = \{(p_i, d_i)\}_i$ where each $d_i \leq T_B$. The length of the browsing session is $|B|$.
Subsequence of an individual browsing session B is a sequence $Q = \{(p_i, d_i)\}_i$ where each delay $d_i \leq T_Q$, and $\{(p_i, d_i)\}_i \subset B$. The subsequence length is $|Q|$.

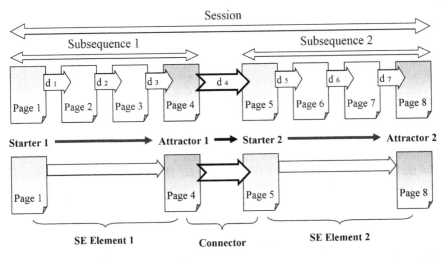

Fig. 8.4 Illustration of the navigational click stream segmentation. Navigation points and segments of click streams constitute the elements of the navigation space. Higher order abstractions of browsing behavior are represented by SE elements and connectors

The sessions correspond to the bursts of human activity in a web environment. These activity segments are followed by the longer inactivity delays. During the duration of a session users execute tasks of various complexities which can be further divided into the subtasks represented by the subsequences. Delays between the subsequences are shorter than the session delays. For instance, in a single session user logins into a system (subsequence 1), locates and downloads a document (subsequence 2), and performs a search for an internal resource (subsequence 3). Then leaves the web environment and carries out an offline task (e.g., fills in the downloaded document using information contained in the searched resource). Later on returns to the web environment, and in the following session locates and completes an online form, and uploads the created document. This relatively common example of a human interaction with a web environment consists of two session; the first having three subsequences, and the second only one.

Important issue is determining the appropriate values for delays T_B and T_Q that segment the user activity into sessions and subsequences. The former research [18] indicated that student browsing sessions last on average 25.5 min. However, we adopt the average maximum attention span of 1 h as a value for T_B. If the user's browsing activity was followed by a period of inactivity greater than 1 h, it is considered a single session, and the following activity comprises the next session.

Value of T_Q is determined dynamically and computed as an average delay in a browsing session: $T_Q = \frac{1}{N} \sum_{i=1}^{N} d_i$. If the delays between page views are short, it is useful to bound the value of T_Q from below. This is preferable in environments with frame-based and/or script generated pages where numerous logs are recorded in a rapid transition. Since our situation contained both cases, we adjusted the value of T_Q by bounding it from below by 30 s:

$$T_Q = max \left(30, \frac{1}{N} \sum_{i=1}^{N} d_i \right). \qquad (8.1)$$

Using the mentioned primitives we define navigation space and subspace as follows.

Definition 8.2 (Navigation Space and Subspace).
Navigation space is a triplet $\mathcal{G} = (\mathcal{P}, \mathcal{B}, \mathcal{Q})$ where $\mathcal{P}$ is a set of points (e.g., URLs), $\mathcal{B}$ is a set of browsing sessions, and $\mathcal{Q}$ is a set of subsequences.
Navigation subspace of $\mathcal{G}$ is a space $A = (D,H,K)$ where $D \subseteq \mathcal{P}$, $H \subseteq \mathcal{B}$, and $K \subseteq \mathcal{Q}$; denoted as $A \subseteq \mathcal{G}$.

The navigation space incorporates the navigation points and the temporal segments of logged sequences. It is often the case that web portals employ various automated monitoring tools, are scanned by web crawlers and spiders from search engines, and, unfortunately, frequently attacked by malicious software agents. All this traffic is recorded in logs. Thus the navigation space contains both human and machine generated traffic. It is practical to divide the navigation space into subspaces based on the nature of the traffic; for example, human navigation subspace and machine navigation subspace. Different spaces may have distinctively different topological and/or temporal characteristics. While human navigation subspace may be utilized for exploration of human dynamics, the machine navigation subspace may provide valuable information for defense against attackers. In the further text we primarily focus on the human navigation (sub)space.

Definition 8.3 (Starter, Attractor, Singleton).
Let $B = \{(Q_i, d_i)\}_i^M$ be a browsing session, and $Q_i = \{(p_{ik}, d_{ik})\}_k^N$ be its subsequence.
Starter is the point p_1 of the first pair element of subsequence Q_i or session B with length greater that 1. Set of starters is denoted as S.
Attractor is the point p_l of the last pair element of subsequence Q_i or session B with length greater that 1; $l \equiv N$ or $l \equiv M$. Set of attractors is denoted as A.
Singleton is a point p such that there exist a browsing session B or subsequence Q_i where $|B| = 1$ or $|Q_i| = 1$, and $(p, d) \in B$ or $(p, d) \in Q_i$. Set of singletons is denoted as Z.

The starters, attractors, and singletons encompass the particular navigation points. The starters are the initial points of subsequences and sessions. They represent the initial navigation elements of user actions. The attractors are the terminal points of subsequences and sessions and are regarded as the users' targets. Consider the following segment of browsing behavior. A user starts at the 'welcome' page, then follows the link to the 'announcements' page, and there he/she clicks on the 'security updates' link. After reading the latest security announcements, and determining that none of the listed issues apply to his/her system, user leaves the session. In this example the user initiated the session from the 'welcome' page and targeted the 'security updates'. Hence the starter is the 'welcome' page and the attractor is the 'security updates' page. Singletons relate to the single user actions such as use of hotlists (e.g., history or bookmarks) [19]. Note that a single point p can be starter, attractor, and/or singleton.

Definition 8.4 (SE Elements and Connectors).
Let $B = \{(Q_i, d_i)\}_i$ be a browsing session and Q_i, Q_{i+1} be consecutive subsequences $Q_i \rightarrow Q_{i+1}$ of B, $Q_i = \{(p_{ik}, dp_{ik})\}_k^N$, $Q_{i+1} = \{(p_{i+1l}, dp_{i+1l})\}_l^M$.
SE element (start-end) of a subsequence Q_i is a pair $SE_i = (p_{i1}, p_{iN})$.
Connector of subsequences Q_i and Q_{i+1} is a pair $C_i = (p_{iN}, p_{i+1,1})$.

The SE elements and connectors allow as to observe higher order abstractions of users' elemental and complex browsing patterns. The SE elements outline the abstractions of browsing subgoals. Using the example from the former paragraph, the SE element pair is ('welcome', 'security updates') pages. From the initial navigation point, users can follow various navigational pathways to reach the target. Focusing on the starting and ending points of user actions eliminates the variance of navigational choices. The connectors indicate the links between the elemental browsing patterns, thus enable us to elucidate formation of more complex behavioral patterns as interconnected sequences of the elemental patterns.

8.5.2 Navigation Space and Subspace Extraction

8.5.2.1 Session Extraction

Preprocessed and databased web logs did not contain referrer information. Temporal sequences were reconstructed by ordering the logs originating from the unique IP addresses according to the time-stamp information. Time differences between the consecutive logs constituted the delays between transitions. Ordered log sequences from the specific IP addresses were divided into the browsing sessions as described in Definition 8.1. Session divisor was the predetermined user inactivity period ds_i greater than $T_B = 1$ h.

It is noticeable (see Table 8.3) that user sessions on the corporate intranet were on average longer (approx. 48.5 min) than those of students (approx. 25.5 min) reported in [18]. Average number of 156 sessions per IP address, and large variation in the maximum and minimum numbers of sequences from distinct IP addresses, indicate that association of particular users with the distinct IP addresses is relevant only for registered static IP addresses.

Table 8.3 Observed basic session data statistics

Sessions	3,454,243
Unique sessions	2,704,067
Average sessions per day	9,464
Average session length	36 [transitions]
Average session duration	2,912.23 [s] (48 min 32 s)
Average dp_i delay per session	81.55 [s] (1 min 22 s)
Average sessions per IP address	156
Maximum	1,553
Minimum	1

8.5.2.2 Subsequence Extraction and Human Navigation Subspace

Recorded session sequences were analyzed for subsequences as specified in Definition 8.1. Segmentation of sessions into subsequences was according to the dynamically obtained value of the delay separator T_Q expressed in (8.1).

It has been observed that sessions contained machine generated subsequences. As seen in the histogram of average delays between subsequences (Fig. 8.5a), there was a disproportionally large number of sessions with average delays between subsequences around 30 min and 1 h. This is indicated by the spikes in Fig. 8.5a. Detailed view (see subcharts of Fig. 8.5a) revealed that the variation in the average delay between subsequences was approximately ±3 s. The observed temporal variation significantly correlates with the peak average subsequence duration (Fig. 8.5b). It is highly unlikely that human generated traffic would produce this precision.

The primary target of our investigation is the human navigation subspace. The machine generated traffic pollutes the data and should be filtered. We filtered two main groups of the machine generated subsequences: login subsequences and subsequences with the delay periodicity around 30 min and 1 h.

Every user is required to login into intranet in order to access the services and resources. The login procedure involves validation and generates several log records with 0 delays. The records vary depending on whether the login was successful or unsuccessful. In both cases the log records and the login related subsequences can be clearly identified and filtered.

The second group of machine generated traffic are the subsequences with periodicity of 30 min and 1 h. Direct way of identifying these subsequences is to search for the sessions with only two subsequences having less than 1 s (or 0 s) duration (machines can generate requests fast and local intranet servers are capable of responding within milliseconds) and delay ds_i between the subsequences within the intervals: 1,800 and 3,600 ± 3 s. It has been discovered that substantial number of such sessions contained relatively small number (170) of unique subsequences. Furthermore, these subsequences contained only 120 unique URLs. The identified subsequences and URLs were considered to be machine generated and filtered from further analysis. Moreover, the subsequences with SE elements containing the identified URLs were also filtered (Table 8.4).

Filtering of the detected machine generated subsequences and their URLs significantly reduced the total number of subsequences – by 56.97% (from

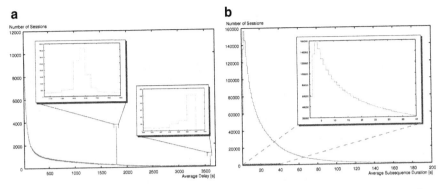

Fig. 8.5 Histograms: (**a**) average delay between subsequences in sessions, (**b**) average subsequence duration. There are noticeable spikes in chart (**a**) around 1,800 s (30 min) and 3,600 s (1 h). The detailed view is displayed in subcharts. Temporal variation of spikes is approximately 3 s. This well corresponds to the peak average subsequence duration displayed in chart (**b**). The spikes with relatively accurate delays between subsequences are due to the machine generated traffic

Table 8.4 Observed basic subsequence data statistics		
	Subsequences	7,335,577
	Valid subsequences	3,156,310
	Filtered subsequences	4,179,267
	Unique subsequences	3,547,170
	Unique valid subsequences	1,644,848
	Average subsequences per session	3
	Average subsequence length	4.52 [transitions]
	Average subsequence duration	30.68 [s]
	Average ds_i delay	388.46 [s] (6 min 28 s)

7,335,577 to 3,156,310), as well as the number of unique subsequences – by 46.37% (from 3,547,170 to 1,644,848). Since the login sequences were also filtered, the number of subsequences per session decreased at least by 1. Reduction also occurred in the session lengths due to the filtering of identified invalid URLs. The filtering did not significantly affect the duration of subsequences because the logs of machine generated subsequences occurred in rapid transitions with almost 0 durations and delays. It is noticeable that the average subsequence duration (30.68 s) is approximately equal to the chosen lower bound for ds_i (30 s).

8.5.3 Analysis of Human–Web Interactions

Extracted navigation space and subspace serve as a base for exploration of user browsing behavior. Its specific topological elements, together with the defined metrics, enable us to elucidate vital behavioral and usability characteristics. We start with the analysis of the principal navigation points and then proceed to the investigation of higher order abstractions. We infer relevant common and particular behavioral and usability attributes.

8.5.3.1 Starter, Attractor, and Singleton Analysis

The point characteristics of a navigation space highlight the initial and the terminal targets of knowledge worker activities, and also the single-action behaviors. It is evident that the knowledge worker navigation subspace is substantially smaller, in this respect, than the observed complete navigation space. Reduction of starters and attractors is approximately 67.4% (from 7,335,577 to 2,392,541), and singletons 57.56% (from 1,326,954 to 763,769). The unique valid sets of starters (115,770), attractors (288,075), and singletons (57,894) are very small in comparison to the set of unique URLs (3,015,848) in the navigation space (see Tables 8.2 and 8.5).

Knowledge workers utilized a small spectrum of starting navigation points and targeted relatively small number of resources during their browsing. The set of starters, i.e., the initial navigation points of knowledge workers' (sub-)goals, was approximately 3.84% of the total navigation points. Although the set of unique attractors, i.e., (sub-)goal targets, was approximately three times higher than the set of initial navigation points, it is still relatively minor portion (approx. 9.55% of unique URLs). Knowledge workers aimed at relatively few resources.

Few resources were perceived of value to be bookmarked. Number of unique single user actions was minuscule. Single actions, such as use of hotlists [19], followed by delays greater than 1 h are represented by the singletons. The unique singletons accounted for only 1.92% of navigation points. Small number of starters and/or attractors was perceived useful and bookmarked; then accessed directly in the following browsing experiences. Only about ten navigation points were found substantially useful by users to be included in their hotlists and recurrently accessed.

Knowledge workers had focused interests and exhibited minuscule exploratory behavior. A narrow spectrum of starters, attractors, and singletons was frequently used. Substantial segment of the navigation point set has been only occasionally accessed. The histograms and quantile characteristics of starters, attractors, and singletons (see Fig. 8.6) indicate that higher frequency of occurrences is concentrated to relatively small number of elements. Approximately ten starters and singletons, and fifty attractors were very frequent. The quantile analysis (Fig. 8.6) reveals that ten starters (approx. 0.0086% of the unique valid starters) and singletons (approx. 0.017% of the unique valid singletons), and fifty frequent attractors (approx. 0.017% of the unique valid attractors) accounted for about 20% of total occurrences.

Table 8.5 Statistics for starters, attractors, and singletons

	Starters	Attractors	Singletons
Total	7,335,577	7,335,577	1,326,954
Valid	2,392,541	2,392,541	763,769
Filtered	4,943,936	4,943,936	563,185
Unique	187,452	1,540,093	58,036
Unique valid	115,770	288,075	57,894

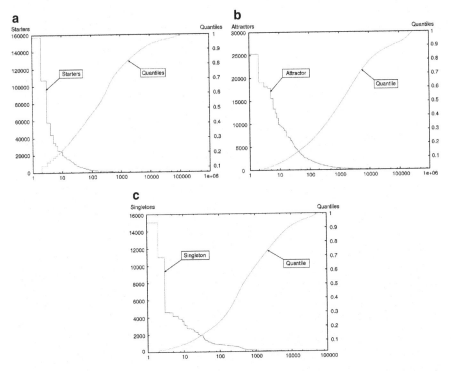

Fig. 8.6   Histograms and quantiles: (**a**) starters, (**b**) attractors, and (**c**) singletons. Right y-axis contains a quantile scale. X-axis is in a logarithmic scale

Knowledge workers were generally more familiar with the starting navigation points rather than the targets. In other words, they knew where to start and were familiar with the traversal path to the target (instead of just utilizing shortcuts such as bookmarks). Smaller number of starters repeats substantially more frequently than the adequate number of attractors. The starter–attractor ratio was around 1:10 (with respect to the comparable frequency of use). Approximately one hundred starters and one thousand attractors were relatively frequent. One hundred starters (approx. 0.086% of the unique valid starters) and one thousand attractors (approx. 0.35% of the unique valid attractors) constituted about 45% and 48% of total occurrences, respectively.

8.5.3.2   SE Element and Connector Analysis

These components signify higher order abstractions of user behavior. The SE elements represent the starting and the ending points of subsequences, or corresponding elemental patterns. The connectors delineate transitions between pattern primitives. Complex abstract browsing patterns are exposed as the sequences of SE elements interconnected by connectors.

Table 8.6 Statistics for SE elements and connectors

	SE elements	Connectors
Total	7,335,577	3,952,429
Valid	2,392,541	2,346,438
Filtered	4,943,936	1,605,991
Unique	1,540,093	1,142,700
Unique valid	1,072,340	898,896

Extraction of the SE elements of subsequences and the connectors between subsequences was relatively straightforward. The SE elements and connectors also undergone filtering based on the detected machine generated log records and associated URLs. If the invalid URL was present in at least one element of a pair, the respective SE element and/or connector was marked as invalid and excluded from analysis.

There was a noticeable reduction of SE elements and connectors in the knowledge worker navigation subspace due to the filtering (see Table 8.6). Number of SE elements decreased by 67.4% (from 7,335,577 to 2,392,541) and connectors by 40.63% (from 3,952,429 to 2,346,438). Similarly, reduction is evident in the number of unique SE elements (30.37%: from 1,540,093 to 1,072,340) and connectors (21.34%: from 1,142,700 to 898,896).

Frequent users knew their targets and navigational paths to reach them. Duration of subsequences in sessions was short – with the peak in the interval of two to 5 s (see histogram in Fig. 8.5b). During such short period users were able to navigate through four to five pages on average (see Table 8.6) in order to reach the target. Since there was approximately 1 s per page transition, there was virtually no time to thoroughly scan the page. Therefore it is reasonable to assume the knowledge workers knew where the next navigational point was located on the given page and proceed directly there.

Session objective was accomplished via few subgoals. Average session (after filtering) contained three subsequences (see Table 8.6) where each subsequence can be considered a separate action and/or subgoal. Average knowledge worker spent about 30 s to reach the subgoal/resource, and additional 6.5 min before taking another action. Considering the number of unique valid subsequences (about 1.6 million) the complete population of users had relatively wide spectrum of browsing patterns. However, the narrow explored intranet space of a single user suggests large diversification.

Small number of SE elements and connectors was frequently repetitive. Histogram and quantile charts in Fig. 8.7 depict re-occurrence of SE elements and connectors. Approximately six hundred SE elements and four hundred connectors were frequent (refer to the left histogram curves of Fig. 8.7). These six hundred SE elements (approx. 0.056% of the unique valid SE elements) and four hundred connectors (approx. 0.0445% of the unique valid connectors) accounted for about 20% of total observations (see the right quantile curves of Fig. 8.7).

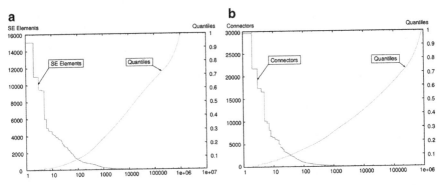

Fig. 8.7 Histograms and quantiles: (**a**) SE elements, and (**b**) connectors. Right y-axis contains a quantile scale. X-axis is in a logarithmic scale

Knowledge workers formed elemental and complex browsing patterns. Strong repetition of the SE elements indicates that knowledge workers often initiated their browsing actions from the same navigation point and targeted the same resource. This underlines the elemental pattern formation. Relatively small number of elemental browsing patterns was frequently repeated. Re-occurrence of connectors suggests that after completing a browsing sub-task, by reaching the desired target, they proceeded to the frequent starting point of following sub-task(s). Frequently repeating elemental patterns interlinked with frequent transitions to the other elemental sub-task highlights formation of more complex browsing patterns. Although the number of highly repetitive SE elements and connectors was small, knowledge workers exposed a spectrum of behavioral diversity in elemental as well as more complex behavioral patterns.

8.6   Modeling

Approaches to modeling human–web interactions often utilize statistical modeling methods or empirical studies on click stream data [20]. Significant attention has been devoted to modeling navigational transitions with predictive capabilities [21]. Markov models have been frequently used due to their predictive accuracies [22], however, higher-order models become exceedingly complex and computationally expensive. Similar complications rise when utilizing adaptive learning strategies [23] at the processing stages where large data volumes still remain. Relaxation of computational complexity of such models has been attempted by focusing only on the frequently occurring patterns [24]. Effective solution to the inherent drawbacks of these methods requires deeper understanding of human dynamics in web environments.

  Early models of human dynamics assumed random nature of human actions that can be well approximated by Poisson processes. However, recent elucidation of temporal dynamics of human information access in web environments revealed that the individual human actions follow non-Poisson statistics characterized by heavy tails [15, 16]. Similar results have been reported from workload studies of search engines and server systems [25, 26]. The progressive trend in modeling human–web interactions focuses on capturing the long tail characteristics [27].

8.6.1 Modeling Long Tails of Human–Web Interactions

The term *long tail* colloquially refers to a feature of statistical distributions where the *head* contains a small number of high frequency elements that gradually progresses to the *long tail* of low frequency elements. The mass of a long tail can substantially outweigh the mass of a head. Numerous aspects of human dynamics have been observed to display such characteristics.

The former analysis of navigation space topological features indicates that the long tail characteristics are evident in knowledge worker browsing behavior. All histograms of starters, attractors, and singletons show long tails. The elemental behavioral abstractions, that is the SE elements, and their connectors, throughout which users form more complex behavioral patterns, equally display long tails. Furthermore, even the complete sessions have this attribute. (Note that the histogram charts have x-axis in a logarithmic scale. It allows us to observe the details of heads of distributions.)

If the long tails are the common denominator of human browsing behavior in web environments, what is the underlying functional law that accurately captures it?

Conventionally, the heavy tails in human dynamics have been modeled by power distribution [16, 28], lognormal and Pareto distributions [29], or Zipf distribution [30]. Temporal decay of web site visitation has been reported to follow the power-law $P(\tau) \sim \tau^{-\alpha}$ with $\alpha \approx 1.2 \pm 0.1$ [15]. Similar results have been reported for timing of web site visitation by a single user: $\alpha \approx \frac{3}{2}$ [16]. The distribution of delays between sending two consecutive emails by a single user have been suitably modeled by the power-law with $\alpha \approx 1$. These distributions display linear dependency in a log–log plot. However, certain empirical observations exhibited distinctive non-linear log–log tendency – such as time distribution of two consecutive electronic transactions made by a stock broker (modeled by a power-law with the exponential cutoff $P(\tau) \sim \tau^{-1.3} \exp(\frac{-\tau}{\tau_0})$ in [16]). The results of our analysis suggest better and more accurate novel distribution.

The novel distribution that efficiently captures the long tail features of a human browsing behavior in web environments is derived from the analysis of log–log plots. Figure 8.8a shows a log–log plot of attractor histogram. It is evident that the curve has a quadratic shape. Plots of other histograms have the same quadratic appearance. Nonlinearity is the reason why power-law distribution (and other well known long tail distributions) is unsuitable since it only captures linear dependency. Models employing conventional distributions may display systematic deviations.

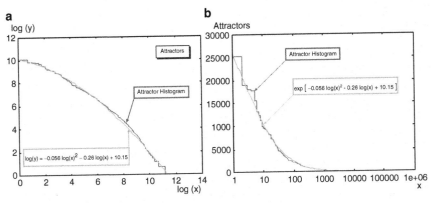

Fig. 8.8 Long tail analysis in attractor histogram: (**a**) log–log plot, (**b**) normal plot with x-axis in a logarithmic scale. Log–log plot clearly shows inverted quadratic characteristics. The distribution is well approximated by the LPE p.d.f. function $f(x) = \exp\left[-0.056\log(x)^2 - 0.26\log(x) + 10.15\right]$

Expressing the quadratic characteristics of a log–log plot in an analytic form leads to the formula:

$$\log(y) = \sum_{i=0}^{2} \theta_i \log(x)^i.$$ (8.2)

Eliminating the logarithm on the left-hand-side of the equation, and presenting the generalized polynomial form results in the following expression:

$$f(x; \theta) = \exp\left[\sum_{i=0}^{n} \theta_i \log(x)^i\right].$$ (8.3)

Naturally, even more generalized form can be obtained by not limiting i to the non-negative integers, but considering it to be a real, $i \in R$.

The derived log-polynomial-exponential (LPE) function (8.3) appropriately represents the observed long tail dynamics of user browsing behavior. Although the general n-th order polynomial can be considered, the second order form was sufficient for modeling our observations (see Fig. 8.8b). When using the second order polynomial form, the common concave shape depicted in Fig. 8.8a suggests that the quadratic term will always be negative, $\theta_2 \in R^-$, and the offset at the origin always positive, $\theta_0 \in R^+$. The estimation of parameters ` can be done by applying various statistical inference techniques.

It can be noticed that LPE p.d.f. (8.3) is base independent and can clearly be utilized for modeling linear log–log dependencies (then the second and higher order terms of the polynomial will be zero; $\theta_i = 0, i \geq 2$). Thus it is well suited for approximating the formerly reported empirical results of human temporal dynamics. Furthermore, it is more general and has significant approximating power.

8.7 Applications

Findings from analysis and modeling of human–web interactions have a wide practical applicability. Knowledge of browsing and behavioral characteristics of web users is beneficial in designing better e-commerce sites [31], enterprise web portals [32], search engines [33], communications [34], web-based platforms for networking and collaboration [35], and many other domains and technologies. Among the most attractive application areas of human–web interaction research are recommender systems and collaborative filtering engines [36, 37].

The purpose of recommender and collaborative filtering systems is relatively clear. They offer recommendations to users. Commonly, recommendations are provided on-the-fly while user is engaged in the browsing session. Every web user has been most likely exposed to recommendations of various kinds. When you search for information using a search engine, the results contain not only suggestions on where to find the information you are looking for, but also related advertisements. When you are shopping on the web, you might be recommended to buy also other related products or goods. When you listen to music or watch video clip on the web, the system will suggests you similar songs or clips. When you are interacting on a networking site, you will be recommended to check out other friends-of-a-friend. These are all examples of recommendations in web based environment.

Recommendation systems and collaborative filtering engines are automated systems for proposing online suggestions to the users. While the recommender systems utilize similarities between items or historical data, the collaborative filtering engines leverage correlations among like-minded users. Distinctive boundaries between the systems have been becoming increasingly fuzzy in the recent development and technological trends.

We present a novel application of the demonstrated behavioral and usability findings. The findings from the analyzed large scale organizational intranet portal are utilized in designing the browsing assistance system. The system helps users navigate in the web environment. It offers suggestions on the potential resources of interest based on the browsing characteristics of the users and the usability aspects of the web environment. It improves users' navigation and usability of web-based environment. The system is scalable and well suited for large scale organizational systems.

Progress in advancing internal organizational information systems has been inadequate. Knowledge-intensive organizations increasingly rely on advanced information technology and infrastructure [38]. Information systems should facilitate improved operating efficiency of organizations and their members [39]. This necessitates well deployed organizational intranet portals [40,41]. Improved usability and efficiency of web-based organizational information systems bring economic benefits to organizations and time benefits to users.

8.7.1 Conceptualization

We expand the formerly introduced analytic framework for the concepts utilized in design of the browsing assistance system. Presented definitions are accompanied by intuitive and illustrative explanations. This helps to understand and comprehend the concept at both practical and higher order abstract levels.

In Analysis section we defined several navigation points: starters, attractors, and singletons. A single starter can be used for navigating to numerous different attractors. Analogously, from a single attractor, users can transition to several different starters that are the initial points of the following subtasks. To observe the multitudes of navigational and transitional pathways, we define the starter and attractor mappings.

Definition 8.5 (Starter and Attractor Mappings).
Let $B = \{(Q_i, d_i)\}_i$ be a browsing session with consecutive subsequences Q_i and Q_{i+1}.
Starter–attractor mapping $\omega : S \to A$ is a mapping where for each starter $s \in S$, $\omega(s)$ is a set of attractors of the subsequences Q_i having starter s.
Attractor–starter mapping $\psi : A \to S$ is a mapping where for each attractor $a \in A$ of the subsequences Q_i, $\psi(a)$ is a set of starters of the existing consecutive subsequences Q_{i+1}.

The starter–attractor mapping underlines the range of different attractors the users accessed when initiating their browsing interactions from the given starter. It does not quantify the number of available links on the starter page. Instead, it exposes the range of detected abstract browsing patterns: starter $\to$ set of attractors. Between the starter and attractor may be several intermediate pages in the observed subsequences. The starter–attractor mapping outlines an important 'long-range' browsing pattern indicator. On the other hand, the attractor–starter mapping delineate an important 'close-range' interaction pattern indicator: attractor $\to$ set of starters. The transition from the attractor to the next starter is direct. The attractor–starter mapping relates more closely to the spectrum of links exposed on the given attractor page (static or dynamic) and/or utilization of hotlists.

Definition 8.6 (Top Sets).
Let ω be a starter–attractor mapping and ψ be an attractor–starter mapping. Top-n sets $\omega^{(n)}(s) \subseteq \omega(s)$ and $\psi^{(n)}(a) \subseteq \psi(a)$ are the ordered sets of the first n points $p \in \omega^{(n)}(s)$ and $p \in \psi^{(n)}(a)$ selected with respect to an ordering defined by a function $f : \Phi \to \Re$; where Φ is either/or $S \cup A$, $S \times A$, $A \times S$.

The top sets describe the sampling from the image sets of starter and attractor mappings with respect to an ordering function. They extract a subset of image set containing a number of highest ranking elements. Consider for example a starter s with $\omega(s) = \{a_1, \ldots, a_x\}, x \in N$. Top-n set $\omega^{(n)}(s) = \{a_1, \ldots, a_n\}, n \leq x$, can be the selection of the first n attractor points according to a ranking function f defining ordering on the set $S \cup A$. Various ordering functions can be defined. A relative frequency of occurrences of points a_i can be a simple and suitable ordering function, for instance.

8.7.2 System Design

It is often beneficial to account for relevant a priori knowledge when designing a system. The conceptual design of the presented system efficiently employs valuable information obtained from the analysis of knowledge worker browsing interactions on a large corporate intranet portal. The observations have pertinent implications to the architecture of the assistance system.

8.7.2.1 A Priori Knowledge of Human–Web Interactions

Exploratory analysis of knowledge worker browsing behavior and usability of the organizational information system highlighted numerous relevant features. Several features are directly or indirectly applicable to the browsing assistance system design. Following is the concise list of the important observations.

- Knowledge workers form repetitive browsing and behavioral patterns.
- Complex system interaction tasks are divided into three subtasks on average.
- General browsing strategy can be expressed as: knowledge of the starting point and familiarity with the navigational pathway to the target.
- Extended use of the information system leads to the habitual interaction behavior.
- Knowledge workers navigate rapidly in the subsequences – within seconds.
- Users have relatively short attention span for elemental tasks – approximately 7 min on average.
- Knowledge workers utilize a small set of starting navigation points and target small number of resources.

The knowledge workers have generally focused browsing interests. Their browsing tasks are mainly related to their work description. Thus, they effectively utilize only relatively small set of resources from the large pool of available ones. Knowledge workers browsing habitually focuses on the initial navigation points and traversal path to the desired resource. As they get used to the system, the navigation from starter to attractor is progressively rapid.

8.7.2.2 Strategic Design Factors

The essential requirements on the recommendation algorithm for intranet browsing assistance system under consideration fall into three main categories:

1. **Recommendation Quality** The algorithm should provide reasonably accurate and suitable recommendations.

2. **Diverse User Population Accountability** While focusing on the local knowledge workers, the algorithm should encompass diversity in the user population.
3. **Computational Efficiency and Scalability** The algorithm should be computationally efficient and scalable in the dimensions of user population and resource number.

Adequate coverage of these three domains demands formulating effective strategies for algorithm design. In devising the strategic elements we utilize the findings of the human–system interactions on a large organizational intranet portal. They provide actionable a priori knowledge. Building upon these observations enables us to determine the core strategic design factors.

Exploit Starters and Attractors for Assistance Services The starters and attractors should be the primary navigation points for appropriate assistance services. The observed knowledge workers browsing strategy relies on knowing the right starters for reaching their goals. The attractors are the desired targets and transition initiators to the subsequent starters. These are the navigation points where users pay the most attention to the content, and spend their time at. The intermediate points between starters and attractors in the subsequences are just passage points. They are passed through relatively rapidly – within seconds. Thus, the users do not pay sufficient attention to the content of these pages and proceed straight to the known link in the navigational pathway to the target. If the assistance service is provided on these pages, it is unlikely the users would notice it; not to mention use it within such a short time. It would simply be an inefficient use of computing resources.

Provide Recommendations on Relevant Attractors and Consecutive Starters Effective browsing assistance services should aim at satisfying the objective navigational needs of the users. Rather than focusing at predicting the next page in user's navigation stream, it is of higher benefit to users to be offered direct access to the desired resource. Thus, users can skip all the essentially unwanted transitional pages and reach the desired resource immediately. This potentially saves users' time, servers' computational resources, and network bandwidth. The former strategic point proposes to provide assistance services only at the starter and attractor pages. When a user reaches the starter, his/her desired target is the corresponding attractor. Analogously, when a user arrives at the attractor, he/she would like to transit to the appropriate starter. Hence, the effective browsing assistance service should be recommending the suitable attractors and starters.

Limit the Prediction Depth to Less Than Three Levels There is essentially no need to go beyond three levels of depth in predicting the appropriate attractors and starters. This implies from the empirical evidence obtained when analyzing knowledge workers' browsing interactions. Knowledge workers divided their browsing tasks into three subtasks–on average. Their browsing sessions thus contained three subsequences. Each subsequence has its starter s_i and attractor a_i. Consider the following generic session:

$$s_1 \xrightarrow{1} a_1, s_2 \xrightarrow{2} a_2, s_3 \xrightarrow{3} a_3,$$

where the numbers above the right arrows denote the depth. Assuming the user is at the beginning of a session, s_1, the desired elements in the first depth level are: a_1, s_2; in the second level: a_2, s_3, and in the third: only a_3. The recommendation set $r = \{a_1, s_2, a_2, s_3, a_3\}$ would be sufficient for the whole session, in principle. Hence, to cover the generic session, it is sufficient to limit the prediction depth to less than or equal to three. It may be practical to focus just on the next level, since when the user reaches the desired attractor or starter, the recommendations on the next level attractors or starters will be provided again. This strategic design consideration may lead to computationally more efficient and scalable algorithms.

Fast responsiveness of the assistance system should be also be among the high priority issues. It has been observed that knowledge workers have relatively short attention span in electronic environments. Extended waiting times may result in negative browsing experiences. The secondary effect of unfavorable experiences leads to relatively low usability perceptions. The responsiveness factor directly relates to the computational efficiency. The recommendation algorithm of the assistance system should be computationally inexpensive.

8.7.3 Recommendation Algorithm Derivation

The design of the recommendation algorithm for browsing assistance system utilizes the presented strategic concepts and accounts for the essential system requirements. The recommendations are provided on the starter and attractor pages. The system aims at supplying a list viable resources comprising of both starter and attractor pages. The resource recommendations are based on the first level predictions.

The recommendation algorithm has several phases. First, it identifies the navigation point a user has reached. If the point is starter and/or attractor it proceeds to the generation of the initial recommendation set. The initial recommendation set is generated in two stages (see Fig. 8.9). In the first stage, a set of top-n elements according to the appropriate starter–attractor or attractor–starter mappings is generated. The selected top-n points are used as seeds for the second stage expansion, again with respect to the suitable starter–attractor or attractor–starter mappings. The two-stage process produces the initial set of $n + n{\cdot}m$ elements. The initial set contains an appropriate mix of starters and attractors. The final recommendation set is selected from the initially generated set. The elements in the initial set are ranked with respect to the ordering function, and a number of the highest ranking points is chosen.

Recall that a navigation point can be starter, attractor, singleton, simple point, or any multiple combination of these. The two stage generation of the initial recommendation set varies depending on whether the detected navigation point is starter, attractor, or both. If the point is both starter and attractor, it is prioritized as starter. The details of the algorithm for the relevant cases (starter and attractor) are described in the following paragraphs.

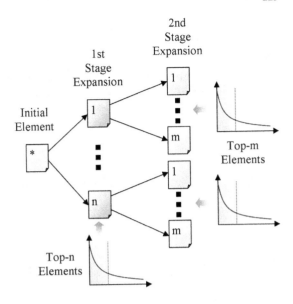

Fig. 8.9 Illustration of the two-stage generation of the initial recommendation set

Assume the reached navigation point is a starter s. The algorithm maps the starter s to a set of attractors $\omega(s)$ according to the starter–attractor mapping ω. Top-n attractors are selected from the set $\omega(s)$. The selection is done with respect to the suitable ranking/ordering function. The selected top-n attractors in $\omega^{(n)}(s)$ are used for generating additional n sets by attractor–starter mapping. The corresponding set of top-m starters $\psi^{(m)}(a_i)$ is obtained for each attractor $a_i \in \omega^{(n)}(s)$. A subset of $\psi(a_i)$, with cardinality m, is chosen according to the ordering function. The two-stage process, outlined as follows:

$$s \longrightarrow \omega^{(n)}(s) \longrightarrow \bigcup_{a_i \in \omega^{(n)}(s)} \psi^{(m)}(a_i), \tag{8.4}$$

leads to the initial recommendation set $r(s)$ containing $n(1 + m)$ elements:

$$r(s) = \omega^{(n)}(s) \cup \left(\bigcup_{a_i \in \omega^{(n)}(s)} \psi^{(m)}(a_i) \right). \tag{8.5}$$

The initial recommendation set $r(s)$ is intentionally larger than the required final recommendation set. Hence, the set $r(s)$ undergoes further selection. A subset of w elements is chosen – again according to the proper ordering function f:

$$r^{(w)}(s) = \left[\omega^{(n)}(s) \cup \left(\bigcup_{a_i \in \omega^{(n)}(s)} \psi^{(m)}(a_i) \right) \right]_{\triangleright f}. \tag{8.6}$$

Analogous process is repeated when a user reaches an attractor navigation point. Given the attractor a, the top-n set $\psi^{(n)}(a)$ is generated according to the attractor–starter mapping ψ. Sampling of $\psi(a)$ is done with respect to the given ordering. This is the first stage expansion. The obtained top-n set $\psi^{(n)}(a)$ is used for the second stage expansion. The corresponding sets of top-m attractors $\omega^{(m)}(s_i)$ are derived for each starter $s_i \in \psi^{(n)}(a)$. The two-stage processing:

$$a \longrightarrow \psi^{(n)}(a) \longrightarrow \bigcup_{s_i \in \psi^{(n)}(a)} \omega^{(m)}(s_i), \tag{8.7}$$

forms the initial recommendation set $r(a)$ with $n(1+m)$ elements:

$$r(a) = \psi^{(n)}(a) \cup \left(\bigcup_{s_i \in \psi^{(n)}(a)} \omega^{(m)}(s_i) \right). \tag{8.8}$$

The acquired initial recommendation set $r(a)$ is correspondingly sampled for a subset of top w elements – according to the ordering function f. The resulting final recommendation set $r^{(w)}(a)$ is obtained:

$$r^{(w)}(a) = \left[\psi^{(n)}(a) \cup \left(\bigcup_{s_i \in \psi^{(n)}(a)} \omega^{(m)}(s_i) \right) \right]_{\triangleright f}. \tag{8.9}$$

An important element of the algorithm is the right choice of the ordering function f. The function should provide qualitatively appropriate ranking of the navigation points. In addition, it should be computationally inexpensive in order to enable on-the-fly recommendations and scalability of the algorithm.

A suitable ordering function is a relative frequency. The navigation points are evaluated according to their relative utilization frequency detected during the knowledge worker interactions. This facilitates the reuse of the analytic data and efficient implementability. It also permits easy extensions to various domains of definition. As knowledge workers utilize the intranet portal resources more frequently, the relative use frequency becomes more accurate and convergent.

Multiple categories and multiplicity of navigation points (see Definition 8.6) present a slight difficulty. The sets of starters, attractors, and singletons are not necessarily disjunct. This rises an important question: how to compute the relative frequency of a point that has been detected as starter, attractor, and singleton (or any valid combination of these)? A simple and effective solution to this problem is to compute the average of the applicable relative frequencies:

$$f(p) = avrg(f_S(p) + f_A(p) + f_Z(p)); \quad f_S(p) \neq 0, \ f_A(p) \neq 0, \ f_Z(p) \neq 0, \tag{8.10}$$

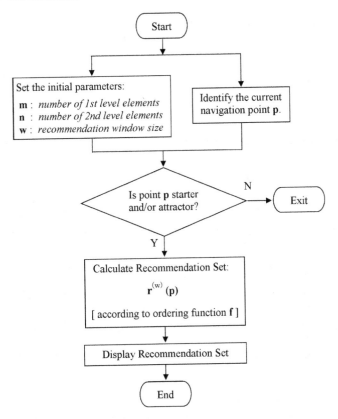

Fig. 8.10   Intuitive flowchart presentation of recommendation algorithm

where f_S denotes the starter relative frequency, f_A stands for the attractor relative frequency, and f_Z indicates the singleton relative frequency. This evaluation accounts for the average combined relative frequency value of a point.

At this point we are ready to present the complete algorithm. Simplified, but intuitively understandable, flowchart illustration of the derived recommendation algorithm for browsing assistance system is presented in Fig. 8.10. At the beginning, the user's reached navigation point p is examined. If the point p is neither starter nor attractor, the algorithm exits. In parallel with the point examination, the initial parameters are set:

m – the first level expansion range
n – the second level expansion range
w – the recommendation window size

If the point p has been detected to be the starter, the algorithm calculates the appropriate recommendation set $r^{(w)}(p)$ according to Eq. 8.6. This applies also to the case where point p is both: starter and attractor. The point p is then preferentially treated as a starter. If the current navigation point p is identified as attractor, the algorithm calculates the recommendation set $r^{(w)}(p)$ differently – according to Eq. 8.9. The averaged relative frequency ordering function (8.10) is employed in all cases. The obtained recommendation set r of the size w is then suitably presented to the user on-the-fly at the given page p.

8.7.4 System Evaluation

The presented recommendation algorithm has been evaluated using the processed data of the large-scale target intranet portal. The main goal of the evaluation has been to examine the correctness of the algorithm's recommendations given the actual interactions of knowledge workers during their browsing experiences. The recommendation correctness of the algorithm has been tested for various sizes of the recommendation window.

Individual users were associated with the distinct IP addresses. The set of detected unique IP addresses contained both statically and dynamically assigned addresses. Smaller number of the distinct IP addresses were static and larger number of the addresses were dynamic. This was due to widespread use of dynamic addressing in the organization. It should be noted that the exact identification of the individual users is generally not possible for dynamically assigned IP addresses. However, the detected IP address space proportionally corresponded to the number of portal users.

We identified IP addresses with more than fifty sessions originating from them. This represents approximately at least once per week interaction activity on the intranet portal. There were 8,739 such IPs. A random sample of subsequences originating from these addresses was obtained. Ten subsequences were selected from each IP address. The test points were selected from the subsequence samples. If the test point was a starter, the desired target was the corresponding attractor of the original subsequence. In case of the attractor test point, the desired target was the starter of the consecutive subsequence. The testing set consisted of the pairs (p, y): point $p \rightarrow$ desired target y. The cardinality of the testing set was 87,390.

Given a navigation point p_i in the testing set $\{(p_i, y_i)\}_i$, the introduced algorithm generated recommendation set $r^{(w)}(p_i)$. The generated recommendation set $r^{(w)}(p_i)$ was scanned for the corresponding desired target element y_i. If the set $r^{(w)}(p_i)$ contained the actual desired point y_i, the recommendation was considered correct, otherwise it was considered incorrect. The correctness of the recommendation algorithm was measured by a simple indicator function of y_i on $r^{(w)}(p_i)$.

The recommendation correctness of the introduced algorithm was evaluated for different sizes of the recommendation window $w \in\ <1, 30>$. The range $<1, 10>$ was examined with the increment one, and the range $<10, 30>$ with the increment five. The first and the second stage expansion parameters were set to five:

Correctness [%]

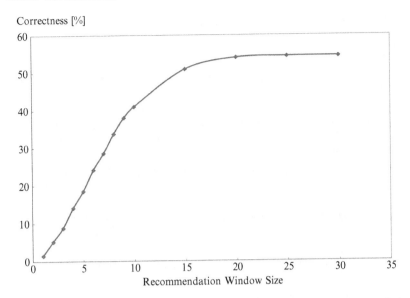

Recommendation Window Size

Fig. 8.11   Recommendation correctness evaluated for varying size of recommendation window

$m = n = 5$. Thus, the cardinality of the initial recommendation set r was thirty; $|r| = n(1 + m) = 30$. Top-w candidates, $r^{(w)}$, were selected from the initial recommendation set according to the averaged combined relative frequency (8.10). The obtained correctness results are graphically presented in Fig. 8.11.

The recommendation performance of the derived algorithm was rising approximately linearly up to the window size ten. In this range the correctness, as a function of window size w, indicated the steepest gain. At the window size ten, $w = 10$, the correctness was approximately 41% – which is significant. Then the recommendation correctness of the algorithm started saturating. The saturating range is noticeable between the window size values of ten and twenty, $w \in < 10, 20 >$. The recommendation correctness at $w = 20$ was over 54%. The performance of the algorithm started stabilizing for window size values greater than twenty. The performance gains in the window size interval $w \in < 20, 30 >$ were relatively minor.

The evaluation results indicate that the appropriate size of the recommendation window is between ten and twenty, $w \in < 10, 20 >$. The performance of the algorithm in this range is around 50%, and the number of recommended items is not excessive. The range provides sufficient space for adjustability according to other characteristics of user interactions. Users with short attention span may prefer ten recommended elements, whereas more exploratory users may appreciate larger number of recommendations – possibly up to twenty. The adjustments of recommendation window size may be managed by users directly, or by adaptive methods.

8.8 Conclusions and Future Trends

World wide web has evolved during the past few decades into a global medium. It transcends organizational and national boundaries. Growing number of businesses are establishing their global web presence. They are also building their internal web enabled information systems and portals. The web functions as an important commercial, communication, and collaboration platform. Increasing number of people interact with web based environments on a daily basis. It is natural that human–web interaction research is gaining the eminent position in this evolving climate.

The viewpoint on human–web interaction research presented in this work highlights its evolutionary spiral perspective through which it moves toward higher levels. One loop in the spiral incorporates five essential domains: data collection, (pre-)processing, analysis, modeling, and applications. Although this image portrays a sequential nature of the progress, achievements in each domain provide valuable knowledge and feedback to both the consecutive and all the others domains.

Elucidation of human–web interactions starts with collecting timely and reliable data. Approaches to data collection are wide-ranging and each one has its own advantages and disadvantages. The practical trend favors the approaches that do not recognizably interfere with users; and that enable scalable automated acquisition of data. Server-side web logs, described in section two, belong to this category. The data collection process is independent of users' local conditions and is performed directly by the web server. Acquired data is hardly ever perfect and requires preprocessing before it can be used in the further stages. The preprocessing primarily focuses on removing records of machine generated traffic, irrelevant logs, and extracting applicable information into the form that facilitates further operations on the data. The pertinent issues in this domain have been addressed in section four. Prepared data is used in analysis of human–web interactions. The analytic framework introduced in section five utilizes temporal segmentation of users' interactions into sessions and subsequences. It enables observation of topological and temporal aspects of human navigation space, identification of essential navigational points and abstractions. The analysis of human–web interactions revealed evident long tail characteristics. The novel accurate model of the long tail features is given in section six. In the final stage of this work we presented a practical applicability of the research framework. The findings were applied to the design of efficient browsing assistance system for large scale web portals.

The future of web inevitably leads to more user-conscious, user-oriented, and user-friendly environments. The environments that adjust automatically, on-the-fly, and optimally to users' conditions and tendencies. This necessitates deeper understanding of elemental aspects of human behavior in digital environments, more sophisticated and efficient behavioral models; and advanced data acquisition, analysis, and application tools. Reaching for these targets will inevitably lead to deeper interdisciplinary collaboration.

References

1. T. Berners-Lee and R. Cailliau. Worldwideweb: Proposal for a hypertext project. http://www. w3.org/Proposal.html, November 1990.
2. P. Géczy, S. Akaho, N. Izumi, and K. Hasida. Human web behavior mining. In *Proceedings of WWW/Internet*, pp. 163–170, Vila Real, Portugal, 2007.
3. J. Grudin. Three faces of human-computer interaction. *Annals of the History of Computing*, 27:46–62, 2005.
4. K. Hassanein and M. Head. Manipulating perceived social presence through the web interface and its impact on attitude towards online shopping. *International Journal of Human-Computer Studies*, 65(8):689–708, 2007.
5. S. AlShaali and U. Varshney. On the usability of mobile commerce. *Intl. J. Mobile Communication*, 3:29–37, 2005.
6. M. Petre, S. Minocha, and D. Roberts. Usability beyond the website: an empirically-grounded e-commerce evaluation for the total customer experience. *Behaviour and Information Technology*, 25:189–203, 2006.
7. Y-H. Park and P.S. Fader. Modeling browsing behavior at multiple websites. *Marketing Science*, 23:280–303, 2004.
8. R.J.K. Jacob and K.S. Karn. Eye tracking in human-computer interaction and usability research: Ready to deliver the promises. In J. Hyona, R. Radach, and H. Deubel, Eds., *The Mind's Eye: Cognitive and Applied Aspects of Eye Movement Research*, pp. 573–605, Elsevier Science, Amsterdam, 2003.
9. L.A. Granka, T. Joachims, and G. Gay. Eye-tracking analysis of user behavior in www search. In *Proceedings of The 27th SIGIR*, pp. 478–479, Sheffield, United Kingdom, 2004.
10. P. van Schaik and J. Ling. Using on-line surveys to measure three key constructs of the quality of human-computer interaction in web sites: psychometric properties and implications. *International Journal of Human-Computer Studies*, 59(5):545–567, 2003.
11. R. Benbunan-Fich. Using protocol analysis to evaluate the usability of a commercial web site. *Information and Management*, 39:151–163, 2001.
12. K.L. Norman and E. Panizzi. Levels of automation and user participation in usability testing. *Interacting with Computers*, 18:246–264, 2006.
13. J.W. Palmer. Web site usability, design, and performance metrics. *Information Systems Research*, 13:151–167, 2002.
14. A.-L. Barabasi. The origin of bursts and heavy tails in human dynamics. *Nature*, 435:207–211, 2005.
15. Z. Dezso, E. Almaas, A. Lukacs, B. Racz, I. Szakadat, and A.-L. Barabasi. Dynamics of information access on the web. *Physical Review*, E73:066132(6), 2006.
16. A. Vazquez, J.G. Oliveira, Z. Dezso, K.-I. Goh, I. Kondor, and A.-L. Barabasi. Modeling bursts and heavy tails in human dynamics. *Physical Review*, E73:036127(19), 2006.
17. P. Géczy, S. Akaho, N. Izumi, and K. Hasida. Knowledge worker intranet behaviour and usability. *Int. J. Business Intelligence and Data Mining*, 2:447–470, 2007.
18. L. Catledge and J. Pitkow. Characterizing browsing strategies in the world wide web. *Computer Networks and ISDN Systems*, 27:1065–1073, 1995.
19. M.V. Thakor, W. Borsuk, and M. Kalamas. Hotlists and web browsing behavior–an empirical investigation. *Journal of Business Research*, 57:776–786, 2004.
20. R.E. Bucklin and C. Sismeiro. A model of web site browsing behavior estimated on clickstream data. *Journal of Marketing Research*, 40:249–267, 2003.
21. Mei-Ling Shyu, Choochart Haruechaiyasak, and Shu-Ching Chen. Mining user access patterns with traversal constraint for predicting web page requests. *Knowledge and Information Systems*, 10(4):515–528, 2006.
22. M. Deshpande and G. Karypis. Selective Markov models for predicting web page accesses. *ACM Transactions on Internet Technology*, 4:163–184, 2004.
23. I. Zukerman and D.W. Albrecht. Predictive statistical models for user modeling. *User Modeling and User-Adapted Interaction*, 11:5–18, 2001.

24. J. Jozefowska, A. Lawrynowicz, and T. Lukaszewski. Faster frequent pattern mining from the semantic web. *Intelligent Information Processing and Web Mining, Advances in Soft Computing*, pp. 121–130, 2006.

25. C. Bedue, R. Baeza-Yates, B. Ribeiro-Neto, A. Ziviani, and N. Ziviani. Modeling performance-driven workload characterization of web search systems. In *Proceedings of CIKM*, pp. 842–843, Arlington, USA, 2006.

26. B. Schroeder and M. Harchol-Balter. Web servers under overload: How scheduling can help. *ACM Transactions on Internet Technology*, 6:20–52, 2006.

27. P. Géczy, S. Akaho, N. Izumi, and K. Hasida. Long tail attributes of knowledge worker intranet interactions. In P. Perner, Ed., *Machine Learning and Data Mining in Pattern Recognition*, pp. 419–433, Springer-Verlag, Heidelberg, 2007.

28. A. Vazquez. Exact results for the Barabasi model of human dynamics. *Physical Review Letters*, 95:248701(6), 2005.

29. A.B. Downey. Lognormal and Pareto distributions in the internet. *Computer Communications*, 28:790–801, 2005.

30. J. Leskovec, J. Kleinberg, and C. Faloutsos. Graphs over time: Densification laws, shrinking diameters and possible explanations. In *Proceedings of KDD*, pp. 177–187, Chicago, Illinois, USA, 2005.

31. W.W. Moe. Buying, searching, or browsing: Differentiating between online shoppers using in-store navigational clickstream. *Journal of Consumer Psychology*, 13:29–39, 2003.

32. R. M. Dewan, M. L. Freimer, A. Seidmann, and J. Zhang. Web portals: Evidence and analysis of media concentration. *Journal of Management Information Systems*, 21(2):181–199, 2004.

33. E. Agichtein, E. Brill, and S. Dumais. Improving web search ranking by incorporating user behavior information. In *Proceedings of The 29th SIGIR*, pp. 19–26, Seattle, Washington, USA, 2006.

34. S.J. Stolfo, S. Hershkop, C-W. Hu, W-J. Li, O. Nimeskern, and K. Wang. Behavior-based modeling and its application to email analysis. *ACM Transactions on Internet Technology*, 6:187–221, 2006.

35. R. Mak and J. Walton. The collaborative information portal and NASA's mars rover mission. *IEEE Internet Computing*, 9(1):20–26, 2005.

36. G. Adomavicius and A. Tuzhilin. Toward the next generation of recommender systems: A survey of the state-of-the-art and possible extensions. *IEEE Transactions on Knowledge and Data Engineering*, 17:734–749, 2005.

37. R. Jin, L. Si, and C. Zhai. A study of mixture models for collaborative filtering. *Information Retrieval*, 9:357–382, 2006.

38. M. Alvesson. *Knowledge Work and Knowledge-Intensive Firms*. Oxford University Press, Oxford, 2004.

39. T. H. Davenport. *Thinking for a Living - How to Get Better Performance and Results from Knowledge Workers*. Harvard Business School Press, Boston, 2005.

40. H. Collins. *Enterprise Knowledge Portals*. Amacom, New York, NY, USA, 2003.

41. D. Sullivan. *Proven Portals: Best Practices for Planning, Designing, and Developing Enterprise Portal*. Addison-Wesley, Boston, MA, USA, 2004.

Chapter 9
Web Recommender Agents with Inductive Learning Capabilities

Domenico Rosaci

Abstract The activity of generating Web recommendations has been based in the past mainly on content-based and collaborative-filtering algorithms, that exploit a pre-fixed user's profile to compare the interests of a user with the content of a Web site and with the profiles of other users. However, some recent proposals introduced the possibility to automatically construct the user's profile by software agents able to monitor "over the shoulders" the user's behaviour. This way, the profile can contain some useful information about not only the user's interest but also the user's behaviour. For instance, in the CILIOS approach recently presented, the user's profile contains a logic program, automatically constructed by a neural network-based approach, that represents causal implications about events belonging to the user's environment. In this paper we propose to use the logic knowledge extracted by CILIOS to support Web recommendation activities. A new type of agent, called CILWEB, is provided with both the CILIOS inductive learning capability and an additional implication-based recommendation algorithm. The introduction of the implication-based recommendations gives to the CILWEB agent the capability of better performing with respect to the traditional recommendation systems, as it is shown by some experimental results.

9.1 Introduction

Web Recommender Systems support Web activities of a user providing him/her with useful suggestions about objects, products, or services which he/she might be interested in. Usually, recommender systems are intelligent applications which help the user to identify the Web pages which could meet his/her interest, or the products of an e-shop site that he/she might want to visit, or other similar contents.

D. Rosaci (✉)
DIMET Department, University Mediterranea of Reggio Calabria, Via Graziella Feo di Vito, 89100 Reggio Calabria, Italy
e-mail: domenico.rosaci@unirc.it

R. Chbeir et al., *Emergent Web Intelligence: Advanced Information Retrieval*, Advanced Information and Knowledge Processing, DOI 10.1007/978-1-84996-074-8_9,
© Springer-Verlag London Limited 2010

For instance, recommender systems are probably among the most prominent applications for improving the performances of e-commerce sites. Indeed, the catalogues of the e-stores are becoming very large, as well as the number of online customers. In this context, recommender systems play a key role to help the users in the decision-making process where they want to choose one item amongst a potentially overwhelming set of alternative products or services. For this reason, recommender systems are more and more used to recommend movies, books, CDs, news, travels, financial services, etc. Moreover, besides on the e-commerce, they have a similar impact on other Web domains, such as e-learning, e-government and cultural services, which involve large communities of users and large sets of items.

9.1.1 Agent-Based Recommender Systems: a Brief Overview

A large number of different recommender systems [4,11,30,43] have been proposed in the last years to support users' Web activities. Generally, they are partitioned in three main categories [10], namely: (i) *Content-based* recommender systems, that suggest to a user the items which appear the most similar to those he/she has already accessed in the past; (ii) *Collaborative Filtering* recommender systems, that suggest to a user items which have been also considered by similar users; (iii) *Hybrid* recommender systems, that exploit both content-based and collaborative filtering techniques to generate recommendations (e.g., a Web site can generate suggestions considering user's personal interests and user's commonalities among other known users). In these situations, hybrid recommender systems have been usually recognized as the most promising solution. In fact, hybrid recommender systems generally produce a higher number of relevant recommendations with respect to both purely content-based and collaborative filtering systems. One common thread in recommender systems research is the need to combine recommendation techniques to achieve peak performance. It is worth to point out that all of the known recommendation techniques have strengths and weaknesses, and many approaches proposed in the literature have chosen to combine techniques in different ways. Therefore, different recommendation techniques have been presented, exploiting different types of hybridization techniques [10].

The recommender techniques described above are basically conceived for generating recommendations for a user that visits a Web site having a number of different items. Therefore the recommendations are generated based on the items that the users have accessed on the given site.

However nowadays a different type of recommender system is quickly emerging. This kind of system considers the users' interests with respect to all the sites they have visited in the past. A new, promising solution to implement recommender systems dealing with different Web sites is represented by the Multi-Agent Systems (MASs). The main component of a MAS is the *software information agent*, which is an application capable to autonomously and proactively perform some tasks on the behalf of its human user. An agent can be thus exploited as a client by the user, which observes the user's behaviour during his navigation and in this way it is capable to build a model which represents the user's interests with respect to all the visited Web sites. To this purpose, agent-based systems exploit in their recommendation algorithms an internal representation (profile) of the user. Specifically, each user is associated to a software agent which monitors his/her Web activities. When the user accesses a Web site, his/her agent exploits the profile in the interaction with the site. In particular, the agent can use both content-based and collaborative filtering techniques to provide recommendations to the user by comparing the user's profile with the content of the site (resp. the profile of the other visitors of the site) to generate content-based recommendations (resp. collaborative filtering recommendations). We note that these systems try to be unobtrusive, avoiding to directly pose annoying questions to the human user but, on the contrary, directly learning his/her preferences by observing his/her behaviour.

9.1.2 Our Contribution: Recommender Agents That Automatically Learn Users' Interests and Behaviour

In the context described above, an important issue arises in order to design Web recommender agents actually autonomous and proactive. Indeed, it has been widely recognized that this kind of software agent, besides of determining the categories of interest for its human owner, should be able to capture the owner's behavior, i.e., it should learn *causal implications* among events that could happen in the agent's environment [9, 44, 53]. For instance, if an agent is associated to a human owner that buys a book only if the book is offered with a discount, the relationship between the event "the book is offered with a discount" and the event "the agent buys a book" should be represented in the agent's profile. In [44], a multi-agent framework is presented, called CILIOS, able of inducing logical rules representing causal implications by means of a connectionist representation, based on neural-symbolic networks. This mechanism exploits a new profile representation, that allows a more rich description of user's interests and behaviour with respect to the traditional user profile representations. CILIOS derives from [15] the idea of using a neural symbolic network for representing a logic program. The use of the approach presented in [15] gives, on one hand, the possibility to represent an initial background knowledge by a neural-symbolic network. Such a network can be trained for refining the initial knowledge by means of a supervised learning phase that exploits, as training set, the actual user's behaviour. On the other hand, the choice of this approach allows the obtained knowledge, represented by the network weights, to be re-translated into the symbolic form for making it understandable. Finally, the so obtained symbolic knowledge can be object of a reasoning phase that generates useful deductions.

    In this work we propose to apply the CILIOS approach to implement an agent-based Web Recommender System, called *Connectionist Inductive Web* (CILWEB). A CILWEB agent is able to automatically learn the behaviour of its human user and the operations that he/she performs. In particular, we propose to use the causal implications extracted by CILWEB to suggest to the user the next items to visit.

More in particular, when the CILWEB client is exploited by a human user to access a Web site, the associated agent suggests to the user some links that could be interesting for him/her, based on:

- The contents pointed by the links. For instance, the human user could be interested in books, and the agent detects some links to contents regarding books. In this case, the agent suggests these links, following a typical content-based recommender behaviour.
- The opinion of other similar users. The agent detects the users most similar to its human owner and then suggests to the owner the items most accessed by these users, following a collaborative-filtering behaviour.
- The causal implications learnt by the agent. For instance, suppose that the agent has learnt that the user generally visits a page relative to cellular phones after visiting a page relative to hardware components. In this case, if the human owner has just visited a page relative to hardware components, then the agent could suggest him/her some links to pages relative to cellular phones. We call *implication-based* this type of suggestions.

The first two features (content-based and collaborative filtering suggestions) are directly inherited by CILIOS. The third feature (implication-based suggestions) is a novel contribution introduced in CILWEB. At the best of our knowledge, none of the recommender systems proposed in the past generates recommendations based on causal implications. We show in Section 9.6 that the introduction of implication-based recommendations significantly improves the quality of the suggestions.

It is important to point out that the current version of CILWEB has been developed and tested on dedicated XML Web pages, using a common dictionary shared by all the agents involved in the system. Indeed, the system is suitable to generate recommendations in the context of a virtual Web community of users, such as an e-commerce or an e-learning community, but it is not possible at the moment to apply it to the whole World Wide Web. We are studying in our ongoing research the possibility to extend CILWEB to classical Web pages, without the necessity of a common dictionary. Another important remark is that the use of neural network is appositely proposed for making possible to learn causal implications by examples. In fact, a part of the knowledge we extract by CILWEB (that relative to causal implications) is not implicit in Web pages but depends on the actual behaviour of the human user when accessing the pages. Therefore, it is necessary to have a framework able to induce logical rules by examples.

Figure 9.1 graphically shows how CILWEB works. Each user is provided with a CILWEB agent, that provides him/her with useful recommendations during his navigation. To this purpose, each CILWEB agent is composed of four modules, three of which are dedicated to compute a different type of recommendations, while the fourth module allows to automatically built the agent personal ontology. In particular, the modules called *CB recommender* and *CF recommender* compute content-based and collaborative filtering recommendations, respectively,

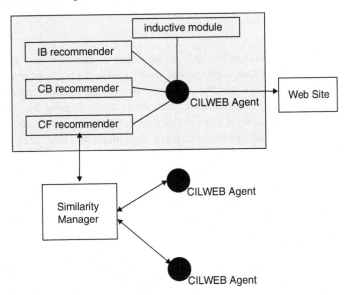

Fig. 9.1 The CILWEB architecture

using the approach proposed in [44]. In order to compute the collaborative filtering recommendations, the CF recommender interacts with a central *similarity manager*, that is a unit able to compute the similarities between the agent ontologies, exploiting the methodology described in [44]. Finally, the module called *IB recommender* compute the implication-based recommendations, using the algorithm presented in Section 9.5.

It is important to remark that the agent internally stores the user's profile, and this private information is not sent either to the site or another agent (differently from the case of a spyware). Actually, the agent itself computes the content-based recommendations comparing (on the client side) its internal profile with the content of the visited site. Regarding the collaborative filtering recommendation, the agent profile is sent only to the central unit called "similarity manager" that compares this profile with those of the other agents, and we can suppose that the communication between client agent and similarity manager is performed in a secure way, using a secure communication protocol.

In Section 9.2 we discuss some related work about existing recommendation techniques for supporting Web users. Section 9.3 introduces the knowledge representation model exploited in CILWEB. In Section 9.4, we describe the CILIOS method for building agent profiles containing causal implications by using neural-symbolic networks, that is the core of CILWEB. In Section 9.5 we present our implication-based recommendation algorithm. Then, in Section 9.6 we present an experimental evaluation of CILWEB in comparison with other well-known recommender systems. Finally, in Section 9.7 we draw our conclusions.

9.2 Related Work

The most effective recommender systems proposed in the past use, besides of content-based algorithms that compare the user's profile with a site content, also collaborative-filtering algorithms that, in order to provide recommendations to a given user, exploit information coming from other users. Among the others, we discuss below some of the most known collaborative-filtering recommendation algorithms. For further information about these algorithms, the interested users can see [33]. We remark that the performances of the systems described below are measured by using three widely accepted accuracy measures, namely *Precision, Recall,* and *F-Measure.* Precision is defined as the share of the recommendations actually used by the user among those suggested by the system; vice versa, Recall is the share of the recommendations suggested by the system among those chosen by the user. F-Measure represents the harmonic mean between Precision and Recall (see [49] for details about these measures).

Markov Model [36] The Markov Model (hereafter *MM*) can be adopted as a clickstream-based collaborative filtering approach. Clickstream-based Collaborative Filtering approaches (hereafter *CCF*) are presently receiving a great attention in the context of Web personalization. They are prediction models that can recommend to a user the next Web pages to visit. These models are trained offline and, then, are used online for deriving recommendations. *MM* has generally a high Precision; however, this is obtained by slightly sacrificing Recall; this behaviour is motivated by the fact that algorithms underlying *MM* are not particularly suited to operate on sparse data that are very common in this application context. This problem is partially overcome by adopting the so called multi-order mixed Markov Models.

Association Rule Model [1] The Association Rule Model (hereafter *ARM*) is a *CCF* approach. It is often applied for finding frequent product sets in e-commerce and for exploiting the detected information to suggest to users the next pages of an e-commerce site to visit. If compared with *MM*, *ARM* generally shows a higher Recall but a lower Precision.

Sequential Association Rule Model [51] The Sequential Association Rule Model (hereafter *SARM*) has been conceived as an evolution of *ARM*. Unlike association rule, sequential association rule is a relatively frequent sequence of transactions, where each transaction is a set of items. The support calculation is different in the association rule and sequential association rule. The former is transaction-based, while the latter is sequence-based. Suppose that a customer has two transactions buying the same item. In association rule, the customer contributes to the support count of that item by two, whereas it counts only once in the support counting in sequential association rule. Specifically, while *ARM* considers sequences of temporal contiguous pages, the sequences which *SARM* operates on can comprise not contiguously accessed pages. Due to this characteristic, *SARM* can improve the accuracy of obtained results; more specifically, the value of F-Measure it obtains is generally higher than that characterizing *MM* and *ARM*.

Hybrid Approach [33] In [33] a technique capable of combining *MM, ARM* and *SARM* is presented. It considers a Web log file storing information about the Web pages visited by users and applies a suitable machine learning algorithm on it to determine an optimal sequence of application of *MM, ARM* and *SARM*; in other words, it aims at finding a sequential combination of *MM, ARM* and *SARM* that maximizes the overall accuracy. As claimed by the authors, this approach achieves a better recall than *ARM* and *SARM* and shows a precision comparable with *MM*.

Besides of the above techniques, generally used also in absence of agent technology, a relevant number of recommender systems based on the use of software agents has been proposed in the last five years. Among the others, we describe below some well-known proposals.

Push!Music [31] It is a model where media (e.g., music files) are autonomous entities that carry their own individual information. In this context, the authors explores how collaborative filtering-like behaviour could emerge out of large ensembles of interacting agents, which are distributed over mobile devices in social networks. A *context* is defined in the form of a stream of media, e.g., a playlist, which a user experiences over time. In this natural context agents could "socialize" with each other. It is also in this context that the user would be exposed to the media content, and vice versa. The main hypothesis is that agents can feel a sense of similarity towards each other based on their contextual experiences with other agents.

IMPLICIT [6] It is a recommender system which combines multi-agent systems and traditional recommender system techniques. IMPLICIT uses a search engine in order to obtain a certain number of suggestions for any entered keyword. Personal agents communicate and collaborate in order to produce suitable recommendations in the context of the current community. The search engine results are thus complemented with the recommendations produced by the agents and this helps to add personalization without decreasing significantly the number of the pages. IMPLICIT attempts to learn the user interests and preferences from the observations of his behaviour.

SUGGEST [45] It supports user navigation on the Web by dynamically generating links to pages that have not yet been visited by a user and might be potentially interesting for him/her. It is also capable of managing dynamic Web sites. In order to carry out its task, SUGGEST builds and maintains historical information about user behaviour by means of an incremental graph partitioning algorithm. To extract information about navigational patterns, SUGGEST exploits an algorithm that models the usage information as a complete graph. The so constructed graph is then partitioned by using a clustering algorithm, in order to find groups of strongly correlated pages. The algorithm is a modified version of the well-known incremental connected components algorithm. After the clustering step, a suggestion list is constructed in a straightforward manner, by finding the cluster which has the largest intersection with the page window correspondent to the current session.

C-Graph [8] This approach proposes an agent model, able to support the navigation of a Web user, by providing him/her with useful suggestions. The C-Graph agent, during the navigation of a site, carries out two activities at the same time: the first is providing the user with a set of recommendations to support his navigation, while the second is monitoring the user behaviour for learning his preferences and encoding such a new knowledge into the ontology. A key issue which is faced concerns with the model used for representing the user ontology, that is capable of embedding both concepts of interest for him/her and the correlations he/she perceives.

CBCF [35] (Content-Boosted Collaborative Filtering) It uses a content-based predictor to enhance existing user data, to exploit collaborative filtering to generate personalized suggestions. The content-based approach views content information as text documents, and user ratings as one of six class labels. The collaborative filtering component uses a neighborhood-based algorithm, where a subset of users similar to the active users, and a weighted combination of their ratings is exploited to generate recommendations for the active user.

X-Compass [25] It is an XML-based agent model for supporting a user during his activities on the Web. For this purpose, X-Compass constructs and manages a user profile; such an activity is performed automatically, by monitoring the behaviour of a user during his accesses to Web pages. This profile represents user interests, as well as some relationships existing among them.

Similarities and Differences with CILWEB All the aforementioned systems exploits, similarly to CILWEB, an internal profile for storing information relative to the user. Moreover, all these systems provide both content-based and collaborative-filtering recommendations. However, none of these systems represents in the user's profile causal implications between actions performed by the user, while CILWEB introduces the representation of implications by a logic program that is automatically built by the agent exploiting a neural network-based inductive learning. Moreover, the systems described above do not provide the possibility to change the structure of the inferred relationships, that have an a-priori, fixed schema, while our system is able to learn general relationships, whose structure can continuously change with the learning activity, involving new terms and new links between terms. More in particular, the use of neural networks as learning engine provides CILWEB with the possibility to learn a large set of relationships, as guaranteed by the theoretical foundations of the neural network framework.

9.3 CILWEB Knowledge Representation: Ontology and Agent Profile

In our framework, each agent stores a personal profile, while the whole community of agents share a global ontology. The global ontology is necessary to fix all the possible concepts represented in the systems, while each personal profile identifies the concepts of interests for just that agent, as well as the existing relationships between the concepts. The profile stores two main categories of information. First, it represents the interests of the user, i.e., those concepts that he/she considers the most attractive when navigating on the Web. The notion of *concept* plays a key role in knowledge representation of information agents, where they are generally studied under the subject of *ontologies*. Therefore we need to briefly deal with such a subject to clearly introduce concepts in our framework.

9.3.1 Ontology

In the context of an application domain a concept could be a term that abstractly describes a collection of objects, e.g., *computer*, or it could denote a *predicate*, that is a relationship between concepts as, for instance, *buy(buyer, seller)*, or it could indicate an *action*, e.g., *pay*. In any case, the set of concepts that are used in relation to a given reality is the result of an operation called *conceptualization*, that consists in choosing the most suitable concepts to describe that reality. When a conceptualization has been chosen, it is necessary to provide a *description* of such a conceptualization. That is, a concept has to be associated with a string identifier, called *concept name*, and with a *meaning* that defines the semantics of the concept, expressed in a given language (natural or mathematical). A description of a conceptualization is called *ontology* [28]. Many formalisms exist in the literature for representing ontologies. In Cooperative Agent Systems ontologies are often considered as collection of conceptual schemas representing the different terms that can compose an agent message [2, 46]. As an example, in the well-known JAva DEvelopment Framework (JADE) [32] (a middleware that is fully compliant with the standard defined by FIPA [21]), an ontology is an extension of the basic class *ontology*, that can contain different categories of elements as predicates, terms, concepts, actions, etc. The User Modeling instead considers as ontology models those languages that have been developed for representing the semantic of Web resources, and that show the capability of modeling semi-structured data. This is the case of XML (eXtensible Markup Language) [50], a markup language standard developed by the W3C (World-Wide Web Consortium) for facilitating information exchange. Another well-known standard is the Ontology Web Language (OWL) [40], that has been conceived for defining and instantiating Web ontologies. An OWL ontology may include descriptions of classes, properties and their instances, and the OWL semantics specifies how to derive logical consequences from a given ontology. Other examples of ontology languages are the Ontology Markup Language (OML) [39], DAML + OIL [12] and the Semantic Web Rule Language (SWRL) [47].

In this paper we adopt an abstract notion of *concept*, that is independent from any actual implementation. In the CILWEB environment, a concept simply identifies a category of objects (texts, images, media, etc.) contained in Web pages. In its turn, a concept instance is an actual object contained in Web pages. We assume that all the objects contained in the pages of a Web site are collected in a *site catalogue*. Consequently, each concept instance is an item of the site catalogue and therefore we will use the terms *item* and *concept instance* interchangeably. Its actual implementation thus depends on the ontology language used to develop the Web pages of the site.

```
<?xml version="1.0" encoding="ISO-8859-1"?>
  <bookstore xmlns:xsi=
  "http://www.w3.org/2001/XMLSchema-instance"
  xsi:noNamespaceSchemaLocation="bookstore.xsd">
    <bookseller> John Smith </bookseller>
    <book book-id="carrie">
      <title>Carrie</title>
      <author>Stephen King</author>
      <note>First Edition</note>
      <quantity>10</quantity>
      <price>20.75</price>
    </book>
    <book book-id="darktower">
      <title>The Dark Tower</title>
      <author>Stephen King</author>
      <quantity>6</quantity>
      <price>19.90</price>
    </book>
  </bookstore>
```

Fig. 9.2   An example of CILWEB site

The current version of CILWEB has been developed for supporting users that navigate on XML Web sites, and exploits a common ontology implemented by an XML schema. In this case, concepts are elements of the XML schema and concept instances are instances of the XML elements. As an example, consider the Web page whose XML code is shown in Fig. 9.2. This page contains an instance of the concept *bookstore*, that represents an on-line store of books. Such a concept is defined in the XML ontology contained in the XML-schema document "bookstore.xsd", that is shown in Fig. 9.3. As we can see, the element bookstore contains a sub-element *bookseller*, that represents the owner of the bookstore, and a list of sub-elements *book*, where each book contains a title, an author, a quantity and a price. In particular, the concept instance of the bookstore represented in the Web page of Fig. 9.2 represents a bookstore whose seller is John Smith and that contains the two books of Stephen King titled "Carrie" and "The Dark Tower".

Although we have observed over the last years an important evolution towards the standardization of agent communication languages (ACL's), as KQML [20] and FIPA ACL [21], it is worth to point out that the focus of these standards is mainly on the syntax of messages and the semantics of performatives, while the semantics of the content is specified by the ontology. This means that, in order to correctly understand the content of a message, the receiving agent has to understand the concepts contained in the ontology of the sending agent. In a MAS, this is possible if either all the agents share the same ontology, or every agent knows each other's ontology. However, none of these situations are desirable, since: (i) every agent generally deals with its own particular task and thus requires its own specialized ontology; (ii) making every agent of an open MAS, whose size can quickly increase in time, always acquainted with every other agent's ontology would lead to a untenable situation.

```
<?xml version="1.0" encoding="ISO-8859-1" ?>
<xs:schema xmlns:xs="http://www.w3.org/2001/XMLSchema">
  <xs:element name="bookstore">
    <xs:complexType>
      <xs:sequence>
        <xs:element name="bookseller" type="xs:string"/ >
        <xs:element name="book" maxOccurs="unbounded">
          <xs:complexType>
            <xs:sequence>
              <xs:element name="title" type="xs:string"/>
              <xs:element name="author" type="xs:string"/>
              <xs:element name="note" type="xs:string"
              minOccurs="0"/>
              <xs:element name="quantity"
              type="xs:positiveInteger"/>
              <xs:element name="price" type="xs:decimal"/>
            </xs:sequence>
            <xs:attribute name="book-id" type="xs:ID"/>
          </xs:complexType>
        </xs:element>
      </xs:sequence>
    </xs:complexType>
  </xs:element></xs:schema>
</xs:schema>
```

Fig. 9.3 An example of XML schema ontology

A possible way to solve the difficulties of an agent in understanding the messages coming from other agents having different ontologies is offered by the *semantic negotiation* [5, 17, 18, 29, 52]. This is a process by which agents of a community try to reach mutually acceptable definitions (i.e., mutually acceptable agreements on terms).

Regarding this issue, in this paper we assume that all the agents in CILWEB uses the same common ontology and consequently share the same concepts. This is clearly a simplification that is not suitable for open multi-agent systems, as remarked above. However, in this paper we specifically deal with the problem of generating recommendations for Web users, that is orthogonal to the ontology issues that we have discussed in this section, and the assumption of a common ontology does not imply any loss of generality in the approach.

9.3.2   User Profile

The profile of a user is a data structure that stores all the concepts of the common ontology in which the user has been interested during his navigation on different Web sites. In particular, the profile associates with each concept two numerical values, namely: (i) an *interest rate*, denoted by ir, that quantitatively represents the interest rate that the user gives to that concept and (ii) a *last date*, denoted by ld, that represents the last date on which the user has shown interest in that concept. The interest rates will be used by the system in order to select the more interesting concepts for the user, while the last date values allow to periodically prune from the profile those concepts no longer accessed by the user. More formally:

Definition 9.1 (User Profile). A *user profile* is a set of l triplets $\langle c, ir, ld \rangle$, where l is the number of concepts contained in the profile, c is a concept, ir is the interest of the user in c and ld is the last date on which the user accessed c.

Analogously to other user modeling approaches (e.g., [25, 42]), the CILWEB agent computes the interest rate ir associated with each concept c by measuring the no-idle time t spent by the user on the instances of that concept during his navigation. The value t is considered as a rough measure of the user's interest in the concept and it is strictly related to the characteristics of the exploited device. We also consider, in order to better evaluate the interest of the user in the concept, the possible actions that he/she can perform on the concept instances.

More in detail, since the user can store, print or simply read the Web page that contains c, this is taken into account by weighting ir with a coefficient ρ_a for each action a, where $a = 1$ (resp. $a = 2$, $a = 3$) represents the action of printing (resp. storing, visiting).

The ir of a concept that has not never accessed by the user is equal to 0. When the user accesses to an instance of the concept, and he/she spends a time t on this instance, possibly performing an action a, then the value of the ir associated to the concept is updated by using the following formula:

$$ir = \begin{cases} (ir + \frac{t}{T} \times \rho_a)/2 \, , & \text{if } t < T \\ (ir + \rho_a)/2 \, , & \text{elsewhere} \end{cases} \tag{9.1}$$

In words, ir is computed as the mean value between the previous value of ir and the new contribution given by the current access. This contribution is assumed to be maximum, i.e., equal to 1, if the time spent by the user on the concept instance reaches a threshold value T (where T is an integer value greater than 0). Otherwise, it is equal to the ratio $\frac{t}{T} \times \rho_a$, weighted by the parameter ρ_a to take into account the importance of the action performed by the user. The value of ρ_a ranges in the interval $[0,1]$, where 0 means "no importance" and 1 means "maximum importance". Both the threshold T and the parameters ρ_a are stored into the agent, and they can be set by the user.

The agent also stores, for each concept c, the last date of access ld. This value is used by the agent itself to periodically decrease the ir value of the no longer visited concepts, based on the temporal distance from the last date ld.

9.3.3 The CILWEB Ontology Implementation

In the current implementation of CILWEB, the common ontology is realized as an XML-Schema document, where each element represents a *concept*. All the sites

```
<?xml version="1.0" encoding="ISO-8859-1" ?>
  <xs:schema xmlns:xs="http://www.w3.org/2001/XMLSchema">
    <xs:element name="hyperlink">
      <xs:complexType>
        <xs:sequence>
          <xs:element name="textURL" type="string">
          <xs:element name="destinationConcept"
          type="conceptType">
          <xs:element name="destinationURL"
          type="anyURI">
        </xs:sequence>
      </xs:complexType>
    </xs:element></xs:schema>
  </xs:schema>
```

Fig. 9.4   An XML schema implementation of a hyperlink

of the CILWEB community are XML sites that contains instances of concepts that belong to the ontology. The mechanism for accessing a concept is as follows. Each Web page p of a site contains some *hyperlinks* represented by pairs (s, d), where s and d are instances of concepts present in the common ontology. We say that a user, that is visiting the Web page, *accesses* the concept instance d when he/she clicks on a hyperlink (s, d) present in the page.

The hyperlinks have been implemented by using the XML-Schema element *hyperlink* represented in Fig. 9.4. Such an element is composed of three sub-elements, namely: (i) a *textURL* that contains the textual description of the hyperlink (e.g., "Anna Karenina"), (ii) a *destinationConcept* that represents the concept which the hyperlink refers to (e.g., *book*), and (iii) the *destinationURL* that contains the actual URL pointed by the hyperlink.

This implementation of a hyperlink allows the client agent to automatically detect the concept to which the hyperlink points, and therefore understand the interest of the agent. Note that the type *conceptType* associated to the *destinationConcept* of the hyperlink in Fig. 9.5 is an XML schema element that represents at a top level all the concepts contained in the XML ontology. This is obtained in the XML schema by using a *restriction* construct. If the XML ontology contains n different concepts, say $c1, c2, \ldots, cn$, then the element *conceptType* is expressed as in Fig. 9.5, stating that an instance of *conceptType* is an instance of $c1$, or an instance of $c2, \ldots$, or an instance of cn.

9.3.4   Causal Implications

Generally, a user navigates on the Web following some habitual behaviour. For example, the user *John* might be accustomed to read each morning at home, on an online newspaper, at first pages relative to world news and then news about sports. However, the user *John* does not read about sports if he has yet read news about

```
<?xml version="1.0" encoding="ISO-8859-1" ?>
<xs:schema xmlns:xs="http://www.w3.org/2001/XMLSchema">
  <xs:element name="conceptType">
    <xs:simpleType>
      <xs:restrictionBase="string">
        <xs:enumeration value= "c1"/ >
        <xs:enumeration value= "c2"/ >
        ...
        <xs:enumeration value= "cn"/ >
      </xs:restriction>
    </xs:simpleType>
  </xs:element></xs:schema>
</xs:schema>
```

Fig. 9.5 An XML schema implementation of a concept type

finance. In other words, such a user accesses a page relative to the concept "sports" only in the morning at home after having previously visited a page relative to the concept "world" and he has not previously accessed a page relative to the concept "finance". As another example, the same user might be accustomed to visit a Web site dealing with musical events (i.e., relative to the concept "music") only if it is not at the office.

Roughly speaking, in the reality of an agent there exist some situations that may happen or not. In order to represent such situations, we use propositional objects, that we call *events*, following [34]. In our framework, an event can represent the user's access to a page relative to a given concept, and we denote this event with the same name of the concept. For instance, we can use the event *finance* to represent the fact that the user accessed to a page relative to the concept "finance".

Often, we want also to represent an event that is the *negation* of another event. We represent this kind of situation by an event $\neg e$ that is the *classical negation* of e. If e is an event, the classical negation of e, denoted by $\neg e$, means that the negation of e happens. For instance, we represent the fact that the user is not at home by the event $\neg home$.

A CILWEB agent is generally able to determine if an event is happened or not. However, in other cases, we want to represent the fact that *there is no evidence for the agent that an event happens*. For instance, if the agent has been activated just now, it is not able to determine if its user has previously visited the financial page on the newspaper. To model this kind of situations, we use the *default negation*. If e is an event, the default negation of e, denoted by $\sim e$, means that e is assumed to be *false* by default. For instance $\sim finance$ means that the agent is not able to determine if its user previously accessed to financial pages.

Extended Logic Programming [27] is a formalism to represent logical rules that deal with both classical and default negation. Moreover, there exist some relationships between events that can be represented by logical rules. For instance, suppose to represent the situation described above: *John* reads sports pages if he has already read pages about world news and he has not previously read pages about finance. We can model such a situation in two different ways, depending on the meaning that we give to the negative condition "John has not previously read pages about finance". As a first possibility, we can mean: "There is no evidence that John has previously read pages about finance". In this case, we use the rule: *sports* ← *world*, ∼ *finance*. Note that if the agent has not information about the event *finance*, in this representation it supposes that *finance* is false by default. However, as a second possibility, we could choose that we have to explicitly prove that *finance* is false in order to derive *sports*. In this case, if we do not have information about *finance*, we do not derive *sports*. The rule that we use in this situation is *sports* ← *world*, ¬*finance*. It is worth pointing out that the rules representing causal implications are intrinsically dynamic, in the sense that they change with time. It is thus important to have a mechanism for inducing these rules by observing the user behaviour, as we will see in the following.

Definition 9.2. A clause k is a triple (*head,body,∼ body*), where *head* is an event and $body = \{a_1, a_2, ..., a_n\}$ and $\sim body = \{a_{n+1}, \sim a_{n+2}, ..., \sim a_m\}$ are two sets of events. Such a clause represents a propositional rule of the form: $head \leftarrow a_1, a_2, ..., a_n, \sim a_{n+1}, \sim a_{n+2}, ..., \sim a_m$. This notation means that, if both $a_1, a_2, ..., a_n$ are proved to be *true*, and $a_{n+1}, a_{n+2}, ..., a_m$ are assumed to be *false* by default, then *head* is to be proved. □

Generally, in representing an agent ontology, we have to consider a (finite) set of clauses, that form an *extended logic program*. The semantics of extended programs is an extension of the stable model semantics [7] and it is represented by the *answer sets* [27]. For understanding the semantics of such a kind of program, firstly consider the case of a program formed by clauses that do not have any classical negative event, i.e., a program with only default negation. This program is called a *general logic program*.

Definition 9.3. Let $\mathcal{P}$ a general logic program. We call *Herbrand base* [7] of $\mathcal{P}$, denoted by $\mathcal{B}_{\mathcal{P}}$, the set of events occurring in $\mathcal{P}$. An *interpretation* of $\mathcal{P}$ is a function mapping each event in $\mathcal{B}_{\mathcal{P}}$ to {*true, false*}. A *Herbrand Model* for $\mathcal{P}$ is an interpretation making *true* all the clauses of the program. A Herbrand model $\mathcal{M}$ of $\mathcal{P}$ is minimal if no proper subset of $\mathcal{M}$ is a Herbrand model of $\mathcal{P}$. □

Definition 9.4. Let $\mathcal{P}$ be a general logic program. The *Immediate Consequence Operator* is the mapping $\mathcal{T}_{\mathcal{P}}:2^{\mathcal{B}_{\mathcal{P}}} \leftarrow 2^{\mathcal{B}_{\mathcal{P}}}$ defined as follows. Let $\mathcal{I}$ an interpretation of $\mathcal{P}$, then $\mathcal{T}_{\mathcal{P}}(\mathcal{I}) = \{e \in \mathcal{B}_{\mathcal{P}} | e \leftarrow e_1, ..., e_n$ is a clause of $\mathcal{P}$ and $\{e_1, ..., e_n\} \subseteq \mathcal{I}\}$, where $\sim e_j$ is mapped to *false* (resp. *true*) by $\mathcal{I}$ iff e_j is mapped to *true* (resp. *false*) by $\mathcal{I}$. □

Definition 9.5. Let $\mathcal{T}$ be a mapping and let α be an ordinal successor. We define $\mathcal{T} \uparrow \alpha = \mathcal{T}(\mathcal{T} \uparrow (\alpha - 1))$ and $\mathcal{T} \uparrow -1 = \mathcal{T}$. Let $\mathcal{P}$ be a general logic program. Assuming that $\mathcal{B}_{\mathcal{P}}$ is finite, there is some $n \in \omega$ ($\omega = \{1, 2, ...\}$), such that $\mathcal{T}_{\mathcal{P}} \uparrow n = \mathcal{T}_{\mathcal{P}} \uparrow (n + 1)$. We define the *Least Fixpoint* $\mathcal{T}_{\mathcal{P}} \uparrow \omega$ of $\mathcal{P} = \mathcal{T}_{\mathcal{P}} \uparrow n$. □

A general program that does not contain *negative events* ∼e has exactly one minimal Herbrand model, that is identical to the least fixpoint $\mathcal{T}_{\mathcal{P}} \uparrow \omega$. Programs with negative events may have several Herbrand models. In [26], the definition of *stable model* is introduced for providing a semantic for a general logic program. The intuition behind this definition is as follows: consider a rational agent with a set of premises $\mathcal{P}$. We search for sets of interpretation of $\mathcal{P}$ that can be considered as sets of *belief* that the rational agent might hold. To this purpose, consider an interpretation $\mathcal{I}$. Then, any clause of $\mathcal{P}$ that has an event $\sim e$ in its body, when $e \in \mathcal{I}$, is useless, and may be removed from $\mathcal{P}$. Moreover, any event $\sim e$, when $e \notin \mathcal{I}$, is trivial, and may be deleted from the clauses in which it appears in $\mathcal{P}$. This yields a simplified (positive) program $\mathcal{P}_\mathcal{I}$ and if $\mathcal{I}$ happens to be precisely the set of events that follows logically from $\mathcal{P}_\mathcal{I}$, then the set $\mathcal{I}$ is *stable* and represents a set of belief for the rational agent. More formally:

Definition 9.6. Let $\mathcal{P}$ be a general logic program. Given a set $\mathcal{I}$ of events from $\mathcal{P}$, let $\mathcal{P}_\mathcal{I}$ be the (positive) program obtained from $\mathcal{P}$ by deleting (i) each clause that has a negative event $\sim e$ in its body, with $e \in I$, and (ii) the negative events in the bodies of the remaining clauses. □

The program $\mathcal{P}_\mathcal{I}$ is positive (i.e., does not contain any negative event) and thus it has a unique minimal Herbrand Model $\mathcal{M}$ [19]. We say that $\mathcal{M}$ is a stable model if it coincides with $\mathcal{I}$.

Definition 9.7. Let $\mathcal{P}$ be a general logic program. A Herbrand interpretation $\mathcal{I}$ of $\mathcal{P}$ is called *stable* iff $T_{\mathcal{P}_\mathcal{I}}(I) = \mathcal{I}$. □

A general program is *well behaved* if it has exactly one stable model. In a well behaved general program, an event e is *true* or *false*, depending on whether e belongs or not to the unique stable model of the program. Now, we characterize some general logic programs that are well-behaved, and that are called *acceptable programs*.

Definition 9.8. A *level mapping* for a program $\mathcal{P}$ is a mapping $||: \mathcal{B}_\mathcal{P} \rightarrow \mathcal{N}$ of events to natural numbers. We denote by $|\ e\ |$ the *level* of e, for $e \in \mathcal{B}_\mathcal{P}$, and $|\sim e| = |\ e\ |$. □

Definition 9.9. Let $\mathcal{P}$ be a general logic program, $||$ a mapping for $\mathcal{P}$ and $\mathcal{I}$ a model for $\mathcal{P}$. $\mathcal{P}$ is called *acceptable* w.r.t. $||$ and $\mathcal{I}$ if, for every clause $e \leftarrow a_1, a_2, ..., a_n$ in $\mathcal{P}$, the following implication holds, for $1 \leq i \leq n$:

$if\ \mathcal{I} \models \wedge_{j=1}^{i-1} a_j \Longrightarrow |\ e\ | > |\ a_i\ |,$

where $\models$ means "is a model". $\mathcal{P}$ is called *acceptable* if it is acceptable w.r.t. some level mapping and a model of $\mathcal{P}$. □

Definition 9.10. For each acceptable general program $\mathcal{P}$, the function $T_\mathcal{P}$ has a unique fixpoint. The sequence of all $T_\mathcal{P} \uparrow m(i)$, $m \in \mathcal{N}$, converges to this fixpoint $T_\mathcal{P} \uparrow \omega(i)$ (which is identical to the stable model of $\mathcal{P}$), for each $i \in \mathcal{B}_\mathcal{P}$. □

The semantics of extended programs is an extension of the stable model semantics [7] and is represented by the *answer sets*. A *well behaved* extended program has exactly one answer set, and an event e is *true, false* or *unknown* depending on whether its answer set contain e, $\neg e$ or neither. If a program does not contain classical negation, then its answer sets are exactly the same as its stable models [27]. Formally:

Definition 9.11. Let $\mathcal{P}$ be an extended logic program. Given a set $\mathcal{I}$ of events from $\mathcal{P}$, let $\mathcal{P}_{\mathcal{I}}$ the extended program obtained from $\mathcal{P}$ by deleting (i) each clause that has a negative event $\sim e$ in its body, with $e \in I$, and (ii) the negative events in the bodies of the remaining clauses.   □

$\mathcal{P}_{\mathcal{I}}$ is called, after its inventors, the *Gelfond-Lifschitz Reduction* of $\mathcal{P}$ w.r.t. $\mathcal{I}$. The answer set of $\mathcal{P}_{\mathcal{I}}$ is unique and it is defined as follows:

Definition 9.12. Let $\mathcal{P}$ be an extended logic program and let $\mathcal{P}_{\mathcal{I}}$ be the Gelfond-Lifschitz Reduction of $\mathcal{P}$ w.r.t. the event set $\mathcal{I}$. The *answer set* of $\mathcal{P}_{\mathcal{I}}$ is the smallest subset of $\mathcal{B}_{\mathcal{P}}$ such that: (i) for any clause $b \leftarrow a_1, a_2, ..., a_n$ of $\mathcal{P}_{\mathcal{I}}$, if $a_1, ..., a_n \in \mathcal{P}_{\mathcal{I}}$ then $b \in \mathcal{P}_{\mathcal{I}}$, and (ii) if $\mathcal{P}_{\mathcal{I}}$ contains a pair of complementary events then $\mathcal{P}_{\mathcal{I}} = \mathcal{B}_{\mathcal{P}}$.   □

Now, we define the answer set of an extended logic program $\mathcal{P}$ as follows.

Definition 9.13. Let $\mathcal{P}$ be an extended logic program and let $\mathcal{P}_{\mathcal{I}}$ be the Gelfond-Lifschitz Reduction of $\mathcal{P}$ w.r.t. the event set $\mathcal{I}$. Let $\mathcal{I}^+$ the answer set of $\mathcal{P}_{\mathcal{I}}$. $\mathcal{I}$ is an answer set of $\mathcal{P}$ iff $\mathcal{I} = \mathcal{I}^+$.   □

If an extended logic program does not contain classical negation, it is a general logic program. In this case, its answer sets are identical to its stable models. However, it is worth pointing out that the absence of an event e in the stable model of a general program means that e is *false* (by default), while the absence of both e and $\neg e$ in the answer set of an extended program means that we do not know nothing about e. Some extended logic programs can be easily reduced to general logic programs. Consider an extended logic program $\mathcal{P}$, and an event set $\mathcal{I}$ of this program. For each negative event $\neg e \in \mathcal{I}$, consider a positive event e^P that does not occur in $\mathcal{P}$. e^P is called the *positive form* of e. We call *positive form* of $\mathcal{I}$, denoted by $\mathcal{I}^*$, the set of the positive forms of all the events of $\mathcal{I}$, and we call the *positive form* of the program $\mathcal{P}$ the program obtained from $\mathcal{P}$ by replacing all the negative events $\neg e$ of each clause of $\mathcal{I}$ by its positive form. Then we define the notion of *consistent answer set*.

Definition 9.14. Let $\mathcal{P}$ be an extended logic program and let $\mathcal{I}$ a consistent event set of $\mathcal{P}$, i.e., an event set that does not contain any contradiction. $\mathcal{I}$ is an answer set of $\mathcal{P}$ iff $\mathcal{I}^*$ is a stable model of $\mathcal{P}^*$.   □

Definition 9.15. An extended logic program $\mathcal{P}$ is called *acceptable* if its positive form $\mathcal{P}^*$ is acceptable.   □

Acceptable extended programs [22] have a unique answer set.

9.4 Connectionist Representation of Agent's Profile

It has been proved [14] that neural networks can be used to learn clauses of extended general programs and that they are capable of computing the answer set of the program if this latter is acceptable (see Definition 9.15 for remembering the meanings of acceptable program).

9.4.1 Neural Networks That Learn Functions

A standard feedforward neural network is composed by a set of N nodes $\mathcal{N}$ and a set of M arcs $\mathcal{A}$. The nodes are partitioned into three groups, called *layers*: a set of I nodes $\mathcal{N}_\mathcal{I}$ called *input layer*, a set of H nodes $\mathcal{N}_\mathcal{H}$, called *hidden layer* and a set of O nodes $\mathcal{N}_\mathcal{O}$, called *output layer*. Each node of the output layer is connected with all the nodes of the hidden layer, and each node of the hidden layer is connected with all the nodes of the input layer. A real value W_{ij}, called *weight*, is associated with the arc from the node j to the node i. The network is used for representing a real function. Each input layer node is associated with an input (real) value and each output layer node is associated with an output (real) value of the function. The output values are computed by the network, by using the input values. Hidden layer nodes are associated with intermediate results of the computation. The network computes the output values as follows: both each hidden and output layer node n is provided with the same function a, that is called *activation function*, and with a parameter θ_n, that is called *bias*. Each hidden layer node j computes its associated hidden value $h_j = a(\sum_{i=1}^{I} W_{ji} \cdot I_i - \theta_h)$, where i is an input layer node, i.e., by computing the weighted sum of the input values I_i using the weights associated to all the connections between each input layer node i and the hidden layer node j. Analogously, each output layer node j computes its associated output value $o_j = a(\sum_{h=1}^{H} W_{oh} \cdot H_h - \theta_o)$, where h is an hidden layer node, i.e., by computing the weighted sum of the hidden values H_h using the weights associated to all the connections between each hidden layer node h and the output node o.

9.4.2 Neural Networks That Learn Extended Logic Programs

Several authors [15, 41, 48] suggested that symbolic knowledge can be represented by a connectionist system, as a neural network, in order to build effective learning system. In particular, in [15], it is proved that, for each extended logic program $\mathcal{P}$, there exists a feedforward neural network $\mathcal{N}$ with exactly one hidden layer and semi-linear activation functions, that is equivalent to $\mathcal{N}$ in the sense that $\mathcal{N}$ computes $T_\mathcal{P}$. Authors give the following constructive definition of $\mathcal{N}$.

Definition 9.16 ([15]). Let $\mathcal{P}$ an acceptable extended program. The *neural network* $\mathcal{N}$ associated to $\mathcal{P}$ is defined as follows. For each clause c

$$b^c \leftarrow a_1^c, a_2^c, ..., a_n^c, \sim a_{n+1}^c, \sim a_{n+2}^c, ..., \sim a_m^c$$

of $\mathcal{P}$, a node n_i^c in the input layer of $\mathcal{N}$ is associated with each event a_i^c, $i = 1, ..., m$ of the clause's body, a node n_b^c in the output layer of $\mathcal{N}$ is associated with the event b^c of the clause's head and a node n_h^c in the hidden layer of $\mathcal{N}$ is associated with the clause. If an event appears in more than one clause, only a node is associated to it in the network. A node can assume a value belonging to the interval $[-1,1]$, as the result of the bipolar semi-linear activation function $a(x) = \frac{1}{1+e^{-\beta x}}$. A *minimum activation value* A_m, $0 < A_m < 1$ is defined, representing the minimum activation for a node to be considered *true*, and a *maximum activation value* A_M, $-1 < A_M < 0$ is also defined, representing the maximum activation for a node to be considered *false*. Thus, the state of a node is *false* if the result of its input function belongs to the interval $[-1, A_M]$, the state is *true* if the input function produces a value belonging to $[A_m, 1]$. Weights and biases computed by the algorithm do not allow the network to present activations in the range $[A_M, A_m]$. An input node has a fixed value, *true* or *false*. By setting an input node a equal to *true*, we add the fact $a \leftarrow$ to the network. By setting an input node a equal to *false*, we mean that there is no evidence that a is *true*, that is we represent the default negation of a. Note that, in order to mean that a is *false* in the strong sense, we have to explicitly add the fact $\neg a \leftarrow$ to the network, by introducing the input node $\neg a$ and setting it to *true*. An arc (n_h^c, n_b^c) with weight W is introduced from the hidden layer node to the output node, an arc (n_i^c, n_h^c), $i = 1, ..., n$ with weight W is introduced from each input layer node corresponding to an event not negated by default to the hidden layer node, and an arc (n_i^c, n_h^c), $i = n + 1, ..., m$ with weight $-W$ is introduced from each input layer node corresponding to an event negated by default to the hidden layer node.   □

As an example, suppose that the agent's ontology has to represent the background knowledge relative to a user that accesses to a page relative to a book only if the content of the book is not annoying and the book is considered interesting. More in particular, for the user the book is considered interesting if there is no evidence that the book belongs to the category "Fantasy", and it is considered as not annoying if it is interesting and there is no evidence that it is too long. This situation can be represented by the following logic program, where each meaning has an intuitive meaning.

$$k_1 : Book \leftarrow Interesting, \neg Annoying \tag{9.2}$$

$$k_2 : \neg Annoying \leftarrow Interesting, \sim TooLong \tag{9.3}$$

$$k_3 : Interesting \leftarrow \sim Fantasy \tag{9.4}$$

The rules above can be applied for each link to a page relative to the concept "Book", present in the page that the user is currently visiting, in order to decide if the link has to be suggested or not to the human owner.

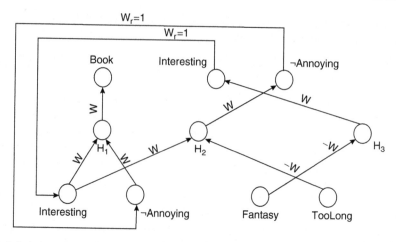

Fig. 9.6 A recurrent neural network associated to a logic program

The neural network that represents this program, built by following Definition 9.16, is shown in Fig. 9.6. Note that in this example, the nodes *Interesting* and *¬Annoying* appear both in the input and the output layer. This happens because the associated events appear both in the body and in the head of some clauses. The network can compute in one step the operator $T_P(\mathbf{i})$. In order to compute the upward powers $T_P^m(\mathbf{i})$ of $T_P(\mathbf{i})$ it is necessary to iterate the computation of $T_P(\mathbf{i})$. To this purpose, an arc for each pair of homonym nodes is introduced, from the input layer node to the corresponding (homonym) output layer node. The weight $W_r = 1$ is associated to each of these arcs, obtaining a (partial) recurrent neural network. A recurrent neural network can be used for performing *deduction*, in the sense that it can compute the (unique) fixed point $T_P^\infty(\mathbf{i})$ of an acceptable extended logic program. Hence, a neural network may be fruitfully exploited for encoding the clauses of the program P contained in an agent ontology. When the agent initially starts to monitor the activities of its owner, the program P can be viewed as a *background knowledge* relative to the agent's owner.

In [15], a translation method for computing the values of W as well as the values of the bias associated to each hidden and output layer node, is also presented. We report a short description of this method in the Appendix.

Two relevant cases can be studied, relative to the knowledge refinement process. The first case corresponds to the application of a reasoning process to the refined knowledge by the agent. The second case deals with the induction process. We analyze these cases in the following two paragraphs.

9.4.2.1 Induction

It is possible that the agent observes a correlation between events, i.e., independently from the knowledge encoded in the ontology, a state configuration of events is produced after another configuration of events happens. This is the core of the induction process, because in this situation the agent has to learn the causal implication between events directly from the observation. For instance, suppose that the agent observes that the event *Interesting* becomes true when both *Fantasy* and *TooLong* happen. This can happen, for instance, due to a direct decision of the human owner that choose to visit a link relative to a book in the category "Fantasy" and having a long content. By applying the rules contained in the background knowledge, after having assigned to both the input nodes *Fantasy* and *TooLong* the value *true*, we derive for *Interesting* the value *false*. However, the direct observation of the human behaviour detects the event *Interesting* is true. The agent could suppose that there exists a causal implication between the pair of events (*Fantasy, TooLong*) and the event *Interesting* and, as consequence, that it is necessary to modify the topology of the neural network for taking into account this fact. This modification can be automatically performed by applying to the neural network a *constructive learning algorithm*. Constructive Learning Algorithms are capable to obviate the need of an *a priori* choice of the network topology, but instead adaptively adding neurons as needed for improving classification accuracy [41]. Therefore, they are suitable to train an initial neural network, representing an initial background knowledge as, for instance, that depicted in Fig. 9.6. There exist many different constructive neural network learning algorithm, as the M-Tiling described in [54] and the Pyramid proposed in [23], or the Dynamic Node Creation Method presented in [3]. As an example, the Dynamic Node Creation Method adds fully connected nodes to the hidden layer of a feed forward neural network architecture trained using the Back Propagation algorithm. Training starts with an initial number of nodes in the hidden layer, and proceeds until the functional mapping is learned or the error ceases to descend and a new hidden node is added. After addition of a new node both the weights involving the new nodes and previous weights are retrained. If we apply the Dynamic Node Creation algorithm to the network in Fig. 9.6, by presenting it the pattern composed by the inputs *Book = false*, *Interesting = false*, ¬*Annoying = false*, *TooLong = true*, *Fantasy = true* and the outputs *Book = false*, *Interesting = true*, ¬*Annoying = false*, by setting a tolerance for the overall error equal to 0 (i.e., we want to obtain a perfect mapping between input an output), the algorithm verifies that, by using the three neurons of the initial configuration the error is over the tolerance, due to the fact that the network produces *Interesting = false*. As a consequence, a hidden node is added to the network, and this node is connected with all the input and the output nodes. Then, the backpropagation algorithm is applied to the network. The new network that we obtain is described in Fig. 9.7, where we have omitted to depict the arcs (*Interesting*, H_4), (¬*Annoying*, H_4), ($H4$, *Book*) that are resulted equal to 0 at the end of the computation, and then are not influent. The backpropagation algorithm computes also the weights $W1 = W2 = 4.63$, $W3 = 4.57$. The refined knowledge is numerically encoded in the weights of the network; in order to make clearly understandable such a knowledge, we need to transform it in an equivalent symbolic format. Several approaches to the problem of extracting symbolic knowledge from a trained neural network have been proposed in the literature [13,41]. In particular,

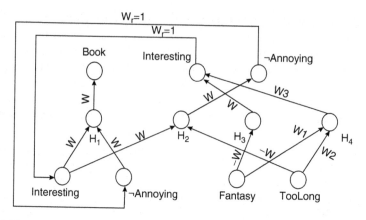

Fig. 9.7 The neural network representing a refinement of the agent's background knowledge

in [13], an approach for extracting an extended logic program from a trained neural network, is presented. We briefly describe this approach in the following Section 9.4.3.

Finally, it is important to briefly discuss the possibility that the network produces a stable output "by itself", if it is not activated. This possibility is often referred as the case of the "echo states". We remark that the possible presence of echo states in the neural network does not generate any problem in our approach, since the output of the network is used only in the case the network has been activated, after the learning phase. In other words, a network which has not been yet trained by examples does not produce any rules for the system.

9.4.3 Knowledge Extraction from Neural Networks

This subsection focuses on the problem of extracting symbolic knowledge from trained neural networks. In other words, we will analyze how finding a logical representation for a given neural network. The extraction process is necessary to give an explanation of the results derived from the learning. Indeed, the logic representation extracted by the neural network, obtained from inductive learning with examples, can be added to an existing background and represents a refinement of such an initial knowledge.

The knowledge acquired by a neural network during its training phase is encoded in the networks architecture and in the values of its weights and thresholds. Given a particular set of weights and thresholds, resulting from a training process on a neural network, the *extraction problem* can be defined as follows: Find for each input vector i, all the outputs o_j in the corresponding output vector o such that the activation of o_j is greater than A_m, where A_m is the minimum activation function defined in Section 9.4.2 (in this case, we say that output neuron o_j is *active* for input vector i).

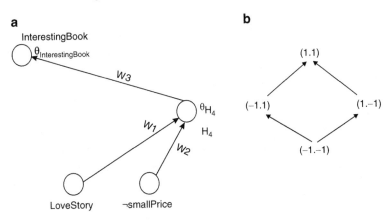

Fig. 9.8 (a) A single hidden layer neural network and (b) the ordering of the set of its input vector

For example, consider a network with input neurons a and b. If $i = (1, -1)$ activates output neuron c, then we derive the rule $c \leftarrow a \sim b$. As a result, if the input vector i has length p, there are $2p$ possible input vectors to be checked. We want to find the activation value of o_j, $Act(o_j) = h(\sum_{i=1}^{r} W_{ji} \cdot H_i - \theta_{o_i})$, such that $Act(o_j) > A_m$. Considering the monotonically crescent characteristic of the activation function $h(x)$ and given that $0 < A_m < 1$ and $\beta > 0$, we can rewrite $h(x) > A_m$ as $x > h^{-1}(A_m)$, that is we can say that o_j is active for i iff $\sum_{i=1}^{r} W_{ji} \cdot H_i > A_m + \theta_{o_i}$.

For instance, applying this approach to the simple network of Fig. 9.8a, we see that the output *Interesting* is active for the input *Fantasy* $= TooLong = 1$, and then we extract the rule *Interesting* $\leftarrow$ *Fantasy, TooLong*. We can easily see that no other rules can be extracted from this network, without checking all the other input configurations. In fact, since $W_1, W_2 > 0$, it is easy to verify that the ordering of Fig. 9.8b on the set of input vectors $I = [Fantasy, TooLong]$ holds with respect to the output *Interesting* of the network. The ordering says that the activation of the output is maximum for $I = [1, 1]$ and minimum if $I = [-1, -1]$. Therefore, the activation value of *Interesting* is governed by this ordering.

This example helps us to understand that, in the case of a *positive* neural network, that is a network whose weights have all a positive value, it is easy to find an ordering on the set of input vectors I with respect to the set of output vectors O and that it is possible to exploit such information for extracting symbolic knowledge from the network. The ordering can help to reduce the search space, since we can safely avoid checking irrelevant input vectors, in the sense that those vectors that are not checked would not generate new rules, as in the case of the example above. Notice that in the worst case we still have to check 2^n input vectors, where i is the number of input nodes, and in the best case we only need to check one input vector (either the minimum or the maximum element in the ordering).

While the knowledge extraction problem can be efficiently solved, in many cases, in presence of positive networks, it becomes more difficult in the case of networks having some negative weights. The approach presented in [13] gives an algorithm that solve the extraction problem for non positive networks that present a "regularity". They define *regular networks* those networks either with all the weights from the hidden layer to each output neuron positive or with all of them negative. For a regular network N they define a Transformation Algorithm that generates a positive network equivalent to N, and therefore they propose a Knowledge Extraction Algorithm based on the Transformation Algorithm. They also define an extraction algorithm for network that are not regular, but in this case the algorithm is not *complete*, in the sense that it is not sure that all the possible rules encoded in the network will be extracted. The formalization of the Knowledge Extraction problem is complex enough, and it is out of the scope of this paper. For more details, we refer the interested reader to the paper [13].

9.5 Implication-Based Web Recommendations

In this section we describe an algorithm that exploits causal implications learnt by a CILWEB agent in order to generate suggestions for its human owner.

The idea underlying this algorithm is that the use of causal implications extracted by the CILWEB system can extend the set of recommendations usually generated by content-based (CB) and collaborative filtering (CF) approaches. In [44], it is shown that the agent ontologies built by using the CILIOS approach can be effectively used for generating both CB and CF recommendations. More in particular, if a is an agent visiting the site s, then CB recommendations can be generated by finding all the items contained in s which are instances of concepts belonging to the a's ontology. Moreover, the CF recommendations can be generated by determining the set AS of the agents having the ontologies most similar to that of a. Then, the CF recommendations are composed by the items of s most accessed by the agents of AS. Then, the CILIOS approach presented in [44] does not introduce any contributions regarding to the exploited recommendation algorithms, that consist of the traditional content-based and collaborative filtering approaches. The contribution of CILIOS is focused on the automatically building of a new type of agent ontology, and on the possibility of adapting the traditional algorithms to this ontology. To make possible this adaptation, CILIOS provides a way of determining inter-ontology similarities between agents, taking into account all the ontology components as concepts, categories, events and causal implications.

Instead, the algorithm proposed in this section allows to compute a new type of recommendations, called *implication-based recommendations*. An implication-based recommendation suggests some links to the user, such that each link contains items joined by a causal implication with other items previously visited by the user.

Implication-based recommendations cannot be determined by traditional recommendation algorithms, that consider only users and items in their computation. We note that in the actual behaviour of Web users, causal implications assume a main role in determining users' actions. Indeed, a user often chooses to visit an item belonging to an item category x only because he/she follows a habitual behaviour that leads him/her to be interested in that category when he/she has previously visited another category y, without considering the absolute interest he/she has for x. In other words, the user could generally have a little interest in items of category y, but this interest can drastically increase when he/she has previously visited items belonging to the category y. Therefore, if we use a purely content-based approach in the situation of a user that visits the site after having accessed items of y, the generally low interest for x does not lead the approach to suggest items of x, while an implication-based approach is able to suggest them.

To understand how a causal implication generates a relationship between items, and to show how the algorithm works, consider as example that a CILWEB agent accesses the Web page reported in Fig. 9.9, dealing with the Italian writer Dante Alighieri.

This page contains some links to other page, and each link is classified by the agent on the basis of an existing ontology as shown in Table 9.1, where for each link is reported the associated concept in the ontology. Also suppose that the current

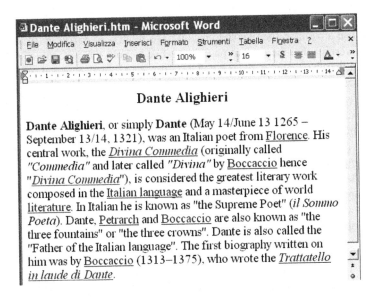

Fig. 9.9   A Web page about Dante

Table 9.1   Links and concepts in Dante Web page

Link name	Concept
Firenze	Birthplace
Divina commedia	Dante_Book
Petrarch	Petrarch
Boccaccio	Boccaccio
Italian language	Language
Literature	Literature
Trattatello	Boccaccio_Book

page is associated with the concept *Dante*, and that the concepts *Dante*, *Petrarch* and *Boccaccio* are sub-concepts of the more general concept *Author* (where the concept *a* is a sub-concept of the concept *b* is all the instances of *a* are also instances of *b*). Finally, suppose that:

- For each concept, an event having the same name of the concept is defined in the agent's profile. We call C-events such type of events associated with concepts.
- The events *PC*, *palmtop* and *cell* are also defined, representing the fact the owner uses as device a personal computer or a palmtop or a cellular phone, respectively. We call NC-events this second type of events, that are not associated to concepts.

Finally, consider that the following rules are contained in the agent's profile:

$$r_1 : Birthplace \leftarrow Author, \neg palm, \neg cell \tag{9.5}$$

$$r_2 : Petrarch \leftarrow Dante, \neg cell \tag{9.6}$$

stating that the agent's owner: (i) when he/she visits a page relative to an *Author* and he/she does not use either a palmtop or a cellular, visits the page relative to the author's *Birthplace* and (ii) if he/she visits a page relative to *Dante* and he/she does not use a cellular, then he/she visits a page relative to *Petrarch*. In this case, the agent verifies that the current page is relative to both the concepts *Author* and *Dante* and that the events *palm* and *cell* are false, and in consequence suggests the two links Florence (relative to the concept Birthplace) and *Petrarch* (relative to the concept *Petrarch*).

This example helps us to understand the steps composing our implication-based recommendation algorithm that are executed by a recommender agent each way his human owner visits a Web page. Consider that the agent, before to execute the algorithm, computes two sets of recommendations, called *CBR* and *CFR*, that contains Content-Based and Collaborative-Filtering recommendations, respectively. These two sets are built exploiting the CILIOS approach described in [44]. Our algorithm computes an additional set, called *IBR*, that contains Implication-Based Recommendations, following the steps formally described below.

1. Let P be the logic program contained in the agent ontology, let E be the set of events and let L be the set of the links present in the visited Web page.
2. Assign a state to each literal lit_e associated to an event $e \in E$. The literal lit_e is set to *true* if e is happened, is set to false otherwise.
3. Computes the unique answer set A_P of P.
4. Select all the literals $r_1, r_2, \ldots, r_n \in A_P$ such that the event associated to r_i is a C-event.
5. Build the set of links $L = \{l_1, l_2, \ldots, l_m\}$ such that $l_i \in L$ and the concept c_i associated to l_i belongs to A_P.
6. Compute the set $IBR = L - CBR \bigcup CFR$.

The last row of the algorithm above avoids that the algorithm recommends a link that has been already computed either in content-based or in collaborative filtering recommendations. This way, the implication-based recommendations contained in *IBR* can be considered as additional suggestions that the agent is able to compute besides content-based and collaborative filtering recommendations.

9.6   Evaluation of CILWEB

In this section we describe a set of experiments performed to real users, in order to evaluate the advantages deriving from the introduction of implication-based recommendations. To this purpose, we compared the performances of CILWEB and those of other well-known techniques in the field of Collaborative Filtering Recommendation Systems (CFRS). CFRS are Recommendation Systems that require each user to specify his ratings about system recommendations; after this, they recognize commonalities among users on the basis of their ratings and generate new recommendations taking into account inter-user comparisons.

In our experiments we used a set of 50 CILWEB agents, each associated to a human user and provided with a CILWEB profile. Each agent has a background knowledge containing some rules involving both C-events and NC-events (see Section 9.5). We used a common ontology composed by 130 concepts, each of which representing a different Web categories (as *Book*, *CD*, *Literature*, etc.), denoted by $g_1, g_2, \ldots, g_{130}$ (see Section 9.3). The chosen value for the number of concepts was due to a typical dimension of a common ontology in a medium-size virtual community, as in e-commerce or e-learning. Therefore each agent contains in its profile a logic program that can be represented, following the methodology described in Section 9.4.2, by a three layers neural network having an input layer with 150 nodes, where 130 of these nodes are associated to Web categories and 20 nodes are associated to NC-events. In particular, each node i, $i = 1, \ldots, 130$ of the input layer is associated to the Web category g_i and receives a boolean input equal to 1 if the user has clicked on a link belonging to g_i, -1 otherwise. Instead, each node i, $i = 131, \ldots, 150$, of the input layer is associated to an NC event and receives an input equal to 1 if the associated event is happened, -1 otherwise.

Analogously, the output layer of the network is composed by 130 nodes, where each node j is associated to the Web category g_i and yields a boolean output that, when its is equal to 1, represents the prediction that the user will click on a link belonging to g_i. For each of our 50 agents, we have represented by the neural network a different set of rules, by using the translation algorithm presented in Section 9.4.2 for inserting the necessary hidden nodes into the hidden level, and consequently setting the initial weights and biases. Then, we have trained this network by using the Dynamic Node Creation algorithm and a training set composed by 2,156 patterns. Each pattern represents a Web session performed by a user, and it is composed by 150 input $i_1, i_2, \ldots, i_{150}$ and 130 output $o_1, o_2, \ldots, o_{130}$.

An agent a is able to give a recommendation to its associated user u, in the sense that, when the user clicks on a link for visiting a Web page, the agent automatically proposes a number of Web categories that u should consider interesting to visit.

We note that initially the agent profiles are empty, before to begin the learning phase, and that any pre-determined relationship has been inserted.

The recommendation is generated on the basis of three different contributions, namely:

- Content-based recommendations, computed as described in the CILIOS approach [44]. Roughly speaking, the set CBR of these recommendations is computed by selecting, among all the links present in the visited Web-page, those links associated to those concepts having the best interest rates (see Section 9.3).
- Collaborative filtering recommendations, already computed as in the CILIOS approach. In particular, the set of CFR recommendations is computed by selecting, among all the links present in the visited Web-page, those links associated to those concepts in which the agents most similar to a are best interested. The computation of the most similar agents is performed by using the similarity metrics described in [44].
- Implications-based recommendations, computed as described in Section 9.5. CILWEB agents generate its predictions about the future pages for a user on the basis of the last 15 pages visited by this user, using the 150 input neurons of the associated neural-network. If the user has chosen in the last 15 clicks, one or more times, a page belonging to the group g_k, the input of the node i_k of the network is set equal to *true*, it is set equal to *false* otherwise.

In this section, we quantitatively compare the effectiveness of this Multi-Agent System based on CILIOS Architecture with:

(i) Four of the most used collaborative-filtering approaches, namely the Markov Model (MM) [16], the Association Rule (AR) Model [37], the Sequential Association Rule (SAR) Model [38], and the hybrid model (H) [33], that exploits different combinations of MM, AR and SAR.[1] These approaches are not based on ontologies, but the similarities between users are computed only comparing the choices made in the past in selecting Web pages:
(ii) A CFRS based on ontology, i.e., X-COMPASS (X-C) [24]
(iii) The CILIOS Approach [24]

Analogously to CILWEB, we have considered a set of 50 agents for all of the above approaches, that support the same 50 users considered by CILWEB. The performance metrics, precision, recall and F-measure, are used for measuring the approaches effectiveness. In order to measure the performance of the approaches in the experiments, accordingly with [33], a session data set is divided into a training and a test set. The training set is used to generate the user models underlying each approach (for instance, for training the neural networks of the CILWEB agents), while the test set is treated as current session data and used to evaluate the models. Each session s, composed by 170 group of links, in the test set is divided, as in the training set, into two parts. The first 60 values in s are treated as an active session

---

[1] The interested reader can found some details about these collaborative filtering techniques in [33].

and are used for making predictions, while the remaining portion of the session is used to evaluate the prediction models. We define *active session window*, denoted by as_s, as the portion of a users active session used by an approach for prediction. The remaining portion of the session is denoted by $output_s$. Each approach takes as_s as an input and makes a prediction. We denote the recommended pages as $P(as_s)$. Then precision, recall, and the F-measure can be represented as follows.

$$Pre(P(as_s)) = \frac{|P(as_s) \cap output_s|}{|P(as_s)|} \qquad (9.7)$$

$$Rec(P(as_s)) = \frac{|P(as_s) \cap output_s|}{|test_s|} \qquad (9.8)$$

$$F(P(as_s)) = \frac{2 * Rec(P(as_s)) * Pre(P(as_s))}{Rec(P(as_s)) + Pre(P(as_s))} \qquad (9.9)$$

For all the methods, the exploited training data set contains a total of 2,258 session records, having the same structure described above relatively to the neural network training. The exploited test sets contains 613 patterns having the same structure. All the values used above are comparable with those used for similar experiments in the literature, as in [33]. Figure 9.10 presents the results obtained on this data set by an agent that uses our approach and those obtained by the approaches MM, AR, SAR, HYBRID, CILIOS and X-COMPASS, in terms of average precision, average recall and average F-measure, respectively. Each average has been evaluated by considering all the single results obtained in each session s.

These results show that CILWEB performs better, in the average, than all the other systems, presenting the highest precision, recall and F-Measure. The advantage is quantified in above 24% of precision with respect to CILIOS (that is the second best performer in precision), in above 29% of recall with respect to CILIOS and X-COMPASS (second best performers in recall) and in above 24% of F-Measure with respect to CILIOS (second best performer in F-Measure).

We easily argue that the advantages in terms of performances are due to the introduction of the implication-based recommendations, since the only difference

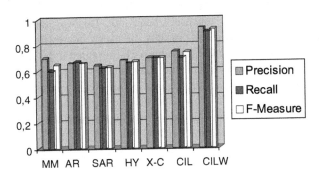

Fig. 9.10 Comparison between recommendation methods

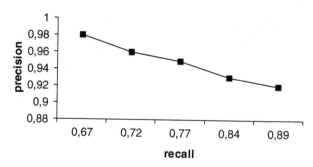

Fig. 9.11 Recall vs Precision in CILWEB

between CILIOS and CILWEB is represented by the set of implication-based recommendations computed by CILWEB and not provided by CILIOS.

It is also interesting to examine the relationship between recall and precision, represented in Fig. 9.11. We have determined this relationship varying the total number of recommendations that the system is able to generate. When this number increases, the recall increases too, since the number of relevant recommendations becomes higher, while the precision decreases. We note that the decrement of the precision caused by an increment of the recall is small enough, passing from a precision equal to 0.98 (in correspondence to a recall equal to 0.67) to a precision equal to 0.92 (corresponding to a recall equal to 0.89). This behaviour is very satisfactory, since we can choose to increase the number of provided (relevant) recommendations without producing a too drastic reduction of the precision.

9.7 Conclusions

The activity of generating Web recommendations has been based in past recommender systems on content-based and collaborative-filtering algorithms, that exploit a user profile to compare the interests of a user with the content of a Web site and with the profiles of other users. However, some recent proposals introduced more sophisticated user profiles automatically constructed by software agents able to monitor "over the shoulders" the user's behaviour. This way, the profile can contain some useful information about not only the user's interest but also the user's behaviour. For instance, in the CILIOS approach presented in [44], the user's profile contains a logic program, automatically constructed by a neural network-based approach, that represents causal implications about events belonging to the user's environment. In this paper we propose to use the logic knowledge extracted by CILIOS to support Web recommendation activities. A new type of agent, called CILWEB, is provided with both the CILIOS inductive learning capability and an additional implication-based recommendation algorithm. The introduction of the implication-based recommendation gives to the CILWEB agent the capability of performing better with respect to the traditional recommendation systems, as it is shown by some experimental results.

Appendix: The Rules-Network Translation Method

Given a general logic program $\mathcal{P}$, let q denote the number of clauses C_l ($1 \leq l \leq q$) occurring in $\mathcal{P}$; m, the number of literals occurring in P; A_m, the minimum activation for a neuron to be considered *active* (or *true*); A_M, the maximum activation for a neuron to be considered *not active* (or *false*); $h(x) = \frac{2}{1+e^{-\beta \cdot x}} - 1$, the bipolar semi-linear activation function, where β is the steepness parameter (that defines the slope of $h(x)$); W (resp. $-W$), the weight of connections associated with positive (resp. negative) literals; θ_l, the threshold of hidden neuron N_l associated with clause C_l; θ_A, the threshold of output neuron A, where A is the head of clause C_l; k_l, the number of literals in the body of clause C_l; p_l, the number of positive literals in the body of clause C_l; n_l, the number of negative literals in the body of clause C_l; μ_l, the number of clauses in P with the same atom in the head for each clause C_l; $max_P(k_1, \ldots, k_q, \mu_1, \ldots, \mu_q)$, the greatest element among all ks and μs of $\mathcal{P}$. Now, assume that the literals of P are numbered from 1 to m such that the input and output layers of N are vectors of maximum length m, where the i-th neuron represents the i-th literal of P. Assume, for mathematical convenience and without loss of generality, that $A_M = -A_m$. The translation ia realized by executing the following steps:

1. Calculate $max_{\mathcal{P}}(k_1, \ldots, k_q, \mu_1, \ldots, \mu_q)$ of $\mathcal{P}$.
2. Calculate $A_m > \frac{max_P(k_1,\ldots,k_q,\mu_1,\ldots,\mu_q)-1}{max_{\mathcal{P}}(k_1,\ldots,k_q,\mu_1,\ldots,\mu_q)+1}$.
3. Calculate $W \geq \frac{2}{\beta} \cdot \frac{ln(1+A_m)-ln(1-A_m)}{max_P(k_1,\ldots,k_q,\mu_1,\ldots,\mu_q)\cdot(1-A_m)+A_m+1}$.
4. For each clause C_l of $\mathcal{P}$ of the form $A \leftarrow L_1, \ldots, L_k$ ($k \geq 0$):

   (a) Add a neuron N_l to the hidden layer of N.
   (b) Connect each neuron L_i ($1 \leq i \leq k$) in the input layer to the neuron N_l in the hidden layer. If L_i is a positive literal then set the connection weight to W; otherwise, set the connection weight to $-W$.
   (c) Connect the neuron N_l in the hidden layer to the neuron A in the output layer and set the connection weight to W.
   (d) Define the threshold θ_l of the neuron N_l in the hidden layer as $\theta_l = \frac{(1+A_m)(k_l-1)}{2} \cdot W$.
   (e) Define the threshold θ_A of the neuron A in the output layer as $\theta_A = \frac{(1+A_m)(1-\mu_l)}{2} \cdot W$.

5. Set $h(x)$ as the activation function of the neurons in the hidden and output layers of N. In this way, a gradient descent learning algorithm, such as backpropagation, can be applied on N efficiently.
6. If N ought to be fully connected, set all other connections to zero.

Example 9.1. As an example of neural network representation of a program, consider the case of the network of Fig. 9.6, representing the background knowledge

Table 9.2 Neural network parameters k, p, n and μ

i:	1	2	3
k_i	2	2	1
p_i	2	1	0
n_i	0	1	1
μ_i	1	2	1

Table 9.3 Node biases

n:	H_1	H_2	H_3	MakeO	Interesting	$\neg$ Annoying
θ_n	3.375	3.375	0	0	0	0

of the agent *John*, as described above. For this case, we have $q = 3$, $m = 5$ and the other parameters set as in Table 9.2. Consequently, $max_P(k_1, k_2, k_3, \mu_1, \mu_2, \mu_3) = 2$.

Therefore, we have $A_m > 0.333$. Then, supposing to choose $A_m = 0.5$, we have $W \geq \frac{4.394}{\beta}$ and then, choosing $\beta = 1$, we choose to set $W = 4.5$. The biases have the values shown in Table 9.3. We also use, as function $h(x)$ of both the hidden and the output nodes, the standard bipolar semi-linear function $h(x) = \frac{2}{1+e^{-\beta \cdot x}} - 1$. This network, given any initial activation in the (recursive) input layer nodes *Interesting* and *¬Annoying*, always converges to the following state: *Book = true, Interesting = true, ¬Annoying = true, TooLong = false, Fantasy = false.* For instance, if we initially set all the inputs equal to -0.8, corresponding to set *Interesting = false, ¬Annoying = false, TooLong = false, Fantasy = false*, we can compute the hidden nodes' values $H1 = h(-4.5 \cdot 0.8 - 4.5 \cdot -0.8 - 3.375) = -0.999$, $H2 = h(4 \cdot -0.8 - 4 \cdot -0.8 - 3.375) = -0.936$, $H3 = h(-4 \cdot -0.8) = 0.922$ and then the network yields the output nodes' values *Book* $= h(4.5 \cdot -0.999) = -0.977$ (corresponding to the logic value *false*), *¬Annoying* $= h(4.5 \cdot -0.936) = -0.970$ (corresponding to the logic value *false*) and *Interesting* $= h(4.5 \cdot 0.922) = 0.969$ (corresponding to the logic value *true*). As you can see in Fig. 9.6, the change of the value of *Interesting* has effect on the network input, due to the presence of recursive arcs from the output to the input layer: we have thus to re-compute the values $H1 = h(4.5 \cdot 0.969 + 4.5 \cdot -0.970 - 3.375) = -0.934$ and $H2 = h(4.5 \cdot 0.969 - 4.5 \cdot -0.8 - 3.375) = 0.979$, and then we have *Book* $= h(4.5 \cdot -0.934) = -0.977$ (corresponding to the logic value *false*), *¬Annoying* $= h(4.5 \cdot 0.979) = 0.976$ (corresponding to the logic value *true*). Finally, we have to execute another computation, since the value of *¬Annoying* is changed, where we obtain $H1 = h(4.5 \cdot 0.969 + 4.5 \cdot 0.976 - 3.375) = 0.991$ and *Book* $= h(4.5 \cdot 0.991) = 0.977$ (corresponding to the logic value *true*) and thus the final, stable, outputs are *Book = true, ¬Annoying = true* and *Interesting = true*. Remember that the input *Fantasy* and *TooLong*, that are not recursive, have the fixed state *false*.

References

1. R. Agrawal, T. Imieliński, and A. Swami. Mining association rules between sets of items in large databases. In *SIGMOD '93: Proceedings of the 1993 ACM SIGMOD international conference on Management of data*, pages 207–216, New York, NY, USA, 1993. ACM.
2. G. Antoniou, E. Franconi, and F. van Harmelen. Introduction to semantic web ontology languages. In *Reasoning Web, Proceedings of the Summer School, Malta, 2005*. Springer, 2005.
3. T. Ash. Dynamic node creation in backpropagation networks. *Connection Science*, 1:365–375, 1989.
4. S. Berkovsky, T. Kuflik, and F. Ricci. Mediation of user models for enhanced personalization in recommender systems. *User Model. User-Adapt. Interact.*, 18(3):245–286, 2008.
5. Robbert-Jan Beun, Rogier M. van Eijk, and Huub Prust. Ontological feedback in multiagent systems. In *AAMAS '04: Proceedings of the Third International Joint Conference on Autonomous Agents and Multiagent Systems*, pages 110–117, Washington, DC, USA, 2004. IEEE Computer Society.
6. A. Birukov, E. Blanzieri, and P. Giorgini. Implicit: A recommender system that uses implicit knowledge to produce suggestions. In *Workshop on Multi-Agent Information Retrieval and Recommender Systems at the Nineteenth International Joint Conference on Artificial Intelligence (IJCAI-05)*, Edinburgh, Scotland, 2005.
7. G. Brewka and T. Eiter. Preferred answer sets for extended logic programs. *Artificial Intelligence*, 109:297–356, 1999.
8. F. Buccafurri, G. Lax, D. Rosaci, and D. Ursino. A user behavior-based agent for improving web usage. In *Proceedings of the International Conference on Ontologies, Databases and Applications of Semantics Conference (ODBASE 2002)*, Lecture Notes in Computer Science, pages 1168–1185, Irvine, CA, USA, 2002. Springer-Verlag.
9. F. Buccafurri, D. Rosaci, G.M.L. Sarné, and D. Ursino. An agent-based hierarchical clustering approach for e-commerce environments. In *Proceedings of the 3th E-Commerce and web Technologies (EC-Web 2002)*, Lecture Notes in Computer Science, pages 115–118, Aix-en-Provence, France, 2002. Springer-Verlag.
10. Robin Burke. Hybrid recommender systems: Survey and experiments. *User Modeling and User-Adapted Interaction*, 12(4):331–370, 2002.
11. L.-S. Chen, F.-H. Hsu, M.-C. Chen, and Y.-C. Hsu. Developing recommender systems with the consideration of product profitability for sellers. *Inf. Sci.*, 178(4):1032–1048, 2008.
12. DAML + OIL URL. http://www.daml.org. 2005.
13. A.S. d'Avila Garcez, K. Broda, and D.M. Gabbay. Symbolic logic extraction from trained neural networks: A sound approach. *Artificial Intelligence*, 125:155–207, 2001.
14. A.S. d'Avila Garcez, K. Broda, and D.M. Gabbay. *Neural-Symbolic Learning Systems*. Springer-Verlag, 2002.
15. A.S. d'Avila Garcez and G. Zaverucha. The connectionist inductive learning and logic programming system. *Applied Intelligence*, 11(1):59–77, 1999.
16. M. Deshpande and G. Karypis. Selective markov models for predicting web page accesses. *ACM Trans. Inter. Tech.*, 4(2):163–184, 2004.
17. J. van Diggelen, R.J. Beun, F. Dignum, R.M. van Eijk, and J.-J. Ch. Meyer. Optimal communication vocabularies and heterogeneous ontologies. In R.M. van Eijk, M.-P. Huget, and F. Dignum, editors, *Developments in Agent Communication*, LNAI 3396, pages 76–90, Berlin, Heidelberg, New York, Tokyo, 2004. Springer Verlag.
18. David W. Embley. Toward semantic understanding: an approach based on information extraction ontologies. In *ADC '04: Proceedings of the 15th Australasian Database Conference*, pages 3–12, Darlinghurst, Australia, Australia, 2004. Australian Computer Society, Inc.
19. M.H. Van Enden and R.A. Kowalski. The semantics of predicate logic as a programming language. *Journal of the ACM*, 23(4):733–742, 1976.
20. T. Finin, R. Fritzson, D. McKay, and R. McEntire. KQML as an agent communication language. In *Proceedings of the 3rd International Conference on Information and Knowledge Management (CIKM'94)*, pages 456–463, Gaithersburg, Maryland, USA, 1994. ACM Press.

21. http://www.fipa.org, 2003.
22. M. Fitting. Metric methods: three examples and a theorem. *Journal of Logic Programming*, 21(2):113–127, 1994.
23. S. Gallant. *Neural Networks and Expert Systems*. MIT Press, 1996.
24. S. Garruzzo, S. Modafferi, D. Rosaci, and D. Ursino. X-compass: An xml agent for supporting user navigation on the web. In *FQAS '02: Proceedings of the 5th International Conference on Flexible Query Answering Systems*, pages 197–211, London, UK, 2002. Springer-Verlag.
25. Salvatore Garruzzo, Stefano Modafferi, Domenico Rosaci, and Domenico Ursino. X-compass: An xml agent for supporting user navigation on the web. In *FQAS '02: Proceedings of the 5th International Conference on Flexible Query Answering Systems*, pages 197–211, London, UK, 2002. Springer-Verlag.
26. M. Gelfond and V. Lifschitz. The stable model semantics for logic programming. In *Proceedings of the Logic Programming Symposium*, 1988.
27. M. Gelfond and V. Lifschitz. Classical negations in logic programs and disjunctive databases. *New Generation Computing*, 9(4,4):365–386, 1991.
28. T.R. Gruber. A translation approach to portable ontologies. *Knowledge Acquisition*, 5(2): 199–220, 1993.
29. R. Guha. Semantic Negotiation: Co-identifying objects across data sources. In *AAAI '04 Spring Symposium Series: Proceedings of the Semantic Web Services*, 2004.
30. M.-H. Hsu. A personalized english learning recommender system for esl students. *Expert Syst. Appl.*, 34(1):683–688, 2008.
31. Mattias Jacobsson, Mattias Rost, and Lars Erik Holmquist. When media gets wise: Collaborative filtering with mobile media agents. In *IUI '06: Proceedings of the 11th International Conference on Intelligent User Interfaces*, pages 291–293, New York, NY, USA, 2006. ACM Press.
32. http://jade.tilab.com/, 2004.
33. D. Kim, V. Atluri, M. Bieber, N. Adam, and Y. Yesha. A clickstream-based collaborative filtering personalization model: towards a better performance. In *WIDM '04: Proceedings of the 6th annual ACM international workshop on Web information and data management*, pages 88–95, New York, NY, USA, 2004. ACM Press.
34. R.A. Kowalski and M. Sergot. A logic-based calculus of events. *New Generation Computing*, 4:67–95, 1986.
35. Prem Melville, Raymod J. Mooney, and Ramadass Nagarajan. Content-boosted collaborative filtering for improved recommendations. In *Eighteenth National Conference on Artificial Intelligence*, pages 187–192, Menlo Park, CA, USA, 2002. American Association for Artificial Intelligence.
36. S.P. Meyn and R.L. Tweedie. *Markov Chains and Stochastic Stability*. Cambridge University Press, 2008.
37. B. Mobasher, R. Cooley, and J. Srivastava. Automatic personalization based on web usage mining. *Comm. of the ACM*, 43(8):142–151, 2000.
38. B. Mobasher, H. Dai, T. Luo, and M. Nakagawa. Effective personalization based on association rule discovery from web usage data. In *WIDM '01: Proceedings of the ACM international workshop on Web information and data management*, pages 9–15. ACM Press, 2001.
39. OML URL. http://www.ontologos.org/oml/. 2005.
40. OWL URL. http://www.w3.org/tr/owl-features/. 2005.
41. R. Parekh and V. Honavar. Constructive theory refinement in knowledge-based neural networks. In *Proceedings of the Int. Joint Conference on Neural Networks*, pages 2318–2323, Anchorage, AK, USA, 1998.
42. Jeffrey Parsons, Paul Ralph, and Katherine Gallager. Using viewing time to infer user preference in recommender systems. In *AAAI Workshop on Semantic Web Personalization - SWP 2004*, pages 413–421, 2004.
43. P. Pu, L. Chen, and P. Kumar. Evaluating product search and recommender systems for e-commerce environments. *Electronic Commerce Research*, 8(1–2):1–27, 2008.
44. D. Rosaci. Cilios: Connectionist inductive learning and inter-ontology similarities for recommending information agents. *Inf. Syst.*, 32(6), 2007.

45. Fabrizio Silvestri, Ranieri Baraglia, Paolo Palmerini, and Massimo Serranó. On-line generations of suggestions for web users. *Journal Of Digital Information Management (JDIM)*, 2(2):104–108, 2004.
46. M.P. Singh and M.N. Huhns. *Service-Oriented Computing:Semantics, Processes, Agents*. John Wiley and Sons, 2005.
47. SWRL URL. http://www.w3.org/swrl/. 2005.
48. G.G. Towell and J.W. Shavlik. Knowledge-based artificial neural networks. *Artificial Intelligence*, 70(1):119–165, 1994.
49. C.J. Van Rijsbergen. *Information Retrieval*. Butterworth, 1979.
50. W3C Recommendation URL. http://www.w3.org. 2005.
51. Y. Wang, Z. Li, and Y. Zhang. Mining sequential association-rule for improving web document prediction. In *ICCIMA '05: Proceedings of the Sixth International Conference on Computational Intelligence and Multimedia Applications*, pages 146–151, Washington, DC, USA, 2005. IEEE Computer Society.
52. Andrew B. Williams. Learning to share meaning in a multi-agent system. *Autonomous Agents and Multi-Agent Systems*, 8(2):165–193, 2004.
53. M. Wooldridge. *Reasoning about rational agents*. MIT Press, 2000.
54. J. Yang, R. Parekh, and V. Honavar. Mtiling - a constructive neural network learning algorithm for multi-category pattern classification. In *Proceedings of the World Congress on Neural Networks'96, San Diego, CA*, pages 182–187, 1996.

Chapter 10
Capturing the Semantics of User Interaction: A Review and Case Study

Donn Morrison, Stéphane Marchand-Maillet, and Eric Bruno

Abstract In many retrieval domains there exists a problematic gap between what computers can describe and what humans are capable of perceiving. This gap is most evident in the indexing of multimedia data such as images, video and sound where the low-level features are too semantically deficient to be of use from a typical users' perspective. On the other hand, users possess the ability to quickly examine and summarise these documents, even subconsciously. Examples include specifying relevance between a query and results, rating preferences in film databases, purchasing items from online retailers, and even browsing web sites. Data from these interactions, captured and stored in log files, can be interpreted to have semantic meaning, which proves indispensable when used in a collaborative setting where users share similar preferences or goals. In this chapter we summarise techniques for efficiently exploiting user interaction in its many forms for the generation and augmentation of semantic data in large databases. This user interaction can be applied to improve performance in recommender and information retrieval systems. A case study is presented which applies a popular technique, latent semantic analysis, to improve retrieval on an image database.

10.1 Introduction

The growth of the internet and the technology explosion have contributed to a high demand for new methods of information filtering and retrieval. The amount of multimedia content created daily is accelerating to a point where management, annotation and retrieval is becoming problematic. Increasingly, research is moving towards exploiting *crowdsourcing* to better aid filtering and retrieval. Crowdsourcing is a moniker that describes the outsourcing of a problem or task to a large number of users in an attempt at finding a solution [29]. Although the definition lends itself to

D. Morrison (✉), S. Marchand-Maillet, and E. Bruno
Computer Vision and Multimedia Laboratory, Computer Science Department,
University of Geneva, CH-1211 Geneva, Switzerland
e-mail: {donn.morrison,stephane.marchand-maillet,eric.bruno}@unige.ch

R. Chbeir et al., *Emergent Web Intelligence: Advanced Information Retrieval*, Advanced
Information and Knowledge Processing, DOI 10.1007/978-1-84996-074-8_10,
© Springer-Verlag London Limited 2010

an explicit arrangement of the distribution of problem workload, such as the Netflix Prize [43], it also covers implicitly sourced user-power, where tasks are less defined and subtle, an example being the reCAPTCHA effort to fight spam while helping optical character recognition in book scanning [52]. In this chapter we discuss different types of crowdsourcing used in retrieval and recommender systems.

Information retrieval of multimedia documents including text, video, images and sound is a rapidly growing research area with problems spanning disciplines from psychology (user behaviour) to mathematics (optimisation) and computer science (algorithms and data mining). Arguably, the central concern is twofold. First, there exists the burden of "information overload," a term first coined in Alvin Toffler's 1970 book *Future Shock*, which describes the problem of having too much information to process efficiently [16, 51]. The massive (and ever increasing) amount of multimedia data on the internet creates the need for efficient filtering methods in order to present documents to relevant users and users to relevant documents. This problem is common in domains from information retrieval where users are searching for documents in a large database to recommendation systems where users rate movies or books in order to be given suggestions matching their history and profile. Recommending too many items to a user causes information overload, and often too many choices stagnates purchasing or interest. Therefore, only a select number of relevant items should be presented to the user to stimulate interest (Fig. 10.1).

Fig. 10.1 *Information overload:* How do you find new music compatible with your tastes? (image taken from http://www.flickr.com/photos/ario/190168823/ and used with permission under the Creative Commons license http://creativecommons.org/licenses/by-nc-sa/2.0/deed.en)

The problem requires a method of filtering information such that the user does not have to navigate and browse large lists of items in order to find things he or she may be interested in. This is where *collaborative filtering* (CF) and *recommender systems* (RS) have fundamental roles to play. Collaborative filtering is a popular method employed by recommender systems that builds user profiles based on ratings given to items in the system. Similar users can be grouped based on similar ratings, and unrated items can then be recommended to users.

The corresponding problem in information retrieval is the *semantic gap*. This oft cited term [8, 14, 30, 38, 61] describes the gap between the low-level information computers can describe (or summarise) and the high-level concepts which humans can perceive. *What is it that tells us that an image of a person wearing a ski mask running from a bank most probably signifies a robbery?* Certainly, algorithms can be trained to recognise this specific imagery, but this is only one of endless possibilities of high-level semantic information extracted from a document. There would need to exist a recogniser for every possible scenario. One can make the humorous reference to hiring one doctoral student to build a recogniser for every concept [50], but the reality is that without some mapping from syntax to semantics, this has been (and still is) the most followed path (Fig. 10.2).

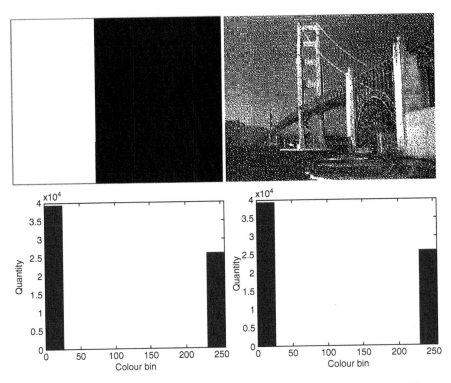

Fig. 10.2 An illustration of the semantic gap in image retrieval: the two images contain different semantic content but identical low-level content (the 256-bin histograms)

An emerging way to alleviate the problems caused by the semantic gap is to use crowdsourcing as a way to supplement the missing semantic information. Inferred semantic relationships can take many forms, but the more popular can be categorised as: browsing logs, where users casually peruse a document collection with no formal information need; click-through data, where information is sought but evidence of interest (the "click") may not always imply relevance [9, 62]; and relevance feedback judgements, where the user has a definite query and explicitly rates search results with respect to relevance in order to refine that query [35, 39]. Manually providing semantic data is also common, such as manual tagging of documents with keywords. However, in this chapter we focus on the less intrusive ways of collecting user interaction, as it is important for the users to feel free to operate naturally, without spending time consciously annotating and entering data.

Both information overload and the semantic gap have much to gain from user involvement when the data can be collected and processed effectively. The relatively new social web and the growth of user-driven content and collaboration is fuelling new research on the efficient use of user interaction data. For some time now, it has been shown that user browsing habits and general web trends can be extracted from web server logs [4, 42, 65]. These methods are now being applied to collections of multimedia documents lacking semantic metadata, web search result click-through [9], and virtually any area where user interaction can be harvested. A number of novel methods of extracting explicit user interaction data have been documented recently in the literature. For example, Ahn et al. [54] procured incentive to label images on the internet using a game-based approach which paired random users together to find agreement on semantic labels. A highest score list secured bragging rights as the motivation. Other similarly spawned crowdsourcing games from the same scientists include Peekaboom (object recognition) [56] and Phetch (image retrieval) [55]. Likewise, in the LabelMe project [46], incentive for researchers to use a region-level labelled image database encourages participation in the labelling process itself. While explicit user involvement such as these can potentially yield higher quality semantic data, the drawback is that the incentive must pass a certain threshold of enough users to make the collection technique worthwhile.

This problem motivates research in collecting implicit or *functional-based* user involvement data. This approach puts the generation of interaction data at a level where the users do not feel like they are performing a task because the user interaction is engineered to be subtle. Examples include the aforementioned long-term learning of relevance feedback or click-through data in information retrieval systems. Here the user is performing a functional task such as searching for a document; a side effect is that the user may select relevant documents or specify which examples are relevant to further refine the query. Associations can then be assumed on the keywords used in the query and the documents examined. Similarly, if a user is browsing a document database, a browsing strategy may afford a certain amount of semantic data, such as browsing a random sampling by concept (e.g., lizards of South America). The exact semantic labelling of such data may be more difficult, but it can also be useful to view this data as a graph of semantic similarity on the document database where the nodes denote documents and weighted edges semantic similarity.

This chapter is organised as follows. In Section 10.2, we review past works highlighting the main concepts of extracting and exploiting semantic data from user interaction. The survey is divided into the two distinct yet closely related topics: collaborative filtering and long-term learning. For each topic, we show the commonalities across the literature and summarise shortcomings. Next, in Section 10.3, we show how both applications of user interaction are related, and that ultimately the problem can be abstracted such that the presented methods work in both domains, depending only on the interpretation of the semantics. Next, a case study showing an example of long-term learning is given in Section 10.4. Here we demonstrate a simple example of how semantic concepts can be extracted from accumulated relevance feedback using latent semantic analysis. The results are applied to an image database to aid retrieval. Finally, the chapter ends with a discussion on similarities between and the drawbacks associated with each application of user interaction, followed by a conclusion.

10.2   Survey of Collaborative Filtering and Long-Term Learning

The following survey attempts to clearly present to the reader the main approaches and methodologies employed in the literature to date. While far from an exhaustive review of the two domains, it is hoped that it is sufficient to provide a starting point to those commencing study in collaborative filtering or long-term learning. A specific goal has been the review of more recent approaches, while also highlighting the main foundational studies on which they are built.

10.2.1   Collaborative Information Filtering

Collaborative information filtering describes the process of accumulating and propagating user judgements, normally for use in a recommender system where users are interested in purchasing and rating items such as movies, books, and other products. In order to better target users by recommending items relevant to their profiles, predictions must be made using historical data.

Collaborative filtering originated in the early 1990s from an influential paper by Goldberg et al. [17]. They devised an e-mail filtering system that allowed users to filter messages based on the reactions of other users to those messages. For example, if Alice and Bob replied to similar types of messages, Alice could save time by reading only the messages that Bob had replied to. The system, called *Tapestry*, also allowed filtering of e-mail by traditional content-based methods, using keywords contained in the messages. Thus, a user could enter a query such as "Find all messages replied to by Alice and Bob containing the words *bricks* and *small*."

Data collected from collaborative filtering, and within the larger context of the recommender system, falls into two categories: *implicit* and *explicit* data [25].

Implicitly collected data relies on users interacting with the system, but not explicitly rating items. Ratings, normally on a scale of *like* or *dislike*, can be inferred from this user interaction. For example, a customer purchasing an item generally implies a positive sentiment towards the item [24, 28]. However, this data has a certain ambiguity to it, because user behaviour can be unpredictable and we lack a certain cognitive basis for the inference. Conversely, explicit rating data is where users are consciously assigning relevance or sentiment towards items. An example is the rating of films, books, or jokes on websites [24]. This data has a greater inter-user bias because users rate items differently, but is less ambiguous than its counterpart.

Two major issues which must be overcome in collaborative filtering are data sparsity and computational scalability. Sparsity is a side effect of having many users and many items. Users will normally only rate a very small subset of the items, even through implicit means. Rarely will an item be rated by every user, and rarely will a user rate every item. This leads to a large amount of sparsity in the resulting dataset – typically more than 95% [13, 43, 48, 59]. Normally the user rating vectors are represented as a matrix, called the *user-item matrix*, and sparsity is seen as missing values, or zero-valued ratings (see Fig. 10.3). Sparsity leads to problems such as reduced recommendation quality and reduced coverage [48].

Scalability becomes a problem because as the number of users and items in a recommender system grows, complexity in computing similarities also becomes difficult. In order to recommend and predict ratings quickly, many current recommender systems require processing to be done offline [6, 13, 36].

Having matured for more than a decade since Goldberg's initial study, techniques for predicting ratings based on previous user interaction can be easily categorised into two distinct types: *model-based* and *memory-based* approaches. Model-based approaches involve the construction of a model based on training examples. Predictions can be quickly made by querying the model with the item. Memory-based

User

Item	u_1	u_2	u_3	u_4	u_5	u_6	u_7	u_8	u_9	u_{10}	...	u_K
i_1	1	0	1	0	1	0	0	0	1	0	...	0
i_2	0	0	0	0	0	0	0	0	0	0	...	1
i_3	0	0	0	0	0	0	0	0	0	0	...	1
i_4	0	1	0	0	0	1	0	1	0	1	...	0
i_5	0	0	1	0	0	0	0	0	0	0	...	0
i_6	0	0	0	0	1	0	0	0	0	1	...	0
i_7	1	0	0	1	0	0	0	1	0	0	...	0
i_8	0	0	0	0	0	0	0	0	0	1	...	1
i_9	0	0	0	0	0	1	1	0	0	0	...	0
⋮	⋮	⋮	⋮	⋮	⋮	⋮	⋮	⋮	⋮	⋮	⋱	⋮
i_N	1	0	0	0	1	0	1	0	1	0	...	0

Fig. 10.3 An example of user-item matrix sparsity for implicit rating data. A value of 1 signifies that user u_a purchased item i_j. Zeros are treated as missing values for explicit ratings [28]

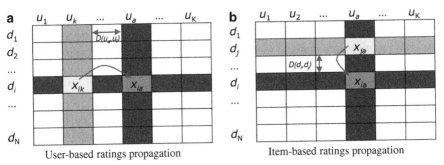

Fig. 10.4 An example of user- and item-based similarities used in memory-based collaborative filtering techniques. Rows d_{1-N} represent the items and columns u_{1-K} represent the users of the system and $D(d_i, d_j)$ and $D(u_a, u_k)$ are the distances between items d_i, d_j and users u_a, u_k respectively

approaches, on the other hand, store generated similarities and for each prediction, look up and recommend the closest matches. Both approaches involve some degree of offline processing. Model-based approaches require models to be updated each time ratings or items are added. The same applies to memory-based collaborative filtering, only it is the similarities that must be updated when new ratings or items become available. Model- and memory-based approaches can be further divided into *user-based*, *item-based*, and hybrid methods which attempt to unify the two.

User-based collaborative filtering finds users that have similar rating profiles to the active user and attempts to predict ratings for items which the active user has not rated. Conversely, item-based collaborative filtering takes a list of items rated by the current user and finds other similar items. In this way, the user can be recommended items based on what is in their online shopping cart or what they have purchased previously.

Another important distinction between user- and item-based CF is the type of rating which is desired. In user-based CF, we are looking for a prediction of how much a user will like a certain item. In item-based CF, we are looking for the top-N items to recommend to a user [48]. Figure 10.4a and b illustrate these differences.

10.2.1.1 Memory-Based Approaches

The GroupLens project [44], founded in the early 1990s, implemented a collaborative filtering system for recommending Usenet news articles. The memory-based approach found similarity between users and recommended unread articles to users based on these similarities. An explicit rating system was implemented in the user interface, which allowed users to rate the current article with a stroke of a key. The group now has several areas of study including MovieLens for movie recommendation, which allows researchers to use the database of film ratings, WikiLens, community maintained recommender systems [16], and MetaLens, a recommender system combining multiple sources of information for film recommendations [49].

Generally, for an active user a, a profile is learned and relevant items are recommended based on similarities to other users in the system. Correlation between users can be measured in many ways, for example, the Pearson correlation between users a and i:

$$P_{a,i} = \bar{x}_a + \frac{\sum_{u=1}^{n} [(x_{u,i} - \bar{x}_u) \cdot w_{a,u}]}{\sum_{u=1}^{n} w_{a,u}} \tag{10.1}$$

$$w_{a,u} = \frac{\sum_{i=1}^{m} [(x_{a,i} - \bar{x}_a)]}{\sqrt{\sum_{i=1}^{m} (x_{a,i} - \bar{x}_a)^2 \sum_{i=1}^{m} (x_{u,i} - \bar{x}_u)^2}} \tag{10.2}$$

where n is the number of users and m is the number of items. Similarly, cosine similarity

$$D_{a,i} = \frac{x_a \cdot x_i}{||x_a|| \cdot ||x_i||}, \tag{10.3}$$

where x_a denotes the ratings vector for user a, are often used.

The authors of [3] combined the properties of content-based and collaborative-based methods for the recommendation of web pages to users of the *Fab* system. By using the two modalities, they were able to alleviate the problem of having no ratings for a specific web page as well as having no content for a specific web page: if the system lacked data from one modality, the algorithm would fall back to using the other modality. The behaviour was not explicitly defined for when both modalities were missing. Users were not recommended pages they had already visited, and no more than one page per site was recommended in a batch.

Herlocker et al. [23] reviewed design choices for memory-based collaborative filtering in explicit ratings scenarios such as film, book, product review sites. They reviewed similarity measures, neighbour selection such as correlation weight thresholding or maximum neighbours, and rating combination methods. They concluded by recommending Pearson correlation as the similarity measure, at least for ratings data on a discreet scale. They also pointed out the importance of using significance weights to reduce neighbours with small numbers of overlapping ratings.

Walker et al. [57] provided a brief review and implemented user-based recommender system for web pages called *Altered Vista* in an educational domain. A similarity index was generated using Pearson correlation over users who have rated at least two or more items and neighbours were only selected if they have a correlation of at least 0.50. A total of 242 items were rated by 63 users, yielding a total of 934 ratings and a sparsity of 94%. The authors noted a strong positive rating bias, and cited it as the reason for an increase of error after limiting the size of the user neighbourhood.

Attempts have also been made to combine user- and item-based predictions which arguably improves performance by taking into consideration both modes simultaneously. For example, Wang et al. [58] used a combination of user- and item-based similarities in an attempt to reduce sparsity and predict ratings. Using the cosine similarity measure in both user- and item-based domains, they attempted to fuse predictions using a probabilistic framework based on controllable parameters which determined the importance of the different modes of data. In addition, they also took advantage of less similar users and items to smooth the ratings vectors.

10.2.1.2   Model-Based Approaches

Unlike their memory-based counterparts, model-based approaches attempt to build a predictive or generative model in order to make relevance predictions for items towards a specific user. Memory-based approaches offer limited room for improvement, as they are inherently based on similarity measures which have matured. It has been noted that memory-based methods are more prone to data sparsity, lack an aspect of learning and therefore cannot generalise, and are computationally intractable for very large datasets [28]. In comparison, model-based methods promise a greater diversity in approaches, improved scalability and in some cases, inherent treatment of sparsity [28, 48, 59].

Billsus and Pazzani [5] demonstrated a probabilistic user model based on a Simple Bayesian Classifier (SBC) for predicting user interest in text documents based on previous ratings. A trivial extension to the SBC was made in which the way per feature biases are treated was based on a threshold. If the expected information gain of a certain feature passes the threshold (0.1), the system used a Laplace correction for the estimate, otherwise, it used a very low constant in place of a zero probability, virtually masking the feature, avoiding the case where the joint probability score would become zero. The system was per-user; it did not cross-correlate user ratings for predictions.

Wang et al. [59] introduced a relevance model based on the principles relevance and non-relevance of documents in text retrieval which demonstrates how user- and item-based models are simply "different factorisations with different independence assumptions." The study also attempted to alleviate data sparsity by applying a linear interpolation smoothing to each item and user vector. Using implicitly gathered ratings from the Audioscrobbler community comprising 428 users, 516 items, and sparsity of 96.86%, the authors reported results on parity with the item-based top-N SUGGEST algorithm [13].

In [53], Masao et al. demonstrated relevance models in a user-based collaborative filtering setting. The authors described their Polya model, which is based on a Dirichlet compound multinomial distribution. Using a database of Wikipedia articles, the authors considered user edits on an article as an implicit positive rating on that article. They combined information retrieval and collaborative filtering such that a document in information retrieval corresponds to an item in collaborative filtering, and the words of the document correspond to the ratings of an item. The authors reported that their Polya model has comparable performance to state-of-the-art item-based collaborative filtering techniques.

Latent variable and factor models, born out of latent semantic analysis (LSA) for text retrieval in the early 1990s [10], have been extensively used in the collaborative filtering domain. For instance, Sarwar et al. [48] conducted a study using singular value decomposition (SVD) for top-N item recommendation. The study focused primarily on dimension reduction for collaborative filtering. They used SVD to calculate the predicted rating of a user on an item as well as finding item neighbours in the reduced space for top-N recommendations. To tackle sparsity they calculated a filled-in user-item matrix based on naive recommendations and subsequently factored and obtained a reduced rank approximation of the original matrix. As we will see in the case study in Section 10.4, the decomposition if a matrix A is formulated as:

$$A = U \Sigma V^T, \tag{10.4}$$

where the resulting matrices U, Σ, and V^T contain the eigenvectors of AA^T, the squares of the eigenvalues of $A^T A$, and the eigenvectors of $A^T A$, respectively. To calculate a prediction from the rank-k approximation of the original matrix, the dot product of the cth row of U and pth column of V^T were calculated, and the user average $\bar{C}$ was then added:

$$C_{P_{prod}} = \bar{C} + \left(U_k \cdot \sqrt{\Sigma_k}^T \right)(c) \cdot \left(\sqrt{\Sigma_k} \cdot V^T \right)(p). \tag{10.5}$$

For recommendation generation a neighbourhood was found for a user and the most frequently purchased items by the users' neighbours were recommended. Experiments centred around the use of the MovieLens dataset, sampled to contain 100,000 ratings from 943 users on 1,682 items, with a sparsity of 94%. Another experiment with 6,502 users purchasing 23,554 items yielding 97,045 ratings in total (sparsity 99.4%) was also carried out, although this data was not used for rating prediction. Using precision and recall as evaluation metrics, they found that performance was significantly worse for the very sparse purchase dataset and comparable using the MovieLens dataset. Experiments were also performed in order to find an optimal low-rank approximation, yielding optimal performance at $k = 20$ for film ratings and a linear improvement with the increase of k for purchase history, signifying that perhaps very sparse purchase histories are more difficult to group into coherent clusters.

In their paper, Marlin and Zemel [36] introduced a multiple multiplicative factor (MMF) model to generate item recommendations. This approach differs from other latent variable models in that it multiplies the factor distributions:

$$P(\mathbf{Z} = \mathbf{z}|\eta) = \prod_{k=1}^{K} P(Z_k = z_k|\eta_k). \tag{10.6}$$

According to the authors, the multiplicative formulation allows for predictions for specific dimensions to be determined by a subset of the active factors and yields a "sharper predicted distribution" in contrast to mixture models where the distributions are averaged. Furthermore, the authors claim of a complete vector having influence over a rated item differs from traditional aspect models where the influence is characterised by only one latent variable. The MMF was adapted to CF by treating the latent factors Z_k as "user attitudes" and data vectors $\mathbf{x^n}$ as user rating profiles. The authors conducted experiments on the EachMovie and MovieLens datasets, containing 35,000 users on 1,600 films, and 6,000 users on 3,500 films, respectively.[1] The results showed improvement over other approaches such as a Pearson-based K-nearest neighbour, multinomial and multinomial mixture models, and user rating profile models. A noted drawback was that the model was very complex during the learning and inference phases.

Hofmann, who first proposed a probabilistic analogue to LSA,[2] modified the traditional probabilistic latent semantic analysis (pLSA) algorithm for use in a film recommender system [28]. The premise of the study was that memory-based techniques were insufficient in several ways: accuracy, lack of generalisation, inability to scale to large datasets, and inability to tailor for specific tasks. Hofmann's user-based approach assumed independence between users and items by making use of a latent variable Z with states z, one for each of the total possible user-item pairs (u, y). The total number of states z was limited to k, which can be seen as analogous to the number of singular values retained in a low-rank approximation with SVD. These variables z, in effect were the number of overlapping *user communities* modelled by the system:

$$P(u|y; \theta) = \sum_z P(y|z)P(z|u) \tag{10.7}$$

The latent variables z, which generated the user ratings, were optimised using a *tempered* version of the expectation-maximisation algorithm [12, 27], which attempts to reduce model overfitting. Thus, the model generation consisted of estimating the priors in the E-step:

$$P(z|u, y; \hat{\theta}) = \frac{\hat{P}(y|z)\hat{P}(z|u)}{\sum_{z'} \hat{P}(y|z')\hat{P}(z'|u)} \tag{10.8}$$

and the M-step, which updates $P(y|z)$ and $P(z|u)$ based on the new distributions calculated in the E-step:

$$P(y|z) = \frac{\sum_{(u,y'):y'=y} Q^*(z; u, y, \hat{\theta})}{\sum_{(u,y)} Q^*(z; u, y, \hat{\theta})} \tag{10.9}$$

$$P(z|u) = \frac{\sum_{(u',y):u'=u} Q^*(z; u, y, \hat{\theta})}{|\{\langle u', y \rangle : u' = u\}|}. \tag{10.10}$$

Where $Q^*(z; u, y)$ is a variational probability distribution for every observed pair. While the above model was sufficient for predicting whether a user will purchase an item, the model had to be extended for user ratings, and a new observed variable v was introduced which represented the rating scale ([0–5]), however we shall omit

---

[1] Sparsity values were not given for the subsampled datasets, but only users with more than 20 ratings were considered.

[2] See [26] for details.

the details here. The pLSA model was tested on the EachMovie dataset comprising 61,265 users, 1,623 items and over 2.1 million ratings. The author noted a lower mean average error compared to a memory-, user-based approach using the Pearson correlation.

10.2.1.3 Summary

In this section we have introduced memory- and model-based collaborative filtering techniques which include user- and item-based approaches, depending on the intended application in a recommender system. Collaborative filtering, in its early conception, took advantage of memory-based approaches which grouped similar users and items in order to propagate rating predictions onto unrated items. Soon after, researchers began to see the benefits of using model-based approaches, but both approaches are still used today.

Because of the commercial aspect, large ratings datasets have been available for some time (as opposed to databases of relevance feedback histories, as we will see in the Section 10.2.2). Due to privacy implications, virtually all are released in an anonymous version with any personally identifiable material removed. Such freely available databases include the *Jester Online Joke Recommendation System* dataset [18], the *EachMovie* dataset [37], the *MovieLens* dataset [44], the *BookCrossing* dataset [66], and the more recently released dataset for the *Netflix Prize* [43].

Sparsity and complexity are the two major issues faced when building a collaborative filtering system. Many studies attempt to explicitly treat sparsity before any predictions are made. Sparsity is related to two other problems in collaborative filtering. These are the cold start problem and the few ratings problem. The cold start issue presents itself when a new recommender system is deployed and there are no user ratings to make predictions. The few ratings problem is where user has not rated many items, so item and rating predictions for this user will normally be of poor quality.

10.2.2 Long-Term Learning of Relevance Feedback

The overall goal of long-term learning is to improve information retrieval on a database. This result, however, can be realised in several ways. The semantic data extracted from past relevance feedback sessions can be used to propagate annotations images in the database, either from a training set or a representative pre-annotated portion of the database. If the annotations are language-based, such as keywords, these can be indexed directly for later keyword-based queries.

Relevance feedback (RF) is a method of allowing the user to iteratively refine a query by marking relevant and irrelevant examples. The most popular method, Rocchio's formula, was introduced in 1971 [45]. A query is modified based on relevant and irrelevant examples such that

$$q' = \alpha q + \beta \frac{1}{|R|} \sum_{d_j \in R} d_j - \gamma \frac{1}{|R|} \sum_{d_j \in R} d_j, \qquad (10.11)$$

where d is the document in relevance space R, q is the original query, weighted by α, and β, γ weight positive and negative examples. Typically, relevance feedback simply uses a discreet rating scale. Following a query, a rating $r_i \in \{-1, 0, +1\}$ can be assigned where -1 signifies non-relevance to the query, 0 denotes an unrated document, and $+1$ signifies relevance to the query. Accommodating a gradient or fuzzy scale [60], where a user rates a document between a minimum and maximum of relevance, for example between 1 and 5 with 5 being most relevant, is also common, however it has been argued that increasing the number of choices available to the user can inhibit ratings and pronounce the ratings bias problem where users inherently rate documents differently [2].

Many variations have appeared in the literature since Rocchio but it was only until recently that research began focusing on using long-term learning on cumulative relevance feedback instances [22, 39, 61]. Although the historical data provided by relevance feedback is used extensively in the following literature, the actual relevance feedback algorithms and techniques in the short-term sense are not reviewed here. For a thorough review on relevance feedback for short-term learning, the reader is directed to both [47] and Chapter 10 of [2] which specifically covers user interfaces and interaction.

Due to the complex nature of the problem, many areas have been explored to bridge the semantic gap using long-term learning. The core idea is to extend the traditional relevance feedback model such that it persists over future queries. The motivation behind this idea can be seen in the probability distribution that emerges from user interaction. In many natural settings, including human interaction, a power law distribution is observed (see Fig. 10.5). In information retrieval, it has been shown that this distribution, also known as the 80–20 rule, yields queries in

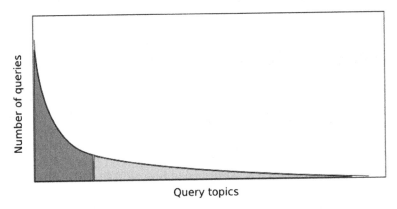

Query topics

Fig. 10.5 An illustrative example of the long tail of user queries in an information retrieval system. The majority of the searches comprise only a small portion of the distribution, leaving a tail composed of infrequent searches

which the most frequent fall in the first 20% and the less frequent are distributed along the *long tail* – the last 80% [1]. If 80% of users search for 20% of the information, there is a large amount of duplication involved, allowing subsequent query sessions to be more efficient and accurate.

Compared with collaborative filtering, the user interaction data associated with long-term learning is somewhat different. The aforementioned categories of implicit and explicit data do not fit well with the relevance feedback model. This is because in relevance feedback, the user is approaching the system from a functional perspective. This *functional-based* user involvement is both implicit and explicit in the sense that the user is not cognitively rating the documents for any purpose other than the current query session, yet there is still an explicit rating of similarity between rated documents and the query. However, in the context of long-term learning, we feel that this data falls more into the category of implicit data, so we shall refer to it accordingly. Click-through data, on the other hand, is more obviously viewed as implicit because the user will be browsing search results by clicking on relevant documents. These click-throughs can be readily compared to purchases in collaborative filtering, where a purchase infers some positive endorsement.

Long-term learning suffers from sparsity and scalability in much the same way as collaborative filtering. The number of documents in a database is normally very large, and there can be a large number of users as well. Yet for an average query, the user may find the desired document after specifying only a few relevant and non-relevant examples. This can be akin to a user in CF who has only purchased a handful of items, so arguably the sparsity problem is amplified.

As with CF, problems with scalability result when the number of documents and relevance feedback sessions grows such that offline processing is required to update models in order to make swift similarity judgements in the semantic space during a query. This is especially evident with latent semantic analysis (LSA) based approaches, which normally rely heavily on singular value decomposition (SVD) to realise semantic propagation.

The survey that follows has been grouped into approaches to facilitate easier perusal.

10.2.2.1 Rule-Based Approaches

The Viper group from the University of Geneva produced one of the first studies which examined long-term learning to aid future queries [39, 40]. The authors analysed the logs of image queries using the *GIFT (GNU Image Finding Tool)* demonstration system over a long period of time and used this information to update *tf-idf* (term frequency-inverse document frequency) feature weightings in the low-level feature space via an adaptation of Rocchio's algorithm. Images were paired based on two rules: images sharing similar features and also marked relevant have a high weight while images sharing similar features but marked both relevant and irrelevant should have a low weight (indicating a semantic disagreement). The authors alluded similarities to market basket analysis where a query session is synonymous to a purchase basket, and relationships between items (images) build the purchase (query). Two factors were introduced to manage the relevance feedback information. The first being a measure of the difference between the positively and negatively rated marks for each feature and the second re-weighting the positively and negatively marked features differently such that the ratio is scaled non-linearly.

In [64], the authors developed a retrieval system employing both short-term and long-term learning of relevance feedback. A rule-based approach was used to group positive and negative examples for the current session based on past groupings. Working under the constraint that the sets must maintain concept distinction, past RF sessions would aid future queries by locating the closest concept grouping. If concept distinction is broken, where non-orthogonal concepts exist within the data, the system falls back to an initialised state for the current query, relying solely on short-term relevance feedback.

10.2.2.2   Transformation of Feature Vectors

Long-term learning can also be used to reweight low-level feature vectors used in the retrieval engine rather than modifying the query vector. For example, the authors of [31] demonstrated a document transformation algorithm for long-term learning of click-through data for web search engines. Document transformation changes the representation of documents permanently [7] by considering each document vector as a sum of the original document terms in addition to a learned part. The learned part is updated based on past relevance feedback sessions. The authors used a collection of 4,100 referer logs from a university web server as click-through data, but it is unclear how irrelevant documents were counted, as the data did not come from a search engine which would have had a view of the complete result set for each query.

In another example, Wenyin et al. [61] described an approach for automatic image annotation by long-term learning. As a user browses an image database using a content-based retrieval system, iteratively providing relevance feedback, the system permanently updates weights associated with indexed image keywords. Unannotated images are annotated using the new image as a query and taking the keywords from the top N results. The performance of the system was evaluated on a database of 12,200 images, in 122 classes, mostly from the Corel database. Artificial relevance feedback data was collected by selecting the relevant and non-relevant images in the top 100 results. Using 0% and 10% initial annotations on these images, the authors tested the accuracy of the semi-automatic annotation. After 20 iterations of relevance feedback, the accuracy over 122 classes was roughly 68%. Accuracy was calculated by comparing the newly annotated images with the ground truth images.

In [8], long-term user interaction with a relevance feedback system was used to make better semantic judgements on unlabelled images for the purpose of image annotation. Cord et al. postulated that relationships between images which are created during relevance feedback can denote similar or dissimilar concepts. The authors tried to learn semantic space by augmenting feature vectors around a group of concept points. These concept points are calculated by computing the centre of gravity on labelled feature vectors. The idea is to increasingly cluster the vectors around the concept centres as users interact with the system. In their experiments, labels were randomly generated for a database containing 6,000 images from 50 concepts from the Corel dataset. For each session, 50 positive and 50 negative labels were created, yielding a density of 1.6% (98.4% sparsity). The authors found increases in mean average precision as well as computation time over traditional approaches.

10.2.2.3 Latent-Variable Approaches

As we have seen for many collaborative filtering approaches, latent-variable approaches such as latent semantic analysis (LSA), traditionally used in text retrieval, have also been explored for long-term learning. The model is adapted such that the terms become the images and the documents become the query sessions, with all instances of relevance feedback combined into one vector. The matrix representation remains the same; however, each element takes a value of 1, 0, or -1, depending on the relevance of the image with respect to the query (this will be further detailed in the case study of Section 10.4).

In [22], the authors aimed to improve image retrieval performance using LSA adapted from text retrieval. For images with no previous relevance feedback judgements, the system falls back to the low-level feature space to create a pseudo-document, or pseudo-relevance feedback based on low-level feature similarities with other documents. The authors performed a validation experiment on image databases consisting of both texture and segmentation data from the MIT and UCI repositories.[3] A total of 640 images from 15 semantic categories were used from the MIT repository and 2,310 images from the seven class UCI repository. Random queries were created and two sessions of relevance feedback were conducted to generate the historical information to be processed by LSA. Dimension reduction for SVD was fixed at $k = 100$. From experiments on different levels of data, they concluded that LSA is robust to a lack of data quality but is highly dependent on the sparsity of interaction data.

Singular value decomposition was used to generate a semantic space using patterns of relevance feedback in [21]. Low-level features were used in conjunction with the long-term relevance feedback data to improve performance in the MiAlbum image retrieval system. Artificial relevance feedback data was generated by running simulated queries on a database of categorised images and using the positive and negative examples taken from the top three relevant and top three non-relevant results respectively. A support vector machine was used for the short-term learning, classifying the images in the reduced semantic space created by the decomposition. As in [30], the authors attempted to show a theoretical upper bound on the amount of relevance feedback required to minimise the number of disagreements (mistakes) between the system and the user. A database of 10,000 images over 79 semantic

---

[3] http://archive.ics.uci.edu/ml/

categories from the Corel dataset was used. The semantic space is continually updated as the system is used, however, no mention was made of images which are unlabelled by users during relevance feedback. They noted that the main issue in augmenting the semantic space is the estimation of the rank of the reduced semantic space, represented as k in the singular value decomposition, and is closely related to the number of semantic classes in the database. This was also noted in [21,38].

Koskela and Laaksonen [32] use long-term learning in their PicSOM retrieval system. PicSOM is based on multiple parallel tree-structured self-organising maps (SOMs) and uses MPEG7 content descriptors for features. The authors claimed that by the use of SOMs the system automatically picks the most relevant features. As in [22], the authors used the interactions as documents and the images as words from the vocabulary for LSA. They noted that the relevance feedback information provided by the users is similar to hidden annotations. Using the Corel dataset (59,995 images, 6,897 annotated positively, 317 sessions) with a ground truth set of 6 classes, the authors reported a significant increase in performance over a standard low-level feature approach.

Morrison et al. [38] clustered images using singular value decomposition based on historical patterns of relevance feedback. These clusters were used to improve image retrieval in a content-based retrieval setting. Citing previous works showing success using latent semantic analysis, they used this technique in experiments on both real and artificial datasets in an attempt to determine the validity of previous studies which use only artificial relevance feedback data. Among topics discussed in the study are the optimal rank of the approximated image-session matrix, which is confirmed to relate directly to the number of discernible concepts in the underlying data. Average precision was highest when the decomposition was cropped at $k = 10$ singular values, which matched the number of concepts in the image database. They concluded that for the purposes of model and parameter selection, artificial data can be useful when real-world data is difficult to collect. The authors reflected that their study did not consider the power-law distribution, which normally accompanies user interaction.

Franco and Lumini [15] constructed a retrieval system employing short- and long-term learning. All past relevance feedback sessions, dubbed the "global query space," were grouped into Karhunen–Loève (KL) subspaces by selecting the first k eigenvectors derived from the KL transformation of the original space. The parameter k, they noted, is bounded by both the feature space and the number of samples. Their MKL transform (mixture of KL), a generalised version of the KL transform, was built using relevant and irrelevant image subspaces, called regions. Relevant regions comprise images rated as relevant in the first relevance feedback iteration, and similarly for non-relevant images. Although computationally complex, the MKL space is updated by merging the new space derived from the most recent RF iteration into the set of global spaces already collected. For their evaluations, the authors conducted experiments on three image databases and demonstrated improvement in retrieval accuracy with the long-term learning approach compared to retrieval without. Sparsity is not explicitly treated, but the system does fall back into a content-based mode if the relevant space is not sufficiently populated.

10.2.2.4 Statistical Approaches

In [14], the authors combined relevance feedback-based long-term user interactions with content-based features to build semantic similarities between images for use in later retrieval sessions. The similarity model between the request and target images are refined during a standard relevance feedback process for the current session. This refinement and fusion is facilitated by a *barycenter*. The paper also discussed the problems with asymmetrical learning, where the irrelevant images are marked irrelevant by the user for a variety of reasons, whereas relevant images are marked relevant only because they relate semantically to the query. Therefore, the authors reduced the relevance of irrelevant images during the fusion of feedback stages. The long-term similarity measure is applied at the end of each retrieval session. An experiment was conducted to verify the system using a database of 1,200 colour images. The authors reported a significant increase in accuracy even after few uses. The paper concluded with a note that the system does not support a multiple user scenario, also suggesting that it may be helpful to explore usage on a large database.

In [19] introduced an active learning approach to long-term learning where a kernel matrix is updated with new user labels after each retrieval session. A rule-based merging of the kernel matrix and the most recent relevance feedback session allowed positively labelled images to become more similar, and images labelled positively and negatively to become less similar. Long-term learning data is synthetically generated using the ground truth categories. 50 examples are labelled over 10 simulated retrieval sessions. The approach was evaluated on an database containing 6,000 images from the Corel collection over 11 categories. The proposed method outperformed basic and support vector machine-based (SVM) active learning mechanisms. A low-rank approximation of the full kernel matrix via QR decomposition was proposed to handle large databases linearly.

The authors of [34] gathered real-world user relevance feedback in their long-term learning system. They proposed a Min/Max strategy that attempts to minimise the distance between similar images and maximise the distance between dissimilar images in the geometric vector space. Their regularised distance metric learning learns the distance metric associated with semantic categories. Because the algorithm is computing feature vector distances, the system is scalable in the sense that adding more images and relevance judgements only linearly increases the complexity.

Similarly, in [33], a statistical correlation model was built to create semantic relationships between images based on the co-occurrence frequency that a set of images are rated relevant to a query. These relationships were fused with low-level features to propagate the annotations onto unseen images. The long-term similarity measure is applied at the end of each retrieval session. An experiment was conducted to verify the system using a database of 1,200 images. Approximately 3,000 image query sessions with relevance feedback were recorded by having two users query twice for each of 20 keywords and provide relevance feedback on the query. Retrieval precision was averaged over each subject and the authors report an increase from 10% to 40% for the top 10 images, and 4.6% to 18.5% for the top 100 images.

Graph-based methods are also commonly used to represent user interaction. Craswell and Szummer [9] used Markov random walks on a large bipartite click graph of keyword-based queries and images collected from a popular online search engine. The click-through data was regarded as soft relevance feedback data where a click signifies relevance to the query (supposedly by having browsed the resulting thumbnails). By following walks either backward or forward from the query on the graph, document clusters could be found for associated search keywords.

10.2.2.5   Summary

In this section we have reviewed the literature on long-term learning of relevance feedback. Long-term learning of user interaction is a useful tool to help bridge the semantic gap, propagate semantic knowledge over a document database, and improve retrieval precision and recall on subsequent queries.

It should be apparent that the majority of these studies share common traits. First, due to the difficulty in acquiring large amounts of relevance feedback for image databases, there is a general trend to use artificial data, often generated based on ground-truth concepts (image categories). Typically, the system picks a set number of relevant and irrelevant images from a random query for a specific image [8, 14, 19, 21, 22, 38]. In general, data sparsity is a realised constraint and labelled data constitutes between 0.01% and 5% of the image database, which tends to agree with the few studies that do investigate real-world data [34, 38]. Unlike the many collaborative filtering datasets available for research, access to large volumes of user searches is generally restricted to big search engine companies such as Google, Yahoo, and Microsoft. Despite growing privacy concerns, and some bungled data releases,[4] there is growing collaboration between academia and big search engine companies [9].

The second trait is that most studies in long-term learning have only looked at orthogonal query concepts. In other words, only very simple queries are assumed, where inherent concepts do not overlap and are separable. In a real world setting, this is rarely the case. For example, topics are usually separated according to preselected image categories such as "horse," "dog,", "sunset,", "elephant," etc. In this case, it is assumed the user is always searching for at most one concept. But if the user decides to search for images of horses that also contain dogs, traditional orthogonal models are suddenly insufficient.

---

[4] In August 2006, AOL Research released millions of anonymous search histories only to have some queries subsequently linked to at least one individual by identifiable keywords [20]. Later, in October 2006, security researchers reversed the anonymous Netflix movie ratings data by cross-referencing ratings and dates with publicly available data on IMDB.com [41].

10.3   Unifying Interaction Domains

Having introduced formative and recent works as well as the fundamental properties of both interaction domains, we now summarise the commonalities between the two to demonstrate that work in one domain is easily transferred to the other. Information retrieval has traditionally been viewed from a content-based perspective, naturally because the documents can only be represented by their derived features. Although we have seen that the field is active with respect to exploiting user interaction, it can be argued that not enough emphasis is being put on these approaches. Users play a very important role in the information retrieval life cycle, and therefore information derived from these interactions should be considered carefully. Recommender systems, being at a much younger age due to their birth alongside the internet, have clearly benefited from the close-knit underlying social networking systems and online communities. In this sense, research in this field is very active, due mostly to the economic incentive of recommending products to customers.

10.3.1   Propagation of Interaction Data

Collaborative filtering in recommender systems and long-term learning in retrieval systems share a common trait which is the propagation of high-level information across items. In long-term learning, the goal is to propagate relevance judgements for documents with respect to a query or high-level concept. Although the system may have many users, typically there is no distinction between which users made which queries. A retrieval system does not need to make a distinction between users because the goal is to predict documents that are relevant to semantically similar queries. In a system which does in fact allow for some personalisation, this would be represented as another modality, and models would require adaptation.

Contrast this to recommender systems, where each user has a specific profile. In this domain this information is very important, and allows the comparison of profiles to make predictions on unrated items. The propagation that is occurring here is that of predictions on items for a specific user.

Looking at both domains within the context of the representation of user interaction, the documents in information retrieval can be seen as the items in a recommender system, and the query sessions analogous to the users, with one small exception: when new item ratings are recorded, the data becomes less sparse. However, when new queries are recorded, sparsity remains constant and redundancy is increased. Further, an indication of relevance in information retrieval is analogous to a rating in recommender systems.

10.3.2   Dealing with Sparsity

As we have seen, sparsity is a problem that dramatically affects performance in both domains. It is inherently related to the cold start problem where the system is not able to make predictions or suggest relevant documents when there is no data available on which to base them. Sparsity is most evident when an item or document has never been rated; this item has no link through user profiles or queries and therefore cannot be recommended based only on user interaction. In long-term learning, we can deal with sparsity by introducing a concept called pseudo-relevance-feedback, where semantic similarity is initially assumed based on low-level feature distances to other documents. Another approach sees semantically ambiguous documents highlighted (perhaps mixed into the search results) so that the interaction required to disambiguate them are more likely to be found. If the user never sees a document, it will never be rated.

Low-level features and meta-data can also be used to alleviate sparsity in collaborative filtering where we have some information on the items being rated: genre, style, cost, size, weight, etc. These high- and low-level features can take the place of user ratings if properly accounted for, say by a weighting scheme similar to that aforementioned. Of course, the problem with assuming too much from low-level features is that these systems will then be inferring semantic information where none exists.

10.3.3   On Types of User Interaction

The user interaction data gathered from recommender and information retrieval systems has inherent differences. Although an information retrieval system can build a database of explicit user judgements on similarity between images, this is rarely the case. When it is the case [63], it is arguably unscalable to large databases and a burden on the users of the system. Therefore it is most common for user interaction data to come from implicit means, and as we have seen, this comes from actual use of the retrieval system itself in the form of functional-based interaction. This functional scenario allows the data to be captured without being any more of a burden than a user would normally experience. This functional implicit interaction, however, is in fact a hybrid of implicit and explicit interaction. It is explicit because the user is explicitly providing a judgement on an item's relevance to a query; and it is implicit because relevance feedback is just one of the stages of a state-of-the-art information retrieval system, and it can be assumed that the user does not regard the process as providing data to aid queries in the longer term. The fact that historical relevance feedback judgements are used in the long term rather than discarded after each session does not affect the user.

Recommender systems have much more flexibility in this regard, affording both implicit and explicit interaction, depending on the application domain. Implicit data, collected from actions such as purchases allows inference of taste towards items.

From an explicit perspective, recommender systems have a unique position where users feel motivated to rate items, either from feeling a completeness for rating their entire film collection or a satisfaction that by rating items they will improve the system's ability to suggest new items of interest.

10.3.4 Underlying Relationship to the Power Law Distribution

In long-term learning, the observed power law distribution, where the top N queries constitute the majority of the interaction data, is directly exploited to make subsequent queries more accurate. If a query lies in the first 20% of this distribution, there is a high likelihood that it can be used in the future. The effectiveness of this is reduced as we traverse the distribution along the long tail of infrequent queries.

In a recommender system, the power law plays another role and is exploited differently. Many collaborative filtering systems acknowledge that it is in fact the long tail – the 80% of infrequent ratings – that are of high value. Simply suggesting the most popular items will not win over many users. As [24] remarked, suggesting bananas to shoppers may be accurate, but many shoppers will have already known about bananas, so it is more useful to suggest items they may not be familiar with.

10.4 Long-Term Learning in Image Retrieval: A Case Study

In this section we introduce an example case study for improving image retrieval using long-term learning. The example is not meant to be extensive, but does take principles from the state-of-the-art. Suppose we wish to improve retrieval accuracy on a frequently queried image database. We can imagine that the current retrieval algorithm employs a similarity measure over a colour-based low-level feature vector and also allows users to specify relevance feedback iteratively until the desired image has been found. The details of the low-level features and the exact implementation of the similarity measure and relevance feedback algorithm are not discussed here, since we wish to demonstrate the long-term learning aspect on relevance feedback data using latent semantic analysis. Specifically, we want to show how many relevance feedback sessions are necessary before a good average precision is achieved.

Because LSA traditionally works with term-document matrices in text retrieval, we shall adapt this for our relevance feedback data, as has been shown in [21, 22]. Thus, the terms become the images and the documents become the relevance feedback data. In this way, each instance of relevance feedback can be thought of as a document containing occurrences of images as terms. Some "documents" may share terms, meaning an image has been marked relevant in more than one query. However, unlike text documents, an image can only occur at most once in a session.

Query session

	q_1	q_2	q_3	q_4	q_5	q_6	q_7	q_8	q_9	q_{10}	$\cdots$	q_m
d_1	0	1	−1	0	0	1	0	0	1	1	...	0
d_2	−1	0	1	1	0	0	0	0	0	0	...	1
d_3	0	0	0	0	0	0	0	0	0	0	...	−1
d_4	0	−1	1	0	1	−1	1	−1	0	−1	...	0
d_5	1	0	0	0	0	0	0	1	0	0	...	0
d_6	1	0	0	0	−1	0	0	0	0	1	...	0
d_7	−1	0	−1	−1	0	0	0	1	0	0	...	0
d_8	0	0	0	0	0	0	0	0	0	1	...	−1
d_9	0	0	0	0	0	1	1	1	0	0	...	0
$\vdots$	$\vdots$	$\vdots$	$\vdots$	$\vdots$	$\vdots$	$\vdots$	$\vdots$	$\vdots$	$\vdots$	$\vdots$	$\ddots$	$\vdots$
d_n	0	−1	1	1	0	0	−1	0	1	0	...	0

(Image label on left: **Image**)

Fig. 10.6 An example image-session matrix

10.4.1 Formulation

Suppose the image database exists containing n images (d_{1-n}) and m query sessions (q_{1-m}) representing the instances of relevance feedback. We can formulate a matrix A of size $n \times m$ where each element

$$a_{ij} = \begin{cases} 1 & \text{where image } d_i \text{ is relevant to query } q_j \\ -1 & \text{where image } d_i \text{ is not relevant to query } q_j \\ 0 & \text{no relevance between } d_i \text{ and } q_j. \end{cases}$$

One will then arrive at a representation such as that in Fig. 10.6. As we can see, the representation is very similar to the example user-item matrix in Section 10.2.1 (Fig. 10.3) except here we are allowing for negative ratings.

10.4.2 Latent Semantic Analysis

Latent semantic analysis, primarily used in text retrieval, uses at its core singular value decomposition [11]. Given a sparse $m \times n$ term-document matrix A, a decomposition $A = U \Sigma V^T$ is calculated, normally through a QR decomposition, which yields U ($m \times n$), the term-concept matrix, Σ ($n \times n$), a diagonal matrix containing the singular values in decreasing order, and V^T ($n \times n$), the concept-document matrix.

Normally, a form of dimension reduction is then applied, often referred to as *rank lowering*, where only the top k singular values are retained, and the original matrix can be approximated by multiplying the three components

$$A_k = U_k \Sigma_k V_k^T. \tag{10.12}$$

This dimension reduction has the effect of causing zero valued entries in the original matrix A to become non-zero. By multiplying either the term-concept matrix U or the concept-document matrix V by the diagonal matrix Σ and their respective transposes, one determines directly a term-term (or document-document) similarity matrix in this new rank-k approximated semantic space:

$$T_{sim} = U_k \Sigma_k^2 U_k^T, \tag{10.13}$$

and

$$D_{sim} = V_k \Sigma_k^2 V_k^T. \tag{10.14}$$

Our decision to use latent semantic analysis over classical supervised classification approaches comes from the fact that LSA is very good at discovering underlying concepts in data without the need of having these categories defined initially. LSA is also naturally suited for dealing with the term-document matrix because the derived semantic classes are orthogonal. A problem does arise, however, when there are many overlapping semantic classes. Singular value decomposition is not well suited for this problem. In this case study, the semantic classes are assumed (and generated) to be non-overlapping.

10.4.3 Database

As we have seen from previous work, exploitation of user interaction can help bridge the semantic gap by making available the underlying semantic knowledge expressed by users during image retrieval sessions. However, as we have discussed in Section 10.2.2, real-world user interaction data is often difficult and time-consuming to acquire. Therefore, in the interest of the demonstration, we will simulate the relevance feedback by sampling from a uniform distribution relevance examples from each image category in the database.

The image database used in the following experiments is a subset of the Corel collection. 2,000 images from 20 categories (100 images per category) were selected.[5] Figure 10.7 shows a random sampling from the dataset. Next, artificial relevance feedback sessions were created based on the same image categories.

First, a ground truth image-session matrix is generated based on the underlying image categories. This matrix is much like the representation in Fig. 10.6, but the relevance feedback judgements for each query are complete. In other words, with respect to each query concept, every image in the database is rated as either relevant or irrelevant. This matrix will no doubt be highly redundant, but it is only

---

[5] Image categories used are: *colors_and_textures, cougars, creative_crystals, creative_textures, cuisine, desserts, dolphins_and_whales, elephants, endangered_species, everyday_objects, fabulous_fruit, fireworks, fitness, flowering_potted_plants, flowers_closeup, foxes_and_coyotes, frost_textures, fruits_and_nuts, fungi, hawks_and_falcons.*

Fig. 10.7 Example images randomly sampled from the 20 categories. Not all categories may be represented

the basis for computing an artificially sparse image-session matrix. We generated a mask of uniform noise thresholded at a coverage percentage. For example, noise generated at a coverage percentage of 99% would randomly delete 99% of the elements in the image-session matrix, simulating the sparsity normally seen. This deletion is realised through matrix multiplication, where a matrix of uniform noise N_c thresholded at coverage c (such that each element $n_{ij} = \{0, 1\}$) is multiplied element-by-element with the complete image-session matrix A:

$$A_{sparse} = N_c A \qquad (10.15)$$

10.4.4 Experiments

The goal of the experiments is to determine a suitable amount of relevance feedback data so that average precision is sufficient in a retrieval setting. For the experiments, we fixed the simulated sparsity at 99.0% to closely model a real-world scenario. The average precision is a function of the number of retrieval sessions. Recall that average precision is defined as

$$\mathrm{AP} = \frac{\sum_{r=1}^{N} (P(r) \times \mathrm{rel}(r))}{\text{total relevant documents}} \qquad (10.16)$$

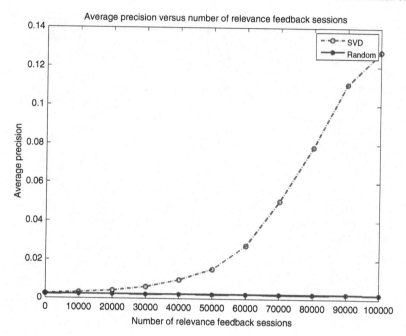

Fig. 10.8 Average precision versus the number of relevance feedback sessions with fixed $k = 20$ and 99.0% sparsity

where r is the rank of the document, N denotes the total documents received, rel() denotes binary relevance, and $P()$ precision.

Figure 10.8 shows the average precision plotted against a random retrieval for comparison. There is an exponential increase in average precision with a linear increase in the number of relevance feedback sessions. Due to the high sparsity, we do not see much improvement over random until after 60,000 relevance feedback sessions.

Figure 10.9 shows an example image similarity matrix as per Eq. 10.13. The categories are well grouped, despite the very high sparsity. Singular value decomposition performs well when redundant examples are given.

10.4.5 Discussion

This case study provided a brief example of using latent semantic analysis for grouping historical relevance feedback sessions to aid image retrieval. Sparsity poses a large problem in this domain, but this can be offset by gathering a large amount of long-term user interaction from image queries. In retrieval systems where hundreds of thousands of images queries are performed each day, the improvement in retrieval would be significant.

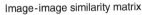

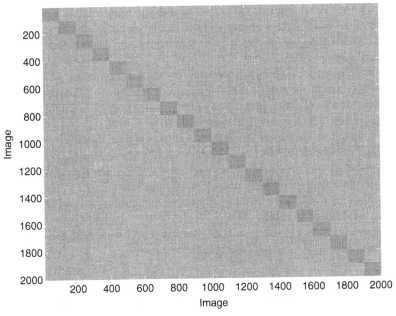

Fig. 10.9 Image similarity matrix with fixed $k = 20$ and 99.0% sparsity at 90,000 relevance feedback sessions

10.5 Conclusion

In this chapter we have attempted to unify two domains, *collaborative filtering* for recommender systems and *long-term learning* for information retrieval, under the umbrella of crowdsourcing for information gain. We highlighted examples from recent literature which show how the problem of information overload can be eased by collaborative filtering approaches. Likewise, the problematic semantic gap in information retrieval can also be narrowed by collecting and mining relevance feedback histories.

We examined the different types of user interaction data that exist within the two domains: implicit data, such as item purchases or click-through in information retrieval; explicit data, where users make a conscious effort to rate items for future gain; and a type of hybrid of the two which is unique to relevance feedback in information retrieval: functional-based data, where a user is performing a task which involves a cognitive aspect and a side effect is usable semantic information. In addition, we looked at how both domains must deal with inherent data sparsity due to a lack of ratings in collaborative filtering and a lack of relevance feedback judgements in information retrieval.

By perusing the literature, we extracted the fundamentals from each domain. In collaborative filtering, techniques are broadly divided into memory- and model-based approaches, while the recommender systems in which they are used decide whether the recommendations must be user- or item-based. Research in long-term learning tends to favour analogues to model-based approaches in collaborative filtering, yielding techniques such as feature transforms, rule-based, and latent-variable models.

The underlying principle of the propagation of semantic data was also discussed, and how it relates to the cold start problem in both domains, and the problem where a user has little or no item ratings in a recommender system. Scalability was also briefly explored, which is an often overlooked factor.

The long tail, or the power law distribution, a term describing the exponentially decreasing popularity of items in recommender systems and user queries in information retrieval was examined. Recommender systems often have much more to gain by exploiting the long tail, rather than recommending the most popular items. On the other hand long-term learning in information retrieval focuses on exploiting duplicity in frequent searches.

It is hoped that the chapter serves as a starting point for students and researchers beginning study in the growing field of either domain.

Acknowledgements This research was funded by the Swiss National Science Foundation (NSF) through IM2 (Interactive Multimedia Information Management).

References

1. Chris Anderson, *The long tail*, Wired Magazine **12** (2004), no. 10.
2. Ricardo Baeza-Yates and Neto-Ribeiro Berthier, *Modern information retrieval*, Addison-Wesley, Essex, England, 1999.
3. Marko Balabanović and Yoav Shoham, *Fab: content-based, collaborative recommendation*, Commun. ACM **40** (1997), no. 3, 66–72.
4. Pierre Baldi, Paolo Frasconi, and Padhraic Smyth, *Modeling the internet and the web: Probabilistic methods and algorithms*, John Wiley & Sons, West Sussex, England, 2003.
5. Daniel Billsus and Michael Pazzani, *Learning probabilistic user models*, Proceedings of the Workshop on Machine Learning for User Modeling (Chia Laguna, IT), 1997.
6. C. Boutilier, R. Zemel, and B. Marlin, *Active collaborative filtering*, In Proceedings of the Nineteenth Annual Conference on Uncertainty in Artificial Intelligence, 2003, pp. 98–106.
7. T. Brauen, *Document vector modification*, The SMART Retrieval System (G. Salton, ed.), Prentice Hall, New Jersey, 1971, pp. 456–484.
8. M. Cord and P. H. Gosselin, *Image retrieval using long-term semantic learning*, IEEE International Conference on Image Processing, 2006.
9. Nick Craswell and Martin Szummer, *Random walks on the click graph*, In Proceedings of SIGIR 2007, 2007.
10. S. Deerwester, S. Dumais, T. Landauer, G. Furnas, and R. Harshman, *Indexing by latent semantic analysis*, Journal of the American Society of Information Science **4** (1990), 391–407.
11. Scott C. Deerwester, Susan T. Dumais, Thomas K. Landauer, George W. Furnas, and Richard A. Harshman, *Indexing by latent semantic analysis*, Journal of the American Society of Information Science **41** (1990), no. 6, 391–407.
12. A. P. Dempster, N. M. Laird, and D. B. Rubin, *Maximum likelihood from incomplete data via the em algorithm*, Journal of the Royal Statistical Society. Series B (Methodological) **39** (1977), no. 1, 1–38.

13. Mukund Deshpande and George Karypis, *Item-based top-N recommendation algorithms*, ACM Trans. Inf. Syst. **22** (2004), no. 1, 143–177.
14. J. Fournier and M. Cord, *Long-term similarity learning in content-based image retrieval*, 2002.
15. Annalisa Franco and Alessandro Lumini, *Mixture of KL subspaces for relevance feedback*, Multimedia Tools Appl. **37** (2008), no. 2, 189–209.
16. Dan Frankowski, Shyong K. Lam, Shilad Sen, F. Maxwell Harper, Scott Yilek, Michael Cassano, and John Riedl, *Recommenders everywhere: the wikilens community-maintained recommender system*, WikiSym '07: Proceedings of the 2007 international symposium on Wikis (New York, NY, USA), ACM, 2007, pp. 47–60.
17. David Goldberg, David Nichols, Brian M. Oki, and Douglas Terry, *Using collaborative filtering to weave an information tapestry*, Commun. ACM **35** (1992), no. 12, 61–70.
18. Ken Goldberg, Theresa Roeder, Dhruv Gupta, and Chris Perkins, *Eigentaste: A constant time collaborative filtering algorithm*, Information Retrieval **4** (2001), no. 2, 133–151.
19. P.-H. Gosselin and M. Cord, *Semantic kernel learning for interactive image retrieval*, IEEE International Conference on Image Processing (Genoa, Italy), IEEE, sept. 2005.
20. Katie Hafner, *Tempting data, privacy concerns; researchers yearn to use AOL logs, but they hesitate*, Web site: The New York Times, August 23, 2006. Retrieved on 2006-09-13. http://www.nytimes.com/2006/08/23/technology/23search.html
21. Xiaofei He, O. King, Wei-Ying Ma, Mingjing Li, and Hong-Jiang Zhang, *Learning a semantic space from user's relevance feedback for image retrieval*, Circuits and Systems for Video Technology, IEEE Transactions on **13** (2003), no. 1, 39–48.
22. D. Heisterkamp, *Building a latent-semantic index of an image database from patterns of relevance feedback*, 2002.
23. Jon Herlocker, Joseph A. Konstan, and John Riedl, *An empirical analysis of design choices in neighborhood-based collaborative filtering algorithms*, Inf. Retr. **5** (2002), no. 4, 287–310.
24. Jonathan L. Herlocker, Joseph A. Konstan, Loren G. Terveen, and John T. Riedl, *Evaluating collaborative filtering recommender systems*, ACM Trans. Inf. Syst. **22** (2004), no. 1, 5–53.
25. Will Hill, Larry Stead, Mark Rosenstein, and George Furnas, *Recommending and evaluating choices in a virtual community of use*, CHI '95: Proceedings of the SIGCHI conference on Human factors in computing systems (New York, NY, USA), ACM Press/Addison-Wesley Publishing Co., 1995, pp. 194–201.
26. Thomas Hofmann, *Probabilistic latent semantic analysis*, Proc. of Uncertainty in Artificial Intelligence, UAI'99 (Stockholm), 1999.
27. Thomas Hofmann, *Unsupervised learning by probabilistic latent semantic analysis*, IEEE Trans. on PAMI **25** (2000).
28. Thomas Hofmann, *Latent semantic models for collaborative filtering*, ACM Trans. Inf. Syst. **22** (2004), no. 1, 89–115.
29. Jeff Howe, *The rise of crowdsourcing*, Wired Magazine **14** (2006), no. 06.
30. Takeo Kanade and Shingo Uchihashi, *User-powered "content-free" approach to image retrieval*, Proceedings of International Symposium on Digital Libraries and Knowledge Communities in Networked Information Society 2004 (DLKC04), 2004, pp. 24–32.
31. Charles Kemp and Kotagiri Ramamohanarao, *Long-term learning for web search engines*, PKDD '02: Proceedings of the 6th European Conference on Principles of Data Mining and Knowledge Discovery (London, UK), Springer-Verlag, 2002, pp. 263–274.
32. Markus Koskela and Jorma Laaksonen, *Using long-term learning to improve efficiency of content-based image retrieval*, 2003.
33. M. Li, Z. Chen, and H. Zhang, *Statistical correlation analysis in image retrieval*, 2002.
34. Rong Jin Luo Si, Steven C. H. Hoi, and Michael R. Lyu, *Collaborative image retrieval via regularized metric learning*, ACM Multimedia Systems Journal (MMSJ), Special Issue on Machine Learning Approaches to Multimedia Information Retrieval **12** (2006), no. 1, 34–44.
35. Stéphane Marchand-Maillet and Eric Bruno, *Exploiting user interaction for semantic content-based image retrieval*, Tech. report, Computer Vision and Multimedia Laboratory, Computing Centre, University of Geneva, 2003.

36. Benjamin Marlin and Richard S. Zemel, *The multiple multiplicative factor model for collaborative filtering*, ICML '04: Proceedings of the twenty-first international conference on Machine learning (New York, NY, USA), ACM, 2004, p. 73.
37. P. McJones, *EachMovie collaborative filtering dataset*, Website: http://www.research.compaq. com/SRC/eachmovie/, 1997, DEC (now Compaq) Systems Research Center.
38. Donn Morrison, Stéphane Marchand-Maillet, and Eric Bruno, *Semantic clustering of images using patterns of relevance feedback*, Proceedings of the 6th International Workshop on Content-based Multimedia Indexing (London, UK), June 18-20 2008.
39. Henning Müller, Wolfgang Müller, David McG. Squire, Stéphane Marchand-Maillet, and Thierry Pun, *Long-term learning from user behavior in content-based image retrieval*, Tech. report, Université de Genève, 2000.
40. Henning Müller, Thierry Pun, and David Squire, *Learning from user behavior in image retrieval: Application of market basket analysis*, Int. J. Comput. Vision **56** (2004), no. 1-2, 65–77.
41. Arvind Narayanan and Vitaly Shmatikov, *How to break anonymity of the netflix prize dataset*, 2006.
42. O. Nasraoui, C. Cardona, C. Rojas, and F. Gonzalez, *Mining evolving user profiles in noisy web clickstream data with a scalable immune system clustering algorithm*, 2003.
43. Netflix, *The Netflix Prize*, Web site: http://www.netflixprize.com/, 2006.
44. P. Resnick, N. Iacovou, M. Suchak, P. Bergstorm, and J. Riedl, *GroupLens: An Open Architecture for Collaborative Filtering of Netnews*, Proceedings of ACM 1994 Conference on Computer Supported Cooperative Work (Chapel Hill, North Carolina), ACM, 1994, pp. 175–186.
45. J. J. Rocchio, *Relevance feedback in information retrieval*, The SMART Retrieval System (G. Salton, ed.), Prentice Hall, New Jersey, 1971, pp. 456–484.
46. Bryan C. Russell, Antonio Torralba, Kevin P. Murphy, and William T. Freeman, *LabelMe: A database and web-based tool for image annotation*, Int. J. Comput. Vision **77** (2008), no. 1–3, 157–173.
47. Ian Ruthven and Mounia Lalmas, *A survey on the use of relevance feedback for information access systems*, Knowl. Eng. Rev. **18** (2003), no. 2, 95–145.
48. B. Sarwar, G. Karypis, J. Konstan, and J. Riedl, *Application of dimensionality reduction in recommender systems–a case study*, 2000.
49. J.B. Schafer, J.A. Konstan, and J. Riedl, *The view through metalens: Usage patterns for meta-recommendation system*, IEE Proceedings Software **151** (2004), 267–279.
50. Cees Snoek, *Content-based video indexing*, Presentation given at Summer School on Multimedia Semantics (SSMS'07), Glasgow, UK, 2007, Slides URL: http://www.dcs.gla.ac.uk/ssms07/ teaching-material/SSMS2007_CeesSnoek-part2.pdf.
51. Alvin Toffler, *Future shock*, Random House, New York City, NY, USA, 1970.
52. Carnegie Mellon University, *reCAPTCHA*, Web site: http://recaptcha.net/, 2007.
53. Masao Utiyama and Mikio Yamamoto, *Relevance feedback models for recommendation*, Proceedings of the 2006 Conference on Empirical Methods in Natural Language Processing (EMNLP 2006), 2006, pp. 449–456.
54. Luis von Ahn and Laura Dabbish, *Labeling images with a computer game*, CHI '04: Proceedings of the SIGCHI conference on Human factors in computing systems (New York, NY, USA), ACM Press, 2004, pp. 319–326.
55. Luis von Ahn, Shiry Ginosar, Mihir Kedia, Ruoran Liu, and Manuel Blum, *Improving accessibility of the web with a computer game*, CHI '06: Proceedings of the SIGCHI conference on Human Factors in computing systems (New York, NY, USA), ACM, 2006, pp. 79–82.
56. Luis von Ahn, Ruoran Liu, and Manuel Blum, *Peekaboom: a game for locating objects in images*, CHI '06: Proceedings of the SIGCHI conference on Human Factors in computing systems (New York, NY, USA), ACM, 2006, pp. 55–64.
57. A. Walker, M. M. Recker, K. Lawless, and D. Wiley, *Collaborative information filtering: a review and an educational application*, International Journal of Artificial Intelligence in Education **14** (2004), 1–26.

58. Jun Wang, Arjen P. de Vries, and Marcel J. T. Reinders, *Unifying user-based and item-based collaborative filtering approaches by similarity fusion*, SIGIR '06: Proceedings of the 29th annual international ACM SIGIR conference on Research and development in information retrieval (New York, NY, USA), ACM, 2006, pp. 501–508.

59. Jun Wang, Arjen P. de Vries, and Marcel J.T. Reinders, *A user-item relevance model for log-based collaborative filtering*, Proc. of European Conference on Information Retrieval (ECIR 2006), London, UK, 2006.

60. Yu Wang, Mingyue Ding, Chengping Zhou, and Ying Hu, *Interactive relevance feedback mechanism for image retrieval using rough set*, Know.-Based Syst. **19** (2006), no. 8, 696–703.

61. L. Wenyin, S. Dumais, Y. Sun, H. Zhang, M. Czerwinski, and B. Field, *Semi-automatic image annotation*, 2001.

62. Gui-Rong Xue, Hua-Jun Zeng, Zheng Chen, Yong Yu, Wei-Ying Ma, WenSi Xi, and WeiGuo Fan, *Optimizing web search using web click-through data*, CIKM '04: Proceedings of the thirteenth ACM international conference on Information and knowledge management (New York, NY, USA), ACM, 2004, pp. 118–126.

63. Alexei Yavlinsky and Daniel Heesch, *An online system for gathering image similarity judgements*, MULTIMEDIA '07: Proceedings of the 15th international conference on Multimedia (New York, NY, USA), ACM, 2007, pp. 565–568.

64. Tomohiro Yoshizawa and Haim Schweitzer, *Long-term learning of semantic grouping from relevance-feedback*, MIR '04: Proceedings of the 6th ACM SIGMM international workshop on Multimedia information retrieval (New York, NY, USA), ACM, 2004, pp. 165–172.

65. Osmar R. Zaïane, Man Xin, and Jiawei Han, *Discovering web access patterns and trends by applying OLAP and data mining technology on web logs*, Advances in Digital Libraries, 1998, pp. 19–29.

66. Cai-Nicolas Ziegler, Sean M. McNee, Joseph A. Konstan, and Georg Lausen, *Improving recommendation lists through topic diversification*, WWW '05: Proceedings of the 14th international conference on World Wide Web (New York, NY, USA), ACM, 2005, pp. 22–32.

Chapter 11
Analysis of Usage Patterns in Large Multimedia Websites*

Rahul Singh and Bibek Bhattarai

Abstract User behavior in a website is a critical indicator of the web site's usability and success. Therefore an understanding of usage patterns is essential to website design optimization. In this context, large multimedia websites pose a significant challenge for comprehension of the complex and diverse user behaviors they sustain. This is due to the complexity of analyzing and understanding user-data interactions in media-rich contexts. In this chapter we present a novel multi-perspective approach for usability analysis of large media rich websites. Our research combines multimedia web content analysis with elements of web-log analysis and visualization/visual mining of web usage metadata. Multimedia content analysis allows direct estimation of the information-cues presented to a user by the web content. Analysis of web logs and usage-metadata, such as location, type, and frequency of interactions provides a complimentary perspective on the site's usage. The entire set of information is leveraged through powerful visualization and interactive querying techniques to provide analysis of usage patterns, measure of design quality, as well as the ability to rapidly identify problems in the web-site design. Experiments on media rich sites including the SkyServer – a large multimedia web-based astronomy information repository demonstrate the efficacy and promise of the proposed approach.

11.1 Introduction

The success of a website depends on users finding the information they seek. Understanding usage patterns is therefore a key step in optimizing web-site design and determining its usability. In general, user behavior for large websites is

---

*Jim Gray from Microsoft Research played a significant role in formulating some of the ideas involved in this chapter and in terms of overall advice and encouragement for this research. This work would not have happened without his participation.

R. Singh (✉) and B. Bhattarai
San Francisco State University, San Francisco, USA
e-mail: rsingh@cs.sfsu.edu

R. Chbeir et al., *Emergent Web Intelligence: Advanced Information Retrieval*, Advanced   301
Information and Knowledge Processing, DOI 10.1007/978-1-84996-074-8_11,
© Springer-Verlag London Limited 2010

complex and difficult to characterize. Advances in web-site design have further complicated this challenge due to two primary factors. *First* websites today are increasingly *media rich* in that, their content is expressed not just through text but through images, various forms of graphics, and even video and audio. Unlike text, the semantic content of media is much harder to discern algorithmically (the so-called signal-to-symbol-gap). This complicates analyzing the content of web-pages which in turn impacts reasoning about its usage. *Second*, many websites have started to support interaction modalities that extend beyond static browsing and link following. Examples of such user-data interaction modalities include Java-script enabled click-able images, click-able maps, and parametric and SQL-based database queries. For example, all of the aforementioned interaction modalities are supported in SkyServer [1], a media rich scientific (astronomy) website as well as more general websites such as CNN and Amazon. The presence of such diverse interaction modalities require development of new techniques to understand what information the user may have been looking for and determine how successfully/efficiently the information needs were satisfied.

The success of any website depends on users satisfying their information needs (finding the information they seek). Website usability can therefore be thought of as a measure of the ease with which users satisfy their information goals. Clearly, without the ability to survey the users, questions of usability and information goals can not be answered with certainty. Unfortunately, it is difficult to conduct such surveys once a site is live. Thus automated methods need to be developed that, given usage patterns, can estimate user information goals and measure how easily the structure of a site enables the fulfillment of these goals.

At the state-of-the art, techniques for usage analysis can be grouped into two broad categories; those that are based on the analysis of web-logs [7, 9, 11, 16, 19–21, 26, 28–32] and those that try to analyze the content of web-pages to model usage [2, 4–6, 12, 15]. Given a partially conducted transaction, web-log mining techniques seek to determine which page will be accessed next. The obvious way to approach this problem is to first extract patterns from the logs and then build a predictive model. Some of the strategies that have been proposed for model construction include the use of Markov models [9, 31], collaborative filtering [26], and various forms of association rule mining [20, 21, 30]. In contrast techniques that try to model usage through web-content analysis try to extract the information goal(s) for a browsing pattern based on web-content. Typically, such techniques do not use the information provided by the usage log. For example, they do not analyze the usage patterns by considering temporal information available in the logs.

Each of the aforementioned approaches has important limitations that impact their efficacy in real-world settings. For instance, usage-log mining provides information about how users are traversing the website. However, it cannot provide information either about the putative information goals underlying the user-behavior or about the extent to which the user information goals are satisfied. Consequently usage-log mining is, by itself, inadequate for assessing usability. A stark example of this can be obtained by considering the two actual users sessions from the SkyServer website [1] shown in Fig. 11.1. Log analysis shows that both user sessions followed

---

User Session 1:

P1: http://skyserver.sdss.org/dr2/en/

  P2: http://skyserver.sdss.org/dr2/en/sdss/

    P3: http://skyserver.sdss.org/dr2/en/sdss/data/data.asp

      P4: http://skyserver.sdss.org/dr2/en/sdss/instruments/instruments.asp

User Session 2:

P1: http://skyserver.sdss.org/dr2/en/

  P2: http://skyserver.sdss.org/dr2/en/sdss/

    P3: http://skyserver.sdss.org/dr2/en/sdss/data/data.asp

Fig. 11.1 Two user sessions on the Skyserver. Web-log analysis can identify the similarity in the usage patterns while web-content analysis can provide cues to the underlying information goals that were being pursued

the similar browsing path, namely "P1, P2, P3, P4" for session-1 and "P1, P2, P3" for session-2. Log analysis also shows that user-1 left the site after visiting the page *instruments.asp*, while user-2 left from the *data.asp* page. But, log analysis can not address the question as to why both users followed similar paths but chose different pages to exit the site. Further it can not tell us what the possible information goals were which could have lead to the observed behavior or whether the user goals were satisfied at all.

In contrast to log analysis, content-based methods are based on the intuition that web content has a significant impact on the user navigation choices. These methods therefore seek to explain the user behavior based on the content of the pages visited. Content based techniques, such as [4, 5], require a fundamental model of user behavior. An important framework in this context is that of *information foraging theory* [23]. The basic idea of information foraging theory is that in a web site, the user makes traversal decisions looking for information that would satisfy his or her information goal. Thus, the traversal history and the content of pages visited can be representative of the user information need. However, by focusing solely on page content, methods based on this framework run the risk of missing important contextual information available through web-logs, such as load patterns, temporal sequencing of the usage patterns, source of requests etc.

In recent research, attempts have been made to analyze the web-content output by web servers with the goal of providing a summarized and high-level perspective of web usage [22]. While sharing many of our goals, especially in terms of information presentation, the research in [22] focuses on server analytics. It therefore discounts modeling the perceptual aspects of user-behavior and its potential impact on usage patterns. Research in the area of adaptive hypermedia [3] also shares many of our goals. Adaptive hypermedia systems try to adapt aspects of the system to user characteristics including user goals, knowledge, and background [18]. Such systems typically include three important components: (1) a domain model, which specifies the conceptual design of the application, (2) a user model which contains information about the user, and (3) an adaptation model defining how the adaptation of the system is performed. Majority of adaptive hypermedia systems use an overlay model of user knowledge [18], where an estimation of user knowledge for each domain model is stored. An alternative is the historic model which utilizes user history of page visits. This assumes that past user behavior is a reliable indicator of future user actions. Another strategy is to build a model using data from a group of users and then use the model to make predictions about individual users. Different machine learning and statistical techniques have been utilized to build such models including [33]: linear models, TFIDF-models, Markov models, neural networks, clustering methods, rule induction, and Bayesian networks. One of the main problems in constructing such predictive models has been the collection of training data containing information about non-observable user characteristics such as user intention, user information needs, and interruptability. Experience sampling is one possible way to collect such information. In it, users are asked to reveal unobservable characteristics underlying their behavior during the course of activity. This information is subsequently used to build the predictive models. An overview of different experience sampling strategies and their comparison through user studies is provided in [17]. In yet other research, attempts have also been made to directly obtain information about information usage by user eye-tracking (in the specific context of perusing web-search results) [8]. Availability of additional information available through methods such as experience sampling or sensor-based monitoring of the physical user context can undoubtedly aid user-context modeling. However, deploying such solutions in real-world settings can be complicated either due to lack of access to users or due to privacy concerns.

The research presented in this chapter brings together and builds on many of the aforementioned ideas conceptually and technically. On the conceptual side, we combine web-page content with information from web-logs and contextual metadata about usage patterns. On the technical side, we consider both textual content as well as media-based content in web-pages during information goal determination as well as usage-flow modeling. Further, in our approach different forms of user-data interactions are accounted for (beyond users following static links). Finally, our research not only emphasizes the algorithmic aspects of usage analysis, but also demonstrates the role powerful visualization-query-exploration interfaces can play in utilizing human-machine synergy towards addressing this problem.

We begin this chapter by presenting an overview of the proposed approach in Section 11.2. This is followed in Section 11.3 by a description of the Skyserver, which is a large media-rich website and constitutes our primary experimental testbed. Section 11.4 outlines the proposed approach. Experiments and case studies are presented in Section 11.5. The chapter is concluded in Section 11.6 by reiterating the fundamental ideas behind our solution methodology and by outlining its broad applicability in designing and analyzing modern web-based information systems.

11.2 Overview of the Proposed Approach

Our approach involves two aspects. The first deals with the issue of user goal determination based on the observed usage patterns and multimedia page content and connectivity analysis. The second addresses the problem of presenting to webdesigners and administrators, the considerable amount of contextual information related to usage patterns which is available from usage logs (such as access statistics, the distribution of geographical origin of activities, distribution of sessions durations, distribution of unique users over location or time, etc.) in a manner that is easy to interact with and assimilate. The integration of these perspectives has not found prominence in prior research efforts. However, this is crucial, since the identification of interesting/important usage patterns requires both modeling user behavior as well as the ability to interpret metadata related to usage patterns [5]. Thus the proposed approach brings together content and usage-pattern-based information goal determination with visualization and visual data mining of contextual metadata related to usage-patterns. By correlating these perspectives, user actions can be decomposed in terms of the following intuitive characteristics: *who, when, where*(pertaining to the spatial-temporal distribution of usage patterns and analyzed through visualization and visual mining of contextual metadata obtained from usage-logs), *what, how* (pertaining to user actions and obtainable through logs and content analysis), and *why* (related to the discerned user information goal – which provides a possible explanation of the user behavior). The interplay of these factors is graphically illustrated in Fig. 11.2.

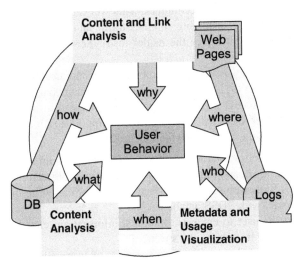

Fig. 11.2 Interplay of the three major concepts underlying the proposed method: content analysis (determining the core information content perused by the user), information goal determination (putatively explaining the user information need), and usage analysis and visualization (providing the analyst with analytical and contextual evidence on the usage patterns and the usability of the web-site)

We use ideas based on information foraging theory [23] to develop an explanatory model of user behavior. A key distinction of our work from prior research lies in the analysis of multimedia page content in estimating the information goals underlying the user behavior. Once the information goals are determined, an analysis of the linkage structure of the site provides the shortest path from the start page to the page(s) containing the information goal(s). If analysis of the usage logs show that multiple sessions diverge from this path, it may indicate a potential usability problem (such as critical links not clearly presented). The overall approach thus encompasses the following steps:

- Web content analysis to extract information goal related to the web session.
- Calculation of the overall user flow on the site for the extracted information goal. This provides a *simulated model* of how traffic on the site may be expected to behave for the specific information goals.
- Computation and comparison of the optimal (shortest) path with the path chosen by the user(s) to analyze usability and if/how the web-design may be improved to optimize access to information.
- Integrated visualization of the above information with contextual metadata extracted from the web logs.

11.3   Introduction to the Skyserver

The SkyServer website [1] constitutes the primary test-bed for development, testing, and validation of the proposed techniques. This website provides a large, media-rich real-world repository sustaining complex traffic and user-behavior patterns. In this section, we briefly introduce the reader to SkyServer and highlight its main characteristics.

SkyServer provides access to a large volume of astronomical data from the Sloan Digital Sky Survey (SDSS) [27]. The information is presented using text and a large number of images. Access to the information is provided through standard web browsers. The SkyServer website is designed to support a rich set of interactions between the user and the data [27], which include:

- Simple point-and-click interaction allows user to click on images of various different celestial object and retrieve data related to those objects.
- Text and GUI SQL web service interface where user can write their own query to access interact with SDSS database.
- Tools that let the user to enter astronomical information related to a particular object and retrieve its images and spectra.
- Skyserver is designed to support a diverse set of users starting from students learning astronomy at school level to scientists and professional astronomers. It should be noted that SkyServer is a *very* large website, offering views and data for over 80 million astronomical phenomena, totaling over one-and-a-half terabytes. The usage log data analyzed as part of this research is approximately 35 gigabytes and spans a timeline from May 2003 to October 2004.

11.4   Analysis of Usage Patterns

As the first step in the proposed approach, the content of the web-log is analyzed to derive contextual information that is important for understanding usage patterns. Dynamic content requests which culminate in an *Http GET* request or an *XMLHttp* request are recorded in the usage logs. Therefore these results can be reconstructed and analyzed. Web-log analysis begins with a data preprocessing step, where the data is scrubbed and validated. The preprocessing step is followed by *user delineation* and *user session definition*. These steps are elaborated below:

- *Definition of unique users:* Central to web usage analysis is the idea that users are discrete entities that exhibit (possibly multiple groups of) self-similar behavior in consuming web content. To categorize the behaviors, it is essential to identify each user. Prior work also explores the concerns regarding what constitutes a distinct user [25]. We define a unique user as having a distinct value for IP address and user-agent.
- *Definition of user sessions:* Studies have shown that user sessions are typically delimited by a timeout value of 25 min [24]. Based on these observations we use a timeout threshold of 30 min. For each discovered session, we cache the starting time of each session and the duration of the session as a whole.

These steps are followed by analysis of the web content. In this step we first extract the information stored in each page of the website. The process begins by constructing a sitemap for the website based on URL analysis. The site connectivity information is stored in an adjacency matrix. Subsequently, the text and media-based content in the site is analyzed. Using this information in the next stage, the putative information goals corresponding to the traversal pattern are identified. This is followed by the simulation of the user-flow. Finally this information is combined with metadata related to the usage patterns and presented using an interactive visualization interface. Using this interface the usability of the site can be analyzed.

11.4.1 Analysis of Text-Based Web-Content

The two most frequent media for most websites are text and images and therefore we focus on these in our analysis. Textual content is analyzed using a grammarless statistical method, which includes stemming and stop word filtering. First, the text-based content of each web page in the website is extracted and a vector of all unique terms present in the website constructed. Using the terms vector and the web pages connectivity information we construct the *term-page matrix*, TP_{TFIDF},

$$TP_{TFIDF}(i, j) = TFIDF(t_i, p_j) \qquad (11.1)$$

In this matrix, the determination of the importance of a term t in a page p *is obtained* using its normalized TFIDF (Term-Frequency-Inverted-Document-Frequency) value. This is a standard approach in text analysis, which essentially gives higher weight to more informative terms. The normalized TFIDF formulation used by us takes the length of the page into consideration for calculation of a term's importance and is defined as:

$$TFIDF = \left(\frac{tf}{N_{term}} \right) \times \log_2 \left(\frac{N_{page}}{df} \right)$$ (11.2)

In Eq. (11.2), tf is the frequency count of term in a given page, N_{term} is total number of terms in the page, N_{page} is total number of documents in the collection, and df is the frequency count of pages in which the term occurs and which *link to*, or *are linked from* the page of interest. This helps avoid the effect of unwanted terms by using a smaller, relevant document set as a background set.

11.4.2 Analysis of Image-Based Web-Content

After the text-based information content of a site has been captured, the next challenge is to represent its image-based content. In the case of web-pages the problem of determining the information corresponding to an image can be ameliorated by associating with the image, key snippets of proximal text. This brings up two sub-problems. First, the possible variability of semantics of an image (in terms of the text associated with the image) needs to be captured. This situation can arise when an image is used in multiple contexts. Second, the visual importance of an image has to be captured so that terms associated with highly prominent images receive greater weight as compared to terms associated with less prominent images. Solving these problems require the ability to describe and compare images.

In order to achieve these goals, we use color-texture analysis. Our approach uses the JSEG [10] color/texture analysis algorithm to identify textures within the image. Texture characterization is done with Grey-Level Co-occurrence Matrices (GLCM) [13]. We use eight vectors as the offset parameter for GLCM, and measure four statistical properties for each co-occurrence matrix: energy, entropy, contrast, and homogeneity. In addition, we generate a six-bit color histogram for each texture. Relative size, energy, entropy, contrast, homogeneity, and the color histogram are combined to create feature vector which is then used to describe each image in the web-site. Given two images represented by texture-color feature vector, their similarity is computed as the Pearson's distance between the vectors. A score of 1.0 indicates identical images and low scores indicate highly dissimilar images. If any specific image appears in two different pages, these pages have an image-semantic-based relationship. Consequently, the information from both pages contributes to the definition of the semantics associated with this image.

After image-based analysis is completed, key-terms from text proximal to images are used to describe the semantics associated with images while the term-frequency matrix captures the semantics of textual content of the website. Next, the information in the term-frequency matrix is combined with the image semantics to obtain a unified semantics representation of the entire information in the website. This is done by re-weighting terms associated with images in the term-frequency matrix. The amount by which the weight values are adjusted is directly proportional to the size and complexity of the corresponding image. Such an adjustment is justified by the specificities of the human visual perception of images; an image with more texture (complexity) exhibits more information to the human eye than, for instance, an image of the same size but containing only single texture (such as an image with a uniform background of a single color).

11.4.3   Information Goal Extraction

For the extraction of the information goal, we first extract a list of terms from each page that is visited during the given session. The importance of each term in the list is calculated as summation of its TFIDF values across the pages visited in the session. Before summation, the TFIDF value of each term is multiplied by the importance value assigned to each page. For example, if we have a model where the final page in the session is accorded the greatest importance, then the terms appearing in the final page will be given greater weight as compared to appearing in other pages. Conversely, a model which weights all pages in a session equally can also be used. Finally, the term list is sorted and the 20 most important terms used as a summary of the user information goals. The specific number of terms used to summarize the user information goals is essentially a parameter which can be varied during analysis. Our choice of 20-terms was driven by the goals of obtaining a reasonable coverage of putative information goals without, at the same time, overwhelming the analysis with terms that may not be significant user goals.

To implement this idea, first a usage adjacency matrix U is constructed; if in a session a user visited the link from page i to page j then the matrix U is defined as shown in Eq. (11.3).

$$U(i, j) = \begin{cases} 1.0 : \textit{user visits page} \\ 0.0 : \textit{otherwise} \end{cases} \quad (11.3)$$

Next, the vector $I = \{I_p\}$ consisting of importance values corresponding to each page p in the site is constructed. In defining I, different weighting schemes may be used as described earlier. For instance, all pages can be weighted equally, or be weighted in incremental order (progressively increasing the importance value), or the final page can be weighted the highest (remaining pages weighted equally). Subsequently, the list of terms related to given session is obtained by multiplying TP_{TFIDF} with U and the vector I.

$$L = TP_{TFIDF} \times U \times I \quad (11.4)$$

Finally, the term weights are sorted to identify the top most informative terms.

11.4.4 Content-Based Usage Analysis

The first step in usage analysis involves computing the user flow through the website for a given information goal. Determining the user flow provides a probabilistic model of how other users with similar information goal behave, given the site structure and content. Our approach is based on the idea of information scent [23], which posits that users anticipate the information stored in distal page by looking at the text or graphical snippets (the *information scent*) present on the link pointing to the distal page. Consequently, given a specific information goal, links having information scent that strongly correlates with the information goal have a greater probability of being followed. The user flow is determined as follows:

- *Calculation of Information Correlation:* We calculate the correlation between users' information goal and information stored in a link by computing the normalized sum of the TFIDF value of all the terms that are present in *both* the URL and in the information goal as shown in Eq. (11.5). In cases where text is absent in the hyperlink, the title of the distal page is utilized in calculating the correlation. In Eq. (11.5), $C(l)$ is the correlation for link l, and t_{val} denotes the TFIDF value of term t in page P. Term t is also present in the information goal G.

$$C(l) = \frac{\sum_{tval} \forall t \in l, t \in G}{\sum_{i=1}^{n} t_i \forall t_i \in P} \tag{11.5}$$

- *User Flow Calculation:* The user flow is computed by simulating usage through an activation function A. The total percentage of users at a given time in a page depends on total information correlation value (IC) for all the links pointing to the page. The dampening factor α represents the fraction of users that can leave the website from any given page. The value of α can is determined based on site characteristics or by using the law of surfing [14].

$$A(t) = (\alpha \times IC \times A(t-1)) + E \tag{11.6}$$

In Eq. (11.6) E is the source activation vector and simulates users flowing through the links from the entry (or start) page of the usage pattern. The initial activation vector $A(1) = E$ and the final activation vector $A(n)$ gives the percentage of users in each node of the website after n iterations through the activation function.

- *Shortest Path Computation and Comparison:* Our underlying assumption is that the shortest path represents the most optimal (direct) path to the desired information goal. Thus, comparison of actual user paths with the shortest path provides cues to how well the links are organized in the website. For instance, repeated deviation of users from the shortest path may indicate usability issues such as an important link getting obfuscated due to design of the site. To compare a user-path with the optimal path we use a simple greedy strategy. We start the comparison from final page of the optimal path and seek to find a match starting with the final page of the user-path and moving backwards to the start page. For every mismatch we assign a score of -1 and if a matching page is found we assign a score of $+1$ and mark the matching page. In the next iteration the page prior to the final page of the shortest path is considered and compared with the pages in the user path starting with the page prior to the matched page in the previous iteration and moving backwards. Again for each mismatched page, a score of -1 is assigned. The process is iterated until all pages in the shortest path have been sequentially compared with the pages in the user path. At the end the sum of scores over all the pages is calculated. The difference between this score and the shortest path length gives the measure of similarity between the user path and the optimal path. A score equal to length of shortest path means that the user path was identical to the shortest (most optimal path), while a score less than length of shortest path means user path differed from the shortest path.

As an example, consider the user-path and shortest path showed in Fig. 11.3, where the pages in the user-paths are labeled as *A, B, C, D* and *E*, and the pages in the shortest path labeled as *I, II* and *III* respectively. We weight the final page with the highest importance and therefore start from page *III* of shortest path and compare it with pages in users' path starting from page *E* to *A*. As page *III* matches with page *E*, we assign the score of $+1$ and mark page *E* as "matched". In next iteration we will take page *II* and start comparison from page *D* since page *E* is already matched. Page *II* matches with page *D*, we assign the score of $+1$ and mark page *D* as "matched". We now take page *I* and start comparing from page *C*. We find two mismatches at page *C* and page *B*, thus mismatch score of -1 will be assigned to each page. Finally page *I* matches with page *A* we assign $+1$ score to page *A*. The total score is then: $(+1) + (-1) + (-1) + (+1) + (+1) = 1$. This captures the fact that the user did not visit the direct link between page *A* and page *D*, but instead took the path page B– page C– page D.

Users' Path:

A: http://skyserver.sdss.org/dr2/en/

  B: http://skyserver.sdss.org/dr2/en/sdss/

    C: http://skyserver.sdss.org/dr2/en/sdss/release/

      D: http://skyserver.sdss.org/dr2/en/sdss/pubs/

        E: http://skyserver.sdss.org/dr2/en/sdss/dr2paper/

Shortest Path:

I: http://skyserver.sdss.org/dr2/en/

  II: http://skyserver.sdss.org/dr2/en/sdss/pubs/

    III: http://skyserver.sdss.org/dr2/en/sdss/dr2paper/

Fig. 11.3 Comparison between the path taken by a user and the optimal (shortest) path to the same information content

11.4.5 Contextual Metadata Extraction and Visualization

Obtaining a holistic understanding of usage patterns in a large website like the SkyServer requires combining the aforementioned analysis with contextual metadata associated with usage patterns. In our approach to this issue the basic principle lies in encouraging human-machine synergy by taking advantage of the human skills of domain expertise, contextual reasoning, pattern detection, hypotheses formulation, exploration, and sense-making. The process is facilitated through an integrated visualization-query-exploration interface (Fig. 11.4). The interface is *reflective*, which means that making a change in one of the components propagates the change to all other components. This interface also follows a direct manipulation paradigm. Perceiving a pattern of interest, a user can directly interact and explore the information. As a manipulation occurs in one of the information "views", its effects are appropriately reflected in the other views, thereby helping in understanding the relationships present in the data and its ultimate assimilation.

One of the features that the interface offers is the ability to directly correlate different aspects of information derived from the usage-logs. The correlation domains include: browsers (web agents), page, entry page, exit page, date, session duration, day of the week, month and hour. The correlation ranges include: *user sessions, user session duration, hits,* and *unique users*. The user can choose to chart any domain as the independent variable and any range as the dependent variable. For instance, a user can select an arbitrary slice of time (e.g. 2 weeks, 1 year, or 3 years) and

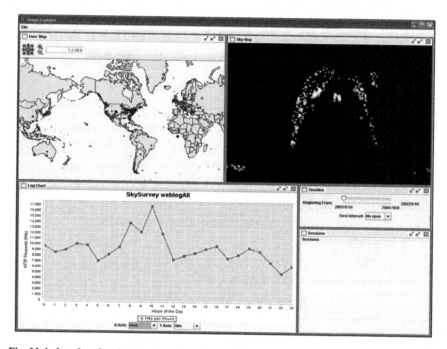

Fig. 11.4 Interface for visualization of contextual metadata

constrain the spatial information and log information accordingly. This mechanism can be used, for example to obtain a temporal distribution of the data as well as discern complex patterns such as recurring events or the influence of specific time periods on usage patterns. The visualization emphasizes the specific perspectives of *location* and *time* for analyzing the log data. Bearing in mind the cautions of [25] (with regards to user identity), we search for evidence of the location of the user by extracting information from various trustworthy web references, whenever possible. By visualizing this information on an interactive map, the user can explore the geographical distribution of the traffic (e.g. hits, sessions, visitors, etc.) is coming from. Further, by making the size of the dots proportional to the traffic volume, highly active sites/users can be easily identified.

A final component in the visualization shown in Fig. 11.4 (top right) is specific to astronomical data: in this part web pages about galaxies and stars are projected on a Cartesian map of the night sky. This provides a context-sensitive (astronomical) perspective of the data. This view is also reflected on the other views of the data.

In Figs. 11.5 and 11.6, we show further snapshots of the visualization interface Fig. 11.5 depicts the visualization of a user session. In this visualization, a directed graph is used to represent a subset of the web structure that is related to the user session being explored. For a given user session, the specific information being displayed include: (1) the path followed by user, (2) the shortest path as obtained after analysis with the proposed approach, and (3) the predicted user flow based on the specific information goal. Further, orange colored circles represent the web pages that have some relevance to the user goal and the red rectangular bars represent the total percentage of users that visit the page (based on the user flow). The orange directed lines (solid) linking the circles represents the direction of the user flow. Similarly, the green directed lines (dotted) and blue directed lines (dashed) represent the actual users' paths and system-computed shortest path, respectively. Pages that the user visits during the session, but are not present in the user flow graph, are represented by green squares. The same is true for blue triangles that represent the page that is present only in shortest computed path.

The visualization is interactive and dynamic, thus allowing researchers to explore the information and analysis. For instance, when a mouse pointer is moved over a square in the graph, information about the page (link information and thumbnail image of web-page) and percentage of user flow distribution in the page displayed as tool tip. The tool tip for the final page of a session also displays the match/mismatch score between user path and shortest path. This visualization provides a powerful tool that interfaces with the algorithmic aspects of our methodology and helps web designers rapidly analyze a user session to find, for example:

- The difference between the user path and the optimal path
- Page(s) where the user path diverges from the optimal path
- The predicted user flow for the information goal extracted

This allows web designers to rapidly identify the pages that have erroneous correlation value, driving users away from their goal. The system also provides the option to visualize users' paths, users flow graph, and the shortest path separately.

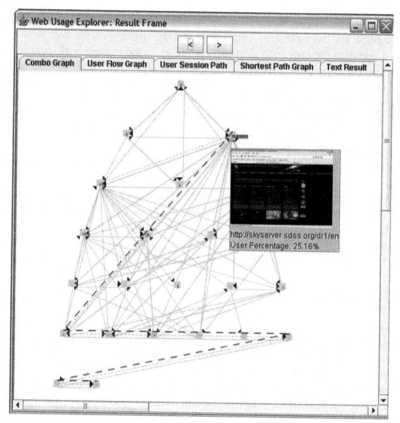

Fig. 11.5 Visualization support for usage analysis: The snapshot of the interface depicted in this figure shows the user session (Green dotted line), related shortest path (Blue dashed line) and user flow (Orange solid line). For a detailed discussion of the data depicted in this figure, the reader is referred to the case study in Section 11.5, where the user misses the optimal path to the information goal

The visualization framework also supports display and interaction with other types of contextual metadata relevant to the usage patterns. For instance, it is helpful to know where the majority of the website traffic comes from and which specific utilities/tools/functionality of the web-site are used the most. Such insights can be, for instance, help to address localization issues and system performance decisions such as scheduling system downtimes, or deciding where to place a redundant server for best workload distribution. Figure 11.6 presents a snapshot of one such visualization of the web traffic directed to a specific substructure of the Sky Server website (the search and query tools) with regards to the location of the internet service providers of the client. As this example illustrates, one of the search tools on Sky Server, *shownearest.asp*, is by far the most heavily used utility. The map also shows that the majority of the usage comes from the US costal regions (west coast not shown) and from around the Great Lakes.

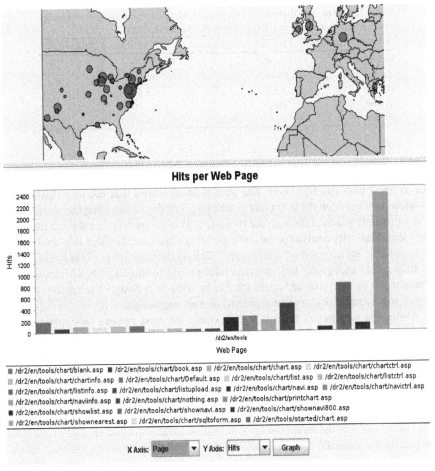

Fig. 11.6 Visualization of contextual metadata showing spatial distribution of the hits (top) and usage distribution for specific tools on the website (bottom)

11.5   Case Studies and Experiments

We begin with a case study involving a subset of the usage data from the SkyServer logs. The study starts with the data and visual interface shown in Fig. 11.4. Using the interactive interface, a visualization of the hits per month reveals that the month of April 2004 was very busy for the given usage-data sample; contributing 28.57% of the traffic between May 2003 and October 2004. We select, without loss of generality, traffic from Oxford, England which is shown on the map as a listed observatory. With these constraints, the system reveals four user sessions, one of which is long enough to have a meaningful information goal. This session starts from the index page, then browses to a spatial search page and executes three dynamic queries, each looking for a galaxy at specific points in the sky. The information goals predicted

Table 11.1 The comparative contribution of text-only content and text and image content to the user flow to select pages of the Skyserver website

Website subsections	Text only correlation (%)	Text/Image correlation (%)
Index page	25.16	25.29
Tools	33.06	28.81
Help	1.65	1.55
Traffic	0.00	4.10
Project	0.00	0.38

by our approach consist of the dynamic query results and static web page terms. Figure 11.5 shows the user flow (solid line), the user session path (dotted line), and the shortest path (dashed line). The visualization shows that the user missed the shortest path between the index and search pages of the site and that the search page was ultimately reached through the tool page. This is typical of a possible usability problem. Manually analyzing the corresponding pages, we find that the "tool-page" link visually dominates the "search-page" link on the index page. This causes users to follow the "tool-page" link and thus take a longer, indirect path. This case study illustrates how the proposed approach can be used by a designer to rapidly and interactively identify and correct problems in web-site design.

Using the parameters from this case study, we next present an experiment to evaluate the difference in the quality of results obtained by incorporating text-and-image information versus text-only information (see Table 11.1). When text-only information is used, no user flow is obtained for the (image rich) *traffic* and *project* subsections of the website, as they have no textual correlation with the information goal. In contrast, when *both* text and image-based information is considered, the activation function generates user flow to the traffic and project sections. This is due to the contribution of the image-based information to the information goal(s) and consequently the usage flow. It is interesting to note that the user flow simulation results obtained by incorporating both image and textual information, are supported by actual usage patterns from the logs and therefore constitute a more accurate model than what is possible with text dominated methods such as [4, 5].

Two related questions arise in the context of contrasting the multimedia content analysis strategy with a text-only approach. *First*, what is the impact of considering image content on information goals as compared with a text-only approach? *Second*, are there extreme cases where multimedia analysis can correctly identify information terms (goals) that could be totally missed in a text-only analysis?

We investigate these questions using data from the user sessions shown in Fig. 11.7. The results obtained from analyzing these user sessions are, based on our experience, representative for user sessions which involve media (image)-rich pages. The detailed results are presented in Table 11.2 and Fig. 11.8. For this specific user session, the terms *famous*, *place*, and *tool-title* are the top three goal terms in both text-only and text-and-image analysis. Table 11.2 shows that these terms have a reduced mean relevance using text-only analysis when compared with multimedia analysis. This is due to the fact that images contribute to increasing the relevance of these terms.

1: http://skyserver.sdss.org/dr1/en/tools

  2: http://skyserver.sdss.org/dr1/en/tools/places

    3: http://skyserver.sdss.org/dr1/en/tools/places/page1.asp

Fig. 11.7 A user session on the Skyserver used for analyzing the advantages of multimedia (text and image) analysis as opposed to text-only analysis

Table 11.2 Examples of changes in term relevance scores when multimedia (text and image) analysis is used instead of text-only analysis of the user session shown in Fig. 11.7

Term	Mean relevance for text-only analysis	Mean relevance for text-and-image analysis
Famous	0.0274	0.0369
Place	0.0272	0.0368
Tool-title	0.1000	0.1054

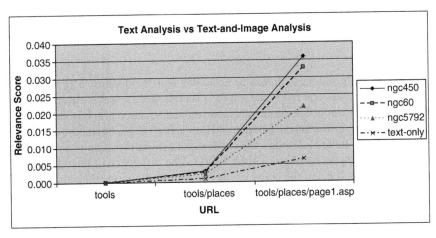

Fig. 11.8 Term relevance scores using the proposed multimedia content analysis approach versus text-only analysis of the pages

The extreme case is observed for the information goal terms *ngc450*, *ngc60* and *ngc5792*, which are names of galaxies prominently displayed on *page1.asp* (the third and final page visited in the session). The relevance scores of these terms are plotted across the session in Fig. 11.8 using both text-only and multimedia (text and image) analysis (proposed method). The reader may note that in the case of text-only analysis these terms have nearly negligible relevance values, since they only occur as image captions. In contrast, with the proposed method, the relevance values of these terms are significantly higher.

In the final experiment we perform a side-by-side comparison of information goal prediction for the user session shown in Fig. 11.9 using the proposed approach

1: http://skyserver.sdss.org/dr1/en/proj/challenges

2: http://skyserver.sdss.org/dr1/en/proj/challenges/hii

3: http://skyserver.sdss.org/dr1/en/proj/challenges/hii/characteristics.asp

4: http://skyserver.sdss.org/dr1/en/proj/challenges/hii/query.asp

5: http://skyserver.sdss.org/dr1/en/proj/challenges/hii/identifying.asp

6: http://skyserver.sdss.org/dr1/en/proj/challenges/hii/catalogs.asp

Fig. 11.9 A user session on the Skyserver used for comparing the proposed method with the IUNIS algorithm

Table 11.3 Comparison with the IUNIS algorithm

Proposed approach		IUNIS	
Terms	Mean relevancy (%)	Terms	Mean relevancy (%)
Region	14.44	Schema	0.19
Hii	14.26	Browser	0.16
Challenge	10.32	Query	1.04
Catalog	8.53	Drl	0.00
Write	8.14	sdss	1.09

and the IUNIS algorithm [4]. It may be noted that both methods use a TFIDF-based measure to calculate term relevance and the term relevance scores are averaged over all pages in the session. Therefore the fundamental distinction is in how these methods account for non-textual information and how actual usage patterns are accounted in the analysis. Table 11.3 shows the top five putative information goals as determined by the proposed method and by IUNIS. The difference in the relevance of the terms obtained using the above methods is stark; the terms ranked as the top five terms by our approach have a significantly higher mean relevance score as compared with terms determined using IUNIS. Since the relevance of a term in a page is the TFIDF-based importance of the term, this indicates a weakness of IUNIS in that information goals identified by it can have low relevance (TFIDF scores). To understand why the IUNIS algorithm picks such terms we note that in highly interlinked websites like the Skysever, contents of nodes with large fan-in receive higher activation weights in INUIS even if they are not important in terms of the actual user goals. Thus terms with low relevancy-scores can get identified, incorrectly, to be important.

11.6 Conclusions

This chapter presents novel approach for usability analysis of large websites. We propose three fundamental extensions to the state-of-the art. First, we emphasize an integrative solution to this challenge that leverages and correlates information in web-logs, the content of web pages, and contextual metadata to understand usage patterns. Second, we develop techniques that are capable of discerning information goals by taking into account information in the web-pages that may be expressed textually or through media such as images. Finally, we emphasize the role powerful visualization techniques can play, not only by enabling human machine synergy in analyzing complex patterns, but also by acting as the unification point around which the various analysis strategies can be brought together. Case studies and experiments conducted on real-world data from the SkyServer illustrate the efficacy of these ideas and their promise in developing a new generation of usage analysis strategies.

Acknowledgements The authors thank Mike Wong for his participation in parts of this project and to Jay Kim for help in formatting. This work was funded in part by a Microsoft unrestricted research grant to RS.

References

1. Sloan Digital Sky Survey project's website SkyServer: "http://skyserver.sdss.org/"
2. Blackmon M. H., Polson P. G., Kitajima M. Repairing Usability Problems Identified by the Cognitive Walkthrough for the Web. ACM CHI, pp. 497–504, 2003
3. Brusilovsky P., Adaptive Hypermedia, User Modeling and User Adapted Interactions, 11: pp. 87–110, 2001
4. Chi E. H., P. L. Pirolli, Chen K., Pitkow J. Using Information Scent to Model User Information Needs and Actions on the Web. ACM CHI, pp. 490–497, 2001
5. Chi E. H., Rosien A., Supattanasiri G., Williams A., Royer C., Chow C., Robles E., Dalal B., Chen J., Cousins S. The Bloodhound Project: Automating Discovery of Web Usability Issues using the InfoScent Simulator. ACM CHI, pp. 1323–1332, 2003
6. Cooley, R. The Use of Web Structure and Content to Identify Subjectively Interesting Web Usage Patterns. 2003 ACM Transactions on Internet Technology 3(2), pp. 93–116, 2003
7. Cooley, R., Mobasher B., Srivastava, J. Web Mining: Information and Pattern Discovery on the World Wide Web. Proceedings of the 9th IEEE International Conference on Tools with Artificial Intelligence (ICTAI'97), pp. 558–567, 1997
8. Cutrell, E. and Guan, Z., "What are you looking for?: an eye-tracking study of information usage in web search". Proceedings of the SIGCHI Conference on Human Factors in Computing Systems, pp. 407–416, 2007
9. Deshpande M., Karypis G., "Selective Markov Models for Predicting Web Page Access", ACM Transactions on Internet Technology, 4(2), 163–184, 2004
10. Deng Y., and Manjunath B. S., Unsupervised segmentation of color-texture regions in images and video, IEEE Transactions on Pattern Analysis and Machine Intelligence, vol. 23, no. 8, pp. 800–810, 2001
11. Ding, C. and Zhou, J., "Improving website search with server log analysis and multiple evidence combination", International Journal of Web and Grid Services 3(2), pp. 103–127, 2007
12. Heer, J. and Chi, E. H. Identification of Web User Traffic Composition and Multimodal Clustering and Information Scent, Proc. Of the Workshop on Web Mining, SIAM Conference on Data Mining, pp. 51–58, 2001
13. Howarth P., Rüger S., Evaluation of Texture Features for Content-based Image Retrieval, Lecture Notes in Computer Science, Volume 3115, pp. 326–334, 2004
14. Huberman B., Pirolli P., Pitkow G., Lukose R., Strong Regularities in World Wide Web Surfing, Science, 280, pp. 95–97, 1998

15. Jin, X., Zhou, Y., Mobasher, B. Web Usage Mining Based on Probabilistic Latent Semantic Analysis. Proceedings ACM Special Interest Group on Knowledge Discovery and Data Mining, pp. 197–205, 2004

16. Joshi K., Joshi A., Yesha Y., Krishnapuram R., "Warehousing and mining Web logs", 2nd international workshop on Web information and data management, pp. 63–68, 1999

17. Kapoor, A. and Horvitz, E. "Experience sampling for building predictive user models: a comparative study" Proceeding of the Twenty-Sixth Annual SIGCHI Conference on Human Factors in Computing Systems, pp. 657–666, 2008

18. Kravčík, M. and Gašević, D. "Adaptive hypermedia for the semantic web", Proceedings of the Joint international Workshop on Adaptivity, Personalization &Amp; the Semantic Web, pp. 3–10, 2006

19. Masseglia F., Poncelet P., Teisseire M., Using data mining techniques on Web access logs to dynamically improve hypertext structure, ACM SIGWEB Newsletter, vol. 8 no. 3, pp. 13–19, October 1999

20. Mobasher B., Dai H., Luo T., Nakagawa M., "Effective Personalization Based on Association Rule Discovery from Web-Usage Data", ACM Workshop on Web Information and Data Management, pp. 9–15, 2001

21. Nanopoulos A., Katsaros D., and Manolopoulos Y., "Effective Prediction of Web-User Access: A Data Mining Approach", WEBKDD 2001

22. Norguet, J., Zimányi, E., and Steinberger, R., "Semantic analysis of web site audience". ACM Symposium on Applied Computing pp. 525–529, 2006

23. Pirolli P. L., and Card S. K. (1999) Information foraging. Psychological Review. 106: pp. 643–675

24. Pirolli, P., Pitkow, J. and Rao, R. Silk from a sow's ear: Extracting usable structures from the web. ACM CHI, pp. 118–125, 1996

25. Pitkow, J. Characterizing browsing strategies in the World-Wide Web. Computer Networks and ISDN Systems, 27(6) pp. 1065–1073, 1995

26. Shardanand U., Maes P., "Social Information Filtering: Algorithms for Automating Word of Mouth", ACM CHI, pp. 210–217, 1995

27. Szalay A. S., Gray J., Thakar A. R., Kunszt P. Z., Malik T., Raddick J., Stoughton C., vandenBerg J. The SDSS SkyServer - Public Access to the Sloan Digital Sky Server Data. ACM SIGMOD pp. 570–581, 2002

28. Wang X., Abraham A., and Smith K., "Intelligent web traffic mining and analysis", Journal of Network and Computer Applications, Volume 28, Issue 2, pp. 147–165, 2005

29. White, R. W. and Morris, D., "Investigating the querying and browsing behavior of advanced search engine users", Proceedings of the 30th Annual international ACM SIGIR Conference on Research and Development in information Retrieval, pp. 255–262, 2007

30. Yang H., Parthasarathy S., "On the Use of Constrained Associations for Web Log Mining", Lecture Notes in Computer Science, 2703, pp. 100–118, 2003

31. Yang Q., Zhang H., Li T., "Mining Web Logs for Prediction Models in WWW Caching and Prefetching", Proceedings of the seventh ACM SIGKDD international conference on Knowledge discovery and data mining, pp. 473–478, 2001

32. Zaïane O., Xin M., Han J., "Discovering Web Access Patterns and Trends by Applying OLAP and Data Mining Technology on Web Logs", Advances in Digital Libraries, p. 19, April 22–24, 1998

33. Zukerman, I. and Albrecht, D. W. 2001. Predictive Statistical Models for User Modeling. User Modeling and User-Adapted Interaction 11, 1–2, pp. 5–18, 2001

Chapter 12
An Adaptation Framework for Web Multimedia Presentations

S. Benbernou, M.S. Hacid, A. Makhoul, and A. Mostefaoui

Abstract A multimedia document is composed of several media-objects that are presented to user/application with respect to certain spatio-temporal relationships defined over them (called also multimedia presentation). In Web environments, those media objects could be located onto different servers and hence pose the problem of delivering multimedia documents with respect to those constrains. In many situations, it is not always possible to support the presentation spatio-temporal constraints. This is due to noisy problems such as low bandwidth, or user preferences/profile as the lack of audio devise. One interesting alternative consists in adapting the presentation by substituting media elements by others media that are semantically equivalent. This adaptation is not obvious and could lead, if it is not carried out carefully, to a misunderstood presentation. This paper deals with the problem of finding adequate multimedia presentation that fulfils spatio-temporal constraints. More precisely, we first propose a spatio-temporal algebra for the composition of multimedia presentations. Secondly, we present a semantic adaptation strategy by means of substitution of media elements that preserves presentation semantics.

S. Benbernou
Computer Science Department, University Paris Descartes, 45 Rue des Saints Pères, 75270 Paris 06
e-mail: salima.benbernou@parisdescartes.fr

M.S. Hacid
Computer Science Department, University of Lyon1, 43 bld du 11 Novembre 1918, 69220 Villeurbanne, France
e-mail: mshacid@liris.cnrs.fr

A. Makhoul and A. Mostefaoui (✉)
Computer Science Laboratory (LIFC), University of Franche-Comte, Rue Engel-Gros BP 527, 90016 Belfort, Cedex, France
e-mail: abdallah.makhoul,ahmed.mostefaoui@univ-fcomte.fr

R. Chbeir et al., *Emergent Web Intelligence: Advanced Information Retrieval*, Advanced Information and Knowledge Processing, DOI 10.1007/978-1-84996-074-8_12,
© Springer-Verlag London Limited 2010

12.1 Introduction

Nowadays many web applications (especially those that are web 2.0 and web 3.0 compliant) make use of complex composite multimedia document. In fact, the growing capabilities of today's computers and the "democratisation" of multimedia devises (webcam, phone camera, etc.) have made it possible to create, manipulate, publish and access advanced multimedia content. The latter consists in a collection of different types of media objects (text, video, audio, images, 3D animation, etc.) that are displayed to the end user in accordance to a certain structural and temporal relationships defined over them. This is what we call *multimedia presentation*. Many recent web applications, ranging from professional applications (digital libraries, medical databases, ...) to general public applications (distance learning, e-commerce, ...) use the multimedia presentation paradigm. Let us consider, for illustration purposes, the example of an e-commerce application. Actually, presenting a product in a web application goes beyond a classical presentation that consists in a picture associated with an explicative text to include advanced video, presenting the product in all its faces, sophisticated 3D animation for virtual clothes trying on for instance, elaborated audio for user interaction, etc.

To get a comprehensive meaning, a multimedia presentation must contains, in addition to the different media objects that compose it, specified synchronized information describing explicitly when and where each object has to be presented in the *playout* of the presentation, e.g., documents written in Synchronised Multimedia Integration Language (SMIL) [1]. It is a common experience that the management of multimedia presentations poses a number of challenges due in particular to the end-user context (e.g., reduced display devise, limited network bandwidth, resource constrained environment, etc.). Hence, a multimedia presentation needs to be adapted in order to fulfil the context requirements and without explicitly providing different versions for each case. However, this adaptation is not straightforward and must be carried out with respect to the semantic of the presentation on one hand and to the user context constraints on the other hand. To illustrate, let us introduce the following motivating example.

12.1.1 Motivation

We consider an e-learning application in which a chemistry course is made available for web students. Such a course (see Fig. 12.1) is composed of several different objects: (a) a video, noted v, showing the chemical reaction at its different phases, a 3D animation, noted a presenting this reaction at the molecular level, a set of slides, noted s, explaining the chemical formulas and finally an audio object, noted d, reporting the teacher explanation.

Let us assume that this course is accessed by a student through its PDA for instance and due to surrounding noises or lack of loudspeaker, he is not able to hear the teacher explanation. In this case, from the point of view of the system, two scenarios

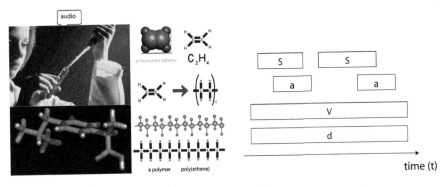

Fig. 12.1 Example of a multimedia presentation with its spatio-temporal constraints

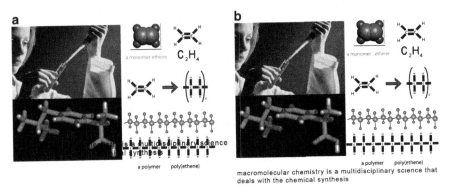

Fig. 12.2 (a) Invalid adaptation; (b) valid adaptation

are possible: (a) it delivers the presentation with the risk of deteriorating its semantic (the meaning of the course); or (b) does not deliver the presentation because it could not meet the user requirement.

Another scenario is possible in which an adaptation of the multimedia presentation is made in a way that both its semantic is preserved and the user constraint is supported. We illustrate the adaptation mechanism in this example by replacing the audio objects by anther *semantically equivalent* object that could be displayed to the user. Here, the audio object is replaced by a text transcribing the teacher explanation. However, this substitution introduces new spatial and temporal constraints on the presentation that the system must take into account. For instance, as reported in Fig. 12.2, the colour of the text, its position as well as its font size should take into account the spatial constraints introduced by the other object composing the presentation. This substitution, as shown in the example, could lead to a misunderstood content if it is not carried out carefully by respecting the new introduced spatial as well as temporal constraints.

12.1.2 Contributions

Our objective in this work is to provide a general framework for the adaptation of multimedia presentation, which could be seen as a web service. More precisely, we present a spatio-temporal model that is based on interval algebra to check the structural and temporal constraints of adapted presentation. Our contribution is twofold:

- Firstly we studied a novel spatio-temporal model, based on Interval algebra proposed by Allen [2]. We extended the interval relations from monodirectional ones to 3D ones (one temporal and two spatial). With this new model, we can easily handle the presentations constraints as well as user constraints.
- Secondly, a framework of multimedia adaptation including substitution is presented. After finding alternatives for each media-object, based on user's context, the substitution of the undesired element by another one is achieved regarding the alternative set. The framework handles then possible spatio-temporal conflicts that can arise after the substitution as shown in the above example.

The rest of this paper is organized as follows: An overview of some existing multimedia models is given in Section 12.2. In Section 12.3, a spatio-temporal representation is proposed. A spatio-temporal reasoning approach on the proposed model is given in Section 12.4. In Section 12.5 we present a framework for multimedia adaptation by substitution. First based on [3] we provide a augmentation model and secondly the substition step is described in more details. The conflict aspects are discussed in Section 12.6.

12.2 Related Work

Research works dealing with multimedia models for presentation adaptation that we are aware of are SMIL [1], AHM [4], TIEMPO [5], $Z_Y X$ [6] and other adaptations schemes [3, 12, 19].

The Synchronized Multimedia Integration Language (*SMIL*) [1], is designed by the W3C group. It integrates a set of multimedia objects into a synchronized multimedia presentation. It is an interval-based temporal model. Each media-element is represented by a temporal interval, which can be coordinated by the use of schedule elements. We distinguish the parallel (par) and sequential (seq) elements. In SMIL the placement of presentation components in spatial dimension is an absolute positioning. Due to the switch element, SMIL allows author to specify a set of alternative elements from which only one element should be chosen. Thus the switch element allows the static adaptation.

The Amsterdam Hypermedia Model (*AHM*) [4] is a combination of the two models, CWI Multimedia Interchange Format (CMIF) [10] and Dexter Hypertext Reference Model [11]. The first one specifies the spatial/temporal constraints of the presentation, and the second supports links and interaction models. It is considered as interval based model. The AHM provides an absolute spatial model.

Spatial relationships between components are defined by the use of channels, which determine the position and extent of the media. AHM can specify alternatives by grouping media items of the same media type.

The Temporal integrated model to present multimedia objects *TIEMPO* [5] is a flexible document model. A media object is modeled by a temporal space, a presentation interval and a projection. The temporal space represents the content and the layout information associated with the media object. The presentation interval represents the duration for which the media object is presented. The projection describes which and how many data units of the temporal space are presented per second in the presentation element. TIEMPO has an interval-based temporal model, and the temporal specification is based on interval operators without considering event-based. It supports an absolute spatial model describing the position, the size and the overlapping between media-elements.

The $Z_Y X$ multimedia model [6] emphasizes reuse, adaptation and presentation neutrality. It is possible to reuse media objects, document fragments, and entire document. It has a tree structure, where elements of the presentation are nodes of this tree. Each element contains binding points, which each point can bind to another variable element of the presentation. It presents operators, selectors, projectors and interaction elements. The element of $Z_Y X$ can be annotated by a set of attributes that describes its content. Similar to SMIL, $Z_Y X$ can be considered as temporal interval-based approach. It presents temporal operator (parallel, sequential, etc.) elements to determine the temporal relationships between the presentation elements. For the spatial model, $Z_Y X$ uses spatial projectors to define the layout of elements. It is defined as an absolute positioning. For the adaptation of multimedia presentation, the model $Z_Y X$ offers two elements: switch and query. The switch element as in SMIL model, allows the alternatives at the authoring time before the presentation. This element describes the static adaptability of $Z_Y X$. The dynamic multimedia adaptation of $Z_Y X$ is represented by the query element. When the document is selected to presentation the query element is evaluated and it is replaced by the fragment best matching the metadata annotated to the element.

The shortcoming of these models is the lack of use of spatial/temporal constraints especially in the adaptation by substitution. For the spatial model all the discussed models use an absolute positioning, that allows only one spatial presentation. We can not change their positions which is necessary in the adaptation phase particularly the adaptation by substitution because elements do not have necessarily the same size.

In our framework we consider all possible relations. We unified the spatial and temporal multimedia models on a one spatio-temporal model based on interval algebra that gives the necessar flexibility to the document and uses all interval relations.

12.3 Spatio-Temporal Representation

In this section after overviewing some preliminaries and the temporal representation, we suggest the underlying spatio-temporal model for our framework.

12.3.1 Preliminaries

In multimedia presentation, a *spatial model* is used to represent the position of media-objects on the screen and the spatial relationships between them. We distinguish three popular spatial models [6]: absolute positioning, directional relations [12] and topological relations [13], which are used in geographic databases to answer queries of region relations. A *temporal model* is also needed to define the temporal features of the presentation. There are four types of temporal models [14], time point-based models, event-based models, Interval-based models and script based-models.

Based on these models, the adaptation could be made on a multimedia presentation. We distinguish three kind of existing adaptation models: (1) *scenario adaptation* is used to adapt automatically the spatial/temporal constraints between media elements [15], (2) *structure adaptation* is involved when adapting the content media while distorting the element structure [16–20], for instance a text can be transformed into different formats (PDF, PS, ...) by loosing some aesthetic characteristics. (3) *Adaptation by substitution* is needed when the quality of a media element becomes very weak and it is impossible to present it, or to matching the user's preferences. It consists on replacing this element by something else semantically correct and that can be from a different type.

12.3.2 Temporal Representation

12.3.2.1 Interval-Based Temporal Reasoning

Allen [2] proposed an algebra for presenting and reasoning about temporal relations between events represented as intervals. The basis of this algebra is the set of thirteen temporal relations that can be held between events (see Fig. 12.3). A graphical notation called *"scenario"* is used in which nodes represent events and directed edges are possible temporal relations. Peter Van Beek [21] has defined a consistent scenario as *"a labeling of the graph where every label is a singleton and it is possible to map the vertices to a time line and have the single relations between vertices hold"*. Furthermore, Allen introduced a table of transitivity between the thirteen relations in order to ensure the constraint propagation. The construction of this table is based on the composition ";" between the relations [2].

12.3.2.2 Conceptual Neighborhoods

Freska [22] introduced the notion of conceptual neighborhood between interval relations. He defined three types *A*, *B* and *C* of conceptual neighborhood based on transformations. For example A-transformation moves one binding point of the first

Relation (r) x r y	Graphic x ◄──► y ▭	Converse (r^{-1}) $y\ r^{-1}\ x$
before (b) (<)	◄──► ▭	after (bi) (>)
meets (m)	◄──►▭	met (mi)
overlaps (o)	◄─▢─►	overlapped by (oi)
during (d)	▢◄──►▢	contains (di)
starts (s)	▢◄──►▭	started by (si)
finishes (f)	▭◄──►▢	finished by (fi)
equal (e)(=)	▢◄──►▢	equal (e)(=)

Fig. 12.3   Conceptual neighborhood

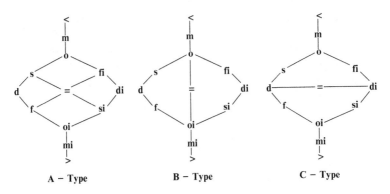

Fig. 12.4   Conceptual neighborhood

interval in one direction. The conceptual neighborhoods are defined by graphs as shown in Fig. 12.4. In this paper, we used the A-Type.

Definition 12.1 (Neighbors). Two relations are neighbors iff they are connected by an edge of the conceptual neighborhood graph. For example "<" and "m" are neighbors.

Definition 12.2 (Conceptual Distance d). The conceptual distance between two relations is the length of the shortest path which relates both of them in the conceptual neighborhood graph.

12.3.3 Spatio-Temporal Representation

We have seen in the previous section that in multimedia presentations the spatial and temporal models are often analyzed separately. In our framework, we extend 1-D temporal relations to 3-D spatio-temporal relations based on Interval Algebra. Hence, we propose a framework that integrates both the spatial and temporal models.

12.3.3.1 Interval-Based Spatio-Temporal Model

Several types of relations such as temporal, topological (inside, overlap...), directional (left, northeast...), have been defined and used in a wide range of models. Our goal is to unify the spatial and temporal relations, by extending the interval relation-based reasoning, as a way for enabling three dimensions reasoning (two spatials and one temporal).

Definition 12.3 (1-D Relation). One-dimensional relation is a relation between two objects over one dimension, where each object is represented by one interval, and related with interval relations.

Definition 12.4 (N-D Relation). The relation between two objects in N-D dimensions corresponds to the combination of N 1-D relations. Thus, an N-D relation is defined as an N-uplet of 1-D projections to N axes.

Definition 12.5 (Spatio-Temporal Relation). A spatio-temporal relation is a tuple (R_x, R_y, R_t) Where R_x, R_y and R_t are defined as 1-D relation, corresponding respectively to projections over x, y and t (time) axis.

Figure 12.5 shows an example of multimedia presentation represented over the temporal and spatial dimensions.

For instance, let us consider the example depicted in Fig. 12.5, representing multimedia document. Instead of having absolute coordinates, we have T1 (d_i, b, m) I, where d_i, b and m stand for R_x, R_y and R_t respectively. The latters are obtained by projecting objects to different axis.

Definition 12.6 (Undefined Relation $\perp$). If it does not exist any information about the relation between objects, we use the undefined one $\perp$, such that for all relation r: d $(\perp, r) = \infty$, $(\perp ; r) = \perp$, $(r ; \perp) = \perp$, $(\perp ; \perp) = \perp$ and $\perp^{-1}) = \perp$.

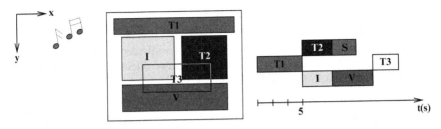

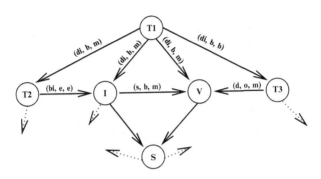

Fig. 12.5 Spatio-temporal representation of multimedia document

Fig. 12.6 A VSTCN representation of a multimedia document

For example, In Fig. 12.5 we have S ($\perp$, $\perp$, s) V and I ($\perp$, $\perp$, m) S, where S represents an audio element that does not have a spatial feature. Let us note R to be the set of all possible 1-D relations, R = {b, m, o, s, e, d, f, f_i, d_i, s_i, o_i, m_i, b_i, $\perp$}.

12.3.3.2 Spatio-Temporal Model

The relations defined above can serve to present spatio-temporal constraints of multimedia presentations.

Definition 12.7 (Variable Spatio-Temporal Constraints Network VSTCN).
VSTCN is a Directed Acyclic Graph (DAG), g = < N, E, λ, μ > such that N represents the set of nodes, E represents a set for edges, λ: E $\rightarrow$ $2^{R \times R \times R}$ is a function from arcs to spatio-temporal relations and μ: N $\rightarrow$ A assigns one of alternatives to a selected node, where A designates the set of alternatives that can be affected to this node.

A multimedia presentation can be represented as a VSTCN where node labels represent media-objects and edge labels are the spatio-temporal constraints between these objects. Figure 12.6 shows a part of spatio-temporal constraints network of the above example.

12.4 Spatio-Temporal Reasoning

Similar to the temporal reasoning, the spatio-temporal scenario is represented as a graph where vertices represent objects and to every directed edge is assigned a subset of possible spatio-temporal relation.

Example. Let us assume having three objects A, B and C. they are related with A (b, o, o) B and B (b, si, m) C. Because we don't have knowledge about the relation between A and C, every component R_x, R_y and R_t is setting to R. we can find three feasible relations between A and C that provide consistent scenarios. R (A, C) can be one of the three following relations: (b, d, b), (b, f_i, b) or (b, o, b). Next we define Spatio-Temporal operators applied to Spatio-Temporal relations.

Definition 12.8 (Spatio-Temporal Inverse Relation). We define the inverse of spatio-temporal relation as the inverse of every component of this relation. $[(R_1, R_2, R_3)]^{-1} = (R_1^{-1}, R_2^{-1}, R_3^{-1})$.

Example: $(b, d_i, e)^{-1} = (b_i, d, e)$.

Definition 12.9 (Closest Function C). C: $R \times P(R) \to R$ is a function that returns the closest relation from an element of the partition P(R) to a selected relation. Let $A \in P(R)$ and $\alpha \in R$, $C(\alpha, A) = \beta \Leftrightarrow \forall r \in A$, $d(\alpha, \beta) < d(\alpha, r)$, where d is a conceptual distance defined in the previous section.

Example: $C(b, \{m, o, d\}) = m$.

Definition 12.10 (Spatio-Temporal Composition). We define a spatio-temporal composition between two Spatio-Temporal relations as the composition of every component of these relations. Let $(\alpha, \alpha', \alpha'')$ and $(\beta, \beta', \beta'') \in R^3$.$[(\alpha, \alpha', \alpha'') ; ((\beta, \beta', \beta'')] = [\{\alpha ; \beta\}, \{\alpha' ; \beta'\}, \{\alpha'' ; \beta''\}]$.

Example: $[(b, o, o) ; (b, s, m)] = [\{b\}, \{d, f, o\}, \{b\}] = \{(b, d, b), (b, f_i, b), (b, o, b)\}$.

Definition 12.11 (Spatio-Temporal Closest Function *STC*). *STC* : $R^3 \times [P(R)]^3 \to R^3$ is a function that returns the closest spatio-temporal relation. Let $(\alpha, \alpha', \alpha'') \in R^3$ and $(A, A', A'') \in [P(R)]^3$. *STC* $[(\alpha, \alpha', \alpha''), (A, A', A'')] = [C(\alpha, A), C(\alpha', A'), C(\alpha'', A'')]$.

After the definition of a Spatio-Temporal multimedia presentation model, we propose in the next section a method for Multimedia adaptation by substitution based on this suggested model.

12.5 Framework for Multimedia Adaptation by substitution

The adaptation by substitution consists in replacing a media-object by another, which is not necessarily of the same type, when it looses its effective quality, or to matching the user's preferences. We will distinguish between two steps, *augmentation* and *substitution* as defined in [3]. The augmentation step identifies alternative elements according to semantic constraints, while the substitution step chooses an alternative (from those found in the augmentation step), according to user's context, and studies its impacts on the presentation after the substitution. The objective of our approach is to propose a complete declarative way for the representation of spatio-temporal composition of objects.

12.5.1 Augmentation

The basis of this process is to get semantically sound alternatives. As we consider *dynamic* adaptation, the augmentation step exploites metadata annotated with media elements in querying multimedia databases, and selects elements that are compatible to some predefined semantic constraints (subjects, duration, . . .). Next we define semantic constraints and provide an augmentation model.

12.5.1.1 Media-Element

A media-element can be either discret (e.g., image, text) or continuous (e.g., video, audio). To receive potential alternatives, every media-element is annotated with metadata which could be exploited in querying databases. In our case, metadata is descriptive, it contains keywords about elements that are called properties of the media-element (e.g., subjects, duration, . . .).

Let M be the set of all media-elements.

Definition 12.12 (Subjects *Subj*). $\forall$ m $\in$ M, the function *Subj* (m): M $\rightarrow$ Characters, returns a set of subjects associated with m.

Definition 12.13 (Duration *Dur*). $\forall$ m $\in$ M the function *Dur*(m): M $\rightarrow$ Integer is a function that returns the duration.

We can define other properties, which the strictness of alternatives depends on. The more metadata is closed to element's content the more alternatives are strict.

12.5.1.2 Semantic Constraints

We define semantic constraints as relationships that must be satisfies between the initial element and its alternatives. A similarity relation is then needed.

Remark. Subjects of continuous media-elements can change along time. To get a strict similarity, we define subject for every temporal interval. The discrete elements are represented as one interval with one subject.

Definition 12.14 (Similarity *Sim*). (*Sim* , M) is an equivalence relation on M defined as: $\forall$ m1, m2 $\in$ M, m1 *Sim* m2 $\Leftrightarrow$

$$Subj\,(m1) = Subj\,(m2) \land Dur\,(m1) = Dur\,(m2).$$

We introduce interval similarity that ensures the similarity of two media-elements in a selected temporal interval.

Definition 12.15 (Interval Similarity *IntSimil*). $\forall$ m_1, m_2 $\in$ M, *IntSimil* (m_1, m_2, T) is true iff *Subj* (m_1) = *Subj* (m_2) during T.

The information synchronization is very important between the initial element and its alternatives. We define flow information synchronization that ensures the same flow of information after a selected interval.

Definition 12.16 (Flow Information Synchronization *FIS*). m_1, m_2 $\in$ M have the same flow of information after an interval T, *FIS* (m_1, m_2, T) is true iff

$$\forall \text{ T'} / \text{ (T' bi T} \vee \text{T' m T), } [IntSimil\ (m_1, m_2, \text{T}) \wedge IntSimil\ (m_1, m_2, \text{T'})].$$

12.5.1.3 Augmentation Model

By using metadata, the augmentation process queries multimedia databases. Let Q be the answer of a query. It finds potential alternatives. Each element of the query that is similar to the initial media-element m, is added to a set $A\ (m)$ called semantic alternatives of m.

12.5.2 *Substitution*

The substitution process controls the dynamic adaptation. We distinguish two parts in this process. The first one is related to maintaining information about time presentation and selecting an alternative that is the best choice to the presentation state. The second part deals with the substitution step, where the chosen alternative in the selection step replaces the initial element.

12.5.2.1 Selection Model

In the previous section we found a set of alternatives $A\ (m)$ from which the replacement element will be chosen. Before selecting an element from the set A, the current state of the initial element is needed. Let Ti be the set of temporal intervals.

Definition 12.17 (Current Interval CurrInt). *CurrInt* (m):M$\rightarrow$*Ti* is a function that returns the current interval of m played in the actual presentation.

Remark. $\forall$ m $\in$ M, If it is in inactive state, *CurrInt* (m) returns the first interval of m. The $Z_Y X$ model provides the reusability of media-elements by means of spatial and temporal selectors. In our case we define a temporal interval selector.

Definition 12.18 (Temporal Interval Selector *TISEL*). Let m ∈ M, and T ∈ *Ti* we define *TISEL*(m, T): M × *Ti* → M is a function that returns the part of m after the selected interval.

The objective of the adaptation by substitution is to respond to user's profile, thus the selected alternative must be compatible with that profile.

Definition 12.19 (User's Profile *UP*). *UP* designates a set of constraints imposed by the user during the presentation of the multimedia document.

The selected alternative must respond to *UP* and continue the same flow of information where the initial element is interrupted. The selection approach is presented by the Algorithm 12.1. After the selection of *m'* as an alternative of *m*, the next step is to replace *m* by *m'* and study its impacts on the consistency and the understanding of the presentation.

Algorithm 12.1 Select an alternative

Require: *m : M* // initial element,
    A (m) // set of alternatives.
Ensure: *m' : M* // selected alternative.
    T ← *CurrInt(m)*
2: **for** every element e_i ∈ *A(m)* **do**
      if (*e_i* responds *UP* ∧ *FIS* (*m*, e_i, T)) **then**
4:       *m' = TISEL* (*e_i*, T)
        SKIP for
6:    **end if**
    end for

12.5.2.2 Substitution Model

We find a virtual spatio-temporal relation that can hold between m and m' before assigning m' to the corresponding node N, then we change all the existing spatio-temporal constraints between N and remaining nodes on the VSTCN representing the document. Media element is represented spatially by its minimum bounding rectangle, so an alternative can have different length and width of the original one. To find the spatio-temporal relation between the alternative and the initial element, first the temporal relation between these two elements is set to equal (e) because they considered the same duration. Then, we assume that the two elements have the same spatial starting point which means R_x and R_y are either s, e or s_i, depending on the size of the alternative.

Remark. If one of those elements (original or its alternative) is an audio element, the relation between these elements will be (⊥, ⊥, e) because audio elements have no spatial representation. Algorithm 12.2 finds the spatio-temporal relation R (m', m).

After finding the virtual relation that exists between m' and m, we assign m' to the node instead of m, then we find the new relations by means of the spatio-temporal closest function to ensure as much as possible the semantic of the presentation. These steps are given by the Algorithm 12.3.

Algorithm 12.2 Find the spatio-temporal relation

Require: m : M,
    m': M.
Ensure: R (m', m) = Spatio-Temporal relation between m and m'.
    if ((m ∨ m') = audio element)) **then**
        R (m', m) ←(⊥,⊥, e)
3:    **else** R_t (m', m)← e
    if width (m')< width (m) **then**
        R_x (m', m)←s
6:    **end if**
    if (width (m')= width (m)) **then**
        R_x (m', m)←e
9:    **end if**
    if (width (m')> width (m)) **then**
        R_x (m', m)←s_i
12:   **end if**
    if (height (m')< height (m)) **then**
        R_y (m', m)←s
15:   **end if**
    if (height (m')= height (m)) **then**
        R_y (m', m)←e
18:   **end if**
    if (height (m')> height (m)) **then**
        R_y (m', m)←s_i
21:   **end if**
    end if

Algorithm 12.3 New presentation generation

Require: VSTCN: old multimedia document
    R (m', m) : spatio-temporal relation.
Ensure: VSTCN: new multimedia document.
    // suppose N_i is the node for which new element m' is assigned to//
    N_i, N_k : N
    N_i ← m'
    for every node N_k ! = N_i **do**
        R (N_i, N_k) ← STC (R (N_i, N_k), [R (m', m) ; R (N_i, N_k)])
4: **end for**

Example

Let us illustrate by the example introduced in Section 12.1. Figure 12.7 shows a spatio-temporal representation of the studied document and the corresponding VSTCN.

Let us assume due to a noisy problem we substitute the video V by one of its alternatives I1 (series of images). The virtual relation between I1 and V are shown in Fig. 12.8, $R(I1, V) = (s_i, s, e)$.

Then we have:

$$R(I1, T) = STC(R(V, T), [R(I1, V); R(V, T)]).$$
$$= STC((m, s, d_i), [(s_i, s, e); (m, s, d_i)]).$$
$$= STC((m, s, d_i), [\{d_i, f_i, o\}, \{s\}, \{d_i\}]).$$
$$= (o, s, d_i).$$
$$R(I1, I) = STC(R(V, I), [R(I1, V); R(V, I)]).$$
$$= (s_i, b, m).$$

The temporal relations between objects are still the same. The new obtained VSTCN and its spatio-temporal are depicted in Fig. 12.9.

After the replacement it may occur conflicts that can disrupt the presentation.

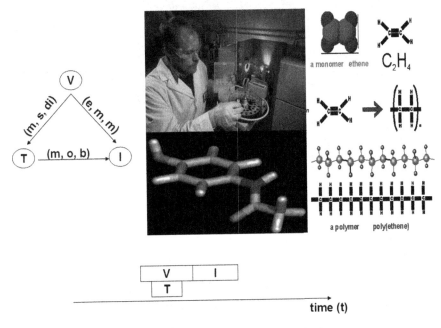

Fig. 12.7 Spatio-temporal network and representation before substitution

Fig. 12.8 Relation between the original and its alternative element

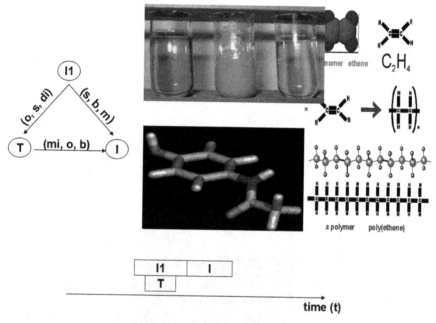

Fig. 12.9 Spatio-temporal network and representation after substitution

12.6 Conflicts

We define conflict as a state where the existed constraints between media elements lead to inconsistent presentation. This conflict may occur after the replacement of an element by its alternative. We distinguish two types of conflicts *temporal* and *spatial*.

12.6.1 *Temporal Conflict*

The temporal conflict is represented by the overlapping between two audios. In a multimedia presentation the permitted temporal relation that can hold between two audios is one of the set Rc = $\{b, m, m_i, b_i\}$. After substituting an element in the document, we must check the temporal conflict. If the new element is an audio, then we change the temporal relation with other audios if it is not included in the set Rc. We choose the closest relation of Rc, to keep as possible the semantics of the presentation. After changing this relation we must find again all the relations issued from the new element. These steps are depicted in Algorithm 12.4.

Algorithm 12.4 Temporal conflict detection

Require: VSTCN: old multimedia document.
Ensure: temporal conflict checking. // suppose N_i is assigned a new audio element//
    N_i, N_k : N
    for every node N_k ! $= N_i$ **do**
      if N_k is an audio **then**
        if $R_t (N_i, N_k) \notin$ Rc **then**
          $R_t (N_i, N_k) = C (R_t(N_i, N_k),$ Rc$)$
5:      **end if**
      end if
      for every node N_j / $(N_j$! $= N_i) \wedge (N_j$! $= N_k)$ **do**
        $R_t (N_i, N_j) \leftarrow C (R_t (N_i, N_j), [R_t (N_i, N_k) ; R_t (N_k, N_j)])$
      end for
10: **end for**

12.6.2 *Spatial Conflict*

The spatial conflict is represented by the prohibition of the spatial overlapping between elements. For instance, if a part of a text is covered, it becomes unreadable. To eliminate this conflict it is sufficient to have one of the three relations R_x, R_y or R_t an element of the set Rc. If we don't have a temporal overlapping, this means that the two elements never will be presented at the same time on the screen. In addition, if one of the spatial relations R_x or R_y belongs to the set Rc, then the spatial intersection will be null. If none of the three relations belongs to Rc, we must determine which relation we want to change with the minimum loss of semantics, by defining a new distance: *set conceptual distance* as a distance of a relation to a set of relations.

Definition 12.20 (Set Conceptual Distance D). D: R $\times$ P(R)$\rightarrow$ N is a function which returns the distance of a relation $\alpha \in$ R to a set of relations A $\in$ P(R), defined by D$(\alpha, A) = d(\alpha, C (\alpha, A))$.

Now we compute $D(R_x, Rc)$ and $D(R_y, Rc)$ the relation that has the shortest distance to Rc. We change it by its closest relation in the set Rc.

In the previous example we saw that T becomes understanding after the substitution of V by I1. Figure 12.10 shows this document after the resolution of spatial conflict.

Algorithm 12.5 depicts the steps for detecting spatial conflict.

Algorithm 12.5 Detect spatial conflict

Require: VSTCN: old multimedia document.
Ensure: test the document for Spatial conflict. // suppose N_i is assigned a new text element//
    $N_i, N_k : N$
    for every node $N_k \; ! = N_i$ **do**
      if N_k is a text **then**
        if $R_x (N_i, N_k) \notin Rc \wedge R_y (N_i, N_k) \notin Rc \wedge R_t (N_i, N_k) \notin Rc$ **then**
          $D(R_a, Rc) = \min (D(R_x, Rc), D(R_y, Rc))$ // a = x or y.
          $R_a (N_i, N_k) = C (R_a(N_i, N_k), Rc)$
5:      **end if**
      end if
      for every node $N_j \; / (N_j \; ! = N_i) \wedge (N_j \; ! = N_k)$ **do**
        $R (N_i, N_j) \leftarrow STC (R (N_i, N_j), [R (N_i, N_k) ; R (N_k, N_j)])$
      end for
10: **end for**

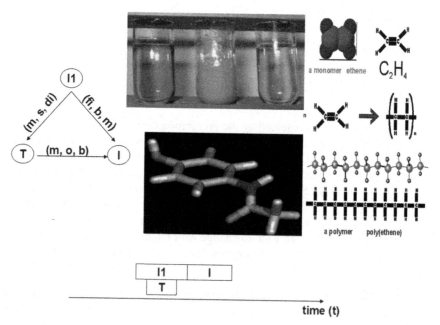

Fig. 12.10 Resolve spatial conflict

12.7   Conclusion and Perspectives

Multimedia document is characterized by spatial/temporal and interaction models describing relationships between different media-elements. To obtain more flexible documents, in this paper we provide a Spatio-Temporal model based on interval algebra introduced by J.Allen. An extension of 1-D relation to 3-D permits the representation of spatio-temporal relationships between media-objects.

A framework for multimedia adaptation by substitution is proposed. It is based on two steps, Augmentation and Substitution. The first one deals with finding alternatives for media-elements that are semantically closed. Therefore we define semantic constraints between media-elements. The second step substitutes the unwanted media by its alternative taking into account the spatio-temporal coherence of the presentation. However, our model lacks the interaction. In our future work we shall provide interaction model defining links from and to media-objects. Furthermore to give more precision to the position of element we will define strong and weak relations. these relations can lead us to resolve other conflicts.

Finaly we notice that, the flexibility of our model encloses the three diferent types of adaptation (scenario, structure, and substitution). For example, a simple transformation of temporal relations between objects can resolve the screen size constraint (e.g., from overlap to meet). On another way, if a video in colors can't be palyed face to narrow bandwidth, first it can be transformed to black and white (structure adaptation), before getting the final solution which is the substitution, if the structure adaptation can't offense the constraint.

References

1. W3c 2001, synchronized multimedia integration language, recommendation disponible en ligne http://www.w3.org/tr/smil20/,2001.
2. Allen J. Maintaining knowledge about temporal intervals. *communications of the ACM*, Vol. 26(11):832–843, 1983.
3. Klas W. Boll S. and Wandel J. A cross-media adaptation strategy for multimedia presentations. *proc.ACM Multimedia99*, 1999.
4. Hardman L. Modelling and authoring hypermedia documents. *Phd thesis, University of Amsterdam, Netherlands*, 1998.
5. Wirag S. Specification and scheduling of adaptive multimedia documents. *Technical Report 1999/04, University of Stutgart, Computer Science Department*, 1999.
6. Klas W. Boll S. Zyx a multimedia document model for reuse and adaptation of multimedia content. *proc. ACM Multimedia99*, TKDE 13(3):361–382, 2001.
7. Sébastien Laborie, Jérome Euzenat, and Nabil Layaida. Multimedia document summarization based on a semantic adaptation framework. *Proceedings of the 2007 international workshop on Semantically aware document processing and indexing*, pages 87–94, 2007.
8. Sébastien Laborie and Jérome Euzenat. An incremental framework for adapting the hypermedia structure of multimedia documents. *Advances in Semantic Media Adaptation and Personalization, Springer Berlin/Heidelberg*, pages 157–176, 2008.
9. Christian Timmerer Dietmar Jannach, Klaus Leopold and Hermann Hellwagner. A knowledge-based framework for multimedia adaptation. *Applied Intelligence, Springer*, 24(2):109–125, 2006.

10. Bulterman D.C.A. User-centred abstractions for adaptive hypermedia presentations. *In proc. ACM Multimedia98, Bristol, UK,* 1998.

11. Halsz F.G. and Schwartz M. The dexter hypertext reference model. *Communications of the ACM,* 31(7):836–852, 1994.

12. Papidias D. and Sellis T. Qualitative representation of spatial knowledge in 2d space. *VLOB,* 3(4):479–516, 1994.

13. Egenhofer M. and Franzosa R. Point-set topological spatial relations. *Int. Journal of Geographical Information Systems,* 5(2):161–174, 1991.

14. Boll S. Zyx, towards flexible multimedia document models for reuse and adaptation. *PHD Thesis, University of Vienna, Austria,* 2001.

15. Gomaa A. Adam N. and Atluri V. Adapting spatial constraints of composite multimedia objects to achieve universal access. *Cimic Rutgers,* 2004.

16. Qiu M. Zhang K., Kong J. and Song G. Multimedia layout adaptation through grammatical specifications. *(c) springer-Verlag,* 2004.

17. Brever EA. Fox A., Gribble SD. and Amir E. Adapting to network and client variability via on-demand dynamic distallation. *Proceedings of the seventh international ACM conference on ASPLOS; Cambridge MA,* 1996.

18. Deffner B. Busse I. and Schulzrinne H. Dynamic qos control of multimedia applications based on rtp. *Computer communications,* 19(1):49–58, 1996.

19. Wang L. Kazantzidis M. and Gerla M. On fairness and efficiency of adaptive audio application layers for multi-hop wirless networks. *IEEE MOMUC99,* pages 357–362, 1999.

20. B. Prabhakaran. Adaptive multimedia presentation strategies. *Multimedia Tools Application,* 12(2/3):281–298, 2000.

21. Van Beek P. Reasoning about qualitative temporal information. *Artificial Intelligence,* 58:297–326, 1992.

22. Freska C. Temporal reasoning based on semi-intervals. *Artificial intelligence,* 54:199–227, 1996.

Chapter 13
A Multifactor Secure Authentication System for Wireless Payment

Sugata Sanyal, Ayu Tiwari, and Sudip Sanyal

Abstract Organizations are deploying wireless based online payment applications to expand their business globally, it increases the growing need of regulatory requirements for the protection of confidential data, and especially in internet based financial areas. Existing internet based authentication systems often use either the Web or the Mobile channel individually to confirm the claimed identity of the remote user. The vulnerability is that access is based on only single factor authentication which is not secure to protect user data, there is a need of multifactor authentication. This paper proposes a new protocol based on multifactor authentication system that is both secure and highly usable. It uses a novel approach based on Transaction Identification Code and SMS to enforce another security level with the traditional Login/password system. The system provides a highly secure environment that is simple to use and deploy with in a limited resources that does not require any change in infrastructure or underline protocol of wireless network. This Protocol for Wireless Payment is extended as a two way authentications system to satisfy the emerging market need of mutual authentication and also supports secure B2B communication which increases faith of the user and business organizations on wireless financial transaction using mobile devices.

13.1 Introduction

Online banking, one of the fastest growing internet based activity which increases flexibility to the users to make their utility payments world wide and also increases the business of the organizations universally. It is so popular that the

S. Sanyal
School of Technology and Computer Science, Tata Institute of Fundamental Research (TIFR), Mumbai, India
e-mail: sanyal@tifr.res.in

A. Tiwari (✉) and S. Sanyal
Indian Institute of Information Technology (IIIT), Allahabad (UP), India
e-mail: ayu.tiwari@gmail.com; ssanyal@iiita.ac.in

R. Chbeir et al., *Emergent Web Intelligence: Advanced Information Retrieval*, Advanced Information and Knowledge Processing, DOI 10.1007/978-1-84996-074-8_13,
© Springer-Verlag London Limited 2010

criminals are well aware of it and it is major revenue making source for criminals. The fundamental requirement of any online banking applications is a security to protect users confidential data. Financial institutions providing online services and offering Internet-based products should use secure and efficient methods of authentication to protect data of their customers. Accessing today's web-based services always requires a username and password to authenticate the user identity. This is a significant vulnerability since the password can be captured by the man in the middle attack and later used for making illegal access to the users account. The user authentication method used by current online payment systems is not adequate and secure. Thus it is possible for an unscrupulous user to use credit card number or account details stolen from valid user. Financial agencies considered single-factor authentication is not sufficient for user authentication and insecure for high-risk financial transactions which involve access to customer information or the online fund transfer to other parties using web browsers or cell phones/PDA [32,33].

The single factor authentication does not support all the security requirements, major drawbacks of single factor authentication are:

1. System relies on password authentication only.
2. Easily deducible with public domain cracking software utilities.
3. Weakness of the system: Password is encrypted and Needs to traverse insecure medium (Interception and decryption).
4. This makes it vulnerable to passive attacks.
5. Rigid and strict password requirements, so difficult to remember passwords and this leads to storing of an e-copy of the password on the computer at easily accessible locations.

In order to support our claim single factor authentication is vulnerable to various attacks. We would like to highlight the key points of the published guidelines of FFIEC (Federal Financial Institutions Examination Council). The FFIEC Council is a formal interagency body empowered to prescribe uniform principles, standards, and report forms for the federal examination of financial institutions. They introduced a various points related to need of stronger authentication for Internet banking services as mentioned in [14]:

• Financial institutions must use the guidance by FFIEC for evaluating and implementing authentication systems and practices.
• Financial institutions thus offering internet based products must have reliable and secure methods to authenticate users.
• Risk assessment must be conducted to identify types and levels of risk associated with their particular internet finance related product.

So, we need Multifactor Authentication technique to secure our web transactions and to increase faith of users on mobile financial transactions. In this proposed work we are introducing new authentication system which is secure and highly usable, based on multifactor authentication approach. It uses a novel approach to create an authentication system based on TICs (Transaction Identification code) and SMS to enforce an extra security level over the traditional login in a username/password context. Al-Qayedi et al.[1] have also proposed the use of SMS to implement secure login session but have not used TICs in their protocol. TICs are user specific unique transaction identification codes which are issued by banks or financial institutions to their users. This code is similar to One Time Password (OTP) but provide more secure authentication to the transactions and one TIC code is used only once. This work also suggests an encryption/decryption technique that would be used to keep TICs as secret codes on cell phones/PDA. The user can easily pick up a TIC (from the stored list of TICs) to initiate secure web transaction using cell phones/PDAs, instead of remembering and typing a complicated TIC code in each transaction. This protocol is extended to introduce mutual authentication by two way authentication system, i.e., the company or service provider is authenticated to the user along with the authentication of user to the financial institution. In two way authentication business organizations can also adopt this proposed system for their B2B mutual communication. The proposed protocol can also implemented in B2B communication with very slight modification to it. It enforces the strong security over the existing system to protect the business communication over the insecure networks.

The paper is structured as follows: Section 13.2 reviews the related work on e-payment systems. Section 13.3 introduces the Multifactor authentication approach. Section 13.4 presents our protocol for Wireless Payment including the system design and architecture for secure web authentication. Section 13.5 presents the architecture of the two way authentication scheme and its functional components. In Section 13.6, we discuss some implementation issues. In Section 13.7, security analysis demonstrates the resistance of the protocol against various internet threats. Section 13.8 shows various advantages of this new system followed by some conclusion in Section 13.9.

13.2 Background and Related Work

According to Gao et al. [11], mobile payment refers to wireless-based electronic payment for m-commerce to support point-of-sale/point-of-service (POS) payment transactions using mobile devices. In general, m-payment systems can be used by wireless-based merchants, content vendors and information and service providers to process and support payment transactions driven by wireless-based commerce applications. As discussed in [33], the existing m-payment systems can be classified into three major types. The first type is account-based payment systems which can be mobile phone-based, smart card or credit-card m-payment systems [10, 12, 16, 18, 21]. Second type of m-payment system refers to the mobile POS payment systems by which customers can purchase products on vending machines or at retail stores with their mobile devices. The third type is E-wallets or E-cash which stores digital cash, which has been transferred from a credit card, debit card or virtual check inside their e-wallets. This payment system is designed to complement existing credit and debit card systems for mobile users and can be either automated POS payments or attended POS payments [16, 21]. An example of mobile POS payment system is Ultras M-Pay (http://www.ultra.si/).

13.2.1 Secure Electronic Transaction (SET)

The Secure Electronic Transaction is an open protocol specification developed for credit card transactions over internet. Although SET has been designed to operate in a wired infrastructure [15,22,25] its transaction flow and implementation of security are of interest to us since it can also be employed in a wireless scenario [15]. As referred to [15] basic transaction flow under SET protocol is:

1. The consumer accesses the merchant's web site, browses the goods on display and selects what he or she wants and gets the total cost of all chosen items including taxes and shipping costs.
2. The system asks for payment method and the consumer chooses to pay through a credit card using SET.
3. Digital Wallet is special software used to enter credit card information.
4. After getting details of customer payment the merchant contacts the merchants Bank for customer authorization and payment.
5. Merchant Bank will contact the customers Bank for the same and get approval of payment.
6. Merchant will notify, if transaction is successful.
7. A few seconds later, there is a confirmation to the customer that this order has been processed.

SET is a good example of a protocol which does not provide secure user authentication. Generally, implementation of SET uses SSL-based methods, which is not completely secure [2].

Some disadvantages of SET are:

1. SET is designed for wired networks and does not meet all the challenges of wireless network.
2. SET protocol worked in the traditional model of payment data , so an end-to-end security mechanism was required.
3. Direction of transaction flow in SET. In SET transactions are carried out between Customer Agent and Merchant. It is vulnerable to attacks like transaction/balance modification by Merchant.
4. The transaction flow is from Customer to Merchant so all the details of the users credit cards/debit cards must flow via the merchants side. It increases the users risk, since data can be copied and used later to access a customer account without authorization.
5. There is no notification to the Customer from the customers Bank after the successful transfer. The user has to logon to their Bank online portal in order to get transaction and payment detail.
6. SET is only for card (credit or debit) based transactions. Account based transactions are not included.

13.3   Multifactor Authentication Approach

Multifactor Authentication is a technique for users to authenticate themselves using two or more authentication, generally this method has been implemented for large devices which are more capable in terms of power and processing capabilities, some commonly available systems uses combination of something the user possesses such as a security token (e.g., USB dongle or security smart card), and something the user knows (e.g., password). Another very popular multifactor authentication technique is Biometrics. The major draw back of Biometric approaches is that it requires large systems to implement with very high power and processing capability with high implementation and deployment cost.

The proposed work suggests that Multifactor Authentication technique can be implemented in secure web transactions using cell phones. The best way to implement the multifactor authentication approach without any extra hardware and extra cost is to use two separate communication channels to confirm the identity of the user.

13.3.1   Multifactor Authentication Techniques

In the present work, we propose a multifactor authentication technique based on TICs and SMS confirmation.

13.3.1.1   TIC Authentication

TIC code authenticates the wireless transaction to allow server access. It is a technique which verifies both the user and the ongoing transaction. A TIC code certifies that the current transaction has been initiated by the right person and that its a valid user who is trying to access his/her account.

TIC codes are:

- Issued by the Bank or Financial Institution to its customers.
- A 32 bit or 64 bit Pseudo Randomly generated code which are assigned to the customers.
- May be a complicated digit sequence or combination of numeric and alpha numeric characters.
- One time code, each transaction will use unique TIC code for authentication.

The TIC codes are most sensitive data for any financial transactions, so we are storing TICs in encrypted format on users cell phone. The key to decrypt the TIC before making any online web transaction is a local password on cell phone and only valid cell phone owner will know the password. This password is a local password and user can change it easily time to time to keep protection. The Bank or Financial institutions are responsible for TIC generation and distribution to their customers.

The TIC generation logic is strictly confidential and limited to the only responsible authorized staff of the organization. The financial organizations will also maintain the authentication server to record the issued TICs to the users and matches the same code for each receive transaction and cancel the used TIC after successful transaction, so that each TIC will be used only once [30] also recommended that financial institutions should decide the validity time period for TICs according to its standard organizational issuing policies, this method decrease the risk of fraud with the very old TICs.

13.3.1.2 SMS Authentication

The Bank or Financial institution stores user cell number to send SMS to their customers for their transaction confirmation. Cellular network uses separate channel to send and receive SMS over wireless medium [1]. Here we assume that users carry their cell phone with them regularly and therefore can receive the short message and reply SMS to confirm or deny their financial transaction. As a result, only valid users will receive SMS from the authentication server. After getting the SMS, a user can acknowledge the choices. When the authentication server receives "YES" it knows that the user is valid and that the user has approved their initiated transaction.

So, Multifactor Authentication is used to verify the user and the transaction by using following steps as referred to [30]:

1. *Web-Based Basic Authentication* Firstly, the user will access web server using their assigned web-based username/password for basic authentication.
2. *TIC Authentication* After successful authentication of the user using username/password, the web server will demand for a TIC code from the web user as a second authentication when user will initiate any financial transaction. Now user will decrypt and insert one time TIC code to uniquely identify his/her transaction and prove his/her identity to the web Authentication server.
3. *SMS Confirmation* After the successful TIC code authentication, the third authentication will take place, a SMS confirmation is a final approval to their initiated online transactions.

The security of the system also depends on the security of the messages sent by SMS and WAP, which are encrypted and protected with A5/3 Algorithm [13]. The user will get a SMS with the required details which are essential to identify and recognize the users initiated transaction. By this SMS, a user will confirm their transaction by "YES" or "NO". Transaction will be committed on server only if the user chooses "YES" and Rollback in case of "NO". As refer to [30], in next section, we are focusing on proposed protocol based on above recommended authentication techniques.

13.4   Secure Web Authentication Protocol

The data flow and architecture, based on Multifactor Authentication techniques, is described in this section.

13.4.1   Architecture of Secure Web Authentication Protocol

Figure 13.1 shows high level architecture of protocol for a secure web authentication using small wireless mobile devices like cell phone/PDA. Figure 13.2 shows more detailed pictorial representation of transactions of protocol.

The basic function of this protocol starts when user initiates payment or fund transfer process using their cell phone/ PDA. It is highly recommended to use separate authentication server to implement the protocol and increase security. Step by step processes of using the proposed system are given below:

1. User will get their secure login/password details from bank or financial institution when they make contract with financial institution to open their account. Financial Institution is also responsible to distribute the TICs to their customers, authorized person will make initial setup to their customers cell phones/PDA and install TIC codes with internal encryption.

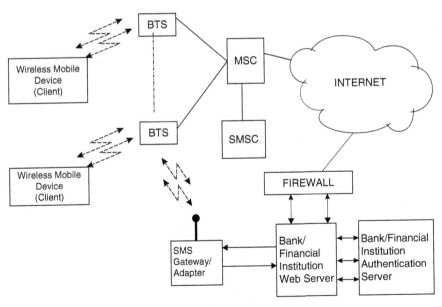

BTS – Base Transceiver Station, MSC –Mobile Switching Centre, SMSC – Short Message Service Centre.

Fig. 13.1 Architecture of multifactor secure Web authentication protocol using mobile devices

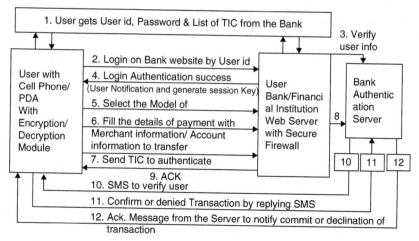

Fig. 13.2 Multifactor secure Web authentication protocol – transaction flow

2. The user will login using a Username/Password on Bank web server through GPRS connection and web-based username/password is a basic authentication used to identify the user to the web server.

3. After successful basic authentication the user will get an option to initiate transaction with a welcome message and secure session id. We have considered three modes of payment: Credit Card, Electronic transfer and Debit Card.

4. The user will select mode of payment. In case of credit card based payment protocol demand valid credit card number.

5. The user will insert the details of payment by filling in a simple form with details such as the merchants account number, invoice number or account number to which an amount has to be transferred.

6. User can not submit online transaction without TIC code. As we have already mentioned in Section 13.3.1, TIC is a one time code and user will insert a TIC code from the stored list of TIC codes. Note that TICs are password protected on the cell phone and this password will be used to open the list of TIC codes and decrypt the selected one before using it in ongoing transaction.

7. Complete transaction with an attached TIC will be further encrypted and submitted to the server for processing. Here we are suggesting hybrid encryption technique to encrypt the transaction details, more details on cryptography implemented in the proposed system are mentioned in Section 13.2.1.

8. On the server side, banks authentication server decrypts the received transaction and extracts a TIC code. The server verifies the TIC sent by the user by comparing it to its stored list of TICs in the user account information at the server database. If both TICs matched, it cancels the used TIC from its database and goes to the next step. If no TIC matched with the database then the authentication server will deny any further user transaction and transmit an appropriate error message to the user.

9. If TIC authentication is successful, a authorization server will generate a text SMS and send to the SMS Gateway/Adapter to transmit it over the cellular network. Cellular network uses SMSC as a backbone device of the network to deliver a SMS to the user cell phone. The user will acknowledge to the server to verify his/her web transaction.

10. The user will confirm his/her initiated transaction by replying a SMS with "YES", or deny it by choosing "NO", by sending a confirmation SMS.

In the above module all the transactions from client to server or vice versa are strictly in an encrypted format. An Encryption and decryption module is installed on the users cell phone/PDA and on server side environment. Moreover, unlike SET, at no stage does the user have to supply personal information to the merchant. The cryptography module is discussed in more detail in next subsection.

13.4.2   Cryptography and Key Management

The most effective solution for secure communication over wireless networks is to employ an end-to-end security approach. End to end security can be achieved with the help of strong cryptography techniques. Public key encryption techniques is very popular encryption method and used in many application areas like application data security, operating systems security, network security and Digital Rights Management (DRM) are some examples. Internet Engineering Task Force (IETF) is an organization formed to decide standards for Internet and mobile platforms for cellular network environment. Public Key Infrastructure (PKI) is also widely accepted in cellular network environment to make secure communication in wireless networks. As mentioned in [20] public-key encryption needs more computation and processing time in comparison of symmetric-key encryption. Therefore, public-key encryption is not always suitable in large amount of data communication. However, public-key encryption is used to exchange a symmetric key, which can be later used for further encryption of data. This approach uses combination of above two techniques in encryption and adopted by various security protocols and it is called hybrid encryption schemes [17, 20, 27].

AES Rijndael Encryption Algorithm has been referred in the proposed system [8, 29]. AES Rijndael algorithm uses iterated block cipher, it produces output after multiple transformation of input block and cipher key. It supports variable-length block using variable-length keys; a 128, 192, or 256-bit key which can be used to encrypt data blocks that are 128, 192, or 256 bits long. All nine combinations of key and block lengths are possible [8, 29]. AES Rijndael algorithm was designed to have the following characteristics:

- Algorithm is secure against all known attacks.
- It perform operations at good speed over huge platforms, code is also small.
- Design is simple.

The AES Rijandael implementation was taken from the Legion of the Bouncy Castle cryptographic package [6] which provides a Java implementation for the algorithm.We have used block size of 16 bytes processed with 128-bit keys: this proved to be the best combination for operation on J2ME devices due to the speed and memory limitation of such devices [31].

13.4.2.1   Cipher Key Management

Securing the communication between client and server is our primary concern. For this reason we have implemented a hybrid encryption scheme over wireless medium. As referred to [31], we have used a session-key management mechanism where the encryption/decryption keys are randomly generated for every client session. This mechanism works as follows: the server uses a 128-bit key. At the start of user session the server randomly generates one secret key (128 bits) and stores it in the users specific entry in the database. The server then encrypts the session key using the client's 128 bit shared secret logic known to the client and the server. Session key is transmitted to the client after encryption.

A TIC code is used to encrypt all the transaction details of the customer before submission to the server, and then the TIC code itself is encrypted with a secret key which is generated by the server and transmitted to the user after a successful login.The client decrypts this secret key and uses this further to encrypt the TIC code before transmission to the server. On server side same secret key is stored which decrypts the TIC code, then matches the TIC code with the issued TICs to the customer If this TIC matches with the database then it will be next used to decrypt the other transaction details which were encrypted by an identical TIC at the user end otherwise transaction would be denied.

Another important issue that must be addressed is securing the storage of the shared secret on the client and server. On the server, this shared secret is stored in the database, which we have assumed to be secured by the database management system, operating system with secure firewalls and other computer security policies. Reference [31], also explain that securing the shared secret on the client machine involves big risk since these are small devices that can even be stolen. We used the following mechanism to protect the shared secret on the client environment:The shared secret key is stored in an encrypted format on the cell phone/PDA, in the Keys Java class in the application's JAR file. As shown in Fig. 13.3, the shared secret is encrypted by the client's 128 bits pin code, since AES requires that the key length is 128 bits [31].

In case of the banking application, at the time of subscription to the mobile banking service, it is the responsibility of the service manager to encrypt the shared secret with the client's pin code when the application is distributed, and to store the shared secret on the mobile phone/PDA.Furthermore, to enhance the security of code on the client, the Java classes in the MIDlet JAR file are obfuscated to protect the code from byte code de-compilers. The obfuscator we used is the Retroguard obfuscator v1.1 [7].

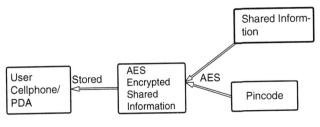

Fig. 13.3 Storing of shared information on client environment

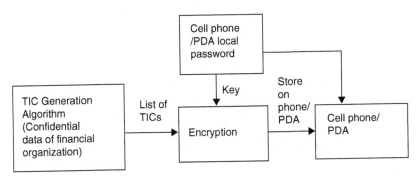

Fig. 13.4 TIC protection at client environment

In proposed protocol TIC codes are most sensitive data which are stored on cell phone/PDA. To maintain the security we have proposed that TICs are stored on the cell phone/PDA in an encrypted format and password protected as shown in Fig. 13.4. The user will insert local password of TICs to open the list of TICs and can select any TIC from the list to initiate financial transaction. This selection of TIC automatically decrypts the selected TIC and displays it on the users screen. This selection will also remove the selected TIC from the list of TICs at client environment. Local password of TIC is the key for decryption of TIC and known to the user only. Even the server at the financial institution is unaware of this key. It can be changed at any moment according to the convenience of the user. The local Encryption and decryption of TIC is also based on the AES symmetric key algorithm. AES cryptographic algorithm is best suited for the small devices; it enhanced the performance of cryptographic processing speed over small hand held devices instead of degrading the device performance.

However, there are several instances when we require a two-way authentication. In the following section we present the protocol for mutual authentication [30].

13.5 System for Two Way Authentication

After having analyzed the Secure Electronic Transaction (SET), on-line payments [2, 15, 16] and having taken into consideration the constraints of the wireless infrastructure, we developed the secure protocol for Wireless Payment, supportive of one-way authentication in the previous section. In reference to [10], we extend the protocol to support two-way authentication in the present section. In this architecture (Fig. 13.5) we have considered five major components with certain roles:

1. *User*   A user is a valid account holding customer of the bank.
2. *Customer Agent* (CA)   A CA is a software module which is running on the customers mobile device.
3. *Merchant Agent (MA)*   An MA is an online service provider and merchant website by which users do online purchasing.
4. *Customers Bank*   This is the bank at which the user has a valid account, it also contains the authentication server necessary to authenticate the user.
5. *Merchant Bank*   This is the bank in which the merchant has a valid account, the merchant Bank is also responsible for authenticating the merchant.

As referred to [15, 30] the two way Authentication protocol functions when the Merchant and Customer perform some commerce and Merchant generates an invoice statement for Customer to settle payment and it performs all authentication process for the other party. To implement the present scenario we have assumed all the participating financial institutions has business contract and bound with legal terms and conditions to give services to their customers. Figure 13.5, demonstrates the step by step flow of the payment transactions.

1. The MA generates an invoice and sends the Merchants encrypted banking information and authentication certificate with the invoice details to the CA.
2. The CA requests for authentication of Merchant to its Bank with the Merchant bank details, the merchant account details and a Merchant authentication certificate provided by the MA.

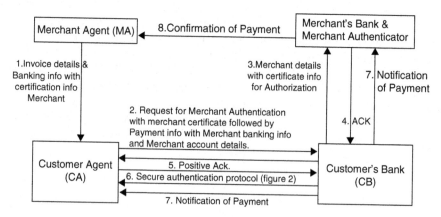

Fig. 13.5 Protocol for wireless payment: two way authentication system

3. The Customer Bank forwards the Merchant details with the authentication certificate to the Merchant bank for authentication of the merchant.
4. The Merchant Bank sends a positive or a negative acknowledgement to the Customer Bank which confirms the validity of the Merchant or invalidates the Merchant.
5. In case of validation, the Customers bank sends a Positive ACK to the CA and goes to step 6. If the Merchant certificate is not valid, the Customer Bank will notify the CA with that information. If Customer Bank receives a negative or suspicious acknowledgement of the Merchant it simply rejects the user transaction with valid security reason.
6. To initiate a payment process, secure web authentication protocol will be used to authenticate the customer. As mentioned in Section 13.4.1, secure web authentication protocol includes TIC validation and SMS confirmation as a part of secure customer authentication.
7. After getting a successful SMS confirmation from the customer, the Customer Bank will start transferring of amount to the Merchant Bank and after successful transfer also generate a payment notification for the Merchant Bank as well as to the customer with the required transaction detail.
8. As a final step Merchant bank will send a confirmation of the received payment from the customer to the MA with relevant details, such as invoice number, customer id and amount received. So that, the Merchant can shipped the purchased goods to the customer.

Protocol for secure web authentication secures the financial transactions between customer and customers Bank and preserves customers confidential data from the third party. As referred to [10] we also do not route payment transaction data via the MA. As a result, the security of the system is less susceptible to attack. Customer payment information and personal data are no longer available to the merchant directly and thus those details cannot be altered by the merchant.

In the next subsection we have presented complete transaction flow of the protocol, which is presented in the form of sequence diagrams. These details are required in order to perform a complete threat analysis of the proposed system.

13.5.1 Transaction Flow of Protocol

There are four sequence diagrams to demonstrate the step by step transaction flow of the proposed system. We have considered five major components in describing transaction flow of proposed system:

1. Customer Agent (CA)
2. Customer Bank (CB)
3. Customer Bank Authentication Server (CBAS)
4. Merchant Bank (MB)
5. Merchant Agent (MA)

13.5.1.1 First Authentication of User to the Bank Authentication Server

1. The user (CA) visits the website of the merchant to purchase goods online and chooses a payment option from the website.
2. The merchant web server (MA) generates invoice details and the merchant bank information with the merchant authorization certificate and sends to the CA in an encrypted format. We have discussed an encryption/decryption technique in Section 13.4.2. The same technique is useful to transmit merchant certificate information in an encrypted manner so that no one but CA can use it for merchant authentication. Note that cell phone has standard encryption/decryption capabilities to access and transfer data over the wireless cellular networks.
3. The user (CA) generates http request to their bank web server to initiate payment transaction.
4. The CB web server displays secure login page to logon on the web server.
5. The user can login using their user id and secret password known to them. Before transmitting users login details from client to server they will be encrypted using public key cryptography which is implemented on bank server by standard security mechanism. For more information on the public key cryptography refer to [17, 30].
6. The user details will be forwarded to the bank authentication server. Note that to maintain strong security mechanism we have recommended that the bank should maintain separate authentication server.
7. At authentication server users login data will be decrypted and matched with the secure database records of the customer. On success it generates random session key which will be encrypted by shared secret logic as mentioned in Section 13.4.2.
8. The customer bank (CB) will send general textual welcome message and session id to track the user session with the secret session key received from CBAS to the user (CA). If the user authentication fails then it sends invalid login message to the user.

   After successful login two way authentications take place as mentioned in Section 13.5.1.2.

13.5.1.2 Two Way Authentication – Authentication of Merchant to the Customer

9. The user (CA) will send the request to the users bank for merchant authentication before making payment to MB. The CA will forward received merchant details to authenticate the merchant.
10. Here we have assumed that the customer banks (CBs) and the merchant banks (MBs) have business model and they are linked to each other with the legal terms and conditions with standard policies decided by their business organizations. So, the CB will make a request to the merchant's bank to authenticate the merchant. Each merchant has legal authorization certificate which has been

issued by their banks or some centralized financial institutions to authenticate the merchant services.

11. The MB will acknowledge a request for the merchant authentication after matching details of merchant provided by the CB. Acknowledgement may be positive or negative depending on the validity of the merchant certificate.

12. The CB will forward the received acknowledgement of the merchant authentication to the user (CA). Note that if MB would provide negative acknowledgement then the CB simply terminates the user transaction with valid security reason and if CB receives positive acknowledge from the MB then it is assumed that the merchant is valid and user can go forward to make payment.

To initiate payment it will run multifactor secure web authentication protocol as mentioned in Figs. 13.1 and 13.2. Detailed explanation of the transaction flows of this protocol is mentioned in Section 13.5.1.3.

13.5.1.3   Second Authentication of User to the Bank Authentication Server

13. The user (CA) will select the mode of payment to make payment. Here we have considered three basic modes of payment: Electronic Transfer, Credit Card or Debit Card.

14. Selection of payment method generates an entry form with appropriate fields.

15. The user will fill the details of transaction by filling simple entries like amount, account number to which amount has to be transferred, if there is a merchant payment it automatically selects invoice number and other merchant details which was given by the merchant.

16. The user (CA) will insert the TIC code by opening the list of TICs stored at client environment. Note that:

- The TICs are stored on the cell phone/PDA in an encrypted format and password protected.
- The user will insert local password of TICs to open the list of TICs and can select any TIC from the list.
- This selection of TIC automatically decrypts the selected TIC and displays it on the user's screen. This selection will also remove the selected TIC from the list of TICs at client environment.
- Local password of TICs is a key for decryption of TIC and known to the user only, even server at financial institution is unaware of this key.
- Transmission of TIC from CA to CB is strictly in an encrypted format as referred to Section 13.4.2.

17. The bank server will forward the received TIC to the CBAS for TIC authentication and CBAS decrypts the received encrypted TIC to match with its database.

18. The CBAS server will match the received TIC with the assigned list of TICs to the user. If the match succeeds it delete the used TIC from its database and send message to the CB server. On unsuccessful match it sends denial message to the bank server.

19. If a received TIC matches with the assigned list of TICs to the user, the bank server generates acknowledgement to the user with message to wait for a SMS. If TIC does not match with the users assigned list of TICs then it denies the current transaction and sends a message to the user that transaction is cancelled because of invalid TIC.

After successful match of the TIC the user is free to close the current user session or make new financial transaction. The next step is SMS confirmation, the authentication server will generate a SMS destined to the user, as discussed in Section 13.5.1.4.

13.5.1.4 Third Authentication of the User and Transaction by SMS Confirmation to the Bank Authentication Server

20. The CBAS will send a SMS with transaction details for the confirmation of transaction by the user.
21. The user will reply to SMS by choosing "YES" or "NO". A SMS reply "YES" means user is valid and confirming their transaction. A SMS reply "NO" means user is denying their transaction.
22. If the bank authentication server receives "YES" from the user's SMS confirmation, it generates a notification of payment to the user and commits the users transaction.
23. The bank server will also send a notification of payment to the MB with invoice number and other required customer information.
24. The MB is responsible for sending notification of payment received from the customer to the merchant. Notification includes details of payment like invoice number and other required customer information.
25. If the CBAS receives "NO" from user's SMS, it immediately rolls back the current user transaction and sends a notification of cancellation of transaction to the CA.

Communication between the Customer Bank and the Merchant Bank is also online exchange of data which involves risk of many types on internet based attacks. In order to make secure communication between the two business entities we must maintain secure channel with strong security credentials. Although in present scenario organizations are actively participating in implementation of security to protect their B2B communication, also organizations are very much aware of time to time improvement of their security system to protect their confidentiality. A suggested protocol in Section 13.4.1 can also be implemented in B2B communication but without SMS confirmation module. If the business units use TIC codes as a special one-time token to uniquely authenticate their every mutual transaction, they will get more secure financial transaction over the existing one. Bank servers have strong processing unit and large storage capabilities, so there is no restriction to maintain TICs in their database. It is recommended that banks should use separate TIC format to authenticate their B2B transactions. When bank initiate fund transfer to other bank it will insert TIC code as a one time token in their transactions and encrypt the complete financial details and transmit it to the server of other banking unit. At the server side it decrypts the received transaction and compares the TIC with the stored TICs in their database corresponding to bank branch who initiated the transaction. On each successful transaction both the business unit will cancel the used TIC from their database. Business organizations can easily implement this protocol with their existing infrastructure without replacing any of their existing security models and use existing encryption/decryption techniques which they have been using so far in their mutual communication, only addition of one field for TIC code is required to implement the proposed system. There is no SMS confirmation required because it is not feasible to implement in B2B communication, as well as there are very less chances of fraud or unauthorized access to the business data. Business units are generally trusted parties and bound in legal terms and conditions of association of financial authority.

The two-way authentication protocol addresses several shortcomings of the SET:

- Data that is vital for the user is never available to the merchant in an unencrypted manner and merchant will not have access to any customers confidential information.
- Secure Credit Card based transaction supported over SET. Only Credit Card owner can initiate transaction, if any unauthorized person gains access to your Credit Card information and try to initiate transaction with your Credit Card number then this protocol will deny this transaction because TIC authentication and SMS confirmation would not be present in fraudulent transaction.
- Set supports only card based financial transactions but using this protocol users are free to make direct account based fund transfer using Electronic Transfer.

Protocol is secure from various internet based attacks and also protects users from unauthorized access if they lost their cell phone or their phone is stolen. The detail security analysis of the system is mentioned in Section 13.7.

The actual implementation requires elaboration of some specific technologies which are discussed in the next section.

13.6 Implementation Issues

J2ME is the preferred development platform the portability of Java code, the Java phone can process data locally which reduces the network traffic, and the capability to establish a new security policy on the client that will encrypted only sensitive data rather than encrypting complete transaction data. It also makes effective power utilization in limited power devices [19]. Also, J2ME mobile information device applications (MIDlets) can make use of, the WAP to perform HTTP network connection, without requiring TCP/IP [31]. J2ME provides a feasible solution to the traditional security gap in the WAP gateway. The security gap is due to the security protocol conversion mechanism; the security gap is between WAP gateway with the secure sockets layer (SSL) encryption and the WAP wireless transport layer security (WTLS) encryption protocols. Due to this protocol conversion data would be available in an unencrypted format during the switching process of protocols, which increases the risks to the confidentiality of data in the gateway [28, 30, 31].

13.6.1 J2ME Overview

J2ME provides the ability of servers to accept a new set of clients: cell phones, two-way pagers, and palmtops. These devices can be programmed using the mobile information device profile (MIDP), a set of Java APIs which, together with the connected limited device configuration (CLDC) provide a complete Java runtime environment [19, 26]. The J2ME supports many powerful features of the Java programming language as a light-weight virtual machine (KVM), it also provides a secure and easy execution environment for mobile devices [19].

13.6.2 Simulation

Our simulation of client applications have used Sun J2ME Wireless Toolkit consisting of build tools, utilities and a device emulator. It also includes the standard APIs like Limited Device Configuration (CLDC), Mobile Information Device Profile (MIDP), Wireless Messaging API (WMA), PDA Optional Packages for the J2ME Platform, J2ME Web Services Specification, etc. The authentication server is based on J2EE technology with web server Apache Tomcat and database Oracle 9i with Jserver capabilities.

13.6.2.1 Session Management

Various strategies have been developed to track client sessions on HTTP, a stateless protocol; the most popular of these are the use of cookies and URL rewriting [31]. The Java Servlet API are used to create the HttpSession object, which maintain session for each user at web server. We have used cookies to keep track on user sessions. To group HTTP request or response in a current active sessions cookie interchange mechanism is used. Each MIDlet client request to the web server explicitly contains a session cookie back. Server creates a new session using the HttpSession object, it sends the JSESSIONID cookie in the "SET-COOKIE" response header. The MIDlet client uses getHeaderField method on the HttpConnection object to extract the coookie, and use it further with the every HTTP request to keep track on session [31].

The initial setup of the cell phone/ PDA to connect with the bank financial server includes the Customer Agent (CA) installation with shared secret key. Once a phone is active to connect to the server user can store the TIC codes. The bank authority is responsible for TIC codes generation at the financial institution server and distribution of TICs to the customer and encryption of TICs before storing them on the client environment. TIC codes are pseudo random codes and can be generated with pseudo random number generation algorithm as mentioned in [23,24,30]. TIC generation logic is strictly confidential at the web authentication server and we are assuming that the banks will update TIC generation data regularly and time to time improve TIC generation algorithms to maintain confidentiality. Users demand for TICs as per their requirement as suggested in Sections. 13.3.1 and 13.4.1. The authorized person of the financial institution is responsible for the distribution of TICs to the user cell phone via simple data cable and distribution process includes the encryption of TICs for security reasons. At server side, we have assumed that TICs are stored in database and there is a strong security of Database management system (supported by Oracle 9i) and operating system with secure firewalls to protect server side data.

The small cost analysis of the proposed system shows that implementation of this protocol will not increase expenses of users significantly. This protocol can be easily implemented and executed on the current expenses charged by financial institution to the users to perform online payments or with very less addition to the current charge of online payment. Basically, cost model of the suggested protocol depends mostly on the policies that financial institutions adopt for implementing this protocol. Implementation does not require many infrastructure change or wireless protocol modifications so it will not put extra cost to the financial institutions or wireless network service providers.

13.7   Analysis of Various Internet Threats

The proposed protocol is capable of handling various internet threats like phishing, loss of cell phone, etc. In this section we present a detailed analysis of our system under various threats. In each case we analyze the information that an attacker may have and the specific points in the protocol where the attacker would fail to proceed with a fraudulent transaction.

13.7.1   Security Against Phishing

Phishing fraud has become a popular technique for user identity theft. Phishers fraudulently acquire sensitive information of users such as passwords and credit card details to gain unauthorized access to the user's confidential financial data and perform illegal transfer of funds. Phishing is generally carried out using email or an instant message or via phone contact.once this information is acquired, the phishers may use a person's details to create fake accounts in a victim's name, ruin a victim's credit, or even prevent victims from accessing their own accounts.

The protocol proposed in this paper is secure against phishing attacks. A multifactor secure protocol for user authentication has capability to secure the user data and maintain integrity, confidentiality and access control from malware access. To understand the origin of this security we have considered below scenarios.

13.7.1.1 If Phishers Fraudulently Acquires User ID and Secret Password

This is a general scenario of phishing attacks by which the attacker gets secret password of the user account and falsely accesses the user account to perform illegal transfer of fund. The proposed protocol shows that in the present case our protocol protects the users account and private data. The attacker would not be able to perform any illegal action, because of:

1. Figure 13.6 shows the first authentication of the user. As mentioned in step 5 of Fig. 13.6, the user has to produce login id and secret password to logon on bank server. If phisher fraudulently acquires the users account password then he successfully achieves the authentication of step 5 and subsequently step 6, steps 7 and step 8 of Fig. 13.6. If organizations would rely on only user name and password authentication then any unauthorized person can easily acquires the

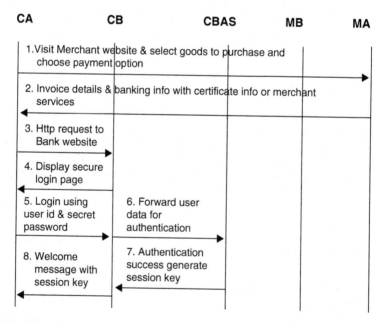

Fig. 13.6 First authentication of user to the bank

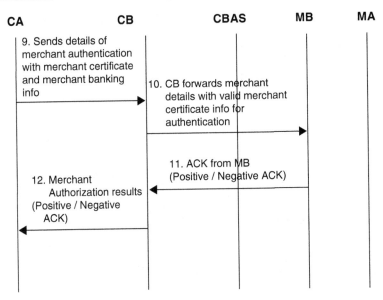

Fig. 13.7 Two way authentication

control of user financial account by means of some phishing attack. To avoid this situation we have proposed additional authentication system – The TIC verification and authentication to protect users accounts from various phishing attacks (Fig. 13.7).

2. In reference to Fig. 13.8 which shows the Second authentication of the user, any transaction trying to access user account has to produce one time valid TIC code to the web authentication server according to steps 16 and 17 of Fig. 13.4. At step 17 the authentication server would deny the falsely going transaction if it does not find a valid TIC code from the user.

3. TIC codes are secret codes issued to valid account holders and TICs are not publicly accessible. It is a one time code for each online transaction and it is randomly generated in nature so any phisher can not guess the next TIC code of user account.

13.7.1.2   Transmission of TICs Over Insecure Channel

In Fig. 13.8, step 16 shows that a TIC code transmission from the users cell phone/PDA to the web authentication server is strongly in encrypted format. So, it would not be easy for phishing attackers to decrypt a TIC code to access the users private information. Encryption techniques are discussed in more detail in Section 13.4.2. Moreover, one TIC is used only once and then discarded.

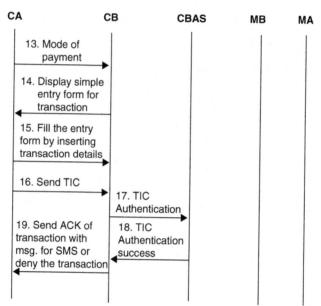

Fig. 13.8 Second authentication of user to the bank

13.7.1.3 If Phisher Fraudulently Acquire User's Secret Password and also One TIC Code by Some Phishing Technique

This is an extreme scenario of phishing attack in the present system by which attacker gets the secret password of the user account with one TIC code and falsely accesses user account to perform illegal transfer of fund. This protocol is safe in this extreme situation and protects users confidentiality.

1. There is another major security factor of the presented protocol to protect users from this extremely vulnerable condition. The system is secure in this condition by multifactor authentication technique as mentioned in step 20 of Fig. 13.9.
2. In Fig. 13.9 of Section 13.5 shows third authentication of the user to the bank by SMS confirmation. A SMS confirmation is a next factor which saves the user information from malicious access of unauthorized users in this extreme situation. At step 21 in Fig. 13.9 by replying "NO" to SMS confirmation the user can deny unauthorized access of account and take necessary action of changing of passwords and secure their confidential information from attackers.
3. The TIC codes are pseudo random in nature so, if phishing attacker gets one TIC code sample by some phishing technique, the phisher can not generate next TIC code because TIC generation logic is strictly confidential at web authentication server and we have assumed that banks and financial institutions are responsible for time to time updating of TIC generation data and upgrading of TIC generation algorithms.

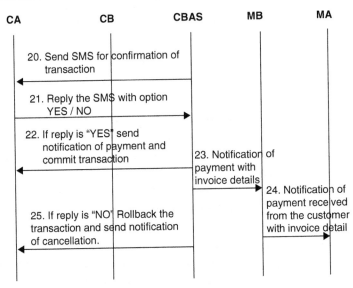

Fig. 13.9 Third authentication of user to the bank by SMS confirmation

4. If the user is getting continuous SMSs for web transaction confirmations which have not been initiated by them, the user can notify to the bank or financial institution and get replacement of all previously issued TIC codes to the user.

13.7.2   Security Against Virus Attack on Cell Phones and PDAs

Mobile wireless devices, like cell phones and PDAs, are also vulnerable to hackers and viruses. Popular viruses "Cabir" and "CommWarrior.A," could scan users address book and phone numbers and transmit from mobile phones and BlackBerrys by using Bluetooth or via messages services without the knowledge of user [3–5].

The proposed system is secure against mobile device virus attacks on the users cell phone. The system is secure from the various virus attacks by the following points:

1. The users always carry their cell phone with them so a SMS confirmation will not be present in case of malicious transaction raised by any unauthorized user, who has gained access to the users confidential data through virus attacks.
2. The TICs are stored in an encrypted format and password protected, so the person who has gained information illegally will still be unable to decrypt the TICs and virus attacks would not be able to disturb the users data.
3. It is always recommended that to prevent inadvertently downloading a mobile device virus through a Bluetooth connection, check the access permissions on

your Bluetooth settings and turn off user devices Bluetooth connection when they are not using it. The users can also use antivirus software on some mobile platforms to protect themselves from viruses.

13.7.3 User Session Hijacking

An attack in which all users activities or operations are closely monitored by using malicious software ("malware") is known as user session hijacking. Session hijacking malware can be reside users local computer, or remote as part of a "man-in-the-middle" attack. To overcome this threat proposed secure protocol provides security at the following steps:

1. In Fig. 13.6 first authentication of the user to the bank, after successful completion of step 5 and 6 authentication server creates a session id as mentioned in steps 7 and 8 of Fig. 13.6. This session key would be transferred to the user in an encrypted manner to create a secure session. Further Http requests from user should use session id to make request to the server. If the server receives unauthorized Http request which does not contain the session id generated by it, then the service would be rejected.
2. The TIC codes are pseudo randomly generated by confidential algorithm; it is a complicated code which can not be easily predicted by any person. The TIC codes, which are one time code for each transaction, are cancelled by the web authentication server from the database after each successful transaction. So, if a man in the middle attacks on the user session to monitor user activities then he will get a TIC that has already been cancelled.
3. Sensitive and confidential transaction information would be encrypted before transmission over the channel. As mentioned at step 16 in Fig. 13.8, TIC transmission over the user session is also in strongly encrypted format and secret encryption key is uniquely generated by the web authentication server as shown at steps 7 and 8 of Fig. 13.6.
4. We have used 128-bit shared secret logic between server and client to transmit unique secret key to the client on every login. So, there is no need to transmit this shared logic over the insecure medium since it is known at both ends.
5. Another factor of security is a SMS confirmation as mentioned in Fig. 13.9. A SMS does not route on the same channel which has been used in online web transaction. A SMS uses control channels over cellular networks. Security of the system also depends on the security of the messages sent by SMS, which are encrypted with A5/3 Algorithm [13].

13.7.4   Cell Phone/PDA Theft

A major drawback of handheld devices is that they can be lost or stolen. If user's phone is lost or stolen, the user can suspend their wireless service to protect themselves against unauthorized access and charges. However, it is entirely possible that an unauthorized person may try to initiate a transaction with lost/stolen cell phone. This protocol protects the user from this contingency due to the following reasons.

1. Due to above reason we assume people lose their mobile phones, they are typically reported lost and deactivated. Once deactivated, the user will no longer be able to receive SMS messages destined for user.
2. Another important issue of security is that if some person has stolen users cell phone/PDA then that thief does not know the local password of stored TICs of users cell phone/PDA. If the users bank account password is known to thief still he/she can not misuse the users account because thief has no access to the TIC codes which are stored in an encrypted format with password protection.
3. If the users cell phone/PDA is lost or stolen it is strongly recommended that the user should take necessary action of deactivation and make immediate request to the bank for cancellation of the entire issued TICs to the user.

In addition to the above scenarios we have also considered some cases which should be addressed in real implementations to maintain the reliability of the system.

13.7.5   Issues

We have considered below scenarios to address the various issues of real implementation of the system:

13.7.5.1   If Merchant Has Generated Invoice Details and Customer Did Not Transfer the Payment or Merchant Bank Did Not Receive the Payment

Our background study shows that SET protocol is a popular protocol for online payment. Our proposed work also shows that this protocol can be extended for the wireless networks and mobile devices. We referred SET strategy which is also applicable to this proposed system.

The bank confirms the successful completion of the transaction by sending them a reference/transaction number for audit purposes. At the end of the day, it also sends each merchant a database of the transactions which had transpired during the day [15, 22]. The merchant would verify a received payment from the customers everyday and dispatch the purchased goods after transfer of full payment from the customer including taxes and shipping costs.

13.7.5.2 If Customer Has Transferred the Payment and Customer Did Not Receive the Purchased Goods

Another important issue is after transfer of payment if customer did not receive the purchased goods. To avoid the possible of this case we have used the two way authentication protocol as mentioned in Fig. 13.7, which authenticates the merchant and their services. Merchant authentication shows that merchant is valid and bound in legal terms and conditions of association to banking authority and it is secure for customer to do commerce with authorized merchant.

13.7.5.3 If Cell Phone Has Been Stolen, How Stored Passwords Are Secured on Hand Held Devices

If the cell phone has been stolen and the thief tries to break the security password of TICs then the thief would not be able to easily break the security password because it is restricted by J2ME security model. The class loader in CLDC is a built-in "bootstrap", we can not replace or override or change configuration of class loader. The user define class loaders can be eliminated by "Sandbox" security model restrictions [9].

When a MIDlet needs to store persistent information, it can use new record store. All the persistent storages are shared by all Midlets installed on the device, the TIC's are stored in an encrypted format with the secret key known to the user which is the password of TIC's. A secret shared logic is also stored after encryption as mentioned in Section 13.4.2. This secret logic is stored in MIDlet after encryption with pin code which is protected by the MIDlet security features. In MIDP 2.0 a MIDlet suite can save data in a persistent storage area. The storage unit in J2ME CLDC is the record store. Each MIDlet suite can have one or more record stores; these are stored on the persistent storage of the device. A MIDlet is restricted by one protection domain defined by AMS (Application Management Software) to authenticate the origin of a MIDlet: The authenticated MIDlet is qualified as trusted, otherwise, it will be qualified as mistrusted. So, un-trusted applications require that sensitive APIs can only be accessed through user permission.

13.7.5.4 If SMS Is Delayed or Destroyed due to Network Congestion

While it is expected that to implement a functional m-commerce system it is a fundamental requirement that we have a fast and congestion free connectivity of wireless cellular network, we still consider the scenario of a SMS being lost. In order to address this extreme situation we have implemented user session life time till TIC verification and successful ACK from the bank.

The user session starts after successful login using user id/password and user can logout to terminate the session after TIC validation and after getting an ACK from the bank. A SMS uses a different channel of cellular network, so there is no need to maintain the user session till the SMS confirmation. The bank authentication server notifies the user via SMS regarding the confirmation of payment transfer. If SMS is delayed and bank authentication server did not receive any SMS confirmation response in the pre-decided time interval, then the bank authentication server will resend a SMS to the customer for the confirmation of the pending transaction. It is entirely possible that the bank will receive more than one acknowledgement for the same transaction. In this case it simply rejects the duplicate one. If the acknowledgement does not come through after a specified length of time, or after a specified number of SMS has been sent, then the authentication server would assume that the user is not interested in the transaction and would roll back the actions taken with respect to that transaction.

13.8   Advantages

Major advantages of the proposed protocols are:

1. It implements Multifactor Authentication in existing available infrastructure and wireless protocols.
2. Privacy at every point over the insecure network. System maintains end to end security in communication.
3. It supports mutual authentication to authenticate both the parties.
4. No need of any customization or modification to the existing network protocols.
5. Hybrid Encryption is used to protect data over insecure channel.
6. Protection against lost or stolen devices.
7. System is secure against unauthorized use of Credit Cards. Provides safeguard over the existing card based payment system.
8. Protocol is secure against the man-in-the-middle attack.
9. Business units can also adopt this protocol to secure their B2B communication with very slight modification to this protocol.
10. Application layer security solution for wireless payment system, with the existing network and physical layer security.

13.9   Conclusion

Enterprises are increasingly taking advantage of wireless networks to expand their business and make mode of payment easy and reachable to every user. However, financial transactions over these networks are vulnerable to various type of frauds and attacks which introduce significant security concerns, especially as enterprises must not only authenticate their customers and transactions, but must also implement a mechanism for authentication of merchant or business organization. To address this requirement we have introduced the application level security solution, secure web authentication protocol is a multifactor authentication protocol. Protocol is extended as a Two Way Authentication to support mutual authentication and also suggested that same solution can also be implemented to secure B2B communication with very small modification to the protocol. Proposed system is secure against internet based attacks. It is also secure in case of lost or theft of mobiles devices. The protocol can be implemented within limited resources of a Java MIDP device, without any modification to the existing communication protocols or wireless network infrastructure.

References

1. W. Adi, A. Mabrouk, A. Al-Qayedi, A. Zahro: (2004), Combined Web/Mobile Authentication for Secure Web Access Control, Wireless communications and Networking conference, IEEE Communications Society, pp. 677–681. March 2004.
2. L. Albert, K. C. Kaya: (2001), CONSEPP: CONvenient and Secure Electronic Payment Protocol Based on X9.59, 17th Annual Computer Security Applications Conference, New Orleans, Louisiana, IEEE press, pp. 286–295, December 2001.
3. Article: Helping Consumers Prepare to Avoid Potential Threats: (2006) http://www.educause.edu/ir/library/pdf/CSD4433.pdf
4. Article: Cybersecurity a private affair: (March 2007) http://searchsecurity.techtarget.com/qna
5. Article: http://news.zdnet.com
6. Article: Legion of the Bouncy Castle http://www.bouncycastle.org
7. Article: RetroGuard for Java Obfuscator http://www.retrologic.com
8. J. Daemen and V. Rijmen Rijndael: (2001), The advanced encryption standard, In Dr. Dobb's Journal, Volume 26 Issue 3, pp. 137–139, March 2001.
9. M. Debbabi, M. Saleh, C. Talhi and S. Zhioua: (2006) Security Evaluation of J2ME CLDC Embedded Java Platform, Journal of Object Technology, volume.5, Issue 2, pages 125–154, March-April 2006 http://www.jot.fm/issues/issues20063/article2
10. A. Fourati, H.K.B. Ayed, F. Kamoun, A. Benzekri: (2002), A SET Based Approach to Secure the Payment in Mobile Commerce, In Proceedings of 27th Annual IEEE Conference on Local Computer Networks, Florida, pp. 136–140, November 2002.
11. J. Gao, J. Cai, K. Patel, and S.Shim: (2005), Wireless Payment, Proceedings of the Second International Conference on Embedded Software and Systems (ICESS05), China, pp. 367–374, December 2005.
12. Stephan Gro, Sabine Lein, Sandra Steinbrecher: (2005) A Multilateral Secure Payment System for Wireless LAN Hotspots, Trust, Privacy and Security in Digital Business: Second International Conference, TrustBus 2005, Copenhagen, Denmark, Book Title:TrustBus, Publisher Springer, pp. 80–89, August 2005.
13. GSM calls even more secure - thanks to new A5/3 Algorithm ETSI: (2002), http://www.cellular.co.za
14. Guidelines: Authentication in an Internet Banking Environment, Federal Financial Institutions Examination Council, Arlington, October 2005, http://www.ffiec.gov
15. J. Hall, S. Kilbank, M. Barbeau, E. Kranakis: (2001), WPP: A Secure Payment Protocol for Supporting Credit- and Debit-Card Transactions over Wireless Networks, IEEE International Conference on Telecommunications (ICT), Bucharest, Romania, Volume 1, June 2001.
16. Huang Z., Chen K.: (2002), Electronic Payment in Mobile Environment, In Proceedings of 13th International Workshop on Database and Expert Systems Applications (DEXA'02), France, pp. 413–417, September 2002.
17. Jablon David P.: Integrity, Sciences, Inc. Westboro, MA, ACM SIGCOMM, September, 2005, Strong Password - Only Authenticated Key exchange, Computer Communication Review, Vol. 26, pp. 5–26, September 2005.

18. S. Kungpisdan, B. Srinivasan and P.D. Le: (2004), A Secure Account-Based Mobile Payment Protocol, Proceedings of the International Conference on Information Technology: Coding and Computing, IEEE CS press, Las Vegas USA, volume 1, pp. 35–39. April 2004.
19. Lawton G.: (2002), Moving Java into Mobile Phones, IEEE Computer, Vol. 35, Issue 6 pp. 17–20, June 2002.
20. E. Limor: (2002), Using Public Key Cryptography in Mobile Phones, white paper, VP Research, Discretix Technologies Ltd. 2002, http://www.discretix.com
21. Y.B. Lin, M.F. Chang, H. C.H. Rao: (2000), Mobile prepaid phone services, IEEE Personal Communications, vol. 7, pp. 6–14, June 2000.
22. MasterCard Inc.: (1997), SET Secure Electronic Transaction Specification, Book 1: Business Description, MasterCard Inc., May 1997, http://www.win.tue.nl
23. Mitzenmacher M., Upfal E.: (2005), Probability and Computing: Randomized Algorithms and Probabilistic Analysis, Cambridge University Press, New York, NY., 2005.
24. Motwani R., Raghavan P: (1995), Randomized Algorithms, Cambridge University Press, New York, 1995.
25. V. Pasupathinathan, J. Pieprzyk, H. Wang and J.Y. Cho: (2006), Formal Analysis of Card-based Payment Systems in Mobile devices, Fourth Australasian Information Security Workshop, Conferences in Research and Practice in Information Technology, Vol. 54, pp. 213–220, January 2006.
26. Vartan Proumian: (2002) Wireless J2ME Platform Programming, Sun Micro system press, Java Series, Prentice Hall PTR, April 2002.
27. Halevi Shai, Krawczyk Hugo: (1999), Public-key cryptography and password protocols, Proceedings of the 5th ACM conference on Computer and communications security, San Francisco, Vol. 2, Issue 3, pp. 230–268, November 1998.
28. Soriano M. and Ponce D.: (2002), A Security and Usability Proposal for Mobile Electronic Commerce, IEEE Communication Magazines, Volume 40, Issue 8, pp. 62–67, August 2002.
29. William Stallings: (2003) Cryptography and Network Security Third edition, Pearson Education, 2003.
30. Ayu Tiwari, Sudip Sanyal, Ajith Abraham, Sugata Sanyal and Svein Knapskog: (2007) A Multifactor Security Protocol For Wireless Payment-Secure Web Authentication using Mobile Devices, IADIS International Conference, Applied Computing 2007, Salamanca, Spain, pp. 160–167, February 2007.
31. Itani Wassim and Kayssi Ayman I.: (2004), J2ME End-to-End Security for M-Commerce, Journal of Network and Computer Applications, Volume 27 Issue 1, pp. 13–32, January 2004.
32. White paper: AEP Smartgate Security, Strong Multi Factor User Authentication for secure information sharing, white paper, AEP Networks, December 1998, http://www.aepnetworks.com/products/downloads
33. White paper: Enhanced Online Banking Security, Zero Touch Multi-Factor Authentication, November 2006, http://www.entrust.com/resources/download.cfm/22600/EfraudWhitePaper.pdf

Chapter 14
A Lightweight Authentication Protocol for Web Applications in Mobile Environments

Francesco Buccafurri and Gianluca Lax

Abstract User's authentication over insecure networks like the Internet is frequently required to be based just on username and password due to the simplicity and the convenience of such a mechanism. A number of password authentication schemes have been proposed in the literature with different robustness against possible attacks. Moreover, the issue of saving power and requiring reduced computation resources without loss of security, is rapidly increasing its importance mainly due to the emergence of ubiquitous (mobile) Web applications, where the user works on wireless devices possibly with limited computation capacities and poor energy autonomy. In this paper we give a significant contribution towards the above direction, by proposing a new authentication scheme requiring neither cryptographic algorithms nor one-way hash functions, as all the methods existing in the literature do, but resisting all the major known attacks, thus improving the state of the art on the authentication schemes in mobile environments.

14.1 Introduction

One of the most convenient and simplest methods to access remote applications over insecure networks is the use of password authentication schemes. A very typical example of the above scenario is the emerging setting of ubiquitous mobile Web applications, like m-commerce activities, e-government services and so on. In this case, besides the problem of network insecurity, which is intrinsic in the Internet, another issue has to be taken into account: The user works on wireless devices that might have very limited computation capacities and very poor energy autonomy. As a consequence, the robustness of the adopted password authentication scheme against possible attacks is not the only issue to be considered, even though still important.

F. Buccafurri (✉) and G. Lax
DIMET, University of Reggio Calabria, via Graziella, Località Feo di Vito,
89122 Reggio Calabria, Italy
e-mail: bucca@unirc.it; lax@unirc.it

R. Chbeir et al., *Emergent Web Intelligence: Advanced Information Retrieval*, Advanced
Information and Knowledge Processing, DOI 10.1007/978-1-84996-074-8_14,
© Springer-Verlag London Limited 2010

Indeed, the problem of extending as much as possible the battery autonomy as well as the possibility of executing the authentication process even in case of severe limitations of computation resources are attracting the interest of researchers, who in the last years have tried to improve the efficiency of password authentication schemes, first by proposing one-way-hash-function-based approaches [23, 31] instead of cryptographic-algorithm-based ones [11, 35, 40, 42], and also by reducing the number of times the hash function has to be computed [25, 36]. However, despite different robustness features, no significant distance in terms of efficiency exists among the state-of-the-art techniques, which all rely on one-way hash functions, whose computational requirements cannot allow us to define them as lightweight solutions, thus suitable to the mobile setting we are referring to in this work.

The net contribution of this paper is the proposal of a new authentication scheme requiring neither cryptographic algorithms nor one-way hash functions, relying on a very light and original computation mechanism of pseudo-random number generation, but guaranteeing at least the same security level as the state-of-the-art techniques, thus representing a step ahead in the field of authentication schemes in mobile environments.

The structure of the paper is the following. The next section introduces some basic issues and notations used throughout the paper. Among them, Section 14.2.2 describes in general how a password authentication scheme works as well as possible attacks which can treat it. Before presenting our proposal we include in Section 14.3 a deep overview on the existing techniques, analyzing both strong and weak points of them, in order to prepare the comparison of our technique with the state of the art that we give during its presentation. The proposal consists of two main issues, related each other, that are the password authentication protocol and the pseudo-random number generator (i.e., PRNG). The former is dealt with in Section 14.4, the latter in Section 14.6. Both the presented techniques are deeply analyzed from the security point of view in Sections 14.5 and 14.7, respectively. Section 14.8 concludes the paper.

14.2 Preliminary Notions and Notations

In this section, we introduce some important issues that will be dealt with throughout the paper. These regard hash functions, cryptographic hash functions, pseudo-random-number generators, password authentication schemes and typical attacks on these schemes. Finally, we introduce the notations used in the paper.

14.2.1 Hash Functions and PRNGs

A *hash function* is a procedure or a mathematical function used to map a large set of valid potential inputs to a much smaller range of hash values. They are mostly used to speed up table lookup or data comparison tasks. An example of hash function is CRC (Cyclic Redundancy Check) [13] that is widely used in error-detection contexts, both for its effectiveness to detect many kinds of errors and for its efficiency, since a simple shift register circuit can be constructed to compute it in hardware [30]. CRC is computed to produce a n-bit string, named *checksum*, starting from an arbitrary length string, called *frame*, such that also a slight change of the frame produces a different checksum. The checksum is computed as the rest of the binary division with no carry bit (it is identical to XOR), of the frame, by a predefined *generator polynomial*, a $(n + 1)$-bit string representing the coefficients of a polynomial with degree n. CRC is thus parametric w.r.t. the generator polynomial and for this reason there are many kinds of CRCs. For example, the most frequently used are CRC32 or CRC64, that generate a checksum of length 32 and 64 bits, respectively. Obviously, the higher the checksum length, the better the effectiveness of CRC in error-detecting is. Beside dependence on the generator-polynomial length, CRC is parametric w.r.t. the value of its coefficients. Consequently, the goodness of CRC strictly depends also on the latter parameter. There are many standard generator polynomials. In Fig. 14.1 a simple example of CRC computation is shown. Therein, given the frame $\langle 1010100 \rangle$ and the generator polynomial $\langle 1101 \rangle$, the generated checksum is $\langle 010 \rangle$.

Cryptographic hash functions (also called one-way hash functions) are strongly related to hash functions. They take a message of any length as input and produce a fixed length string as output that is named *digest*. The digest is a concise representation, a digital fingerprint, of the message from which it was computed. Among other properties, cryptographic hash functions must satisfy the *collision-resistant* property: it should be unfeasible for an attacker to find a message such that its digest equals a given value. Cryptographic hash functions are exploited in a number of applications like message integrity verification, password verification, commitment scheme, authentication scheme, where finding a message that matches a given digest, that is finding collisions, could be used by an attacker to break the application. For this reason the robustness of the above property is essential. Examples of cryptographic hash functions typically used are SHA-1 [29] and RIPEMD-160 [8].

A *pseudo-random number generator* (PRNG) is an algorithm to generate a sequence of pseudo-random numbers (i.e., PRNs) showing the same properties as random numbers. The sequence is not truly random because it can be determined by the knowledge of the PRNG's state. A PRNG starts from an arbitrary starting state, called *seed*, and always produces the same sequence whenever it is initialized with the same seed. The maximum length of the sequence before it begins to repeat is named *period* and is determined by the seed's size. In particular, if the seed contains

```
1010100   Frame
1101      Generator polynomial
01111
1101
001000
1101
0010      Checksum
```

Fig. 14.1 An example of CRC computation

n bits, the period can be no longer than 2^n. Pseudo-random numbers (*PRNs*) are very important in the practice of cryptography. For example, RC4 [34] generates a pseudo-random stream of bits which, for encryption, is combined with the plain text using XOR.

14.2.2 Password Authentication Schemes and Attacks

Password authentication schemes are protocols used to authenticate a user to a server over an insecure network. They are usually composed of three phases, the *registration phase*, the *login phase*, and the *authentication phase*. In the registration phase, the user sends a request registration to the server through a secure channel and they agree on the user's ID and password. In the login phase, the user submits his identity ID and an identification code to the server to access services. In the authentication phase, the server verifies the validity of the login request. Moreover, password authentication schemes usually also provide a *password change phase* allowing the user to set a new password.

Typical attacks on password authentication schemes are the following.

Replay Attack   An intercepted login request is maliciously repeated by an adversary trying to impersonate the legal user.

Denial-of-Service Attack   An attacker provides false verification information of a user in the password change phase in such a way that the user will not be able to login anymore.

Server-Spoofing Attack   The adversary pretends to be the server in order to obtain precious login information by the user.

Stolen-Verifier Attack   The adversary, who have stolen the password-verifier (usually hashed passwords) from the server, uses it to impersonate the legal user.

Password-Guessing Attack   It can be of three types [7]:

1. *Detectable on-line*, which requires participation of the server to check the validity of a guess password.
2. *Undetectable on-line*, where an attacker attempts to use a guessed password and verifies the correctness of his guess by observing the response of the server.
3. *Off-line*, in which the adversary guesses a password and verifies his guess off-line, since no participation of the server is required. If his guess fails he tries again with another password, until he finds the proper one. Usually this type of attack exploits the fact that most passwords have very low entropy.

We conclude this section by defining in Table 14.1 some notations that will be used throughout this paper. Observe that, for the sake of presentation, we denote by U not only the human actor of the authentication protocol but also the client machine he uses to run all the user-side operations.

Table 14.1 Notations

U	The user
S	The remote server
ID	The user's identifier
PW	The user's password
x	The long secret key of S
H	A cryptographic hash function
$seed$	Seed of the PRNG
PRN_t	The tth PRN generated by the PRNG
$\oplus$	XOR operation
$\wedge$	AND operation
$\vee$	OR operation
$\|$	Concatenation operation

14.3   An Overview on the Previous Literature

There is a large literature on password authentication schemes. The milestone is represented by the Lamport's scheme [22], which exploits cryptographic hash function to generate one-time passwords against replay attacks. Since then, a number of schemes more and more secure and efficient have been proposed. They can be classified into three types, namely, RSA-based schemes, ElGamal-based schemes, and Hash-based schemes. The methods belonging to the first two types usually exploit smart cards in order to implement RSA [33] public key cryptosystems [11,35,40,42] and ElGamar's [10] public key cryptosystems [1,14,17,21], respectively. To reduce the high computational cost of RSA-based and ElGamar-based schemes, many techniques based on cryptographic hash function, highly more efficient than the above ones, have been proposed. Now we describe the most important methods belonging to the third type, i.e., based on hash function, since our proposal belongs to this class. The reader can find in [39] a rich survey on password authentication schemes.

In the scheme proposed in [38], U delivers his ID to S in the registration phase, and receives the password $PW = H(ID\|x)$. Recall that x, as indicated in Table 14.1, is a server-side randomly chosen value with a sufficiently large numbers of bits, classically used for avoiding off-line password guessing attacks by dramatically enlarging the search space used by the attacker to invert the digest. To login, U sends $\langle ID, R = H(T \oplus PW), T \rangle$ to S, where T is the current timestamp. Then, S checks whether T is a valid timestamp and whether the computed $H(T \oplus H(ID\|x))$ is equal to R. If both the checks succeed, the login request is accepted. This scheme does not allow the user to choose or change his password.

In [15], the registration phase expects that U chooses PW and submits $H(PW)$ to S, which replies by providing an ID and the value $H(ID \oplus x) \oplus H(PW)$. In the login phase, U sends $\langle ID, R = H(ID \oplus x) \oplus H(PW) \oplus T, T \rangle$ to S. S checks whether T is a valid timestamp and whether the computed value $H(ID \oplus x) \oplus H(PW) \oplus T$ is equal to R. If both the checks succeed, the login request is accepted.

In [32], the access to the server is controlled by a combination of the user's ID and password, this latter is considered to be a secret value that only the user and the server know. U submits his ID and PW to the server in the registration phase. To login, U sends a randomly generated value RC to S (Step 1) and receives another randomly generated value RS (Step 2). Then, he submits $\langle ID, H(H(ID||PW)||RC||RS)\rangle$ as a login request. The server verifies the validity of the received one-time authentication token, and grants or denies the access. Furthermore, [32] provides a password change phase. When U wants to change his PW to PW', first he runs Step 1 and Step 2 as above. Then, he computes $T = H(H(ID||PW)||RC||RS))$ and $T' = H(H(ID||PW)||(RC + 1)||RS))$ and submits $\langle ID, T, H(ID||PW') \oplus T'\rangle$ to S. The server verifies the validity of the received T and, only in this case, changes the stored password digest to $H(ID||PW')$ obtained by the XOR between the third item of the message and T'.

The authors of [23] proved that the scheme proposed in [32] is vulnerable to a password guess attack, by means of which an attacker can easily obtain the user's password. This guessing attack is performed as follows. The adversary intercepts the items ID, RC, RS, and $H(ID||PW)$ exchanged between U and S over an insecure network. Then, he can guess a candidate password PW' and calculate $T' = H(H(ID||PW')||RC||RS)$. If T' is equal to T, the user's password is guessed. Otherwise, the adversary tries the next candidate password. Since most user's passwords are meaningful (in dictionary) or short string (less than 8 bytes size) to be easy memorized, the guessing attack is computationally feasible. Once the adversary obtains the user's password, he can impersonate U to login. To remedy the guessing attack, the authors of [23] propose an improved scheme. This latter expects that U sends $\langle ID, RC \oplus H(ID||PW)\rangle$ in Step 1, thus receiving $RS \oplus H(ID||PW)$ from S in Step 2, in such a way that the adversary cannot obtain RC and RS without knowing $H(ID||PW)$.

Later, [19] found that the improved scheme proposed in [23] is still vulnerable to the off-line guessing attack. Indeed, the adversary who has intercepted $\langle ID, RC \oplus H(ID||PW), RS \oplus H(ID||PW)\rangle$, and $H(H(ID||PW)||RC||RS)$, can guess a password PW' and then compute $HPW' = H(ID||PW'), RC' = RC \oplus H(ID||PW) \oplus HPW'$, and $RS' = RS \oplus H(ID||PW) \oplus HPW'$. If $H(H(ID||PW')||RC'||RS')$ equals the intercepted $H(H(ID||PW)||RC||RS)$, the adversary has correctly guessed the password. In addition, [19] showed that the scheme proposed in [23] also suffers from the denial-of-service attack and the stolen-verifier attack [5, 24]. Indeed, the denial-of-service attack is performed by randomly modifying the third item of the message $\langle ID, T, H(ID||PW') \oplus T'\rangle$ sent from U to S in the password change phase of [23]. In this case, S verifies successfully the validity of the received T and changes the stored password digest to the random value of the (modified) third item. From now on, U's subsequent login requests will be denied. Concerning the stolen-verifier attack, if PW is a weak password and the verifier $H(ID||PW))$ is stolen, the adversary can exploit the off-line guessing attack to guess PW.

In [41], the authors proposed a password change phase and claimed that their scheme is secure against the password guessing attack, the replay attack, the server spoofing attack, and the modification attack. In their scheme to change the U's password to PW_n, U sends $\langle ID, H(ID||PW) \oplus RC, H(ID||PW_n) \oplus RC\rangle$ to S. Next, the server S replies with $\langle H(ID||PW) \oplus RS, H(H(ID||PW)||RCS||RC)\rangle$, where RC, RS, and RCS are suitably obtained according to the Diffie-Hellman key agreement scheme [6]. Next, U sends $\langle ID, H(H(ID||PW)||RCS||RS) \oplus H(ID||PW_n)\rangle$ to S. The server uses the previously obtained $H(ID||PW_n)$ to retrieve $H(H(ID||PW)||RCS||RS)$ from the second item of the last received message and uses the stored verifier $H(ID||PW)$, the previously computed RCS, and RS to compute $H(H(ID||PW)||RCS||RS)$. If this value is equal to the retrieved one, S updates the stored verifier to $H(ID||PW_n)$.

Unfortunately, [20] found that the protocol proposed in [41] is still vulnerable to a denial-of-service attack exploiting the linearity of the XOR operation and working as follows. In the first step, the adversary replaces the transmitting $H(ID||PW_n) \oplus RC$ with $(H(ID||PW_n)\oplus RC)\oplus E$, where E is a randomly chosen. Then, S retrieves RC and, subsequently, $H(ID||PW_n) \oplus E$ in place of $H(ID||PW_n)$ due to the XOR linearity (indeed, $((H(ID||PW_n)\oplus RC)\oplus E)\oplus RC = H(ID||PW_n)\oplus E)$. Moreover, in the third step, the adversary replaces $H(H(ID||PW)||RCS||RS) \oplus H(ID||PW_n)$ with $(H(H(ID||PW)||RCS||RS) \oplus H(ID||PW_n)) \oplus E$. Again, due to the XOR linearity, the last item is equal to $H(H(ID||PW)||RCS||RS) \oplus (H(ID||PW_n) \oplus E)$. As a consequence, since the value computed by S corresponds to the retrieved one, S changes the stored verifier to $H(ID||PW_n) \oplus E$, which clearly does not equal the actual one sent from U, whose login will be denied in the future. To solve this drawback, the authors of [20] proposed an improved version of such a protocol fundamentally based on the sending of the ciphered digest of the new password as an authentication code (MAC).

Recently, [31] has proposed a protocol to provide remote user authentication based on a combination of cryptographic hash functions and the Diffie–Hellman key agreement scheme. However, [28] has shown that this proposal suffers from the off-line password-guessing attack when a server impersonation attack is performed. This fact allows an attacker to impersonate a legal server in order to obtain enough information from the interchanged message to perform an off-line password-guessing attack.

14.4   The Authentication Protocol

According to the general scheme, our password authentication protocol is divided into three phases, namely registration, login, and authentication phase, to which the password change phase is added. Here, we assume both the user and the server are able to generate a sequence $PRN_0, PRN_1, \ldots$ of pseudo-random numbers depending on an initial seed according to a suitable PRNG. We remark that the aim of our proposal is to design a scheme that allows us to run the whole authentication process which, from the client-side point of view, has a very low power consumption and relies on very poor computational resources. As a consequence, even though any enough secure PRNG could be in principle adopted, we look for a very efficient yet secure PRNG. In Section 14.6 we propose a suitable PRNG, that meets the above requirements more than those existing in the literature. The efficiency requirements here recalled have to drive the definition of all the components of our password authentication protocol. As shown in Section 14.3, all the existing schemes use at least cryptographic hash functions both in the authentication phase and in the password change phase (if any). We overcome this efficiency drawback by using only CRC (see Section 14.2) that is much faster than cryptographic hash functions.[1] In particular, both the authentication and login phases do not use explicitly CRC, but rely on the PRN generator that, as illustrated in Section 14.6, does it. Beside this, they use only standard boolean operations. Concerning the password change phase, CRC is explicitly used as a *MAC* combined again with standard boolean operations. Observe that since CRC is not cryptographic (i.e., it is feasible to find collisions) and suffers from the well-known vulnerability arising from its linearity[2] [3, 37], it is certainly not enough to substitute the cryptographic hash function used in a given classic approach by CRC. Therefore, the usage of CRC needs a non-trivial ad-hoc designing of the proposed schemes able to compensate the weakness of CRC.

At this point we are ready to present how our protocol works.

The Registration Phase In the registration phase the user U submits his identity to the server S for registration. In particular, the user chooses an identifier ID and a password PW that are submitted to S through a secure channel. The server verifies the uniqueness of ID, computes $HPW = H(PW||x)$ (we recall that, according to the notation introduced in Table 14.1, x is the long secret of S), and stores the couple ID and HPW into the verification table along with a random number $seed$ that will be used for $PRNs$ generation. Then, S delivers $seed$ to U. The registration phase is concluded. Observe that, in this phase (and also in the next ones), the server is aware about U's password PW. However, as done also by other schemes, [31,32,38], PW is processed on-the-fly and never stored by S in order to prevent stolen-verifier attacks.

The Login Phase In the login phase, the user logins to the server. U computes $PW \oplus PRN_c$, where PRN_c is the next pseudo-random number (as usually in PRNG schemes, the already used numbers are discarded), and submits $\langle ID, P = PW \oplus PRN_c, c \rangle$ to S. Observe that since PRN_c is random, PW cannot be snooped by an attacker. S first computes PRN_c by using c and the initial seed $seed$. It is worth noting that the need of $seed$ at each step occurs only in the most general case, since the PRNG scheme might allow us to compute the next number just on the basis of a dynamic seed derived from the initial one – this is the case of our PRNG scheme, as described in Section 14.6. At this point the server computes

---

[1] For completeness, we have also performed some experiments comparing the efficiency of CRC (64 bits) computation with SHA-1. The experimental results show that CRC is one magnitude order faster than SHA-1. Indeed, computing 10^9 CRC hashes required about 300 s, whereas SHA-1 took about 3,800 s.

[2] It holds that CRC(a XOR b) =CRC(a) XOR CRC(b), that is the checksum of the XOR of two numbers is equal to the XOR of the checksums of the two numbers.

$PW' = P \oplus PRN_c$ and goes to the authentication phase (the next one) only if $H(PW'||x)$ coincides to the U's password digest HPW stored in the verification table (otherwise the authentication phase is stopped with failure response).

The Authentication Phase   The authentication phase is divided into two steps:

Step 1 (Server Authentication) S sends $A = PRN_{c+1} \oplus PRN_{c+2}$ to U in order to authenticate itself (note that we need to send at least two xored PRNs in order not to disclose any PRN). U computes independently $PRN_{c+1} \oplus PRN_{c+2}$ and compares it to A. If they differ, then U halts the authentication phase since he cannot trust S. Otherwise, the protocol goes to Step 2.

Step 2 (User Authentication) U replies with $\langle ID, A = PRN_{c+2} \oplus PRN_{c+3} \rangle$. Finally, S computes independently $PRN_{c+2} \oplus PRN_{c+3}$ and compares it with A. In case they coincide, the server grants the access to U. Otherwise, the access is denied.

As observed earlier, all the PRNs used in the phases presented above, that is, PRN_c, PRN_{c+1}, PRN_{c+2}, and PRN_{c+3}, are discarded by both the user and the server in order to prevent replay attacks. As a consequence, in the next valid pseudo-random number will be PRN_{c+4}.

Figure 14.2 summarizes the messages exchanged between user and server in the login and the authentication phases.

Password Change Phase   When the user wants to change his current password PW to a new password PW_n, he has to run the password change phase. This is divided into the following three steps, summarized in Fig. 14.3:

Step A U submits the four-item message $\langle ID, PW \oplus PRN_c, c, PW_n \oplus PRN_{c+1} \rangle$ to S, where PRN_c is again the next pseudo-random number.

Step B   After verifying the validity of the second item in the same way as described in the authentication protocol, S retries PW_n from the fourth item. Then, S generates an authentication code MAC [20] by computing a (non-cryptographic) hash over PW_n. MAC is used to guarantee and verify the integrity of PW_n and is computed as $MAC = CRC(PW_n)$. Next, S sends $(MAC \wedge PRN_{c+1}) \oplus PRN_{c+2}$ and $(MAC \vee PRN_{c+1}) \oplus PRN_{c+3}$ to U, where, we recall, symbols $\wedge$ and $\vee$ denote

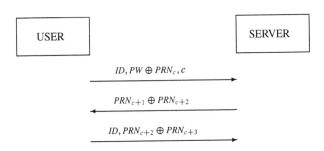

Fig. 14.2   The login and the authentication phases

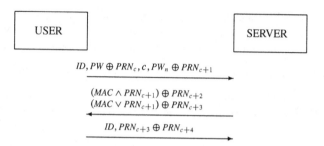

Fig. 14.3 The password change phase

the AND and OR operations, respectively. We remark that the choice of CRC instead of a cryptographic hash function is coherent with the efficiency requirements characterizing our proposal. However, our solution does not coincide with a trivial substitution of cryptographic hash function with CRC in the classical password change approach. Indeed, as shown in Section 14.5, it would result in a very insecure approach just because of the linearity of CRC.

Step C U independently computes MAC and verifies that the received messages are equals to those he obtains by using the PRNs autonomously generated. In this case, U replies by sending $\langle ID, PRN_{c+3} \oplus PRN_{c+4} \rangle$, thus authorizing S to replaces the old-password digest with the new one in the verification table.

Finally, the used *PRN*s are discarded by both S and U.

14.5 Security Analysis of the Proposed Protocols

In this section, we will show that our protocol can resist to the most common types of attacks, introduced in Section 14.2.

Replay Attacks   The attacker intercepts $\langle ID, P = PW \oplus PRN_c \rangle$ sent by U to S in the login phase and sends it to the server as login request trying to impersonate U. If PRN_c has been already used by U, then clearly the server denies the access. Otherwise, the attacker cannot generate the correct response $B = PRN_{c+2} \oplus PRN_{c+3}$ needed in Step 2 of the authentication phase, which requires the knowledge of U's seed. Moreover, since the messages exchanged between U and S in all the phases change at every login request, the attacker has no advantage from intercepting and replaying them to the other party.

Password Guessing Attacks   Detectable on-line guessing attacks are contrasted by forcing the server to wait an appropriate time at the login phase before replying with an invalid login request message. This dramatically reduces the number of password guessing trials an attacker can do. Undetectable on-line guessing attacks are contrasted by our technique since it satisfies the requirement of fresh and authentic login requests, as required in [7]. Finally, our scheme withstands off-line guessing attacks since the attacker cannot verify off-line the correctness of a password guessing trial. Indeed, to perform an off-line guessing attack, the attacker should know PRN_c at the login phase and this is not the case since no PRN is disclosed.

Server Spoofing Attacks   After verifying the correctness of a login request containing PRN_c, only the real server can reply correctly with $PRN_{c+1} \oplus PRN_{c+2}$ at Step 1 of the authentication phase, thus achieving the correct server authentication.

Stolen Verifier Attacks   An attacker who steals the hashed passwords HPW from the verification table of S must guess the user's password PW. However, since the server stores the digest of $PW||x$, it is unfeasible for an attacker to guess PW even when PW is weak (thus easily guessed by a dictionary attack).

Denial-of-Service Attack   As already described in the discussion about the weakness of the proposals [23, 41] (see Section 14.3), this attack aims to tamper the password change phase in order to make it impossible for U to login to S. To break our password change phase, the attacker should suitably change both the fourth item of the message sent in Step A of the password change phase, namely PW_n, and the MAC of Step B. However, both the items are ciphered (by the PRNs), so that no *ad-hoc* change can be done. Moreover, differently from [41], our protocol is designed in such a way that XOR and CRC linearity cannot be exploited by an attacker. Indeed, the deny-of-service attack presented in [20] (here described at the end of Section 14.3) fails in our case since in the first item of Step B $((MAC \wedge PRN_{c+1}) \oplus PRN_{c+2}) \oplus E \neq ((MAC \oplus E) \wedge PRN_{c+1}) \oplus PRN_{c+2}$ (the same argumentation can be done also for the second item of Step B reporting the same expression as above with the only differences that the AND operation is replaced by the AND one, and PRN_{c+2} is replaced by PRN_{c+3}). In sum we obtain a robust protocol overcoming the linearity-weakness of CRC by avoiding to use the boolean operator XOR, that is linear too. However, the usage of either AND or OR, would result in weakening the checksum MAC. Indeed, the expression $(MAC \wedge PRN_{c+1})$ disables the effect of MAC on the bits of PRN_{c+1} with value 0, since they are invariant (in the worst case of PRN_{c+1} composed of only 0s, MAC is irrelevant). However, the expression $(MAC \vee PRN_{c+1})$ has a specular behavior, so that those bits of PRN_{c+1} that are missed in the previous expression (i.e., those with value 0) become now relevant and vice versa. This way, no information is loss. Observe that the combination of AND and OR does not allow the attacker to reconstruct the XOR (in order to exploit its linearity), since PRNs used as a cipher in the two expressions $((MAC \wedge PRN_{c+1}) \oplus PRN_{c+2})$ and $((MAC \vee PRN_{c+1}) \oplus PRN_{c+3})$ are different (namely, PRN_{c+2} and PRN_{c+3}).

14.6   Pseudo Random Number Generation

The aim of our proposal is to design a scheme that allows us to run the whole client-side authentication process with a very low power consumption and relying on very poor computational resources. As a consequence the choice of the PRNG is a crucial step. In this section we propose a new PRNG that meets the above efficiency requirements more than those existing in the literature [2, 16, 26] and offers a high security level. Indeed we use neither encryption nor cryptographic hash functions.

We start by giving in the next section a brief overview of our PRNG. The single components are then illustrated in the sequel of the paper.

14.6.1   Overview of the Method

The proposed pseudo-random number generator is based on the following elements:

1. An initial seed s consisting of a k-bit string
2. A *basic* function $\mathcal{B}$ to obtain a k-bit string from another k-bit string
3. A (non-cryptographic) hash function $\mathcal{H}$

The scheme to generate pseudo-random numbers PRNs is shown in Fig. 14.4. In particular, by computing $\mathcal{B}(s)$ we obtain a new seed s_1 that is recorded in place of s. Starting from s, it is possible to create a chain of values $s_1, ..., s_n$ such that $s_{i+1} = \mathcal{B}(s_i)$ for $i > 1$. Since the function $\mathcal{B}$ is used to generate a new seed, it is important that its *periodicity*, that is the value j such that $s_j = s$, is as large as possible, hopefully 2^k (i.e., the upper bound).

Once the new seed s_1 is generated, we compute $PRN_1 = \mathcal{H}(s_1)$. The following elements PRN_i, such that $i > 1$, are obtained by iterating the above procedure.

An important issue regards the hash function to be used. In our approach, the strongness of cryptographic hash function is not necessary. We just require that given $PRN_i = \mathcal{H}(s_i)$, it is unfeasible for the attacker to guess s_i from the knowledge of PRN_i (we define *weak one-wayness* such a property). On the contrary, for a cryptographic hash function it is required the infeasibility of finding any y (possibly

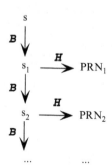

Fig. 14.4 Pseudo-random number generation scheme

different from s) such that $PRN = \mathcal{H}(y)$. In order to reach the goal of computationally weak one-wayness of the hash function, a possible strategy is to design a hash function producing a large number of collisions and, thus, a sufficiently large research space.

Finally, we stress again that our approach does not consist simply in the substitution of a non-cryptographic hash function in place of a cryptographic one in a typical pseudo-random number generation scheme. It is intuitive to understand that this would result in a very insecure approach just because of the weakness of the hash function itself. We have designed thus a new weak hash function and, coherently, a new scheme guaranteeing the security of the approach.

14.6.2 Pseudo-Random Number Generation Scheme

In this section we give the definitions of the elements composing the pseudo-random number generation scheme, that are the *basic function* $\mathcal{B}$ and the *hash function* $\mathcal{H}$, we study some their important properties, and, finally, we deal with the problem of the definition of the *initial seed* s. Observe that the choice of the basic function and the hash function cannot proceed orthogonally. Since the non-secret result is the composition of the two functions, we have to avoid that they are based on the same elementary operations, giving useful information to the attacker to proceed by cryptanalysis techniques. To prevent this, as we will explain in the following sections, the basic function is based on string reverse and sum, whereas the hash function is based on XOR and shift.

In the following, we denote by $x^k = (x_0, \ldots, x_{k-1})$ a k-bit string, where x_j, such that $0 \le j \le k-1$, is its jth bit and by $\widetilde{x}^k = (x_{k-1}, \ldots, x_0)$ the k-bit-reverse string. Moreover, $x^k + 1$ denotes the k-bit string representing the number obtained by summing x^k thought as a binary number and 1 (in 2^k-modulo arithmetic). For example, given $x^3 = 111$, $x^3 + 1$ represents the string 000, since $(111 + 001)(\text{mod } 1000) = 000(\text{mod } 1000)$. Finally, we denote by 1^k (0^k, resp.) the k-bit string composed of all 1s (0s, resp.).

Now we define the basic function $\mathcal{B}$ allowing us to generate the sequence of seeds used in the scheme. The function is defined as follows.

Definition 14.1. Given a k-bit string s^k, then $\mathcal{B}(s^k) = \widetilde{s}^k + 1$.

In words, $\mathcal{B}(s^k)$ is obtained by reversing the string s^k and, then, by summing 1 (modulo 2^k). For example, given $s^3 = 011$, then $x = \mathcal{B}(s^3) = 111$ and $\mathcal{B}(x) = 000$.

As required in Section 14.6.1 since this function allows us to have a new seed at each generation, it is important that its period is as large as possible, hopefully it should be 2^k. This means that, starting from a k-bit string s^k it is possible to generate $2^k - 1$ different new seeds before re-obtaining s^k. It is easy to note that such a requirement is satisfied whether k is chosen odd (i.e., $k \text{ mod } 2 \ne 0$). For example, for $k = 1$ we have period 2 (we generate the trivial sequence $\langle 0, 1 \rangle$), for $k = 3$ the period is 2^3 (the sequence $\langle 000, 001, 101, 110, 100,$ $010, 011, 111 \rangle$), and so on, whereas for example for $k = 2$ the period is 3 ($\langle 00, 01, 11 \rangle$) and for $k = 4$ it is just 7 instead of 16 (the obtained sequence is $\langle 0000, 0001, 1001, 1010, 0110, 0111, 1111 \rangle$).

Consider now the hash function $\mathcal{H}$. As observed in Section 14.6.1, our proposal is based on the usage of a non-cryptographic hash function able to guarantee a weak one-wayness, obtained by the generation of a large number of collisions.

The first question is understanding if some already existing weak hash function can be used for our purpose. A good candidate could be CRC, already presented in Section 14.2. CRC satisfies the one-way requirement introduced in Section 14.6.1. Indeed, given a k-bit frame s^k and its w-bit checksum c^w computed by CRC, there are 2^{k-w} collisions, that is there exist 2^{k-w} k-bit strings s_i^k such that $\mathrm{CRC}(s_i^k) = c^w$. We may vary k in order to increase the number of collisions generated by CRC to any value to the goal of making practically infeasible a brute-force attack attempting to find the original frame s^k.

Beside these nice features, CRC is not immune from malicious attacks exploiting its linearity w.r.t. XOR (this weakness has been widely documented in the literature and already exploited in some application contexts, like Wep [3, 37]). As already mentioned in Section 14.4, it holds that $\mathrm{CRC}(a\ \mathrm{XOR}\ b) = \mathrm{CRC}(a)\ \mathrm{XOR}$ $\mathrm{CRC}(b)$, that is the checksum of the XOR of two numbers is equal to the XOR of the checksums of the two numbers. In our case, this property of CRC could be in principle exploited by an attacker to obtain the hash of the ith seed of an user (i.e., $PRN_i = \mathrm{CRC}(s_i^k)$) starting from the knowledge of (1) the hash of the jth seed of the user and (2) the XOR between s_i^k and s_j^k (this issue is analyzed in Section 14.7.4).

Moreover, observe that the basic function operates a reverse of the string at each step just to introduce a suitable "noise", moving away its behavior from the pure XOR (that would allow the attack described above). The simple increment (the simplest basic function that one could imagine), behaves exactly as a XOR every time the sum does not produce carry (i.e., every two steps). The introduction of the reverse is vanished whenever the string is palindromic. However, as we will show in Section 14.7.3, this problem does not produce any worry, since the attacker cannot realistically guess that a seed is palindromic (according to a probabilistic argumentation), and, anyway (as an optimization), such rare palindromic seeds can be discarded after their generation. Unfortunately, it is easy to verify that the introduction of the reverse operation, even though benefic, is not enough. Indeed, every two steps, the "noise" introduced by the reverse operation is *quasi*-cancelled. We use the prefix *quasi* because the basic function includes also the increment at each step.

We need thus to construct a new hash function not suffering from the above problem, and preserving the other nice features of CRC. The idea is to apply a cyclic right shift to each seed before calculating the CRC value. But, clearly, the number of such shifts cannot be equal for each seed, otherwise the prediction described above can be identically applied. The solution we adopt is that the number of cyclic right shifts applied on a given seed s_i^k is equal to the number of 1s occurring in the seed itself. We denote by $\overrightarrow{s}_i^k$ the resulting k-bit string.

Now we are ready to define our hash function $\mathcal{H}$.

Fig. 14.5 An instantiation
of the scheme

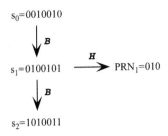

Definition 14.2. Given a k-bit string s_i^k, then $\mathcal{H}(s_i^k) = \mathrm{CRC}(\overrightarrow{s}_i^k)$.

For example, given the initial 7-bit seed $s_0 = \langle 0010010 \rangle$, after the reverse $\langle 0100100 \rangle$ and the increment we obtain $s_1 = \mathcal{B}(s_0) = \langle 0100101 \rangle$. Hence we compute $\overrightarrow{s}_1 = \langle 1010100 \rangle$ by applying three cyclic right shifts and then we calculate $\mathrm{CRC}(\overrightarrow{s}_1) = \langle 010 \rangle$ (details about how to do the latter computation have been provided in Fig. 14.1). Finally the seed is updated to $s_2 = \langle 1010011 \rangle$. A schematization of this example is given in Fig. 14.5.

In the definition of $\mathcal{H}$ we have to preserve the property of the basis function of generating 2^k different seeds. In other words, we have to guarantee that two different seeds do not collide into the same value after the shifting. This can be easily proven. Indeed, suppose that $\overrightarrow{s}_i^k = \overrightarrow{s}_j^k$ with $i \neq j$ and $i, j < 2^k$. Let u be the number of 1s in $\overrightarrow{s}_i^k$ (and, consequently, also in $\overrightarrow{s}_j^k$). Now, shifting both numbers by u left circular shifts, we obtain s_i^k and s_j^k, respectively, with $s_i^k = s_j^k$ by construction. We have shown that $s_i^k \neq s_j^k$ because basic function period is 2^k, thus consequently $\overrightarrow{s}_i^k \neq \overrightarrow{s}_j^k$.

14.7   Security Analysis of the Proposed PRN Generator

In this section we analyze the robustness of the proposed pseudo-random number generation scheme both by statistical analysis of randomness of generated numbers and by examining possible strategies followed by an attacker to guess future random numbers. For the sake of simplicity, the analysis is done assuming the seed length $k = 511$ and PRNs have size 64 bits. Observe that we analyze the security of our PRNG assuming the worst case in which all the PRNs are disclosed to the attacker. This is clearly in favor of security, since in our password authentication scheme PRNs never are transmitted in plain.

14.7.1 Number Randomness Validation

According to the German Federal Office for Information Security (BSI) [4] that established opportune criteria for quality of deterministic random number generators,

Table 14.2 The results of the test T3

T3									
Run length 1		Run length 2		Run length 3		Run length 4		Run length 5	
Ex. 2,267–2,733	Ob. 2,508	Ex. 1,079–1,421	Ob. 1,227	Ex. 502–748	Ob. 628	Ex. 233–402	Ob. 335	Ex. 90–223	Ob. 166

we demonstrate that our generation scheme is at least in class K2. Following the qualitative intuitive description reported in [12], schemes in K2 generate random numbers *having similar statistical properties to random numbers which have been generated by an ideal random number generator*. Membership to class K2 is characterized by the passing of five specific statistical tests. Such tests, whose validity is well-known [9, 18, 27], are: the *monobit* test T1 (equal numbers of 1s and 0s in the sequence), *poker test* T2 (a special instance of the chi-squared test), *runs test* T3 (counts the frequency of runs of various lengths), *long runs test* T4 (checks whether there exists any run of length 34 or greater) and the *autocorrelation test* T5.

We have generated a sequence (of 20,000 bits, the required size) of numbers by means of our scheme and we have performed successfully the five tests above. In detail, the sequence passed the monobit test since the measured result 10,035 lies in the allowed interval (that is from 9,654 to 10,346). The result of the poker test has been 34.1 (it must range from 1.03 to 57.4). Test T3 (run test) refers to a maximum subsequence of 0s or 1s occurring in succession. The sequence passes the run test if the number of occurrences of run lengths lies within the permitted intervals. In Table 14.2 the results obtained (denoted by Ob.) as well as the expected intervals (denoted by Ex.) for several run lengths are reported. These results are referred to runs of 0s, but valid results have been measured also for runs of 1s. The sequence passed test T4 (long run test), since no sequence of length 34 occurred. Finally, the results measured for the autocorrelation test (with shift τ from 1 to 5,000) have been always in the expected interval (that is from 2,326 to 2,674).

14.7.2 Brute Force Attack

Consider a brute-force attack conducted knowing some pseudo-random numbers (that are the PRN_i of the scheme) already used by the user. The attacker has to guess the original seed s_i such that $\mathscr{H}(s_i) = PRN_i$.

Since the hash function maps in an uniform way all the $2^{511}s_i$ in the set of $2^{64}PRN_i$, the probability of attack success is $(2^{511}/2^{64})^{-1} = 2^{-447}$, since the attacker has $= 2^{447}$ potential solutions. The attacker conducts the attack by computing $\overrightarrow{PRN_i}$, that can be obtained by applying l cyclic left shifts to PRN_i, where l is the number of 1s occurring in PRN_i itself (we recall that this issue has been described in Section 14.6.2). Now, he must find the original seed s_i such that $PRN_i = \mathrm{CRC}(\overrightarrow{s}_i)$. He will find $2^{511}/2^{64} = 2^{447}$ potential solutions, and the jth solution is $j \cdot p_{crc} + \vec{s}_i$, where $0 \le j \le 2^{447} - 1$, p_{crc} is the generator polynomial of CRC and the symbols $\cdot$ and $+$ denote the standard multiplication and addition between numbers, respectively.

We remark that, if the value $\bar{s}$ chosen by the attacker (among the 2^{447} found) differs from the actual s_i (i.e., the current seed of the fraud victim), then the probability that $\mathcal{H}(\mathcal{B}s) = PRN_{i+1}$ is $\frac{1}{2^{64}}$. In words, chosen s by the attacker, the probability that the next pseudo-random number generated starting from s equals the one actually used by the user (i.e., PRN_{i+1}) is the same as guessing PRN_i with no background knowledge. Thus, these results should discourage the attacker from trying to break the scheme.

Now consider the case the attacker knows a sequence C of c consecutive pseudo-random numbers spent by the victim. By a brute force the attacker should test $2^{(64/2)*c}$ seeds to find a seed $\bar{s}$ such that it produces such a sequence C.

Observe that, since our generation scheme produces a mapping between a set of 2^{511} bit strings and a set of 2^{64} numbers, till c is less than $511/64 - 1 \approx 7$, the probability to guess also the next pseudo-random number of the victim is again 2^{-64}. For higher c, this probability becomes 1 but the number of seeds to test is really too large (about 2^{224}).

14.7.3 Palindrome-Based Attack

As described at the beginning of Section 14.6.1, our generation scheme needs an initial seed s^k, a k-bit string where k is a parameter suitably fixed. The robustness of the scheme depends on both the length and the value of the initial seed. In the previous sections we have already shown some requirements k has to satisfy. A first requisite, motivated in Section 14.6.2, is that k is odd, in order to guarantee that the basic-function period is 2^k. The natural way to set the initial seed is clearly its random generation. Nothing seems to dissuade from this simple and effective approach. However, the problem introduced in Section 14.6.2 about the bad behaviour of palindromic seeds, forces us to understand whether a random generation of a seed can (probabilistically) result in such a bad situation.

Concerning this issue, since the probability that a randomly generated k-bit string, with $k \bmod 2 \ne 0$, is palindromic is $2^{-\frac{k-1}{2}}$, then we can state that the probability that a randomly generated seed is palindromic is actually negligible for sufficiently large k. For example, if $k = 511$, then the probability of having a palindromic initial seed is 2^{-255}. This result gives us the hint to justify what we have claimed in Section 14.6.2, about the robustness of our scheme w.r.t. the risks introduced by the potential occurrence of palindromic seeds.

14.7.4 CRC-Linearity-Based Attack

In Section 14.6.2, we have noted that every two steps, the "noise" introduced by the reverse operation is *quasi*-cancelled. To understand how this could be exploited for an attack, we observe that when a seed s_i^k has both the left-most and the right-most bit 0 (i.e., every four steps), the attacker knows that s_i^k XOR $s_{i+2}^k = 10^{k-2}1$ (we recall that $10^{k-2}1$ denotes a k-bit string of the form $1 \cdots 1$, with $k - 2$ 0s). Thus, the CRC of s_{i+2}^k is easily predictable by exploiting the above property. This behavior can be generalized also for other bit configurations. It is easy to see that if s_i^k is of the form $00 \cdots 01$, then we expect that the XOR with the seed generated two steps ahead is of the form $10^{k-3}11$. Again, if s_i^k is of the form $10 \cdots 00$, then we expect that the XOR with s_{i+2}^k is of the form $110^{k-3}1$. Finally, if s_i^k is of the form $10 \cdots 01$, then we expect that the XOR with s_{i+2}^k is of the form $110^{k-4}11$. This is a symptom of the alternating destructive effect of the reverse operation and, further, of the general invariance of the internal part of the seed, when the basic function is applied. Observe that this negative effect is maximum whenever the seed is palindromic, because the effect of the reverse is null also on a single step.

The next theorem gives us the probabilistic support that a quasi-random generation of the initial seed prevents this drawback for its entire lifetime.

Theorem 14.1. *Let t and k be two positive integers such that $t < 2^{\frac{k-4}{2}}$. Let s^k be a k-bit seed of the form $10c^j d^{k-4-2j} e^j 00$, where c^j and e^j are j-bit strings, d^{k-4-2j} is a $(k - 4 - 2j)$-bit string containing at least one 0 and $j = \lceil log_2 t \rceil + 1$. It holds that the sequence $S^t = \langle s_0^k, \ldots, s_t^k \rangle$ such that $s_0^k = \mathscr{B}(s^k)$ and $s_r^k = \mathscr{B}(s_{r-1}^k)$ for $1 \leq r \leq t$ does not contain any seed of the form $10f^{k-4}01$, where f is a $(k - 4)$-bit string.*

Proof. Let i be the maximum number such that, for each $h < i$, it results that the 2 left-most bits of s_{h+1}^k coincide with the 2 left-most bits of $\widetilde{s}_h^k$. In words, i represents a step until which the increment, at each step, does not modify the 2 left-most bits of the current seed. The portion of the sequence S^k bounded by i is obtained in the following way: $s_0^k = \widetilde{s}^k + 1 = 00 \cdots 01 + 1 = 00 \cdots 10$, $s_1^k = \widetilde{s}_0^k + 1 = 01 \cdots 01$, $s_2^k = 10 \cdots 11$, $s_3^k = 11 \cdots 10$, $s_4^k = 01 \cdots 00$, $s_5^k = 00 \cdots 11$, $s_6^k = 11 \cdots 01$, and $s_7^k = 10 \cdots 00$. Since s_7^k has the same form of s_0^k, the sequence will cycle among seeds having these structures until the above assumption is valid. We show that $i \geq t$. This implies that the theorem statement holds, since, as shown above, no bad seed is generated before the step i. We prove that $i \geq t$ by contradiction. Hence, suppose that $i < t$. By hypothesis, we know that d^{k-4-2j} contains at least one 0, say o_1. Let p_1 the distance (in terms of positions) of such bit o_1 from the right-most bit of s^k. Again, by hypothesis, $p_1 > 2 + j$. In order the carry generated at the ith step to be propagated to the 2 left-most bits of s_i^k, it is necessary that the bit o_1 is first set to 1, and then reset again. Let t_1 be the number of steps after which o_1 is set and let t_2 be the number of steps (starting from t_1) after which o_1 is reset. Observe that at step t_1, when the carry reaches o_1, all the $p_1 - 1$ right-most bits of $s_{t_1}^k$ are reset. It results that $t_1 + t_2 \leq i$. However, $t_2 \geq 2^{p_1} - 1$, since at least $2^{p_1} - 1$ steps are needed in order the last $p_1 - 1$ bits of $s_{t_2}^k$ to become all 1. Thus, $t > t_2 \geq 2^{p_1} - 1 \geq 2^{j+2} > 2^j$. But, by hypothesis $j = \lceil log_2 t \rceil + 1$ and, consequently it results $t < 2^j$. We have thus reached a contradiction (i.e., both $t > 2^j$ and $t < 2^j$). This proves that $i \geq t$ that implies the theorem statement. The proof is thus concluded.   ∎

The theorem states that (i) fixing both the first and the last two bits of the initial seed (to 10 and 00, respectively), and (ii) ensuring that the seed contains an internal centered range whose bounds are distant $\lceil log_2 t \rceil + 1$ from the bottom (and the top) of the seed itself such that at least one 0 occurs in this interval, then it results that for at least t applications of the basic function (thus, at least for the next t generations), we do not generate bad seeds (i.e., seeds of the form $10 \cdots 01$). For example, in order to have the above property for the first $t = 50,000$ generations, it suffices to set the initial seed to $10 s_1^{17} s^{k-38} s_2^{17} 00$, where s_1^{17}, s_1^{17} and s^{k-38} are randomly generated, with the only constraint that s^{k-38} contains at least one 0. It is easy to verify that the probability that a randomly generated string s^{k-38} does not satisfies the above requirement is $\frac{1}{2^{k-38}}$ (thus the blind random generation could be also accepted). For example in the case $k = 511$ this probability is $\frac{1}{2^{473}}$.

Once the above requirements are satisfied, those attacks that exploits the linearity of CRC results unsuccessful.

14.8 Conclusions

In this paper we have proposed a new password authentication scheme that can be used for secure authentication in mobile Web environments where the aspects of computational resource limitation and power consumption are crucial. Both the authentication protocol and the PRNG here presented are very efficient since they use neither encryption nor cryptographic hash functions. Therefore, the paper proposes a net contribution, since we have argued that we do not have to pay any price in terms of security (for the considered applications) in order to have this gain of computational simplicity.

References

1. A. K. Awasthi and S. Lal. A remote user authentication scheme using smart cards with forward secrecy. *IEEE Transactions on Consumer Electronics*, 49(4):12461248, 2003.
2. L Blum, M Blum, and M Shub. A simple unpredictable pseudo random number generator. *SIAM J. Comput.*, 15(2):364–383, 1986.
3. Nikita Borisov, Ian Goldberg, and David Wagner. Intercepting mobile communications: the insecurity of 802.11. In *MobiCom '01: Proceedings of the 7th annual international conference on Mobile computing and networking*, pages 180–189, New York, NY, USA, 2001. ACM Press.
4. Bundesamt für Sicherheit in der Informationstechnik. http://www.bsi.de/english/index.htm.

5. Chien-Ming CHEN and Wei-Chi KU. Stolen-verifier attack on two new strong-password authentication protocols. *IEICE transactions on communications*, 85(11):2519–2521, 2002.

6. Whitfield Diffie and Martin E. Hellman. New directions in cryptography. *IEEE Transactions on Information Theory*, IT-22(6):644–654, 1976.

7. Yun Ding and Patrick Horster. Undetectable on-line password guessing attacks. *ACM Operating Systems Review*, 29(4):77–86, 1995.

8. Hans Dobbertin, Antoon Bosselaers, and Bart Preneel. RIPEMD-160: A strengthened version of RIPEMD. In *Fast Software Encryption*, pages 71–82, 1996.

9. Y. Dodge. A natural random number generator. *International Statistical Review*, 64(3): 329–343, 1996.

10. T. ElGamal. A public key cryptosystem and a signature scheme based on discrete logarithms. *IEEE Transactions on Information Theory*, 31(4):469–472, 1985.

11. Lei Fan, Jian-Hua Li, and HongWen Zhu. An enhancement of timestamp-based password authentication scheme. *Computers & Security*, 21(7):665–667, 2002.

12. Functionality Classes and Evaluation Methodolog for Deterministic Random Number Generators (AIS 20, Version 2.0, 2 December 1999). http://www.bsi.de/zertifiz/zert/interpr/ais20e. pdf.

13. John R. Hill. A table driven approach to cyclic redundancy check calculations. *SIGCOMM Comput. Commun. Rev.*, 9(2):40–60, 1979.

14. M. S. Hwang and L. H. L. A new remote user authentication scheme using smart cards. *IEEE Transactions on Consumer Electronics*, 46(1):28–30, 2000.

15. Min-Shiang Hwang, Cheng-Chi Lee, and Yuan-Liang Tang. A simple remote user authentication scheme. *Mathematical and Computer Modelling*, 36:103–107, 2002.

16. R. Impagliazzo, L. A. Levin, and M. Luby. Pseudo-random generation from one-way functions. In *STOC '89: Proceedings of the twenty-first annual ACM symposium on Theory of computing*, pages 12–24, New York, NY, USA, 1989. ACM.

17. C. W. Lin J. J. Shen and M. S. Hwang. A modified remote user authentication scheme using smart cards. *IEEE Transactions on Consumer Electronics*, 49(2):414–416, 2003.

18. John R. Koza. Evolving a computer program to generate random numbers using the genetic programming paradigm. In *Proceedings of the Fourth International Conference on Genetic Algorithms*, pages 37–44, 1991.

19. Wei-Chi Ku, Chien-Ming Chen, and Hui-Lung Lee. Weaknesses of lee-li-hwang's hash-based password authentication scheme. *SIGOPS Oper. Syst. Rev.*, 37(4):19–25, 2003.

20. Wei-Chi Ku and Hao-Chuan Tsai. Weaknesses and improvements of yang-chang-hwang's password authentication scheme. *Informatica, Lith. Acad. Sci.*, 16(2):203–212, 2005.

21. M. Kumar. New remote user authentication scheme using smart cards. *IEEE Trans. Consumer Electronic*, 50(2):597–600, 2004.

22. L. Lamport. Password authentication with insecure communication. *Communications of the ACM*, 24(11):770–772, Nov. 1981.

23. Cheng-Chi Lee, Li-Hua Li, and Min-Shiang Hwang. A remote user authentication scheme using hash functions. *SIGOPS Oper. Syst. Rev.*, 36(4):23–29, 2002.

24. Chun-Li LIN, Hung-Min SUN, and Tzonelih HWANG. Attacks and solutions on strong-password authentication. *IEICE transactions on communications*, 84(9):2622–2627, 2001.

25. Min-Hui Lin and Chin-Chen Chang. A secure one-time password authentication scheme with low-computation for mobile communications. *SIGOPS Oper. Syst. Rev.*, 38(2):76–84, 2004.

26. Makoto Matsumoto and Takuji Nishimura. Mersenne twister: a 623-dimensionally equidistributed uniform pseudo-random number generator. *ACM Trans. Model. Comput. Simul.*, 8(1):3–30, 1998.

27. Ueli M. Maurer. A universal statistical test for random bit generators. *J. Cryptol.*, 5(2):89–105, 1992.

28. J. Munilla and A. Peinado. Off-line password-guessing attack to peyravian-jeffries's remote user authentication protocol. *Comput. Commun.*, 30(1):52–54, 2006.

29. NIST/NSA. Fips 180-2 secure hash standard (SHS). NIST/NSA, aug 2002.

30. W.W. Peterson. Error-correcting codes. M.I.T. Press and John Wiley & Sons, 1961.

31. Mohammad Peyravian and Clark Jeffries. Secure remote user access over insecure networks. *Computer Communications*, 29(5):660–667, 2006.
32. Mohammad Peyravian and Nevenko Zunic. Methods for protecting password transmission. *Computers & Security*, 19(5):466–469, 2000.
33. R. L. Rivest, A. Shamir, and L. Adleman. A method for obtaining digital signatures and public-key cryptosystems. *Commun. ACM*, 26(1):96–99, 1983.
34. R.L. Rivest. The RC4 Encryption Algorithm. RSA Data Security, Inc., Mar 1992.
35. Jau-Ji Shen, Chih-Wei Lin, and Min-Shiang Hwang. Security enhancement for the timestamp-based password authentication scheme using smart cards. *Computers & Security*, 22(7):591–595, 2003.
36. Akihiro SHIMIZU. *A One-Time Password Authentication Method*. PhD thesis, Kochi University of. Technology, 2003.
37. Adam Stubblefield, John Ioannidis, and Aviel D. Rubin. A key recovery attack on the 802.11b wired equivalent privacy protocol (wep). *ACM Trans. Inf. Syst. Secur.*, 7(2):319–332, 2004.
38. Hung-Min Sun. An efficient remote use authentication scheme using smart cards. *IEEE Transactions on Consumer Electronics*, 46(4):958–961, 2000.
39. Chwei-Shyong Tsai, Cheng-Chi Lee, and Min-Shiang Hwang. Password authentication schemes: Current status and key issues. *International Journal of Network Security*, 3(2):101–115.
40. R. C. Wang C. C. Yang and T. Y. Chang. An improvement of the yang-shieh password authentication schemes. *Applied Mathematics and Computation*, 162:13911396, 2005.
41. Chou Chen Yang, Ting Yi Chang, and Min-Shiang Hwang. Security of improvement on methods for protecting password transmission. *Informatica, Lith. Acad. Sci.*, 14(4):551–558, 2003.
42. W.H. Yang and S.P. Shieh. Password authentication schemes with smart card. *Computer & Security*, 18(8):727–733, 1999.

Chapter 15
Developing Access Control Model of Web OLAP over Trusted and Collaborative Data Warehouses

Somchart Fugkeaw, Jarernsri L. Mitrpanont, Piyawit Manpanpanich, and Sekpon Juntapremjitt

Abstract This paper proposes the design and development of Role- based Access Control (RBAC) model for the Single Sign-On (SSO) Web-OLAP query spanning over multiple data warehouses (DWs). The model is based on PKI Authentication and Privilege Management Infrastructure (PMI); it presents a binding model of RBAC authorization based on dimension privilege specified in attribute certificate (AC) and user identification. Particularly, the way of attribute mapping between DW user authentication and privilege of dimensional access is illustrated. In our approach, we apply the multi-agent system to automate flexible and effective management of user authentication, role delegation as well as system accountability. Finally, the paper culminates in the prototype system A-COLD (Access Control of web-OLAP over multiple DWs) that incorporates the OLAP features and authentication and authorization enforcement in the multi-user and multi-data warehouse environment.

15.1 Introduction

Data warehousing technology has played a significant role in the decision support scenarios. The manager performs an analytical query from the data warehouse using Online Analytical Processing (OLAP) tool. Analysts and decision-makers can also

S. Fugkeaw
Thai Digital ID Co., Ltd. Bangkok, 10500, Thailand
e-mail: somchart@thaidigitalid.com

J.L. Mitrpanont
Faculty of ICT, Mahidol University, Bangkok, 10400, Thailand
e-mail: itjlm@mahidol.ac.th

P. Manpanpanich
Thai Digital ID Co., Ltd. Bangkok, 10500, Thailand
e-mail: piyawit@thaidigitalid.com

S. Juntapremjitt
Whitehat Certified Co., Ltd. Bangkok, 10310, Thailand
e-mail: sekpon@whitehatpro.com

R. Chbeir et al., *Emergent Web Intelligence: Advanced Information Retrieval*, Advanced
Information and Knowledge Processing, DOI 10.1007/978-1-84996-074-8_15,
© Springer-Verlag London Limited 2010

use OLAP to perform What-If Analysis to access the effect of hypothetical scenarios [15] and to support multidimensional view of data as well. The data warehouse is typically modeled in a multidimensional view upon the dimensional axis and factual data. The data contained in the data warehouse is somehow critical for the certain group of users. The right for access in viewing the dimensional schema should be properly specified according to the level of privilege. A set of security controls has been established to protect this crucial asset. Normally, the user and password accounts are widely used for an authentication control. However, this technique may not be secure enough as it uses only one factor authentication (i.e., user account and password) for the very sensitive data (e.g., financial data, strategic data, complex environment). These data involve many levels of users and multiple sources of these data.

At present, the security issue has received much attention and been considered one of the necessary factors for designing data warehouses.

In fact, the access control management in DW that needs the fine consolidation of the access control policies from the operational data sources is very difficult due to heterogeneous schema, exhaustive monitoring, and difficult control of autonomous data sources. The traditional approach to the authorization mostly involves the authenticating user against the access control list of the target resource. However, when there are large numbers of users it can be complex to manage. RBAC is recognized as an effective access control management for large numbers of users because it allocates permissions to roles rather than individuals, and there are typically far fewer roles than users [13].

In this paper, we focus on the design of the two factor authentication and authorization management of the multi-users delegated to the multiple DWs federations. In our design, the users are intended to perform the OLAP query over multiple DWs based on their roles and privileges via the SSO Web OLAP. Technically, the PKI is a key to perform the authentication and authorization. X.509 certificate standard [12] is deployed by means of user certificate for the user identification and X.509 Privilege Management Infrastructure (PMI) is adopted for the authorization after the authentication is done. By this, we define the user privilege for accessing each dimension of several DWs in the Attribute Certificate (AC). The AC enriches the effective control of the Data Warehouse Dimension Hierarchies by specifying the access permission of the dimension level and fact attribute. Our proposed model is thus based on the role-based access control (RBAC) model in handling the concern authentication and authorization management of many levels of users and the privilege to access the dimensional data.

Multi-agent system (MAS) is a technique in the artificial intelligence area focusing on the system where several agents communicate with each other to solve the complex problem. Individual autonomous agents can jointly act as a collective entity through their coordinated interactions, which is known as a multi-agent system [10]. Due to its autonomy and high flexibility of control, it is thus convincing to apply MAS concept to automate the security functions in the distributed systems. Here, we apply MAS concept as a mediator to (1) perform the Web OLAP SSO-authentication control of the relying entities having certificate; (2) apply the dynamic activity-based authorization policy to users; (3) render the client privileges allocated by ACs to the legal DWs; (4) schedule client requests and allocate the OLAP services to multi clients autonomously and dynamically.

The major contributions of the paper are:

1. High modularity and compactness of the DW authentication and authorization system based on a multi-agent modeling
2. Flexible, scalable and more fine-grained access control within DW federations environment
3. Inclusion of intelligent feature of the activity-based policy enforcement to the DW users

The rest of this paper is organized into four additional sections. Section 15.2 presents some works related to our research. Section 15.3 describes the architectural framework of the web OLAP authentication and authorization model based on the PKI, PMI and MAS concept. Section 15.4 details the design and implementation of the proposed model. Finally, Section 15.5 summarizes our research work, reports our current implementation and suggests the future work.

15.2 Related Work

The research works related to the security and access control in database systems have been done so far by a number of publications. The techniques such as K-anonymity for data privacy, Access Control Lists, and database encryption have been introduced to support the database privacy and security. However, the security issue has recently been received an attention by the researchers in the DW area. Thus, the room for this research is large and crucially demanded. However, the security and access control model deployed in database system is not practical for data warehousing system due to the different database schema.

For the works related to DW and OLAP security, most of them focus on the issue of access control, multilevel security, the applications of these aspects to federated databases, applications using commercial tools and so on.

For instance, in [1], authors present an approach of DW security based on metadata. In the model, a different view of data is defined for each user group. This is a simple, yet interesting model for a not complex DW environment because in real situation, a combination of groups and views may occur.

On the other hand, in [2] the authors propose the security model by considering the security measure from the data sources and it is then propagated to DW design. However, the construction of DW requires a more complex stage. Examples of this stage are confidentiality and security constraints of the dimension and fact elements, after the integration of data from multiple sources.

In addition, there are some interesting approaches [4–6] dealing with the access control model for DWs by defining the authorization scheme over the OLAP operations. In [4, 5], the authors present a methodology and language for conceptual modeling of OLAP security. They extend the ADAPTed UML approach to specifying security measures on a multidimensional UML class diagram of OLAP at the conceptual level. This approach points out the crucial requirements for DW security by specifying the proper authorization of users performed via OLAP tools. This approach initially guides our idea for access control model based on the user role consideration.

Recently, in [3] the authors discuss the specific confidentiality problems regarding DWs as well as present an extension of the Unified Modeling Language for specifying security constraints in the conceptual MD modeling. Thus, the security measures are well designed yielding the security of conceptual modeling for the DW schema as early stage of the DW design. The approach is very interesting and practical for fine-grained security of data warehouse. However, in our point of view, many corporates have already deployed their DW projects; and some may not be feasible to redesign the DW and invoke several security and confidentiality constraints into the DW.

To our knowledge, the existing works do not pay attention to the authentication method of the OLAP users; instead, the security measurement is designed and enforced in the DW schema. The authorization is granted according to the user's role registered in the database profile. Additionally, the previous approaches have not directed the core into the management of multiple DW access control.

Our research has been envisioned by the need of the strong authentication and the authorization model to work with several existing data marts or data warehouses. We believe that a strong authentication is vital and should be invoked to the ground design of the access control for a certain kind of OLAP applications (e.g., financial and strategic information.) In fact, such model is highly required for serving the dynamic access control policy for collaborative data warehouse systems which rely on organizations sharing DW resource by means of the analytical query according to the role and privilege that DW owner has specified to the users.

For the prominent examples related to RBAC and X.509 certificate attribute have been discussed in [11,13,14]. In [11], X.509 based identity/attribute certificates and use-condition certificates are used for the access control. In [13, 14], the authors implemented the PERMIS project that provides a policy driven role based access control system based on the X.509 Attribute Certificate. In addition, the model of Secure role based messaging (SRBM) model presented in [9] describe the technique for role-based security that offers distributed key shares, fast membership revocation, mandatory security controls and detection of identity spoofing for distributed security control.

In [8], the concept of Community Authorization Service (CAS) is developed to support authorization in distributed virtual organizations. The authors introduce a trusted third party administered by the virtual organization that performs fine-grain control of community policy.

Because OLAP tools are used to serve a number of users, making sure people see only what they are supposed to see is important. By and large, all established OLAP tools have a security layer that can interact with the common corporate login protocols. There are, however, cases where several organizations need to share the information across the strategic view via the OLAP tool, they may have developed their own user authentication mechanism and have a "single sign-on" policy for accessing several applications seamlessly. For these cases, having a seamless integration between the OLAP tool and the in-house authentication is very promising research area and this inspires our research idea.

In this paper, we apply our authentication and authorization model proposed in [17] to support the Web SSO-OLAP security running over multiple DWs. The security and access control rule are specified in Attribute Certificate and DW Authorization policy based on the multidimensional (MD) schema of the DW. The reason that we adopt the PMI to be an access control model is to engage in the standard authorization model which is appropriate for integration to the authentication infrastructure in the distributed environment. This is applicable to providing more flexibility in managing high trust in the DW federation systems and to supporting fine-grained authorization. In addition, the design of the activity-based policy enforcement is introduced to serve the full accountability of all activities. Finally, the web OLAP tool, A-COLD has been developed to support multi-users with the agent mechanism driven fine-grained access control over multiple data warehouses.

15.3 A Framework of the Proposed Model

15.3.1 Overview of the Proposed Model

Figure 15.1 presents the conceptual view of our proposed model.
The system model consists of four main parts:

1. *User Interface* is designed as a web interface for the client who requests to query several DWs via OLAP tool. In our system, the clients need to authenticate

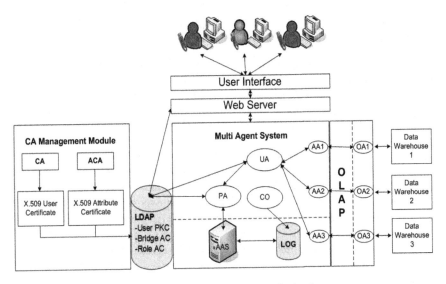

Fig. 15.1 A framework of Web OLAP authentication and authorization

themselves by using the certificate securely stored in a smart card or a token for two-factor authentication before accessing the OLAP. In addition, the single sign-on is required and supported in this process.

2. *CA Management Module* is a component that issues X.509 user certificates and attribute certificates. These certificates are physically stored in the LDAP directory for further authentication and authorization. The management of DW users' privileges is done by the role assignment of ACs issued by the Attribute Certificate Authority (ACA). Attribute Certificate contains version, holder, issuer, signature, serial number, validity period, and attributes. In the attributes field, we can assign type and value to support for the specific role. In our model, there are three certificate types as follows:

(a) Public Key Certificate (PKC) or User Certificate is an X.509 certificate issued by the CA to identify the user of which the public key is bound to a particular distinguished name.

(b) Bridge Attribute Certificate (Bridge AC) is another kind of Attribute Certificate designed to facilitate the mapping between the PKC and Role AC.

(c) Role Attribute Certificate (Role AC) is an attribute certificate that associates user roles with applications.

3. *Multi Agent System (MAS)* is the core part of the proposed model. It acts as a system driver to perform the authentication, authorization, and auditing function for multi-DW and OLAP tool and closely works with the CA management module. The trust and security management of the MAS are also guaranteed by the PKI. At the MAS server, the key pair and certificate are installed to further use for securing and authenticating the communication process among agents. Since MAS is the core trusted entity, all active agents trust all information signed by the MAS key. There are five types of agents:

(a) User Agent (UA) is responsible for validating client certificates, verifying client requests, and obtaining the authorization information from PA and presenting the capability list to the client. Each UA will be dead after a complete logout, or after certain idle period, which is the SSO session timeout value.

(b) Application Agent (AA) is mapped to a particular OLAP Agent (OA) embedded at the OLAP tools. Its job is to authorize requests and communicate to OA according to the dynamic user privilege profile, to schedule the sequence of clients connecting to OLAP applications, and to log on to the OLAP application on behalf of the client.

(c) OLAP Agent (OA) is located at the OLAP engine and mapped to a particular DW as the representative of a DW to support the analytical query requested from UAs, to map the associated DW schema into the defined MD schema, and to support the multiple OLAP queries run over multiple DWs. Each OA is trained to understand the MD structure and each has its own key pair and certificate.

(d) Collector Agent (CO) interfaces with the log server. All entities send activity logs to this agent for recording in the log server.

(e) Policy Agent (PA) figures out the effective capability list for the point of authorization (UA). It combines the capability list obtained from Role AC and Activity Analyzer Server (AAS) to generate the effective capability list for a given user. Therefore the effective capability list at UA to enforce the user sessions is the combination of the static role based obtained from ACs and dynamic capability list.

To enhance the advance access control management, the following two servers are employed to support the activity-based policy enforcement.

(i) Activity Analyzer Server (AAS) performs two functions: analyzing logs and dynamically forming the dynamic capability list for a user based on his/her access request activities and the preventive authorization policy. For example, the preventive authorization policy could define that user privileges will be degraded to 'guest' if it found that he/she requested for over-privilege accesses more than ten times within 20 min. As the capability list is based on user activity, it is dynamic. It is intended to be merged with the administrator-defined capability list from Role AC to generate the effective capability list.

(ii) Log server collects all activity logs from all entities through CO.

4. *Data warehouse* is a server storing the data subject to the business application(s) categorized in the multidimensional view scheme. Data warehouses or data marts are the sources where the OLAP query is run upon to response the analytical query. In our approach, we specify the access control based on the elements of the multidimensional (MD) schema that normally consists of a set of dimensions and fact(s).

15.3.2   Access Control over Multi-data Warehouse

In order to facilitate the access control management of DWs and make the agent understand the component of the schema and even it can map other schema to our scheme, we adopt the MD modeling of [7] that defines the MD schema in terms of object class as follows:

Definition 15.1 (MD Schema:).

1. *Dimension Class* (D) is defined as a tuple D < KA, DA, DL, ARR > where:

   - KA is a key attribute for the class.
   - DA is a set of dimension attributes that is not considered to be a dimension level but characterize the dimension class.
   - DL is a set of dimension levels.
   - ARR represents the order of dimension level (l) that state the partial order for Roll up function: $R_{up}\ l_1 - > l_2$.

2. *Fact Class* (F) is defined as a tuple of < KA, Gran, FA > where:

   - KA is a key attribute for fact.

- Gran is a finite set of base dimension level name (representing by its dimension name) associated to the fact class.
- FA is a set of fact attributes or measures.

An MD Schema S is a tuple $< D, F >$ where D is a finite set of dimension and F is a fact classes constructed from these dimension members.

Access Control Rules (AR):

1. AR can be applied to Dimension Members and their dimension levels (DL).
2. AR is applied to Fact by its attribute (FA).
3. AR can be applied to both Dimensions and Facts.

15.3.2.1 User Authentication and Privileges Authorization Subsystems

Figure 15.2 illustrates relationships among MAS components for the DW authentication and authorization process.

For the authentication process, UA uses the method getUserCert and sends DN and Serial No. of the User Certificate to the LDAP directory, the UA then gets the user certificate to validate the user authentication. The authorization process is initiated by the privilege request of the UA to the PA. Then the PA will look up the user information (of the particular PKC) in the Bridge AC that holds the Attributes of DN (associated to User PKC), and Role ID (associated to Role AC) while the Role AC holds DWid and Group id. These information will be linked to the DW Authorization Policy which is a database specifying the privilege of the specific role for accessing DWs. Finally, PA will realize the proper privileges of the users and the authorization will be assigned thereafter. Figure 15.3 simplifies the attributes used to bind PKCs, Bridge AC, and Role AC.

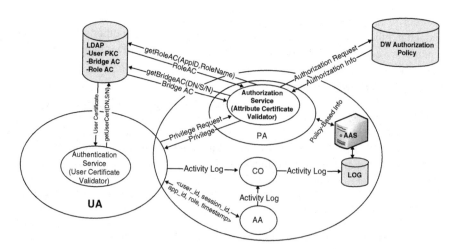

Fig. 15.2 A model of X.509 authentication, RBAC authorization, and activity-based policy

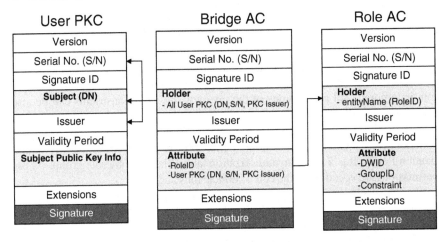

Fig. 15.3   Attribute mapping between PKC, Bridge AC, and Role AC

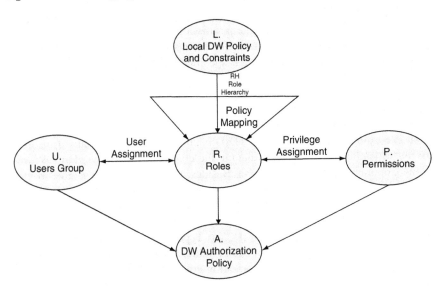

Fig. 15.4   RBAC model for multi-data warehouse

15.3.2.2   DW Policy Mapping

As we consider the peculiarities of DWs and multidimensional modeling, the RBAC is specifically designed to cover the DW schema with respect to the authorization policy.

Figure 15.4 illustrates the distinctive view of the proposed RBAC model working with multi-data warehouse.

The model is adapted from the general RBAC model by Sandhu [16]. It is easily described based on five sets of entities called, local DW Security Policy (L), users

(U), roles (R), permissions (P) and DW Authorization policy (A). The local DW security policy determines the roles and permission (privilege) of the users assigned in many-to-many relationships. DW Role hierarchy (RH) in RBAC is a natural way of organizing roles to reflect the dimensional hierarchy and responsibility. A role of higher user groups can inherit permissions from junior roles, e.g., the manager role incorporates all permissions of the operator role. The constraints can be also specified to establish higher-level organization policy and they can apply to any of the listed components. In order to ease in managing the access control over multiple collaborative warehouses, we map the policies for relying DWs into a DW authorization Policy. It is a set of an authorization tables classified by role groups whose permissions are specified to the cell of dimensions and facts.

For the specific requirement of certain role that requires a more fine-grained access to the instance level, we can define the specific role in the attribute constraints fields of the Role AC. For example, we can set the policy of dimension level of "Region" in the RA dimension in the way that RA operators of each region could only see the information specifically for their work region.

Table 15.1 presents the specific privilege of the roles for the relying DWs. Roles are specified by user group, while the permission of dimension levels and fact attributes of each group are determined. The permission of each dimension and fact is denoted either "Y" or "N" where Y is specified that the access is permitted while "N" is not permitted. Even though the security is not specified in the early state of DW design, our approach allows the security to be specified flexibly via the authorization policy and user authentication.

Based on Table 15.1, organizations are able to share the DW data with one another. For example, CA manager of TDID is allowed to view the data of the ePay DW by which his/her role is equivalent to the ePay Manager of the ePay DW own by the Coporate B, but not vice versa. Besides, the ePay manager is able to view the fact of no. of certificate issued and revoked in the RA DW with the permission of dimension level "RA Type = ePay". This is applicable to the dimension cell value permission. To this end, we specify the constraint atttribute of the Role AC of "ePay Manager" with the value "DWID2.RA Type = ePay". The agents will realize the role specification by taking constraint value, DWid, and Groupid attributes in Role AC connected to the DW Authorization Policy to enforce the access control to the user.

The policy information contained in the database is signed by the MAS key to ensure the integrity. Therefore the AA will need to verify the signature of the database before getting the policy.

The use of Bridge AC makes the system more efficient and flexible in managing the change of role without the modification in application and effect to the users. Only the attributes in Bridge AC and Role AC will be updated upon the change events. A new issuance of Role AC is required when there are no needed role available in the LDAP, otherwise the existing Role ACs will be shared by a user whose role is similar even the different DW. If there is any new role or a need to revoke the existing role, the corresponding role_id in the DW Authorization Policy will be updated.

Table 15.1 DW authorization policy

DW1: TDID CA DW

DWID	GroupID	Time. Year	Time. Quarter	Time. Month	Time. Day	Customer. Type	Customer. Region	Customer. Province	Certificate. Category	Certificate. Type	Certificate. Name	Certificate. DN	Certificate. Group	Promotion. Type	Promotion. Name	Fact. Sales	Fact. Certificate_Issued
1	1(CA Manager)	Y	Y	Y	Y	Y	Y	Y	Y	Y	Y	Y	Y	Y	Y	Y	Y
1	2(CA Administrator)	Y	Y	Y	Y	Y	Y	Y	Y	Y	Y	Y	Y	Y	Y	N	Y
1	3(CA Operator)	Y	Y	Y	Y	Y	Y	Y	Y	Y	Y	Y	N	N	N	N	Y
1	4 (Marketing)	Y	Y	Y	Y	Y	Y	Y	Y	Y	Y	Y	Y	Y	Y	Y	N

DW2: RA DW

DWID	GroupID	Time. Year	Time. Quarter	Time. Month	Time. Day	CA. Type	CA. Clas	CA. Name	RA. Type	RA. Region	RA. Province	RA. Name	Fact. Sales	Fact. Certificate_Issued	Fact. Certificate_Revoked
2	1(CA Manager)	Y	Y	Y	Y	Y	Y	Y	Y	Y	Y	Y	Y	Y	Y
2	2(RA Administrator)	Y	Y	Y	Y	Y	Y	Y	Y	Y	Y	Y	N	Y	Y
2	3(RA Operator)	Y	Y	Y	Y	N	N	N	Y	Y	Y	Y	N	Y	Y
2	4(ePay Manager)	Y	Y	Y	Y	N	N	N	Y	N	N	N	N	Y	Y

(continued)

Table 15.1 (continued)

DW3: ePay DW

DWID	GroupID	Time. Year	Time. Quarter	Time. Month	Time. Day	Customer. Type	Customer. Region	Customer. Province	Customer. Name	Certificate Issuing.CA	Certificate. RA Name	Certificate. Cert Role	Fact. Payment_Fee	Fact. Payment_Amount_by_Payer	Fact No_Failed_Record
3	1(ePay Manager, CA Manager)	Y	Y	Y	Y	Y	Y	Y	Y	Y	Y	Y	Y	Y	Y
3	2(ePay Operator)	Y	Y	Y	Y	Y	Y	Y	Y	Y	Y	N	N	Y	
3	3 (Marketing)	Y	Y	Y	Y	Y	Y	Y	Y	Y	Y	Y	Y	Y	N

As a consequence, our model permits the classification of both role information and users into security classes and the enforcement of RBAC to the granularity. The technique for DW role granting is transparent to the users, only information contained in the certificate and DW access control policies of relying DW domains are managed by the agent systems.

15.3.2.3   Process

In the overall process, there are two major phases: Setup and Runtime. Only when a client signs in to the system, the Setup phase is done for client authentication and UA preparation. Upon receiving an application access request from the client, the Runtime phase starts for access verification and application delegation. All activities of all steps are sent to CO and stored in the log server. The steps are described as follows:

Setup Phase:

[Step1] Two-Factor Authentication: Client uses the smart card or Token (i.e., something you have) in addition to the user account and password (i.e., something you know) to authenticate himself/herself via SSL to the Web Server. This step is normally supported by SSL technology.

[Step 2] MAS Construction: After the successful two-factor authentication, Web Server requests the MAS module to generate a UA. The UA is mapped to the client for managing all of its application requests. Logically, the MAS module, a trusted core component, will generate the UA whenever the client has successfully authenticated to the system. On this ground, this newly-created UA is automatically trusted.

[Step 3] Client Certificate Validation: The UA looks up the LDAP, verifies the authenticity of the client certificate, and checks its validity against a pre-defined policy (e.g. CRL status, specific content rules).

Runtime Phase:

[Step 4] Client Capability Identification: Client capability is dynamically identified on every access request. If the authenticity and validity of the client certificate are ensured, the user will be induced to the profile forming step. UA requests PA for the effective capability list for such a user. Basically, PA will lookup the Bridge AC to find the user role and then traverse to the associated Role AC where the DW privileges of the given role are specified. Then, the PA will get the role and privilege for all DWs of the corresponding user. This information will be combined with the activity based policy information in the AAS to form the capability list and sent to UA. Essentially the capability list contains information about the action/privilege that the user can access to the corresponding DWs.

[Step 5] Application Delegation: Once the UA recognizes an application access request (DW and action) from the client, it will verify such a request against

the client capability list (and maybe some additional policies). If the user is authorized, the UA will then make a request to an appropriate AA to start the new session.

[Step 6] UA Message Delivery: The message that UA sends to the AA includes < user_id, session_id, app_id, privilege, timestamp > where

- User_id is the id of the client or user asking for the request.
- Session_id is the id of communication session of the request (this could be randomly generated at the beginning of the session).
- DW_id is the id of DW which is requested by the user.
- Privilege is the function that the user presents himself/herself to the DW, used together with user_id to obtain proper authorization.
- Timestamp is the time that UA sends the request.

Trust of the UA message is assured by the PKI technique. That is, MAS guarantees the UA message to the AA by signing with its private key. The signed message is then encrypted with the AA's public key to ensure confidentiality. AA automatically trusts the message signed by MAS key since the MAS is a core trusted element. In addition, only legal AA can use its own private key to decrypt the message.

[Step 7] UA Message Verification: Upon receiving a message, AA will acknowledged the UA and verify the trustworthiness of the message by verifying the digital signature signed by MAS in the previous step. AA will send all activities of UA requests to CO for collecting in the log server.

[Step 8] OLAP Coordination: After the process in Step 7 is done, AA will then be responsible for controlling the use of OLAP tool by several users (UAs). AA will sign and pass the request format in Step 6 to OLAP Agent (OA) with the time stamp that AA sends the request.

[Step 9] AA Message Verification: Upon receipt of a message, OA will acknowledge the AA and verify the trustworthiness of the message by verifying the digital signature signed by AA in the previous step. OA will send all activities of AA requests to CO for collecting in the log server.

[Step 10] Multi-data Warehouse Control: After the process in Step 9 is done, OA will then be responsible for accessing data warehouse according to the access control capability list obtained from AA requested by several users (UAs). OA manages the data access queue and check authorization before access data.

15.4 Implementation

15.4.1 Overview of the Implementation

The initial scope of our implementation is to develop the authentication and authorization engines connected to the constructed OLAP tool pulled with several DWs. Our proposed System **A-COLD** (Access Control of web-OLAP over multiple DWs) takes the authentication and authorization properties by leveraging the MAS engine functions. The prototype system is a Java-based API, so it can be embedded into any OLAP application that requires its secure functionality. The OA will communicate between authentication and authorization engines and OLAP tools. They also map and integrate the heterogeneous DW schema to the model that we have defined [7]. However, the first version of our experiment we do not touch on this feature yet. The relational schema of multiple DWs we used for the test.

The test scenario consists of a web server, LDAP directory, Database Oracle 9i. In the experiment, 100 clients are assigned to register for the certificates and key pairs, which are kept in the USB e-token issued by the CA in order to access to the web OLAP connected to multiple DWs autonomously. Figure 15.5 presents the implementation environment of A-COLD.

Not only does the experiment validate the functionality of A-COLD, it also assesses its scalability and reliability. There are two corporate sites that need to share the data access to each DW. A-COLD is a web-based application installed at the TDID site, while all collaborative DWs are connected to the A-COLD engine. Users from both site are able to perform the analytical query based on their roles via this tool by using the token contained the certificate. The system will validate the authorization as described in Section 15.3.

All experiments were run on Intel Pentium hardware with 1.8 GHz processor and 2 GB of RAM runningWindows Server 2003 Enterprise Edition. For the data set, we use three warehouse databases namely, TDID_CA DW, RA data DW, and ePay DW. All DWs are distributed in the different sites and currently available for serving the certification-related service. The following shows the detail of DW schema we used to experiment.

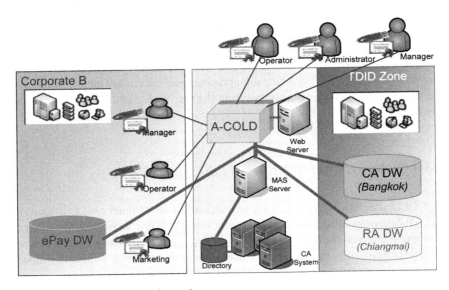

Fig. 15.5 A-COLD implementation environment

TDID CA DW is the data warehouse containing the data about certification services operated by Thai Digital ID Co., Ltd. (TDID). It has two fact attributes < Sales, Certificate Issued > and fours main dimension members:

1. Certificate < Category, Type, DN, Name >
2. Customer < Type, Region, Province >
3. Time < Year, Quarter, Month, Date >, and
4. Promotion < Group, Type, Name >

Registration Authority (RA) DW is the data warehouse that houses the data about RA which is an authority in a network that gets the user requests and then verifies credentials for a digital certificate. It has three fact attributes < Sales, No. of cert issued, No. of Cert Revoked > and three dimension members:

1. CA < Type, Class, Name >
2. RA < Type, Region, Province, Name >, and
3. Time < Year, Quarter, Month, Date >

ePay DW is the data warehouse storing the data about ePayment service run by Corporate B., our partner organization that currently outsources their CA operation service to TDID. ePay DW contains a number of transaction data that customers use to perform inter-bank payment transfer between counterpart companies. It has three measures < Payment Fee, Payment amount by Payer, No. of failed records > and three dimension members:

1. Customer < Name, Type, Region, Province >
2. ePay Certificate < Issuing CA, RA Name, Cert Role >, and
3. Time < Year, Quarter, Month, Date >

Figure 15.6 illustrates the main configuration of the DW Authorization Management System which connects to the OLAP. From this screen, the system administrator can configure the system components including web server, LDAP directory, log server, activity analyzer server, and OLAP server connected to DW servers. Here, we can add any DWs to the profile list and connect them to the authentication pool. To verify the multi-DW authentication process, user access and authorization, the administrator can check all activities from the activity log and event log provided by our system.

15.4.2 Access Control System via the OLAP Tool

A-COLD is a Java Web OLAP that provides a full set of functionality to analyze OLAP data originating from corporate data sources. It is a Web application that is deployed to run on the dedicated Web application server. All authorized users from several organizations can access the tool from their Web browser without downloading any components to their local machines.

Figure 15.7 displays the OLAP screen shot of the TDID CA DW with the user role "CA Operator". The user can perform the analytical query according to

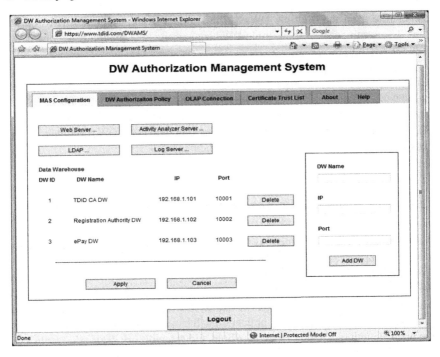

Fig. 15.6   DW authorization management system

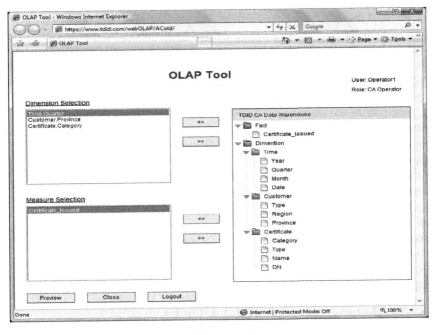

Fig. 15.7   OLAP screen shot for user role "CA Operator"

his/her role from the multiple DWs via this tool with the standard OLAP operations. Users can connect to multiple DWs consecutively without a re-logon via the Web-OLAP tool.

In the experiment, we found that all 100 users are capable to concurrently query via the A-COLD over multiple DWs based on their roles in a functionally accurate and consistent manner. They also satisfy the convenient and flexible feature of the tool by navigating to different DWs without additional re-logon. Based on the trust of certificate issued by the CA, the business partner who is the DW resource provider even ensure the trust of all users access to their systems.

15.4.3 Performance Improvement by Parallel Agent Processing

As we employ the multi agent systems concept, the overall performance of the system is improved by promoting the parallel agent processing. Traditionally, one Application Agent (AA) is mapped to and responsible for an application. As a result, the AA queue creates a bottleneck due to its serial request processing. We introduce parallelism by having multiple AAs dedicated to an application. Each of them maintains its own queue. Initially an application will have only one "original" AA. When the queue length reaches a certain threshold, the AA will fork itself as a "replica" to accept future incoming requests, while the original still serves incoming requests if its queue has available room. Both the original AA and its replicas can do forking. To prevent wasting the resources, each AA replica instance has its own clock counting down; if the timeout is met, it will be expired. The clock will be reset for every request upon arrival. One may notice that the back-end application still processes in serial manner. This is left to the system administrator as it is trivial to establish server load balancing or clustering. Besides, as the serial processing still exists in Policy Agent (PA) and OLAP Agent (OA), which serves AA requests and serve the analytical query from the users, we use the same tactic as applied to AA.

Based on the test scenario, we evaluate the optimum threshold by feeding a number of requests to the system and observe the speed of the total execution time and consider the resource consumption (i.e., CPU and memory usage) to determine the appropriate value of the forking thresholds.

Figure 15.8 illustrates the experimental result of the processing time and resource consumption of the different threshold values.

According to the result, we consider that the forking threshold at 50 requests is an appropriate balance for good processing speed and percentage of CPU usage. Even though the threshold at 25 requests gives a bit better performance speed, it consumes more CPU time since the java thread is generated more. Empirically, we also observed that the memory usage is around 45% which is indifferent for all given thresholds and simulated requests.

Figure 15.9 represents the simulation result which compares the overall processing time between single agent processing (threshold = 0) and multiple agents processing with the forking thresholds at 25, 50, 75, and 100 requests to serve

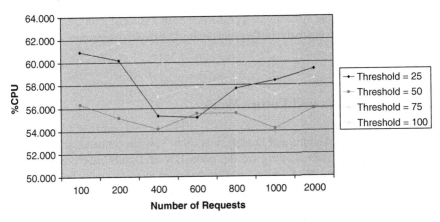

Fig. 15.8 CPU usage versus number of requests of varying thresholds

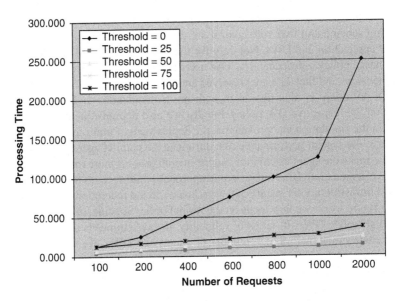

Fig. 15.9 Processing time versus number of requests of varying thresholds

the number of requests as shown in the graph. We evaluate the execution time, starting from UA construction to the sessions that some certain numbers of users successfully connect to the multiple DWs by using the OLAP.

The graph confirms that the computing speed by multiple agents significantly outperforms the single agent processing (threshold = 0). As we simulated a large number of requests upto 2,000 requests, it still yields a reasonable performance.

Ultimately, our proposed system has been proven for its functionality, including access control, OLAP query, and performance. Besides, due to the extensive capability of MAS, the system yields performance that is satisfactory, scalable, and robust. This would bring to the further real deployment to the expansion of a number of DWs and users.

15.5 Conclusion and Future Work

We have presented the idea and implementation of how the authentication, RBAC authorization, and accountability for the multi-DW and multi-user are well supported by the PKI and MAS technique. Our proposed model actually benefits from multi agent systems enabling the high modularity, flexibility, and performance of the authentication and authorization. The impact of the proposed architecture covers a real need of an access control model for multi-DW. In our approach, the user authentication is strongly controlled by the PKCs while the authorization is regarded in terms of DW role based assignment by Role ACs. We proposed the Bridge AC as a mechanism to facilitate the mapping of user identification and role. By this, the updating scheme and user role control are done efficiently without the change on OLAP application and DWs. Not only for the static policy based handling, the activity based policy enforcement by DW users is also taken into account. The access of dimensions and fact data are preserved and well monitored by the agent systems. The OLAP query is thus filtered in both pre-authentication and role verification based on the respective DW policy. Finally, we also demonstrate the advantage of MAS in the simulation and proven that the deployment of multi-agent considerably improves the system performance. We introduce the parallel agent processing technique to make the agent's activities and the overall process more robust and scalable. We have demonstrated that our proposed approach could serve as the efficient access control infrastructure for secure data warehouses in the federation environment.

For future work, we will focus on the formal policy specification and integration for collaborative DWs. In terms of reliability, the system needs to be tested under a real environment with a high number of clients and DWs. We will also consider the design of OLAP feature capable to support "drill-across" over multiple DWs with the consolidated permissions. Finally, our authorization engine will be tested to work with existing commercial OLAP tools.

References

1. N. Katic, G. Quirchmayr, J. Schiefer, M. Stolba, A. Min Tjoa, A prototype model for data warehouse security based on metadata, In Proceedings of 9th International Workshop on Database and Expert Systems Applications (DEXA'98). IEEE Computer Society, 8, Vienna, Austria, 1998. pp. 300–308.
2. A. Rosenthal, E. Sciore, View security as the basic for data warehouse security, In Proceedings of 2nd International Workshop on Design and Management of Data Warehouse, 28, Sweden, 2000, pp. 8.1–8.8.

3. Eduardo Fernández-Medina, Juan Trujillo, Rodolfo Villarroel, Mario Piattini: Developing secure data warehouses with a UML extension. Inf. Syst. 32(6): 826–856 (2007).
4. T. Priebe, G. Pernul, Towards OLAP security design-survey and research issues, In Proceedings of 3rd ACM International Workshop on Data Warehousing and OLAP (DOLAP'00), Washington, DC, USA, 2000, pp. 33–40.
5. T. Priebe, G. Pernul, A pragmatic approach to conceptual modeling of OLAP security, In Proceedings of 20th Int. Conference on Conceptual Modeling, Springer, LNCS 2224, Yokohama, Japan, 2001, pp. 311–324.
6. L. Wang, S. Jajodia, D. Wijesekera, Securing OLAP data cubes against privacy breaches, In Proceedings of IEEE Symposium on Security and Privacy, Berkeley, CA, 2004. pp. 161–178.
7. J. L. Mitrpanont, S. Fugkeaw: Multi-Version and Evolution Support for Multidimensional Database Schema. Databases and Applications 2005 (DBA 2005), Innsbruck, Austria, 2005.
8. L. Pearlman, V. Welch, I. Foster, K. Kesselman and S. Tuecke, "A Community Authorization Service for Group Collaboration", IEEE Workshop on Policies for Distributed Systems and Networks, 2002.
9. G. Zhao, S. Otenko, D. W. Chadwick, Distributed Key Management for Secure Role based Messaging, pp. 132–137, Proc. of International Conference of Advanced Information Networking and Applications (AINA 2006), Vienna, Austria, April, 2006.
10. X. Wang, G. Zhao, X. Zhang, Beihong Jin, An Agent-Based Model For Web Services Transaction Processing, Proc. of International Conference on e-Technology, e-Commerce and e-Service (EEE'05), Beijing, China, March 2005.
11. W. Thompson, W. Johnston, S. Mudumbai, G. Hoo, K. Jackson, and A. Essiari, "Certificate-based access control for widely distributed resources". Proc. of the 8th USENIX Security Symposium, Washington DC, August, 1999.
12. ITU-T Rec. X.509 (2000) ISO/IEC 9594–8 The Directory: Authentication Framework.
13. D.W. Chadwick, A. Otenko, and E. Ball, "Implementing role based access controls using X.509 attribute certificates", IEEE Internet Computing, March 2003.
14. A. Otenko, D.W. Chadwick. "The PERMIS X.509 Role Based Privilege Management Infrastructure", In Proc 7th ACM Symposium On Access Control Models And Technologies (SACMAT 2002), Monterey, CA, USA, pp. 135–140, June 2002.
15. A. Balmin et al. Hypothetical Queries in an OLAP Environment. VLDB (2000), pp. 220–231.
16. R.S. Sandhu, E.J. Coyne, H.L. Feinstein, C.E. Youman.: Role based access control models, IEEE Computer, pp. 38–47 (1996).
17. S. Fugkeaw, P. Manpanpanich, and S. Juntrapremjitt, A Development of Multi-SSO Authentication and RBAC Model in the Distributed Systems, Proceedings of 2nd IEEE International Conference on Digital Information Management (ICDIM 2007), October 2007, Lyon, France, 2007.

Chapter 16
Security in Distributed Collaborative Environments: Limitations and Solutions

Rachid Saadi, Jean-Marc Pierson, and Lionel Brunie

Abstract The main goal of establishing collaboration between heterogeneous environment is to create such as Pervasive context which provide nomadic users with ubiquitous access to digital information and surrounding resources. However, the constraints of mobility and heterogeneity arise a number of crucial issues related to security, especially authentication access control and privacy. First of all, in this chapter we explore the trust paradigm, specially the transitive capability to enable a trust peer to peer collaboration. In this manner, when each organization sets its own security policy to recognize (authenticate) users members of a trusted community and provide them a local access (access control), the trust transitivity between peers will allows users to gain a broad, larger and controlled access inside the pervasive environment. Next, we study the problem of user's privacy. In fact in pervasive and ubiquitous environments, nomadic users gather and exchange certificates or credential which providing them rights to access by transitivity unknown and trusted environments. These signed documents embeds increasing number of attribute that require to be filtered according to such contextual situation. In this chapter, we propose a new morph signature enabling each certificate owner to preserve his privacy by discloses or blinds some sensitive attributes according to faced situation.

16.1 Introduction

Users of Information Technologies are somehow contradictory! On one hand, they want their life easy, so they prefer to access transparently to the large set of information, appliances and devices being in their environment. On the other hand, they

R. Saadi (✉) and L. Brunie
LIRIS Lab, INSA de Lyon, France
e-mail: rachid.saadi@liris.cnrs.fr; lionel.brunie@liris.cnrs.fr

J.-M. Pierson
IRIT Lab, University Paul Sabatier Toulouse, France
e-mail: jean-marc.pierson@irit.fr

R. Chbeir et al., *Emergent Web Intelligence: Advanced Information Retrieval*, Advanced Information and Knowledge Processing, DOI 10.1007/978-1-84996-074-8_16,
© Springer-Verlag London Limited 2010

want to have a clear understanding of what they access and they want to ensure that only the minimum information about themselves is delivered to third parties. They want to be trusted, but are reluctant to trust.

In this chapter, we will explore this contradiction. We will give way to mechanisms that allow a certain balance reachable between paranoia and naiveness.

This goal is large, and we will certainly not address all kind of issues this statement opens. We will focus our propose on trust management in collaborative distributed environments. They witness a growing interests with the meet of web-enhanced information technologies and wireless devices. The anywhere anytime access to information and services is nowadays a must. All the approaches rely on a kind of trust to establish the necessary regulations for authentication, authorization and access control.

While the trust is easy to set up between the known participants of a communication, the evaluation of trust becomes a challenge when confronted with unknown environment. It is more likely to happen that the collaboration in the mobile environment will occur between totally unknown parties. An approach to handle this situation has long been to establish some third parties that certify the identities, roles and/or rights of both participants in a collaboration. In a completely decentralized environment, this option is not sufficient. To decide upon accesses one prefer to rely only on what is presented to him by the other party and by the trust it can establish, directly by knowing the other party or indirectly, and vice versa. Hence a mobile user must for example present a set of certificates known in advance and the visited site may use these certificates to determine the trust he can have in this user and thus potentially allow an adapted access. In this schema the mobile user must know in advance where she wants to go and what she should present as identifications. This is difficult to achieve in a global environment. Moreover, the user likes to be able to have an evaluation of the site she is visiting to allow limited access to her resources. And finally, an user does not want to bother about the management of her security at fine grain while preserving her privacy. Ideally, the process should be automatized.

After exploring related work concerning the management of security issues and trust in collaborative distributed environments in Section 16.3 we motivate on use cases the need for adapted trust mechanisms and access control in Section 16.2. This first part on literature reviews and users' understandings permit to draw the sketch of what is missing and which tools are available to go one step further.

In a second part, we propose an approach where the users can behave as chameleons (Section 16.4) taking the "colors" of their environments enriching their nomadic accesses. It relies on a distrust model (Section 16.5) extended to evaluate the distinct disposition of trust of participants (Section 16.6). Finally we present a certification mechanism (namely X316, Section 16.7) that allows to carry out the trust evaluation together with the roles of the participants while allowing to hide some of its elements, preserving the privacy of its users and adapting to the trustfulness of the environment. We conclude in 16.8 by comparing our approach with existing approaches in terms of interoperability, traceability, mobility, trust propagation, disposition to trust and multiple identifications.

16.2   Uses Cases

16.2.1   Nomadic User

The objective of our research is to extend the access scope for each user inside different sites. These sites are organization, host or domain like universities, restaurants, post offices, airports, etc. The challenge is to allow each mobile user to roam and access inside this environment easily and transparently, by exceeding a certain numbers of barriers like the heterogeneity of the different access policies.

Let's consider the following use case, as illustrated in Fig. 16.1. We have Pr Bob; he is member of University A. This Professor goes to a conference in University B and goes to meeting in University C. He communicates with the different surrounding "objects" (students, professors and resources: Printer, video projector, etc.). In fact, Bob owns a professional card or conference badge that defines his status and contains a picture or fingerprint to identify its holder. This card or badge allows Bob an access inside these universities according to a convention or shared collaboration (the same work group). These Universities do not know the owner of the card, but trust his cards.

If we map this scenario in the mobile distributed environment, universities correspond to sites. A certificate simulates the professional card and the fingerprint or the

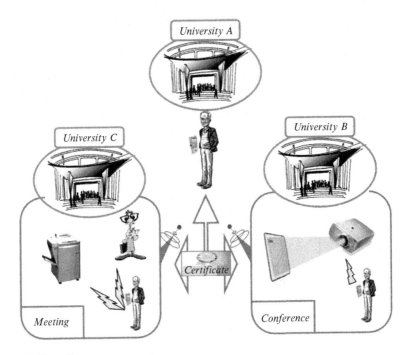

Fig. 16.1 Nomadic user

picture is replaced by an authentication system embedded in the certificate. In this manner, if Bob has the right to access a conference, according to his certificate, he obtains a new temporary certificate (like a badge in a conference). This certificate allows Bob to communicate inside this new site like all members.

The challenge is how each target site can recognize, evaluate the trustworthiness and give then an access to this unknown foreign user?

16.2.2 Private User

Actually all distributed systems (grid, pervasive, etc.) are based on a certification model that embeds in the certificate more and more user information such as: name, birthday, role, public key identifier, etc. Each certificate can thus be used freely by its owner anywhere in the environment.

When a certificate is presented to an organization (see Fig. 16.2), this one should read only relevant information from the certificate. Let's illustrate this by an example:

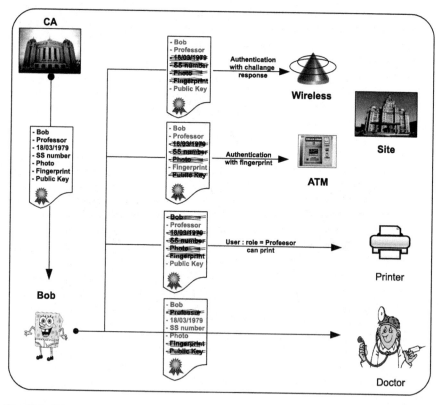

Fig. 16.2 Private user

Bob obtains from his home site a certificate containing his electronic identity with: name, photo, birth-date, marital status, Social Security number, health insurance, job title, and employer. When Bob would like to shop online, he will present from this certificate only needed information (e.g., name) and would not disclose his marital status, birth-date or job information. When Bob visits a doctor he has to provide his name, health insurance information, SS number, etc., but will not declare his job status. Similarly, when Bob wants to buy an alcoholic drink he must prove his age (older than eighteen). So he presents his certificate, showing only his photo and his birth-date and hides all other information.

The problem is: How the certificate format can be adapted according to the user and environment context?

16.3 Related Work

In this section, we will exhibit some works towards the modeling of trust, its evaluation and its granularity in distributed collaborative environments. We also exhibit some works related to access control, focusing on the advances in distributed collaborative environments. Furthermore, we describe some means to aggregate authentication mechanisms in certificates while hiding some parts of the contained information of the certificates.

16.3.1 Trust

In the last decades, trust models such as [1, 13, 40] have defined "trust" as a fundamental aspect for an inter-domain relationship. In the domain of social sciences there has been substantial research into the concept of trust. Some distinguished authors include Luhmann [38], Barber [8], Coleman [23], and Fukuyama [24]. The findings have been applied in areas including economics, finance, management, government, and psychology. In recent years trust has garnered considerable interest in the computer science community as the basis of solutions to various network security issues such as authentication, authorization and access control.

We now delineate some systems discussed in the literature that pertain particularly to trust-based security and access control in pervasive environments.

In [17] Capra describes hTrust, a trust management system targeted towards mobile/pervasive computing. The architecture is decentralized and makes each entity in the network responsible for its own security. The backbone of the system is a trust formation function which forms an opinion about the trustworthiness of an entity based on aggregated trust information that comprises both locally maintained history of direct experiences as well as recommendations received from other entities. In computing trustworthiness, the function allows an entity to assign more weight to its own past experiences, thus preferring trust reflexivity, or assign more weight to recommendations, thus preferring trust transitivity.

The Pervasive Trust Management (PTM) model [5, 7] by Almenarez et al. aims to enable pervasive devices to establish spontaneous relationships in infrastructure-less ad hoc networks. In PTM trust is established between entities either directly or indirectly (through recommendations). The two approaches are considered largely independent of each other. In contrast, Capra's hTrust treats trust formation as a function of both direct experiences and recommendations. When computing trust-worthiness using the indirect approach, PTM assigns weights to the trust values reported by the recommenders which reflect the reliability of the sources. Almenarez et al. also present TrustAC [6], which defines access control policies based on trust values obtained from PTM.

Capra and Musolesi [18] present an autonomic trust prediction model for perva-sive environments. The model requires that each service provider in the environment advertises a service specification which is a promise of a certain quality of service. Given the service specification and the actual quality of service observed in previous interactions with the service provider, the model uses a Kalman filter [35] to assess its trustworthiness for future interactions.

There are a number of other studies that, although do not address pervasive com-puting in particular, have been influential in the area of trust management.

Reference [2] by Abdul-Rahman and Hailes is one of the earlier works to de-scribe a practical model to support trust in electronic communities. Trust Builder [57] by Winslett et al. and Trust-X [12] by Bertino et al. are significant Auto-mated Trust Negotiation systems. Guha et al. [26] describe a set of trust propagation schemes and evaluate them on a large trust network consisting of 800 K trust scores expressed among 130 K people.

To give it precise meaning and to make the concept mathematically manipulable, several authors have proposed formal models of trust.

Marsh [39] was one of the earliest researchers to give a formalism of trust. The model is based on simple linear mathematics. The utility of the model is demon-strated by its application to agents in cooperative situations. Carbone et al. [19] propose a formal model of trust in the context of pervasive computing, which fo-cuses on the aspects of trust formation, evolution and propagation. The model is based on domain theory [48]. Jonker and Treur [20] stress that trust is a function of experiences between two entities over time. Based on this notion they develop formal trust evolution and update functions.

Several authors have employed a graph theoretic approach towards the formal-ization of trust, particularly its evolution and propagation.

Sant and Maple's [47] graph theoretic framework for trust is grounded in the be-lief that trust is not a local but rather a global phenomenon. The authors suggest that it is important to take a global view to ensure an accurate level of trust in networks. Levien's Advogato system [36] shares similarities with that of Sant and Maple.

All these approaches compute trust value resulting from a trust chain as an aver-age value. We believe that this evaluation not sufficient: for instance, it does not take into account some constraints such as the personality and the subjectivity of each node. In Sections 16.5 and 16.6 we will introduce a trust model handling propaga-tion and the disposition to trust of the participants.

In the rest of this related work we introduce how the trust paradigm is fulfilled along different distributed systems.

16.3.2 Distributed and Collaborative Environments

16.3.2.1 Trust Granularity

Aforementioned, the trust is the starting point to establish and build links between the various actors and entities of the environment, namely organizations and users. In distributed environments, trust is used at various levels, and its perception may be different depending on the involved players. Thus, we can identify three trust classes as following:

- **Trust Among Users** Different users need to know each other to establish trust, which be direct or transitive via one or more third parties. In distributed systems, this level of trust has been used mainly in the peer to peer networks and virtual communities under the name of reputation [25] (e.g., facebook, ebay, etc.).

  The reputation is basically defined to evaluate the trustworthiness that can be awarded to an entity based on its references and recommendations of other members of the community.

- **Trust Between Organization and Users** Within an organization, individual members are identified and have a local profile namely students, teachers, secretary, etc. At this level, each members is recognizable and trust each other, due to they belonging to the same organization. This later is considered to be the local authority. Thus each member rely on this authority is rely on any other entity certified by it.

  In this kind of relationship, the notion of delegation is frequently implemented. It has been defined with the aim to broad the scope of security policies to make them more flexible and dynamic. This approach extends the authority by using the propagation of the confidence. Thus, a source of authority may delegate a trust entity to manage certain conduct of its resources. This mechanism is increasingly integrated into the distributed architectures. It allows security policy of involving local users who have the ability to assign more access to resources based on their perception of trust. For example, a visitor who is an outsider of the local site can acquire an access to the Internet or use a printer, if they have a friend (member of the local domain) who have the authority to delegate this access right. Certain systems go further, by proposing a mechanism for multi-level delegation, which can have the right to delegate the delegation it self.

- **Trust Beyond Organizations** This relationship of trust is usually the result of agreements or contracts between the various organizations to develop a collaboration or project for short or long period. This will make it easier for project members belonging to different areas to move and use shared resources within the framework of this alliance. This type of collaboration has emerged under the name of VO: Virtual Organization [43].

The research about the Virtual Organizations began around 1990s. It is a distributed organizational structure which combines several independent organizations. The difficulty of establishing such alliance is due to the constraints imposed by the various administrations that are heterogeneous and potentially conflicting, but with the primary objective to cooperate, while protecting their information systems.

This type of collaboration can be expanded. In this case, trust is treated as a unifying relationship, often located among similar organizations, such as universities, government agencies, schengens statements, and so on.

16.3.2.2 Distributed and Collaborative Systems

The collaboration between organizations is fulfilled between heterogeneous access policy. Among them, three description models are identified:

- Discretionary access control (DAC)
- Mandatory access control (MAC)
- Role based access control (RBAC)

In DAC [27] all permission can be represented by an access matrix, where each row corresponds to a user and each column to a resource. The problem of this model is the difficulties of management, because in pervasive environment, it is not able to put all access control list of a user in a mobile device.

MAC [10] typically deals with data resources, all of them are assigned a label according to a classification, typically security levels like: top secret, secret, confidential, unclassified.

RBAC [46] is based on the concept of roles. A role represents a collection of permissions. In this manner, users are assigned roles according to the tasks they have to perform. During the last decade, the role model-based has emerged as the most suitable for security requirements. Indeed, several alternatives have emerged to improve the basic model by making it more flexible and more responsive to the requirements of the new distributed systems.

The model RB-RBAC (Rule-Based RBAC) [4] introduces the concept of negative authorization to express that an actor is forbidden to play a role if it does not enable certain attributes. The model TRBAC [11] Temporal RBAC, as its name suggests, using the time constraint for allocation of role. In other words, a user can have a role in the morning and another in the afternoon. The model OrBAC [3] (Organization Based Access Control) defines a level of abstraction of the real world, which is the newest and is the most generic possible. its design incorporates a hard definition of context, hierarchical roles and delegation.

A distributed system is typically constructed out of different sites using different access policies. In what follows, we will introduce the major distributed system, which consider the problems of authentication and access control in the new generation of network, such as Pervasive, Grid, etc. and we will detail some security solutions in these environments.

The Shibboleth [49] is developed since 2001, it implements widely used federated identity standards, principally SAML [52], to provide a federated single sign-on and attribute exchange framework. Shibboleth also provides extended privacy functionality allowing the browser user and their home site to control the attributes released to each application. Using Shibboleth enabled access simplifies management of identity and permissions for organizations supporting users and applications. The application modify the known authentication protocol. Sandardly, the resources owner (SOA source of autority) is responsible to authenticate the user request. With Shibboleth, the home user institution (which the user is member), checks the identify of the guest, and transmit the corresponding attributes to the resources providers. Shiboboleth is widely adopted by the academic community, but there is not adapted to trust propagation. In fact, neither mapping concept nor the delegation protocol are enabled for this system.

The project PERMIS [21] (Privilege and Role Management Infrastructure Standards Validation) is an access control system based on the certification mechanism. It has been developed since 2001 by the group "Research Systems Security" at the University of Salford. It implements a system of access control based on the RBAC model using X.509 [30] certificates attributes. The authorizations are represented in XML and stored in an LDAP directory. PERMIS can operate in push or pull mode to retrieve the attributes for authorization. This system implements the concept of static delegation of authority. Thus, the SOA is responsible to define in the authorization, the entities with the right to assigning roles.

However, "DyVOSE" project [55] at the national e-Science Center from the University of Glasgow are working together to integrate a dynamic delegation to PERMIS, which enable creating a chain of delegation with a limited size. The spread of trust addressed by the dynamic delegation represents a major evolution of the PERMIS project. It extends the scope of the access security policies, but is still limited compared to a mapping approach which is applied between different policies.

The access control mechanism Sygn [50] provides a decentralized permission storage and management system in Grid Computing. All permissions in Sygn are encoded in certificates, which are stored by their owners and used when required. Permissions can be created on demand, by the owners of the resources or by administrators to whom this responsibility has been delegated. Sygn allows an efficient decentralized administration of dynamically changing resources and permissions. Sygn avoids the use of centralized and minimizes the use of trusted third parties. However, like PERMIS, the spread of trust remains limited.

Actually, the delegation is considered as a main aspect of Trust in distributed environment. Some certification models use a system of delegation, The delegation gives to users an access for example, through other authorized users [16, 33], or authorized agents [34], etc. This certificate contains the rights of user. The delegation itself is viewed as a right. Only the users with rights to delegate an action can actually delegate that action, and the ability to delegate can itself be delegated. The delegation mechanism is considered to be efficient, but not sufficient alone to perform a broad access. Indeed, the user's scope is restricted to environments where she is locally known. Consequently, she has an access if there is at least one entity that trusts her.

Therefore, to enhance the access scope, a system based on a "Mapping Policy" is implemented for instance in Grid Computing [56]. Pearlman et al. [43] defines a virtual Organisation VO that groups some users and resources, e.g., hosts or storage space. It relies on a centralized server CAS. This server is used to map or convert the local user access to a VO access. Applying this mapping concept seems to be inadequate in the mobile distributed environment. Indeed, the user must have an account in the virtual organisation to obtain a VO certificate, and this certificate does not allow the user to access another VO, but only this one. Moreover, using a centralized server is seen as a drawback. Various projects work to extend the CAS server. They are trying to resolve the scaling issue, by enabling a communication protocols between VOs to manage a decentralized and large access control policy. With this last point, the collaboration between servers CAS is a good approach but remains limited because the interaction is static and can not be spread and evolved dynamically.

Trust-Based Access Control (TrustAC) [6] is a system for ensuring pervasive environments access control using a mechanism for evaluating the trust called PTM [7]. In TrustAC, the user's device is responsible to administrate its own security policy. Each device maintains a list of secure or malicious entities by awarding them a trust degree according to their reputation and recommendations from other users. In contrast to the RBAC model, in this system each user is not linked to a role but to a numeric value bounded between 0 and 1 which corresponds to the degree of trustworthiness within the community. The use of numerical values can manage classes and categories of users (as the model DAC). Thus, like RBAC, each permission is granted to a trust degree and not the individual himself. This allows the implementation of the Mapping by level and reduces the complexity of the mapping security policies. A drawback of TrustAC is that it does not evaluate the organization's identity or the user context (The device used, e.g., PDA, Laptop, etc.).

To summarize this part, we believe that there is a need for enabling the delegation of authority and the propagation of trust, that must take into account the context of usage and allows the users to be recognize in their visited environments as in their own environment. We will present later in Section 16.4 the Chameleon architecture that handle this need.

In the last part of this literature review, we present the certification concept which is considered as the most used tool to ensure security in distributed systems.

16.3.3 Certification Mechanism

The Certification mechanism is a service based on digital signature. It uses the concept of Public Key Infrastructure (PKI) to provide a security privilege based on the trust accorded to the signatory. This mechanism is implemented to authenticate contents of the certificate and to implement a distributed system based on trust.

In the literature, some certification models are standardized and formalized, e.g., PGP(Pretty Good Privacy) [58], SPKI [29], Sygn [50], X509 [30], Akenti [54].

X509 is the most used standard. However, it has first been designed as an identity certificate, and its last extension proposed to extend its scope to attribute certificate. Unfortunately, the usability of the new extension is deemed to be too complex and requires adaptations (depending on security policies, e.g., RBAC), like in PRIMA [37] and PERMIS [21] which adapt the X509 attribute format to extend its capabilities.

SPKI was proposed to become an alternative to X509. SPKI focuses on authorization certificates more than identity certificates. The objective of SPKI is simplicity. Unlike the X509, which is based on ASN 1.0 [31] format, SPKI certificate is described in S-expression [42] offering more flexibility and readability.

These last models of certification have some drawbacks. In fact, all of them identify one user only with her public key using a challenge-response mechanism [22]. But each nomadic user owns multiple devices with different capacity (computing power) and capabilities (biometric identification, memory, . . .). Hence one certificate should embed more than one identification in order to give the user different means to authenticate her certificates. Furthermore, on one hand, the certificate contains more and more information (sensitive or public) and, on the other hand the context of usage is very important in new collaborative distributed environments. The certificate contents should therefore be adaptable (or rather adapted) according to the context.

16.3.4 Morph Mechanism

We define the morph mechanism to perform the certification contextual adaptation. It represents the ability to hide some attributes on a signed message according to context. Steinfeld et al. [53] define this property as CES (Content Extraction Signature): "*A Content Extraction Signature should allow anyone, given a signed document, to extract a publicly verifiable extracted signature for a specified subdocument of a signed document, without interaction with the signer of the original document*".

The most used approach divides the messages into fragments, then signs each one separately. Micaly and Rivest [41] is the first work which introduces the concept of transitive signature. In their algorithm, giving a signature on two graph edges Sig(x,y) and Sig(y,z) (where x, y and z represent subdocuments), a valid signature Sig(x,z) can be computed to hide "y" without accessing the secrete key. Johanson et al. [32] have introduced some improvements by enabling a homomorphic signature. Let a signature Sig(x). Anyone can compute a signature Sig(w) on any subpart w of x obtained by rubbing out some position of x. [14] is the first work which uses homomorphic function property to define a new signature algorithm for morphing certificates.

All previous approaches have a drawback; they define a new algorithm to perform the certificate adaptability, instead of using the existing standard.

[53] exposes a modification of the RSA computing algorithm. Their approach is based on the homomorphic property of RSA, i.e., $h_1^d h_2^d \, modN = (h_1 h_2)^d \, modN$. This algorithm multiplies the RSA sub-messages$_i$ signatures ($h_i^d \, modN$), and checks whether the result is the signature of the hash values products. Their approaches are very useful. However, they are based on mathematical proprieties that address only a specific class of signature algorithm. This constraint reduces the usability scope.

The World Wide Web Consortium "W3C" standard: "XML Digital signature" (XMLDSig) [9] offers the capability to sign different parts of documents. [15] add some elements to the XMLSignature standard to perform the certificate adaptability. These methods are very attractive, but are not appropriate in a certificate model. They treat certificates as any documents, where each one is decomposed into several sub-documents. Consequently, the user is free to disclose or blind any part (e.g certificate identifier). But credential or certificate does not consist of distinct parts, but are rather composed of a single bloc, which contains two sort of fields: **Static field** (e.g., certificate identifier, issuer identity, time of validity, …) that can not be adapted and **Dynamic field** (e.g., user name, user rights, …) that can be hidden on demand depending on the context.

To conclude, the certification mechanism has to be used and standards have to be favored to sign the certificates. The need to handle dynamically the certificate's contents is not covered by the literature. We will later propose a new model of certification in Section 16.7 that finds solutions to the afore mentioned problems.

16.4 The Chameleon Architecture

As illustrated in the first use case, one of the primary characteristics of a collaborative distributed environment is to allow users to roam ubiquitously between disparate administrative domains. As stated before, the issue is how a local site can authenticate and allow access to previously unknown foreign users.

Our Chameleon architecture works as a front-end for each site and controls access to it by foreign users. When a foreign user approaches a site, the chameleon system upon authenticating the user, transforms them into a local user and grants them access. The architecture is named after the animal chameleon which has the ability to transform itself to fit into its environment (see Fig. 16.3).

To set up the Chameleon architecture we define three modules (see Fig. 16.4):

- *PEP "Policy Enforcement Point"* Used to authenticate a user and capture her context
- *PDP: "Policy Decision Point"* Used to evaluate user and provide her an access profile
- *PAP "Policy Access Point"* Used to enable the mapping policy

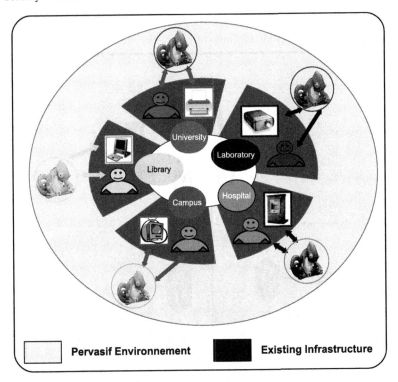

Fig. 16.3 The chameleon

Our architecture allows a user to authenticate on a remote site and to grant her an access to the site without being locally recognized in advance. The architecture is a trust-based access control model that uses the dynamic certification mechanism called "X316" [45] (see Section 16.7).

16.4.1   Selecting a Certificate (Fig. 16.4 Steps 1–3)

We use the certificate model called X316: Morph Access Pass Certificate [45]. The X316 works as a pass, allowing its owner to roam among different sites. Each site issues all its members a Home certificate (H316) that contains the member's local profile and rights. A target site can authenticate the user and attribute them a Trust certificate (T316), if they are approved as trusted.

When a user arrives at a target site, the user's device selects and transmits a valid credential depending on the identity of the target site (hospital, university, airport, etc.). The PEP receives the user credential, and authenticates the certificate owner by selecting an authentication process such as challenge response, biometric, etc.

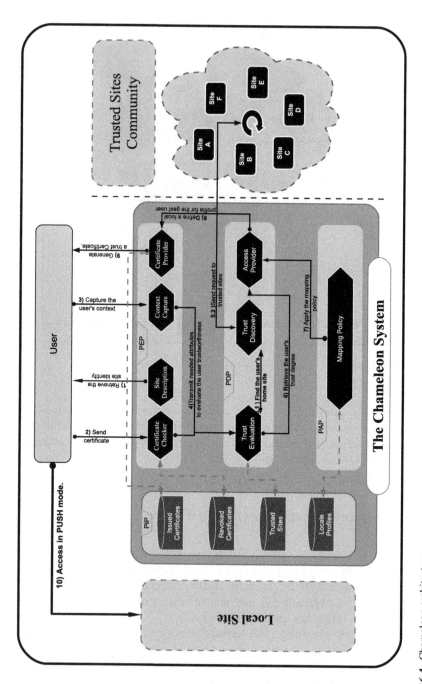

Fig. 16.4 Chameleon architecture

16.4.2 Evaluating the Trustworthiness of a User (Fig. 16.4 Steps 4–6)

Once the user is authenticated, the target site attempts to assign her a profile based on the identity of the certificate issuer. We define a trust model (see Section 16.5) to enable organizations to communicate and share certain information about their members.

Each site administrator builds its local **trust set** which contains all the trusted sites and assigns each one a numerical trust value. When a user arrives at a target site, the PDP of this site requests trusted sites about the user's home site "H". Once H is located, a trust chain is created between the target site and the home site.

In this manner, the environment can be seen as a graph, and we note $T_g(S, E)$ a valued and directed graph such that:

- The nodes of the graph represent the sites of S.
- Each trust relation between two sites is represented by a directed edge e. The set of edges is consequently identified with the set of relations, E.
- Each edge is valued by the distrust degree between the sites represented by the source and destination nodes of this edge.

The evaluation of this path allows the target site to decide if the foreign user can be allowed to access the target site resources. This model, using community collaboration, enables the target site to evaluate the nomadic user in relation to its home site.

We will consider three different acceses: *local, direct and transitive access.*

- A local access is provided by the home site to all registered users (i.e., where they have their accounts and can authenticate themselves).
- A direct access is provided by the PDP module of a site to all users registered in its trusted sites. This direct access is valued by the trust degree between the local and the trusted site.
- A transitive access can be provided by a site to a user who does not belong to a site of its trust set, under a condition that a valid trust chain between one of the user's home sites and trusted sites exists in the graph. This transitive access is valued by the trust propagation degree between these two sites (in case of the existence of several possible chains, the PDP is responsible for choosing the reference chain). To manage the users' access, each site has to define thresholds beyond which access is not allowed (i.e., when trust can not be established anyway).

16.4.3 Attributing an Access Profile (Fig. 16.4 Steps 7–9)

Attributing an access profile to a foreign user requires to first define two constructs: a local profile and a mapping policy.

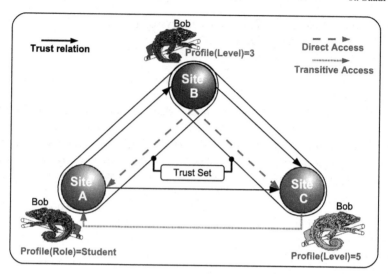

Fig. 16.5 Trust propagation

Once a user is allowed to access a target site, the PAP attributes her a local profile using a mapping policy. Each site defines some external profiles (local profiles), which can be attributed to trusted foreign users. The mapping policy is implemented to find a mapping between the home profile of a foreign user to an analogous local one. Each site creates a mapping table that enables the matching between the different profiles of trusted sites and its own analogous profiles. For example (see Fig. 16.5), a user Bob, having an access profile with level 5 in his home site C wants to access a site B which provides Bob a new access level for instance, level 3.

After having established the global architecture and functions of the Chameleon, we enter now in details in the (dis)trust model that serves as a basis for it.

16.5 The Distrust Model

16.5.1 The Trust Relation

Definition 16.1. *The Trust relation:* Let S denotes a set of sites. Let A and B two sites, $A \in S, B \in S$. If A trusts B then we say that the relation Trust is verified between A and B and we note **A Trust B** A is called the trustor and B the trustee.

We endow the trust relation with the following properties:

- **Reflexivity** $\forall A \in S, A\ Trust\ A$
  Trivially, a site trusts itself.

- **Non-Symmetry** The Trust relation is not symmetric. Indeed, a site is fully responsible for its trust policy and there is no obligation of reciprocity, so we can get
  A *Trust* $B \wedge \neg B$ *Trust* A.
- **Transitivity** The Trust relation is transitive:
  $\forall A, B, C \in S, A$ *Trust* $B \wedge B$ *Trust* $C \Rightarrow A$ *Trust* C
  This property is fundamental for the effectiveness of the proposition. It allows the definition of "trust chains" between sites that do not know each other (see below).

We define a Trust Set of a site A as the set of sites with which A has a direct trust relationship with and can directly evaluate the trustworthiness of each of those sites.

Based on the *Trust* relation, we introduce **the distrust function** t^0, to estimate the level of (dis)trust between two sites.

16.5.2 Distrust Function

Definition 16.2. *Distrust function:* We call distrust function and we note t^0, the function defined as:

$$t^0 : S * S \to \mathbb{N} \quad \text{S: set of sites}$$
$$(A, B) \to d \quad \mathbb{N} : \text{set of natural numbers}$$

$$t^0(A, B) = \begin{cases} +\infty & if \neg(A \ Trust \ B) \\ 0 \le d \le T_A^0 & otherwise \end{cases} \tag{16.1}$$

where d represents **the distrust degree** and T_A^0 denotes the distrust threshold of the site A. The distrust threshold represents the maximum level of distrust beyond which A does not trust B (i.e., over this threshold the relation A Trust B is not verified).

This function quantifies the degree of distrust that the site A shows wrt the site B. When $t^0(A, B)$ increases, the distrust increases (i.e., the trust decreases). As consequences:

- $t^0(A, A) = 0$: any site has a complete trust in itself.
- $t^0(A, B) < t^0(A, C)$: means that the trustor A has a higher trust in B than in C.

The distrust function shows properties related to the properties of the Trust relation.

16.5.2.1 Properties of Distrust Function

Self Trust

$$\forall A \in S, t^0(A, A) = 0$$

Non-commutativity

$$\exists A, B \in S / t^0(A, B) = d_1 \wedge t^0(B, A) = d_2 \wedge d_1 \neq d_2$$
i.e., $t^0(A, B)$ is independent from $t^0(B, A)$.

Composition

Let A, B, C three sites. The **composition** of the distrust degrees $t^0(A, B)$ and $t^0(B, C)$, noted $t^0(A, B) + t^0(B, C)$ is defined as:

$$
\begin{array}{l}
t^0(A, B) \\
\quad + \\
t^0(B, C)
\end{array}
=
\begin{cases}
+\infty & if(t^0(A, B) = +\infty) \vee (t^0(B, C) = +\infty) \\
t^0(A, B) & \\
\quad + & otherwise \\
t^0(B, C) &
\end{cases}
\tag{16.2}
$$

This distrust model allows one to construct a *Trust graph* $T_g(S, E)$. This trust chain is used to decide if a "foreign" user can be allowed to access to the site resources (i.e., to decide if a user who does not own an account of the system can get logged in the system).

To allow foreign user a local access, each site has to define thresholds beyond which access is not permitted.

We distinguish two thresholds:

- Distrust threshold T_A^0: It is defined by the local site 'A' to build up its Trust Set by attributing to each trusted site a distrust value between 0 and the max value T_A^0.
- Global (distrust) threshold θT_A^0: Each trustor A has to define a global threshold, corresponding to the maximum tolerated degree for a transitive access. This value is proportional to the distrust threshold and to the defined maximum authorized chain length L_A starting from A. $\theta T_A^0 = T_A^0 * L_A$.

This distrust model is decentralized. Each site evaluates its distrust threshold independently from other sites. This can lead to a divergence in the evolution of the transitive access. For example: one trustor can value its trustees up to 20 and another can value its trustees up to 500. To smooth these differences, the distrust propagation function is defined to evaluate, for each site, its distrust degree relatively to its distrust threshold.

16.5.2.2 Distrust Propagation Function

Let A, B, C be three sites. The composition of the distrust degrees $t^0(A, B)$ and $t^0(B, C)$, noted $P_B^0(A, C) = t^0(A, B) \oplus t^0(B, C)$ is defined as:

$$P_B^0(A, C) = \begin{cases} +\infty & \text{if}(t^0(A, B) = +\infty) \vee (t^0(B, C) = +\infty) \\ \\ t^0(A, B) \\ + & \text{otherwise} \\ \frac{t^0(B,C)}{T_B^0} * T_A^0 \end{cases} \quad (16.3)$$

Consequently, a site A can allow a foreign user U (registered in C) an access through an intermediary trusted site B.

$$\text{iif } 0 \leq P_B^0(A, C) \leq \theta T_A^0$$

Generalization: Trust Chains

The composition of distrust degrees is generalized to n sites by composing two by two the distrust degrees:
Let A and C be 2 sites of S; let B_1 B_n be n sites of S.
Let us note T = $(B_1, \ldots, B_n)$.
We note $P_T^0(A, C)$ and we call distrust propagation degree between A and C based on T the value:

$$P_T^0(A, C) = t^0(A, B_1) \oplus \cdots \oplus t^0(B_n, C).$$
$$P_\phi^0(A, C) = t^0(A, C)(\text{property}).$$

Theorem 16.1.

$$P_\phi^0(A, C) = +\infty \Leftrightarrow \exists F, G \in (A, B_1, \ldots, B_n, C)/t^0(F, G) = +\infty \quad (16.4)$$

Proof. Trivial by application of the definition of t^0: The composition of distrust degrees equals $+\infty$ if and only if one at least of the distrust degrees equals $+\infty$.

Example

Let's take five sites that build a trust chain (A,B,C,D,E). Suppose a user of the site E wants to access the site A. To decide if this user can be granted an access, A computes $P_{B,C,D}^0(A, E)$ progressively (see Fig. 16.6).
If $P_A = 3 \wedge T_A^0 = 70$ then $\theta T_A^0(B) = 70 * 3 = 210$.
As a consequence, the user of the site E will be allowed to access the site A since:

$$0 \leq (P_{B,C,D}^0(A, E) = 173.3) \leq (\theta T_A^0(B) = 210)$$

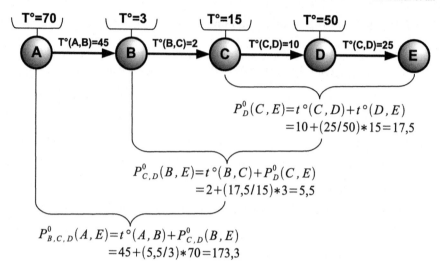

Fig. 16.6 The trust propagation

16.6 Establishing Trust Beliefs Based on Disposition to Trust

As stated beforehand, a site's Trust sSet is composed of the sites that it can evaluate directly for their trustworthiness. In other words the members of the set are those sites with whom the site has a direct trust relationship.

We introduce a novel method for the evaluation of trustworthiness of sites in the Trust Set. The method is composed of the following three steps:

1. Specify the disposition to trust of the local site.
2. Trust sort.
3. Generate the quantitative evaluations of each of the trust set members.

The objective of this method is to allow the creation of trust beliefs that are based not on the disposition to trust of individual administrators but on an uniform disposition to trust of the home site. The result is a set of trust beliefs that are neutral to the disposition to trust of the multiple administrators that contribute to its creation. The trust beliefs are however consistent with an uniform disposition to trust defined for the home site.

16.6.1 Specification of Disposition to Trust

Disposition to trust is the inherent propensity of an individual to trust or distrust others. An individual's disposition to trust does not vary for specific entities but is a stable characteristic of their personality that governs how they view the trustworthiness of every other entity that they encounter. McKnight et al. [28] define disposition to trust as the "extent to which a person displays a tendency to be willing to depend on others across a broad spectrum of situations and persons".

Although, disposition to trust has been discussed in the literature as the characteristic of an individual, for our purpose we propose its definition as the characteristic of an organization. We define a variable d that represents the disposition to trust of an organization. d may be a variable on a range such as 0–9 with 0 representing high disposition to trust and 9 representing low disposition to trust. Low disposition to trust indicates that an individual or in our case an organization is less willing to trust a foreign entity and vice versa. The value of d may be selected after consensus between all the administrators in the organization.

16.6.2   Trust Sort

Instead of assigning trust values to individual nodes, we propose that an administrator perform trust evaluations in relation to other nodes.

As for an example, let's take Alice, Bob and Cathy having some trust relationships. We note that on a range of 0–9, Alice may perceive the trustworthiness of Cathy as 5. Whereas based on similar experiences, Bob may evaluate Cathy's trustworthiness as 8. This difference occurs due to the difference in the disposition to trust of Alice and Bob.

However, if the administrators are required to evaluate the trustworthiness of nodes in relation to other nodes we may have the following scenario. Let's say that Alice rates Cathy as more trustworthy than David. Based on similar experiences with Cathy and David, Bob is also very likely to rate Cathy more trustworthy than David. We make the hypothesis that with this alternate approach we are more likely to have more consistent trustworthiness evaluations.

We call the notion of evaluating nodes in relation to other nodes as "Trust Sort". An administrator is indeed sorting the foreign nodes in terms of their trustworthiness. The result is a sorted list of nodes.

16.6.3   Generation of Quantitative Trust Values

16.6.3.1   A Classification of Sites

We can broadly classify sites into two categories based on their disposition to trust. The first category represents sites that generally exhibit high levels of trust in the members of their trust set. In contrast, the second category represents the sites that are inclined towards low levels of trust in the members of their trust set.

We define a mathematical function $y = f_d(x)$ that we call the BV (**BehaV**ior) function. The function represents a curve in the Cartesian coordinate system.

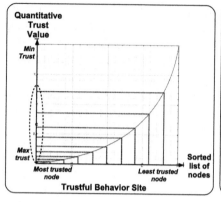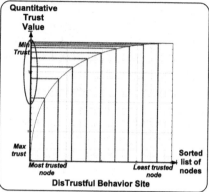

Fig. 16.7 The trust behavior

- The input x is a positive integer that represents the order number of a node in the sorted list. The list is numbered from 1 to n where n is the total number of nodes in the list. The node in position 1 is the most trusted node.
- The output y represents the corresponding quantitative trust value for the node based on the disposition to trust of the local site.

We note that in our model we consider zero as the maximum trust value.

We now present the contrast between sites that exhibit trustful and distrustful disposition to trust or behavior in terms of the BV function.

1. **Class 1 "Sites That Exhibit Trustful Behavior"** This class represents the behavior of sites which are more trusting. We define that this characteristic is represented by the BV function when it takes a hyperbola form. As illustrated in Fig. 16.7 the projections of the x values are gathered closer to the maximum trust value (zero).

2. **Class 2 "Sites That Exhibit Distrustful Behavior"** This class represents the behavior of sites which are less trusting. We define that this characteristic is represented by the BV function when it takes a parabola form. As illustrated in Fig. 16.7 the projections of the x values are gathered closer to the minimum trust value.

16.6.3.2   The Behavior Function

We use a Bezier curve to implement the BV function due to the flexibility it allows in plotting geometric curves.

The Bezier Curve is a parametric form to draw a smooth curve. It is fulfilled through some points $P_0, P_1, \ldots, P_n$, starting at P_0 going towards $P_1, \ldots, P_{n-1}$ and terminating at P_n (see Fig. 16.8).

Fig. 16.8 The Bezier curve

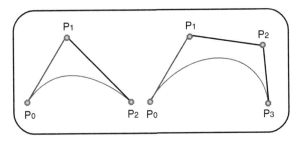

In our model we will use a Bezier curve with three points, which is called a Quadratic Bezier curve. It is defined as follows:

A quadratic Bezier curve is the path traced by the function B(t), given points $P_0, P_1,$ and P_2.

$$B(t) = (1 - t)^2 * P_0 + 2t(1 - t) * P_1 + t^2 * P_2. \tag{16.5}$$

The BV function is expressed by a Bezier curve that passes through three points where:

- The origin point ($P_0(0,0)$)
- The behavior point ($P_1(b_x, b_y)$)
- The threshold point ($P_2(h_x, h_y)$) where the h_x represents the number of sorted site and the h_y represents the trust threshold

As illustrated in Fig. 16.9, by moving the behavior point P_1 inside the rectangle that is defined by P_0 and P_2, we are able to adjust the curvature.

Based on the Bezier curve, let us now define the "BV function".

The BV function describes the trust behavior of a site. It takes the order number of a node in the sorted list (x) and returns the corresponding "Quantitative trust value" (y). To apply the BV function with the Bezier curve, we modify the Bezier curve to obtain the output y as a function of x, instead of taking a temporal variable t as input to compute x and y.

The BV function curve can be drawn through the three points $P_0(0,0)$, $P_1(b_x, b_y)$ and $P_2(h_x, h_y)$ using the Bezier curve as follows:

$$BV : [0, h_x] \longrightarrow [0, h_y]$$
$$X \longrightarrow Y$$

$$BV_{P_1, P_2}(X) = \begin{cases} Y = (h_y - 2b_y)(\propto (X))^2 + 2b_y \propto (X), & \text{if } (h_x \neq 2b_x); \\ Y = \frac{h_y}{h_x}x, & \text{otherwise.} \end{cases}$$

$$Where \propto (X) = \frac{-b_x + \sqrt{b_x^2 - 2b_x * X + h_x * X}}{h_x - 2b_x} \wedge \begin{cases} 0 < X < h_x \\ 0 < b_x < h_x \\ 0 < b_y < h_y \end{cases}$$

$$\tag{16.6}$$

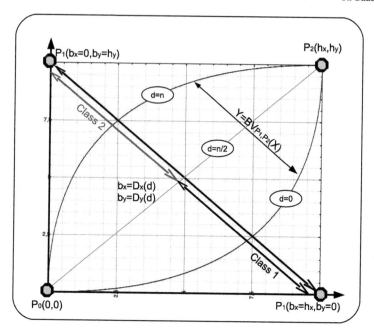

Fig. 16.9 The behavior curve functions

16.6.3.3   The Disposition to Trust Function D

As discussed earlier, the disposition to trust d of a site is given on a range. We now define a function called the D function which operates on the behavior point P_1 to control the curvature of the BV function.

The D function operates on the point P_1. According to the position of the point P_1 the Bezier curve will transition between parabola and hyperbola forms. As illustrated in Fig. 16.9 the first and the last points delimit the curve frame. This frame is a rectangle and it is defined by source point $P_0(0,0)$ and the threshold point $P_2(h_x, h_y)$. The middle point $P_1(b_x, b_y)$ controls site behavior. We assume that this point can move through the second diagonal of the defined rectangle $b_x = \frac{-h_y}{h_x} * b_y + h_y$. We define the Disposition to Trust function D as follows, such that scrolling d between 0 and n gives updated positions for P_1:

$$D : [0, n] \longrightarrow [0, h_x] * [0, h_y]$$
$$d \longrightarrow (b_x, b_y)$$
$$D(d) = \begin{cases} b_x = \frac{-h_x}{n}d + h_x \\ b_y = \frac{h_y}{n}d \end{cases} \quad (16.7)$$

The variable d represents the disposition to trust of a site. The value 0 indicates maximum trustful behavior and n represents maximum distrustful behavior.

16.6.4 Generating Quantitative Trust Values

Given d and the threshold points (P_1, P_2), the BV function is able to assign each site in the sorted list a corresponding quantitative trust value as follows:

1. Specifying the P_1 is fulfilled by selecting the corresponding disposition to trust d between 0 and n.
2. The P_2 point is specified by assigning h_x and h_y the following values:

   - $h_x = $ (Number of trusted sites) $+1$
   - $h_y = T^0$ (the trust threshold)

3. Putting the trusted sites as classified along the abscissa of the BV function.

Example

- Let's consider two sites, where the disposition to trust of each one (the point P_1) is bounded between 0 (very distrustful) and 9 (very trustful):

  - S_1: Trustful site, $d = 1$;
  - S_2: Distrustful site, $d = 8$.

- These sites evaluate five trusted sites (A,B,C,D,E). The threshold point P_2 has the coordinates:
$$h_x = 5 + 1 = 6 \text{ and } h_y = T^0 = 50. \tag{16.8}$$
- The sorted list of both S_1 and S_2 is:
  (high trust)$(+)$. **SiteD. SiteC. SiteE. Site A. SiteB.** $(-)$(low trust)

Thus, by performing the BV function (see Fig. 16.10), we depict in the Table 16.1 the trusted values that would be assigned to each trusted site.

In this section, we illustrated the need to have a means to handle different disposition of trusts in a distributed collaborative environment and we proposed a solution based on simple projection and Bezier curves. This proposal eliminates most of the bias due to the differences in a community in their disposition to trust.

The next section will propose a new model of certificate that allows to embed the trust model, the role/profile mapping facility and different authentication mechanisms while preserving the privacy of its user.

16.7 X316: Morph Access Pass Certificate

In distributed systems, especially in distributed collaborative environments, mobile users gather certificates providing them rights to access unknown and trusted environments. As seen in the second use case, such certificate embeds increasing number of information that leads the certificate provider to adapt existing standards to its requirements. Contrary to existing certificate standards, we aim to provide a flexible

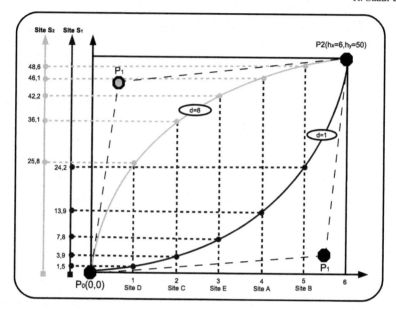

Fig. 16.10 Site classification

Table 16.1 Example of sorting trusted sites

	Site A	Site B	Site C	Site D	Site E
Site S1	13,9	24,2	3,9	1,5	7,8
Site S2	46,1	48,6	36,1	25,8	42,2

format of certificate enabling to disclose, to hide and to cipher any authorized part of a certificate according to the user context, environment and wish. In this section, we define and describe a new certificate model called $X316$ and we supply a security toolbox (i.e., X316 Signature, X316 Encryption and X316 Context) allowing its user for managing her certificate freely according to contextual situation.

Our contribution has an objective to define a very flexible model of certification. It is inspirited by the W3C standards: "XML Digital signature"(XMLDSig). The X316 is designed for a nomadic user. Indeed, unlike other certification systems, the same X316 certificate can be used and authenticated from various devices with different capability and characteristics, and can be generated dynamically along a user trip. In fact, by defining specific tags to delimit the dynamic parts, this certificate acquires the capability to transform and to morph easily its content according to context, situation, and environment.

Therefore, the X316 fulfills three properties:

- Generic structure
- Multi authentication
- Contextual adaptation

The X316 certificate is composed of four parts: Header, Right, Authentication and Signature.

- **HEADER** It identifies the certificate, and is mainly composed of the issuer and the subject.
- **RIGHT** It is a variable part of a certificate, depending on the site's policy. This part contains information about user's profile (e.g., role or access level) and user capabilities (e.g., delegation).
- **AUTHENTICATION** This part permits to identify the owner of the X316. The authenticators are numerous, and related to the variety of devices used in the pervasive environment (PDA, mobile phone, terminals). Facilitating certificates management is fulfilled by embedding several authenticators according to the device's authentication capabilities and the site's security policy. Two ways of authentication have been identified, remote and local authentication [44].
- **SIGNATURE** This part contains the information about the public cipher key and the result of the certificate's signature.

The X316 could be obtained in three different ways (see Fig. 16.11):

- Each site gives a Home Certificate or **H316**, to all its members.
- Each site gives a Roam certificate or **R316**, to a passing user, when it trusts her Home Site. This certificate allows the user to extend her access scope along her trip. The R316 does not provide access, it proves the user rights. This credential type is generated dynamically without user authentication.

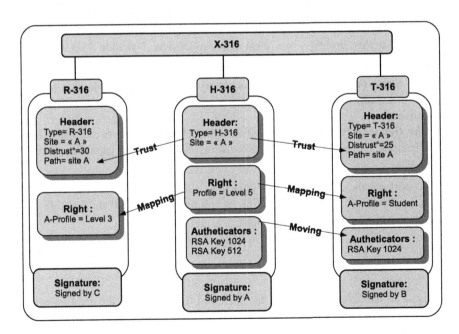

Fig. 16.11 The X316 type

- Each site gives a Trust certificate or **T316**, to a guest, when it trusts her Home Site. Instead of the R316 the T316 provides an access inside the target site and needs user authentication.

In the rest of the section we use this syntax definition to describe each of the X316 parts, where "?" denotes zero or one occurrence; "+" denotes one or more occurrences and "*" denotes zero or more occurrences.

16.7.1 X316 Signature (The Morph Capability)

All standards (e.g., X509 and PGP) use a hash algorithm to obtain a residual value from the certificate data. This value is signed by a private key of the certification authority. Consequently if the content of the certificate is modified, the residual result will be erroneous: The user is not able to adapt her certificate by blinding any information inside.

In our solution, we use a single certificate that mainly contains the user profile, all user access rights and some authentication systems. Yet we define in this model a specific signature method, using specific tags. Thus the user can manage and morph her certificates according to the specific transaction or context. However, some authorized information can be freely masked by the certificate owner far from her home site. In this manner each user extracts a sub-certificate from the original one which only contains needed information for each specific situation.

The challenge is: how each user can customize her static certificates according to a contextual situation?

To solve this problem, we must distinguish The Dynamic Part from the Static Part.

- **The Static Part** is composed of mandatory and non changeable data (ex: the ID of the certificate, the time of validity). These data set up the identity of the certificate.
- **The Dynamic Part** provides sensitive information (e.g., the user name profile, telephone, . . .) and a contextual information (e.g., the device capability, security context, . . .).

To perform the X316 signature algorithm, all dynamic parts in the certificate must be delimited. Thus we define the morph template to perform this signature specification to any types of certificate.

16.7.1.1 Morph Template

The morph template is defined to facilitate and to standardize the creation of the morph signature. Indeed most of certificate formats (X509, PGP, SPKI, etc.) are formatted to express a regular structure and semantic contents. All these standards are conceived to organize in a well-formatted manner. We define the morph template to perform the morph signature process through any certificate formats. The morph template is composed of two sections: The "Credential Type" and the "Dynamic Mask".

- *The Credential Type* The morph signature should be computed through any type of certificate (XML or ANS). This section tells about the type of the signed document. This information is crucial as it defines how it will be parsed.
- *The Dynamic Mask* This section defines the dynamic parts in the signed certificate. For instance, in the X509 certificate, the extensions part or email part can be considered as dynamic parts.

Dynamic Mask Syntax

The dynamic Mask enables to define the parts that are allowed to be hidden. This attribute is expressed by alphanumeric values where:

- The ∗ corresponds to any sequence of alphanumeric values.
- The ? corresponds to one alphanumeric value.
- $(xxx)^{*}$': if the ∗ is put to the power, it implies that the corresponding DP part and all its children parts are considered as a DP parts.

As illustrated in Fig. 16.12, the morph signature has as inputs the certificate and the corresponding template. The morph signature parses the template to recognize the dynamic parts. Then according to the type of the document, the morph signature

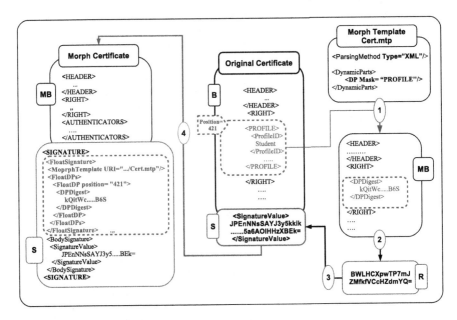

Fig. 16.12 X316 signature

algorithm retrieves all defined dynamic parts and replaces them by their corresponding hash values. Finally, the morph document is generated and the signature can be
computed. Please note that each DP can contain some other DP. In this manner, the
certificate subject is able to hide all the DP parts or a set of sub-parts inside the DP
part. Consequently before computing the global DP part, the digest of all sub DP
parts must be computed recursively. For the sake of clarity, these computed parts
are moved to the float part in the signature (see Fig. 16.12 step 4). To verify the
authenticity of each credential, the remaining DP Digest parts are replaced at their
right position before checking the signature.

16.7.1.2 Float Signature

The Float Signature part is composed of three attributes (Fig. 16.13):

- The Morph Template defines the used template to compute the morph signature.
- The "FloatDP" contains all hidden dynamic parts. Each removable part is defined
  by its corressponding DpDigest value and its position in the original certificate.
- The DP Signature: This optional section allows the certificate user to sign the
  "FloatsDPs" section. This signature permits to check that the X316 is only gen-
  erated by its user.

Example

```
00  <FloatSignature>
01  <MoprphTemplate URI = ``.../X316DP.mtp"/>
02  <FloatDPs>
03    <FloatDP position=``421">
04      <DPDigest>.KQitWc...B6S</DPDigest>
05    </FloatDP>
06  </FloatDPs>
07  <DPSignature>
08    <ds:SignatureMethod Algorithm=``...xmldsig#rsa-sha1"/>
09    <KeyInfo>
10      <KeyValue URI=``#512RSAPubKey">
11    </KeyInfo>
12    <ds:SignatureValue>
13        KU6t7...BFh= </ds:SignatureValue>
14  </DPSignature>
15  </FloatSignature>
```

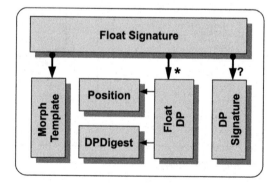

Fig. 16.13 Float signature
part

This example describes the float signature (lines 01–14) with subject signature using the "512RSAPubKey" (line 10).

16.7.2   X316 Encryption

X316 certificate may be transfered along the user travel among different sites where some are trusted and others are not.

Alice wants to access a target site. For her request she must send some sensitive information held in her certificate to the site administrator. Unfortunately she considers the communication protocols unsafe. One solution consists to encrypt these information. If one section in the certificate is ciphered, the scope of the certificate will be limited, allowing only the site that has the cipher key to check the signature.

The morph certificate can solve this problem allowing each user to make safe any information as long as it is delimited by a DP tag. If the certificate is to be transferred to several sites, Alice ciphers the different sensitive information with different keys. Each user can manage her certificate freely; she can cipher any dynamic part, if this one is considered as sensitive.

Therefore, the X316 encryption is defined to allow a user to make confidential any dynamic part inside the certificate. X316 encryption operates like XMLEncryption, with differences. Indeed, the certificate must still be checkable even if some parts are ciphered.

The X316 encryption allows to cipher only the dynamic part. The idea is to put in the cipher part the corresponding hash value of the plain text part. This hash value allows anyone to check the validity of the certificate without knowing the actual content. In fact the morph-transform algorithm replaces all EncryptedDP parts by the corresponding DPDigest of its plain text.

16.7.2.1   X316 Encryption Syntax

```
00  <EncryptedDP>
01     <DPDigest>
02     <ec:EncryptionMethod Algorithm=/>
03     <KeyInfo>
04     <ec:CipherValue>
05  </EncryptedDP>
```

16.7.2.2   EncryptedDP Description

"DPDigest" (Line 01) contains the digest value of the plain text part. When the X316 encryption is used, DPDigest must appear. Indeed the certificate must be checkable by anyone and not only by the recipient.

"EncryptionMethod Algorithm" (Line 02) defines the algorithm used to perform the encryption task. It is defined following W3C recommendation.

The X316 encryption allows using the symmetric and the asymmetric encryption. The difference between these modes is in the "KeyInfo" parameter.

KeyInfo Syntax

```
00   <KeyInfo>
01     <ds:KeyID id= />?
02     <ds:KeyValue>?
03     (<EncryptedKey>
04        <ec:EncryptionMethod Algorithm=/>
05        <KeyInfo>
06        <ec:CipherValue>
07     </EncryptedKey>)?
08   </KeyInfo>
```

KeyInfo Description

The keyInfo contains the description of the key used to cipher the DP part. We define two types of encryption:

- *Symmetric Encryption* In this case, only the KeyId (Line 01) is informed as W3C definition. This identifier allows to recognize and retrieve the used key.
- *Asymmetric Encryption* This mode works with two keys, a public key and a session key (symmetric key). This method of encryption ciphers the plain text with a session key, then, it ciphers it with the public key. Thus, "EncryptedKey" (lines 03–07) are required to inform of the ciphered session key; the line 04 defines the Asymmetric encryption algorithm following W3C recommendation; "KeyInfo" in line 05 defines the public key that is used to cipher the session key. It contains the KeyID (line 01) or the KeyValue (line 02); the line 05 contains the encrypted session key.

Example

We describe here an **asymmetric encryption** using RSA (line 07) with AES (line 04).

```
00   <EncryptedDP>
01     <DPDigest>
02        kQitWcHqiq6rcZopVVpmm/bB6S=
03     </DPDigest>
04     <ec:EncryptionMethod Algorithm=''..#aes128-cbc"/>
05     <KeyInfo>
06        <EncryptedKey>
07        <ec:EncryptionMethod Algorithm=''..xmlenc#rsa-1_5"/>
08        <KeyInfo>
09         <ds:KeyId Id=''YrQkh1zr.2SsoKE1M="/>
10        </KeyInfo>
11        <ec:CipherValue>xizrbc</ec:CipherValue>
```

```
12   </EncryptedKey>
13   </KeyInfo>
14   <ec:CipherValue>
15   G5LyRhgvjChfo0SYiPGWxwPW2
16   </ec:CipherValue>
17 </EncryptedDP>
```

As the "DPDigest" part, the "EncryptedDP" part is placed into the signature float part.

The signature is checked by moving the corresponding "DPDigest" parts to their original positions. Consequently any entity is able to verify the authenticity of the certificate without reading the ciphered part. The entity having the corresponding key can solely decrypt the "CipherValue" part and compare the hash result with the "DPDigest" value to check the validity of the content.

16.7.3 X316 Context

In the X316 framework, the user is allowed to manage her certificate. This procedure is difficult because she must manually choose the corresponding dynamic parts according to context. To help the user we introduce the concept of X316 context. It defines the context profile, e.g., Buying, Selling, Delegation, etc.

Each context profile defines its corresponding parts and indexes the essential parts in the source certificate.

16.7.3.1 X316 Context Syntax

```
00 <X316_Context ID=>
01   <Cx_Profile>
02   <Certificates>
03     (<Certificate>
04       <ID>
05       <Issuer>
06       <Mask>
07         <Value>
08         <Privacy>
09           (<Encryption Digit=>
10             <Subject>
11           </Encryption>)*
12         </Privacy>
13       </Mask>
14     </Certificate>)+
15   </Certificates>
16 </X316_Context>
```

16.7.3.2 X316 Context Description

Each X316 context is defined by a Profile (line 01). Some certificates (lines 02-14) are selected for each context. Each certificate is defined by its ID and a Mask.

The Mask represents the certificate stamp. It is composed of a series of digits (bounded between 0 and n) separated by points, where the nth Mask digit corresponds to the nth DP part (i.e., with respect to its position and order in the certificate) as following:

$$Mask\ digit = \begin{cases} 0 & \text{If the corresponding DP must be hidden} \\ 1 & \text{If the corresponding DP must be disclosed} \\ \geq 2 & \text{If the corresponding DP must be ciphered} \end{cases}$$

In one certificate some DPs parts can be ciphered with different keys. In this case a Mask digit can take several values between 2 and n, where each value (lines 09–12) identifies the entity (subject: line 10) that is able to decipher the encrypted parts.

Example

This example defines a transaction among three actors:
Buyer = "Alice", Seller = "Bob" and the Bank.

- HEADER: ID = "1234" Issuer = "Buyer:Alice" Subject = "Seller:Bob"
- RIGHT:
  - Bob_Profile = "Seller"
  - Capability = Transfer from
    · Alice account **CreditCardNumber = "5487..."** to
    · Bob account BankAccount = "USA ..."
    · the DUE = "400$" for
    · the **OBJECT = "PDA HP HX4700"**.
- AUTHENTICATION: Alice PUBKEY = "RSA 1024".

This certificate must be checked by both Bob and his Bank, but neither Bob should be able to read the Alice "CreditCardNumber", nor the Bank should be able to read the transaction "OBJECT". Therefore in this certificate we define the "CreditCardNumber" and the "OBJECT" as Dynamic Parts. By these means these fields can be secured using the X316 Encryption. The corresponding X316 Context for this transaction follows:

```
00 <X316_Context ID =''3AE456">
01   <Cx_Profile> Buying transaction </Cx_Profile>
02   <Certificates>
03    <Certificate>
04     <ID>1234</ID>
05     <Issuer>Alice</Issuer>
05     <Mask>
06       <Value>2.3</Value>
07       <Privacy>
08         <Encryption Digit=''2">
09           <Subject>Seller's Bank</Subject>
10         </Encryption>
11         <Encryption Digit=''3">
12           <Subject>Seller</Subject>
```

```
13        </Encryption>
14      </Privacy>
15      </Mask>
16    </Certificate>
17  </Certificates>
18 </X316_Context>
```

As illustrated in the X316 context, the first DP "CreditCardNumber" having the first Mask digit = "2" (line 05 and lines 07–09) must be ciphered with the seller's bank key (e.g., Bank's public key). The second DP "OBJECT" corresponding to the mask digit = "3" (line 05 and lines 10–12) must be ciphered with the Seller key (e.g., the session key defined by both Alice and Bob to communicate safely).

16.7.4 Test and Implementation

The X316 signature is more efficient than other approaches. The delimitation of removable parts is fulfilled easily by distinguishing static fields from removable ones. Some tests were implemented to verify the scalability of the X316 morph characteristic: Indeed, as the number of dynamic parts increases, the work to be done to handle encryption and signature increases as well. We selected Visual C# .net for the signature implementation. This ".net" series is very suitable for security programming. It provides a standard and unique API to develop a similar software both for mobile and PC devices. We generated an XML file of 20KByte (it is already a large size for a certificate), and computed the elapsed time to verify the signature by varying the number of dynamic parts (DPs) from 0 to 200. For these tests we have used three type of devices: a smartphone "SPV m3000" (195MHZ CPU), a PDA "HP HX4700" (624MHZ), and a workstation PC intel (3GHZ). The results show that our procedure does not add much work to the devices: As shown in Fig. 16.14, even the SPV M3000 computes the X316 signature within less than 1 s.

16.7.5 X316 Summary

In this section, we have demonstrated the need for a new kind of certificates and we have proposed the X316 certification model. The X316 offers a number of advantages: It allows to embed several authentications into the same certificate, it allows to hide or cypher dynamically parts of the certificate. Moreover, a security toolbox enabling these functionality has been developed and successfully tested.

The algorithm for the computation of the morph signature allowing to hide and cypher parts of a certificate is more general that this scope and can be applied to any kind of digital document appearing in the digital world, from standard XML documents to multimedia documents. We are currently working on this latter adaptation.

R. Saadi et al.

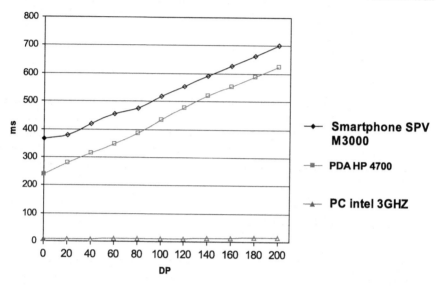

Fig. 16.14 Test and evaluation

16.8 Conclusion and Discussion

After exhibiting some related work and motivation of the need for new research in
the field of security in distributed collaborative environments, we have presented
in this chapter the Chameleon architecture. It allows the user to roam transparently (Table 16.2 C3) in heterogeneous environments (Table 16.2 C1) simply by
using a certification mechanism (X316). The Chameleon using the X316 presents a
number of advantages. Indeed, it consists in a decentralized architecture since each
site, knowing only its neighbors, can perform a large but controlled access to user
communities. Chameleon reduces the human interaction where many security management functions can be processed dynamically. In addition, Chameleon increases
the user rights along her trip without modifying the local site policy by enabling
trust evaluation with corresponding mapping policy (Table 16.2 C4).

We have made the argument that in organizations where there may be multiple
administrators or administrators may change with time, inconsistencies may occur
in the set of trust beliefs of the organization due to variations in the disposition to
trust of the administrators (Table 16.2 C5).

We have presented our access control model based on trust and in the context
of this architecture we have introduced a new method for administrators to establish
the set of trust beliefs which is more likely to be freed from inconsistencies. The key
to this solution is tying the quantification of trust not to the multiple dispositions to
trust of the administrators but to a single disposition to trust of the organization.

Having administrators evaluate the trustworthiness of neighboring nodes in relation to other nodes (trust sort) and using a mapping function (BV function)
for assigning quantitative values are the highlights of the method. One of the

Table 16.2 Comparative of distributed systems

	C1 interoperability of heterogeneous policies	C2 traceability	C3 mobility	C4 trust propagation	C5 disposition to trust	C6 multiple identifications
Shibboleth	Yes	Yes	User	No	No	No
PERMIS	Yes	No	User/service	Delegation	No	No
Sygn	Yes	Yes	User/service	Delegation	No	No
CAS	Yes	No	User/service	Mapping	No	No
TrusrAC	Yes	No	User/service	Trust evaluation	No	No
Chalemeon	Yes	Yes	User/service	Trust evaluation and mapping	Yes	Yes

shortcomings that we recognize in this solution is that the BV function assigns trust values evenly to all the nodes. It doesn't take into consideration that the trust values may not be evenly distributed. Elimination of this shortcoming can be a target for future work.

The certification model is the basis of the authentication in ubiquitous computing. Our model of certificate presents a number of advantages. The X316 provide a hard traceability (Table 16.2 C2) whith embedding a chain of certificates. Furthermore the user can enter unknown sites with various user interfaces (devices) using the same certificate (Table 16.2 C6). We have also introduced a new computing method signature to enrich the certificate adaptability with respect to a contextual situation.

One of the collaborative distributed environments challenges is the fluency of the interaction between the environment and the user. Thanks to the context template with the X316 certificates, we reduce at the minimum the user intervention.

We believe that the proposed method can be adapted to any distributed computing models such as peer-to-peer, ad-hoc networks, grid computing, and pervasive grids.

References

1. A. Abdul-Rahman and S. Hailes. *A distributed Trust Model*. The ACM Workshop on New Security Paradigms, pp 48–60, Sep 1997.
2. Abdul-Rahman A., Hailes S. *Supporting Trust in Virtual Communities*. Hawaii Int. Conference on System Sciences, January 2000.
3. A. Abou El Kalam, R. El Baida, P. Balbiani, S. Benferhat, F. Cuppens, Y. Deswarte, A. Mige, C. Saurel, and G. Trouessin, *Organization Based Access Control*. IEEE 4th International Workshop on Policies for Distributed Systems and Networks. pp 120–131, Jun 2003.
4. M. Al-Kahtani and R. Sandhu, *A Model for Attribute-Based User-Role Assignment*. The 18th Annual Computer Security Applications Conference, pp 353, Dec 2002.
5. F. Almenarez, A. Marin, C. Campo, C. Garcia-Rubio. *PTM: A Pervasive Trust Management Model for Dynamic Open Environments*. In Proc. of the First Workshop on Pervasive Security, Privacy and Trust, PSP'04 in conjunction with Mobiquitous 2004. Boston, MA, USA, August, 2004.

6. F. Almenarez, A. Marin, C. Campo, C. Garcia-Rubio. *TrustAC: Trust-Based Access Control for Pervasive Devices.* Security in Pervasive Computing: Second International Conference, SPC 2005, Boppard, Germany, April 6–8, 2005.

7. F. Almenarez, A. Marin, D. Diaz, and J. Sanchez, *Developing a Model for Trust Management in Pervasive Devices.* In Proc. of the Fourth Annual IEEE International Conference on Pervasive Computing and Communications, 13–17 March, 2006.

8. Bernard Barber. *The Logic and Limits of Trust.* Rutgers University Press, NJ, USA, 1983.

9. M. Bartel, J. Boyer, B. Fox, B. LaMacchia, and E. Simon. *XML-encryption syntax and processing.* In W3C Recommendation. Feb 2002. http://www.w3.org/TR/2002/REC-xmldsig-core-20020212/

10. D. E. Bell. *A Refinement of the Mathematical Model.* Technical Report ESD-TR-278 vol. 3, The Mitre Corp., Bedford, MA, 1973.

11. E. Bertino E, P. A. Bonatti, and E. Ferrari, *TRBAC: A temporal role based access control model.* The fifth ACM workshop on Role-based access control, pp 21–30, Jul 2000.

12. Elisa Bertino, Elena Ferrari, Anna Squicciarini. *Trust-X: A Peer-to-Peer Framework for Trust Establishment.* IEEE Transactions on Knowledge and Data Engineering, 2004.

13. T. Beth, M. Borcherding, and B. Klein. *Valuation of Trust in Open Networks.* The European Symposium on Research in Computer Security, Nov 1994.

14. Stefan Brands. *A technical Overview of Digital Credentials.* Research Report, Feb 2002.

15. L. Bull, P. Stanski, and D. M. Squire. *Content extraction signatures using XML digital signatures and custom transforms on-demand.* In Proceedings of the 12th international Conference on World Wide Web pages 170–177. May 2003.

16. L. Bussard, Y. Roudier, R. Kilian-Kehr, S. Crosta. *Trust and Authorization in Pervasive B2E Scenarios.* 6th Information Security Conference, Oct 2003.

17. Licia Capra. *Engineering Human Trust in Mobile System Collaborations.* In Proc. of the 12th International Symposium on the Foundations of Software Engineering (SIGSOFT 2004), pp. 107–116, November 2004.

18. L. Capra and M. Musolesi. *Autonomic Trust Prediction for Pervasive Systems.* In Proc. of IEEE International Workshop on Trusted and Autonomic Computing Systems (TACS-06), in conjunction with 20th IEEE International Conference on Advanced Information Networking and Applications (AINA 2006), April 2006.

19. Marco Carbone, Mogens Nielsen, and Vladimiro Sassone. *A Formal Model for Trust in Dynamic Networks.* BRICS Report RS-03-4, 2003.

20. Catholijn M. Jonker and Jan Treur. *Formal Analysis of Models for the Dynamics of Trust Based on Experiences.* In Proc. of the 9th European Workshop on Modelling Autonomous Agents in a Multi-Agent World, 1999.

21. D. Chadwick and A. Otenko, *The PERMIS X.509 role based privilege management infrastructure.* The seventh ACM symposium on Access control models and technologies, pp 135–140, 2002.

22. Challenge-response authentication From Wikipedia, the free encyclopedia. http://en.wikipedia.org/wiki/Challenge-response_authentication

23. James Coleman. *Foundations of Social Theory.* Harvard University Press, 1990.

24. Francis Fukuyama. *Trust: The Social Virtues and the Creation of Prosperity.* Free Press, 1995.

25. N. S. Glance, D. Arregui, and M. Dardenne. *Making recommender systems work for organizations.* International Conference on Practical Application of Intelligent Agents and Multi-Agents (PAAM), Apr 1999.

26. R. Guha, Ravi Kumar, Prabhakar Raghavan, and Andrew Tomkins. *Propagation of Trust and Distrust.* In Proceedings of the International World Wide Web Conference, 2004 (WWW2004).

27. M. H. Harrison, W. L. Ruzzo, and J. D. Ullman. *Protection in Operating Systems.* Communications of the ACM, 19(8):461–471, 1976.

28. D. Harrison McKnight, Vivek Choudhury and Charles Kacmar. *Developing and Validating Trust Measures for e-Commerce: An Integrative Typology.* Information Systems Research, September 2002.

29. *ITU-T Simple public key infrastructure* (SPKI) charter, http://www.ietf.org/html.charters/OLD/spki-charter.html.

30. *ITU-T Rec. X.509 (2000)*. ISO/IEC 9594-8 The Directory: Authentication Framework.
31. *ITU-T Rec. X.680 (2002)* ISO/IEC 8824-1:2002, http://asn1.elibel.tm.fr/en/standards/index.htm
32. R. Johnson, D. Molnar, D. Song and D. Wagner, *Homomorphic signature schemes*, Proceeding in Cryptology - CT-RSA 2002, ed. B. Preneel, LNCS 2271, pp. 244–262, 2002.
33. L. Kagal, T. Finin, A. Joshi. *Trust-Based Security in Pervasive Computing Environments*. IEEE Computer, 34(12)154–157, Dec 2001.
34. L. Kagal, T. Finin and Y. Peng, *A Delegation Based Model for Distributed Trust*. Workshop on Autonomy, Delegation, and Control: Interacting with Autonomous Agents, pp 73–80, Aug 2001.
35. R. E. Kalman. *A New Approach to Linear Filtering and Prediction Problems*. Transactions of the ASME - Journal of Basic Engineering, 82(Series D):35-45, 1960.
36. R. Levien and A. Aiken. *Attack Resistant Trust Metrics for Public Key Certification*. In Proc. of the 7th USENIX Security Symposium, pp. 265 -298, January 1998.
37. M. Lorch, D. Adams, D. Kafura, et al. *The PRIMA System for Privilege Management, Authorization and Enforcement*. In Proceedings of the 4th International Workshop on Grid Computing, Nov 2003.
38. Niklas Luhmann. *Trust and Power*. Wiley, Chichester, England, 1979.
39. Marsh, S. *Formalising Trust as a Computational Concept*. Ph.D. Thesis. Department of Mathematics and Computer Science, University of Stirling, Scotland, UK. 1994.
40. S. P. Marsh. *Formalising Trust as a Computational Concept*. PhD thesis, University of Stirling, Apr 1994.
41. S. Micali and R. Rivest L. 2002. *Transitive Signature Schemes*. In Proceedings of the the Cryptographer's Track At the RSA Conference on Topics in Cryptology, Computer Science, vol. 2271. pp 236–243, Feb 2003.
42. X. Orri, J. M. Mas, SPKI-XML Certificate Structure Internet-Draft, Octalis SA, Nov 2001. http://www.ietf.org/internetdrafts/draft-orri-spki-xml-cert-struc-00.txt
43. L. Pearlman, V. Welch, I. Foster, C. Kesselman, and S. Tuecke. *A Community Authorization Service for Group Collaboration*. IEEE 3rd International Workshop on Policies for Distributed Systems and Networks, Jun 2002.
44. R. Saadi, J. M. Pierson, L. Brunie. *(Dis)trust Certification Model for Large Access in Pervasive Environment*. JPCC International Journal of Pervasive Computing and Communications. Volume 1, Issue 4, pp 289–299. Oct 2005.
45. Rachid Saadi, Jean-Marc Pierson and Lionel Brunie. *Context Adapted Certificate Using Morph Template Signature for Pervasive Environments*. The International Symposium on Ubiquitous Computing Systems (UCS 2007), Nov 2007.
46. R. Sandhu, E. J. Coyne, H. L. Feinstein, and al. *Role-Based Access Control Models*. IEEE Computer, 29(2):38–47, 1996.
47. Sant, P. and Maple, C. *A Graph Theoretic Framework for Trust - From Local to Global*. Information Visualization, July 2006.
48. Dana S. Scott. *Domains for Denotational Semantics*. ICALP '82 - LNCS, 140, 1982.
49. *Shibboleth*, url : "http://shibboleth.internet2.edu".
50. L. Seitz, J. M. Pierson and L. Brunie. *Semantic Access Control for Medical Applications in Grid Environments*. A International Conference on Parallel and Distributed Computing, pp 374–383, Aug 2003 *Shibboleth*, url : "http://shibboleth.internet2.edu".
51. N. Shankar, W. Arbaugh. *On Trust for Ubiquitous Computing*. Workshop on Security in Ubiquitous Computing, Sep 2004.
52. *Shibboleth architecture, technical overview*, url: "http://shibboleth.internet2.edu/docs/draft-mace-shibboleth-tech-overview-latest.pdf".
53. R. Steinfeld, L. Bull and Y. Zheng; *Content Extraction Signatures*. In Proceedings of 4th International Conference of Information Security and Cryptology. pages 285–2004. Dec 2001.
54. M. R. Thompson, A. Essiari, and S. Mudumbai 2003. *Certificate-based authorization policy in a PKI environment*. ACM Trans. Inf. Syst. Secur. 6, 4, pp 566–588, Nov 2003.
55. J. Watt and O. Ajayi and J. Jiang and J. Koetsier and R. O. Sinnott. *A Shibboleth-Protected Privilege Management Infrastructure for e-Science Education*, The Sixth IEEE International Symposium on Cluster Computing and the Grid, pp 357–364, 2006.

56. V. Welch, F. Siebenlist, I. Foster, J. Bresnahan, K. Czajkowski, J. Gawor, C. Kesselman, S. Meder, L. Pearlman, S. Tuecke. *Security for Grid Services*. Twelfth International Symposium on High Performance Distributed Computing, Jun 2003.
57. M. Winslett, T. Yu, K. E. Seamons, A. Hess, J. Jacobson, R. Jarvis, B. Smith, L. Yu, *Negotiating trust in the Web*. IEEE Internet Computing, Nov/Dec 2002.
58. P. R. Zimmermann. *The Official PGP User's Guide*. MIT Press, Cambridge, MA, USA, 1995.

Chapter 17
A Low-Cost and Secure Solution for e-Commerce

Marc Pasquet, Delphine Vacquez, and Christophe Rosenberger

Abstract We present in this paper a new architecture for remote banking and e-commerce applications. The proposed solution is designed to be low cost and provides some good guarantees of security for a client and his bank issuer. Indeed, the main problem for an issuer is to identify and authenticate one client (a cardholder) using his personal computer through the web when this client wants to access to remote banking services or when he wants to pay on a e-commerce site equipped with 3D-secure payment solution. The proposed solution described in this paper is MasterCard Chip Authentication Program compliant and was experimented in the project called SOPAS. The main contribution of this system consists in the use of a smartcard with a I2C bus that pilots a terminal only equipped with a screen and a keyboard. During the use of services, the user types his PIN code on the keyboard and all the security part of the transaction is performed by the chip of the smartcard. None information of security stays on the personal computer and a dynamic token created by the card is sent to the bank and verified by the front end. We present first the defined methodology and we analyze the main security aspects of the proposed solution.

17.1 Introduction

Web offers nowadays many services to an individual such as information delivering, online games and also e-commerce. E-commerce is currently one of the most challenging issue in computer science. Many clients buy some products on Internet

---

M. Pasquet (✉) and C. Rosenberger
Laboratoire GREYC, UMR 6072, ENSICAEN, Université de Caen Basse Normandie,
CNRS, 6 boulevard Maréchal Juin, F-14020 Caen, France
e-mail: marc.pasquet@ensicaen.fr; christophe.rosenberger@ensicaen.fr

D. Vacquez
DRI (Department of Industrial Relationships), ENSICAEN, 6 boulevard Maréchal Juin,
F-14020 Caen, France
e-mail: delphine.vacquez@ensicaen.fr

R. Chbeir et al., *Emergent Web Intelligence: Advanced Information Retrieval*, Advanced   455
Information and Knowledge Processing, DOI 10.1007/978-1-84996-074-8_17,
© Springer-Verlag London Limited 2010

by using their smartcards. As for example, in France, 46% of smartcards owners used it for e-commerce in 2006. An important limitation of e-commerce is that many individuals are not confident on the payment process on the Web. Indeed, only three types of information are usually necessary to make an authentication for an e-payment:

- Smartcard number
- Expiration date
- CVX2 number (Visual Cryptogram) on the back of the card

Note that this information can be obtained by looking at the smartcard during less than 1 min. The knowledge of these data is absolutely not a proof you own the smartcard. Fraud exists on e-commere mainly because of this authentication step.

A second limitation concerns the e-commerce architecture to guarantee classical security concepts (confidentiality, authentication, integrity, ...) during the transaction [1, 8]. Many e-payment architectures have been proposed in the last decade [3, 9, 10]. Nethertheless, very few of them have been used in real conditions for e-commerce. The major reason is that the proposed solution must be supported by major card schemes such as Mastercard and Visa. In the following, we present two solutions that were defined within this context.

To limit the risk that the customer can repudiate his payment transaction, a set of companies (Visa, MasterCard, GTE, IBM, Microsoft, Netscape, SAIC, Terisa system, Verisign) have developed, in the eighties one solution call SET (Secure Electronic Transaction) [13]. The customers bank sends him one certificate issued from one CA (Certification authority) of a PKI (Public Key Infrastructure) which is stored on his computer. When he wants to realize a payment on the Web, the customer must sign with the PKI keys [16].

Another solution for electronic payments is 3D secure [18] developed by Visa and used by Mastercard. The commercial trademarks are "Secure Code" for MasterCard and "Verified by Visa" for Visa. The term 3D is the contraction of "Three Domains":

- Acquiring domain (acquiring bank and merchant)
- Issuer domain including the customer authentication
- Interbank field which makes it possible the two other fields to communicate on Internet

The client realizes his purchase on a merchant's Website that is 3D-secure compliant and click on the payment icon ("MasterCard SecureCode" or "Verified by Visa"). He is invited to enter his card scheme, card number and expiration date (see Fig. 17.1). The MPI (Merchant Plug-In) installed in the merchant's website, contacts the Visa or MCI directory to obtain the Internet address of the issuer. Then, using the client's personal computer, the MPI contacts the issuer with a formal PAReq (Payer Authentication Request) message. The client's authentication is under the bank responsibility. When that last task is realized, the bank issuer answers to the MPI of the merchant's website with a formal PARes (Payer Authentication

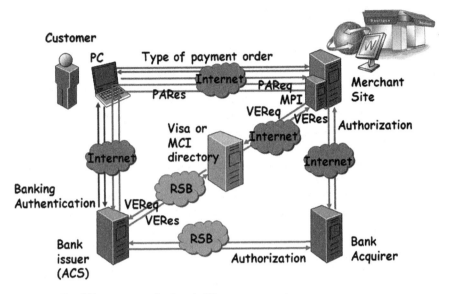

Fig. 17.1   The different communications in 3D-secure payment

Response) message. The MPI sends an authorization request to the acquiring bank which transmits it to the issuer which will answer with an authorization number. The last dialog is realized to be completely EMV compliant (Europay MasterCard and Visa). EMV defines the international standards for chip payment cards. EMV standards are maintained by EMVCo [4].

The most important challenge today in the 3D-secure architecture for a bank issuer, is to authenticate one client with as many guarantees as possible with the lowest cost [17]. In fact, with 3D-secure, the authentication problem from the customer/merchant domain is replaced by the customer/issuing bank domain. Many solutions have been proposed in the literature [5, 14]. The main drawback of these solutions is that they do not exploit the only secure object a client owns that is to say the smartcard.

The goal of the SOPAS project in which we are involved in, is to propose a new e-transaction architecture using the smartcard. The objective is then to develop a secure and a low-cost solution that can be attractive for banks considering security and commercial issues. In this chapter, we detail the SOPAS solution. We show the security analysis we made to validate the proposed architecture and the reasons why we think this solution can be supported by major card schemes.

The chapter is organized as follows. We describe in the second section, the proposed architecture defined within the SOPAS project [12]. In the third section, we focus on the security issues of the proposed solution. Conclusions and perspectives of this work are given in the section four.

17.2 The Proposed Solution

The idea of the SOPAS project is to fulfill two services for one client. The first one is the payment on an e-commerce site equipped with a 3D-secure payment solution. The second service deals with remote banking and concerns the use of a personal computer by a client through the web to access to his bank account and to realize different operations (consultation or bank transfers for example). We think that the proposed solution must allow this last service for economical reasons. A bank could be ready to adopt the solution even it will cost some more money if it can offer an additional service for a client. Remote banking is generally a service that is rarely free for a client. A more secure remote banking could be more expensive for a client but will provide also some more secure e-commerce possibilities. We present in the next subsection some more details on targeted services by the SOPAS project.

17.2.1 Objectives

First, we have in particular to fulfill the client needs to use Internet to carry out its remote banking operations. Today, implemented solutions have the main drawback to be based on a password authentication that is not really secure [15]. Thus, the SOPAS project has two major objectives:

- To gain the user's confidence
- To provide a secure solution whose cost of deployment is as cheap as possible

The client must be able to realize different operations such as those detailed in Table 17.1.

These transactions are very sensitive if we consider the financial impacts of an uncontrolled use. So, before any access to a banking site, a preliminary authentication is required. When the client is authenticated, the remote banking site proposes all the possible operations.

For certain operations realized by the client, it could be necessary:

- To protect against all alterations during the transaction exchanges between the client and the bank
- To guaranty the good achievement of the transaction of a client
- To have the clients agreement proof

Table 17.1 Remote banking operations

Operations	Examples
Standard operations	Consultation, transfer, direct debit
Credits	Consummation credit, real estate credit
Assurance	Assurances subscriptions for cars, home
Saving and Shares	Opening of a saving account, stock buying and selling

All that objectives (authentication, integrity, good achievement and clients agreement proof) can be realized by question/answer mechanisms:

- The bank generates a question and the client uses a personal device to generate an answer to the bank.
- The bank verifies this answer for the authentication process or to validate the transaction.

Second, one client must be able to make a payment on e-commerce websites in an easy and a secure way. We assume here that the merchant is 3D-secure compliant. This is not a strong hypothesis as it is supported by Mastercard and Visa.

17.2.2 General Principles

We propose to use three elements in order to guarantee the client's authentication for remote banking and for 3D-secure compliant e-commerce:

1. *Smartcard* A client is also a cardholder. This smartcard is considered by the banks as to be very secure. It has been personalized by the issuer bank with cryptographic keys to achieve many secure operations. The belonging of this smartcard and the knowledge of the PIN code by the cardholder gives some good guarantees for the bank issuer for the cardholder's authentication.
2. *Personal Device* the personal computer is not a secure environment for a strong authentication of the cardholder. We propose to use a separate device as an interface between the smartcard and the personal computer. This personal device must be very secure and low cost. The solution is here to use a box just equipped with a 2×12 figures screen, a 4×4 buttons keyboard, a card reader without any chip. It is the smartcard itself which pilots directly the personal device by its I2C bus and communicates with the personal computer by its USB bus. This solution is very different than the ones which use a device which is able to compute. Here, the "intelligence" and the security of this personal device is completely delegated to the smartcard. When the smartcard is not connected to the personal device, this one has no secret at all and can be produced everywhere in the world at a very low cost.
3. *CAP (Chip Authentication Program) [11]* CAP provides online chip-based cardholder authentication within the SecureCode program. It encompasses the chip application, the terminal, and the issuer server used in the authentication process, and the interfaces between these components. When the smartcard is inserted in the personal device, the cardholder is invited to enter his PIN code on the keyboard. The PIN code goes directly to the smartcard. The smartcard computes a token that is sent to the bank issuer via the personal device, the computer and the network without any modification.

Such a solution makes it possible to guarantee a complete security of the access to remote bank applications via Internet, ready to develop the confidence of the users.

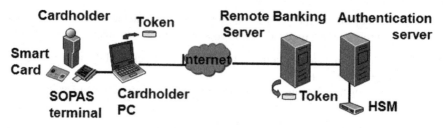

Fig. 17.2 SOPAS solution for remote banking

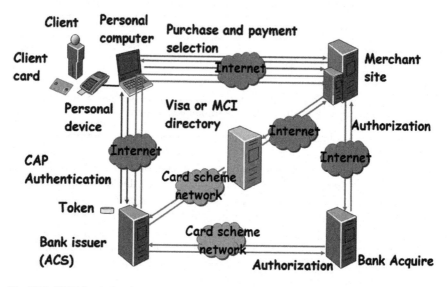

Fig. 17.3 SOPAS solution for e-commerce

Figure 17.2 shows the SOPAS scheme for a remote banking application. The user has a SOPAS smartcard and a SOPAS personal device giving him access to the service. The user proves with the card that he is the legitimate cardholder by entering his PIN code. The card generates a token call "CAP token" which is used as authentication proof by the user to his bank. The generated token is transferred from the card to the user's personal computer via the personal device, then, to the front end of the bank via the Internet network. This device is currently not used to require the user's assent at the time of a significant banking operation (as in case of purchase stock for example). Indeed, the device would make it possible to seal a transaction; this seal is for the bank a proof of the user's assent.

The SOPAS solution is used mainly to authenticate the user to his bank. This solution, based primarily on the concepts of CAP authentication (MasterCard), should moreover be easily transposable everywhere in the world. Figure 17.3 shows the SOPAS solution for e-commerce applications within the 3D secure architecture.

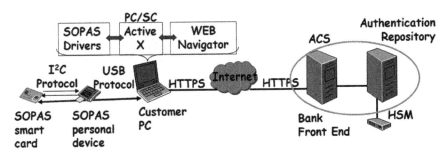

Fig. 17.4   Interface protocols

17.2.3   Interface Protocols

The protocol used for the authentication is of challenge/answer type. The bank sends a random number to the card which turns over a token function of the received random number. This mechanism avoids the attack by replay, contrary to the systems of authentication having a static signature. Figure 17.4 illustrates the communication protocols used with the interfaces of the various entities intervening in the proposed solution.

We can highlight the different parts of the Fig. 17.4:

- The SOPAS Card communicates directly with the personal device (equipped with a keyboard and a LCD screen) by a different interface than which is used to communicate with the personal computer. The protocol used is then I2C [7]. This is particularly important from the security point of view of the solution. This bus makes it possible the card to interact directly with its cardholder by presenting him some information via the LCD screen and while requiring some information (like his PIN code) via the keyboard of the personal device. These two operations thus do not require the intervention of the personal computer which is considered as a non secure element.
- The SOPAS card communicates directly with the user's personal computer with the USB protocol via the personal device.
- The user's personal computer is exchanging information with the front end of the issuer bank using HTTPS protocol because the network is Internet.

17.2.4   Architecture

The following diagram (see Fig. 17.5) details the architecture and the relationships between the card and the personal device. We can observe that the USB and I2C bus allows the card, either to communicate with the customer's personal computer via the USB interface, or to communicate directly with the personal device in order to reach its keyboard and its screen.

Fig. 17.5 SOPAS
architecture

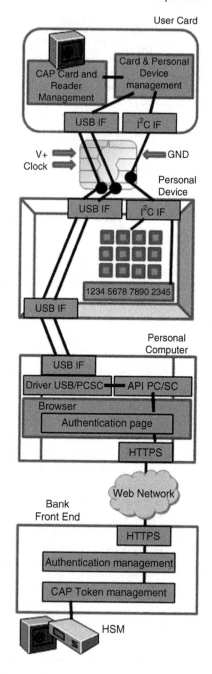

The second circuit (I2C bus) strongly takes part in the security solution. The CAP token is calculated by the card, after the PIN code verification, then sends via the different devices without any modification and controlled by the HSM (Hardware Security Module) connected to the Bank Front End. So, only the two secure devices (Card and HSM) are able to calculate or verify the Token.

17.3 Security Analysis

The objective of this section is to provide an analysis of the SOPAS solution as regarding the security aspects. We study the whole chain in order to determine the potential risks and in order to validate the SOPAS solution. It also provides us to determine some associated countermeasures. This analysis can lead us to possible modifications of the specifications of the final solution. This is particularly justified by different attacks (phishing and pharming) against remote banking services and the different well known attacks in e-commerce and e-payment. We show that these attacks are completely identified within the framework of this analysis. It appears that the SOPAS solution, in addition to being a solution of customer's authentication by his bank, is also a good solution for the bank authentication by the customer, making thus inoperative the previous attacks.

17.3.1 Methodology

To realize that study, we have used the EBIOS method [2]. We used a software tool developed by Central Information Systems Security Division (France) in order to support the EBIOS method. This tool helps the user to produce the risk analysis and management steps according the "five EBIOS steps" method (see Fig. 17.6) and allows all the study results to be recorded and the required summary documents to be produced. The EBIOS tool is open source and free. Different steps are defined in the EBIOS method:

- **Step 1** Context Study: The main purpose is to identify different elements such as targeted system, general information, context of use and involved entities. We have here to determine the security domains linked to the owner of the assets to protect. This essential stage has several objectives:

  1. To present the totality of the security environment in which the target of this study is included
  2. To localize the target of the study in its environment and to define precisely the limits of the security study
  3. To precise the perimeter of the target of the study
  4. To analyze the interfaces and the transactions to allow identifying the assets to protect (the data, the treatments, and the entity of the security target)

Fig. 17.6 EBIOS
methodology

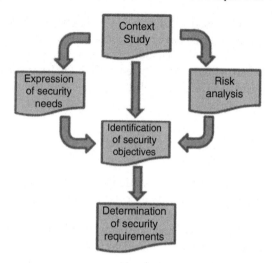

At the end of this first step, the security target is clearly identified, through the
data and transactions which are realized and the entity which are manipulated
there.

- **Step 2**   Expression of security needs on the essential elements: This phase
  makes it possible to estimate the risks, the risk criteria definition, and to express
  the sensitivity of the essential elements face to the respect of the system-targeted
  missions.
- **Step 3**   The purpose here is to identify the risks by studying the threat sources
  then to analysis the risks: study of vulnerabilities and risk evaluation by the
  formalization of threats on the essential elements. The threats are formalized
  by identifying their components (attack methods to which the organization is
  exposed, the elements threatening which can be employed, exploitable vulnerabilities on the entities of the system and their risk level).
- **Step 4**   This phase allows to determine the risk treatments (identification of
  security objectives), the risk acceptance (list of residual risks) and the risk communication (reports produced for every step of the method). The confrontation
  of the threats to the security needs makes it possible to highlight the risks.
- **Step 5**   The purpose is the determination of security requirements. It is a question here of indexing the technical and organizational possible countermeasures
  making it possible to cover, at least partially, these incurred risks.
- **Step 6**   At the end of the method, one particular step can be added. The task
  consists in realizing the list of residual risks starting from the assumption that
  countermeasures can cover only partially the risk.

17.3.2   Hypothesis

In order to proceed the security analysis, we need to make some hypothesis and define its domain.

The card operating system follows the safety requirements evaluated according to the common criteria method [6]. During the personalization of the card, the later remote applet loading is blocked. The card and the personal device are delivered by the bank, and the card delivery follows the standard bank card protocol (security requirement) and is delivered in a face to face situation by the bank. The delivering of the PIN is sent to the cardholder by the standard PIN mailer procedure.

Due to its cost, the personal device is an object which cannot be repaired and which is the subject to a standard exchange in the case of problems (in that eventuality, the material has to be destroyed). The cardholder uses the SOPAS architecture in a personal environment and known conditions in a standard use (for example without a company network environment). The personal computer operating system is an area of risk whose protection is out of the study perimeter. The remote banking server (software and hardware) follows completely the security bank requirements. The bank is supposed to have correctly dimensioned and protected its architecture against mass attacks. The contract aspect between the cardholder and the bank must be reviewed by the bank lawyer and are not covered by this study. The SOPAS smartcard is not only a debit or credit card but includes also a CAP capability. Table 17.2 sums up the different hypothesis for the security analysis.

17.3.3   Results

The total perimeter includes the following security domains: the user, the SOPAS smartcard, the personal device (with its screen and keyboard), the link between the

Table 17.2 Hypothesis

No.	Hypothesis
1	After the initial card personalization, remote applet loading is impossible
2	The card and the personal device are provided by the bank
3	The card OS is "common criteria" compliant
4	The card is delivered in a face to face procedure by the bank, and the PIN is sent by mail in a special letter which occults these numbers
5	The PIN is calculated and is not stored by the personalizing machine
6	A broken personal device will not be repaired (but destroyed) and only exchanged (standard exchange)
7	The cardholder will use the smartcard and the personal device in a home environment
8	The personal computer is a risky zone and is out of the study perimeter
9	The equipments (hardware and software) concerning the bank (ACS and Authentication repository) are compliant with the banking standards

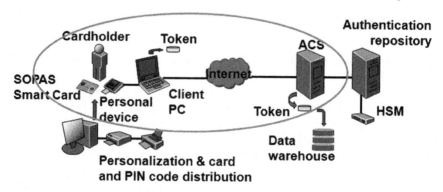

Fig. 17.7 Study perimeter

personal device, the client personal computer, the client personal computer, the bank server, the link between the bank server and the client personal computer. That can be transformed in elementary functional blocks:

- Hardware: personal smartcard, personal computer device, bank servers
- Individual: cardholder
- Organizations: bank, card personalization company
- Networks: USB network, I2C network, Internet
- Software: card operating system, Java card application, Proxy + PC/SC driver, Web browser, bank server, 3D-secure server

These components, directly concerned by the SOPAS solution, appeared in the top left hand in blue in Fig. 17.7. The total perimeter of the study is represented by an ellipse in Fig. 17.7. The red entities inside the perimeter are those whose risks are excluded by the assumptions or whose countermeasures do not concern directly the SOPAS solution. As for example, the SOPAS solution cannot ensure that the personal computer is free from any virus software. We also cannot ensure that remote banking server is suitably configured, dimensioned, ... Nevertheless, for the red elements belonging to the perimeter, the analysis will be able, if necessary, to propose a countermeasure.

The perimeter of this study integrates the data processing sequence of the authentication, from the card to the interface of the banking server. Before using the SOPAS smartcard, procedures of personalization and distribution are necessary. Although, these last do not belong to the perimeter of the SOPAS solution.

The study of the vulnerabilities that we realized enables us to formulate a list of risks associated by the essential elements. The transformation of these risks in scenario makes it possible to better evaluate them and judge their gravity. In this study, we formulated 19 risks. The majority of them concerns the banking data of the user or the technical information allowing the authentication of the customer by his bank.

The incurred risks taken into account in the Ebios list are

- Lost of essential services: the telecommunication network breaks down
- The information system is compromised: interception of the electromagnetic signal coming from the card and the personal device, distance spying, passive listening, stolen document, waste support recovering, divulgation, use of non certified documents, equipment trapping
- Technical failures: hardware and software failures
- Forbidden action: forbidden use of the equipment, deterioration of banking data, software modification, illicit processing of data
- Errors: use errors, abuse of use, identity usurpation, action disavowal

During this study, a certain number of threats have been identified. The threats that have been retained are those which have a direct impact on the authentication mechanism. Additional threats, mainly on the remote banking server (except the authentication function) were sometimes retained because it will have been judged that the SOPAS smartcard and the SOPAS personal device could thwart these last. They are mainly the threats and risks induced by the use of a personal computer to which remote banking services cannot grant its confidence. Indeed, it is not rare that the computer has been infected by a Trojan horse and became victim of the well known technique like the pharming.

It was shown during the study that the SOPAS solution makes it possible to cover the risks thus identified by associating to it a functionality of checking the banking server certificate. That prohibits a fraudulent site to be recognized as being the bank. The user's personal computer not being confident, it is of primary importance so, on one hand, the checking of the server certificate must be embedded in the smartcard and, on the other hand, the result of this checking must be shown on the personal device screen.

Finally, the risk of disavowal an action was retained because the authentication of a user does not have any value of assent on an action realized between the beginning and the end of the connection. This implies the need for the user to sign each remote banking operations (of a sufficient amount). The signature functionality is in fact already present in the SOPAS smartcard but is just used for the user authentication by the bank.

This analysis also showed that, so far as we suppose that the user personal computer is safe (what is not the case but that nevertheless is set as assumption), the encryption of the communications between the SOPAS smartcard and the user personal computer is not necessary. Indeed, the messages forwarding between these two devices are challenge/answer type, and are secure by that way. Coding from beginning to end would be a solution to mitigate the vulnerability of the personal computer which, by the presence of the malevolent programs, could deteriorate the banking data. This solution is however not realistic since at one time or another, the banking data must be posted on the screen of the personal computer.

To conclude this part, the SOPAS smartcard decreases the risks induced by the potential vulnerabilities of the personal computer. Indeed, the secrecies of a connection of the user cannot be recovered any more by a simple keylogger or other spyware and attacks it by replay is not more exploitable. The use of a certificate embedded in the smartcard and the checking of the bank certificate by the SOPAS smartcard could further decrease the risks induced by phishing and pharming techniques. Nevertheless, the use of a personal computer that is not controlled (by the bank) remains the Achilles'heel of this service. Recurring problems here are found: how to protect data in an hostile environment?

17.4 Conclusion and Perspectives

The SOPAS solution is made up of a personal device (card reader, screen and keyboard pilot via the I2C bus by the card) and a smartcard (Multi applicative card with the embedded SOPAS solution and standard EMV), the cost of the card is a little bit more expensive than a standard EMV chip card (6–8 euros) but the personal device is very cheap (10–20 euros). This makes it possible for the bank to deliver cards and personal devices to their clients interested for secure remote banking services and e-commerce.

Thus, the equipped user is able to generate a "CAP token" that he transmits to the bank like an authentication value, when he wishes to reach his remote banking services or to pay on the Web. The bank is convinced to deal with the right person because the smartcard, before generating the token, requires from the customer to enter his PIN code (known only by the card and the cardholder), thus resolving the problem of the CAP token generation.

The security analysis of that solution shows that if we consider the limits created by the use of a unsecure personal computer, the SOPAS approach is a very good and secure solution compared to its deployment price.

There are some perspectives of this work. Two main changes are possible in order to limit the possibility for the user to repudiate his action:

- To oblige the user to sign each remote banking operations (or of a sufficient amount).
- To use different CAP Token generation options: In the Cap protocol, it is optionally possible to include the transaction amount and currency in the CAP transaction. This option is indicated by a flag in the card application, bit 8 of the IAF (Internet Authentication Flags).

Acknowledgments Authors would like to thank all SOPAS project members: Alliansys, Credit Mutuel, Cartes Bancaires, Fime, Gemalto, the Basse-Normandie Region, and the French Ministry of Industry (DGE), for their kind cooperation.

References

1. Anderson, R. (1994) Why Cryptosystems Fail. Communications of the ACM. pp. 32–41 ftp://ftp.cl.cam.ac.uk/users/ rja14/wcf.ps.gz.
2. DCSSI (2004) EBIOSV2: expression of needs and identification of security objectives
3. Ekelhart, A., Fenz, S., Tjoa, A.M., Weippl, E.R. (2007) Security Issues for the Use of Semantic Web in E-Commerce. BIS 2007, LNCS 4439, Springer-Verlag, pp. 1–13.
4. EMVCO (2000) EMV specifications http://www.emvco.com/specifications.cfm
5. Khu-smith, V., Mitchell, C.J. (2003) Enhancing E-commerce Security Using GSM Authentication Vorapranee, EC-Web 2003, LNCS 2738, pp. 7283, Springer-Verlag Berlin Heidelberg.
6. ISO (2006) ISO/CEI 15408 Version 3.1 Common Criteria for Information Technology Security Evaluation.
7. ISO 7816 (1995) Standardization of smartcards.
8. Katsikas, S. K., Lopez, J., Pernul, G. (2005) Trust, Privacy and Security in E-Business: Requirements and Solutions, PCI, Lecture Notes in Computer Science 3746, pp. 548–558, Springer-Verlag Berlin Heidelberg.
9. Kleist, V.F. (2004) A Transaction Cost Model of Electronic Trust: Transactional Return, Incentives for Network Security and Optimal Risk in the Digital Economy. Electronic Commerce Research, vol. 4, pp. 41–57.
10. Konar, D., Mazumdar, C. (2006) An Improved E-Commerce Protocol for Fair Exchange. ICD-CIT 2006, LNCS 4317, Springer-Verlag, pp. 305–313.
11. MasterCard (2004) Chip Authentication Program Functional Architecture.
12. Pasquet, M., Vacquez, D., Rosenberger, C. (2008) "SOPAS: A Low-cost and Secure Solution For E-Commerce", Workshop on Security and High Performance Computing Systems, IEEE High Performance Computing Systems Conference.
13. Pasquet, M., Rosenberger, C., Cuozzo, F. (2008) "Security for electronic commerce", Encyclopedia of Information Science and Technology, 2nd edition, Vol. 4, 14 pages.
14. Payeras-Capell, M.M., Ferrer-Gomila, J.L., Huguet-Rotger, L. (2005) Anonymous Payment in a Fair E-commerce Protocol with Verifiable TTP, TrustBus, Lecture Notes in Computer Science 3592, pp. 60–69, Springer-Verlag Berlin Heidelberg.
15. Pfitzmann, A. (1997) Trusting Mobile User Devices and Security Modules. Computer, pp. 61–68.
16. Rennhard, M., Rafaeli, S., Mathy, L., Plattner, B., Hutchison, D. (2004) Towards Pseudonymous e-Commerce. Electronic Commerce Research, Springer, vol. 4, pp. 83–111.
17. Schlaeger, C., Pernul, G. (2005) Authentication and Authorisation Infrastructures in b2c e-Commerce, EC-Web, Lecture Notes in Computer Science 3590, pp. 306–315, Springer-Verlag Berlin Heidelberg.
18. Visa Corporation. (2001) 3DSecure Functional Specification, Chip Card Specification v1.0.

Chapter 18
Hyperchaotic Encryption for Secure E-Mail Communication

**A.Y. Aguilar-Bustos, C. Cruz-Hernández, R.M. López-Gutiérrez,
E. Tlelo-Cuautle, and C. Posadas-Castillo**

Abstract In this chapter, secure computer communication based on synchronized hyperchaotic maps is presented. In particular, we appeal to model-matching approach from nonlinear control theory to synchronize the outputs of two coupled hyperchaotic Rössler maps. An application to secure e-mail communication for confidential information is given. By using a hyperchaotic encryption scheme, we show that output synchronization of hyperchaotic Rössler maps is indeed suitable for encryption, transmission, and decryption of information.

18.1 Introduction

In order to protect the confidential information for communication and database systems, it is well-known that *cryptography* is a suitable resource [4, 20, 33, 36, 38]. Recently, chaotic encryption to address the secure communication problem has

A.Y. Aguilar-Bustos
Ensenada Technological Institute, Boulevard Tecnológico S.N., México
e-mail: yaveni@hotmail.com

C. Cruz-Hernández (✉)
Electronics and Telecommunications Department, CICESE, Carretera Ensenada-Tijuana No. 3918, Ensenada, B.C. 22860, México
e-mail: ccruz@cicese.mx

R.M. López-Gutiérrez
Engineering Faculty, UABC, Km. 103 Carretera Tijuana-Ensenada, Ensenada, B.C. 22860, México
e-mail: roslopez@uabc.mx

E. Tlelo-Cuautle
Electronics Department, INAOE, Luis Enrique Erro No. 1, Tonantzintla, Puebla 72840, México
e-mail: etlelo@inaoep.mx

C. Posadas-Castillo
Engineering Mechanic and Electric Faculty, UANL, Pedro de Alba S.N., Cd., San Nicolas de los Garza, NL, México
e-mail: cposadas@fime.uanl.mx

R. Chbeir et al., *Emergent Web Intelligence: Advanced Information Retrieval*, Advanced Information and Knowledge Processing, DOI 10.1007/978-1-84996-074-8_18,
© Springer-Verlag London Limited 2010

received a great deal of attention. High sensitivity of chaotic systems to initial conditions and parameters, implies strong cryptographic properties for encryption, which makes them robust against attacks of enemies, spies, interceptors, cryptanalysts, etc.

Most recent publications on secure chaotic communications use analog physical electronic circuits and attempt to develop a real-time system, see, e.g., [9, 11, 12, 14, 15, 21, 22, 29, 43]. Nowadays, most communications is via digital computers and even real-time communication systems are mostly digital not analog.

Synchronization of chaos and hyperchaos has received a lot of attention in last decades [7, 21, 23, 26, 27, 32], this interest increases by practical applications in different fields, particularly in secure communications. Chaos synchronization can be used in different ways for encoding confidential information in private communications. However, in subsequent works, see, e.g., [3, 28, 34] it have been shown that encrypted information by means of comparatively "simple" chaos – with only one positive Lyapunov exponent – does not ensure a sufficient security level. For higher security purpose, *hyperchaotic dynamics* – characterized by more than one positive Lyapunov exponents – are advantageous over simple chaotic dynamics. Two factors of primordial importance in security considerations related to chaotic communication are *(i) the dimension of the attractor* and *(ii) the effort required to obtain the necessary parameters for the matching of a receiver dynamics.*

On the basis of these considerations, one way to enhance the level of encryption security is by applying proper *cryptographic techniques* to the information in *combination with chaotic encryption schemes* [10, 39]. Another way is to encode information by using *high dimensional chaotic attractors,* or *hyperchaotic attractors*, which take advantage of the increased randomness and unpredictably of the higher dimensional dynamics. In this case, one generally encounters *multiple positive Lyapunov exponents.* However, hyperchaos synchronization is a much more difficult problem, see, e.g., [1, 8, 16, 17, 24, 37, 42]. The level of security is also enhanced by using *chaos modeled by delayed differential equations,* such systems have an infinite-dimensional state space, and produce hyperchaotic dynamics with an *arbitrarily large number of positive Lyapunov exponents* [9, 12, 35].

The aim of this chapter is to present a cryptosystem for secure e-mail communications to transmit encrypted audio and image messages, which is based on synchronized hyperchaotic Rössler maps. This objective is achieved by appealing to nonlinear control theory, in particular, we use the model-matching approach given in [2]. This approach presents several advantages over the existing synchronization methods reported in the current literature [2, 21, 23].

We apply output synchronization of hyperchaotic Rössler maps to encrypt, transmit, and decrypt confidential audio and image messages for e-mail communication.

The sections of this chapter are organized as follows: In Section 18.2, secure e-mail computer communication is described. In Section 18.3, the proposed hyperchaotic cryptosystem is presented. In Section 18.4, a brief summary on output synchronization of hyperchaotic maps is provided. By using computer simulations, the approach used is explained by means of the hyperchaotic Rössler map in Section 18.5. An application of output synchronization to secure e-mail communications is illustrated in Section 18.6. The chapter is concluded with some remarks in Section 18.7.

18.2 Description

We describe our hyperchaotic encryption scheme in a current Internet transmission among remote computers. In this scenario, in the transmitter computer and in each receiver computers were installed the output synchronization program (software), the transmission of hyperchaotic encrypted audio and image messages; which are transmitted through common e-mail among computer networks. Such messages are decrypted in an exact fashion in a remote network of the receiver computers. Figure 18.1 illustrates the secure computer communications for real-time digital communication systems via e-mail. The cryptosystem is composed by three processes: (i) hyperchaotic encryption, (ii) hyperchaotic synchronization, and (ii) hyperchaotic decryption. In next sections, we explain each process to achieve the secure computer communications.

18.3 Hyperchaotic Cryptosystem

In this section, a cryptosystem based on synchronized hyperchaotic (three-dimensional) maps is described. The aim is to transmit encrypted messages from computer A to remote computer B (the so-called *authorized* communicating

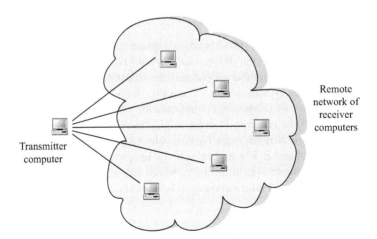

Fig. 18.1 Secure communications among remote computer networks via e-mail

Fig. 18.2 Secure
communication scheme based
on hyperchaotic encryption
for remote computers
A and B

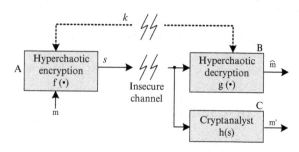

Fig. 18.2 Secure communication scheme based on hyperchaotic encryption for remote computers A and B

computers) as is depicted in Fig. 18.2. A *message m* is to be transmitted over an *insecure* communication channel. To avoid any *unauthorized* computer (intruder) located at the mentioned channel; *m* is encrypted prior to transmission to generate an *encrypted* message *s*,

$$s = f(m, k),$$

by using a hyperchaotic map f on computer A.

The encrypted message s is sent to computer B, where m is *recovered* as $\hat{m}$ from the hyperchaotic decryption g, as

$$\hat{m} = g(s, k).$$

If f and g have used the same *key k*, then at computer B it is possible to obtain $\hat{m} = m$. A *secure* channel (dashed line) is used for transmission of the keys. Generally, this secure communication channel is a courier and is too slow for the transmission of m. Our hyperchaotic cryptosystem is reliable, if it preserves the security of m, i.e., if $m\prime \neq m$ for even the best *cryptanalytic* function h, given by

$$m\prime = h(s).$$

To achieve the proposed hyperchaotic encryption scheme, we appeal to *3D hyperchaotic Rössler map* for encryption/decryption purposes (f and g, respectively). The Rössler map have a number of parameters determining their dynamics; such parameters and initial conditions are the coding "keys", k. We expect that it can perform the objective of the secure communication and the transmitting messages can be recovered at the receiver. In order to guarantee the encryption and decryption, the hyperchaotic Rössler maps have to achieve the so-called *synchronization* on both computers A and B. For such reason, our first problem to solve is to design a control u for hyperchaotic synchronization, which will be shown in next section. In this work, the confidential information m to be sent via e-mail are audio and image messages.

18.4   Output Synchronization of Hyperchaotic Maps

Consider a map defined by

$$P : \begin{cases} x\,(k+1) = f\,(x\,(k)\,,u\,(k))\,, \\ y\,(k) = h\,(x\,(k))\,, \end{cases} \tag{18.1}$$

where the state vector $x \in X$ (an open set in $\mathfrak{R}^n$), the input u is inside an open set U in $\mathfrak{R}$, and the output y belongs to an open set Y in $\mathfrak{R}$. The mappings $f : X \times U \to X$ and $h : X \to Y$ are analytic. In addition, consider the following map, described by

$$M : \begin{cases} x_M\,(k+1) = f_M\,(x_M\,(k)\,,u_M\,(k))\,, \\ y_M\,(k) = h_M\,(x_M\,(k))\,, \end{cases} \tag{18.2}$$

where the state vector $x_M \in X_M$ (an open set in $\mathfrak{R}^{n_M}$), the input $u_M \in U_M$ (an open set in $\mathfrak{R}$), and the output y_M belongs to an open set Y_M in $\mathfrak{R}$. Also, the mappings $f_M : X_M \times U_M \to X_M$ and $h_M : X_M \to Y_M$ are analytic. For certain parameter values, the uncontrolled maps (18.1) and (18.2), i.e., for $u\,(k) = u_M\,(k) = 0$, exhibit *hyperchaotic behavior*; that is, the maps have *multiple positive Lyapunov exponents*. The synchronization problem addressed here is defined as follows.

Definition 18.1 (Output synchronization problem, OP). *[13] The output $y\,(k)$ of the hyperchaotic map (18.1) synchronizes with the output $y_M\,(k)$ of the hyperchaotic map (18.2), if*

$$\lim_{k \to \infty} |y\,(k) - y_M\,(k)| = 0, \tag{18.3}$$

no matter which initial conditions $x\,(0)$ and $x_M\,(0)$ have, and for suitable input sequences $u\,(k)$ and $u_M\,(k)$.

Notice that, we are considering *partial synchronization* between hyperchaotic maps (18.1) and (18.2), which is a substantial difference with other approaches based on complete synchronization.

Figure 18.3 shows the *output synchronization scheme* by using model-matching approach: the *master* is the hyperchaotic map M with state vector x_M, input u_M, and output y_M. The nonlinear function $\phi_M = \phi_M\,(x_M,u_M)$ is the coupling sequence between P and M, which is transmitted through a public channel to the slave, and is used to synchronize the master and slave in the sense of the condition (18.3). The *slave* consists of the hyperchaotic map P and a compensator C. The *compensator* C is utilized to control P with inputs ϕ_M and x, and output u. If the compensator C yields properly the control sequence u, then the *output error synchronization* $e\,(k) = y_E\,(k) = y\,(k) - y_M\,(k)$ *asymptotically converges to zero*.

For secure computer communications based on previous output synchronization scheme between maps P and M: at the hyperchaotic transmitter, the messages are encrypted (by direct modulation, additive masking, or another technique) and sent to the hyperchaotic receiver via a public channel. Finally, the original messages are

Fig. 18.3 Output synchronization scheme by using model-matching approach

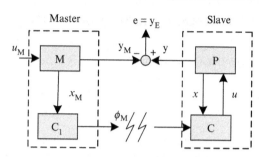

decrypted at the receiver end by using output synchronization. For this purpose, we will use a communication scheme based on *hyperchaotic encryption*, to send audio and image messages.

18.4.1 Model-Matching Problem: a Brief Review

Considering the hyperchaotic maps (18.1) and (18.2), we assume that P evolves in a neighborhood of an equilibrium point x^0; that is, around $\left(x^0, u^0\right) \in X \times U$ such that $f\left(x^0, u^0\right) = x^0$, with $\{u(k) = u^0 : k \geq 0\}$ being a (constant) input sequence. For this sequence there exists another (constant) output sequence $\{y(k) = h\left(x^0\right) = y^0 : k \geq 0\}$. In the same way, let the equilibrium point of M be denoted by x_M^0 around $\left(x_M^0, u_M^0\right) \in X_M \times U_M$. According to Fig. 18.3 we are interested in to design a control u for P which, irrespectively of the initial conditions of P and M, makes the output $y(k)$ of P asymptotically converges to the output $y_M(k)$ produced by M under an arbitrary input $u_M(k)$. This problem is the so-called *discrete-time asymptotic model-matching problem (DAMP)* from nonlinear control theory. Which coincides with the OP, see [2, 21, 23]. In [2] is adopted the following approach: *the DAMP is reduced into a problem of decoupling the output of a suitable auxiliary system from the input u_M to the model M*. In this way, we define an *output error* $y_E(k) = y(k) - y_M(k)$, and we choose $u(k)$ such that $y_E(k)$ is decoupled from $u_M(k)$ for all $k \geq 0$, and converges asymptotically to zero. Such *auxiliary system* is defined as follows

$$E : \begin{cases} x_E(k+1) = f_E(x_E(k), u_E(k), w_E(k)), \\ y_E(k) = h_E(x_E(k)), \end{cases} \tag{18.4}$$

with *auxiliary state vector* $x_E = (x, x_M)^T \in \Re^{n+n_M}$, and *auxiliary inputs* $u_E = u$ and $w_E = u_M$, where

$$f_E(x_E, u_E, w_E) = \begin{pmatrix} f(x, u) \\ f_M(x_M, u_M) \end{pmatrix},$$
$$h_E(x_E) = h(x) - h_M(x_M).$$

Given this system, together with an equilibrium point $x_E^0 = \left(x^0, x_M^0\right)$ it is known that, if the disturbance-decoupling problem with measurement disturbance w_E associated with the system E has a solution on Ω_0^E, an open and dense subset of $X \times X_M \times U \times U_M$, defined around the equilibrium point $\left(x^0, x_M^0, u^0, u_M^0\right)$, then there exists an analytic mapping γ^E defined on Ω_0^E with the property that the control

$$u(k) = \gamma^E\left(x_E(k), w_E(k)\right) = \gamma^E\left(x_E(k), u_M(k)\right) \qquad (18.5)$$

decouples the output y_E of the closed-loop system (18.4)–(18.5) from the disturbance w_E for every initial state of x_E in an open and dense subset of $X \times X_M$ contained in Ω_0^E.

In [2] the OP is treated in terms of a *relative degree* associated with the outputs y and y_M. Thus, the following definitions are introduced. Let f_0, f_{M_0}, and f_{E_0} be the undriven state dynamics $f(\cdot, 0)$, $f_M(\cdot, 0)$, and $f_E(\cdot, 0, 0)$, respectively, and f_0^j, $f_{M_0}^j$, and $f_{E_0}^j$ the j-times iterated compositions of f_0, f_{M_0}, and f_{E_0} with $f_0^0(x) = x$, $f_{M_0}^0(x_M) = x_M$, and $f_{E_0}^0(x_E) = x_E$.

Definition 18.2 ([25]). *The output y of P Eq. (18.1) is said to have a relative degree d in an open and dense subset O of $X \times U$ containing the equilibrium point $\left(x^0, u^0\right)$, if*

$$\frac{\partial}{\partial u}\left[h \circ f_0^l(f(x, u))\right] \equiv 0$$

for all $0 \le l \le d - 1$, for all $(x, u) \in O$, and

$$\frac{\partial}{\partial u}\left[h \circ f_0^d(f(x, u))\right] \ne 0$$

for all $(x, u) \in O$.

A similar definition can be given for the relative degree of M Eq. (18.2), d_M, in an open and dense subset O_M, of $X_M \times U_M$ containing the equilibrium point $\left(x_M^0, u_M^0\right)$.

The following theorem gives necessary and sufficient conditions for the local solvability of the OP.

Theorem 18.1 ([2]). *Consider the maps P Eq. (18.1) and M Eq. (18.2) around, respectively, their equilibria $\left(x^0, u^0\right)$ and $\left(x_M^0, u_M^0\right)$. Suppose that the outputs y of P and y_M of M have finite relative degree d and d_M, respectively defined on O and O_M. Assume that for all $x_E = (x, x_M)^T \in X \times X_M$ and $u_M \in U_M$,*

$$0 \in \text{Im}\left\{h_E \circ f_{E_0}^d\left(f_E(x_E, \cdot, u_M)\right)\right\},$$

where $\text{Im}\{\varphi\}$ denotes the image of φ. Then the OP is locally solvable on Ω_0^E if, and only if,

$$d \le d_M. \qquad (18.6)$$

If the condition (18.6) holds, then from definition of d and d_M, there exists an analytic mapping $\gamma^E : \Re^{n+n_M} \times \Re \times \Re \to \Re$, such that

$$y_E(k + d + 1) = h_E \circ f_{E_0}^d \circ f_E\left(x_E(k), \gamma^E(x_E(k), u_M(k), v(k))\right) = v(k),$$

with $v \in \Re$ an external control, or equivalently we have that,

$$S\left(x(k), \gamma^E(x_E(k), u_M(k), v(k))\right) = v(k) - h \circ f_0^d \circ f(x(k))$$
$$+ h_M \circ f_{M_0}^l \circ f_M(x_M(k), u_M(k)).$$

Where $\gamma^E(x_E, u_M, v)$ is the reverse of $S(x, \cdot)$, that is

$$\gamma^E(x_E(k), u_M(k), v(k)) = S^{-1}\left(\begin{array}{c} x(k), \ v(k) - h \circ f_0^d \circ f(x(k)) \\ + h_M \circ f_{M_0}^l \circ f_M(x_M(k), u_M(k)) \end{array} \right),$$

(18.7)

where the external control is given by

$$v(k) = -\sum_{l=0}^{d} \alpha_l \left[h \circ f_0^l(x(k)) - h_M \circ f_{M_0}^l(x_M(k)) \right].$$ (18.8)

Under the new coordinates

$$(\zeta(x_E), x_M) = \phi(x_E) = \phi(x, x_M),$$

where $\zeta(x_E) = (\zeta_1(x_E), ..., \zeta_{d+1}(x_E))^T$ and $\zeta_i(x_E) = h_{E_i} \circ f_{E_0}^{i-1}(x_E) = \xi_i(x) - h_{M_i} \circ f_{M_0}^{i-1}(x_M)$ for all $i = 1, 2, ..., d + 1$. The closed-loop auxiliary system E, by using the control $u = \gamma^E(x_E, u_M)$ Eqs. (18.7)–(18.8), takes the form

$$\zeta_i(k + 1) = \zeta_{i+1}(k), \qquad i = 1, ..., d,$$
$$\zeta_{d+1}(k + 1) = v(k) = -\alpha_0\zeta_1(k) - \cdots - \alpha_d \zeta_{d+1}(k),$$
$$x_M(k + 1) = f_M(x_M(k), u_M(k)),$$
$$y_E(k) = \zeta_1(k).$$ (18.9)

18.4.2 Output Synchronization

From Eq. (18.5) we can express the control u as follows

$$u(k) = \gamma^E(x(k), x_M(k), u_M(k)) = \gamma^E(x(k), \phi_M(x_M(k), u_M(k))),$$

(18.10)

where the nonlinear function ϕ_M (x_M, u_M) is the coupling sequence to be transmitted from the master M to construct u in C, which solves the OP, see Fig. 18.3. In the context of synchronization, a key observation, provided by the special form in (18.10), is that ϕ_M (x_M, u_M) fixes the coupling sequence to be transmitted to the slave. Next, we rewrite the following procedure to achieve output synchronization between P and M proposed in [2]:

1. Given a hyperchaotic map $x (k + 1) = f (x (k))$, we write it in the forms P Eq. (18.1) and M Eq. (18.2) by adding the control inputs $u (k)$ and $u_M (k)$, respectively.
2. We define properly the outputs y and y_M for P and M, respectively; such that the OP has a solution, that is the condition $d \leq d_M$ holds.
3. We obtain the control u according to Eqs. (18.7)–(18.8).
4. From $u = \gamma^E (x_E, u_M)$, we proceed to identify the coupling sequence $\phi_M (x_M, u_M)$.
5. Once the coupling sequence $\phi_M = \phi_M (x_M, u_M)$ has been decided, then the output y of P can track arbitrary reference signal y_M of M in the sense of condition (18.3).

In next section, we will illustrate the above procedure to synchronize the outputs of two hyperchaotic Rössler maps, which is a necessary condition in secure computer communications for encryption and decryption of confidential information.

18.5 Output Synchronization of Hyperchaotic Rössler Maps

Consider the Rössler map described by [19]:

$$\begin{cases} x_1 (k + 1) = \alpha x_1 (k) (1 - x_1 (k)) - \beta (x_3 (k) + \gamma) (1 - 2x_2 (k)), \\ x_2 (k + 1) = \delta x_2 (k) (1 - x_2 (k)) + \varsigma x_3 (k), \\ x_3 (k + 1) = \eta ((x_3 (k) + \gamma) (1 - 2x_2 (k)) - 1) (1 - \theta x_1 (k)), \end{cases} \tag{18.11}$$

for the parameter values $\alpha = 3.8$, $\beta = 0.05$, $\gamma = 0.35$, $\delta = 3.78$, $\varsigma = 0.2$, $\eta = 0.1$, and $\theta = 1.9$ the uncontrolled Rössler map (18.11) exhibits hyperchaotic behavior. Following Step 1, we add a control input u in (18.11), so we have P for the *slave*,

$$P : \begin{cases} x_1 (k + 1) = \alpha x_1 (k) (1 - x_1 (k)) - \beta (x_3 (k) + \gamma) (1 - 2x_2 (k)) + u (k), \\ x_2 (k + 1) = \delta x_2 (k) (1 - x_2 (k)) + \varsigma x_3 (k), \\ x_3 (k + 1) = \eta ((x_3 (k) + \gamma) (1 - 2x_2 (k)) - 1) (1 - \theta x_1 (k)), \\ \quad y (k) = x_2 (k). \end{cases}$$

$$\tag{18.12}$$

In this way, we propose the Rössler map M for the *master*, described by

$$
M : \begin{cases}
x_{M1}(k+1) = \alpha x_{M1}(k)(1 - x_{M1}(k)) - \beta(x_{M3}(k) + \gamma)(1 - 2x_{M2}(k)) + u_M(k), \\
x_{M2}(k+1) = \delta x_{M2}(k)(1 - x_{M2}(k)) + \varsigma x_{M3}(k), \\
x_{M3}(k+1) = \eta((x_{M3}(k) + \gamma)(1 - 2x_{M2}(k)) - 1)(1 - \theta x_{M1}(k)), \\
y_M(k) = x_{M2}(k),
\end{cases}
$$

(18.13)

in this case, we use $u_M(k) = 0$ to keep the master (18.5) with hyperchaotic behavior. According to the Step 2, we define the outputs $y = x_2$ and $y_M = x_{M2}$ in (18.12) and (18.5), respectively. In this way, the relative degrees of the slave (18.12) and master (18.5) are $d = d_M = 2$, with this, the OP has a solution according to (18.6). Step 3, in order to find the solution u; firstly, we construct the auxiliary system E (18.4) from (18.12) and (18.5), with output given by $y_E = y - y_M = x_2 - x_{M2}$. Defining $\zeta_1 = y_E$, the auxiliary system in new coordinates, is described by

$$
\zeta_1(k+1) = \zeta_2(k),
$$
$$
\zeta_2(k+1) = \zeta_3(k),
$$
$$
\zeta_3(k+1) = -\alpha_2\zeta_3(k) - \alpha_1\zeta_2(k) - \alpha_0\zeta_1(k) = v(k). \tag{18.14}
$$

If we propose the control law according to Eqs. (18.7)–(18.8), then $u(k)$ is given by

$$
u = \frac{1}{\theta}\left(1 - \frac{v + a - b}{c}\right) - (\alpha x_1(1 - x_1) - \beta(x_3 + \gamma)(1 - 2x_2)), \tag{18.15}
$$

where

$$
a = \delta a_1(1 - a_1) + a_2,
$$
$$
\begin{aligned}
a_1 = {} & \delta(\delta x_{M2}(1 - x_{M2}) + \varsigma x_{M3})(1 - (\delta x_{M2}(1 - x_{M2}) + \varsigma x_{M3})) \\
& + \varsigma(\eta((x_{M3} + \gamma)(1 - 2x_{M2}) - 1)(1 - \theta x_{M1})),
\end{aligned}
$$
$$
\begin{aligned}
a_2 = {} & \varsigma[\eta(\eta((x_{M3} + \gamma)(1 - 2x_{M2}) - 1)(1 - \theta x_{M1})) + \gamma) \\
& \times (1 - 2(\delta x_{M2}(1 - x_{M2})) + \varsigma x_{M3})) - 1) \\
& \times (1 - \theta(\alpha x_{M1}(1 - x_{M1}) - \beta(x_{M3} + \gamma)(1 - 2x_{M2}) + u_M))],
\end{aligned}
$$
$$
b = \delta b_1(1 - b_1),
$$
$$
\begin{aligned}
b_1 = {} & \delta(\delta x_2(1 - x_2) + \varsigma x_3)(1 - (\delta x_2(1 - x_2) + \varsigma x_3)) \\
& + \varsigma(\eta((x_3 + \gamma)(1 - 2x_2) - 1)(1 - \theta x_1)),
\end{aligned}
$$
$$
\begin{aligned}
c = {} & \varsigma\eta((\eta((x_3 + \gamma)(1 - 2x_2) - 1)(1 - \theta x_1)) + \gamma) \\
& \times (1 - 2(\delta x_2(1 - x_2) + \varsigma x_3) - 1)).
\end{aligned}
$$

For Step 4; the coupling sequence ϕ_M (x_M, u_M) from (18.5) to (18.12) according to (18.15), is given by

$$\phi_M \left(x_M \left(k \right), u_M \left(k \right) \right) = \alpha_0 x_{M2} \left(k \right) + \alpha_1 \left(\delta x_{M2} \left(k \right) \left(1 - x_{M2} \left(k \right) \right) \right.$$
$$+ \varsigma x_{M3} \left(k \right) \right) + \alpha_2 d + a$$

where

$$d = \delta \left(\delta x_{M2} \left(k \right) \left(1 - x_{M2} \left(k \right) \right) + \varsigma x_{M3} \left(k \right) \right) \left(1 - \left(\delta x_{M2} \left(k \right) \left(1 - x_{M2} \left(k \right) \right) \right.$$
$$\left. + \varsigma x_{M3} \left(k \right) \right) \right) + \varsigma \left(\eta \left(\left(x_{M3} \left(k \right) + \gamma \right) \left(1 - 2 x_{M2} \left(k \right) \right) - 1 \right) \left(1 - \theta x_{M1} \left(k \right) \right) \right).$$

Finally, for Step 5 from Eq. (18.14) we see that the output y of the closed-loop slave P Eq. (18.5) differs from the output y_M of M Eq. (18.12) by a signal y_E obeying the linear difference equation

$$\alpha_2 \, y_E \left(k + 2 \right) + \alpha_1 \, y_E \left(k + 1 \right) + \alpha_0 \, y_E \left(k \right) = 0,$$

where α_0, α_1, and α_2 are constant real coefficients. A proper location of the roots of the polynomial $\alpha_2 \lambda^2 + \alpha_1 \lambda + \alpha_0 = 0$ entails the desired asymptotic behavior $y_E \left(k \right) = 0$, i.e., $y \left(k \right)$ converges to $y_M \left(k \right)$, and therefore the output synchronization condition (18.3) holds. If we choose $\alpha_i = 0.1$, $i = 0, 1, 2$, we assure that the system (18.14) will be exponentially stable and output synchronization condition (18.3) holds. We take the initial conditions $x \left(0 \right) = \left(0.3, 0, 0.05 \right)$ and $x_M \left(0 \right) = \left(0.1, 0.2, -0.1 \right)$ for P and M, respectively. For this hyperchaotic Rössler map was shown in [2] the matching between the outputs $y \left(k \right) = x_2 \left(k \right)$ and $y_M \left(k \right) = x_{M2} \left(k \right)$ after some transient behavior. In next section, we illustrate the encrypted transmission of confidential messages.

18.6 Secure Chaotic Encryption

In this section, we show how output synchronization of two hyperchaotic Rössler maps is used in secure computer communication to send confidential information. In particular, we show a secure e-mail communication schemes to transmit encrypted audio and image messages.

The communication scheme to send confidential messages via e-mail is shown in Fig. 18.4. This cryptosystem uses two transmission lines, in one the coupling sequence $\phi_M \left(k \right) = \phi_M \left(x_M \left(k \right), u_M \left(k \right) \right)$ is transmitted to achieve output synchronization between hyperchaotic transmitter and receiver computers. $\phi_M \left(k \right)$ is only used for fast synchronization and does not contain any information of the confidential message $m \left(k \right)$. While in the second line, we send the encrypted confidential message $m \left(k \right)$, here the nonlinear function $\sigma \left(\cdot, \cdot \right)$ encrypts both the message $m \left(k \right)$ and chaotic output $y_M \left(k \right)$ in the transmitter computer. The encrypted message $s \left(k \right)$

Fig. 18.4 Block diagram for the hyperchaotic encryption to encode, transmit, and decode messages

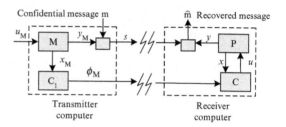

is transmitted to the receiver computer. The nonlinear function for *encryption process* is proposed as follows

$$\sigma\left(y_M, m\right) = s = g_1\left(y_M\right) + g_2\left(y_M\right)m,$$

and the nonlinear function for *decryption process* is given by

$$\lambda\left(y, s\right) = \frac{-g_1\left(y\right)}{g_2\left(y\right)} + \frac{s}{g_2\left(y\right)}.$$

In particular, the *encryption function* installed in the transmitter computer is given by

$$\sigma\left(y_M, m\right) = y_M^3 + \left(1 + y_M^3\right)m = s, \qquad (18.16)$$

and the *decryption function* installed into remote receiver computer is defined by

$$\lambda\left(y, s\right) = \frac{-y^3}{1 + y^3} + \frac{s}{1 + y^3}. \qquad (18.17)$$

The functions (18.16) and (18.17) are implemented for encryption and decryption processes, respectively, see Fig. 18.4.

18.6.1 Communicating Encrypted Audio Messages

Firstly, we use like confidential information $m(k)$ a *voice message*, the transmitted message with the encrypted the information $s(k)$, and at the receiver computer end, the recovered information $\hat{m}(k)$. Figure 18.5 shows the encrypted transmission and recovery when the confidential message $m(k)$ (top of figure) is a voice message, in this case the word "*cuatro*" that means *four* in Spanish. The transmitted hyperchaotic sequence $s(k)$ (middle of figure), and recovered message $\hat{m}(k)$ at the receiver computer (bottom of figure). We can see after brief transient time that the information is recovery faithfully, after a brief transient.

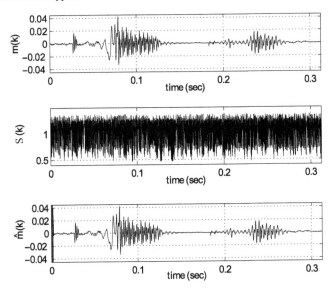

Fig. 18.5 Communication and recovering of confidential message: m (*top of figure*), the original voice message, the hyperchaotic (very complex) sequence s(k) sent to the receiver computer with the encrypted m (*middle of figure*), and the recovered message m (*bottom of figure*)

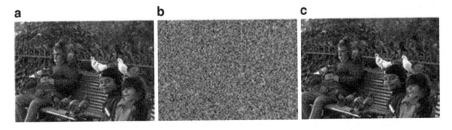

Fig. 18.6 (**a**) Original jpg image message to be sent for computer A, (**b**) hyperchaotic encrypted image through insecure channel, and (**c**) recovered jpg image for computer B

18.6.2   Communicating Encrypted jpg Image Messages

Figure 18.6 shows (a) the original jpg image message in the transmitter computer, (b) the transmitted hyperchaotic encrypted image, and (c) the recovered jpg image into receiver computer.

Remark 18.1. Here the processes of encryption and synchronization are completely separated with no interference between them. So, encrypted message does not interfere with synchronization, therefore not increasing the sensitivity of synchronization to external errors. As a result, the hyperchaotic cryptosystem with two transmission channels gives faster synchronization and high security, see [43].

18.7 Conclusions

In this chapter, we have presented a scheme to achieve output synchronization of hyperchaotic maps via model-matching approach. This method is inspired from nonlinear control theory, which presents the advantage that is systematic, useful to synchronize identical and no identical hyperchaotic systems. We have showed by computer simulations, that this approach is indeed suitable to synchronize two hyperchaotic Rössler maps unidirectionally coupled.

We have applied output synchronization of two hyperchaotic Rössler maps in secure computer communications. In particular, we have presented a hyperchaotic communication scheme to transmit encrypted confidential audio and image messages. As well as, the intrinsic advantages for the encryption presented (the nonlinear function σ and λ), no additive masking by the mentioned schemes, we have increased the security by using complex hyperchaotic transmitted signals. Of course, a complete analysis on security of our cryptosystem will be reported in other side.

Acknowledgements This work was supported by the CONACYT, México under Research Grants No. J49593-Y, 48396-Y and P50051-Y. E. Tlelo-Cuautle was Visiting Researcher at University of California Riverside during 2009–2010 under a sabbatical leave CONACyT grant.

References

1. Aguilar-Bustos A.Y., Cruz-Hernández C.: Synchronization of discrete-time hyperchaotic systems through extended Kalman filtering. Nonlinear Dynamics Systems Theory. **6**, 319–336 (2006)
2. Aguilar-Bustos A.Y., Cruz-Hernández C.: Synchronization of discrete-time hyperchaotic systems: an application in communications. Chaos, Solitons & Fractals. **41**, 1301–1310 (2009)
3. Alvarez G., Montoya F., Romera M., Pastor G.: Breaking parameter modulated chaotic secure communication system. Chaos, Solitons & Fractals. **24**, 783–787 (2004)
4. Charge P., Fournier-Prunaret D., Guglielmi V.: Features analysis of a parametric PWL chaotic map and its utilization for secure transmissions. Chaos, Solitons & Fractals. **38**, 1411–1422 (2008)
5. Chen M., Zhou D., Shang Y.: A sliding mode observer based secure communication scheme. Chaos, Solitons & Fractals. **25**, 573–578 (2005)
6. Chen L.Q.: An open plus closed loop control for discrete chaos and hyperchaos. Phys. Lett. **A281**, 327–333 (2001)
7. Cruz-Hernández C., Nijmeijer H.: Synchronization through filtering. Int. J. Bifurct. Chaos. **10**, 763–775 (2000)
8. Cruz-Hernández C., Posadas C., Sira-Ramírez H.: Synchronization of two hyperchaotic Chua circuits: A generalized Hamiltonian systems approach. Proceedings of the 15th IFAC World Congress, Barcelona, Spain, (2002)
9. Cruz-Hernández C.: Synchronization of time-delay Chua's oscillator with application to secure communication. Nonlinear Dynamics Systems Theory. **4**, 1–13 (2004)
10. Cruz-Hernández C., Serrano-Guerrero H.: Cryptosystems based on synchronized Chua's circuits. Proceedings of the 16th IFAC World Congress, Prague, Czech Republic, (2005)
11. Cruz-Hernández C., López-Mancilla D., García V., Serrano H., Núez R.: Experimental realization of binary signal transmission using chaos. J. Circ. Syst. Comput. **14**, 453–468 (2005)

12. Cruz-Hernández C., Romero-Haros N.: Communicating via synchronized time-delay Chua's circuits. Commun. Nonlinear Sci. Numer. Simul. **13**, 645–659 (2008)
13. Cruz-Hernández C., Martynyuk A.A.: Advances in chaotic dynamics with applications. Series on Stability, Oscillations, and Optimization of Systems, Cambridge Scientific Publishers. London **4** (2009)
14. Cuomo K.M., Oppenheim A.V., Strogratz S.H.: Synchronization of Lorenz-based chaotic circuits with applications to communications. IEEE Trans. Circ. Syst. II. **40**, 626–633 (1993)
15. Dedieu H., Kennedy M.P., Hasler M.: Chaotic shift keying: Modulation and demodulation of a chaotic carrier using self-synchronizing Chuas circuits. IEEE Trans Circ Syst II. **40**, 634–642 (1993)
16. Gao T., Chen Z., Yuan Z., Yu D.: Adaptive synchronization of a new hyperchaotic system with uncertain parameters. Chaos, Solitons & Fractals. **33**, 922–928 (2007)
17. Grassi G.: Observer-based hyperchaos synchronization in cascaded discrete-time systems. Chaos, Solitons & Fractals. **40**, 1029–1039 (2009)
18. Hyun C.H., Kim J.H., Kim E., Park M.: Adaptive fuzzy observer based synchronization design and secure communications of chaotic systems. Chaos, Solitons & Fractals. **27**, 930–940 (2006)
19. Itoh M., Yang T., Chua L.O.: Conditions for impulsive synchronization of chaotic & hyperchaotic systems. Int. J. Bifurct. Chaos. **11**, 551–560 (2001)
20. Kia F., Reza R., Hossein K.: An application of Chen system for secure chaotic communication based on extended Kalman filter and multi-shift cipher algorithm. Commun. Nonlinear Sci. Numer. Simul. **13**, 763–781 (2008)
21. López-Mancilla D., Cruz-Hernández C.: Output synchronization of chaotic systems: model matching approach with application to secure communication. Nonlinear Dynamics Systems Theory. **5**, 141–156 (2005)
22. López-Mancilla D., Cruz-Hernández C.: A note on chaos-based communication schemes. Revista Mexicana de Fsica. **51**, 265–269 (2005)
23. López-Mancilla D., Cruz-Hernández C.: Output synchronization of chaotic systems under non-vanishing perturbations. Chaos, Solitons & Fractals. **37**, 1172–1186 (2008)
24. Mensour B., Longtin A.: Synchronization of delay-differential equations with application to private communication. Phys Lett. **A244**, 59–70 (1998)
25. Monaco S., Normand-Cyrot D.: Minimum phase nonlinear discrete-time systems and feedback stabilization. In Proceedings of the 26th Conference on Decision and Control, Los Angeles, CA, USA, 979-986 (1987)
26. Nijmeijer H., Mareels I.M.Y.: An observer looks at synchronization. IEEE Trans. Circ. Syst. I. **44**, 882–890 (1997)
27. Pecora L.M., Carroll T.L.: Synchronization in chaotic systems. Phys. Rev. Lett. **64**, 821–824 (1990)
28. Pérez G., Cerdeira H.A.: Extracting messages masked by chaos. Phys. Rev. Lett. **74**, 1970–1973 (1995)
29. Posadas-Castillo C., Cruz-Hernández C., López-Mancilla D.: Synchronization of chaotic neural networks: a generalized Hamiltonian systems approach in Hybrid Intelligent Systems, Studies in Fuzziness and Soft Computing. Springer **208** (2007)
30. Posadas-Castillo C., Cruz-Hernández C., López-Gutiérrez R.M.: Synchronization in arrays of chaotic neural networks in Foundations of Fuzzy Logic and Soft Computing, LNAI. Springer **4529** (2007)
31. Posadas-Castillo C., López-Gutiérrez R.M., Cruz-Hernández C.: Synchronization of chaotic solid state Nd:YAG lasers: application to secure communication. Commun. Nonlinear Sci. Numer. Simul. **13**, 1655–1667 (2008)
32. Sira-Ramírez H., Cruz-Hernández C.: Synchronization of chaotic systems: A generalized Hamiltonian systems approach. Int. J. Bifurct. Chaos. **11**, 1381–1395 (2001)
33. Schneier, B.: Applied cryptography: protocols, algorithms, and source code in C. Wiley and Sons, Inc. (1996)
34. Short M., Parker A.T.: Unmasking a hyperchaotic communication scheme. Phys. Rev. **E58**, 1159–1162 (1998)

35. Tamaševičius A., Čenys A., Namajūnas A., Mykolaitis G.: Synchronising hyperchaos in infinitedimensional dynamical systems. Chaos, Solitons & Fractals. **9**, 1403–1408 (1998)
36. Tang F.: An adaptive synchronization strategy based on active control for demodulating message hidden in chaotic signals. Chaos, Solitons & Fractals. **37**, 1090–1096 (2008)
37. Vincent U.E.: Synchronization of identical and non-identical 4-D chaotic systems using active control. Chaos, Solitons & Fractals. **37**, 1065–1075 (2008)
38. Wei-Der C.: Digital secure communication via chaotic systems. Digital Signal Processing (2008)
39. Yang T., Wu C.W., Chua L.O.: Cryptography based on chaotic systems. IEEE Trans. Circ. Syst. I. **44**, 469–472 (1997)
40. Yang Y., Ma X.K., Zhang H.: Synchronization and parameter identification of high-dimensional discrete chaotic systems via parametric adaptive control. Chaos, Solitons & Fractals, **28**, 244–251 (2006)
41. Yan J.J., Yang Y.S., Chiang T.Y., Chen C.Y.: Robust synchronization of unified chaotic via sliding mode control. Chaos, Solitons & Fractals. **34**, 947–954 (2007)
42. Yan Z., Yu P.: Hyperchaos synchronization and control on a new hyperchaotic attractor. Chaos, Solitons & Fractals. **35**, 333–345 (2008)
43. Zhong-Ping J.A.: A note on chaotic on chaotic secure communication systems. IEEE Trans. Circ. Syst. I. **49**, 92–96 (2002)

Index